JOURNAL

OF THE

FEDERAL CONVENTION

JOURNAL

OF THE

FEDERAL CONVENTION

KEPT BY

JAMES MADISON

REPRINTED FROM THE EDITION OF 1840, WHICH WAS PUBLISHED UNDER DIRECTION OF THE
UNITED STATES GOVERNMENT FROM THE ORIGINAL MANUSCRIPTS. A COMPLETE
INDEX SPECIALLY ADAPTED TO THIS EDITION IS ADDED

EDITED BY

E. H. SCOTT

SPECIAL EDITION

THE LAWBOOK EXCHANGE, LTD.
Clark, New Jersey

ISBN 978-1-58477-256-9 (hardcover)
ISBN 978-1-61619-295-2 (paperback)

Lawbook Exchange edition 2003, 2013

The quality of this reprint is equivalent to the quality of the original work.

THE LAWBOOK EXCHANGE, LTD.

33 Terminal Avenue
Clark, New Jersey 07066-1321

*Please see our website for a selection of our other publications
and fine facsimile reprints of classic works of legal history:*
www.lawbookexchange.com

Library of Congress Cataloging-in-Publication Data

United States. Constitutional Convention (1787)
    [Journal of the Federal Convention]
    Journal of the Federal Convention kept by James Madison; edited by E.H. Scott.
      p. cm.
    Originally published: Special ed. Chicago: Scott, Foresman, and Co., 1898.
    Includes bibliographical references and index.
    ISBN 1-58477-256-5 (cloth: acid-free paper)
      1. Constitutional history—United States—Sources. I. Madison, James, 1751-1836. II.
Scott, E. H. (Erastus Howard), 1855-1928. III. Title.

    KF4510 .U538 2002
    342.73'0242—dc21   2002024327

Printed in the United States of America on acid-free paper

JOURNAL

OF THE

FEDERAL CONVENTION

KEPT BY

JAMES MADISON

REPRINTED FROM THE EDITION OF 1840, WHICH WAS PUBLISHED UNDER DIRECTION OF THE
UNITED STATES GOVERNMENT FROM THE ORIGINAL MANUSCRIPTS. A COMPLETE
INDEX SPECIALLY ADAPTED TO THIS EDITION IS ADDED

EDITED BY

E. H. SCOTT

SPECIAL EDITION

CHICAGO:

SCOTT, FORESMAN AND CO.

1898.

PRESS OF
THE HENRY O. SHEPARD CO.,
CHICAGO.

PREFACE.

On the 15th November, 1836, Mrs. MADISON addressed the following letter to the President of the United States:

"MONTPELIER, November 15, 1836.

"Sir: The will of my late husband, JAMES MADISON, contains the following provision:

"'Considering the peculiarity and magnitude of the occasion which produced the Convention at Philadelphia, in 1787, the characters who composed it, the Constitution which resulted from their deliberations, its effects during a trial of so many years on the prosperity of the people living under it, and the interest it has inspired among the friends of free government, it is not an unreasonable inference that a careful and extended report of the proceedings and discussions of that body, which were with closed doors, by a member who was constant in his attendance, will be particularly gratifying to the people of the United States, and to all who take an interest in the progress of political science and the cause of true liberty.

"This provision bears evidence of the value he set on his Report of the Debates in the Convention, and he has charged legacies on them alone to the amount of twelve hundred dollars for the benefit of literary institutions and for benevolent purposes, leaving the residuary net proceeds for the use of his widow."

The President's message in relation to the purchase of the MADISON PAPERS contains the following: "Congress has already, at considerable expense, published in a variety of forms, the naked journals of the Revolutionary Congress, and of the Convention that formed the Constitution of the United States. I am persuaded that the work of Mr. MADISON, considering the author, the subject matter of it, and the circumstances under which it was prepared — long withheld from the public, as it has been, by those motives of personal kindness and delicacy that gave tone to his intercourse with his fellow-men, until he and all who had been participators with him in the scenes he describes have passed away — well deserves to become the property of the nation, and cannot fail, if published and disseminated at the public charge, to confer the most important of all benefits on the present and succeeding generations, accurate knowledge of the principles of their Government, and the circumstances under which they were recommended and embodied in the constitution, for adoption.   ANDREW JACKSON."

The message of the President was referred to the Joint Library Committee, who, on the 24th January, 1837, reported a resolution authorizing that committee " to contract for and purchase, at the sum of thirty thousand dollars, the manuscripts of the late Mr. MADISON, conceding to Mrs. MADISON the right to use copies of the said manuscripts in foreign countries, as she might think fit."

On the 9th July the House of Representatives, after having had under consideration the resolution of the Senate, amended it by changing it into an act, in which form, it was passed, and being concurred in by the Senate and approved by the President on the same day, became a law in the following terms:

"*An act authorizing the printing of the Madison Papers.*

"*Be it enacted by the Senate and House of Representatives of the United States of America in Congress assembled,* That the Joint Committee on the Library be authorized to cause the MADISON PAPERS to be printed and published; and that a sum not exceeding five thousand dollars be appropriated for that purpose out of any money in the Treasury not otherwise appropriated."

On the 28th January, 1839, Mr. WALL of New Jersey, reported to the Senate, a contract made in pursuance of the act of Congress, by Messrs. ROBBINS of Rhode Island, and POPE of Kentucky, the Chairmen of the Joint Library Committee for the publication of the work in its present form, to be executed under the superintendance of Mr. GILPIN, the Solicitor of the Treasury. For this purpose, one of the duplicate manuscript copies, deposited by Mrs. MADISON, was withdrawn by the Library Committee from the Department of State, and delivered to the publishers.

In the publication thus directed it has been deemed to be a primary and indispensable duty to follow the manuscript with scrupulous care. It was not thought proper to admit any note or comment, even explanatory; and all those that are found, were in the manuscript deposited in the Department of State. No alteration of any sort from the copy furnished and revised by Mrs. MADISON, has been permitted, except the correction of a few slight and evident clerical errors, and the insertion of some dates and formal parts of official documents, for which blanks had been left.

CONTENTS.

7

14   CONTENTS.

INTRODUCTION.

NOTE.—The following paper is copied from a rough draught in the handwriting of Mr. Madison. The particular place it was intended to occupy in his works is not designated; but as it traces the causes and steps which led to the meeting of the Convention of 1787, it seems properly to preface the acts of that body. The paper bears evidence, in the paragraph preceding its conclusion, that it was written at a late period of the life of its author, when the pressure of ill health, combined with his great age, in preventing a final revision of it.

As the weakness and wants of man naturally lead to an association of individuals under a common authority, whereby each may have the protection of the whole against danger from without, and enjoy in safety within the advantages of social intercourse, and an exchange of the necessaries and comforts of life; in like manner feeble communities, independent of each other, have resorted to a union, less intimate, but with common councils, for the common safety against powerful neighbours, and for the preservation of justice and peace among themselves. Ancient history furnishes examples of these confederate associations, though with a very imperfect account of their structure, and of the attributes and functions of the presiding authority. There are examples of modern date also, some of them still existing, the modifications and transactions of which are sufficiently known.

It remained for the British Colonies, now United States of North America, to add to those examples, one of a more interesting character than any of them; which led to a system without an example ancient or modern. A system founded on popular rights, and so combining a federal form with the forms of individual republics, as may enable each

29

to supply the defects of the other and obtain that advantage of both.

Whilst the Colonies enjoyed the protection of the parent country, as it was called, against foreign danger, and were secured by its superintending control against conflicts among themselves, they continued independent of each other, under a common, though limited, dependence on the parental authority. When, however, the growth of the offspring in strength and in wealth awakened the jealousy, and tempted the avidity of the parent, into schemes of usurpation and exaction, the obligation was felt by the former of uniting their counsels and efforts, to avert the impending calamity.

As early as the year 1754, indications having been given of a design in the British government to levy contributions on the Colonies without their consent, a meeting of Colonial deputies took place at Albany, which attempted to introduce a compromising substitute, that might at once satisfy the British requisitions, and save their own rights from violation. The attempt had no other effect, than, by bringing these rights into a more conspicuous view, to invigorate the attachment to them, on the one side; and to nourish the haughty and encroaching spirit on the other.

In 1774, the progress made by Great Britain in the open assertion of her pretensions, and the apprehended purpose of otherwise maintaining them by legislative enactments and declarations, had been such that the Colonies did not hesitate to assemble, by their deputies, in a formal Congress, authorized to oppose to the British innovations whatever measures might be found best adapted to the occasion; without, however, losing sight of an eventual reconciliation.

The dissuasive measures of that Congress being without effect another Congress was held in 1775, whose pacific efforts to bring about a change in the views of the other party being equally unavailing, and the commencement of actual hostilities having at length put an end to all hope of reconciliation, the Congress finding, moreover, that the popular voice began to call for an entire and perpetual dissolution of the political ties which had connected them with Great Britain, proceeded on the memorable Fourth of July, 1776, to declare the thirteen Colonies *Independent States.*

During the discussions of this solemn act, a Committee, consisting of a member from each Colony, had been appointed, to prepare and digest a form of Confederation for the future management of the common interests, which had hitherto been left to the discretion of Congress, guided by the exigencies of the contest, and by the known intentions or occasional instructions of the Colonial Legislatures.

It appears that as early as the twenty-first of July, 1775, a plan, entitled "Articles of Confederation and *perpetual* union of the Colonies," had been sketched by Doctor Franklin, the plan being on that day submitted by him to Congress; and though not copied into their Journals, remaining on their files in his handwriting. But notwithstanding the term "perpetual" observed in the title, the Articles provided expressly for the event of a return of the Colonies to a connection with Great Britain.

This sketch became a basis for the plan reported by the Committee on the twelfth of July, now also remaining on the files of Congress in the hand-writing of Mr. Dickinson. The plan, though dated after the Declaration of Independence, was probably drawn up before that event; since the name of Colonies, not States, is used throughout the draught. The plan reported was debated and amended from time to time, till the seventeenth of November, 1777, when it was agreed to by Congress, and proposed to the Legislatures of the States, with an explanatory and recommendatory letter. The ratifications of these, by their delegates in Congress, duly authorized, took place at successive dates; but were not completed till the first of March, 1781, when Maryland, who had made a prerequisite that the vacant lands acquired from the British Crown should be a common fund, yielded to the persuasion that a final and formal establishment of the Federal Union and Government would make a favorable impression, not only on other foreign nations, but on Great Britain herself.

The great difficulty experienced in so framing the Federal system, as to obtain the unanimity required for its due sanction, may be inferred from the long interval, and recurring discussions, between the commencement and completion of the work; from the changes made during its progress; from the language of Congress when proposing it to the States, which dwelt on the impracticability of devising a system acceptable to all of them; from the reluctant assent given by some; and the various alterations proposed by others; and by a tardiness in others again, which produced a special address to them from Congress, enforcing the duty of sacrificing local considerations and favorite opinions to the public safety, and the necessary harmony; nor was the assent of some of the States finally yielded without strong protests against particular Articles, and a reliance on future amendments removing their objections. It is to be recollected, no doubt, that these delays might be occasioned in some degree by an occupation of the public councils, both general and local, with the deliberations and measures essential to a voluntary struggle; but there must have been a balance for these causes in the obvious motives to hasten the establishment of a regular and efficient government; and in the tendency of the crisis to repress opinions and pretensions which might be inflexible in another state of things.

The principal difficulties which embarrassed the progress, and retarded the completion, of the plan of Confederation, may be traced to — first, the natural repugnance of the parties to a relinquishment of power; secondly, a natural jealousy of its abuse in other hands than their own; thirdly, the rule of suffrage among parties whose inequality in size did not correspond with that of their wealth, or of their military or free population; fourthly, the selection and definition of the powers, at once necessary to the federal head, and safe to the several members.

To these sources of difficulty, incident to the formation of all such confederacies, were added two others, one of a temporary, the other of a permanent nature. The first was the case of the Crown lands, so called because they had been held by the British Crown, and being ungranted to individuals when its authority ceased, were considered by the States within whose charters or asserted limits they lay, as devolving on them; whilst it was contended by the others, that being wrested from the dethroned authority by the equal exertions of all, they resulted of right and in equity to the benefit of all. The lands being of vast extent, and of growing value, were the occasion of much discussion and heart-burning; and proved the most obstinate of the impediments to an earlier consummation of the plan of federal government. The State of Maryland, the last that acceded to it, held out as already noticed, till the first of March, 1781; and then yielded only to the hope that, by giving a stable and authoritative character to the Confederation, a successful termination of the contest might be accelerated. The dispute was happily compromised by successive surrenders of portions of the territory by the States having exclusive claims to it, and acceptances of them by Congress.

The other source of dissatisfaction was the peculiar situation of some of the States, which, having no convenient ports for foreign commerce, were subject to be taxed by their neighbours, through whose ports their commerce was carried on. New Jersey, placed between Philadelphia and New York, was likened to a cask tapped at both ends; and North Carolina, between Virginia and South Carolina, to a patient bleeding at both arms. The Articles of Confederation provided no remedy for the complaint; which produced a strong protest on the part of New Jersey, and never ceased to be a source of dissatisfaction and discord, until the new Constitution superseded the old.

But the radical infirmity of the "Articles of Confederation" was the dependence of Congress on the voluntary and simultaneous compliance with its requisitions by so many independent communities, each consulting more or less its particular interests and convenience, and distrusting the compliance of the others.   Whilst the paper emissions of Congress continued to circulate, they were employed as a sinew of war, like gold and silver.   When that ceased to be the case, and the fatal defect of the political system was felt in its alarming force, the war was merely kept alive, and brought to a successful conclusion, by such foreign aids and temporary expedients as could be applied; a hope prevailing with many, and a wish with all, that a state of peace, and the sources of prosperity opened by it, would give to the Confederacy, in practice, the efficiency which had been inferred from its theory.

The close of the war, however, brought no cure for the public embarrassments.   The States, relieved from the pressure of foreign danger, and flushed with the enjoyment of independent and sovereign power, instead of a diminished disposition to part with it, persevered in omissions and in measures incompatible with their relations to the Federal Government, and with those among themselves.

Having served as a member of Congress through the period between March, 1780, and the arrival of peace, in 1783, I had become intimately acquainted with the public distresses and the causes of them.   I had observed the successful opposition to every attempt to procure a remedy by new grants of power to Congress.   I had found, moreover, that despair of success hung over the compromising principle of April, 1783, for the public necessities, which had been so elaborately planned and so impressively recommended to the States.   Sympathizing, under this aspect of affairs, in the alarm of the friends of free government at the threatened danger of an abortive result to the great, and perhaps last, experiment in its favor, I could not be insensible to the obligation to aid as far as I could in averting the calamity. With this view I acceded to the desire of my fellow citizens of the County, that I should be one of its representatives in the Legislature, hoping that I might there best contribute to inculcate the critical posture to which the Revolutionary cause was reduced, and the merit of a leading agency of the State in bringing about a rescue of the Union, and the blessings of liberty staked on it, from an impending catastrophe.

It required but little time after taking my seat in the House of Delegates in May, 1784, to discover, that, however favorable the general disposition of the State might be towards the Confederacy, the Legislature retained the aversion of its predecessors to transfers of power from the State to the Government of the Union; notwithstanding the urgent demands of the Federal Treasury, the glaring inadequacy of the authorized mode of supplying it, the rapid growth of anarchy in the Federal system, and the animosity kindled among the States by their conflicting regulations.

The temper of the Legislature, and the wayward course of its proceedings, may be gathered from the Journals of its sessions in the years 1784 and 1785.

The failure, however, of the varied propositions in the Legislature, for enlarging the powers of Congress; the continued failure of the efforts of Congress to obtain from them the means of providing for the debts of the Revolution, and of countervailing the commercial laws of Great Britain, a source of much irritation, and against which the separate efforts of the States were found worse than abortive; these considerations, with the lights thrown on the whole subject by the free and full discussion it had undergone, led to a general acquiescence in the Resolution passed on the twenty-first of January, 1786, which proposed and invited a meeting of Deputies from all the States, as follows:

" *Resolved*, that Edmund Randolph, James Madison, Jr., Walter Jones, St. George Tucker, and Meriwether Smith, Esquires, be appointed Commissioners, who, or any three of whom, shall meet such Commissioners as may be appointed in the other States of the Union, at a time and place to be agreed on, to take into consideration the trade of the United States; to examine the relative situations and trade of said States; to consider how far a uniform system in their commercial regulations may be necessary to their common interest and their permanent harmony; and to report to the several States such an act, relative to this great object, as, when unanimously ratified by them, will enable the United States in Congress, effectually to provide for the same."

The Resolution had been brought forward some weeks before, on a failure of a proposed grant of power to Congress to collect a revenue from commerce, which had been abandoned by its friends in consequence of material alterations made in the grant by a Committee of the Whole. The Resolution, though introduced by Mr. Tyler, an influential member,—who, having never served in Congress, had more the ear of the House than those whose services there exposed them to an imputable bias,—was so little acceptable, that it was not then persisted in. Being now revived by him, on the last day of the session, and being the alternative of adjourning without any effort for the crisis in the affairs of the Union, it obtained a general vote; less, however, with some of its friends, from a confidence in the success of the experiment, than from a hope that it might prove a step to a more comprehensive and adequate provision for the wants of the Confederacy.

It happened also, that Commissioners, appointed by Virginia and Maryland to settle the jurisdiction on waters dividing the two States, had, apart from their official reports, recommended a uniformity in the regulations of the two States on several subjects, and particularly on those having relation to foreign trade. It appeared at the same time, that Maryland had deemed a concurrence of her neighbours, Delaware and Pennsylvania, indispensable in such a case; who, for like reasons, would require that of their neighbours. So apt and forcible an illustration of the necessity of an uniformity throughout all the States could not but favor the passage of a resolution which proposed a Convention having that for its object.

The Commissioners appointed by the Legislature, and who attended the Convention, were Edmund Randolph, the Attorney of the State, St. George Tucker and James Madison. The designation of the time and place to be proposed for its meeting, and communicated to the States, having been left to the Commissioners, they named, for the time the first Monday in September, and for the place the city of Annapolis, avoiding the residence of Congress, and large commercial cities, as liable to suspicions of an extraneous influence.

Although the invited meeting appeared to be generally favored, five States only assembled; some failing to make appointments, and some of the individuals appointed not hastening their attendance; the result in both cases being ascribed mainly to a belief that the time had not arrived for such a political reform as might be expected from a further experience of its necessity.

But in the interval between the proposal of the Convention and the time of its meeting, such had been the advance of public opinion in the desired direction, stimulated as it had been by the effect of the contemplated object of the meeting, in turning the general attention to the critical state of things, and in calling forth the sentiments and exertions of the most enlightened and influential patriots, that the Convention, thin as it was, did not scruple to decline the limited task assigned to it, and to recommend to the States a Convention with powers adequate to the occasion. Nor had it been unnoticed that the commission of the New Jersey deputation had extended its object to a general provision for the exigencies of the Union. A recommendation for this enlarged purpose was accordingly reported by a committee to whom the subject had been referred. It was drafted by Col. Hamilton, and finally agreed to in the following form:

" To the Honorable, the Legislatures of Virginia, Delaware, Pennsylvania, New Jersey, and New York, the Commissioners from the said States, respectively, assembled at
Annapolis, humbly beg leave to report:

" That, pursuant to their several appointments, they met
at Annapolis, in the State of Maryland, on the eleventh day
of September instant; and having proceeded to a communication of their powers, they found that the States of New
York, Pennsylvania and Virginia, had, in substance, and
nearly in the same terms, authorized their respective Commissioners ' to meet such commissioners as were, or might
be, appointed by the other States of the Union, at such time
and place as should be agreed upon by the said Commissioners, to take into consideration the trade and commerce
of the United States; to consider how far an uniform system
in their commercial intercourse and regulations might be
necessary to their common interest and permanent harmony;
and to report to the several States such an act, relative
to this great object, as, when unanimously ratified by them,
would enable the United States in Congress assembled
effectually to provide for the same.'

"That the State of Delaware had given similar powers
to their Commissioners, with this difference only, that the
act to be framed in virtue of these powers is required to be
reported ' to the United States in Congress assembled, to be
agreed to by them, and confirmed by the Legislature of
every State.'

" That the State of New Jersey had enlarged the object
of their appointment, empowering their commissioners, ' to
consider how far an uniform system in their commercial
regulations, and *other important matters*, might be necessary
to the common interest and permanent harmony of the several States;' and to report such an act on the subject, as,
when ratified by them, ' would enable the United States in
Congress assembled effectually to provide for the exigencies
of the Union.'

" That appointments of Commissioners have also been

made by the States of New Hampshire, Massachusetts, Rhode Island, and North Carolina, none of whom, however, have attended; but that no information has been received by your Commissioners of any appointment having been made by the States of Maryland, Connecticut, South Carolina or Georgia.

"That the express terms of the powers to your Commissioners supposing a deputation from all the States, and having for object the trade and commerce of the United States, your Commissioners did not conceive it advisable to proceed on the business of their mission under the circumstances of so partial and defective a representation.

"Deeply impressed, however, with the magnitude and importance of the object confided to them on this occasion, your Commissioners cannot forbear to indulge an expression of their earnest and unanimous wish, that speedy measures may be taken to effect a general meeting of the States in a future Convention, for the same and such other purposes, as the situation of public affairs may be found to require.

"If, in expressing this wish, or in intimating any other sentiment, your Commissioners should seem to exceed the strict bounds of their appointment, they entertain a full confidence, that a conduct dictated by an anxiety for the welfare of the United States will not fail to receive an indulgent construction.

"In this persuasion, your Commissioners submit an opinion, that the idea of extending the powers of their Deputies to other objects than those of commerce, which has been adopted by the State of New Jersey, was an improvement on the original plan, and will deserve to be incorporated into that of a future Convention. They are the more naturally led to this conclusion, as, in the course of their reflections on the subject, they have been induced to think that the power of regulating trade is of such comprehensive extent, and will enter so far into the general system of the Federal Government, that to give it efficacy, and to obviate questions and doubts concerning its precise nature and limits, may require a correspondent adjustment of other parts of the Federal system.

"That there are important defects in the system of the Federal Government, is acknowledged by the acts of all those States which have concurred in the present meeting. That the defects, upon a closer examination, may be found greater and more numerous than even these acts imply, is at least so far probable, from the embarrassments which characterize the present state of our national affairs, foreign and domestic, as may reasonably be supposed to merit a deliberate and candid discussion, in some mode which will unite the sentiments and councils of all the States. In the choice of the mode, your Commissioners are of opinion, that a Convention of deputies from the different States, for the special and sole purpose of entering into this investigation, and digesting a plan for supplying such defects as may be discovered to exist, will be entitled to a preference, from considerations which will occur without being particularized.

"Your Commissioners decline an enumeration of those national circumstances on which their opinion, respecting the propriety of a future Convention with more enlarged powers, is founded ; as it would be an useless intrusion of facts and observations, most of which have been frequently the subject of public discussion, and none of which can have escaped the penetration of those to whom they would in this instance be addressed. They are, however, of a nature so serious, as, in the view of your Commissioners, to render the situation of the United States delicate and critical, calling for an exertion of the united virtue and wisdom of all the members of the Confederacy.

"Under this impression, your Commissioners, with the most respectful deference, beg leave to suggest their unanimous conviction, that it may essentially tend to advance the interests of the Union, if the States by whom they have been respectively delegated would themselves concur, and use their endeavours to procure the concurrence of the other States, in the appointment of Commissioners, to meet at

Philadelphia on the second Monday in May next, to take into consideration the situation of the United States ; to devise such further provisions as shall appear to them necessary to render the constitution of the Federal Government adequate to the exigencies of the Union ; and to report such an act for that purpose, to the United States in Congress assembled, as, when agreed to by them, and afterwards confirmed by the Legislatures of every State, will effectually provide for the same.

"Though your Commissioners could not with propriety address these observations and sentiments to any but the States they have the honor to represent, they have nevertheless concluded, from motives of respect, to transmit copies of this Report to the United States in Congress assembled, and to the Executives of the other States."

The recommendation was well received by the Legislature of Virginia, which happened to be the *first* that *acted* on it; and the example of her compliance was made as conciliatory and impressive as possible. The Legislature were unanimous, or very nearly so, on the occasion. As a proof of the magnitude and solemnity attached to it, they placed General Washington at the head of the deputation from the State; and as a proof of the deep interest he felt in the case, he overstepped the obstacles to his acceptance of the appointment.

The law complying with the recommendation from Annapolis was in the terms following:

"Whereas, the Commissioners who assembled at Annapolis, on the fourteenth day of September last, for the purpose of devising and reporting the means of enabling Congress to provide effectually for the commercial interests of the United States, have represented the necessity of extending the revision of the Federal system to all its defects; and have recommended that deputies for that purpose be appointed by the several Legislatures, to meet in Convention in the City of Philadelphia, on the second Monday of May next,—a provision which seems preferable to a discussion of the subject in Congress, where it might be too much interrupted by the ordinary business before them, and where it would, besides, be deprived of the valuable counsels of sundry individuals who are disqualified by the constitution or laws of particular States, or restrained by peculiar circumstances, from a seat in that Assembly:

"And whereas, the General Assembly of this Commonwealth, taking into view the actual situation of the Confederacy, as well as reflecting on the alarming representations made from time to time, by the United States in Congress, particularly in their act of the fifteenth day of February last, can no longer doubt that the crisis is arrived at which the good people of America are to decide the solemn question, whether they will, by wise and magnanimous efforts, reap the just fruits of that independence which they have so gloriously acquired, and of that union which they have cemented with so much of their common blood; or whether, by giving way to unmanly jealousies and prejudices, or to partial and transitory interests, they will renounce the auspicious blessings prepared for them by the Revolution, and furnish to its enemies an eventual triumph over those, by whose virtue and valour, it has been accomplished:

"And whereas, the same noble and extended policy, and the same fraternal and affectionate sentiments, which originally determined the citizens of this Commonwealth to unite with their brethren of the other States, in establishing a federal government, cannot but be felt with equal force now, as motives to lay aside every inferior consideration, and to concur in such farther concessions and provisions, as may be necessary to secure the great objects for which that government was instituted, and to render the United States as happy in peace, as they have been glorious in war.

"Be it, therefore, enacted, by the General Assembly of the Commonwealth of Virginia, That seven Commissioners be appointed by joint ballot of both Houses of Assembly, who, or any three of them, are hereby authorized as Deputies from this Commonwealth, to meet such Deputies as may be appointed and authorized by other States, to assemble in Convention at Philadelphia, as above recommended, and to join with them in devising and discussing all such alterations and farther provisions, as may be necessary to render the Federal Constitution adequate to the exigencies of the Union; and in reporting such an act for that purpose, to the United States in Congress, as when agreed to by them, and duly confirmed by the several States, will effectually provide for the same.

"And be it further enacted, That in case of the death of any of the said deputies, or of their declining their appointments, the Executive are hereby authorized to supply such vacancies; and the Governor is requested to transmit forthwith a copy of this act to the United States in Congress, and to the Executives of each of the States in the Union." *

A resort to a General Convention, to re-model the Confederacy, was not a new idea. It had entered at an early date into the conversations and speculations of the most reflecting and foreseeing observers of the inadequacy of the powers allowed to Congress. In a pamphlet published in May, 1781, at the seat of Congress, Pelatiah Webster, an able though not conspicuous citizen, after discussing the fiscal system of the United States, and suggesting, among other remedial provisions, one including a national bank, remarks, that "the authority of Congress at present is very inadequate to the performance of their duties; and this indicates the necessity of their calling a *Continental Convention* for the express purpose of ascertaining, defining, enlarging and limiting, the duties and powers of their Constitution."

On the first day of April, 1783, Colonel Hamilton, in a debate in Congress, observed, "that he wished, instead of

---

* Drawn by J. Madison, passed the House of Delegates November 9th, the Senate November 23d — and Deputies appointed December 4th, 1786.

them (partial Conventions), to see a general Convention take place ; and that he should soon, in pursuance of instructions from his constituents, propose to Congress a plan for that purpose, the object of which would be to strengthen the Federal Constitution." · He alluded probably, to the resolutions introduced by General Schuyler in the Senate, and passed unanimously by the Legislature of New York in the summer of 1782, declaring, that the Confederation was defective, in not giving Congress power to provide a revenue for itself, or in not investing them with funds from established and productive sources ; and that it would be advisable for Congress to recommend to the States to call a general Convention to revise and amend the Confederation." It does not appear, however, that his expectation had been fulfilled.

In a letter to James Madison from R. H. Lee, then President of Congress, dated the twenty-sixth of November, 1784, he says : "It is by many here suggested as a very necessary step for Congress to take, the calling on the States to form a Convention for the sole purpose of revising the Confederation, so far as to enable Congress to execute with more energy, effect and vigor the powers assigned to it, than it appears by experience that they can do under the present state of things." The answer of Mr. Madison remarks : "I hold it for a maxim, that the union of the States is essential to their safety against foreign danger and internal contention ; and that the perpetuity and efficacy of the present system cannot be confided in. The question, therefore, is, in what mode, and at what moment, the experiment for supplying the defects ought to be made."

In the winter of 1784–5, Noah Webster, whose political and other valuable writings had made him known to the public, proposed, in one of his publications, "a new system of government which should act, not on the States, but directly on individuals, and vest in Congress full power to carry its laws into effect."

The proposed and expected Convention at Annapolis, the first of a general character that appears to have been realized, and the state of the public mind awakened by it, had attracted the particular attention of Congress, and favored the idea there of a Convention with fuller power for amending the Confederacy.*

It does not appear that in any of these cases the reformed system was to be otherwise sanctioned than by the Legislative authority of the States; nor whether, nor how far, a change was to be made in the structure of the depository of Federal powers.

The act of Virginia providing for the Convention at Philadelphia was succeeded by appointments from the other States as their Legislatures were assembled, the appointments being selections from the most experienced and highest standing citizens. Rhode Island was the only exception to a compliance with the recommendation from Annapolis, well known to have been swayed by an obdurate adherence to an advantage which her position gave her, of taxing her neighbours through their consumption of imported supplies, an advantage which it was foreseen would be taken from her by a revisal of the Articles of Confederation.

As the public mind had been ripened for a salutary reform of the political system, in the interval between the proposal and the meeting of the Commissioners at Annapolis, the interval between the last event and the meeting of deputies at Philadelphia had continued to develope more and more the necessity and the extent of a systematic provision for the preservation and government of the Union. Among the ripening incidents was the insurrection of Shays, in Massachusetts, against her government; which was with difficulty suppressed, notwithstanding the influence on the insurgents of an apprehended interposition of the Federal troops.

---

* The letters of Wm. Grayson, March 22, 1786, and of James Monroe, of April 28th, 1786, both then members, to Mr. Madison, state that a proposition for such a Convention had been made.

At the date of the Convention, the aspect and retrospect of the political condition of the United States could not but fill the public mind with a gloom which was relieved only by a hope that so select a body would devise an adequate remedy for the existing and prospective evils so impressively demanding it.

It was seen that the public debt, rendered so sacred by the cause in which it had been incurred, remained without any provision for its payment. The reiterated and elaborate efforts of Congress to procure from the States a more adequate power to raise the means of payment, had failed. The effect of the ordinary requisitions of Congress had only displayed the inefficiency of the authority making them, none of the States having duly complied with them, some having failed altogether, or nearly so; while in one instance, that of New Jersey,* a compliance was *expressly* refused; nor was more yielded to the expostulations of members of Congress deputed to her Legislature, than a mere repeal of the law, without a compliance. The want of authority in Congress to regulate commerce had produced in foreign nations, particularly Great Britain, a monopolizing policy, injurious to the trade of the United States, and destructive to their navigation; the imbecility, and anticipated dissolution, of the Confederacy extinguishing all apprehensions of a countervailing policy on the part of the United States. The same want of a general power over commerce led to an exercise of the power, separately, by the States, which not only proved abortive, but engendered rival, conflicting and angry regulations. Besides the vain attempts to supply their respective treasuries by imposts, which turned their commerce into the neighbouring ports, and to coerce a relaxation of the British monopoly of the West India navigation, which was attempted by Virginia,† the States having ports for foreign commerce, taxed and

---

* A letter of Mr. Grayson to Mr. Madison of March 22, 1786, relating the conduct of New Jersey, states this fact.

† See the Journal of her Legislature.

irritated the adjoining States, trading through them, as New York, Pennsylvania, Virginia, and South Carolina. Some of the States, as Connecticut, taxed imports from others, as from Massachusetts, which complained in a letter to the Executive of Virginia, and doubtless to those of other States. In sundry instances, as of New York, New Jersey, Pennsylvania and Maryland, the navigation laws treated the citizens of other States as aliens. In certain cases the authority of the Confederacy was disregarded, as in violation, not only of the Treaty of Peace, but of treaties with France and Holland; which were complained of to Congress. In other cases the Federal authority was violated by treaties and war with Indians, as by Georgia; by troops raised and kept up without the consent of Congress, as by Massachusetts; by compacts without the consent of Congress, as between Pennsylvania and New Jersey, and between Virginia and Maryland. From the Legislative Journals of Virginia it appears, that a vote refusing to apply for a sanction of Congress was followed by a vote against the communication of the compact to Congress. In the internal administration of the States, a violation of contracts had become familiar, in the form of depreciated paper made a legal tender, of property substituted for money, of instalment laws, and of the occlusions of the courts of justice, although evident that all such interferences affected the rights of other States, relatively creditors, as well as citizens creditors within the State. Among the defects which had been severely felt was want of an uniformity in cases requiring it, as laws of naturalization and bankruptcy, a coercive authority operating on individuals, and a guarantee of the internal tranquillity of the States.

As a natural consequence of this distracted and disheartening condition of the Union, the Federal authority had ceased to be respected abroad, and dispositions were shown there, particularly in Great Britain, to take advantage of its imbecility, and to speculate on its approaching downfall. At home it had lost all confidence and credit;

the unstable and unjust career of the States had also for-
feited the respect and confidence essential to order and
good government, involving a general decay of confidence
and credit between man and man.   It was found, moreover,
that those least partial to popular government, or most dis-
trustful of its efficacy, were yielding to anticipations, that
from an increase of the confusion a government might result more congenial with their taste or their opinions; whilst
those most devoted to the principles and forms of Republics
were alarmed for the cause of liberty itself, at stake in the
American experiment, and anxious for a system that would
avoid the inefficacy of a mere confederacy, without passing
into the opposite extreme of a consolidated government.
It was known that there were individuals who had betrayed
a bias towards monarchy, and there had always been some
not unfavorable to a partition of the Union into several
confederacies; either from a better chance of figuring on a
sectional theatre, or that the sections would require stronger
governments, or by their hostile conflicts lead to a monarchical consolidation.   The idea of dismemberment had
recently made its appearance in the newspapers.

Such were the defects, the deformities, the diseases and
the ominous prospects, for which the Convention were to
provide a remedy, and which ought never to be overlooked
in expounding and appreciating the constitutional charter,
the remedy that was provided.

As a sketch on paper, the earliest, perhaps, of a Constitutional Government for the Union (organized into the regular departments, with physical means operating on individuals) to be sanctioned by *the people of the States*, acting
in their original and sovereign character, was contained in
the letters of James Madison to Thomas Jefferson of the
nineteenth of March; to Governor Randolph of the eighth
of April; and to General Washington of the sixteenth of
April, 1787, for which see their respective dates.

The feature, in these letters which vested in the general
authority a negative on the laws of the States, was sug-

gested by the negative in the head of the British Empire, which prevented collisions between the parts and the whole, and between the parts themselves. It was supposed that the substitution of an elective and responsible authority, for an hereditary and irresponsible one, would avoid the appearance even of a departure from Republicanism. But although the subject was so viewed in the Convention, and the votes on it were more than once equally divided, it was finally and justly abandoned, as, apart from other objections, it was not practicable among so many States, increasing in number, and enacting, each of them, so many laws. Instead of the proposed negative, the objects of it were left as finally provided for in the Constitution.

On the arrival of the Virginia Deputies at Philadelphia, it occurred to them, that, from the early and prominent part taken by that State in bringing about the Convention, some initiative step might be expected from them. The Resolutions introduced by Governer Randolph were the result of consultation on the subject, with an understanding that they left all the Deputies entirely open to the lights of discussion, and free to concur in any alterations or modifications which their reflections and judgments might approve. The Resolutions, as the Journals show, became the basis on which the proceedings of the Convention commenced, and to the developements, variations and modifications of which the plan of government proposed by the Convention may be traced.

The curiosity I had felt during my researches into the history of the most distinguished confederacies, particularly those of antiquity, and the deficiency I found in the means of satisfying it, more especially in what related to the process, the principles, the reasons, and the anticipations, which prevailed in the formation of them, determined me to preserve, as far I could, an exact account of what might pass in the Convention while executing its trust; with the magnitude of which I was duly impressed, as I was by the gratification promised to future curiosity by an authentic

4

exhibition of the objects, the opinions, and the reasonings, from which the system of government was to receive its peculiar structure and organization. Nor was I unaware of the value of such a contribution to the fund of materials for the history of a Constitution on which would be staked the happiness of a people great even in its infancy, and possibly the cause of liberty throughout the world.

In pursuance of the task I had assumed, I chose a seat in front of the presiding member, with the other members on my right and left hands. In this favorable position for hearing all that passed, I noted, in terms legible and in abbreviations and marks intelligible to myself, what was read from the Chair or spoken by the members; and losing not a moment unnecessarily between the adjournment and reassembling of the Convention, I was enabled to write out my daily notes during the session, or within a few finishing days after its close, in the extent and form preserved in my own hand on my files.

In the labor and correctness of this I was not a little aided by practice, and by a familiarity with the style and the train of observation and reasoning which characterized the principal speakers. It happened, also, that I was not absent a single day, nor more than a casual fraction of an hour in any day, so that I could not have lost a single speech, unless a very short one.

It may be proper to remark, that, with a very few exceptions, the speeches were neither furnished, nor revised, nor sanctioned, by the speakers, but written out from my notes, aided by the freshness of my recollections. A further remark may be proper, that views of the subject might occasionally be presented, in the speeches and proceedings, with a latent reference to a compromise on some middle ground, by mutual concessions. The exceptions alluded to were,— first, the sketch furnished by Mr. Randolph of his speech on the introduction of his propositions on the 29th day of May ; secondly, the speech of Mr. Hamilton, who happened to call on me when putting the last hand to it, and who acknowledged its fidelity, without suggesting more than a very few verbal alterations which were made ; thirdly, the speech of Gouverneur Morris on the second day of May,* which was communicated to him on a like occasion, and who acquiesced in it without even a verbal change. The correctness of his language and the distinctness of his enunciation were particularly favorable to a reporter. The speeches of Doctor Franklin, excepting a few brief ones, were copied from the written ones read to the Convention by his colleague, Mr. Wilson, it being inconvenient to the Doctor to remain long on his feet.

Of the ability and intelligence of those who composed the Convention the debates and proceedings may be a test ; as the character of the work which was the offspring of their deliberations must be tested by the experience of the future, added to that of nearly half a century which has passed.

But whatever may be the judgment pronounced on the competency of the architects of the Constitution, or whatever may be the destiny of the edifice prepared by them, I feel it a duty to express my profound and solemn conviction, derived from my intimate opportunity of observing and appreciating the views of the Convention, collectively and individually, that there never was an assembly of men, charged with a great and arduous trust, who were more pure in their motives, or more exclusively or anxiously devoted to the object committed to them, than were the members of the Federal Convention of 1787, to the object of devising and proposing a constitutional system which should best supply the defects of that which it was to replace, and best secure the permanent liberty and happiness of their country.

---

* It reads thus in original copy, but probably refers to July 2nd. (Pub. Note.)

DEBATES

FEDERAL CONVENTION OF 1787.

MONDAY, MAY 14TH, 1787,

Was the day fixed for the meeting of the Deputies in Convention, for revising the federal system of government. On that day a small number only had assembled. Seven States were not convened till,

FRIDAY, MAY 25TH.

When the following members appeared:
From

MASSACHUSETTS,	Rufus King.
NEW YORK,	Robert Yates, and
	Alexander Hamilton.
NEW JERSEY,	David Brearly,
	William Churchill Houston, **and**
	William Patterson.
PENNSYLVANIA,	Robert Morris,
	Thomas Fitzsimons,
	James Wilson, and
	Gouverneur Morris.
DELAWARE,	George Read,
	Richard Basset, and
	Jacob Broom.
VIRGINIA,	George Washington,
	Edmund Randolph,
	John Blair,
	James Madison,

                    George Mason,
                    George Wythe, and
                    James McClurg.
NORTH CAROLINA,   Alexander Martin,
                    William Richardson Davie,
                    Richard Dobbs Spaight, and
                    Hugh Williamson.
SOUTH CAROLINA,   John Rutledge,
                    Charles Cotesworth Pinckney,
                    Charles Pinckney, and
                    Pierce Butler.
GEORGIA,   William Few.

Mr. ROBERT MORRIS informed the members assembled, that, by the instruction and in behalf of the deputation of Pennsylvania, he proposed GEORGE WASHINGTON, Esquire, late Commander-in-Chief, for President of the Convention.* Mr. JOHN RUTLEDGE seconded the motion, expressing his confidence that the choice would be unanimous; and observing, that the presence of General WASHINGTON forbade any observations on the occasion which might otherwise be proper.

General WASHINGTON was accordingly unanimously elected by ballot, and conducted to the Chair by Mr. R. MORRIS and Mr. RUTLEDGE; from which, in a very emphatic manner, he thanked the Convention for the honor they had conferred on him; reminded them of the novelty of the scene of business in which he was to act, lamented his want of better qualifications, and claimed the indulgence of the House towards the involuntary errors which his inexperience might occasion.

Mr. WILSON moved that a Secretary be appointed, and nominated Mr. Temple Franklin.

Colonel HAMILTON nominated Major Jackson. On the

---

*The nomination came with particular grace from Pennsylvania, as Doctor Franklin alone could have been thought of as a competitor. The Doctor was himself to have made the nomination of General Washington, but the state of the weather and of his health confined him to his house.

ballot Major Jackson had five votes, and Mr. Franklin two votes.

On reading the credentials of the Deputies, it was noticed that those from Delaware were prohibited from changing the Article in the Confederation establishing an equality of votes among the States.

The appointment of a Committee, on the motion of Mr. C. PINCKNEY, consisting of Messrs. WYTHE, HAMILTON, and C. PINCKNEY, to prepare standing rules and orders, was the only remaining step taken on this day.

MONDAY, MAY 28TH.

In Convention,—From Massachusetts, NATHANIEL GORHAM and CALEB STRONG ; from Connecticut, OLIVER ELLSWORTH ; from Delaware, GUNNING BEDFORD ; from Maryland, JAMES MCHENRY ; from Pennsylvania, BENJAMIN FRANKLIN, GEORGE CLYMER, THOMAS MIFFLIN, and JARED INGERSOLL,—took their seats.

Mr. WYTHE, from the Committee for preparing rules, made a report, which employed the deliberations of this day.

Mr. KING objected to one of the rules in the report authorizing any member to call for the Yeas and Nays and have them entered on the minutes. He urged, that as the acts of the Convention were not to bind the constituents, it was unnecessary to exhibit this evidence of the votes ; and improper, as changes of opinion would be frequent in the course of the business, and would fill the minutes with contradictions.

Colonel MASON seconded the objection, adding, that such a record of the opinions of members would be an obstacle to a change of them on conviction ; and in case of its being hereafter promulged, must furnish handles to the adversaries of the result of the meeting.

The proposed rule was rejected, *nem. con.* The standing rules agreed to were as follows :

RULES.

" A House to do business shall consist of the Deputies of not less than seven States ; and all questions shall be decided by the greater number of these which shall be fully represented. But a less number than seven may adjourn from day to day.

"Immediately after the President shall have taken the Chair, and the members their seats, the minutes of the preceding day shall be read by the Secretary.

" Every member, rising to speak, shall address the President ; and, whilst he shall be speaking, none shall pass between them, or hold discourse with another, or read a book, pamphlet, or paper, printed or manuscript. And of two members rising to speak at the same time, the President shall name him who shall be first heard.

" A member shall not speak oftener than twice, without special leave, upon the same question; and not the second time, before every other who had been silent shall have been heard, if he choose to speak upon the subject.

" A motion, made and seconded, shall be repeated, and, if written, as it shall be when any member shall so require, read aloud, by the Secretary, before it shall be debated; and may be withdrawn at any time before the vote upon it shall have been declared.

" Orders of the day shall be read next after the minutes; and either discussed or postponed, before any other business shall be introduced.

" When a debate shall arise upon a question, no motion, other than to amend the question, to commit it, or to postpone the debate, shall be received.

" A question which is complicated shall, at the request of any member, be divided, and put separately upon the propositions of which it is compounded.

" The determination of a question, although fully debated, shall be postponed, if the Deputies of any State desire it, until the next day.

" A writing which contains any matter brought on to be considered shall be read once throughout, for information; then by paragraphs, to be debated; and again, with the amendments, if any, made on the second reading; and afterwards the question shall be put upon the whole, amended, or approved in its original form, as the case shall be.

" Committees shall be appointed by ballot; and the members who have the greatest number of ballots, although not a majority of the votes present, shall be the Committee. When two or more members have an equal number of votes, the member standing first on the list, in the order of taking down the ballots, shall be preferred.

" A member may be called to order by any other member, as well as by the President; and may be allowed to explain his conduct, or expressions supposed to be reprehensible. And all questions of order shall be decided by the President, without appeal or debate.

" Upon a question to adjourn, for the day, which may be made at any time, if it be seconded, the question shall be put without a debate.

" When the House shall adjourn, every member shall stand in his place until the President pass him."*

A letter from sundry persons of the State of Rhode Island, addressed to the Chairman of the General Convention, was presented to the Chair by Mr GOUVERNEUR MORRIS; and, being read, was ordered to lie on the table for further consideration.

---

* Previous to the arrival of a majority of the States, the rule by which they ought to vote in the Convention had been made a subject of conversation among the members present. It was pressed by Gouverneur Morris, and favored by Robert Morris and others from Pennsylvania, that the large States should unite in firmly refusing to the small States an equal vote, as unreasonable, and as enabling the small States to negative every good system of government, which must, in the nature of things, be founded on a violation of that equality. The members from Virginia, conceiving that such an attempt might beget fatal altercations between the large and small States; and that it would be easier to prevail on the latter, in the course of the deliberations, to give up their equality for the sake of an effective government, than on taking the field of discussion, to disarm themselves of the right, and thereby throw themselves on the mercy of the larger States, discountenanced and stifled the project.

Mr. BUTLER moved that the House provide against interruption of business by absence of members, and against licentious publications of their proceedings. To which was added, by Mr. SPAIGHT, a motion to provide, that, on the one hand, the House might not be precluded by a vote upon any question from revising the subject matter of it, when they see cause, nor, on the other hand, be led too hastily to rescind a decision which was the result of mature discussion. Whereupon it was ordered, that these motions be referred for the consideration of the Committee appointed to draw up the standing rules, and that the Committee make report thereon.

Adjourned till to-morrow, at ten o'clock.

TUESDAY, MAY 29TH.

In Convention,— JOHN DICKINSON, and ELBRIDGE GERRY, the former from Delaware, the latter from Massachusetts, took their seats. The following rules were added, on the Report of Mr. WYTHE, from the Committee —

"That no member be absent from the House, so as to interrupt the representation of the State, without leave.

"That Committees do not sit whilst the House shall be, or ought to be, sitting.

"That no copy be taken of any entry on the Journal during the sitting of the House, without leave of the House.

"That members only be permitted to inspect the Journal.

"That nothing spoken in the House be printed, or otherwise published, or communicated without leave.

"That a motion to reconsider a matter which has been determined by a majority, may be made, with leave, unanimously given, on the same day on which the vote passed; but otherwise, not without one day's previous notice; in which last case, if the House agree to the reconsideration, some future day shall be assigned for that purpose."

Mr. C. PINCKNEY moved, that a Committee be appointed to superintend the minutes.

Mr. G. MORRIS objected to it. The entry of the proceedings of the Convention belonged to the Secretary as their impartial officer. A Committee might have an interest and bias in moulding the entry, according to their opinions and wishes.

The motion was negatived, five Noes, four Ayes.

Mr. RANDOLPH then opened the main business:—

He expressed his regret, that it should fall to him, rather than those who were of longer standing in life and political experience, to open the great subject of their mission. But as the Convention had originated from Virginia, and his colleagues supposed that some proposition was expected from them, they had imposed the task on him.

He then commented on the difficulty of the crisis, and the necessity of preventing the fulfilment of the prophecies of the American downfall.

He observed, that, in revising the Federal system we ought to inquire, first, into the properties which such a government ought to possess; secondly, the defects of the Confederation; thirdly the danger of our situation; and fourthly, the remedy.

1. The character of such a government ought to secure, first, against foreign invasion; secondly, against dissensions between members of the Union, or seditions in particular States; thirdly, to procure to the several States various blessings of which an isolated situation was incapable; fourthly, it should be able to defend itself against encroachment; and fifthly, to be paramount to the State Constitutions.

2. In speaking of the defects of the Confederation, he professed a high respect for its authors, and considered them as having done all that patriots could do, in the then infancy of the science of constitutions, and of confederacies; when the inefficiency of requisitions was unknown — no commercial discord had arisen among any States — no

rebellion had appeared, as in Massachusetts — foreign debts had not become urgent — the havoc of paper-money had not been foreseen — treaties had not been violated — and perhaps nothing better could be obtained, from the jealousy of the States with regard to their sovereignty.

He then proceeded to enumerate the defects:—First, that the Confederation produced no security against foreign invasion; Congress not being permitted to prevent a war, nor to support it by their own authority. Of this he cited many examples; most of which tended to shew, that they could not cause infractions of treaties, or of the law of nations to be punished; that particular States might by their conduct provoke war without control; and that, neither militia nor drafts being fit for defence on such occasions, enlistments only could be successful, and these could not be executed without money.

Secondly, that the Federal Government could not check the quarrel between the States, nor a rebellion in any, not having constitutional power nor means to impose according to the exigency.

Thirdly, that there were many advantages which the United States might acquire, which were not attainable under the Confederation — such as a productive impost — counteraction of the commercial regulations of other nations — pushing of commerce *ad libitum*, &c., &c.

Fourthly, that the Federal Government could not defend itself against encroachments from the States.

Fifthly, that it was not even paramount to the State Constitutions, ratified as it was in many of the States.

3. He next reviewed the danger of our situation and appealed to the sense of the best friends of the United States — to the prospect of anarchy from the laxity of government every where — and to other considerations.

4. He then proceeded to the remedy ; the basis of which he said must be the republican principle.

He proposed, as conformable to his ideas, the following resolutions, which he explained one by one.

1. " Resolved, that the Articles of Confederation ought
to be so corrected and enlarged as to accomplish the objects
proposed by their institution ; namely, " common defence,
security of liberty, and general warfare."

2. " Resolved, therefore, that the rights of suffrage in
the National Legislature ought to be proportioned to the
quotas of contribution, or to the number of free inhabitants,
as the one or the other rule may seem best in different
cases.

3. " Resolved, that the National Legislature ought to
consist of two branches.

4. " Resolved, that the members of the first branch of
the National Legislature ought to be elected by the people
of the several States every ——— for the term of ——— ;
to be of the age of —— years at least ; to receive liberal
stipends by which they may be compensated for the devotion
of their time to the public service ; to be ineligible to any
office established by a particular State, or under the
authority of the United States, except those peculiarly
belong to the functions of the first branch, during the term
of service, and for the space of ——— after its expiration ;
to be incapable of re-election for the space of ——— after
the expiration of their term of service, and to be subject to
recall.

5. " Resolved, that the members of the second branch
of the National Legislature ought to be elected by those of
the first, out of a proper number of persons nominated by
the individual Legislatures, to be of the age of —— years
at least ; to hold their offices for a term sufficient to
ensure their independency ; to receive liberal stipends,
by which they may be compensated for the devotion of
their time to the public service ; and to be ineligible to
any office established by a particular State, or under the
authority of the United States, except those peculiarly
belonging to the functions of the second branch, during
the term of service ; and for the space of ——— after the
expiration thereof.

6. "Resolved, that each branch ought to possess the right of originating acts ; that the National Legislature ought to be empowered to enjoy the legislative rights vested in Congress by the Confederation, and moreover to legislate in all cases to which the separate States are incompetent, or in which the harmony of the United States may be interrupted by the exercise of individual legislation ; to negative all laws passed by the several States contravening, in the opinion of the National Legislature, the Articles of Union, or any treaty subsisting under the authority of the Union ; and to call forth the force of the Union against any member of the Union failing to fulfil its duty under the Articles thereof.

7. "Resolved, that a National Executive be instituted ; to be chosen by the National Legislature for the term of ——— ; to receive punctually, at stated times, a fixed compensation for the services rendered, in which no increase nor diminution shall be made, so as to affect the magistracy existing at the time of increase or diminution ; and to be ineligible a second time ; and that, besides a general authority to execute the national laws, it ought to enjoy the executive rights vested in Congress by the Confederation.

8. "Resolved, that the Executive, and a convenient number of the national Judiciary, ought to compose a Council of Revision, with authority to examine every act of the National Legislature, before it shall operate, and every act of a particular Legislature before a negative thereon shall be final; and that the dissent of the said Council shall amount to a rejection, unless the act of the National Legislature be again passed, or that of a particular Legislature be again negatived by ——— of the members of each branch.

9. "Resolved, that a National Judiciary be established; to consist of one or more supreme tribunals, and of inferior tribunals to be chosen by the National Legislature; to hold their offices during good behaviour, and to receive punctually, at stated times, fixed compensation for their services,

in which no increase or diminution shall be made, so as to affect the persons actually in office at the same time of such increase or diminution. That the jurisdiction of the inferior tribunals shall be to hear and determine, in the first instance, and of the supreme tribunal to hear and determine, in the dernier resort, all piracies and felonies on the high seas; captures from an enemy; cases in which foreigners, or citizens of other States, applying to such jurisdictions, may be interested; or which respect the collection of the national revenue; impeachments of any national officers, and questions which may involve the national peace and harmony.

10. "Resolved, that provision ought to be made for the admission of States lawfully arising within the limits of the United States, whether from a voluntary junction of government and territory, or otherwise, with the consent of a number of voices in the National Legislature less than the whole.

11. "Resolved, that a republican government, and the territory of each State, except in the instance of a voluntary junction of government and territory, ought to be guaranteed by the United States to each State.

12. "Resolved, that provision ought to be made for the continuance of Congress and their authorities and privileges, until a given day after the reform of the Articles of Union shall be adopted, and for the completion of all their engagements.

13. "Resolved, that provision ought to be made for the amendment of the Articles of Union, whensoever it shall seem necessary; and that the assent of the National Legislature ought not to be required thereto.

14. "Resolved, that the legislative, executive, and judiciary powers, within the several States ought to be bound by oath to support the Articles of Union.

15. "Resolved, that the amendments which shall be offered to the Confederation, by the Convention, ought, at a proper time or times, after the approbation of Congress, to

be submitted to an assembly or assemblies of representatives, recommended by the several Legislatures, to be expressly chosen by the people to consider and decide thereon.''

He concluded with an exhortation, not to suffer the present opportunity of establishing general peace, harmony, happiness and liberty in the United States to pass away unimproved.*

It was then resolved, that the House will to-morrow resolve itself into a Committee of the Whole House, to consider of the state of the American Union; and that the propositions moved by Mr. RANDOLPH be referred to the said Committee.

Mr. CHARLES PINCKNEY laid before the House the draft of a federal government which he had prepared, to be agreed upon between the free and independent States of America:

PLAN OF A FEDERAL CONSTITUTION.

We, the people of the States of New Hampshire, Massachusetts, Rhode Island and Providence Plantations, Connecticut, New York, New Jersey, Pennsylvania, Delaware, Maryland, Virginia, North Carolina, South Carolina, and Georgia, do ordain, declare, and establish the following Constitution, for the government of ourselves and posterity.

ARTICLE I.

"The style of this government shall be, The United States of America, and the government shall consist of supreme legislative, executive and judicial powers.

ARTICLE II.

"The legislative power shall be vested in a Congress, to consist of two separate Houses; one to be called the House of Delegates; and the other the Senate, who shall meet on the ———— day of ———— in every year.

---

* This abstract of the speech was furnished to James Madison by Mr. Randolph, and is in his hand-writing.

Article III.

" The members of the House of Delegates shall be chosen every ———— year by the people of the several States; and the qualification of the electors shall be the same as those of the electors in the several States for their Legislatures. Each member shall have been a citizen of the United States for ———— years; and shall be of ———— years of age, and a resident in the State he is chosen for. Until a census of the people shall be taken in the manner hereinafter mentioned, the House of Delegates shall consist of ———— ————, to be chosen from the different States in the following proportions : for New Hampshire, ————; for Massachusetts, ————; for Rhode Island, ————; for Connecticut, ————; for New York, ————; for New Jersey, ————; for Pennsylvania, ————; for Delaware, ————; for Maryland, ————; for Virginia, ————; for North Carolina, ————; for South Carolina ————; for Georgia, ————; and the Legislature shall hereinafter regulate the number of Delegates by the number of inhabitants, according to the provisions hereinafter made, at the rate of one for every ———— thousand. All money bills of every kind shall originate in the House of Delegates, and shall not be altered by the Senate. The House of Delegates shall exclusively possess the power of impeachment, and shall choose its own officers; and vacancies therein shall be supplied by the executive authority of the State in the representation from which they shall happen.

Article IV.

" The Senate shall be elected and chosen by the House of Delegates; which House, immediately after their meeting, shall choose by ballot ———— Senators from among the citizens and residents of New Hampshire; ———— from among those of Massachusetts; ———— from among those of Rhode Island; ———— from among those of Connecticut; ———— from among those of New York; ———— from among those of New Jersey; ———— from among

those of Pennsylvania; ——— from among those of Delaware; ——— from among those of Maryland; ———
from among those of Virginia; ——— from among those
of North Carolina; ——— from among those of South
Carolina; and ——— from among those of Georgia.
The senators chosen from New Hampshire, Massachusetts,
Rhode Island, and Connecticut, shall form one class; those
from New York, New Jersey, Pennsylvania, and Delaware,
one class; and those from Maryland, Virginia, North Carolina, South Carolina, and Georgia, one class. The House
of Delegates shall number these classes one, two, and three;
and fix the times of their service by lot. The first class
shall serve for ——— years; the second for ——— years;
and the third for ——— years. As their times of service
expire, the House of Delegates shall fill them up by
elections for ——— years; and they shall fill all vacancies
that arise from death or resignation, for the time of service
remaining of the members so dying or resigning. Each
Senator shall be ——— years of age at least; and shall
have been a citizen of the United States for four years
before his election; and shall be a resident of the State he
is chosen from. The Senate shall choose its own officers.

ARTICLE V.

" Each State shall prescribe the time and manner of
holding elections by the people for the House of Delegates;
and the House of Delegates shall be the judges of the
elections, returns, and qualifications of their members.

" In each House a majority shall constitute a quorum
to do business. Freedom of speech and debate in the
Legislature shall not be impeached, or questioned, in any
place out of it; and the members of both Houses shall in
all cases, except for treason, felony, or breach of the peace,
be free from arrest during their attendance on Congress,
and in going to and returning from it. Both Houses shall
keep Journals of their proceedings, and publish them, except on secret occasions; and the Yeas and Nays may be

entered thereon at the desire of one ———— of the members present.   Neither House, without the consent of the other, shall adjourn for more than ———— days, nor to any place but where they are sitting.

"The members of each House shall not be eligible to, or capable of holding, any office under the Union, during the time for which they have been respectively elected; nor the members of the Senate for one year after.   The members of each House shall be paid for their services by the States which they represent.   Every bill which shall have passed the Legislature shall be presented to the President of the United States for his revision; if he approves it, he shall sign it; but if he does not approve it, he shall return it, with his objections, to the House it originated in; which House, if two-thirds of the members present, notwithstanding the President's objections, agree to pass it, shall send it to the other House, with the President's objections; where if two-thirds of the members present also agree to pass it, the same shall become a law; and all bills sent to the President, and not returned by him within ———— days, shall be laws, unless the Legislature, by their adjournment, prevent their return; in which case they shall not be laws.

ARTICLE VI.

"The Legislature of the United States shall have the power to lay and collect taxes, duties, imposts, and excises;

To regulate commerce with all nations, and among the several States;

To borrow money and emit bills of credit;

To establish post-offices;

To raise armies;

To build and equip fleets;

To pass laws for arming, organizing, and disciplining the militia of the United States;

To subdue a rebellion in any State, on application of its Legislature;

To coin money, and regulate the value of all coins, and fix the standard of weights and measures;

To provide such dockyards and arsenals, and erect such fortifications as may be necessary for the United States, and to exercise exclusive jurisdiction therein;

To appoint a Treasurer, by ballot;

To constitute tribunals inferior to the Supreme Court;

To establish post and military roads;

To establish and provide for a national university at the seat of government of the United States;

To establish uniform rules of naturalization;

To provide for the establishment of a seat of government for the United States, not exceeding ——— miles square, in which they shall have exclusive jurisdiction;

To make rules concerning captures from an enemy;

To declare the law and punishment of piracies and felonies at sea, and of counterfeiting coin, and of all offences against the laws of nations;

To call forth the aid of the militia to execute the laws of the Union, enforce treaties, suppress insurrections, and repel invasions ;

And to make all laws for carrying the foregoing powers into execution.

" The Legislature of the United States shall have the power to declare the punishment of treason, which shall consist only in levying war against the United States, or any of them, or in adhering to their enemies. No person shall be convicted of treason but by the testimony of two witnesses.

" The proportion of direct taxation shall be regulated by the whole number of inhabitants of every description ; which number shall, within ——— years after the first meeting of the Legislature, and within the term of every ——— year after, be taken in the manner to be prescribed by the Legislature.

" No tax shall be laid on articles exported from the States ; nor capitation tax, but in proportion to the census before directed.

"All laws regulating commerce shall require the assent of two-thirds of the members present in each House. The United States shall not grant any title of nobility. The Legislature of the United States shall pass no law on the subject of religion ; nor touching or abridging the liberty of the press ; nor shall the privilege of the writ of Habeus Corpus ever be suspended, except in case of rebellion or invasion.

"All acts made by the Legislature of the United States, pursuant to this Constitution, and all treaties made under the authority of the United States, shall be the supreme law of the land ; and all judges shall be bound to consider them as such in their decisions.

ARTICLE VII.

"The Senate shall have the sole and exclusive power to declare war ; and to make treaties ; and to appoint ambassadors and other ministers to foreign nations, and judges of the Supreme Court.

"They shall have the exclusive power to regulate the manner of deciding all disputes and controversies now existing, or which may arise, between the States, respecting jurisdiction or territory.

ARTICLE VIII.

"The executive power of the United States shall be vested in a President of the United States of America, which shall be his style ; and his title shall be His Excellency.   He shall be elected for ——— years ; and shall be re-eligible.

"He shall from time to time give information to the Legislature, of the State of the Union, and recommend to their consideration the measures he may think necessary. He shall take care that the laws of the United States be duly executed.   He shall commission all the officers of the United States ; and, except as to ambassadors, other ministers, and judges of the Supreme Court, he shall nominate, and, with the consent of the Senate, appoint, all other officers of the United States. He shall receive public ministers from foreign nations ; and may correspond with the Executives of the different States. He shall have power to grant pardons and reprieves, except in impeachments. He shall be Commander-in-Chief of the army and navy of the United States, and of the militia of the several States ; and shall receive a compensation which shall not be increased or diminished during his continuance in office. At entering on the duties of his office, he shall take an oath faithfully to execute the duties of a President of the United States. He shall be removed from his office on impeachment by the House of Delegates, and conviction in the Supreme Court, of treason, bribery, or corruption. In case of his removal, death, resignation, or disability, the President of the Senate shall exercise the duties of his office until another President be chosen. And in case of the death of the President of the Senate, the Speaker of the House of Delegates shall do so.

ARTICLE IX.

'The Legislature of the United States shall have the power, and it shall be their duty, to establish such courts of law, equity, and admiralty, as shall be necessary.

" The judges of the courts shall hold their offices during good behaviour; and receive a compensation, which shall not be increased or diminished during their continuance in office. One of these courts shall be termed the Supreme Court; whose jurisdiction shall extend to all cases arising under the laws of the United States, or affecting embassadors, other public ministers and consuls; to the trial of impeachment of officers of the United States; to all cases of admiralty and maritime jurisdiction. In cases of impeachment affecting ambassadors, and other public ministers, this jurisdiction shall be original; and in all other cases appellate.

" All criminal offences, except in cases of impeachment

shall be tried in the State where they shall be committed. The trials shall be open and public, and shall be by jury.

ARTICLE X.

" Immediately after the first census of the people of the United States, the House of Delegates shall apportion the Senate by electing for each State, out of the citizens resident therein, one Senator for every ———— members each State shall have in the House of Delegates. Each State shall be entitled to have at least one member in the Senate.

ARTICLE XI.

" No State shall grant letters of marque and reprisal, or enter into treaty, or alliance, or confederation; nor grant any title of nobility; nor, without the consent of the Legislature of the United States, lay any impost on imports; nor keep troops or ships of war in time of peace; nor enter into compacts with other States or foreign powers; nor emit bills of credit; nor make any thing but gold, silver, or copper, a tender in payment of debts; nor engage in war, except for self-defense when actually invaded, or the danger of invasion be so great as not to admit of a delay until the Government of the United States can be informed thereof. And to render these prohibitions effectual, the Legislature of the United States shall have the power to revise the laws of the several States that may be supposed to infringe the powers exclusively delegated by this Constitution to Congress, and to negative and annul such as do.

ARTICLE XII.

" The citizens of each State shall be entitled to all privileges and immunities of citizens in the several States. Any person, charged with crimes in any State, fleeing from justice to another, shall, on demand of the Executive of the State from which he fled, be delivered up, and removed to the State having jurisdiction of the offence.

Article XIII.

"Full faith shall be given, in each State, to the acts of the Legislature, and to the records and judicial proceedings of the courts and magistrates, of every State.

Article XIV.

"The Legislature shall have power to admit new States into the Union, on the same terms with the original States; provided two-thirds of the members present in both Houses agree.

Article XV.

"On the application of the Legislature of a State, the United States shall protect it against domestic insurrection.

Article XVI.

"If two-thirds of the Legislatures of the States apply for the same, the Legislature of the United States shall call a convention for the purpose of amending the Constitution; or, should Congress, with the consent of two-thirds of each House, propose to the States amendments to the same, the agreement of two-thirds of the Legislatures of the States shall be sufficient to make the said amendments parts of the Constitution.

"The ratification of the ————— conventions of ——— States shall be sufficient for organizing this Constitution."

Ordered, that the said draft be referred to the Committee of the Whole appointed to consider the state of the American Union.

Adjourned.

Wednesday, May 30th.

Roger Sherman, from Connecticut, took his seat.

The House went into *Committee of the Whole* on the state of the Union. Mr. Gorham was elected to the Chair by ballot.

The propositions of Mr. RANDOLPH which had been referred to the Committee being taken up, he moved, on the suggestion of Mr. G. MORRIS, that the first of his propositions,—to-wit: *"Resolved, that the Articles of Confederation ought to be so corrected and enlarged, as to accomplish the objects proposed by their institution; namely, common defence, security of liberty, and general welfare,* — should mutually be postponed, in order to consider the three following:

" 1. That a union of the States merely federal will not accomplish the objects proposed by the Articles of Confederation, namely, common defence, security of liberty, and general welfare.

" 2. That no treaty or treaties among the whole or part of the States, as individual sovereignties, would be sufficient.

" 3. That a *national* government ought to be established, consisting of a *supreme* Legislative, Executive and Judiciary "

The motion for postponing was seconded by Mr. G. MORRIS, and unanimously agreed to.

Some verbal criticisms were raised against the first proposition, and it was agreed, on motion of Mr. BUTLER, seconded by Mr. RANDOLPH, to pass on to the third, which underwent a discussion, less, however, on its general merits than on the force and extent of the particular terms *national* and *supreme.*

Mr. CHARLES PINCKNEY wished to know of Mr. RANDOLPH, whether he meant to abolish the State governments altogether.   Mr. RANDOLPH replied, that he meant by these general propositions merely to introduce the particular ones which explained the outlines of the system he had in view.

Mr. BUTLER said, he had not made up his mind on the subject, and was open to the light which discussion might throw on it.   After some general observations, he concluded with saying, that he had opposed the grant of powers to Congress heretofore, because the whole power was vested in

one body.   The proposed distribution of the powers with
different bodies changed the case, and would induce him to
go great lengths.

General PINCKNEY expressed a doubt whether the act of
Congress recommending the Convention, or the commissions
of the Deputies to it, would authorize a discussion of a
system founded on different principles from the Federal
Constitution.

Mr. GERRY seemed to entertain the same doubt.

Mr. GOUVERNEUR MORRIS explained the distinction between a *federal* and a *national, supreme* government; the
former being a mere compact resting on the good faith of
the parties; the latter having a complete and *compulsive*
operation.   He contended, that in all communities there
must be one supreme power, and one only.

Mr. MASON observed, not only that the present Confederation was deficient in not providing for coercion and punishment against delinquent States; but argued very cogently,
that punishment could not in the nature of things be executed on the States collectively, and therefore that such a
government was necessary as could directly operate on
individuals, and would punish those only whose guilt
required it.

Mr. SHERMAN admitted that the Confederation had not
given sufficient power to Congress, and that additional powers were necessary; particularly that of raising money,
which he said would involve many other powers.   He admitted also, that the general and particular jurisdictions
ought in no case to be concurrent.   He seemed, however,
not to be disposed to make too great inroads on the existing system; intimating, as one reason, that it would be
wrong to lose every amendment by inserting such as would
not be agreed to by the States.

It was moved by Mr. READ, and seconded by Mr.
CHARLES COTESWORTH PINCKNEY, to postpone the third
proposition last offered by Mr. RANDOLPH, viz. " that a
national government ought to be established, consisting of

a supreme Legislative, Executive, and Judiciary," in order
to take up the following, viz. "Resolved, that, in order to
carry into execution the design of the States in forming
this Convention, and to accomplish the objects proposed by
the Confederation, a more effective Government, consisting
of a Legislative, Executive, and Judiciary, ought to be
established." The motion to postpone for this purpose was
lost:

Massachusetts, Connecticut, Delaware, South Carolina,
aye — 4; New York, Pennsylvania, Virginia, North Carolina, no — 4.

On the question, as moved by Mr. BUTLER, on the third
proposition, it was resolved, in Committee of Whole, "that
a national government ought to be established, consisting
of a supreme Legislative, Executive, and Judiciary," —
Massachusetts, Pennsylvania, Delaware, Virginia, North
Carolina, South Carolina, aye — 6; Connecticut, no — 1;
New York divided (Colonel HAMILTON, aye, Mr. YATES,
no).

The following Resolution, being the second of those
proposed by Mr. RANDOLPH, was taken up, viz. "*that the
rights of suffrage in the National Legislature ought to be
proportioned to the quotas of contribution, or to the number
of free inhabitants, as the one or the other rule may seem
best in different cases.*"

Mr. MADISON, observing that the words, "*or to the number of free inhabitants,*" might occasion debates which
would divert the Committee from the general question
whether the principle of representation should be changed
moved that they might be struck out.

Mr. KING observed, that the quotas of contribution, which
would alone remain as the measure of representation, would
not answer; because, waiving every other view of the matter, the revenue might hereafter be so collected by the
General Government that the sums respectively drawn from
the States would not appear, and would besides be continually varying.

Mr. MADISON admitted the propriety of the observation, and that some better rule ought to be found.

Colonel HAMILTON moved to alter the resolution so as to read, "that the rights of suffrage in the National Legislature ought to be proportioned to the number of free inhabitants." Mr. SPAIGHT seconded the motion.

It was then moved that the resolution be postponed; which was agreed to.

Mr. RANDOLPH and Mr. MADISON then moved the following resolution: "that the rights of suffrage in the National Legislature ought to be proportioned."

It was moved and seconded to amend it by adding, " and not according to the present system," which was agreed to.

It was then moved and seconded to alter the resolution so as to read, "that the rights of suffrage in the National Legislature ought not to be according to the present system."

It was then moved and seconded to postpone the resolution moved by Mr. RANDOLPH and Mr. MADISON; which being agreed to,—

Mr. MADISON moved, in order to get over the difficulties, the following resolution: "that the equality of suffrage established by the Articles of Confederation ought not to prevail in the National Legislature; and that an equitable ratio of representation ought to be substituted." This was seconded by Mr. GOUVERNEUR MORRIS, and, being generally relished, would have been agreed to; when—

Mr. READ moved, that the whole clause relating to the point of representation be postponed; reminding the Committee that the Deputies from Delaware were restrained by their commission from assenting to any change of the rule of suffrage, and in case such a change should be fixed on, it might become their duty to retire from the Convention.

Mr. GOUVERNEUR MORRIS observed, that the valuable assistance of those members could not be lost without real concern; and that so early a proof of discord in the Convention, as the secession of a State, would add much to the regret; that the change proposed was, however, so fundamental an article in a national government, that it could not be dispensed with.

Mr. MADISON observed, that, whatever reason might have existed for the equality of suffrage when the Union was a federal one among sovereign States, it must cease when a national government should be put into the place. In the former case, the acts of Congress depended so much for their efficacy on the co-operation of the States, that these had a weight, both within and without Congress, nearly in proportion to their extent and importance. In the latter case, as the acts of the General Government would take effect without the intervention of the State Legislatures, a vote from a small State would have the same efficacy and importance as a vote from a large one, and there was the same reason for different numbers of representatives from different States, as from counties of different extents within particular States. He suggested as an expedient for at once taking the sense of the members on this point, and saving the Delaware Deputies from embarrassment, that the question should be taken in Committee, and the clause, on report to the House, be postponed without a question there. This, however, did not appear to satisfy Mr. READ.

By several it was observed, that no just construction of the act of Delaware could require or justify a secession of her Deputies, even if the resolution were to be carried through the House as well as the Committee. It was finally agreed, however, that the clause should be postponed; it being understood that, in the event, the proposed change of representation would certainly be agreed to, no objection or difficulty being started from any other quarter than from Delaware.

The motion of Mr. READ to postpone being agreed to,—

The Committee then rose ; the Chairman reported progress ; and the House, having resolved to resume the subject in Committee to-morrow,—

Adjourned to ten o'clock.

THURSDAY, MAY 31ST.

WILLIAM PIERCE, from Georgia, took his seat.

In the Committee of the Whole on Mr. RANDOLPH'S Resolutions,—The third Resolution, *" that the National Legislature ought to consist of two branches,"* was agreed to without debate, or dissent, except that of Pennsylvania,— given probably from complaisance to Doctor FRANKLIN, who was understood to be partial to a single house of legislation.

The fourth Resolution, first clause, *" that the members of the first branch of the National Legislature ought to be elected by the people of the several States,"* being taken up :

Mr. SHERMAN opposed the election by the people, insisting that it ought to be by the State Legislatures. The people, he said, immediately, should have as little to do as may be about the government. They want information, and are constantly liable to be misled.

Mr. GERRY. The evils we experience flow from the excess of democracy. The people do not want virtue, but are the dupes of pretended patriots. In Massachusetts it had been fully confirmed by experience, that they are daily misled into the most baneful measures and opinions, by the false reports circulated by designing men, and which no one on the spot can refute. One principal evil arises from the want of due provision for those employed in the administration of government. It would seem to be a maxim of democracy to starve the public servants. He mentioned the popular clamor in Massachusetts for the reduction of salaries, and the attack made on that of the Governor, though secured by the spirit of the Constitution itself. He had, he said, been too republican heretofore : he was still, however, republican ; but had been taught by experience the danger of the leveling spirit.

Mr. MASON argued strongly for an election of the larger branch by the people. It was to be the grand depository of the democratic principle of the government. It was, so to speak, to be our House of Commons. It ought to know

and sympathize with every part of the community ; and
ought therefore to be taken, not only from different parts
of the whole republic, but also from different districts of
the larger members of it ; which had in several instances,
particularly in Virginia, different interests and views arising
from difference of produce, of habits, &c. &c.   He admitted
that we had been too democratic, but was afraid we should
incautiously run into the opposite extreme.   We ought to
attend to the rights of every class of the people.   He had
often wondered at the indifference of the superior classes of
society to this dictate of humanity and policy ; considering,
that, however affluent their circumstances, or elevated their
situations, might be, the course of a few years not only
might, but certainly would, distribute their posterity
throughout the lowest classes of society.   Every selfish
motive, therefore, every family attachment, ought to recommend such a system of policy as would provide no less carefully for the rights and happiness of the lowest, than of the
highest, order of citizens.

Mr. WILSON contended strenuously for drawing the
most numerous branch of the Legislature immediately from
the people.   He was for raising the federal pyramid to a
considerable altitude, and for that reason wished to give it
as broad a basis as possible.   No government could long
subsist without the confidence of the people.   In a republican government, this confidence was peculiarly essential.
He also thought it wrong to increase the weight of the
State Legislatures by making them the electors of the
National Legislature.   All interference between the general
and local governments should be obviated as much as possible.   On examination it would be found that the opposition
of States to Federal measures had proceeded much more
from the officers of the States than from the people at large.

Mr. MADISON considered the popular election of one
branch of the National Legislature as essential to every
plan of free government.   He observed, that in some of the
States one branch of the Legislature was composed of men

already removed from the people by an intervening body of electors. That if the first branch of the General Legislature should be elected by the State Legislatures, the second branch elected by the first, the Executive ·by the second together with the first, and other appointments again made for subordinate purposes by the Executive, the people would be lost sight of altogether; and the necessary sympathy between them and their rulers and officers too little felt. He was an advocate for the policy of refining the popular appointments by successive filtrations, but thought it might be pushed too far. He wished the expedient to be resorted to only in the appointment of the second branch of the Legislature, and in the Executive and Judiciary branches of the government. He thought, too, that the great fabric to be raised would be more stable and durable, if it should rest on the solid foundation of the people themselves, than if it should stand merely on the pillars of the Legislatures.

Mr. GERRY did not like the election by the people. The maxims taken from the British constitution were often fallacious when applied to our situation, which was extremely different. Experience, he said, had shown that the State Legislatures, drawn immediately from the people, did not always possess their confidence. He had no objection, however, to an election by the people, if it were so qualified that men of honor and character might not be unwilling to be joined in the appointments. He seemed to think the people might nominate a certain number, out of which the State Legislatures should be bound to choose.

Mr. BUTLER thought an election by the people an impracticable mode.

On the question for an election of the first branch of the National Legislature, by the people, Massachusetts, New York, Pennsylvania, Virginia, North Carolina, Georgia, aye — 5; New Jersey, South Carolina, no — 2; Connecticut, Delaware, divided.

The remaining clauses of the fourth Resolution, relating to *the qualifications of members of the National Legislature,* being postponed, *nem. con.*, as entering too much into detail for general propositions,—

The Committee proceeded to the fifth Resolution, *that the second [or senatorial] branch of the National Legislature ought to be chosen by the first branch, out of persons nominated by the State Legislatures.*

Mr. SPAIGHT contended, that the second branch ought to be chosen by the State Legislatures, and moved an amendment to that effect.

Mr. BUTLER apprehended that the taking so many powers out of the hands of the States as was proposed, tended to destroy all that balance and security of interests among the States which it was necessary to preserve; and called on Mr. RANDOLPH, the mover of the propositions, to explain the extent of his ideas, and particularly the number of members he meant to assign to this second branch.

Mr. RANDOLPH observed, that he had, at the time of offering his propositions, stated his ideas as far as the nature of general propositions required; that details made no part of the plan, and could not perhaps with propriety have been introduced. If he was to give an opinion as to the number of the second branch, he should say that it ought to be much smaller than that of the first; so small as to be exempt from the passionate proceedings to which numerous assemblies are liable. He observed, that the general object was to provide a cure for the evils under which the United States labored; that in tracing these evils to their origin, every man had found it in the turbulence and follies of democracy; that some check therefore was to be sought for, against this tendency of our governments; and that a good Senate seemed most likely to answer the purpose.

Mr. KING reminded the Committee that the choice of the second branch as proposed, (by Mr. SPAIGHT) viz., by the State Legislatures, would be impracticable, unless it was to be very numerous, or *the idea of proportion* among the States was to be disregarded. According to this *idea*, there must be eighty or a hundred members to entitle Delaware to the choice of one of them.

Mr. SPAIGHT withdrew his motion.

Mr. WILSON opposed both a nomination by the State Legislatures, and an election by the first branch of the National Legislature, because the second branch of the latter ought to be independent of both. He thought both branches of the National Legislature ought to be chosen by the people, but was not prepared with a specific proposition. He suggested the mode of choosing the Senate of New York, to wit, of uniting several election districts for one branch, in choosing members for the other branch, as a good model.

Mr. MADISON observed, that such a mode would destroy the influence of the smaller States associated with larger ones in the same district; as the latter would choose from within themselves, although better men might be found in the former. The election of Senators in Virginia, where large and small counties were often formed into one district for the purpose, had illustrated this consequence. Local partiality would often prefer a resident within the county or State, to a candidate of superior merit residing out of it. Less merit also in a resident would be more known throughout his own State.

Mr. SHERMAN favored an election of one member by each of the State Legislatures.

Mr. PINCKNEY moved to strike out the "nomination by the State Legislatures;" on this question—

* Massachusetts, Connecticut, New York, New Jersey, Pennsylvania, Virginia, North Carolina, South Carolina, Georgia, no—9 ; Delaware, divided.

On the whole question for electing by the first branch out of nominations by the State Legislatures—Massachusetts, Virginia, South Carolina, aye—3 ; Connecticut, New York, New Jersey, Pennsylvania, Delaware, North Carolina, Georgia, no—7.

---

* This question is omitted in the printed Journal, and the votes applied to the succeeding one, instead of the votes as here stated.

So the clause was disagreed to, and a chasm left in this part of the plan.

The sixth Resolution, stating the *cases in which the National Legislature ought to legislate*, was next taken into discussion. On the question *whether each branch should originate laws*, there was an unanimous affirmative, without debate. On the question *for transferring all the legislative powers of the existing Congress to this assembly*, there was also an unanimous affirmative, without debate.

On the proposition *for giving legislative power in all cases to which the State Legislatures were individually incompetent*,—Mr. PINCKNEY and Mr. RUTLEDGE objected to the vagueness of the term "*incompetent*," and said they could not well decide how to vote until they should see an exact enumeration of the powers comprehended by this definition.

Mr. BUTLER repeated his fears that we were running into an extreme, in taking away the powers of the States; and called on Mr. RANDOLPH for the extent of his meaning.

Mr. RANDOLPH disclaimed any intention to give indefinite powers to the National Legislature, declaring that he was entirely opposed to such an inroad on the State jurisdictions; and that he did not think any considerations whatever could ever change his determination. His opinion was fixed on this point.

Mr. MADISON said, that he had brought with him into the Convention a strong bias in favor of an enumeration and definition of the powers necessary to be exercised by the National Legislature; but had also brought doubts concerning its practicability. His wishes remained unaltered; but his doubts had become stronger. What his opinion might ultimately be, he could not yet tell. But he should shrink from nothing which should be found essential to such a form of government as would provide for the safety, liberty and happiness of the community. This being the end of all our deliberations, all the necessary means for attaining it must, however reluctantly, be submitted to.

On the question for giving powers, in cases to which the States are not competent—Massachusetts, New York, New Jersey, Pennsylvania, Delaware, Virginia, North Carolina, South Carolina, Georgia, aye—9 ; Connecticut divided, (SHERMAN, no, ELLSWORTH, aye.)

The other clauses, *giving powers necessary to preserve harmony among the States, to negative all State laws contravening, in the opinion of the National Legislature, the Articles of Union,* down to the last clause, (the words, " or any treaties subsisting under the authority of the Union," being added after the words " contravening, &c. the articles of the Union," on motion of Doctor Franklin) were agreed to without debate or dissent.

The last clause of the sixth Resolution, *authorizing an exertion of the force of the whole against a delinquent State,* came next into consideration.

Mr. MADISON observed, that the more he reflected on the use of force, the more he doubted the practicability, the justice and the efficacy of it, when applied to people collectively, and not individually. An union of the States containing such an ingredient seemed to provide for its own destruction. The use of force against a State would look more like a declaration of war than an infliction of punishment; and would probably be considered by the party attacked as a dissolution of all previous compacts by which it might be bound. He hoped that such a system would be framed as might render this resource unnecessary, and moved that the clause be postponed. This motion was agreed to, *nem. con.*

The Committee then rose, and the House adjourned.

FRIDAY, JUNE 1ST.

WILLIAM HOUSTOUN, from Georgia, took his seat.

The *Committee of the Whole* proceeded to the seventh Resolution, *that a National Executive be instituted, to be chosen by the National Legislature for the term of* ———

years, &c., to be ineligible thereafter, to possess the Executive powers of Congress, &c.

Mr. PINCKNEY was for a vigorous Executive, but was afraid the executive powers of the existing Congress might extend to peace and war, &c.; which would render the Executive a monarchy of the worst kind, to wit, an elective one.

Mr. WILSON moved that the Executive consist of a single person. Mr. C. PINCKNEY seconded the motion so as to read "that a National Executive, to consist of a single person, be instituted."

A considerable pause ensuing, and the Chairman asking if he should put the question, Doctor FRANKLIN observed that it was a point of great importance, and wished that the gentlemen would deliver their sentiments on it before the question was put.

Mr. RUTLEDGE animadverted on the shyness of gentlemen on this and other subjects. He said it looked as if they supposed themselves precluded, by having frankly disclosed their opinions, from afterwards changing them, which he did not take to be at all the case. He said he was for vesting the executive power in a single person, though he was not for giving him the power of war and peace. A single man would feel the greatest responsibility, and administer the public affairs best.

Mr. SHERMAN said, he considered the executive magistracy as nothing more than an institution for carrying the will of the legislature into effect; that the person or persons ought to be appointed by and accountable to the legislature only, which was the depository of the supreme will of the society. As they were the best judges of the business which ought to be done by the executive department, and consequently of the number necessary from time to time for doing it, he wished the number might not be fixed, but that the legislature should be at liberty to appoint one or more as experience might dictate.

Mr. WILSON preferred a single magistrate, as giving

most energy, dispatch and responsibility to the office. He did not consider the prerogatives of the British monarch as a proper guide in defining the executive powers. Some of these prerogatives were of a legislative nature; among others, that of war and peace, &c. The only powers he considered strictly executive were those of executing the laws, and appointing officers, not appertaining to, and appointed by, the legislature.

Mr. GERRY favored the policy of annexing a council to the Executive, in order to give weight and inspire confidence.

Mr. RANDOLPH strenuously opposed an unity in the executive magistracy. He regarded it as the fœtus of monarchy. We had, he said, no motive to be governed by the British government as our prototype. He did not mean, however, to throw censure on that excellent fabric. If we were in a situation to copy it, he did not know that he should be opposed to it; but the fixed genius of the people of America required a different form of government. He could not see why the great requisites for the executive department, vigor, dispatch, and responsibility, could not be found in three men as well as in one man. The Executive ought to be independent. It ought, therefore, in order to support its independence, to consist of more than one.

Mr. WILSON said, that unity in the Executive, instead of being the fœtus of monarchy, would be the best safeguard against tyranny. He repeated, that he was not governed by the British model, which was inapplicable to the situation of this country; the extent of which was so great, and the manners so republican, that nothing but a great confederated republic would do for it.

Mr. WILSON's motion for a single magistrate was postponed by common consent, the Committee seeming unprepared for any decision on it; and the first part of the clause agreed to, viz. " that a national Executive be instituted."

Mr. MADISON thought it would be proper, before a choice should be made between a unity and a plurality in the

Executive, to fix the extent of the executive authority; that as certain powers were in their nature executive, and must be given to that department, whether administered by one or more persons, a definition of their extent would assist the judgment in determining how far they might be safely entrusted to a single officer. He accordingly moved that so much of the clause before the Committee as related to the powers of the Executive should be struck out, and that after the words "that a national Executive ought to be instituted," there be inserted the words following, viz. "with power to carry into effect the national laws, to appoint to offices in cases not otherwise provided for, and to execute such other powers, 'not legislative nor judiciary in their nature,' as may from time to time be delegated by the national Legislature." The words "not legislative nor judiciary in their nature," were added to the proposed amendment, in consequence of a suggestion, by General PINCKNEY, that improper powers might otherwise be delegated.

Mr. WILSON seconded this motion.

Mr. PINCKNEY moved to amend the amendment by striking out the last member of it, viz. "and to execute such other powers, not legislative or judiciary in their nature, as may from time to time be delegated." He said they were unnecessary, the object of them being included in the "power to carry into effect the national laws."

Mr. RANDOLPH seconded the motion.

Mr. MADISON did not know that the words were absolutely necessary, or even the preceding words, "to appoint to offices, &c.," the whole being, perhaps, included in the first member of the proposition. He did not, however, see any inconvenience in retaining them; and cases might happen in which they might serve to prevent doubts and misconstructions.

In consequence of the motion of Mr. PINCKNEY, the question on Mr. MADISON's motion was divided; and the words objected to by Mr. PINCKNEY struck out, by the votes of Connecticut, New York, New Jersey, Pennsylvania, Delaware,

North Carolina and Georgia — 7, against Massachusetts, Virginia and South Carolina — 3; the preceding part of the motion being first agreed to, — Connecticut, divided; all the other States in the affirmative.

The next clause in the seventh Resolution, relating to the mode of appointing, and the duration of, the Executive, being under consideration, —

Mr. WILSON said, he was almost unwilling to declare the mode which he wished to take place, being apprehensive that it might appear chimerical. He would say, however, at least, that in theory he was for an election by the peo. ple. Experience, particularly in New York and Massachusetts, showed that an election of the first magistrate by the people at large was both a convenient and successful mode. The objects of choice in such cases must be persons whose merits have general notoriety.

Mr. SHERMAN was for the appointment by the Legislature, and for making him absolutely dependent on that body, as it was the will of that which was to be executed. An independence of the Executive on the supreme Legislature, was, in his opinion, the very essence of tyranny, if there was any such thing.

Mr. WILSON moved, that the blank for the term of duration should be filled with three years, observing, at the same time, that he preferred this short period on the supposition that a re-eligibility would be provided for.

Mr. PINCKNEY moved, for seven years.

Mr. SHERMAN was for three years, and against the doctrine of rotation, as throwing out of office the men best qualified to execute its duties.

Mr MASON was for seven years at least, and for prohibiting a re-eligibility, as the best expedient, both for preventing the effect of a false complaisance on the side of the Legislature towards unfit characters; and a temptation on the side of the Executive to intrigue with the Legislature for a re-appointment.

Mr. BEDFORD was strongly opposed to so long a term as

seven years. He begged the Committee to consider what the situation of the country would be, in case the first magistrate should be saddled on it for such a period, and it should be found on trial that he did not possess the qualifications ascribed to him, or should lose them after his appointment. An impeachment, he said, would be no cure for this evil, as an impeachment would reach misfeasance only, not incapacity. He was for a triennial election, and for an ineligibility after a period of nine years.

On the question, *for seven years,*—New York, New Jersey, Pennsylvania, Delaware, Virgina, aye—5; Connecticut, North Carolina, South Carolina, Georgia, no 4; Massachusetts divided. There being five yeas, four noes, and one divided, a question was asked, whether a majority had voted in the affirmative. The President decided that it was an affirmative vote.

The *mode of appointing* the Executive was the next question.

Mr. WILSON renewed his declarations in favor of an appointment by the people. He wished to derive not only both branches of the Legislature from the people without the intervention of the State Legislatures, but the Executive also, in order to make them as independent as possible of each other, as well as of the States.

Colonel MASON favors the idea, but thinks it impracticable. He wishes, however, that Mr. WILSON might have time to digest it into his own form. The clause " to be chosen by the National Legislature," was accordingly postponed.

Mr. RUTLEDGE suggests an election of the Executive by the second branch only of the National Legislature.

The Committee then rose, and the House adjourned.

SATURDAY, JUNE 2ND.

WILLIAM SAMUEL JOHNSON, from Connecticut, DANIEL OF ST. THOMAS JENIFER, from Maryland, and JOHN LANSING, Jun., from New York, took their seats.

In Committee of the Whole,—It was moved and seconded to postpone the Resolutions of Mr. RANDOLPH respecting the Executive, in order to take up the second branch of the Legislature; which being negatived,—by Massachusetts, Connecticut, Delaware, Virginia, North Carolina, South Carolina, Georgia—7; against New York, Pennsylvania, Maryland—3; the mode of appointing the Executive was resumed.

Mr. WILSON made the following motion, to be substituted for the mode proposed by Mr. RANDOLPH's Resolution, "that the executive magistracy shall be elected in the following manner: That the States be divided into ——— districts and that the persons qualified to vote in each district for members of the first branch of the National Legislature elect ——— members for their respective districts to be electors of the executive magistracy; that the said electors of the executive magistracy meet at ———, and they, or any ——— of them, so met, shall proceed to elect by ballot, but not out of their own body, ——— person– in whom the executive authority of the National Government shall be vested."

Mr. WILSON repeated his arguments in favor of an election without the intervention of the States. He supposed, too, that this mode would produce more confidence among the people in the first magistrate, than an election by the National Legislature.

Mr. GERRY opposed the election by the National Legislature. There would be a constant intrigue kept up for the appointment. The Legislature and the candidates would bargain and play into one another's hands. Votes would be given by the former under promises or expectations from the latter, of recompensing them by services to members of the Legislature or their friends. He liked the principle of Mr. WILSON's motion, but fears it would alarm and give a handle to the State partizans, as tending to supersede altogether the State authorities. He thought the community not yet ripe for stripping the States of their powers, even such as might not be requisite for local purposes. He was for waiting till the people should feel more the necessity of it. He seemed to prefer the taking the suffrages of the States, instead of electors; or letting the Legislatures nominate, and the electors appoint. He was not clear that the people ought to act directly even in the choice of electors, being too little informed of personal characters in large districts, and liable to deceptions.

Mr. WILLIAMSON could see no advantage in the introduction of electors chosen by the people, who would stand in the same relation to them as the State Legislatures; whilst the expedient would be attended to with great trouble and expense.

On the question for agreeing to Mr. WILSON's substitute, it was negatived, — Pennsylvania, Maryland, aye — 2; Massachusetts, Connecticut, New York,* Delaware, Virginia North Carolina, South Carolina, Georgia, no — 8.

On the question, for electing the Executive by the National Legislature, for the term of seven years, it was agreed to, — Massachusetts, Connecticut, New York, Delaware, Virginia, North Carolina, South Carolina, Georgia, aye — 8; Pennsylvania, Maryland, no — 2.

Doctor FRANKLIN moved, that what related to the compensation for the services of the Executive be postponed, in order to substitute, " whose necessary expenses shall be defrayed, but who shall receive no salary, stipend, fee or reward whatsoever for their services." He said, that, being very sensible of the effect of age on his memory, he had been unwilling to trust to that for the observations which seemed to support his motion, and had reduced them to writing, that he might, with the permission of the Committee, read, instead of speaking, them. Mr. WILSON made an offer to read the paper, which was accepted. The following is a literal copy of the paper :

" Sir, it is with reluctance that I rise to express a disapprobation of any one article of the plan for which we are so much obliged to the honorable gentleman who laid it

---

* New York, in the printed Journals, divided.

before us.   From its first reading I have borne a good will
to it, and in general wished it success.   In this particular
of salaries to the Executive branch, I happen to differ : and
as my opinion may appear new and chimerical, it is only
from a persuasion that it is right, and from a sense of duty,
that I hazard it.   The Committee will judge of my reasons
when they have heard them, and their judgment may possibly change mine.   I think I see inconveniences in the
appointment of salaries ; I see none in refusing them, but,
on the contrary, great advantages.

"Sir, there are two passions which have a powerful
influence on the affairs of men.   These are ambition and
avarice ; the love of power, and the love of money.   Separately, each of these has great force in prompting men to
action ; but when united in view of the same object, they
have in many minds the most violent effects.   Place before
the eyes of such men a post of *honor*, that shall be at the
same time a place of *profit*, and they will move heaven and
earth to obtain it.   The vast number of such places it is
that renders the British government so tempestuous.   The
struggles for them are the true sources of all those factions,
which are perpetually dividing the nation, distracting its
councils, hurrying sometimes into fruitless and mischievous
wars, and often compelling a submission to dishonorable
terms of peace.

"And of what kind are the men that will strive for this
profitable pre-eminence, through all the bustle of cabal, the
heat of contention, the infinite mutual abuse of parties,
tearing to pieces the best of characters ?   It will not be
the wise and moderate, the lovers of peace and good order,
the men fittest for the trust.   It will be the bold and
the violent, the men of strong passions and indefatigable
activity in their selfish pursuits.   These will thrust themselves into your government, and be your rulers.   And
these, too, will be mistaken in the expected happiness of
their situation : for their vanquished competitors, of the
same spirit, and from the same motives, will perpetually be

endeavouring to distress their administration, thwart their measures, and render them odious to the people.

" Besides these evils, Sir, though we may set out in the beginning with moderate salaries, we shall find that such will not be of long continuance. Reasons will never be wanting for proposed augmentations. And there will always be a party for giving more to the rulers, that the rulers may be able in return to give more to them. Hence, as all history informs us, there has been in every state and kingdom a constant kind of warfare between the governing and governed, the one striving to obtain more for its support, and the other to pay less. And this has alone occasioned great convulsions, actual civil wars, ending either in dethroning of the princes, or enslaving of the people. Generally, indeed, the ruling power carries its point, the revenues of princes constantly increasing ; and we see that they are never satisfied, but always in want of more. The more the people are discontented with the oppression of taxes, the greater need the prince has of money to distribute among his partizans, and pay the troops that are to suppress all resistance, and enable him to plunder at pleasure. There is scarce a king in an hundred, who would not, if he could, follow the example of Pharaoh, get first all the people's money, then all their lands, and then make them and their children servants for ever. It will be said, that we don't propose to establish kings. I know it ; but there is a natural inclination in mankind to kingly government. It sometimes relieves them from aristocratic domination. They had rather have one tyrant than five hundred. It gives more of the appearance of equality among citizens, and that they like. I am apprehensive, therefore, perhaps too apprehensive, that the government of these States may in future times end in a monarchy. But this catastrophe I think may be delayed, if in our proposed system we do not sow the seeds of contention, faction, and tumult, by making our posts of honor, places of profit. If we do, I fear that, though we do employ at first a number, and not a single person, the number will in time be set aside ; it will only nourish the fœtus of a king, as the honorable gentleman from Virginia very aptly expressed it, and a king will the sooner be set over us.

"It may be imagined by some that this is a Utopian idea, and that we can never find men to serve us in the Executive department without paying them well for their services. I conceive this to be a mistake. Some existing facts present themselves to me, which incline me to a contrary opinion. The high-sheriff of a county in England is an honorable office, but it is not a profitable one. It is rather expensive and therefore not sought for. But yet, it is executed and well executed, and usually by some of the principal gentlemen of the county. In France, the office of Counsellor, or member of their judiciary parliament, is more honorable. It is therefore purchased at a high price: there are indeed fees on the law proceedings, which are divided among them, but these fees do not amount to more than three per cent on the sum paid for the place. Therefore, as legal interest is there at five per cent, they in fact pay two per cent for being allowed to do the judiciary business of the nation, which is at the same time entirely exempt from the burden of paying them any salaries for their services. I do not, however, mean to recommend this as an eligible mode for our Judiciary department. I only bring the instance to show, that the pleasure of doing good and serving their country, and the respect such conduct entitles them to, are sufficient motives with some minds to give up a great portion of their time to the public, without the mean inducement of pecuniary satisfaction.

"Another instance is that of a respectable society who have made the experiment, and practised it with success more than one hundred years. I mean the Quakers. It is an established rule with them, that they are not to go to law; but in their controversies they must apply to their monthly, quarterly, and yearly meetings. Committees of these sit with patience to hear the parties, and spend much time in composing their differences. In doing this, they are supported by a sense of duty, and the respect paid to usefulness. It is honorable to be so employed, but it is never made profitable by salaries, fees or perquisites. And, indeed, in all cases of public service, the less the profit the greater the honor.

" To bring the matter nearer home, have we not seen the great and most important of our offices, that of General of our armies, executed for eight years together without the smallest salary, by a patriot whom I will not now offend by any other praise; and this, through fatigues and distresses, in common with the other brave men, his military friends and companions, and the constant anxieties peculiar to his station? And shall we doubt finding three or four men in all the United States, with public spirit enough to bear sitting in peaceful council for perhaps an equal term, merely to preside over our civil concerns, and see that our laws are duly executed? Sir, I have a better opinion of our country. I think we shall never be without a sufficient number of wise and good men to undertake and execute well and faithfully the office in question.

" Sir, the saving of the salaries that may at first be proposed is not an object with me. The subsequent mischiefs of proposing them are what I apprehend. And therefore it is, that I move the amendment. If it is not seconded or accepted, I must be contented with the satisfaction of having delivered my opinion frankly and done my duty."

The motion was seconded by Col. HAMILTON, with the view, he said, merely of bringing so respectable a proposition before the Committee, and which was besides enforced by arguments that had a certain degree of weight. No debate ensued, and the proposition was postponed for the consideration of the members. It was treated with great respect, but rather for the author of it, than from any apparent conviction of its expediency or practicability.

Mr. DICKINSON moved, " that the Executive be made removable by National Legislature, on the request of a majority of the Legislatures of individual States." It was necessary, he said, to place the power of removing somewhere. He did not like the plan of impeaching the great officers of state. He did not know how provision could be made for removal of them in a better mode than that which he had proposed. He had no idea of abolishing the State governments, as some gentlemen seemed inclined to do. The happiness of this country, in his opinion, required considerable powers to be left in the hands of the States.

Mr. BEDFORD seconded the motion.

Mr. SHERMAN contended, that the National Legislature should have power to remove the Executive at pleasure.

Mr. MASON. Some mode of displacing an unfit magistrate is rendered indispensable by the fallibility of those who choose, as well as by the corruptibility of the man chosen. He opposed decidedly the making the Executive the mere creature of the Legislature, as a violation of the fundamental principle of good government.

Mr. MADISON and Mr. WILSON observed, that it would leave an equality of agency in the small with the great States; that it would enable a minority of the people to prevent the removal of an officer who had rendered himself justly criminal in the eyes of a majority; that it would open a door for intrigues against him in States where his administration, though just, might be unpopular; and might tempt him to pay court to particular States whose leading partizans he might fear, or wish to engage as his partizans. They both thought it bad policy to introduce such a mixture of the State authorities, where their agency could be otherwise supplied.

Mr. DICKINSON considered the business as so important that no man ought to be silent or reserved. He went into a discourse of some length, the sum of which was, that the Legislative, Executive and Judiciary departments ought to be made as independent as possible; but that such an Executive as some seemed to have in contemplation was not consistent with a republic; that a firm Executive could only exist in a limited monarchy. In the British government itself the weight of the Executive arises from the attachments which the Crown draws to itself, and not merely from the force of its prerogatives. In place of these attachments we must look out for something else. One source of stability is the double branch of the Legislature. The division of the country into distinct States formed the other principal source of stability. This division ought therefore to be maintained, and considerable powers to be left with the States. This was the ground of his consolation for the future fate of his country. Without this, and in case of a consolidation of the States into one great republic, we might read its fate in the history of smaller ones. A limited monarchy he considered as *one* of the best governments in the world. It was not *certain* that the same blessings were derivable from any other form. It was certain that equal blessings had never yet been derived from any of the republican forms. A limited monarchy, however, was out of the question. The spirit of the times, the state of affairs forbade the experiment, if it were desirable. Was it possible, moreover, in the nature of things, to introduce it even if these obstacles were less insuperable? A house of nobles was essential to such a government,— could these be created by a breach, or by a stroke of the pen? No. They were the growth of ages, and could only arise under a complication of circumstances none of which existed in this country. But though a form the most perfect, *perhaps*, in itself, be unattainable, we must not despair. If ancient republics have been found to flourish for a moment only, and then vanish forever, it only proves that they were badly constituted; and that we ought to seek for every remedy for their diseases. One of these remedies he conceived to be the accidental lucky division of this country into distinct States; a division which some seemed desirous to abolish altogether.

As to the point of representation in the National Legislature, as it might affect States of different sizes, he said it must probably end in mutual concession. He hoped that each State would retain an equal voice at least in one branch of the National Legislature, and supposed the sums paid within each State would form a better ratio for the other branch than either the number of inhabitants or the quantum of property.

A motion being made to strike out, "on request by a majority of the Legislatures of the individual States," and rejected —(Connecticut, South Carolina and Georgia, being aye; the rest, no,) the question was taken on Mr. DICKIN-SON's motion, "for making the Executive removable by the National Legislature at the request of a majority of State Legislatures," which was also rejected, — all the States being in the negative, except Delaware, which gave an affirmative vote.

The question for making the Executive *ineligible after seven years*, was next taken and agreed to,— Massachusetts, New York, Delaware, Maryland, Virginia, North Carolina, South Carolina, aye — 7; Connecticut, Georgia,* no — 2; Pennsylvania, divided.

Mr. WILLIAMSON, seconded by Mr. DAVIE, moved to add to the last clause the words, "and to be removable on impeachment and conviction of malpractice or neglect of duty;" which was agreed to.

Mr. RUTLEDGE and Mr. C. PINCKNEY moved, that the blank for the number of persons in the Executive be filled with the words, "one person." He supposed the reasons to be so obvious and conclusive in favor of one, that no member would oppose the motion.

Mr. RANDOLPH opposed it with great earnestness, declaring that he should not do justice to the country which sent him, if he were silently to suffer the establishment of a unity in the Executive department. He felt an opposition to it which he believed he should continue to feel as long as he lived. He urged — first, that the permanent temper of the people was adverse to the very semblance of mon-

---

* In the printed Journal, Georgia, aye.

archy; secondly, that a unity was unnecessary, a plurality being equally competent to all the objects of the department; thirdly, that the necessary confidence would never be reposed in a single magistrate; fourthly, that the appointments would generally be in favor of some inhabitant near the centre of the community, and consequently the remote parts would not be on an equal footing. He was in favor of three members of the Executive, to be drawn from different portions of the country.

Mr. BUTLER contended strongly for a single magistrate, as most likely to answer the purpose of the remote parts. If one man should be appointed, he would be responsible to the whole, and he would be impartial to its interests. If three or more should be taken from as many districts, there would be a constant struggle for local advantages. In military matters this would be particularly mischievous. He said, his opinion on this point had been formed under the opportunity he had had of seeing the manner in which a *plurality of military heads* distracted Holland, when threatened with invasion by the imperial troops. One man was for directing the force to the defence of this part, another to that part of the country, just as he happened to be swayed by prejudice or interest.

The motion was then postponed; the Committee rose; and the House adjourned.

MONDAY, JUNE 4TH.

In Committee of the Whole. — The question was resumed on motion of Mr. PINCKNEY, seconded by Mr. WILSON, 'shall the blank for the number of the Executive be filled with a single person?'

Mr. WILSON was in favor of the motion. It had been opposed by the gentleman from Virginia (Mr. RANDOLPH); but the arguments used had not convinced him. He observed that the objections of Mr. RANDOLPH were levelled not so much against the measure itself, as against its unpopularity. If he could suppose that it would occasion a rejection of the plan of which it should form a part, though the part were an important one, yet he would give it up rather than lose the whole. On examination, he could see no evidence of the alleged antipathy of the people. On the contrary, he was persuaded that it does not exist. All know that a single magistrate is not a king. One fact has great weight with him. All the thirteen States, though agreeing in scarce any other instance, agree in placing a single magistrate at the head of the government. The idea of three heads had taken place in none. The degree of power is, indeed, different; but there are no co-ordinate heads. In addition to his former reasons for preferring a unity, he would mention another. The *tranquillity*, not less than the vigor, of the government, he thought, would be favored by it. Among three equal members, he foresaw nothing but uncontrolled, continued and violent animosities; which would not only interrupt the public administration, but diffuse their poison through the other branches of government, through the states, and at length through the people at large. If the members were to be unequal in power, the principal of opposition to the unity was given up. If equal, the making them an odd number would not be a remedy. In courts of justice there are two sides only to a question. In the legislative and executive departments questions have commonly many sides. Each member, therefore, might espouse a separate one, and no two agree.

Mr. SHERMAN. This matter is of great importance, and ought to be well considered before it is determined. Mr. WILSON, he said, had observed that in each State a single magistrate was placed at the head of the government. It was so, he admitted, and properly so; and he wished the same policy to prevail in the Federal Government. But then it should be also remarked, that in all the States there was a council of advice, without which the first magistrate could not act. A council he thought necessary to make the establishment acceptable to the people. Even in Great Britain, the King has a council; and though he appoints it himself, its advice has its weight with him, and attracts the confidence of the people.

Mr. WILLIAMSON asks Mr. WILSON, whether he means to annex a Council.

Mr. WILSON means to have no Council, which oftener serves to cover, than prevent malpractices.

Mr. GERRY was at a loss to discover the policy of three members for the Executive. It would be extremely inconvenient in many instances, particularly in military matters, whether relating to the militia, an army, or a navy. It would be a general with three heads.

On the question for a single Executive, it was agreed to, — Massachusetts, Connecticut, Pennsylvania, Virginia, (Mr. RANDOLPH and Mr. BLAIR, no; Doctor McCLURG, Mr. MADISON and General WASHINGTON, aye; Colonel MASON being no, but not in the House, Mr. WYTHE, aye, but gone home), North Carolina, South Carolina, Georgia, aye, — 7; New York, Delaware, Maryland, no — 3.

The first clause of the eighth Resolution, relating *to a council of revision*, was next taken into consideration.

Mr. GERRY doubts whether the Judiciary ought to form a part of it, as they will have a sufficient check against encroachments of their own department by their exposition of the laws, which involved a power of deciding on their constitutionality. In some States the judges had actually set aside laws, as being against the Constitution. This was done, too, with general approbation. It was quite foreign from the nature of their office to make them judges of the policy of public measures. He moves to postpone the clause, in order to propose, " that the National Executive shall have a right to negative any legislative act, which shall not be afterwards passed by —— parts of each branch of the National Legislature."

Mr. KING seconded the motion, observing that the judges ought to be able to expound the law, as it should come before them, free from the bias of having participated in its formation.

Mr. WILSON thinks neither the original proposition nor the amendment goes far enough. If the Legislative, Executive, and Judiciary ought to be distinct and independent, the Executive ought to have an absolute negative. Without such a self-defence, the Legislature can at any moment sink it into non-existence. He was for varying the proposition, in such a manner as to give the Executive and Judiciary jointly an absolute negative.

On the question to postpone, in order to take Mr. GERRY's proposition into consideration, it was agreed to, — Massachusetts, New York, Pennsylvania, North Carolina, South Carolina, Georgia, aye, — 6; Connecticut, Delaware, Maryland, Virginia, no -- 4.

Mr. GERRY's proposition being now before the Committee, Mr. WILSON and Mr. HAMILTON moved, that the last part of it (viz. " which shall not be afterwards passed by —— parts of each branch of the National Legislature"), be struck out, so as to give the Executive an absolute negative on the laws. There was no danger, they thought, of such a power being too much exercised. It was mentioned by Colonel HAMILTON that the King of Great Britain had not exerted his negative since the Revolution.

Mr. GERRY sees no necessity for so great a control over the Legislature, as the best men in the community would be comprised in the two branches of it.

Doctor FRANKLIN said he was sorry to differ from his colleague, for whom he had a very great respect, on any occasion, but he could not help it on this. He had had some experience of this check in the Executive on the Legislature, under the proprietary government of Pennsylvania. The negative of the Governor was constantly made use of to extort money. No good law whatever could be passed without a private bargain with him. An increase of his salary, or some donation, was always made a condition ; till at last it became the regular practice, to have orders in his favor on the Treasury, presented along with the bills to be signed, so that he might actually receive the former before he should sign the latter. When the Indians were scalping the western people, and notice of it arrived, the concurrence of the Governor in the means of self-defence could not be got, till it was agreed that his estate should be exempted from taxation : so that the people were to fight for the security of his property, whilst he was to bear no share of the burden. This was a mischievous sort of check. If the Executive was to have a Council, such a power would be less objectionable. It was true, the King of Great Britain had not, as was said, exerted his negative since the Revolution ; but that matter was easily explained. The bribes and emoluments now given to the members of parliament rendered it unnecessary, every thing being done according to the will of the ministers. He was afraid, if a negative should be given as proposed, that more power and money would be demanded, till at last enough would be got to influence and bribe the Legislature into a complete subjection to the will of the Executive.

Mr. SHERMAN was against enabling any one man to stop the will of the whole. No one man could be found so far above all the rest in wisdom. He thought we ought to avail ourselves of his wisdom in revising the laws, but not permit him to overrule the decided and cool opinions of the Legislature.

Mr. MADISON supposed, that, if a proper proportion of each branch should be required to overrule the objections of the Executive, it would answer the same purpose as an absolute negative. It would rarely, if ever, happen that the Executive, constituted as ours is proposed to be, would have firmness enough to resist the Legislature, unless backed by a certain part of the body itself. The King of Great Britain, with all his splendid attributes, would not be able to withstand the unanimous and eager wishes of both Houses of Parliament. To give such a prerogative would certainly be obnoxious to the temper of this country,—its present temper at least.

Mr. WILSON believed, as others did, that this power would seldom be used. The Legislature would know that such a power existed, and would refrain from such laws as it would be sure to defeat. Its silent operation would therefore preserve harmony and prevent mischief. The case of Pennsylvania formerly was very different from its present case. The Executive was not then, as now to be, appointed by the people. It will not in this case, as in the one cited, be supported by the head of a great empire, actuated by a different and sometimes opposite interest. The salary, too, is now proposed to be fixed by the Constitution, or, if Doctor Franklin's idea should be adopted, all salary whatever interdicted. The requiring a large proportion of each House to overrule the Executive check, might do in peaceable times ; but there might be tempestuous moments in which animosities may run high between the Executive and Legislative branches, and in which the former ought to be able to defend itself.

Mr. BUTLER had been in favor of a single executive magistrate; but could he have entertained an idea that a complete negative on the laws was to be given him, he certainly should have acted very differently. It had been observed, that in all countries the executive power is in a constant course of increase. This was certainly the case in Great Britain. Gentlemen seemed to think that we had nothing to apprehend from an abuse of the executive power. But why might not a Cataline or a Cromwell arise in this country as well as in others?

Mr. BEDFORD was opposed to every check on the Legislature, even the council of revision first proposed. He thought it would be sufficient to mark out in the constitution the boundaries to the legislative authority, which would give all the requisite security to the rights of the other departments. The representatives of the people were the best judges of what was for their interest, and ought

to be under no external control whatever. The two branches
would produce a sufficient control within the Legislature
itself.

Col. MASON observed that a vote had already passed, he
found — he was out at the time — for vesting the executive
powers in a single person. Among these powers was that
of appointing to offices in certain cases. The probable
abuses of a negative had been well explained by Doctor
FRANKLIN, as proved by experience, the best of all tests.
Will not the same door be opened here? The Executive
may refuse its assent to necessary measures, till new appointments shall be referred to him; and, having by degrees
engrossed all these into his own hands, the American Executive, like the British, will, by bribery and influence, save
himself the trouble and odium of exerting his negative
afterwards. We are, Mr. Chairman, going very far in this
business. We are not indeed constituting a British government, but a more dangerous monarchy, an elective one.
We are introducing a new principle into our system, and
not necessary, as in the British government, where the
Executive has greater rights to defend. Do gentlemen
mean to pave the way to hereditary monarchy? Do they
flatter themselves that the people will ever consent to such
an innovation? If they do, I venture to tell them, they
are mistaken. The people never will consent. And do
gentlemen consider the danger of delay, and the still greater
danger of a rejection, not for a moment, but forever, of the
plan which shall be proposed to them? Notwithstanding
the oppression and injustice experienced among us from
democracy, the genius of the people is in favor of it;
and the genius of the people must be consulted. He
could not but consider the Federal system as in effect
dissolved by the appointment of this Convention to devise
a better one. And do gentlemen look forward to the dangerous interval between extinction of an old, and the
establishment of a new, government; and to the scenes of
confusion which may ensue? He hoped that nothing like

a monarchy would ever be attempted in this country. A
hatred to its oppressions had carried the people through the
late Revolution. Will it not be enough to enable the Executive to suspend offensive laws, till they shall be coolly
revised, and the objections to them overruled by a greater
majority than was required in the first instance? He never
could agree to give up all the rights of the people to a single magistrate. If more than one had been fixed on,
greater powers might have been entrusted to the Executive.
He hoped this attempt to give such powers would have its
weight hereafter, as an argument for increasing the number
of the Executive.

Doctor FRANKLIN. A gentleman from South Carolina,
(Mr. BUTLER) a day or two ago called our attention to the
case of the United Netherlands. He wished the gentleman
had been a little fuller, and had gone back to the original
of that government. The people being under great obligations to the Prince of Orange, whose wisdom and bravery
had saved them, chose him for the Stadtholder. He did
very well. Inconveniences, however, were felt from his
powers; which growing more and more oppressive, they
were at length set aside. Still, however, there was a party
for the Prince of Orange, which descended to his son; who
excited insurrections, spilled a great deal of blood, murdered
the De Witts, and got the powers re-vested in the Stadtholder. Afterwards another prince had power to excite
insurrections, and make the Stadtholdership hereditary.
And the present 'Stadtholder is ready to wade through a
bloody civil war to the establishment of a monarchy. Col.
MASON had mentioned the circumstance of appointing
officers. He knew how that point would be managed. No
new appointment would be suffered, as heretofore in Pennsylvania, unless it be referred to the Executive; so that all
profitable offices will be at his disposal. The first man put
at the helm will be a good one. Nobody knows what sort
may come afterwards. The Executive will be always
increasing here, as elsewhere, till it ends in a monarchy.

On the question for striking out, so as to give the Executive an absolute negative,— Massachusetts, Connecticut, New York, Pennsylvania, Delaware, Maryland, Virginia, North Carolina, South Carolina, Georgia, no — 10.

Mr. BUTLER moved that the Resolution be altered so as to read, " Resolved, that the national Executive have a power to suspend any legislative act for the term of ———."

Doctor FRANKLIN seconded the motion.

Mr. GERRY observed, that the power of suspending might do all the mischief dreaded from the negative of useful laws, without answering the salutary purpose of checking unjust or unwise ones.

On the question for giving this suspending power, all the States, to wit, Massachusetts, Connecticut, New York, Pennsylvania, Delaware, Maryland, Virginia, North Carolina, South Carolina, Georgia, were, no.

On a question for enabling *two-thirds* of each branch of the Legislature to overrule the provisionary check, it passed in the affirmative, *sub silentio;* and was inserted in the blank of Mr. GERRY's motion.

On the question of Mr. GERRY's motion, which gave the Executive alone, without the Judiciary, the revisionary control on the laws, unless overruled by two-thirds of each branch, — Massachusetts, New York, Pennsylvania, Delaware, Virginia, North Carolina, South Carolina, Georgia, aye — 8; Connecticut, Maryland, no — 2.

It was moved by Mr. WILSON, seconded by Mr. MADISON, that the following amendment be made to the last Resolution: after the words " national Executive," to add " and a convenient number of the national Judiciary."

An objection of order being taken by Mr. HAMILTON to the introduction of the last amendment at this time, notice was given by Mr. WILSON and Mr. MADISON, that the same would be moved to-morrow; whereupon Wednesday was assigned to reconsider the amendment of Mr. GERRY.

It was then moved and seconded to proceed to the con-

sideration of the ninth Resolution submitted by Mr. RAN-
DOLPH; when, on motion to agree to the first clause, namely,
"*Resolved, that a national Judiciary be established,*" it
passed in the affirmative, *nem. con.*

It was then moved and seconded, to add these words to
the first clause of the ninth Resolution, namely, "to consist of one supreme tribunal, and of one or more inferior
tribunals;" which passed in the affirmative.

The Committee then rose, and the House adjourned.

TUESDAY, JUNE 5TH.

Governor LIVINGSTON, of New Jersey, took his seat.

In Committee of the Whole. — The words "one or more"
were struck out before "inferior tribunals," as an amendment to the last clause of the ninth Resolution. The clause,
"that the national Judiciary be chosen by the National
Legislature," being under consideration.

MR. WILSON opposed the appointment of Judges by the
National Legislature. Experience showed the impropriety
of such appointments by numerous bodies. Intrigue, partiality, and concealment were the necessary consequences.
A principal reason for unity in the Executive was, that
officers might be appointed by a single, responsible person.

MR. RUTLEDGE was by no means disposed to grant so
great a power to any single person. The people will think
we are leaning too much towards monarchy. He was
against establishing any national tribunal, except a single
supreme one. The State tribunals are most proper to decide in all cases in the first instance.

Doctor FRANKLIN observed, that the two modes of
choosing the Judges had been mentioned, to wit, by
the Legislature, and by the Executive. He wished
such other modes to be suggested as might occur to
other gentlemen; it being a point of great moment.
He would mention one which he had understood was
practised in Scotland. He then, in a brief and en-

tertaining manner, related a Scotch mode, in which the nomination proceeded from the lawyers, who always selected the ablest of the profession, in order to get rid of him, and share his practice among themselves. It was here, he said, the interest of the electors to make the best choice, which should always be made the case if possible.

Mr. MADISON disliked the election of the Judges by the Legislature, or any numerous body. Besides the danger of intrigue and partiality, many of the members were not judges of the requisite qualifications. The legislative talents, which were very different from those of a Judge, commonly recommended men to the favor of legislative assemblies. It was known, too, that the accidental circumstances of presence and absence, of being a member or not a member, had a very undue influence on the appointment. On the other hand, he was not satisfied with referring the appointment to the Executive. He rather inclined to give it to the Senatorial branch, as numerous enough to be confided in; as not so numerous as to be governed by the motives of the other branch; and as being sufficiently stable and independent to follow their deliberate judgments. He hinted this only, and moved that the *appointment by the Legislature* might be struck out, and a blank left, to be hereafter filled on maturer reflection. Mr. WILSON seconds it. On the question for striking out, — Massachusetts, New York, New Jersey, Pennsylvania, Delaware, Maryland, Virginia, North Carolina, Georgia, aye — 9; Connecticut, South Carolina, no — 2.

Mr. WILSON gave notice that he should at a future day move for a reconsideration of that clause which respects "inferior tribunals."

Mr. PINCKNEY gave notice, that when the clause respecting the appointment of the Judiciary should again come before the Committee, he should move to restore the "appointment by the National Legislature."

The following clauses of the ninth Resolution were

agreed to, viz., "*to hold their offices during good behaviour, and to receive punctually, at stated times, a fixed compensation for their services, in which no increase nor diminution shall be made so as to affect the persons actually in office at the time of such increase or diminution.*"

The remaining clause of the ninth Resolution was postponed.

The tenth Resolution was agreed to, viz., "*that provision ought to be made for the admission of States, lawfully arising within the limits of the United States, whether from a voluntary junction of government and territory, or otherwise, with the consent of a number of voices in the national legislature less than the whole.*"

The eleventh Resolution *for guaranteeing to States republican government and territory, &c.*, being read,—

Mr. PATTERSON wished the point of representation could be decided before this clause should be considered, and moved to postpone it; which was not opposed, and agreed to,— Connecticut and South Carolina only voting against it.

The twelfth Resolution, *for continuing Congress till a given day, and for fulfilling their engagements*, produced no debate.

On the question, Massachusetts, New York, New Jersey,* Pennsylvania, Maryland, Virginia, North Carolina, South Carolina, Georgia, aye — 8; Connecticut, Delaware, no — 2.

The thirteenth Resolution, to the effect *that provision ought to be made for hereafter amending the system now to be established, without requiring the assent of the National Legislature*, being taken up,—

Mr. PINCKNEY doubted the propriety or necessity of it.

Mr. GERRY favored it. The novelty and difficulty of the experiment requires periodical revision. The prospect of such a revision would also give intermediate stability to the government. Nothing had yet happened in the States where this provision existed to prove its impropriety.—The proposition was postponed for further consideration;

---

* New Jersey omitted in the printed Journal.

the votes being,— Massachusetts, Connecticut, New York, Pennsylvania, Delaware, Maryland, North Carolina, aye — 7 ; Virginia, South Carolina, Georgia, no — 3.

The fourteenth Resolution, *requiring oath from the State officers to support the National Government,*—was postponed, after a short, uninteresting conversation ; the votes,— Connecticut, New Jersey, Maryland, Virginia, South Carolina, Georgia, aye—6 ; New York, Pennsylvania, Delaware, North Carolina, no—4 ; Massachusetts, divided.

The fifteenth Resolution, for *recommending conventions under appointment of the people to ratify the new Constitution, &c.,* being taken up,—

Mr. SHERMAN thought such a popular ratification unnecessary ; the Articles of Confederation providing for changes and alterations, with the assent of Congress, and ratification of State Legislatures.

Mr. MADISON thought this provision essential. The Articles of Confederation themselves were defective in this respect, resting, in many of the States, on the legislative sanction only. Hence, in conflicts between acts of the States and of Congress, especially where the former are of posterior date, and the decision is to be made by State tribunals, an uncertainty must necessarily prevail ; or rather perhaps a certain decision in favor of the State authority. He suggested also, that, as far as the Articles of Union were to be considered as a treaty only, of a particular sort, among the governments of independent states, the doctrine might be set up that a breach of any one Article, by any of the parties, absolved the other parties from the whole obligation. For these reasons, as well as others, he thought it indispensable that the new Constitution should be ratified in the most unexceptionable form, and by the supreme authority of the people themselves.

Mr. GERRY observed, that in the Eastern States the Confederation had been sanctioned by the people themselves. He seemed afraid of referring the new system to them. The people in that quarter have at this time the wildest ideas of government in the world. They were for abolishing the Senate in Massachusetts, and giving all the other powers of government to the other branch of the Legislature.

Mr. KING supposed, that the last Article of the Confederation rendered the Legislature competent to the ratification. The people of the Southern States, where the Federal Articles had been ratified by the Legislatures only, had since, *impliedly*, given their sanction to it. He thought, notwithstanding, that there might be policy in varying the mode. A convention being a single house, the adoption may more easily be carried through it, than through the Legislatures, where there are several branches. The Legislatures also, being to lose power, will be most likely to raise objections. The people having already parted with the necessary powers, it is immaterial to them, by which government they are possessed, provided they be well employed.

Mr. WILSON took this occasion to lead the Committee, by a train of observations, to the idea of not suffering a disposition in the plurality of States, to confederate anew on better principles, to be defeated by the inconsiderate or selfish opposition of a few States. He hoped the provision for ratifying would be put on such a footing as to admit of such a partial union, with a door open for the accession of the rest.*

Mr. PINCKNEY hoped, that, in case the experiment should not unanimously take place, nine States might be authorized to unite under the same government.

The fifteenth Resolution was postponed, *nem. con.*

Mr. PINCKNEY and Mr. RUTLEDGE moved, that to-morrow be assigned to reconsider that clause of the fourth Resolution which respects the election of the first branch of the National Legislature; which passed in the affirmative,— Connecticut, New York, Pennsylvania, Delaware, Maryland,

---

* This hint was probably meant *in terrorem* to the smaller States of New Jersey and Delaware. Nothing was said in reply to it.

Virginia, aye — 6; Massachusetts, New Jersey, North Carolina, South Carolina, Georgia, no — 5.

Mr. RUTLEDGE having obtained a rule for reconsideration of the clause for establishing *inferior* tribunals under
the national authority, now moved that that part of the
clause in the ninth Resolution should be expunged; arguing, that the State tribunals might and ought to be left in
all cases to decide in the first instance, the right of appeal
to the supreme national tribunal being sufficient to secure
the national rights and uniformity of judgments; that it
was making an unnecessary encroachment on the jurisdiction of the States, and creating unnecessary obstacles to
their adoption of the new system.

Mr. SHERMAN seconded the motion.

Mr. MADISON observed, that unless inferior tribunals
were dispersed throughout the Republic with *final* jurisdiction in *many* cases, appeals would be multiplied to a most
oppressive degree; that, besides, an appeal would not in
many cases be a remedy. What was to be done after improper verdicts, in State tribunals, obtained under the
biassed directions of a dependent judge, or the local prejudices of an undirected jury? To remand the cause for a
new trial would answer no purpose. To order a new trial
at the supreme bar, would oblige the parties to bring up
their witnesses, though ever so distant from the seat of
the court. An effective Judiciary establishment commen-
surate to the Legislative authority, was essential. A government, without a proper Executive and Judiciary, would
be the mere trunk of a body, without arms or legs to act
or move.

Mr. WILSON opposed the motion on like grounds. He
said the admiralty jurisdiction ought to be given wholly to
the National Government, as it related to cases not within
the jurisdiction of particular States, and to a scene in which
controversies with foreigners would be most likely to happen.

Mr. SHERMAN was in favor of the motion. He dwelt

8

chiefly on the supposed expensiveness of having a new set of courts, when the existing State courts would answer the same purpose.

Mr. DICKINSON contended strongly, that if there was to be a National Legislature, there ought to be a National Judiciary, and that the former ought to have authority to institute the latter.

On the question for Mr. RUTLEDGE's motion to strike out " inferior tribunal," it passed in the affirmative,— Connecticut, New York, New Jersey, North Carolina, South Carolina, Georgia, aye — 6; Pennsylvania, Delaware, Maryland, Virginia, no — 4; Massachusetts, divided.

Mr. WILSON and Mr. MADISON then moved, in pursuance of the idea expressed above by Mr. DICKINSON, to add to the ninth Resolution the words following: " that the National Legislature be empowered to institute inferior tribunals." They observed, that there was a distinction between establishing such tribunals absolutely, and giving a discretion to the Legislature to establish or not to establish them. They repeated the necessity of some such provision.

Mr. BUTLER. The people will not bear such innovations. The States will revolt at such encroachments. Supposing such an establishment to be useful, we must not venture on it. We must follow the example of Solon, who gave the Athenians not the best government he could devise, but the best they would receive.

Mr. KING remarked, as to the comparative expense, that the establishment of inferior tribunals would cost infinitely less than the appeals that would be prevented by them.

On this question, as moved by Mr. WILSON and Mr. MADISON,— Massachusetts, New Jersey,* Pennsylvania, Delaware, Maryland, Virginia, North Carolina, Georgia, aye — 8; Connecticut, South Carolina, no — 2; New York, divided.

The Committee then rose, and the House adjourned.

---

* In the printed Journal, New Jersey, no.

WEDNESDAY, JUNE 6TH.

In Committee of the Whole.— Mr. PINCKNEY, according to previous notice, and rule obtained, moved, " that the first branch of the National Legislature be elected by the State Legislatures, and not by the people;" contending that the people were less fit judges in such a case, and that the Legislatures would be less likely to promote the adoption of the new government if they were to be excluded from all share in it.

Mr. RUTLEDGE seconded the motion.

Mr. GERRY. Much depends on the mode of election. In England the people will probably lose their liberty from the smallness of the proportion having a right of suffrage. Our danger arises from the opposite extreme. Hence in Massachusetts the worst men get into the Legislature. Several members of that body had lately been convicted of infamous crimes. Men of indigence, ignorance, and baseness, spare no pains, however dirty, to carry their point against men who are superior to the artifices practised. He was not disposed to run into extremes. He was as much principled as ever against aristocracy and monarchy. It was necessary, on the one hand, that the people should appoint one branch of the government, in order to inspire them with the necessary confidence; but he wished the election, on the other, to be so modified as to secure more effectually a just preference of merit. His idea was, that the people should nominate certain persons, in certain districts, out of whom the State Legislatures should make the appointment.

Mr. WILSON. He wished for vigor in the government, but he wished that vigorous authority to flow immediately from the legitimate source of all authority. The government ought to possess, not only, first, the *force*, but second, the *mind or sense*, of the people at large. The Legislature ought to be the most exact transcript of the whole society. Representation is made necessary only because it is impossible for the people to act collectively. The opposition was to be expected, he said, from the *governments*, not from the citizens of the States. The latter had parted, as was observed by Mr. KING, *with all the necessary powers;* and it was immaterial to them by whom they were exercised, if well exercised. The State officers were to be the losers of power. The people, he supposed, would be rather more attached to the National Government than to the State Governments, as being more important in itself, and more flattering to their pride. There is no danger of improper elections, if made by *large* districts. Bad elections proceed from the smallness of the districts, which give an opportunity to bad men to intrigue themselves into office.

Mr. SHERMAN. If it were in view to abolish the State Governments, the elections ought to be by the people. If the State Governments are to be continued, it is necessary, in order to preserve harmony between the National and State Governments, that the elections to the former should be made by the latter. The right of participating in the National Government would be sufficiently secured to the people by their election of the State Legislatures. The objects of the Union, he thought were few,— first, defence against foreign danger; secondly, against internal disputes, and a resort to force; thirdly, treaties with foreign nations; fourthly, regulating foreign commerce, and drawing revenue from it. These, and perhaps a few lesser objects, alone rendered a confederation of the States necessary. All other matters, civil and criminal, would be much better in the hands of the States. The people are more happy in small than in large States. States, may, indeed, be too small, as Rhode Island, and thereby be too subject to faction. Some others were, perhaps, too large, the powers of government not being able to pervade them. He was for giving the General Government power to legislate and execute within a defined province.

Col. MASON. Under the existing Confederacy, Congress represent the *States*, and not the *people* of the States;

their acts operate on the *States*, not on the *individuals*. The case will be changed in the new plan of government. The people will be represented; they ought therefore to choose the Representatives. The requisites in actual representation are, that the representatives should sympathize with their constituents; should think as they think, and feel as they feel; and that for these purposes they should be residents among them. Much, he said, had been alleged against democratic elections. He admitted that much might be said; but it was to be considered that no government was free from imperfections and evils; and that improper elections in many instances were inseparable from republican governments. But compare these with the advantage of this form, in favor of the rights of the people, in favor of human nature! He was persuaded there was a better chance for proper elections by the people, if divided into large districts, than by the State Legislatures. Paper-money had been issued by the latter, when the former were against it. Was it to be supposed that the State Legislatures, then, would not send to the National Legislature patrons of such projects, if the choice depended on them?

Mr. MADISON considered an election of one branch, at least, of the Legislature by the people immediately, as a clear principle of free government; and that this mode, under proper regulations, had the additional advantage of securing better representatives, as well as of avoiding too great an agency of the State Governments in the general one. He differed from the member from Connecticut, (Mr. SHERMAN,) in thinking the objects mentioned to be all the principal ones that required a national government. Those were certainly important and necessary objects; but he combined with them the necessity of providing more effectually for the security of private rights, and the steady dispensation of justice. Interferences with these were evils which had, more perhaps than anything else, produced this Convention. Was it to be supposed, that republican liberty could long exist under the abuses of it practised in some of the States? The gentleman (Mr. SHERMAN) had admitted, that in a very small State faction and oppression would prevail. It was to be inferred, then, that wherever these prevailed the State was too small. Had they not prevailed in the largest as well as the smallest, though less than in the smallest? And were we not thence admonished to enlarge the sphere as far as the nature of the government would admit? This was the only defence against the inconveniences of democracy, consistent with the democratic form of government. All civilized societies would be divided into different sects, factions, and interests, as they happened to consist of rich and poor, debtors and creditors, the landed, the manufacturing, the commercial interests, the inhabitants of this district or that district, the followers of this political leader or that political leader, the disciples of this religious sect or that religious sect. In all cases where a majority are united by a common interest or passion, the rights of the minority are in danger. What motives are to restrain them? A prudent regard to the maxim, that honesty is the best policy, is found by experience to be as little regarded by bodies of men as by individuals. Respect for character is always diminished in proportion to the number among whom the blame or praise is to be divided. Conscience, the only remaining tie, is known to be inadequate in individuals ; in large numbers, little is to be expected from it. Besides, religion itself, may become a motive to persecution and oppression. These observations are verified by the histories of every country, ancient and modern. In Greece and Rome the rich and poor, the creditors and debtors, as well as the patricians and plebeians, alternately oppressed each other with equal unmercifulness. What a source of oppression was the relation between the parent cities of Rome, Athens, and Carthage, and their respective provinces ; the former possessing the power, and the latter being sufficiently distinguished to be separate objects of it ? Why was America so justly apprehensive of parliamentary injustice ? Because Great Britain had a separate interest, real or supposed, and, if her authority had been admitted, could have pursued that interest at our expense. We have seen the mere distinction of color made, in the most enlightened period of time, a ground of the most oppressive dominion ever exercised by man over man. What has been the source of those unjust laws complained of among ourselves? Has it not been the real or supposed interest of the major number ? Debtors have defrauded their creditors. The landed interest has borne hard on the mercantile interest. The holders of one species of property have thrown a disproportion of taxes on the holders of another species. The lesson we are to draw from the whole is, that where a majority are united by a common sentiment, and have an opportunity, the rights of the minor party become insecure. In a republican government, the majority, if united, have always an opportunity. The only remedy is, to enlarge the sphere, and thereby divide the community into so great a number of interests and parties, that, in the first place, a majority will not be likely, at the same moment, to have a common interest separate from that of the whole, or of the minority ; and in the second place, that in case they should have such an interest, they may not be so apt to unite in the pursuit of it. It was incumbent on us, then, to try this remedy, and, with that view, to frame a republican system on such a scale, and in such a form, as will control all the evils which have been experienced.

Mr. DICKINSON considered it essential, that one branch of the Legislature should be drawn immediately from the people; and expedient, that the other should be chosen by the Legislatures of the States. This combination of the State Governments with the National Government was as politic as it was unavoidable. In the formation of the Senate, we ought to carry it through such a refining process as will assimilate it, as nearly as may be, to the House of Lords in England. He repeated his warm eulogiums on the British Constitution. He was for a strong National

Government; but for leaving the States a considerable
agency in the system. The objection against making the
former dependent on the latter might be obviated by giving
to the Senate an authority permanent, and irrevocable for
three, five or seven years. Being thus independent, they
will check and decide with uncommon freedom.

Mr. READ. Too much attachment is betrayed to the
State Governments. We must look beyond their continuance. A National Government must soon of necessity
swallow them all up. They will soon be reduced to the
mere office of electing the National Senate. He was against
patching up the old Federal system: he hoped the idea
would be dismissed. It would be like putting new cloth on
an old garment. The confederation was founded on temporary principles. It cannot last: it cannot be amended.
If we do not establish a good government on new principles, we must either go to ruin, or have the work to do over
again. The people at large are wrongly suspected of being averse to a General Government. The aversion lies
among interested men who possess their confidence.

Mr. PIERCE was for an election by the people as to the
first branch; and by the States as to the second branch; by
which means the citizens of the States would be represented both *individually* and *collectively*.

General PINCKNEY wished to have a good National Government, and at the same time to leave a considerable share
of power in the States. An election of either branch by the
people, scattered as they are in many States, particularly in
South Carolina, was totally impracticable. He differed
from gentlemen who thought that a choice by the people
would be a better guard against bad measures, than by the
Legislatures. A majority of the people in South Carolina
were notoriously for paper-money, as a legal tender; the
Legislature had refused to make it a legal tender. The
reason was, that the latter had some sense of character, and
were restrained by that consideration. The State Legislatures, also, he said, would be more jealous, and more ready

to thwart the National Government, if excluded from a participation in it. The idea of abolishing these Legislatures would never go down.

Mr. WILSON would not have spoken again, but for what had fallen from Mr. READ; namely that the idea of preserving the State Governments ought to be abandoned. He saw no incompatibility between the National and State Governments, provided the latter was restrained to certain local purposes; nor any probability of their being devoured by the former. In all confederated systems, ancient and modern, the reverse had happened; the generality being destroyed gradually by the usurpations of the parts composing it.

On the question for electing the first branch by the State Legislatures as moved by Mr. PINCKNEY, it was negatived,—Connecticut, New Jersey, South Carolina, aye—3; Massachusetts, New York, Pennsylvania, Delaware, Maryland, Virginia, North Carolina, Georgia, no — 8.

Mr. WILSON moved to reconsider the vote excluding the Judiciary from a share in the revision of the laws, and to add, after "national Executive," the words, "with a convenient number of the national Judiciary;" remarking the expediency of reinforcing the Executive with the influence of that department.

Mr. MADISON seconded the motion. He observed, that the great difficulty in rendering the Executive competent to its own defence arose from the nature of republican government, which could not give to an individual citizen that settled pre-eminence in the eyes of the rest, that weight of property, that personal interest against betraying the national interest, which appertain to an hereditary magistrate. In a republic personal merit alone could be the ground of political exaltation; but it would rarely happen that this merit would be so pre-eminent as to produce universal acquiescence. The executive magistrate would be envied and assailed by disappointed competitors: his firmness therefore would need support. He would not possess

those great emoluments from his station, nor that permanent stake in the public interest, which would place him out
of the reach of foreign corruption. He would stand in need
therefore of being controlled as well as supported. An association of the judges in his revisionary function would
both double the advantage, and diminish the danger. It
would also enable the Judiciary department the better to
defend itself against legislative encroachments. Two objections had been made,— first, that the judges ought not to
be subject to the bias which a participation in the making
of laws might give in the exposition of them; secondly, that
the Judiciary department ought to be separate and distinct from the other great departments. The first objection
had some weight; but it was much diminished by reflecting,
that a small proportion of the laws coming in question
before a judge would be such wherein he had been consulted; that a small part of this proportion would be so
ambiguous as to leave room for his prepossessions; and that
but a few cases would probably arise in the life of a judge,
under such ambiguous passages. How much good, on the
other hand, would proceed from the perspicuity, the conciseness, and the systematic character which the code of
laws would receive from the Judiciary talents. As to the
second objection, it either had no weight, or it applied with
equal weight to the Executive, and to the Judiciary revision of the laws. The maxim on which the objection was
founded, required a separation of the Executive, as well as
the Judiciary, from the Legislature and from each other.
There would, in truth, however, be no improper mixture of
these distinct powers in the present case. In England,
whence the maxim itself had been drawn, the Executive had
an absolute negative on the laws; and the supreme tribunal
of justice (the House of Lords), formed one of the other
branches of the Legislature. In short, whether the object
of the revisionary power was to restrain the Legislature
from encroaching on the other co-ordinate departments, or
on the rights of the people at large; or from passing laws

unwise in their principle, or incorrect in their form; the utility of annexing the wisdom and weight of the Judiciary to the Executive seemed incontestable.

Mr. GERRY thought the Executive whilst standing alone would be more impartial than when he could be covered by the sanction and seduced by the sophistry of the Judges.

Mr. KING. If the unity of the Executive was preferred for the sake of responsibility, the policy of it is as applicable to the revisionary, as to the executive, power.

Mr. PINCKNEY had been at first in favor of joining the heads of the principal departments, the Secretary at War, of Foreign Affairs, &c., in the Council of Revision. He had, however, relinquished the idea, from a consideration that these could be called on by the executive magistrate, whenever he pleased to consult them. He was opposed to the introduction of the judges into the business.

Colonel MASON was for giving all possible weight to the revisionary institution. The executive power ought to be well secured against legislative usurpations on it. The purse and the sword ought never to get into the same hands whether legislative or executive.

Mr. DICKINSON. Secrecy, vigor, and despatch are not the principal properties required in the Executive. Important as these are, that of responsibility is more so, which can only be preserved by leaving it singly to discharge its functions. He thought, too, a junction of the Judiciary to it involved an improper mixture of powers.

Mr. WILSON remarked, that the responsibility required belonged to his executive duties. The revisionary duty was an extraneous one, calculated for collateral purposes.

Mr. WILLIAMSON was for substituting a clause requiring two-thirds for every effective act of the legislature, in place of the revisionary provision.

On the question for joining the judges to the Executive in the revisionary business,— Connecticut, New York, Virginia, aye — 3; Massachusetts, New Jersey, Pennsylvania, Delaware, Maryland, North Carolina, South Carolina, Georgia, no — 8.

Mr. PINCKNEY gave notice, that to-morrow he should move for the re-consideration of that clause in the sixth Resolution adopted by the Committee, which vests a negative in the National Legislature on the laws of the several States.

The Committee rose, and the House adjourned.

THURSDAY, JUNE 7TH.

In Committee of the Whole — Mr. PINCKNEY, according to notice, moved to reconsider the clause respecting the negative on State laws, which was agreed to, and to-morrow fixed for the purpose.

The clause providing for the appointment of the second branch of the National Legislature, having lain blank since the last vote on the mode of electing it, to wit, by the first branch, Mr. DICKINSON now moved, "that the members of the second branch ought to be chosen by the individual Legislatures."

Mr. SHERMAN seconded the motion; observing, that the particular States would thus become interested in supporting the National Government, and that a due harmony between the two governments would be maintained. He admitted that the two ought to have separate and distinct jurisdictions, but that they ought to have a mutual interest in supporting each other.

Mr. PINCKNEY. If the small States should be allowed one Senator only, the number will be too great; there will be eighty at least.

Mr. DICKINSON had two reasons for his motion — first, because the sense of the States would be better collected through their Governments, than immediately from the people at large; secondly, because he wished the Senate to consist of the most distinguished characters, distinguished for their rank in life and their weight of property, and bearing as strong a likeness to the British House of Lords. as possible; and he thought such characters more likely to be selected by the State Legislatures, than in any other mode. The greatness of the number was no objection with him. He hoped there would be eighty, and twice eighty of them. If their number should be small, the popular branch could not be balanced by them. The Legislature of a numerous people ought to be a numerous body.

Mr. WILLIAMSON preferred a small number of Senators, but wished that each State should have at least one. He suggested twenty-five as a convenient number. The different modes of representation in the different branches will serve as a mutual check.

Mr. BUTLER was anxious to know the ratio of representation before he gave any opinion.

Mr. WILSON. If we are to establish a National Government, that government ought to flow from the people at large. If one branch of it should be chosen by the Legislatures, and the other by the people, the two branches will rest on different foundations, and dissensions will naturally arise between them. He wished the Senate to be elected by the people, as well as the other branch; the people might be divided into proper districts for the purpose; and he moved to postpone the motion of Mr. DICKINSON, in order to take up one of that import.

Mr. MORRIS seconded him.

Mr. READ proposed " that the Senate should be appointed by the Executive magistrate, out of a proper number of persons to be nominated by the individual Legislatures." He said, he thought it his duty to speak his mind frankly. Gentlemen he hoped would not be alarmed at the idea. Nothing short of this approach towards a proper model of government would answer the purpose, and he thought it best to come directly to the point at once. His proposition was not seconded nor supported.

Mr. MADISON. If the motion (of Mr. DICKINSON) should be agreed to, we must either depart from the doctrine of proportional representation, or admit into the Senate a very large number of members. The first is inadmissible, being evidently unjust. The second is inexpedient. The use of the Senate is to consist in its proceeding with more coolness, with more system, and with more wisdom, than the popular branch. Enlarge their number, and you communicate to them the vices which they are meant to correct. He differed from Mr. DICKINSON, who thought that the additional number would give additional weight to the body. On the contrary, it appeared to him that their weight would be in an inverse ratio to their numbers. The example of the Roman tribunes was applicable. They lost their influence and power, in proportion as their number was augmented. The reason seemed to be obvious: they were appointed to take care of the popular interests and pretensions at Rome; because the people by reason of their numbers could not act in concert, and were liable to fall into factions among themselves, and to become a prey to their aristocratic adversaries. The more the representatives of the people, therefore, were multiplied, the more they partook of the infirmities of their constituents, the more liable they became to be divided among themselves, either from their own indiscretions or the artifices of the opposite faction, and of course the less capable of fulfilling their trust. When the weight of a set of men depends merely on their personal characters, the greater the number, the greater the weight. When it depends on the degree of political authority lodged in them, the smaller the number, the greater the weight. These considerations might perhaps be combined in the intended Senate; but the latter was the material one.

Mr. GERRY. Four modes of appointing the Senate have been mentioned. First, by the first branch of the National Legislature,— this would create a dependence contrary to the end proposed. Secondly, by the National Executive,— this is a stride towards monarchy that few will think of. Thirdly, by the people; the people have two great interests, the landed interest, and the commercial, including the stockholders. To draw both branches from the people will leave no security to the latter interest; the people being chiefly composed of the landed interest, and erroneously supposing that the other interests are adverse to it. Fourthly, by the individual Legislatures,— the elections being carried through this refinement, will be most like to provide some check in favor of the commercial interest against the landed; without which, oppression will take place; and no free government can last long where that is the case. He was therefore in favor of this last.

Mr. DICKINSON.* The preservation of the States in a certain degree of agency is indispensable. It will produce that collision between the different authorities which should be wished for in order to check each other. To attempt to abolish the States altogether, would degrade the councils of our country, would be impracticable, would be ruinous. He compared the proposed national system to the solar system, in which the States were the planets, and ought to be left to move freely in their proper orbits. The gentleman from Pennsylvania (Mr. WILSON) wished, he said, to extinguish these planets. If the State Governments were excluded from all agency in the national one, and all power drawn from the people at large, the consequence would be that the National Government would move in the same direction as the State Governments now do, and would run into all the same mischiefs. The reform would only unite the thirteen small streams into one great current, pursuing the same course without any opposition whatever. He adhered to the opinion that the Senate ought to be composed of a large number; and that their influence, from family weight and other causes, would be increased thereby. He did not admit that the Tribunes lost their weight in proportion as

---

* It will throw light on this discussion to remark that an election by the State Legislatures involved a surrender of the principle insisted on by the large States, and dreaded by the small ones, namely, that of a proportional representation in the Senate. Such a rule would make the body too numerous, as the smallest State must elect one member at least.

their number was augmented, and gave a historical sketch of this institution. If the reasoning (of Mr. MADISON) was good, it would prove that the number of the Senate ought to be reduced below ten, the highest number of the Tribunitial corps.

Mr. WILSON. The subject, it must be owned, is surrounded with doubts and difficulties. But we must surmount them. The British Government cannot be our model. We have no materials for a similar one. Our manners, our laws, the abolition of entails and of primogeniture, the whole genius of the people, are opposed to it. He did not see the danger of the States being devoured by the National Government. On the contrary, he wished to keep them from devouring the National Government. He was not, however, for extinguishing these planets, as was supposed by Mr. DICKINSON; neither did he, on the other hand, believe that they would warm or enlighten the sun. Within their proper orbits they must still be suffered to act for subordinate purposes, for which their existence is made essential by the great extent of our country. He could not comprehend in what manner the landed interest would be rendered less predominant in the Senate by an election through the medium of the Legislatures, than by the people themselves. If the Legislatures, as was now complained, sacrificed the commercial to the landed interest, what reason was there to expect such a choice from them as would defeat their own views? He was for an election by the people, in large districts, which would be most likely to obtain men of intelligence and uprightness; subdividing the districts only for the accommodation of voters.

Mr. MADISON could as little comprehend in what manner family weight, as desired by Mr. DICKINSON, would be more certainly conveyed into the Senate through elections by the State Legislatures, than in some other modes. The true question was, in what mode the best choice would be made? If an election by the people, or through any other channel than the State Legislatures, promised as uncorrupt and impartial a preference of merit, there could surely be no necessity for an appointment by those Legislatures. Nor was it apparent that a more useful check would be derived through that channel, than from the people through some other. The great evils complained of were, that the State Legislatures run into schemes of paper-money, &c., whenever solicited by the people, and sometimes without even the sanction of the people. Their influence, then, instead of checking a like propensity in the National Legislature, may be expected to promote it. Nothing can be more contradictory than to say that the National Legislature, without a proper check, will follow the example of the State Legislatures; and, in the same breath, that the State Legislatures are the only proper check.

Mr. SHERMAN opposed elections by the people in districts, as not likely to produce such fit men as elections by the State Legislatures.

Mr. GERRY insisted, that the commercial and monied interest would be more secure in the hands of the State Legislatures, than of the people at large. The former have more sense of character, and will be restrained by that from injustice. The people are for paper-money, when the Legislatures are against it. In Massachusetts the county conventions had declared a wish for a *depreciating* paper that would sink itself. Besides, in some States there are two branches in the Legislature, one of which is somewhat aristocratic. There would therefore be so far a better chance of refinement in the choice. There seemed, he thought, to be three powerful objections against elections by districts. First, it is impracticable ; the people cannot be brought to one place for the purpose ; and, whether brought to the same place or not, numberless frauds would be unavoidable. Secondly, small States, forming part of the same district with a large one, or a large part of a large one, would have no chance of gaining an appointment for its citizens of merit. Thirdly, a new source of discord would be opened between different parts of the same district.

9

Mr. PINCKNEY thought the second branch ought to be permanent and independent ; and that the members of it would be rendered more so by receiving their appointments from the State Legislatures. This mode would avoid the rivalships and discontents incident to the election by districts. He was for dividing the States in three classes, according to their respective sizes, and for allowing to the first class three members ; to the second, two ; and to the third, one.

On the question for postponing Mr. DICKINSON's motion, referring the appointment of the Senate to the State Legislatures, in order to consider Mr. WILSON's for referring it to the people, Pennsylvania, aye—1 ; Massachusetts, Connecticut, New York, New Jersey, Delaware, Maryland, Virginia, North Carolina, South Carolina, Georgia, no—10.

Col. MASON. Whatever power may be necessary for the National Government, a certain portion must necessarily be left with the States. It is impossible for one power to pervade the extreme parts of the United States, so as to carry equal justice to them. The State Legislatures also ought to have some means of defending themselves against encroachments of the National Government. In every other department we have studiously endeavoured to provide for its self-defence. Shall we leave the States alone unprovided with the means for this purpose ? And what better means can we provide, than the giving them some share in, or rather to make them a constituent part of, the national establishment ? There is danger on both sides, no doubt ; but we have only seen the evils arising on the side of the State Governments. Those on the other side remain to be displayed. The example of Congress does not apply. Congress had no power to carry their acts into execution, as the National Government will have.

On Mr. DICKINSON's motion for an appointment of the Senate by the State Legislatures,— Massachusetts, Connecticut, New York, Pennsylvania, Delaware, Maryland, Virginia, North Carolina, South Carolina, Georgia, aye—10.

Mr. GERRY gave notice, that he would to-morrow move for a reconsideration of the mode of appointing the National Executive, in order to substitute an appointment by the State Executives.

The Committee rose, and the House adjourned.

FRIDAY, JUNE 8TH.

In Committee of the Whole.—On a reconsideration of the clause giving the National Legislature a negative on such laws of the States as might be contrary to the Articles of Union, or treaties with foreign nations;

Mr. PINCKNEY moved, "that the National Legislature should have authority to negative all laws which they should judge to be improper." He urged that such a universality of the power was indispensably necessary to render it effectual; that the States must be kept in due subordination to the nation ; that if the States were left to act of themselves in any case, it would be impossible to defend the national prerogatives, however extensive they might be, on paper ; that the acts of Congress had been defeated by this means ; nor had foreign treaties escaped repeated violations : that this universal negative was in fact the cornerstone of an efficient national Government ; that under the British Government the negative of the Crown had been found beneficial, and the *States* are more one nation now, than the *colonies* were then.

Mr. MADISON seconded the motion. He could not but regard an indefinite power to negative legislative acts of the States as absolutely necessary to a perfect system. Experience had evinced a constant tendency in the States to encroach on the Federal authority ; to violate national treaties ; to infringe the rights and interests of each other ; to oppress the weaker party within their respective jurisdictions. A negative was the mildest expedient that could be devised for preventing these mischiefs. The existence of such a check would prevent attempts to commit them. Should no such precaution be engrafted, the only remedy would be in an appeal to coercion. Was such a remedy eligible? Was it practicable? Could the national resources, if exerted to the utmost, enforce a national decree against Massachusetts, abetted, perhaps, by several of her neighbours? It would not be possible. A small proportion of the community, in a compact situation, acting on the defensive, and at one of its extremities, might at any time bid defiance to the national authority. Any government for the United States, formed on the supposed practicability of using force against the unconstitutional proceedings of the States, would prove as visionary and fallacious as the government of Congress. The negative would render the use of force unnecessary. The States could of themselves pass no operative act, any more than one branch of a legislature, where there are two branches, can proceed without the other. But in order to give the negative this efficacy, it must extend to all cases. A discrimination would only be a fresh source of contention between the two authorities. In a word, to recur to the illustrations borrowed from the planetary system, this prerogative of the General Government is the great pervading principle that must control the centrifugal tendency of the States ; which, without it, will continually fly out of their proper orbits, and destroy the order and harmony of the political system.

Mr. WILLIAMSON was against giving a power that might restrain the States from regulating their internal police.

Mr. GERRY could not see the extent of such a power, and was against every power that was not necessary. He thought a remonstrance against unreasonable acts of the States would restrain them. If it should not, force might be resorted to. He had no objection to authorize a negative to paper-money and similar measures. When the confederation was depending before Congress, Massachusetts was then for inserting the power of emitting paper-money among the exclusive powers of Congress. He observed, that the proposed negative would extend to the regulations of the militia, a matter on which the existence of the State might depend. The National Legislature, with such a power, may enslave the States. Such an idea as this will never be acceded to. It has never been suggested or conceived among the people. No speculative projector — and there are enough of that character among us, in politics as well as in other things — has, in any pamphlet or newspaper, thrown out the idea. The States, too, have different interests, and are ignorant of each other's interests. The negative, therefore, will be abused. New States, too, having separate views from the old States, will never come into the Union. They may even be under some foreign influence; are they in such case to participate in the negative on the will of the other States?

Mr. SHERMAN thought the cases in which the negative ought to be exercised might be defined. He wished the point might not be decided till a trial at least should be made for that purpose.

Mr. WILSON would not say what modifications of the proposed power might be practicable or expedient. But however novel it might appear, the principle of it, when viewed with a close and steady eye, is right. There is no instance in which the laws say that the individual should be bound in one case, and at liberty to judge whether he will obey or disobey in another. The cases are parallel. Abuses of the power over the individual persons may happen, as well as over the individual States. Federal liberty is to the States what civil liberty is to private individuals; and States are not more unwilling to purchase it, by the necessary concession of their political sovereignty, than the savage is to purchase civil liberty by the surrender of the personal sovereignty, which he enjoys in a state of nature. A definition of the cases in which the negative should be exercised is impracticable. A discretion must be left on one side or the other,— will it not be most safely lodged on the side of the National Government? Among the first sentiments expressed in the first Congress, one was, that

Virginia is no more, that Massachusetts is no more, that Pennsylvania is no more, &c. — we are now one nation of brethren;— we must bury all local interests and distinctions. This language continued for some time. The tables at length began to turn. No sooner were the State Governments formed than their jealousy and ambition began to display themselves; each endeavoured to cut a slice from the common loaf, to add to its own morsel, till at length the Confederation became frittered down to the impotent condition in which it now stands. Review the progress of the Articles of Confederation through Congress, and compare the first and last draught of it. To correct its vices is the business of this convention. One of its vices is the want of an effectual control in the whole over its parts. What danger is there that the whole will unnecessarily sacrifice a part? But reverse the case, and leave the whole at the mercy of each part, and will not the general interest be continually sacrificed to local interests?

Mr. DICKINSON deemed it impossible to draw a line between the cases proper, and improper, for the exercise of the negative. We must take our choice of two things. We must either subject the States to the danger of being injured by the power of the National Government, or the latter to the danger of being injured by that of the States. He thought the danger greater from the States. To leave the power doubtful, would be opening another spring of discord, and he was for shutting as many of them as possible.

Mr. BEDFORD, in answer to his colleague's question, where would be the danger to the States from this power, would refer him to the smallness of his own State, which may be injured at pleasure without redress. It was meant, he found, to strip the small States of their equal right of suffrage. In this case Delaware would have about one-ninetieth for its share in the general councils; whilst Pennsylvania and Virginia would possess one-third of the whole. Is there no difference of interests, no rivalship of commerce, of manufactures? Will not these large States crush the small ones, whenever they stand in the way of their ambitious or interested views? This shows the impossibility of adopting such a system as that on the table, or any other founded on a change in the principle of representation. And after all, if a State does not obey the law of the new system, must not force be resorted to, as the only ultimate remedy in this as in any other system? It seems as if Pennsylvania and Virginia, by the conduct of their deputies, wished to provide a system in which they would have an enormous and monstrous influence. Besides, how can it be thought that the proposed negative can be exercised? Are the laws of the States to be suspended in the most urgent cases, until they can be sent seven or eight hundred miles, and undergo the deliberation of a body who may be incapable of judging of them? Is the National Legislature, too, to sit continually in order to revise the laws of the States?

Mr. MADISON observed, that the difficulties which had been started were worthy of attention, and ought to be answered before the question was put. The case of laws of urgent necessity must be provided for by some emanation of the power from the National Government into each State, so far as to give a temporary assent at least. This was the practice in the Royal Colonies before the Revolution, and would not have been inconvenient if the supreme power of negativing had been faithful to the American interest, and had possessed the necessary information. He supposed that the negative might be very properly lodged in the Senate alone, and that the more numerous and expensive branch therefore might not be obliged to sit constantly. He asked Mr. BEDFORD, what would be the consequence to the small States of a ddissolution of the Union, which seemed likely to happen if no effectual substitute was made for the defective system existing? — and he did not conceive any effectual system could be substituted on any other basis than that of a proportional suffrage. If the large States possessed the avarice and ambition with which they were charged, would the small ones in their neighbourhood be more secure when all control of a General Government was withdrawn?

Mr. BUTLER was vehement against the negative in the proposed extent, as cutting off all hope of equal justice to the distant States. The people there would not, he was sure give it a hearing.

On the question for extending the negative power to all cases, as proposed by Mr. PINCKNEY and Mr. MADISON,— Massachusetts, Pennsylvania, Virginia, (Mr. RANDOLPH and Mr. MASON, no; Mr. BLAIR, Doctor McCLURG and Mr. MADISON, aye; General WASHINGTON not consulted,) aye — 3; Connecticut, New York, New Jersey, Maryland, North Carolina, South Carolina, Georgia, no — 7; Delaware, divided, (Mr. READ and Mr. DICKINSON, aye; Mr. BEDFORD and Mr. BASSET, no).

On motion of Mr. GERRY and Mr. KING, to-morrow was assigned for reconsidering the mode of appointing the national Executive; the reconsideration being voted for by all the States except Connecticut and North Carolina.

Mr. PINCKNEY and Mr. RUTLEDGE moved to add to the fourth Resolution, agreed to by the Committee, the following, viz.: " that the States be divided into three classes, the first class to have three members, the second two, and the third one member, each; that an estimate be taken of the comparative importance of each State at fixed periods, so as to ascertain the number of members they may from time to time be entitled to." The Committee then rose, and the House adjourned.

SATURDAY, JUNE 9TH.

Mr. LUTHER MARTIN, from Maryland, took his seat.

In Committee of the Whole,—Mr. GERRY, according to previous notice given by him, moved " that the national Executive should be elected by the Executives of the States, whose proportion of votes should be the same with that allowed to the States, in the election of the Senate." If the appointment should be made by the National Legislature, it would lessen that independence of the Executive, which ought to prevail; would give birth to intrigue and corruption between the Executive and Legislature previous to the election, and to partiality in the Executive afterwards to the friends who promoted him. Some other mode, therefore, appeared to him necessary. He proposed that of appointing by the State Executives, as most analagous to the principle observed in electing the other branches of the National Government; the first branch being chosen by the *people* of the States and the second by the Legislatures of the States, he did not see any objection against letting the Executive be appointed by the Executives of the States. He supposed the Executives would be most likely to select the fittest men, and that it would be their interest to support the man of their own choice.

Mr. RANDOLPH urged strongly the inexpediency of Mr. GERRY's mode of appointing the National Executive. The confidence of the people would not be secured by it to the National magistrate. The small States would lose all chance of an appointment from within themselves. Bad appointments would be made, the Executives of the States being little conversant with characters not within their own small spheres. The State Executives, too, notwithstanding their constitutional independence, being in fact dependent on the State Legislatures, will generally be guided by the views of the latter, and prefer either favorites within the States, or such as it may be expected will be most partial to the interests of the State. A national Executive thus chosen will not be likely to defend with becoming vigilance and firmness the national rights against State encroachments. Vacancies also must happen. How can these be filled? He could not suppose, either, that the Executives would feel the interest in supporting the national Executive which had been imagined. They will not cherish the great oak which is to reduce them to paltry shrubs.

On the question for referring the appointment of the national Executive to the State Executives, as proposed by Mr. GERRY,— Massachusetts, Connecticut, New York, New Jersey, Pennsylvania, Maryland, Virginia, South Carolina, Georgia, no; Delaware, divided.

Mr. PATTERSON moved, that the Committee resume the clause relating to the rule of suffrage in the National Legislature.

Mr. BREARLY seconds him. He was sorry, he said, that any question on this point was brought into view. It had been much agitated in Congress at the time of forming the Confederation, and was then rightly settled by allowing to each sovereign State an equal vote. Otherwise, the smaller States must have been destroyed instead of being saved. The substitution of a ratio, he admitted, carried fairness on the face of it; but on a deeper examination was unfair and unjust. Judging of the disparity of the States by the quota of Congress, Virginia would have sixteen votes, and Georgia but one. A like proportion to the others will make the whole number ninety. There will be three large States, and ten small ones. The large States, by which he meant Massachusetts, Pennsylvania and Virginia, will carry every thing before them. It had been admitted, and was known to him from facts within New Jersey that where large and small counties were united into a district for electing representatives for the district, the large counties always carried their point, and consequently the States would do so. Virginia with her sixteen votes will be a solid column indeed, a formidable phalanx. While Georgia with her solitary vote, and the other little States, will be obliged to throw themselves constantly into the scale of some large one, in order to have any weight at all. He had come to the Convention with a view of being as useful as he could, in giving energy and stability to the Federal Government. When the proposition for destroying the equality of votes came forward, he was astonished, he was alarmed. Is it fair, then, it will be asked, that Georgia should have an equal vote with Virginia? He would not say it was. What remedy, then? One only, that a map of the United States be spread out, that all the existing boundaries be erased, and that a new partition of the whole be made into thirteen equal parts.

Mr. PATTERSON considered the proposition for a proportional representation as striking at the existence of the lesser States. He would premise, however, to an investigation of this question, some remarks on the nature, structure, and powers of the Convention. The Convention, he said, was formed in pursuance of an act of Congress; that this act was recited in several of the commissions, particularly that of Massachusetts, which he required to be read; that the amendment of the Confederacy was the object of all the laws and commissions on the subject; that the Articles of the Confederation were therefore the proper basis of all the proceedings of the Convention; that we ought to keep within its limits, or we should be charged by our constituents with usurpation; that the people of America were sharp-sighted, and not to be deceived. But the commissions under which we acted were not only the measure of our power, they denoted also the sentiments of the States on the subject of our deliberation. The idea of a National Government, as contradistinguished from a federal one, never entered into the mind of any of them; and to the public mind we must accommodate ourselves. We have no power to go beyond the Federal scheme; and if we had, the people are not ripe for any other. We must follow the people; the people will not follow us. The *proposition* could not be maintained, whether considered in reference to us as a nation, or as a confederacy. A confederacy supposes sovereignty in the members composing it, and sovereignty supposes equality. If we are to be considered as a nation, all State distinctions must be abolished, the whole must be thrown into hotchpot, and when an equal division is made, then there may be fairly an equality of representation. He held up Virginia, Massachusetts and Pennsylvania, as the three large States, and the other ten as small ones; repeating the calculations of Mr. BREARLY, as to the disparity of votes which would take place, and affirming that the small States would never agree to it. He said there was no more reason that a great individual State, contributing much, should have more votes than a small one, contributing little, than that a rich individual citizen should have more votes than an indigent one. If the rateable property of A was to that of B as forty to one, ought A for that reason to have forty times as many votes as B? Such a principle would never be admitted; and if it were admitted would put B entirely at the mercy of A. As A has more to be protected than B, so he ought to contribute more for the common protection. The same may be said of a large State, which has more to be protected than a small one. Give the large States an influence in proportion to their magnitude, and what will be the consequence? Their ambition will be proportionally increased, and the small States will have every thing to fear. It was once proposed by Galloway, and some others, that America should be represented in the British Parliament, and then be bound by its laws. America could not have been entitled to more than one-third of the representatives which would fall to the share of Great Britain,— would American rights and interests have been safe under an authority thus constituted? It has been said that if a national Government is to be formed, so as to operate on the people and not on the States, the Representatives ought to be drawn from the people. But why so? May not a Legislature, filled by the State Legislatures, operate on the people who choose the State Legislatures? Or may not a practicable coercion be found? He admitted that there were none such in the existing system. He was attached strongly to the plan of the existing Confederacy, in which the people choose their legislative representatives; and the Legislatures their federal representatives. No other amendments were wanting than to mark the orbits of the States with due precision, and provide for the use of coercion, which was the great point. He alluded to the hint thrown out by Mr. WILSON, of the necessity to which the large States might be reduced, of confederating among themselves, by a refusal of the others to concur. Let them unite if they please, but let them remember that they have no authority to compel the others to unite. New Jersey will never confederate on the plan before the Committee. She would be swallowed up. He had rather submit to a monarch, to a despot, than to such a fate. He would not only oppose the plan here, but on his return home do every thing in his power to defeat it there.

Mr. WILSON hoped, if the Confederacy should be dissolved, that a *majority*,— nay, a *minority* of the States would unite for their safety. He entered elaborately into the defence of a proportional representation, stating for his first position, that, as all authority was derived from the people, equal numbers of people ought to have an equal number of representatives, and different numbers of people, different numbers of representatives. This principle had been improperly violated in the Confederation, owing to the urgent circumstances of the time. As to the case of A and B stated by Mr. PATTERSON, he observed, that, in districts as large as the States, the number of people was the best measure of their comparative wealth. Whether, therefore, wealth or numbers was to form the ratio it would be the same. Mr. PATTERSON admitted persons, not property, to be the measure of suffrage. Are not the citizens of Pennsylvania equal to those of New Jersey? Does it require one hundred and fifty of the former to balance fifty of the latter? Representatives of different districts ought clearly to hold the same proportion to each other, as their respective constituents hold to each other. If the small States will not confederate on this plan, Pennsylvania, and he presumed some other States, would not confederate on any other. We have been told that each State being sovereign, all are equal. So each man is naturally a sovereign over himself, and all men are therefore naturally equal. Can he retain this equality when he becomes a member of civil government ? He cannot. As little can a sovereign State, when it becomes a member of a federal government. If New Jersey will not part with her sovereignty, it is vain to talk of government. A new partition of the States is desirable, but evidently and totally impracticable.

Mr. WILLIAMSON illustrated the cases by a comparison of the different States to counties of different sizes within the same State ; observing that proportional representation was admitted to be just in the latter case, and could not, therefore, be fairly contested in the former.

The question being about to be put, Mr. PATTERSON hoped that as so much depended on it, it might be thought best to postpone the decision till to-morrow ; which was done, *nem. con.*

The Committee rose, and the House adjourned.

MONDAY, JUNE 11TH.

Mr. ABRAHAM BALDWIN, from Georgia, took his seat.

In Committee of the Whole,—The clause concerning the rule of suffrage in the National Legislature, postponed on Saturday, was resumed.

Mr. SHERMAN proposed, that the proportion of suffrage in the first branch should be according to the respective numbers of free inhabitants ; and that in the second branch, or Senate, each State should have one vote and no more. He said, as the States would remain possessed of certain individual rights, each State ought to be able to protect itself ; otherwise, a few large States will rule the rest. The House of Lords in England, he observed, had certain particular rights under the Constitution, and hence they have an equal vote with the House of Commons, that they may be able to defend their rights.

Mr. RUTLEDGE proposed, that the proportion of suffrage in the first branch should be according to the quotas of contribution. The justice of this rule, he said, could not be contested. Mr. BUTLER urged the same idea ; adding that money was power ; and that the States ought to have weight in the government in proportion to their wealth.

Mr. KING and Mr. WILSON,* in order to bring the question to a point, moved, " that the right of suffrage in the first branch of the National Legislature ought not to be according to the rule established in the Articles of Confederation, but according to some equitable ratio of representation." The clause, so far as it related to suffrage in the first branch, was postponed, in order to consider this motion.

Mr. DICKINSON contended for the *actual* contributions of the States, as the rule of their representation and suffrage in the first branch. By thus connecting the interests of the States with their duty, the latter would be sure to be performed.

Mr. KING remarked, that it was uncertain what mode might be used in levying a national revenue; but that it was probable, imposts would be one source of it. If the *actual* contributions were to be the rule, the non-importing States, as Connecticut and New Jersey, would be in a bad situation, indeed. It might so happen that they would have no representation. This situation of particular States had been always one powerful argument in favor of the five *per cent.* impost.

The question being about to be put, Doctor FRANKLIN said, he had thrown his ideas of the matter on a paper, which Mr. WILSON read to the Committee, in the words following:

Mr. CHAIRMAN,—It has given me great pleasure to observe, that, till this point, the proportion of representation, came before us, our debates were carried on with great coolness and temper. If any thing of a contrary kind has on

---

* In the printed Journal Mr. Rutledge is named as the seconder of the motion.

this occasion appeared, I hope it will not be repeated; for
we are sent here to *consult*, not to *contend*, with each other;
and declarations of a fixed opinion, and of determined resolution never to change it, neither enlighten nor convince
us.   Positiveness and warmth on one side naturally beget
their like on the other, and tend to create and augment discord and division, in a great concern wherein harmony and
union are extremely necessary to give weight to our councils, and render them effectual in promoting and securing
the common good.

"I must own, that I was originally of opinion it would
be better if every member of Congress, or our national
Council, were to consider himself rather as a representative
of the whole, than as an agent for the interests of a particular State; in which case the proportion of members for each
State would be of less consequence, and it would not be very
material whether they voted by States or individually.   But
as I find this is not to be expected, I now think the number
of representatives should bear some proportion to the number of the represented; and that the decisions should be by
the majority of members, not by the majority of the States.
This is objected to from an apprehension that the greater
States would then swallow up the smaller.   I do not at
present clearly see what advantage the greater States could
propose to themselves by swallowing up the smaller, and
therefore do not apprehend they would attempt it.   I recollect that, in the beginning of this century, when the union
was proposed of the two kingdoms, England and Scotland,
the Scotch patriots were full of fears, that unless they had
an equal number of representatives in Parliament, they
should be ruined by the superiority of the English.   They
finally agreed, however, that the different proportions of
importance in the union of the two nations should be
attended to, whereby they were to have only forty members
in the House of Commons, and only sixteen in the House
of Lords.   A very great inferiority of members!   And yet
to this day I do not recollect that anything has been done

in the Parliament of Great Britain to the prejudice of Scotland; and whoever looks over the lists of public officers, civil and military, of that nation, will find, I believe, that the North Britons enjoy at least their full proportion of emolument.

"But, sir, in the present mode of voting by States, it is equally in the power of the lesser States to swallow up the greater; and this is mathematically demonstrable. Suppose, for example, that seven smaller States had each three members in the House, and the six larger to have, one with another six members, and that, upon a question, two members of each smaller State should be in the affirmative, and one in the negative, they would make:— affirmatives, 14; negatives, 7; and that all the larger States should be unanimously in the negative, they would make, negatives, 36; in all, affirmatives, 14, negatives, 43.

"It is, then, apparent, that the fourteen carry the question against the forty-three, and the minority overpowers the majority, contrary to the common practice of assemblies in all countries and ages.

"The greater States, sir, are naturally as unwilling to have their property left in the disposition of the smaller, as the smaller are to have theirs in the disposition of the greater. An honorable gentleman has, to avoid this difficulty, hinted a proposition of equalizing the States. It appears to me an equitable one, and I should, for my own part, not be against such a measure, if it might be found practicable. Formerly, indeed, when almost every province had a different constitution, some with greater, others with fewer, privileges, it was of importance to the borderers, when their boundaries were contested, whether, by running the division lines, they were placed on one side or the other. At present, when such differences are done away, it is less material. The interest of a State is made up of the interests of its individual members. If they are not injured, the State is not injured. Small States are, more easily well and happily governed than large ones. If, therefore, in

10

such an equal division, it should be found necessary to diminish Pennsylvania, I should not be averse to the giving a part of it to New Jersey, and another to Delaware. But as there would probably be considerable difficulties in adjusting such a division; and, however equally made at first, it would be continually varying by the augmentation of inhabitants in some States, and their fixed proportion in others, and thence frequently occasion new divisions I beg leave to propose, for the consideration of the Committee, another mode, which appears to me to be as equitable, more easily carried into practice, and more permanent in its nature.

"Let the weakest State say what proportion of money or force it is able and willing to furnish for the general purposes of the Union:

"Let all the others oblige themselves to furnish each an equal proportion:

"The whole of these joint supplies to be absolutely in the disposition of Congress:

"The Congress in this case to be composed of an equal number of delegates from each State:

"And their decisions to be by the majority of individual members voting.

" If these joint and equal supplies should, on particular occasions, not be sufficient, let Congress make requisitions on the richer and more powerful States for further aids, to be voluntarily afforded, leaving to each State the right of considering the necessity and utility of the aid desired, and of giving more or less as it should be found proper.

"This mode is not new. It was formerly practiced with success by the British government with respect to Ireland and the Colonies. We sometimes gave even more than they expected, or thought just to accept; and in the last war, carried on while we were united, they gave us back in five years a million sterling. We should probably have continued such voluntary contributions, whenever the occasions appeared to require them for the common good of the Empire. It was not till they chose to force us, and to deprive us of the merit and pleasure of voluntary contributions, that we refused and resisted. These contributions, however, were to be disposed of at the pleasure of a government in which we had no representative. I am, therefore, persuaded, that they will not be refused to one in which the representation shall be equal.

"My learned colleague (Mr. WILSON) has already mentioned, that the present method of voting by States was submitted to originally by Congress under a conviction of its impropriety, inequality, and injustice. This appears in the words of their resolution. It is of the sixth of September, 1774. The words are:

"Resolved, that in determining questions in this Congress each Colony or Province shall have one vote; the Congress not being possessed of, or at present able to procure, materials for ascertaining the importance of each Colony."

On the question for agreeing to Mr. KING's and Mr. WILSON's motion, it passed in the affirmative,—Massachusetts, Connecticut, Pennsylvania, Virginia, North Carolina, South Carolina, Georgia, aye — 7; New York, New Jersey, Delaware, no — 3; Maryland, divided.

It was then moved by Mr. RUTLEDGE, seconded by Mr. BUTLER, to add to the words, "equitable ratio of representation," at the end of the motion just agreed to, the words "according to the quotas of contribution." On motion of Mr. WILSON, seconded by Mr. PINCKNEY, this was postponed; in order to add, after the words, "equitable ratio of representation," the words following: "in proportion to the whole number of white and other free citizens and inhabitants of every age, sex and condition, including those bound to servitude for a term of years, and three-fifths of all other persons not comprehended in the foregoing description, except Indians not paying taxes, in each State" —this being the rule in the act of Congress, agreed to by eleven States, for apportioning quotas of revenue on the

States, and requiring a census only every five, seven, or ten years.

Mr. GERRY thought property not the rule of representation. Why, then, should the blacks, who were property in the South, be in the rule of representation more than the cattle and horses of the North?

On the question,—Massachusetts, Connecticut, New York, Pennsylvania, Maryland, Virginia, North Carolina, South Carolina, Georgia; aye — 9; New Jersey, Delaware, no — 2.

Mr. SHERMAN moved, that a question be taken, whether each State shall have one vote in the second branch. Every thing, he said, depended on this. The smaller States would never agree to the plan on any other principle than an equality of suffrage in this branch. Mr. ELLSWORTH seconded the motion. On the question for allowing each State one vote in the second branch,—Connecticut, New York, New Jersey, Delaware, Maryland, aye — 5; Massachusetts, Pennsylvania, Virginia, North Carolina, South Carolina, Georgia, no — 6.

Mr. WILSON and Mr. HAMILTON moved, that the right of suffrage in the second branch ought to be according to the same rule as in the first branch.

On this question for making the ratio of representation, the same in the second as in the first branch, it passed in the affirmative,— Massachusetts, Pennsylvania, Virginia, North Carolina, South Carolina, Georgia, aye — 6; Connecticut, New York, New Jersey, Delaware, Maryland, no — 5.

The eleventh Resolution, for guaranteeing republican government and territory to each State, being considered, the words " or partition," were, on motion of Mr. MADISON, added after the words " voluntary junction,"—Massachusetts, New York, Pennsylvania, Virginia, North Carolina, South Carolina, Georgia, aye — 7; Connecticut, New Jersey, Delaware, Maryland, no — 4.

Mr. READ disliked the idea of guaranteeing territory. It abetted the idea of distinct States, which would be a perpetual source of discord.   There can be no cure for this evil but in doing away States altogether, and uniting them all into one great society.

Alterations having been made in the Resolution, making it read, "that a Republican constitution, and its existing laws, ought to be guaranteed to each State by the United States," the whole was agreed to, *nem. com.*

The thirteenth Resolution, for amending the national Constitution, hereafter, without consent of the national Legislature, being considered, several members did not see the necessity of the Resolution at all, nor the propriety of making the consent of the National Legislature unnecessary.

Col. MASON urged the necessity of such a provision. The plan now to be formed will certainly be defective, as the Confederation has been found on trial to be.   Amendments, therefore, will be necessary; and it will be better to provide for them in an easy, regular and constitutional way, than to trust to chance and violence.   It would be improper to require the consent of the National Legislature, because they may abuse their power, and refuse their assent on that very account.   The opportunity for such an abuse may be the fault of the Constitution calling for amendment.

Mr. RANDOLPH enforced these arguments.

The words, "without requiring the consent of the National Legislature," were postponed.   The other provision in the clause passed, *nem. con.*

The fourteenth resolution, requiring oaths from the members of the State Governments to observe the national Constitution and laws, being considered, —

Mr. SHERMAN opposed it, as unnecessarily intruding into the State jurisdictions.

Mr. RANDOLPH considered it necessary to prevent that competition between the national Constitution and laws, and those of the particular States, which had already been felt. The officers of the States are already under oath to the

States. To preserve a due impartiality they ought to be equally bound to the National Government. The national authority needs every support we can give it. The Executive and Judiciary of the States, notwithstanding their nominal independence on the State Legislatures, are in fact so dependent on them, that unless they be brought under some tie to the National System, they will always lean too much to the State systems, whenever a contest arises between the two.

Mr. GERRY did not like the clause. He thought there was as much reason for requiring an oath of fidelity to the States from national officers, as *vice versa.*

Mr. LUTHER MARTIN moved to strike out the words requiring such an oath from the State officers, viz.: "within the several States," observing, that if the new oath should be contrary to that already taken by them, it would be improper; if coincident, the oaths already taken will be sufficient.

On the question for striking out as proposed by Mr. L. MARTIN,— Connecticut, New Jersey, Delaware, Maryland, aye — 4; Massachusetts, New York, Pennsylvania, Virginia, North Carolina, South Carolina, Georgia, no — 7.

Question on the whole Resolution as proposed by Mr. RANDOLPH,— Massachusetts, Pennsylvania, Virginia, North Carolina, South Carolina, Georgia, aye — 6; Connecticut, New York, New Jersey, Delaware, Maryland, no — 5.

The Committee rose, and the House adjourned.

TUESDAY, JUNE 12TH.

In Committee of the Whole,— The question was taken on the fifteenth Resolution, to wit, referring the new system to the people of the United States for ratification. It passed in the affirmative,— Massachusetts, Pennsylvania,* Virginia, North Carolina, South Carolina, Georgia, aye —

----

* Pennsylvania omitted in the printed Journal. The vote is there entered as of June 11th.

6; Connecticut, New York, New Jersey, no — 3; Delaware, Maryland, divided.

Mr. SHERMAN and Mr. ELLSWORTH moved to fill the blank left in the fourth Resolution, for the periods of electing the members of the first branch, with the words, " every year;" Mr. SHERMAN observing that he did it in order to bring on some question.

Mr. RUTLEDGE proposed " every two years."

Mr. JENIFER proposed, " every three years;" observing that the too great frequency of elections rendered the people indifferent to them, and made the best men unwilling to engage in so precarious a service.

Mr. MADISON seconded the motion for three years. Instability is one of the great vices of our republics to be remedied. Three years will be necessary, in a government so extensive, for members to form any knowledge of the various interests of the States to which they do not belong, and of which they can know but little from the situation and affairs of their own. One year will be almost consumed in preparing for, and traveling to and from the seat of national business.

Mr. GERRY. The people of New England will never give up the point of annual elections. They know of the transition made in England from triennial to septennial elections, and will consider such an innovation here as the prelude to a like usurpation. He considered annual elections as the only defence of the people against tyranny. He was as much against a triennial House, as against a hereditary Executive.

Mr. MADISON observed, that if the opinions of the people were to be our guide, it would be difficult to say what course we ought to take. No member of the Convention could say what the opinions of his constituents were at this time; much less could he say what they would think, if possessed of the information and lights possessed by the members here; and still less, what would be their way of thinking six or twelve months hence. We ought to con-

sider what was right and necessary in itself for the attain-
ment of a proper government.   A plan adjusted to this
idea will recommend itself.   The respectability of this Convention will give weight to their recommendation of it.
Experience will be constantly urging the adoption of it;
and all the most enlightened and respectable citizens will
be its advocates.   Should we fall short of the necessary
and proper point, this influential class of citizens will be
turned against the plan, and little support in opposition to
them can be gained to it from the unreflecting multitude.

Mr. GERRY repeated his opinion, that it was necessary
to consider what the people would approve.   This had been
the policy of all legislators.   If the reasoning (of Mr.
MADISON) were just, and we supposed a limited monarchy
the best form in itself, we ought to recommend it, though
the genius of the people was decidedly adverse to it, and,
having no hereditary distinctions among us, we were destitute of the essential materials for such an innovation.

On the question for the triennial election of the first
branch,— New York, New Jersey, Pennsylvania, Delaware,
Maryland, Virginia, Georgia, aye — 7; Massachusetts, (Mr.
KING, aye, Mr. GORMAN, wavering) Connecticut, North
Carolina, South Carolina, no — 4.

The words requiring members of the first branch to be
of the age of ———— years were struck out,—Maryland
alone, no.

The words " *liberal compensation for members*," being
considered, Mr. MADISON moved to insert the words, " and
fixed."   He observed that it would be improper to leave the
members of the National Legislature to be provided for by
the State Legislatures, because it would create an improper
dependence; and to leave them to regulate their own wages
was an indecent thing, and might in time prove a dangerous one.   He thought wheat, or some other article of which
the average price, throughout a reasonable period preceding, might be settled in some convenient mode, would form
a proper standard.

Colonel MASON seconded the motion; adding, that it would be improper, for other reasons, to leave the wages to be regulated by the States,—first, the different States would make different provision for their representatives, and an inequality would be felt among them, whereas he thought they ought to be in all respects equal; secondly, the parsimony of the States might reduce the provision so low, that, as had already happened in choosing delegates to Congress, the question would be, not who were most fit to be chosen, but who were most willing to serve.

On the question for inserting the words, " and fixed,"— New York, New Jersey, Pennsylvania, Delaware, Maryland, Virginia, North Carolina, Georgia, aye — 8; Massachusetts, Connecticut, South Carolina, no — 3.

Doctor FRANKLIN said, he approved of the amendment just made for rendering the salaries as fixed as possible; but disliked the word " *liberal.*" He would prefer the word "moderate," if it was necessary to substitute any other. He remarked the tendency of abuses, in every case, to grow of themselves when once begun; and related very pleasantly the progression in ecclesiastical benefices, from the first departure from the gratuitous provision for the apostles, to the establishment of the papal system. The word " liberal" was struck out, *nem. con.*

On the motion of Mr. PIERCE, that the wages should be paid out of the National Treasury, Massachusetts, New Jersey, Pennsylvania, Delaware, Maryland, Virginia, North Carolina, Georgia, aye —8; Connecticut, New York, South Carolina, no — 3.

Question on the clause relating to term of service and compensation of the first branch,— Massachusetts, New Jersey, Pennsylvania, Delaware, Maryland, Virginia, North Carolina, Georgia, aye — 8; Connecticut, New York, South Carolina, no — 3.

On a question for striking out the " *ineligibility* of members of the National Legislature to *State offices,*"— Connecticut, New York, North Carolina, South Carolina, aye—

4; New Jersey, Pennsylvania, Delaware, Virginia, Georgia. no — 5; Massachusetts, Maryland, divided.

On the question for agreeing to the clause as amended, — Massachusetts, New York, New Jersey, Pennsylvania, Delaware, Maryland, Virginia, North Carolina, South Carolina, Georgia, aye — 10; Connecticut, no — 1.

On a question for making members of the National Legislature *ineligible* to any office under the National Government for the term of three years after ceasing to be members,— Maryland, aye — 1; Massachusetts, Connecticut, New York, New Jersey, Pennsylvania, Delaware, Virginia, North Carolina, Georgia, no — 10.

On the question for such ineligibility for one year,— Massachusetts, Connecticut, New Jersey, Pennsylvania, Delaware, Virginia, North Carolina, South Carolina, aye — 8; New York, Georgia, no — 2; Maryland, divided.

On the question moved by Mr. PINCKNEY for striking out "incapable of re-election into the first branch of the National Legislature for ———— years, and subject to recall," agreed to, *nem. con.*

On the question for striking out from the fifth Resolution the words requiring members of the Senatorial branch to be of the age of ———— years at least,— Connecticut, New Jersey, Pennsylvania, aye — 3; Massachusetts, New York, Delaware, Maryland, Virginia, South Carolina, no — 6; North Carolina, Georgia, divided.

On the question for filling the blank with "thirty years," as the qualification, it was agreed to,— Massachusetts, New York, Pennsylvania, Maryland, Virginia, North Carolina, South Carolina, aye — 7; Connecticut, New Jersey, Delaware, Georgia, no — 4.

Mr. SPAIGHT moved to fill the blank for the duration of the appointments to the second branch of the National Legislature, with the words, "seven years."

Mr. SHERMAN thought seven years too long. He grounded his opposition, he said, on the principle, that if they did their duty well, they would be re-elected; and if they acted amiss, an earlier opportunity should be allowed for getting rid of them. He preferred five years, which would be between the terms of the first branch and of the Executive.

Mr. PIERCE proposed three years. Seven years would raise an alarm. Great mischiefs have arisen in England from their Septennial Act, which was reprobated by most of their patriotic statesmen.

Mr. RANDOLPH was for the term of seven years. The democratic licentiousness of the State Legislatures proved the necessity of a firm Senate. The object of this second branch is, to control the democratic branch of the National Legislature. If it be not a firm body, the other branch, being more numerous, and coming immediately from the people, will overwhelm it. The senate of Maryland, constituted on like principles, had been scarcely able to stem the popular torrent. No mischief can be apprehended, as the concurrence of the other branch, and in some measure of the Executive, will in all cases be necessary. A firmness and independence may be the more necessary, also, in this branch, as it ought to guard the Constitution against encroachments of the Executive, who will be apt to form combinations with the demagogues of the popular branch.

Mr. MADISON considered seven years as a term by no means too long. What we wished was, to give to the government that stability which was every where called for, and which the enemies of the republican form alleged to be inconsistent with its nature. He was not afraid of giving too much stability, by the term of seven years. His fear was, that the popular branch would still be too great an overmatch for it. It was to be much lamented that we had so little direct experience to guide us. The Constitution of Maryland was the only one that bore any analogy to this part of the plan. In no instance had the Senate of Maryland created just suspicions of danger from it. In some instances, perhaps, it may have erred by yielding to the House of Delegates. In every instance of their opposition to the measures of the House of Delegates, they had had with them the suffrages of the most enlightened and impartial people of the other States, as well as of their own. In the States, where the Senates were chosen in the same manner as the other branches of the Legislature, and held their seats for four years, the institution was found to be no check whatever against the instabilities of the other branches. He conceived it to be of great importance that a stable and firm government, organized in the republican form, should be held out to the people. If this be not done, and the people be left to judge of this species of government by the operations of the defective systems under which they now live, it is much to be feared, the time is not distant, when, in universal disgust, they will renounce the blessing which they have purchased at so dear a rate, and be ready for any change that may be proposed to them.

On the question for "seven years," as the term for the second branch,— New Jersey, Pennsylvania, Delaware, Maryland, Virginia, North Carolina, South Carolina, Georgia, aye— 8; Connecticut, no—1; Massachusetts, (Mr. Gorham and Mr. King, aye; Mr. Gerry and Mr. Strong, no) New York, divided.

Mr. BUTLER and Mr. RUTLEDGE proposed that the members of the second branch should be entitled to no salary or compensation for their services. On the question,*—Connecticut Delaware, South Carolina, aye — 3; New York, New Jersey, Pennsylvania, Maryland, Virginia, North Carolina, Georgia, no — 7; Massachusetts, divided.

It was then moved, and agreed, that the clauses respecting the stipends and ineligibility of the second branch be the same as of the first branch,— Connecticut disagreeing to the ineligibility. It was moved and seconded, to alter the ninth Resolution, so as to read, " that the jurisdiction of the supreme tribunal shall be, to hear and determine, in the dernier resort, all piracies, felonies, &c."

---

* It is probable the votes here turned chiefly on the idea that if the salaries were not here provided for, the members would be paid by their respective States.

It was moved and seconded, to strike out, "all piracies and felonies on the high seas," which was agreed to.

It was moved, and agreed, to strike out, "all captures from an enemy."

It was moved, and agreed, to strike out, "other States," and insert, "two distinct States of the Union."

It was moved, and agreed, to postpone the consideration of the ninth Resolution, relating to the Judiciary.

The Committee then rose, and the House adjourned.

WEDNESDAY, JUNE 13TH.

In Committee of the Whole,—The ninth Resolution being resumed,—

The latter part of the clause relating to the jurisdiction of the national tribunals, was struck out, *nem. con.*; in order to leave full room for their organization.

Mr. RANDOLPH and Mr. MADISON then moved the following resolution respecting a national Judiciary, viz.: "that the jurisdiction of the National Judiciary shall extend to cases which respect the collection of the national revenue, impeachments of any national officers, and questions which involve the national peace and harmony." Agreed to.

Mr. PINCKNEY and Mr. SHERMAN moved to insert after the words, "one supreme tribunal," the words, "the judges of which to be appointed by the National Legislature."

Mr. MADISON objected to an appointment by the whole Legislature. Many of them are incompetent judges of the requisite qualifications. They were too much influenced by their partialities. The candidate who was present, who had displayed a talent for business in the legislative field, who had, perhaps, assisted ignorant members in business of their own, or of their constituents, or used other winning means, would, without any of the essential qualifications for an expositor of the laws, prevail over a competitor not having these recommendations, but possessed of every necessary accomplishment.   He proposed that the appointment should be made by the Senate, which, as a less numerous and more select body, would be more competent judges, and which was sufficiently numerous to justify such a confidence in them.

Mr. Sherman and Mr. Pinckney withdrew their motion, and the appointment by the Senate was agreed to *nem. con.*

Mr. Gerry moved to restrain the Senatorial branch from originating money bills.   The other branch was more immediately the representatives of the people, and it was a maxim, that the people ought to hold the purse-strings. If the Senate should be allowed to originate such bills, they would repeat the experiment, till chance should furnish a set of Representatives in the other branch who will fall into their snares.

Mr. Butler saw no reason for such a discrimination. We were always following the British Constitution, when the reason of it did not apply.   There was no analogy between the House of Lords and the body proposed to be established.   If the Senate should be degraded by any such discriminations, the best men would be apt to decline serving in it, in favor of the other branch.   And it will lead the latter into the practice of tacking other clauses to money bills.

Mr. Madison observed, that the commentators on the British Constitution had not yet agreed on the reason of the restriction on the House of Lords, in money bills. Certain it was, there could be no similar reason in the case before us.   The Senate would be the representatives of the people, as well as the first branch.   If they should have any dangerous influence over it, they would easily prevail on some member of the latter to originate the bill they wished to be passed.   As the Senate would be generally a more capable set of men, it would be wrong to disable them from any preparation of the business, especially of that which was most important, and, in our republics, worse prepared than any other.   The gentleman, in pursuance of his principle, ought to carry the restraint to the *amendment*, as well as the originating of money bills ; since an addition of a given sum would be equivalent to a distinct proposition of it.

Mr. KING differed from Mr. GERRY, and concurred in the objections to the proposition.

Mr. READ favored the proposition, but would not extend the restraint to the case of amendments.

Mr. PINCKNEY thinks the question premature. If the Senate should be formed on the *same* proportional representation as it stands at present, they should have equal power; otherwise, if a different principle should be introduced.

Mr. SHERMAN. As both branches must concur, there can be no danger, whichever way the Senate may be formed. We establish two branches in order to get more wisdom, which is particularly needed in the finance business. The Senate bear their share of the taxes, and are also the representatives of the people. 'What a man does by another, he does by himself,' is a maxim. In Connecticut both branches can originate, in all cases, and it has been found safe and convenient. Whatever might have been the reason of the rule as to the House of Lords, it is clear that no good arises from it now even there.

General PINCKNEY. This distinction prevails in South Carolina, and has been a source of pernicious disputes between the two branches. The Constitution is now evaded by informal schedules of amendments, handed from the Senate to the other House.

Mr. WILLIAMSON wishes for a question, chiefly to prevent re-discussion. The restriction will have one advantage; it will oblige some member in the lower branch to move, and people can then mark him.

On the question for excepting money-bills, as proposed by Mr. GERRY, — New York, Delaware, Virginia, aye — 3; Massachusetts, Connecticut, New Jersey, Maryland, North Carolina, South Carolina, Georgia, no — 7.

The Committee rose, and Mr. GORHAM made report, which was postponed till to-morrow, to give an opportunity for other plans to be proposed — the Report was in the words following:

1. Resolved, that it is the opinion of this Committee, that a national Government ought to be established, consisting of a supreme Legislative, Executive and Judiciary.

2. Resolved, that the National Legislature ought to consist of two branches.

3. Resolved, that the members of the first branch of the National Legislature ought to be elected by the people of the several States for the term of three years, to receive fixed stipends by which they may be compensated for the devotion of their time to the public service, to be paid out of the National Treasury: to be ineligible to any office established by a particular State, or under the authority of the United States, (except those peculiarly belonging to the functions of the first branch,) during the term of service, and under the national Government for the space of one year after its expiration.

4. Resolved, that the members of the second branch of the National Legislature ought to be chosen by the individual Legislatures; to be of the age of thirty years at least; to hold their offices for a term sufficient to ensure their independence, namely, seven years; to receive fixed stipends by which they may be compensated for the devotion of their time to the public service, to be paid out of the National Treasury; to be ineligible to any office established by a particular State, or under the authority of the United States, (except those peculiarly belonging to the functions of the second branch,) during the term of service, and under the national Government for the space of one year after its expiration.

5. Resolved, that each branch ought to possess the right of originating acts.

6. Resolved, that the National Legislature ought to be empowered to enjoy the legislative rights vested in Con-

gress by the Confederation; and moreover to legislate in all cases to which the separate States are incompetent, or in which the harmony of the United States may be interrupted by the exercise of individual legislation; to negative all laws passed by the several States contravening, in the opinion of the National Legislature, the Articles of Union, or any treaties subsisting under the authority of the Union.

7. Resolved, that the rights of suffrage in the first branch of the National Legislature, ought not to be according to the rule established in the Articles of Confederation, but according to some equitable ratio of representation, namely, in proportion to the whole number of white and other free citizens and inhabitants, of every age, sex and condition, including those bound to servitude for a term of years, and three-fifths of all other persons, not comprehended in the foregoing description, except Indians not paying taxes, in each State.

8. Resolved, that the right of suffrage in the second branch of the National Legislature, ought to be according to the rule established for the first.

9. Resolved, that a National Executive be instituted, to consist of a single person; to be chosen by the National Legislature, for the term of seven years; with power to carry into execution the national laws; to appoint to offices in cases not otherwise provided for; to be ineligible a second time; and to be removable on impeachment and conviction of malpractices or neglect of duty; to receive a fixed stipend by which he may be compensated for the devotion of his time to the public service, to be paid out of the National Treasury.

10. Resolved, that the national Executive shall have a right to negative any legislative act, which shall not be afterwards passed by two-thirds of each branch of the national Legislature.

11. Resolved, that a national Judiciary be established, to consist of one supreme tribunal, the Judges of which shall be appointed by the second branch of the national

11

Legislature, to hold their offices during good behaviour, and to receive punctually, at stated times, a fixed compensation for their services, in which no increase or diminution shall be made, so as to affect the persons actually in office at the time of such increase or diminution.

12. Resolved, that the national Legislature be empowered to appoint inferior tribunals.

13. Resolved, that the jurisdiction of the national Judiciary shall extend to all cases which respect the collection of the national revenue, impeachments of any national officers, and questions which involve the national peace and harmony.

14. Resolved, that provision ought to be made for the admission of States lawfully arising within the limits of the United States, whether from a voluntary junction of government and territory, or otherwise, with the consent of a number of voices in the national Legislature less than the whole.

15. Resolved, that provision ought to be made for the continuance of Congress and their authorities and privileges, until a given day, after the reform of the Articles of Union shall be adopted, and for the completion of all their engagements.

16. Resolved, that a republican constitution, and its existing laws, ought to be guaranteed to each State by the United States.

17. Resolved, that provision ought to be made for the amendment of the Articles of Union, whensoever it shall seem necessary.

18. Resolved, that the Legislative, Executive and Judiciary powers within the several States ought to be bound by oath to support the Articles of Union.

19. Resolved, that the amendments which shall be offered to the Confederation by the Convention ought, at a proper time or times after the approbation of Congress, to be submitted to an assembly or assemblies recommended by the several Legislatures, to be expressly chosen by the people to consider and decide thereon.

THURSDAY, JUNE 14TH.

Mr. PATTERSON observed to the Convention, that it was the wish of several Deputations, particularly that of New Jersey, that further time might be allowed them to contemplate the plan reported from the Committee of the Whole, and to digest one purely federal, and contradistinguished from the reported plan. He said, they hoped to have such an one ready by to-morrow to be laid before the Convention; and the Convention adjourned that leisure might be given for the purpose.

FRIDAY, JUNE 15TH.

In Convention,—Mr. PATTERSON laid before the Convention the plan which he said several of the Deputations wished to be substituted in place of that proposed by Mr. RANDOLPH. After some little discussion of the most proper mode of giving it a fair deliberation, it was agreed, that it should be referred to a Committee of the Whole; and that, in order to place the two plans in due comparison, the other should be recommitted. At the earnest request of Mr. LANSING and some other gentlemen, it was also agreed that the Convention should not go into Committee of the Whole on the subject till to-morrow; by which delay the friends of the plan proposed by Mr. PATTERSON would be better prepared to explain and support it, and all would have an opportunity of taking copies.*

---

* This plan had been concerted among the Deputation, or members thereof, from Connecticut, New York, New Jersey, Delaware, and perhaps Mr. MARTIN, from Maryland, who made with them a common cause, though on different principles. Connecticut and New York were against a departure from the principle of the Confederation, wishing rather to add a few new powers to Congress than to substitute a National Government. The States of New Jersey and Delaware were opposed to a National Government, because its patrons considered a proportional representation of the States as the basis of it. The eagerness displayed by the members opposed to a National Government, from these different motives, began now to produce serious anxiety for the result of the Convention. Mr. DICKINSON said to Mr. MADISON, " You see the consequence of pushing things too far. Some of the members from the small States wish for two branches in the General Legislature, and are friends to a good National Government; but we would sooner submit to foreign power, than submit to be deprived in both branches of the legislature, of an equality of suffrage, and thereby be thrown under the domination of the larger States."

The propositions from New Jersey, moved by Mr. PATTERSON, were in the words following:

1. Resolved, that the Articles of Confederation ought to so be revised, corrected and enlarged, as to render the Federal Constitution adequate to the exigencies of government, and the preservation of the Union.

2. Resolved, that, in addition to the powers vested in the United States in Congress, by the present existing Articles of Confederation, they be authorized to pass acts for raising a revenue, by levying a duty or duties on all goods or merchandizes of foreign growth or manufacture, imported into any part of the United States; by stamps on paper, vellum or parchment; and by a postage on all letters or packages passing through the general post-office; to be applied to such Federal purposes as they shall deem proper and expedient; to make rules and regulations for the collection thereof; and the same, from time to time, to alter and amend in such manner as they shall think proper; to pass acts for the regulation of trade and commerce, as well with foreign nations as with each other; provided that all punishments, fines, forfeitures and penalties, to be incurred for contravening such acts, rules and regulations, shall be adjudged by the common law Judiciaries of the State in which any offence contrary to the true intent and meaning of such acts, rules, and regulations, shall have been committed or perpetrated, with liberty of commencing in the first instance all suits and prosecutions for that purpose in the Superior common law Judiciary in such State; subject, nevertheless, for the correction of all errors, both in law and fact, in rendering judgment, to an appeal to the Judiciary of the United States.

3. Resolved, that whenever requisitions shall be necessary, instead of the rule for making requisitions mentioned in the Articles of Confederation, the United States in Congress be authorized to make such requisitions in proportion to the whole number of white and other free citizens and inhabitants, of every age, sex, and condition, including

those bound to servitude for a term of years, and three-fifths of all other persons not comprehended in the forego-ing description, except Indians not paying taxes; that, if such requisitions be not complied with, in the time specified therein, to direct the collection thereof in the non-comply-ing States; and for that purpose to devise and pass acts directing and authorizing the same; provided, that none of the powers hereby vested in the United States in Congress, shall be exercised without the consent of at least ———— States; and in that proportion, if the number of confed-erated States should hereafter be increased or dimin-ished.

4. Resolved, that the United States in Congress be authorized to elect a Federal Executive, to consist of ———— persons, to continue in office for the term of ———— years; to receive punctually, at stated times, a fixed compensation for their services, in which no increase nor diminution shall be made so as to affect the persons composing the Execu-tive at the time of such increase or diminution; to be paid out of the Federal treasury; to be incapable of holding any other office or appointment during their time of service, and for ———— years thereafter: to be ineligible a second time, and removeable by Congress, on application by a majority of the Executives of the several States; that the Executive, besides their general authority to execute the Federal acts, ought to appoint all Federal officers not other-wise provided for, and to direct all military operations; pro-vided, that none of the persons composing the Federal Executive shall, on any occasion, take command of any troops, so as personally to conduct any military enterprise, as General, or in any other capacity.

5. Resolved, that a Federal Judiciary be established, to consist of a supreme tribunal, the Judges of which to be appointed by the Executive, and to hold their offices during good behaviour; to receive punctually, at stated times, a fixed compensation for their services, in which no increase nor diminution shall be made so as to affect the persons

actually in office at the time of such increase or diminution. That the Judiciary so established shall have authority to hear and determine, in the first instance, on all impeachments of Federal officers; and by way of appeal, in the dernier resort, in all cases touching the rights of ambassadors; in all cases of captures from an enemy; in all cases of piracies and felonies on the high seas; in all cases in which foreigners may be interested; in the construction of any treaty or treaties, or which may arise on any of the acts for the regulation of trade, or the collection of the Federal revenue; that none of the Judiciary shall, during the time they remain in office, be capable of receiving or holding any other office or appointment during their term of service, or for ———— thereafter.

6. Resolved, that all acts of the United States in Congress, made by virtue and in pursuance of the powers hereby, and by the Articles of Confederation, vested in them, and all treaties made and ratified under the authority of the United States, shall be the supreme law of the respective States, so far forth as those acts or treaties shall relate to the said States or their citizens; and that the Judiciary of the several States shall be bound thereby in their decisions, anything in the respective laws of the individual States to the contrary notwithstanding: and that if any State, or any body of men in any State, shall oppose or prevent the carrying into execution such acts or treaties, the Federal Executive shall be authorized to call forth the power of the Confederated States, or so much thereof as may be necessary, to enforce and compel an obedience to such acts, or an observance of such treaties.

7. Resolved, that provision be made for the admission of new States into the Union.

8. Resolved, that the rule for naturalization ought to be same in every State.

9. Resolved, that a citizen of one State committing an offence in another State of the Union, shall be deemed

guilty of the same offence as if it had been committed by a
citizen of the State in which the offence was committed.*

Adjourned.

SATURDAY, JUNE 16TH.

In Committee of the Whole, on the Resolutions proposed
by Mr. PATTERSON and Mr. RANDOLPH,— Mr. LANSING called
for the reading of the first Resolution of each plan, which
he considered as involving principles directly in contrast.
That of Mr. PATTERSON, says he, sustains the sovereignty of
the respective States, that of Mr. RANDOLPH destroys it.
The latter requires a negative on all the laws of the particular States, the former only certain general power for the
general good. The plan of Mr. RANDOLPH in short absorbs
all power, except what may be exercised in the little local
matters of the States which are not objects worthy of the
supreme cognizance. He grounded his preference of Mr.
PATTERSON's plan, chiefly, on two objections to that of Mr.
RANDOLPH,—first, want of power in the Convention to
discuss and propose it ; secondly, the improbability of its
being adopted.

1. He was decidedly of opinion that the power of the
Convention was restrained to amendments of a Federal
nature, and having for their basis the Confederacy in being.
The acts of Congress, the tenor of the acts of the States,
the commissions produced by the several Deputations, all
proved this. And this limitation of the power to an amendment of the Confederacy marked the opinion of the States,
that it was unnecessary and improper to go further. He
was sure that this was the case with his State. New York

---

*This copy of Mr. Patterson's propositions varies in a few clauses from that in
the printed Journal furnished from the papers of Mr. Brearly, a colleague of Mr.
Patterson. A confidence is felt, notwithstanding, in its accuracy. That the copy in
the Journal is not entirely correct, is shown by the ensuing speech of Mr. Wilson
(June 16), in which he refers to the mode of removing the Executive " by impeachment and conviction " as a feature in the Virginia plan forming one of its contrasts
to that of Mr. Patterson, which proposed a removal " on application of a majority of
the Executives of the States." In the copy printed in the Journal, the two modes are
combined in the same clause ; whether through inadvertence, or as a contemplated
amendment does not appear.

would never have concurred in sending Deputies to the
Convention, if she had supposed the deliberations were to
turn on a consolidation of the States, and a National Government.

2. Was it probable that the States would adopt and
ratify a scheme, which they had never authorized us to
propose, and which so far exceeded what they regarded as
sufficient? We see by their several acts, particularly in
relation to the plan of revenue proposed by Congress in
1783, not authorized by the Articles of Confederation, what
were the ideas they then entertained. Can so great a
change be supposed to have already taken place? To rely
on any change which is hereafter to take place in the sentiments of the people, would be trusting to too great an
uncertainty. We know only what their present sentiments
are. And it is in vain to propose what will not accord with
these. The States will never feel a sufficient confidence in
a General Government, to give it a negative on their laws.
The scheme is itself totally novel. There is no parallel to
it to be found. The authority of Congress is familiar to
the people, and an augmentation of the powers of Congress
will be readily approved by them.

Mr. PATTERSON said, as he had on a former occasion
given his sentiments on the plan proposed by Mr. RAN-
DOLPH, he would now, avoiding repetition as much as possible, give his reasons in favor of that proposed by himself.
He preferred it because it accorded, —first, with the powers
of the Convention; secondly, with the sentiments of the
people. If the Confederacy was radically wrong, let us
return to our States, and obtain larger powers, not assume
them ourselves. I came here not to speak my own sentiments, but the sentiments of those who sent me. Our
object is not such a government as may be best in itself,
but such a one as our constituents have authorized us to
prepare, and as they will approve. If we argue the matter
on the supposition that no confederacy at present exists, it
cannot be denied that all the States stand on the footing of

equal sovereignty. All, therefore, must concur before any can be bound. If a proportional representation be right, why do we not vote so here? If we argue on the fact that a Federal compact actually exists, and consult the articles of it, we still find an equal sovereignty to be the basis of it. He reads the fifth Article of the Confederation, giving each State a vote; and the thirteenth, declaring that no alteration shall be made without unanimous consent. This is the nature of all treaties. What is unanimously done, must be unanimously undone. It was observed (by Mr. WILSON) that the larger States gave up the point, not because it was right, but because the circumstances of the moment urged the concession. Be it so. Are they for that reason at liberty to take it back? Can the donor resume his gift without the consent of the donee? This doctrine may be convenient, but it is a doctrine that will sacrifice the lesser States. The larger States acceded readily to the Confederacy. It was the small ones that came in reluctantly and slowly. New Jersey and Maryland were the two last; the former objecting to the want of power in Congress over trade; both of them to the want of power to appropriate the vacant territory to the benefit of the whole. If the sovereignty of the States is to be maintained, the representatives must be drawn immediately from the States, not from the people; and we have no power to vary the idea of equal sovereignty. The only expedient that will cure the difficulty is that of throwing the States into hotchpot. To say that this is impracticable, will not make it so. Let it be tried, and we shall see whether the citizens of Massachusetts, Pennsylvania and Virginia accede to it. It will be objected, that coercion will be impracticable. But will it be more so in one plan than the other? Its efficacy will depend on the quantum of power collected, not on its being drawn from the States, or from the individuals; and according to his plan it may be exerted on individuals as well as according to that of Mr. RANDOLPH. A distinct Executive and Judiciary also were equally provided by his plan. It is urged, that two

branches in the Legislature are necessary. Why? For the
purpose of a check. But the reason for the precaution is
not applicable to this case. Within a particular State, where
party heats prevail, such a check may be necessary. In
such a body as Congress it is less necessary; and, besides,
the Delegations of the different States are checks on each
other. Do the people at large complain of Congress? No.
What they wish is, that Congress may have more power.
If the power now proposed be not enough, the people hereafter will make additions to it. With proper powers Congress will act with more energy and wisdom than the
proposed National Legislature; being fewer in number, and
more secreted and refined by the mode of election. The
plan of Mr. RANDOLPH will also be enormously expensive.
Allowing Georgia and Delaware two representatives each in
the popular branch, the aggregate number of that branch
will be one hundred and eighty. Add to it half as many
for the other branch, and you have two hundred and seventy
members, coming once at least a year, from the most distant
as well as the most central parts of the Republic. In the
present deranged state of our finances, can so expensive a
system be seriously thought of? By enlarging the powers
of Congress, the greatest part of this expense will be saved,
and all purposes will be answered. At least a trial ought
to be made.

Mr. WILSON entered into a contrast of the principal
points of the two plans, so far, he said, as there had been
time to examine the one last proposed. These points
were:— 1. In the Virginia plan there are *two*, and in some
degree three, branches in the Legislature; in the plan from
New Jersey there is to be a *single* Legislature only. 2.
Representation of the people at large is the basis of one;
the State Legislatures the pillars of the other. 3. Proportional representation prevails in one, equality of suffrage in
the other. 4. A single Executive Magistrate is at the head
of the one; a plurality is held out in the other. 5. In the
one, a majority of the people of the United States must pre-

vail; in the other, a minority may prevail.   6. The National Legislature is to make laws in all cases to which the separate States are incompetent, &c.; in place of this, Congress are to have additional power in a few cases only.   7. A negative on the laws of the States; in place of this, coercion to be substituted.   8. The Executive to be removable on impeachment and conviction, in one plan; in the other, to be removable at the instance of a majority of the Executives of the States.   9. Revision of the laws provided for, in one; no such check in the other.   10. Inferior national tribunals, in one; none such in the other.   11. In the one, jurisdiction of national tribunals to extend, &c.; an appellate jurisdiction only allowed in the other.   12. Here, the jurisdiction is to extend to all cases affecting the national peace and harmony; there, a few cases only are marked out.   13. Finally, the ratification is, in this, to be by the people themselves; in that, by the legislative authorities, according to the thirteenth Article of the Confederation.

With regard to the *power of the Convention*, he conceived himself authorized to *conclude nothing*, but to be at liberty to *propose any thing*.   In this particular, he felt himself perfectly indifferent to the two plans.

With *regard to the sentiments of the people*, he conceived it difficult to know precisely what they are.   Those of the particular circle in which one moved were commonly mistaken for the general voice.   He could not persuade himself that the State Governments and sovereignties were so much the idols of the people, nor a National Government so obnoxious to them, as some supposed.   Why should a National Government be unpopular?   Has it less dignity?   Will each citizen enjoy under it less liberty or protection?   Will a citizen of *Delaware* be degraded by becoming a citizen of the *United* States?   Where do the people look at present for relief from the evils of which they complain?   Is it from an internal reform of their governments?   No, sir.   It is from the national councils that relief is expected.   For these reasons, he did not fear that the people would not follow us into a National Government; and it will be a further recommendation of Mr. RANDOLPH's plan, that it is to be submitted to *them*, and not to the *Legislatures*, for ratification.

Proceeding now to the first point on which he had contrasted the two plans, he observed, that, anxious as he was for some augmentation of the Federal powers, it would be with extreme reluctance, indeed, that he could ever consent to give powers to Congress. He had two reasons, either of which was sufficient,— first, Congress, as a legislative body, does not stand on the people; secondly, it is a *single* body.

1. He would not repeat the remarks he had formerly made on the principles of representation. He would only say, that an inequality in it has ever been a poison contaminating every branch of government. In Great Britain, where this poison has had a full operation, the security of private rights is owing entirely to the purity of her tribunals of justice, the judges of which are neither appointed nor paid by a venal parliament. The political liberty of that nation, owing to the inequality of representation, is at the mercy of its rulers. He means not to insinuate that there is any parallel between the situation of that country and ours, at present. But it is a lesson we ought not to disregard, that the smallest bodies in Great Britain are notoriously the most corrupt. Every other source of influence must also be stronger in small than in large bodies of men. When Lord Chesterfield had told us that one of the Dutch provinces had been seduced into the views of France, he need not have added, that it was not Holland, but one of the *smallest* of them. There are facts among ourselves which are known to all. Passing over others, we will only remark that the *Impost*, so anxiously wished for by the public, was defeated not by any of the *larger* States in the Union.

2. *Congress is a single Legislature.* Despotism comes on mankind in different shapes, sometimes in an Executive,

sometimes in a military one. Is there no danger of a Legislative despotism? Theory and practice both proclaim it. If the Legislative authority be not restrained, there can be neither liberty nor stability; and it can only be restrained by dividing it within itself, into distinct and independent branches. In a single House there is no check, but the inadequate one, of the virtue and good sense of those who compose it.

On another great point, the contrast was equally favorable to the plan reported by the Committee of the Whole. It vested the Executive powers in a single magistrate. The plan of New Jersey, vested them in a plurality. In order to control the Legislative authority, you must divide it. In order to control the Executive you must unite it. One man will be more responsible than three. Three will contend among themselves, till one becomes the master of his colleagues. In the triumvirates of Rome, first, Cæsar, then Augustus, are witnesses of this truth. The Kings of Sparta, and the Consuls of Rome, prove also the factious consequences of dividing the Executive magistracy. Having already taken up so much time, he would not, he said, proceed to any of the other points. Those on which he had dwelt are sufficient of themselves; and on the decision of them the fate of the others will depend.

Mr. PINCKNEY. The whole comes to this, as he conceived. Give New Jersey an equal vote, and she will dismiss her scruples, and concur in the National system. He thought the Convention authorized to go any length, in recommending, which they found necessary to remedy the evils which produced this Convention.

Mr. ELLSWORTH proposed, as a more distinctive form of collecting the mind of the Committee on the subject, "that the Legislative power of the United States should remain in Congress." This was not seconded, though it seemed better calculated for the purpose than the first proposition of Mr. PATTERSON, in place of which Mr. ELLSWORTH wished to substitute it.

Mr. RANDOLPH was not scrupulous on the point of power. When the salvation of the Republic was at stake, it would be treason to our trust, not to propose what we found necessary. He painted in strong colours the imbecility of the existing confederacy, and the danger of delaying a substantial reform. In answer to the objection drawn from the sense of our constituents, as denoted by their acts relating to the Convention and the objects of their deliberation, he observed, that, as each State acted separately in the case, it would have been indecent for it to have charged the existing Constitution, with all the vices which it might have perceived in it. The first State that set on foot this experiment would not have been justified in going so far, ignorant as it was of the opinion of others, and sensible as it must have been of the uncertainty of a successful issue to the experiment. There are reasons certainly of a peculiar nature, where the ordinary cautions must be dispensed with; and this is certainly one of them. He would not, as far as depended on him, leave anything that seemed necessary, undone. The present moment is favourable, and is probably the last that will offer.

The true question is, whether we shall adhere to the Federal plan, or introduce the National plan. The insufficiency of the former has been fully displayed by the trial already made. There are but two modes by which the end of a General Government can be attained: the first, by coercion, as proposed by Mr. PATTERSON's plan; the second, by real legislation, as proposed by the other plan. Coercion he pronounced to be *impracticable, expensive, cruel to individuals.* It tended, also, to habituate the instruments of it to shed the blood, and riot in the spoils, of their fellow citizens, and consequently trained them up for the service of ambition. We must resort therefore to a *national legislation over individuals;* for which Congress are unfit. To vest such power in them would be blending the Legislative with the Executive, contrary to the received maxim on this subject. If the union of these powers, heretofore, in

Congress has been safe, it has been owing to the general impotency of that body.   Congress are, moreover,not elected by the people, but by the Legislatures, who retain even a power of recall.   They have therefore no will of their own; they are a mere diplomatic body, and are always obsequious to the views of the States, who are always encroaching on the authority of the United States.   A provision for harmony among the States, as in trade, naturalization, &c.; for crushing rebellion, whenever it may rear its crest; and for certain other general benefits, must be made.   The powers for these purposes can never be given to a body inadequate as Congress are in point of representation, elected in the mode in which they are, and possessing no more confidence than they do: for notwithstanding what has been said to the contrary, his own experience satisfied him, that a rooted distrust of Congress pretty generally prevailed.   A National Government alone, properly constituted, will answer the purpose; and he begged it to be considered that the present is the last moment for establishing one.   After this select experiment, the people will yield to despair.

The Committee rose, and the House adjourned.

MONDAY, JUNE 18TH.

·In Committee of the Whole, on the propositions of Mr. PATTERSON and Mr. RANDOLPH,— On motion of Mr. DICKINSON, to postpone the first Resolution in Mr. PATTERSON's plan, in order to take up the following, viz.: " that the Articles of Confederation ought to be revised and amended, so as to render the Government of the United States adequate to the exigencies, the preservation, and the prosperity of the Union,"— the postponement was agreed to by ten States; Pennsylvania, divided.

Mr. HAMILTON had been hitherto silent on the business before the Convention, partly from respect to others whose superior abilities, age and experience, rendered him unwilling to bring forward ideas dissimilar to theirs; and partly from his delicate situation with respect to his own State, to whose sentiments, as expressed by his colleagues, he could by no means accede. The crisis, however, which now marked our affairs, was too serious to permit any scruples whatever to prevail over the duty imposed on every man to contribute his efforts for the public safety and happiness. He was obliged, therefore, to declare himself unfriendly to both plans. He was particularly opposed to that from New Jersey, being fully convinced, that no amendment of the Confederation, leaving the States in possession of their sovereignty, could possibly answer the purpose. On the other hand, he confessed he was much discouraged by the amazing extent of country, in expecting the desired blessings from any general sovereignty that could be substituted. As to the powers of the Convention, he thought the doubts started on that subject had arisen from distinctions and reasonings too subtle. A *federal* government he conceived to mean an association of independent communities into one. Different confederacies have different powers, and exercise them in different ways. In some instances, the powers are exercised over collective bodies, in others, over individuals, as in the German Diet; and among ourselves, in cases of piracy. Great latitude, therefore, must be given to the signification of the term. The plan last proposed departs, itself, from the *federal* idea, as understood by some, since it is to operate eventually on individuals. He agreed, moreover, with the honorable gentleman from Virginia (Mr. RANDOLPH), that we owed it to our country, to do, on this emergency, whatever we should deem essential to its happiness. The States sent us here to provide for the exigencies of the Union. To rely on and propose any plan not adequate to these exigencies, merely because it was not clearly within our powers, would be to sacrifice the means to the end. It may be said, that the *States* cannot *ratify* a plan not within the purview of the Article of the Confederation providing for alterations and amendments.

But may not the States themselves, in which no constitutional authority equal to this purpose exists in the Legislatures, have had in view a reference to the people at large? In the Senate of New York, a proviso was moved, that no act of the Convention should be binding until it should be referred to the people and ratified; and the motion was lost by a single voice only, the reason assigned against it being, that it might possibly be found an inconvenient shackle.

The great question is, what provision shall we make for the happiness of our country? He would first make a comparative examination of the two plans — prove that there were essential defects in both — and point out such changes as might render a *national one* efficacious. The great and essential principles necessary for the support of government are: 1. An active and constant interest in supporting it. This principle does not exist in the States, in favor of the Federal Government. They have evidently in a high degree, the *esprit de corps*. They constantly pursue internal interests adverse to those of the whole. They have their particular debts, their particular plans of finance, &c. All these, when opposed to, invariably prevail over, the requisitions and plans of Congress. 2. The love of power. Men love power. The same remarks are applicable to this principle. The States have constantly shown a disposition rather to regain the powers delegated by them, than to part with more, or to give effect to what they had parted with. The ambition of their demagogues is known to hate the control of the General Government. It may be remarked, too, that the citizens have not that anxiety to prevent a dissolution of the General Government, as of the particular governments. A dissolution of the latter would be fatal; of the former, would still leave the purposes of government attainable to a considerable degree. Consider what such a State as Virginia will be in a few years, a few compared with the life of nations. How strongly will it feel its importance and self-sufficiency! 3. An habitual attachment

12

of the people. The whole force of this tie is on the side of the State Government. Its sovereignty is immediately before the eyes of the people; its protection is immediately enjoyed by them. From its hand distributive justice, and all those acts which familiarize and endear a government to a people, are dispensed to them. 4. *Force*, by which may be understood a *coercion of laws* or *coercion of arms*. Congress have not the former, except in few cases. In particular States, this coercion is nearly sufficient; though he held it, in most cases, not entirely so. A certain portion of military force is absolutely necessary in large communities. Massachusetts is now feeling this necessity, and making provision for it. But how can this force be exerted on the States collectively? It is impossible. It amounts to a war between the two parties. Foreign powers also will not be idle spectators. They will interpose; the confusion will increase; and a dissolution of the Union will ensue. 5. *Influence*,— he did not mean corruption, but a dispensation of those regular honors and emoluments which produce an attachment to the government. Almost all the weight of these is on the side of the States; and must continue so as long as the States continue to exist. All the passions, then, we see, of avarice, ambition, interest, which govern most individuals, and all public bodies, fall into the current of the States, and do not flow into the stream of the General Government. The former, therefore, will generally be an overmatch for the General Government, and render any confederacy in its very nature precarious. Theory is in this case fully confirmed by experience. The Amphictyonic Council had, it would seem, ample powers for general purposes. It had, in particular, the power of fining and using force against, delinquent members. What was the consequence? Their decrees were mere signals of war. The Phocian war is a striking example of it. Philip at length, taking advantage of their disunion, and insinuating himself into their councils, made himself master of their fortunes. The German confederacy affords another lesson. The authority of

Charlemagne seemed to be as great as could be necessary. The great feudal chiefs, however, exercising their local sovereignties, soon felt the spirit, and found the means, of encroachments, which reduced the Imperial authority to a nominal sovereignty. The Diet has succeeded, which, though aided by a Prince at its head, of great authority independently of his imperial attributes, is a striking illustration of the weakness of confederated governments. Other examples instruct us in the same truth. The Swiss Cantons have scarce any union at all, and have been more than once at war with one another. How then are all these evils to be avoided ? Only by such a complete sovereignty in the General Government as will turn all the strong principles and passions above-mentioned on its side. Does the scheme of New Jersey produce this effect ? Does it afford any substantial remedy whatever ? On the contrary it labors under great defects, and the defect of some of its provisions will destroy the efficacy of others. It gives a direct revenue to Congress, but this will not be sufficient. The balance can only be supplied by requisitions; which experience proves cannot be relied on. If States are to deliberate on the mode, they will also deliberate on the object of the supplies, and will grant or not grant, as they approve or disapprove of it. The delinquency of one will invite and countenance it in others. Quotas too, must, in the nature of things, be so unequal, as to produce the same evil. To what standard will you resort? Land is a fallacious one. Compare Holland with Russia; France, or England, with other countries of Europe; Pennsylvania with North Carolina,— will the relative pecuniary abilities, in those instances, correspond with the relative value of land? Take numbers of inhabitants for the rule, and make like comparison of different countries, and you will find it to be equally unjust. The different degrees of industry and improvement in different countries render the first object a precarious measure of wealth. Much depends, too, on *situation*. Connecticut, New Jersey, and North Carolina, not

being commercial States, and contributing to the wealth of
the commercial ones, can never bear quotas assessed by the
ordinary rules of proportion.   They will, and must, fail in
their duty.   Their example will be followed,— and the
union itself be dissolved.   Whence, then, is the national
revenue to be drawn?   From commerce; even from exports,
which, notwithstanding the common opinion, are fit objects
of moderate taxation; from excise, etc., etc.—These, though
not equal, are less unequal than quotas.   Another destructive ingredient in the plan is that equality of suffrage
which is so much desired by the small States.   It is not in
human nature that Virginia and the large States should
consent to it; or, if they did, that they should long abide
by it.   It shocks too much all ideas of justice, and every
human feeling.   Bad principles in a government, though
slow, are sure in their operation, and will gradually destroy
it.   A doubt has been raised whether Congress at present
have a right to keep ships or troops in time of peace.   He
leans to the negative.   Mr. PATTERSON's plan provides no
remedy.   If the powers proposed were adequate, the organization of Congress is such, that they could never be properly
and effectually exercised.   The members of Congress, being
chosen by the States and subject to recall, represent all the
local prejudices.   Should the powers be found effectual, they
will from time to time be heaped on them, till a tyrannic
sway shall be established.   The General power, whatever
be its form, if it preserves itself, must swallow up the state
powers.   Otherwise, it will be swallowed up by them.   It
is against all the principles of a good government, to vest the
requisite powers in such a body as Congress.   Two sovereignties cannot co-exist within the same limits.   Giving powers
to Congress must eventuate in a bad government, or in no
government.   The plan of New Jersey, therefore, will not do.
What, then, is to be done?   Here he was embarrassed.   The
extent of the country to be governed discouraged him.   The
expense of a General Government was also formidable;
unless there were such a diminution of expense on the side

of the State Governments, as the case would admit. If they were extinguished, he was persuaded that great economy might be obtained by substituting a General Government. He did not mean, however, to shock the public opinion by proposing such a measure. On the other hand, he saw no *other* necessity for declining it. They are not necessary for any of the great purposes of commerce, revenue, or agriculture. Subordinate authorities, he was aware, would be necessary. There must be district tribunals; corporations for local purposes. But *cui bono* the vast and expensive apparatus now appertaining to the States? The only difficulty of a serious nature which occurred to him, was that of drawing representatives from the extremes to the centre of the community. What inducements can be offered that will suffice? The moderate wages for the first branch could only be a bait to little demagogues. Three dollars, or thereabouts, he supposed, would be the utmost. The Senate, he feared, from a similar cause, would be filled by certain undertakers, who wish for particular offices under the government. This view of the subject almost led him to despair that a republican government could be established over so great an extent. He was sensible, at the same time, that it would be unwise to propose one of any other form. In his private opinion, he had no scruple in declaring, supported as he was by the opinion of so many of the wise and good, that the British Government was the best in the world; and that he doubted much whether any thing short of it would do in America. He hoped gentlemen of different opinions would bear with him in this, and begged them to recollect the change of opinion on this subject which had taken place, and was still going on. It was once thought that the power of Congress was amply sufficient to secure the end of their institution. The error was now seen by every one. The members most tenacious of republicanism, he observed, were as loud as any in declaiming against the vices of democracy. This progress of the public mind led him to anticipate the time, when others as well as himself, would join in the praise bestowed by Mr. NECKAR on the British Constitution, namely, that it is the only government in the world "which unites public strength with individual security." In every'community where industry is encouraged, there will be a division of it into the few and the many. Hence, separate interests will arise. There will be debtors and creditors, &c. Give all power to the many, they will oppress the few. Give all power to the few, they will oppress the many. Both, therefore, ought to have the power, that each may defend itself against the other. To the want of this check we owe our paper-money, instalment laws, &c. To the proper adjustment of it the British owe the excellence of their Constitution. Their House of Lords is a most noble institution. Having nothing to hope for by a change, and a sufficient interest, by means of their property, in being faithful to the national interest, they form a permanent barrier against every pernicious innovation, whether attempted on the part of the Crown or of the Commons. No temporary Senate will have firmness enough to answer the purpose. The Senate of Maryland which seems to be so much appealed to, has not yet been sufficiently tried. Had the people been unanimous and eager in the late appeal to them on the subject of a paper emission, they would have yielded to the torrent. Their acquiescing in such an appeal is a proof of it. Gentlemen differ in their opinions concerning the necessary checks, from the different estimates they form of the human passions. They suppose seven years a sufficient period to give the Senate an adequate firmness, from not duly considering the amazing violence and turbulence of the democratic spirit. When a great object of government is pursued, which seizes the popular passions, they spread like wild-fire and become irresistible. He appealed to the gentlemen from the New England States, whether experience had not there verified the remark. As to the Executive, it seemed to be admitted that no good one could be established on republican principles. Was not this giving up the merits of the question; for can there be a good government without a good Executive? The English model was the only good one on this subject. The hereditary interest of the King was so interwoven with that of the nation, and his personal emolument so great, that he was placed above the danger of being corrupted from abroad; and at the same time was both sufficiently independent and sufficiently controlled, to answer the purpose of the institution at home. One of the weak sides of republics was their being liable to foreign influence and corruption. Men of little character, acquiring great power, become easily the tools of intermeddling neighbours. Sweden was a striking instance. The French and English had each their parties during the late revolution, which was effected by the predominant influence of the former. What is the inference from all these observations? That we ought to go as far, in order to attain stability and permanency, as republican principles will admit. Let one branch of the Legislature hold their places for life, or at least during good behaviour. Let the Executive, also, be for life. He appealed to the feelings of the members present, whether a term of seven years would induce the sacrifices of private affairs which an acceptance of public trust would require, so as to ensure the services of the best citizens. On this plan, we should have in the Senate a permanent will, a weighty interest which would answer essential purposes. But is this a republican government, it will be asked? Yes, if all the magistrates are appointed and vacancies are filled by the people, or a process of election originating with the people. He was sensible that an Executive, constituted as he proposed would have in fact but little of the power and independence that might be necessary. On the other plan of appointing him for seven years, he thought the Executive ought to have but little power. He would be ambitious, with the means of making creatures; and as the object of his ambition would be to *prolong* his power, it is probable that in case of war he would avail himself of the emergency, to evade or refuse a degradation from his place. An Executive for life has not this motive for forgetting his fidelity, and will therefore be a safer depository of power. It will be objected, probably, that such an Executive will be an *elective monarch*, and will give birth to the tumults which characterize that form of government. He would reply, that *monarch* is an indefinite term. It marks not either the degree or duration of power. If this Executive magistrate would be a monarch for life, the other proposed by the Report from the Committee of the Whole would be a monarch for seven years. The circumstance of being elective was also applicable to both. It had been observed by judicious writers, that elective monarchies would be the best if they could be guarded against the *tumults* excited by the ambition and intrigues of competitors. He was not sure that tumults were an inseparable evil. He thought this character of elective monarchies had been taken rather from particular cases, than from general principles. The election of Roman Emperors was made by the *army.* In *Poland* the election is made by great rival *princes*, with independent power, and ample means of raising commotions. In the German Empire, the appointment is made by the Electors and Princes, who have equal motives and means for exciting cabals and parties. Might not such a mode of election be devised among ourselves, as will defend the community against these effects in any dangerous degree ? Having made these observations, he would read to the Committee a sketch of a plan which he should prefer to either of those under consideration. He was aware that it went beyond the ideas of most members. But will such a plan be adopted out of doors ? In return he would ask, will the people adopt the other plan ? At present they will adopt neither. But he sees the Union dissolving, or already dissolved — he sees evils operating in the States which must soon cure the people of their fondness for democracies — he sees that a great progress has been already made, and is still going on, in the public mind. He thinks, therefore, that the people will in time be unshackled from their prejudices ; and whenever that happens, they will themselves not be satisfied at stopping where the plan of Mr. RANDOLPH would place them, but be ready to go as far at least as he proposes. He did not mean to offer the paper he had sketched as a proposition to the Committee. It was meant only to give a more correct view of his ideas, and to suggest the amendments which he should probably propose to the plan of Mr. RANDOLPH, in the proper stages of its future discussion. He reads his sketch in the words following : to wit.

"I. The supreme Legislative power of the United States of America to be vested in two different bodies of men ; the one to be called the Assembly, the other the Senate ; who together shall form the Legislature of the United States, with power to pass all laws whatsoever, subject to the negative hereafter mentioned.

"II. The Assembly to consist of persons elected by the people to serve for three years.

"III. The Senate to consist of persons elected to serve during good behaviour ; their election to be made by electors chosen for that purpose by the people. In order to this, the States to be divided into election districts. On the death, removal or resignation of any Senator, his place to be filled out of the district from which he came.

"IV. The supreme Executive authority of the United States to be vested in a Governor, to be elected to serve during good behaviour; the election to be made by Electors chosen by the people in the Election Districts aforesaid. The authorities and functions of the Executive to be as follows: to have a negative on all laws about to be passed, and the execution of all laws passed; to have the direction of war when authorized or begun; to have, with the advice and approbation of the Senate, the power of making all treaties; to have the sole appointment of the heads or chief officers of the Departments of Finance, War, and Foreign Affairs; to have the nomination of all other officers (ambassadors to foreign nations included,) subject to the approbation or rejection of the Senate; to have the power of pardoning all offences except treason, which he shall not pardon without the approbation of the Senate.

" V. On the death, resignation, or removal of the Governor, his authorities to be exercised by the President of the Senate till a successor be appointed.

" VI. The Senate to have the sole power of declaring war; the power of advising and approving all treaties; the power of approving or rejecting all appointments of officers, except the heads or chiefs of the Departments of Finance, War, and Foreign Affairs.

" VII. The supreme Judicial authority to be vested in Judges, to hold their offices during good behaviour, with adequate and permanent salaries. This court to have original jurisdiction in all causes of capture, and an appellative jurisdiction in all causes in which the revenues of the General Government, or the citizens of foreign nations, are concerned.

" VIII. The Legislature of the United States to have power to institute courts in each State for the determination of all matters of general concern.

" IX. The Governor, Senators, and all officers of the United States, to be liable to impeachment for mal-, and corrupt conduct; and upon conviction to be removed from office, and disqualified for holding any place of trust or profit: all impeachments to be tried by a Court to consist of the Chief ———, or Judge of the Superior Court of Law of each State, provided such Judge shall hold his place during good behaviour and have a permanent salary.

" X. All laws of the particular States contrary to the Constitution or laws of the United States to be utterly void; and the better to prevent such laws being passed, the Governor or President of each State shall be appointed by the General Government, and shall have a negative upon the laws about to be passed in the State of which he is the Governor or President.

" XI. No State to have any forces land or naval; and the militia of all the States to be under the sole and exclusive direction of the United States, the officers of which to be appointed and commissioned by them."

On these several articles he entered into explanatory observations* corresponding with the principles of his introductory reasoning.

The Committee rose, and the House adjourned.

TUESDAY, JUNE 19TH.

In Committee of the Whole, on the propositions of Mr. PATTERSON,—The substitute offered yesterday by Mr. DICKINSON being rejected by a vote now taken on it, — Connecticut, New York, New Jersey, Delaware, aye—4 ; Massachusetts, Pennsylvania, Virginia, North Carolina, South Carolina, Georgia, no—6 ; Maryland, divided,—Mr. PATTERSON's plan was again at large before the Committee.

Mr. MADISON. Much stress has been laid by some gentlemen on the want of power in the Convention to propose any other than a *federal* plan. To what had been answered by others, he would only add, that neither of the characteristics attached to a *federal* plan would support this objection. One characteristic was that in a *federal* government the power was exercised not on the people *individually*, but on the people *collectively*, on the States. Yet in some instances, as in piracies, captures, &c., the existing Confederacy, and in many instances the amendments to it proposed

---

*The speech introducing the plan, as above taken down and written out, was seen by Mr. HAMILTON, who approved its correctness, with one or two verbal changes, which were made as he suggested. The explanatory observations which did not immediately follow, were to have been furnished by Mr. H., who did not find leisure at the time to write them out, and they were not obtained. Judge Yates, in his notes, appears to have consolidated the explanatory with the introductory observations of Mr. HAMILTON (under date of July 19th, a typographical error). It was in the former, Mr. MADISON observed, that Mr. HAMILTON, in speaking of popular governments, however modified, made the remark attributed to him by Judge Yates, that they were " *but pork still, with a little change of sauce.*"

by Mr. Patterson, must operate immediately on individuals.   The other characteristic was that a *federal* government derived its appointments not immediately from the
people, but from the States which they respectively composed.   Here, too, were facts on the other side.   In two of
the States Connecticut and Rhode Island, the Delegates to
Congress were chosen, not by the Legislatures, but by the
people at large ; and the plan of Mr. Patterson intended
no change in this particular.

It had been alleged (by Mr. Patterson), that the Confederation, having been formed by unanimous consent,
could be dissolved by unanimous consent only.   Does
this doctrine result from the nature of compacts ?   Does
it arise from any particular stipulation in the Articles
of Confederation ?   If we consider the Federal Union as
analagous to the fundamental compact by which individuals compose one society, and which must, in its
theoretic origin at least, have been the unanimous act of
the component members, it cannot be said that no dissolution of the compact can be effected without unanimous
consent.   A breach of the fundamental principles of the
compact by a part of the society, would certainly absolve
the other part from their obligations to it.   If the breach of
any article by *any* of the parties, does not set the others at
liberty, it is because the contrary is *implied* in the compact
itself, and particularly by that law of it which gives an
indefinite authority to the majority to bind the whole, in all
cases.   This latter circumstance shows, that we are not to
consider the Federal Union as analagous to the social compact of individuals : for if it were so, a majority would have
a right to bind the rest, and even to form a new Constitution
for the whole ; which the gentleman from New Jersey
would be among the last to admit.   If we consider the
Federal Union as analogous, not to the social compacts
among individual men, but to the Conventions among
individual States, what is the doctrine resulting from these
Conventions ?   Clearly, according to the expositors of the

law of nations, that a breach of any one article by any one party, leaves all the other parties at liberty to consider the whole convention as dissolved, unless they choose rather to compel the delinquent party to repair the breach. In some treaties, indeed, it is expressly stipulated, that a violation of particular articles shall not have this consequence, and even that particular articles shall remain in force during war which is in general understood to dissolve all subsisting treaties. But are there any exceptions of this sort to the Articles of Confederation ? So far from it, that there is not even an express stipulation that force shall be used to compel an offending member of the Union to discharge its duty. He observed, that the violations of the Federal Articles had been numerous and notorious. Among the most notorious was an act of New Jersey herself ; by which she *expressly refused* to comply with a constitutional requisition of Congress, and yielded no further to the expostulations of their Deputies, than barely to rescind her vote of refusal, without passing any positive act of compliance. He did not wish to draw any rigid inferences from these observations. He thought it proper, however, that the true nature of the existing Confederacy should be investigated, and he was not anxious to strengthen the foundations on which it now stands.

Proceeding to the consideration of Mr. PATTERSON's plan, he stated the object of a proper plan to be twofold,— first, to preserve the Union ; secondly, to provide a Government that will remedy the evils felt by the States, both in their united and individual capacities. Examine Mr. PATTERSON's plan, and say whether it promises satisfaction in these respects.

1. Will it prevent the violations of the law of nations and of treaties which, if not prevented, must involve us in the calamities of foreign wars ? The tendency of the States to these violations has been manifested in sundry instances. The files of Congress contain complaints, already from almost every nation with which treaties have

been formed. Hitherto indulgence has been shown to us. This cannot be the permanent disposition of foreign nations. A rupture with other powers is among the greatest of national calamities. It ought, therefore, to be effectually provided, that no part of a nation shall have it in its power to bring them on the whole. The existing Confederacy does not sufficiently provide against this evil. The proposed amendment to it does not supply the omission. It leaves the will of the States as uncontrolled as ever.

2. Will it prevent encroachments on the Federal authority ? A tendency to such encroachments has been sufficiently exemplified among ourselves, as well as in every other confederated republic, ancient and modern. By the Federal Articles, transactions with the Indians appertain to Congress, yet in several instances the States have entered into treaties and wars with them. In like manner, no two or more States can form among themselves any treaties, &c., without the consent of Congress : yet Virginia and Maryland, in one instance — Pennsylvania and New Jersey in another — have entered into compacts without previous application or subsequent apology. No State, again, can of right raise troops in time of peace with the like consent. Of all cases of the league, this seems to require the most scrupulous observance. Has not Massachusetts, notwithstanding, the most powerful member of the Union, already raised a body of troops? Is she not now augmenting them, without having even deigned to apprise Congress of her intentions? In fine, have we not seen the public land dealt out to Conneticut to bribe her acquiescence in the decree constitutionally awarded against her claim on the territory of Pennsylvania? For no other possible motive can account for the policy of Congress in that measure. If we recur to the examples of other confederacies, we shall find in all of them the same tendency of the parts to encroach on the authority of the whole. He then reviewed the Amphictyonic and Achæan confederacies, among the ancients, and the Helvetic, Germanic, and Belgic, among

the moderns ; tracing their analogy to the United States in the constitution and extent of their federal authorities ; in the tendency of the particular members to usurp on these authorities, and to bring confusion and ruin on the whole. He observed, that the plan of Mr. PATTERSON, besides omitting a control over the States, as a general defence of the Federal prerogatives, was particularly defective in two of its provisions.   In the first place, its ratification was not to be by the people at large; but by the *Legislatures.*   It could not, therefore, render the acts of Congress, in pursuance of their powers, even legally *paramount* to the acts of the States.   And in the second place, it gave to the Federal tribunal an appellate jurisdiction only even in the criminal cases enumerated.   The necessity of any such provision supposed a danger of undue acquittal in the State tribunals,—of what avail would an appellate tribunal be after an acquittal?   Besides, in the most, if not all, of the States, the Executives have, by their respective *Constitutions,* the right of pardoning,— how could this be taken from them by a legislative ratification only?

3. Will it prevent trespasses of the States on each other?   Of these enough has been already seen.   He instanced acts of Virginia and Maryland, which gave a preference to their own citizens in cases where the citizens of other States are entitled to equality of privileges by the Articles of Confederation.   He considered the emissions of paper-money, and other kindred measures, as also aggressions.   The States, relatively to one another, being each of them either debtor or creditor, the creditor States must suffer unjustly from every emission by the debtor States. We have seen retaliating acts on the subject, which threatened danger, not to the harmony only, but the tranquillity of the Union.   The plan of Mr. PATTERSON, not giving even a negative on the acts of the States, left them as much at liberty as ever to execute their unrighteous projects against each other.

4. Will it secure the internal tranquillity of the States

themselves? The insurrections in Massacnusetts admonished all the States of the danger to which they were exposed. Yet the plan of Mr. PATTERSON contained no provisions for supplying the defect of the Confederation on this point. According to the republican theory, indeed, right and power being both vested in the majority, are held to be synonymous. According to fact and experience, a minority may, in an appeal to force, be an overmatch for the majority; — in the first place, if the minority happen to include all such as possess the skill and habits of military life, with such as possess the great pecuniary resources, one-third may conquer the remaining two-thirds; in the second place, one-third of those who participate in the choice of rulers, may be rendered a majority by the accession of those whose poverty disqualifies them from a suffrage, and who, for obvious reasons, must be more ready to join the standard of sedition than that of established government; and, in the third place, where slavery exists, the republican theory becomes still more fallacious.

5. Will it secure a good internal legislation and administration to the particular States? In developing the evils which vitiate the political system of the United States, it is proper to take into view those which prevail within the States individually, as well as those which affect them collectively; since the former indirectly affect the whole, and there is great reason to believe that the pressure of them had a full share in the motives which produced the present Convention. Under this head he enumerated and animadverted on, — first, the multiplicity of the laws passed by the several States; secondly, the mutability of their laws; thirdly, the injustice of them; and fourthly, the impotence of them; — observing that Mr. PATTERSON'S plan contained no remedy for this dreadful class of evils, and could not therefore be received as an adequate provision for the exigencies of the community.

6. Will it secure the Union against the influence of foreign powers over its members? He pretended not to

say that any such influence had yet been tried; but it was naturally to be expected that occasions would produce it. As lessons which claimed particular attention, he cited the intrigues practiced among the Amphictyonic confederates, first by the Kings of Persia, and afterwards fatally, by Philip of Macedon; among the Achæans, first by Macedon, and afterwards, no less fatally, by Rome; among the Swiss, by Austria, France and the lesser neighbouring powers; among the members of the Germanic body, by France, England, Spain and Russia; and in the Belgic republic, by all the great neighbouring powers.　The plan of Mr. PATTERSON, not giving to the general councils any negative on the will of the particular States, left the door open for the like pernicious machinations among ourselves.

7. He begged the smaller States, which were most attached to Mr. PATTERSON's plan, to consider the situation in which it would leave them.　In the first place they would continue to bear the whole expense of maintaining their Delegates in Congress.　It ought not to be said, that, if they were willing to bear this burthen, no others had a right to complain.　As far as it led the smaller States to forbear keeping up a representation, by which the public business was delayed, it was evidently a matter of common concern.　An examination of the minutes of Congress would satisfy every one, that the public business had been frequently delayed by this cause; and that the States most frequently unrepresented in Congress were not the larger States.　He reminded the Convention of another consequence of leaving on a small State the burden of maintaining a representation in Congress.　During a considerable period of the war, one of the Representatives of Delaware, in whom alone, before the signing of the Confederation, the entire vote of that State, and after that event one half of its vote, frequently resided, was a citizen and resident of Pennsylvania, and held an office in his own State incompatible with an appointment from it to Congress.　During another period, the same State was represented by three

13

Delegates, two of whom were citizens of Pennsylvania, and
the third a citizen of New Jersey. These expedients must
have been intended to avoid the burden of supporting Delegates from their own State. But whatever might have
been the cause, was not in effect the vote of one State
doubled, and the influence of another increased by it? In
the second place the coercion on which the efficacy of
the plan depends can never be exerted but on themselves.
The larger States will be impregnable, the smaller only can
feel the vengeance of it. He illustrated the position by
the history of the Amphictyonic confederates; and the ban
of the German Empire. It was the cob-web which could
entangle the weak, but would be the sport of the strong.

8. He begged them to consider the situation in which
they would remain, in case their pertinacious adherence to
an inadmissible plan should prevent the adoption of any
plan. The contemplation of such an event was painful;
but it would be prudent to submit to the task of examining
it at a distance, that the means of escaping it might be the
more readily embraced. Let the union of the States be
dissolved, and one of two consequences must happen.
Either the States must remain individually independent
and sovereign; or two or more confederacies must be formed
among them. In the first event, would the small States be
more secure against the ambition and power of their larger
neighbours, than they would be under a General Government pervading with equal energy every part of the Empire,
and having an equal interest in protecting every part against
every other part? In the second, can the smaller expect
that their larger neighbours would confederate with them
on the principle of the present Confederacy, which gives to
each member an equal suffrage; or that they would exact
less severe concessions from the smaller States, than are
proposed in the scheme of Mr. RANDOLPH.

The great difficulty lies in the affair of representation;
and if this could be adjusted, all others would be surmount-
able. It was admitted by both the gentlemen from New

Jersey, (Mr. BREARLY and Mr. PATTERSON,) that it would not be *just to allow Virginia*, which was sixteen times as large as Delaware, an equal vote only. Their language was, that it would not be *safe for Delaware* to allow Virginia sixteen times as many votes. The expedient proposed by them was, that all the States should be thrown into one mass, and a new partition be made into thirteen equal parts. Would such a scheme be practicable? The dissimilarities existing in the rules of property, as well as in the manners, habits and prejudices, of different States, amounted to a prohibition of the attempt. It had been found impossible for the power of one of the most absolute princes in Europe (the King of France,) directed by the wisdom of one of the most enlightened and patriotic ministers (Mr. Neckar) that any age has produced, to equalize, in some points only, the different usages and regulations of the different provinces. But admitting a general amalgamation and repartition of the States to be practicable, and the danger apprehended by the smaller States from a proportional representation to be real,—would not a particular and voluntary coalition of these with their neighbours, be less inconvenient to the whole community, and equally effectual for their own safety? If New Jersey or Delaware conceived that an advantage would accrue to them from an equalization of the States, in which case they would necessarily form a junction with their neighbours, why might not this end be attained by leaving them at liberty by the Constitution to form such a junction whenever they pleased? And why should they wish to obtrude a like arrangement on all the States, when it was, to say the least, extremely difficult, would be obnoxious to many of the States, and when neither the inconvenience, nor the benefit of the expedient to themselves, would be lessened by confining it to themselves? The prospect of many new States to the westward was another consideration of importance. If they should come into the Union at all, they would come when they contained but few inhabitants. If they should be entitled to vote according to their proportion of inhabitants, all would be right and safe. Let them have an equal vote, and a more objectionable minority than ever, might give law to the whole.

On a question of postponing generally the first proposition of Mr. PATTERSON's plan, it was agreed to,— New York and New Jersey only being, no.

On the question, moved by Mr. KING, whether the Committee should rise, and Mr. RANDOLPH's proposition be reported without alteration, which was in fact a question whether Mr. RANDOLPH's should be adhered to as preferable to those of Mr. PATTERSON,— Massachusetts, Connecticut, Pennsylvania, Virginia, North Carolina, South Carolina, Georgia, aye — 7; New York, New Jersey, Delaware, no — 3; Maryland, divided.

Mr. RANDOLPH's plan was reported from the Committee [q. v. June 13th] being before the house, and —

The first Resolution, "that a national Government ought to be established, consisting, &c.," being taken up,

Mr. WILSON observed that, by a national Government, he did not mean one that would swallow up the State Governments, as seemed to be wished by some gentlemen. He was tenacious of the idea of preserving the latter. He thought, contrary to the opinion of Colonel HAMILTON, that they might not only subsist, but subsist on friendly terms with the former. They were absolutely necessary for certain purposes, which the former could not reach. All large governments must be subdivided into lesser jurisdictions. As examples he mentioned Persia, Rome, and particularly the divisions and subdivisions of England by Alfred.

Colonel HAMILTON coincided with the proposition as it stood in the Report. He had not been understood yesterday. By an abolition of the States, he meant that no boundary could be drawn between the National and State Legislatures; that the former must therefore have indefinite authority. If it were limited at all, the rivalship of the States would gradually subvert it. Even as corporations, the extent of some of them, as Virginia, Massachusetts, &c., would be formidable. As *States*, he thought they ought to be abolished. But he admitted the necessity of leaving in them subordinate jurisdictions. The examples of Persia and the Roman Empire, cited by Mr. WILSON, were, he thought, in favor of his doctrine, the great powers delegated to the Satraps and Proconsuls having frequently produced revolts and schemes of independence.

Mr. KING wished, as every thing depended on this proposition, that no objection might be improperly indulged against the phraseology of it. He conceived that the import of the term "States," "sovereignty," "*national*," "federal," had been often used and implied in the discussions inaccurately and delusively. The States were not "sovereigns" in the sense contended for by some. They did not possess the peculiar features of sovereignty,— they could not make war, nor peace, nor alliances, nor treaties. Considering them as political beings, they were dumb, for they could not speak to any foreign sovereign whatever. They were deaf, for they could not hear any propositions from such sovereign. They had not even the organs or faculties of defence or offence, for they could not of themselves raise troops or equip vessels, for war. On the other side, if the union of the States comprises the idea of a confederation, it comprises that also of consolidation. A union of the States is a union of the men composing them, from whence a *national* character results to the whole. Congress can act alone without the States; they can act, and their acts will be binding, against the instructions of the States. If they declare war, war is *de jure* declared; captures made in pursuance of it are lawful; no acts of the States can vary the situation or prevent the judicial consequences. If the States, therefore, retained some portion of their sovereignty, they had certainly divested themselves of essential portions of it. If they formed a confederacy in some respects, they formed a nation in others. The Convention could clearly deliberate on and propose any alterations that Congress

could have done under the Federal Articles. And could
not Congress propose, by virtue of the last Article, a change
in any article whatever,—and as well that relating to the
equality of suffrage, as any other? He made these remarks
to obviate some scruples which had been expressed. He
doubted much the practicability of annihilating the States;
but thought that much of their power ought to be taken
from them.

Mr. MARTIN said, he considered that the separation from
Great Britain placed the thirteen States in a state of nature
towards each other; that they would have remained in that
state till this time, but for the Confederation; that they
entered into the Confederation on the footing of equality;
that they met now to amend it, on the same footing; and
that he could never accede to a plan that would introduce
an inequality, and lay ten States at the mercy of Virginia,
Massachusetts and Pennsylvania.   '

Mr. WILSON could not admit the doctrine that when the
colonies became independent of Great Britain, they became
independent also of each other. He read the Declaration
of Independence, observing thereon, that the *United Colonies* were declared to be free and independent States; and
inferring, that they were independent, not *individually* but
unitedly, and that they were confederated, as they were
independent States.

Colonel HAMILTON assented to the doctrine of Mr.
WILSON. He denied the doctrine that the States were
thrown into a state of nature. He was not yet prepared to
admit the doctrine that the Confederacy could be dissolved
by partial infractions of it. He admitted that the States
met now on an equal footing, but could see no inference
from that against concerting a change of the system in this
particular. He took this occasion of observing, for the
purpose of appeasing the fear of the small States, that two
circumstances would render them secure under a national
Government in which they might lose the equality of rank
which they now held: one was the local situation of the

three largest States, Virginia, Massachusetts and Pennsylvania. They were separated from each other by distance of place, and equally so, by all the peculiarities which distinguish the interests of one State from those of another. No combination, therefore, could be dreaded. In the second place, as there was a gradation in the States, from Virginia, the largest, down to Delaware, the smallest, it would always happen that ambitious combinations among a few States might and would be counteracted by defensive combinations of greater extent among the rest. No combination has been seen among the large counties, merely as such, against lesser counties. The more close the union of the States, and the more complete the authority of the whole, the less opportunity will be allowed to the stronger States to injure the weaker.

Adjourned.

WEDNESDAY, JUNE 20TH.

In Convention,— Mr. WILLIAM BLOUNT, from North Carolina, took his seat.

The first Resolution of the Report of the Committee of the Whole being before the House —

Mr. ELLSWORTH, seconded by Mr. GORHAM, moves to alter it, so as to run "that the government of the United States ought to consist of a supreme Legislative, Executive and Judiciary." This alteration, he said, would drop the word *national*, and retain the proper title "the United States." He could not admit the doctrine that a breach of any of the Federal Articles could dissolve the whole. It would be highly dangerous not to consider the Confederation as still subsisting. He wished, also, the plan of the Convention to go forth as an amendment of the Articles of the Confederation, since, under this idea the authority of the Legislatures could ratify it. If they are unwilling, the people will be so too. If the plan goes forth to the people for ratification, several succeeding conventions within the States would be unavoidable. He did not like these conventions. They were better fitted to pull down than to build up constitutions.

Mr. RANDOLPH did not object to the change of expression, but apprised the gentleman who wished for it, that he did not admit it for the reasons assigned; particularly that of getting rid of a reference to the people for ratification.

The motion of Mr. ELLSWORTH was acquiesced in, *nem. con.*

The second Resolution, "that the national legislature ought to consist of two branches," being taken up, the word "national" struck out, as of course.

Mr. LANSING observed, that the true question here was, whether the Convention would adhere to, or depart from, the foundation of the present confederacy; and moved, instead of the second Resolution, "that the powers of legislation be vested in the United States in Congress." He had already assigned two reasons against such an innovation as was proposed,—first, the want of competent powers in the Convention; secondly, the state of the public mind. It had been observed by (Mr. MADISON), in discussing the first point, that in two States the Delegates to Congress were chosen by the people. Notwithstanding the first appearance of this remark, it had in fact no weight, as the Delegates, however chosen, did not represent the people, merely as so many individuals; but as forming a sovereign State. Mr. RANDOLPH put it, he said, on its true footing, namely that the public safety superseded the scruple arising from the review of our powers. But in order to feel the force of this consideration, the same impression must be had of the public danger. He had not himself the same impression, and could not therefore dismiss his scruple. Mr. WILSON contended, that, as the Convention were only to recommend, they might recommend what they pleased. He differed much from him. Any act whatever of so respectable a body must have a great effect; and if it does not succeed will be a source of great dissensions. He admitted that there was no certain criterion of the public mind on the subject. He therefore recurred to the evidence of it given by the opposition in the States to the scheme of an Impost. It could not be expected that those possessing sovereignty could ever voluntarily part with it. It was not to be expected from any one State, much less from thirteen. He proceeded to make some observations on the plan itself, and the arguments urged in support of it. The point of representation could receive no elucidation from the case of England. The corruption of the boroughs did not proceed from their comparative smallness; but from the actual fewness of the inhabitants, some of them not having more than one or two. A great inequality existed in the counties of England. Yet the like complaint of peculiar corruption in the small ones had not been made. It had been said that Congress represent the State prejudices,—will not any other body whether chosen by the Legislatures or people of the States, also represent their prejudices? It had been asserted by his colleague (Colonel HAMILTON), that there was no coincidence of interests among the large States that ought to excite fears of oppression in the smaller. If it were true that such a uniformity of interests existed among the States, there was equal safety for all of them whether the representation remained as heretofore, or were proportioned as now proposed. It is proposed that the General Legislature shall have a negative on the laws of the States. Is it conceivable that there will be leisure for such a task? There will, on the most moderate calculation, be as many acts sent up from the States as there are days in the year. Will the members of the General Legislature be competent judges? Will a gentleman from Georgia be a judge of the expediency of a law which is to operate in New Hampshire? Such a negative would be more injurious than that of Great Britain heretofore was. It is said that the National Government must have the influence arising from the grant of offices and honors. In order to render such a government effectual, he believed such an influence to be necessary. But if the States will not agree to it, it is in vain, worse than in vain, to make the proposition. If this influence is to be attained, the States must be entirely abolished. Will any one say, this would ever be agreed to? He doubted whether any General Government, equally beneficial to all, can be attained. That now under consideration, he is sure, must be utterly unattainable. He had another objection. The system was too novel and complex. No man could foresee what its operation will be, either with respect to the General Government, or the State Governments. One or other, it has been surmised, must absorb the whole.

Col. MASON did not expect this point would have been reagitated. The essential differences between the two plans had been clearly stated. The principal objections against that of Mr. RANDOLPH were, the *want of power*, and the *want of practicability*. There can be no weight in the first, as the fiat is not to be *here*, but in the people. He thought with his colleague (Mr. RANDOLPH,) that there were, besides certain crises, in which all the ordinary cautions yielded to public necessity. He gave as an example, the eventual treaty with Great Britain, in forming which the Commissioners of the United States had boldly disregarded the improvident shackles of Congress; had given to their country an honorable and happy peace, and, instead of being censured for the transgression of their powers, had raised to themselves a monument more durable than brass. The *impracticability* of gaining the public concurrence, he thought, was still more groundless. Mr. LANSING had cited the attempts of Congress to gain an enlargement of their powers, and had inferred from the miscarriage of these attempts, the hopelessness of the plan which he (Mr. LANSING) opposed. He thought a very different inference ought to have been drawn, viz. that the plan which Mr. LANSING espoused, and which proposed to augment the powers of Congress, never could be expected to succeed. He meant not to throw any reflections on Congress as a body, much less on any particular members of it. He meant, however, to speak his sentiments without reserve on this subject; it was a privilege of age, and perhaps the only compensation which nature had given for the privation of so many other enjoyments; and he should not scruple to exercise it freely. Is it to be thought that the people of America, so watchful over their interests, so jealous of their liberties, will give up their all, will surrender both the sword and the purse, to the same body,—and that, too, not chosen immediately by themselves? They never will. They never ought. Will they trust such a body with the regulation of their trade, with the regulation of their taxes, with all the other great powers which are in contemplation? Will they give unbounded confidence to a secret Journal,— to the intrigues, to the factions, which in the nature of things appertain to such an assembly? If any man doubts the existence of these characters of Congress, let him consult their Journals for the years '78, '79, and '80. It will be said, that if the people are averse to parting with power, why is it hoped that they will part with it to a national Legislature? The proper answer is, that in this case they do not part with power: they only transfer it from one set of immediate representatives to another set. Much has been said of the unsettled state of the mind of the people. He believed the mind of the people of America, as elsewhere, was unsettled as to some points, but settled as to others. In two points he was sure it was well settled,— first, in an attachment to republican government; secondly, in an attachment to more than one branch in the Legislature. Their constitutions accord so generally in both these circumstances, that they seem almost to have been preconcerted. This must either have been a miracle, or have resulted from the genius of the people. The only exceptions to the establishment of two branches in the Legislature are the State of Pennsylvania, and Congress; and the latter the only single one not chosen by the people themselves. What has been the consequence? The people have been constantly averse to giving that body further powers. It was acknowledged by Mr. PATTERSON, that his plan could not be enforced without military coercion. Does he con-

sider the force of this concession? The most jarring ele-
ments of nature, fire and water themselves, are not more
incompatible than such a mixture of civil liberty and military execution.   Will the militia march from one State into
another, in order to collect the arrears of taxes from the
delinquent members of the Republic?   Will they maintain
an army for this purpose?   Will not the citizens of the
invaded State assist one another, till they rise as one man
and shake off the Union altogether?   Rebellion is the only
case in which the military force of the State can be properly
exerted against its citizens.   In one point of view, he was
struck with horror at the prospect of recurring to this expedient.   To punish the non-payment of taxes with death was
a severity not yet adopted by despotism itself; yet this
unexampled cruelty would be mercy compared to a military
collection of revenue, in which the bayonet could make no
discrimination between the innocent and the guilty.   He
took this occasion to repeat, that, notwithstanding his solici-
tude to establish a national Government, he never would
agree to abolish the State Governments, or render them
absolutely insignificant.   They were as necessary as the
General Government, and he would be equally careful to
preserve them.   He was aware of the difficulty of drawing
the line between them, but hoped it was not insurmountable.
The convention, though comprising so many distinguished
characters, could not be expected to make a faultless Government.   And he would prefer trusting to posterity the
amendment of its defects, rather than to push the experiment too far.

Mr. LUTHER MARTIN agreed with Colonel MASON, as to
the importance of the State Governments: he would support them at the expense of the General Government, which
was instituted for the purpose of that support.   He saw no
necessity for two branches; and if it existed, Congress
might be organized into two.   He considered Congress as
representing the people, being chosen by the Legislatures,
who were chosen by the people.   At any rate, Congress

represented the Legislature; and it was the Legislatures, not the people, who refused to enlarge their powers. Nor could the rule of voting have been the ground of objection, otherwise ten of the States must always have been ready to place further confidence in Congress. The causes of repugnance must therefore be looked for elsewhere. At the separation from the British Empire, the people of America preferred the establishment of themselves into thirteen separate sovereignties, instead of incorporating themselves into one. To these they look up for the security of their lives, liberties, and properties; to these they must look up. The Federal Government they formed to defend the whole against foreign nations in time of war, and to defend the lesser States against the ambition of the larger. They are afraid of granting power unnecessarily, lest they should defeat the original end of the Union; lest the powers should prove dangerous to the sovereignties of the particular States which the Union was meant to support; and expose the lesser to being swallowed up by the larger. He conceived also that the people of the States, having already vested their powers in their respective Legislatures, could not resume them without a dissolution of their Governments. He was against conventions in the States — was not against assisting States against rebellious subjects — thought the *federal* plan of Mr. PATTERSON did not require coercion more than the *national one*, as the latter must depend for the deficiency of its revenues on requisitions and quotas — and that a national judiciary, extended into the States, would be ineffectual, and would be viewed with a jealousy inconsistent with its usefulness.

Mr. SHERMAN seconded and supported Mr. LANSING's motion. He admitted two branches to be necessary in the State Legislatures, but saw no necessity in a confederacy of States. The examples were all of a single council. Congress carried us through the war, and perhaps as well as any government could have done. The complaints at present are, not that the views of Congress are unwise or un-

faithful, but that their powers are insufficient for the
execution of their views. The national debt, and the want
of power somewhere to draw forth the national resources,
are the great matters that press. All the States were sensible of the defect of power in Congress. He thought
much might be said in apology for the failure of the State
Legislatures, to comply with the Confederation. They
were afraid of leaning too hard on the people by accumula-
ting taxes; no *constitutional* rule had been, or could be
observed in the quotas; the accounts also were unsettled,
and every State supposed itself in advance, rather than in
arrears. For want of a general system, taxes to a due
amount had not been drawn from trade, which was the most
convenient resource. As almost all the States had agreed
to the recommendation of Congress on the subject of an
impost, it appeared clearly that they were willing to trust
Congress with power to draw a revenue from trade. There
is no weight, therefore, in the argument drawn from a distrust of Congress; for money matters being the most important of all, if the people will trust them with power as to
them, they will trust them with any other necessary powers. Congress, indeed, by the Confederation, have in fact
the right of saying how much the people shall pay, and to
what purpose it shall be applied; and this right was
granted to them in the expectation that it would in all cases
have its effect. If another branch were to be added to
Congress, to be chosen by the people, it would serve to
embarrass. The people would not much interest themselves in the elections, a few designing men in the large
districts would carry their points; and the people would
have no more confidence in their new representatives than
in Congress. He saw no reason why the State Legislatures should be unfriendly, as had been suggested, to Congress. If they appoint Congress, and approve of their measures, they would be rather favourable and partial to them.
The disparity of the States in point of size he perceived
was the main difficulty. But the large States had not yet

suffered from the equality of votes enjoyed by the smaller ones. In all great and general points, the interests of all the States were the same. The State of Virginia, notwithstanding the equality of votes, ratified the Confederation without even proposing any alteration. Massachusetts also ratified without any material difficulty, &c. In none of the ratifications is the want of two branches noticed or complained of. To consolidate the States, as some have proposed, would dissolve our treaties with foreign nations, which had been formed with us, as *confederated* States. He did not, however, suppose that the creation of two branches in the Legislature would have such an effect. If the difficulty on the subject of representation cannot be otherwise got over, he would agree to have two branches, and a proportional representation in one of them, provided each State had an equal voice in the other. This was necessary to secure the rights of the lesser States; otherwise three or four of the large States would rule the others as they please. Each State, like each individual, had its peculiar habits, usages, and manners, which constituted its happiness. It would not, therefore, give to others a power over this happiness, any more than an individual would do, when he could avoid it.

Mr. WILSON urged the necessity of two branches; observed, that if a proper model was not to be found in other confederacies, it was not to be wondered at. The number of them was small, and the duration of some at least short. The Amphictyonic and Achæan were formed in the infancy of political science; and appear, by their history and fate, to have contained radical defects. The Swiss and Belgic confederacies were held together, not by any vital principle of energy, but by the incumbent pressure of formidable neighbouring nations. The German owed its continuance to the influence of the House of Austria. He appealed to our own experience for the defects of our confederacy. He had been six years, of the twelve since commencement of the Revolution, a member of Congress, and had felt all its weaknesses.   He appealed to the recollection of others, whether, on many important occasions, the public interest had not been obstructed by the small members of the Union.   The success of the Revolution was owing to other causes, than the constitution of Congress.   In many instances it went on even against the difficulties arising from Congress themselves.   He admitted that the large States did accede, as had been stated to the Confederation in its present form.   But it was the effect of necessity not choice. There are other instances of their yielding, from the same motive, to the unreasonable measures of the small States. The situation of things is now a little altered.   He insisted that a jealousy would exist between the State Legislatures and the General Legislature ; observing, that the members of the former would have views and feelings very distinct in this respect from their constituents.   A private citizen of a State is indifferent whether power be exercised by the General or State Legislatures, provided it be exercised most for his happiness.   His representative has an interest in its being exercised by the body to which he belongs.   He will therefore view the National Legislature with the eye of a jealous rival.   He observed that the addresses of Congress to the people at large had always been better received, and produced greater effect, than those made to the Legislatures.

On the question for postponing, in order to take up Mr. LANSING'S proposition, "to vest the powers of legislation in Congress,"— Connecticut, New York, New Jersey, Delaware, aye — 4; Massachusetts, Pennsylvania, Virginia, North Carolina, South Carolina, Georgia, no — 6; Maryland, divided.

On motion of the Deputies from Delaware, the question on the second Resolution in the Report from the Committee of the Whole, was postponed till to-morrow.

Adjourned.

THURSDAY, JUNE 21ST.

In Convention,—Mr. JONATHAN DAYTON, from New Jersey, took his seat.

The second Resolution in the Report from the Committee of the Whole, being under consideration,—

Doctor JOHNSON. On a comparison of the two plans which had been proposed from Virginia and New Jersey, it appeared that the peculiarity which characterized the latter was its being calculated to preserve the individuality of the States. The plan from Virginia did not profess to destroy this individuality altogether; but was charged with such a tendency. One gentleman alone (Colonel HAMILTON), in his animadversions on the plan of New Jersey, boldly and decisively contended for an abolition of the State Governments. Mr. WILSON and the gentleman from Virginia, who also were adversaries of the plan of New Jersey, held a different language. They wished to leave the States in possession of a considerable, though a subordinate, jurisdiction. They had not yet, however, shewn how this could consist with, or be secured against, the general sovereignty and jurisdiction which they proposed to give to the National Government. If this could be shewn, in such a manner as to satisfy the patrons of the New Jersey propositions, that the individuality of the States would not be endangered, many of their objections would no doubt be removed. If this could not be shewn, their objections would have their full force. He wished it, therefore, to be well considered, whether, in case the States, as was proposed, should retain some portion of sovereignty at least, this portion could be preserved, without allowing them to participate effectually in the General Government, without giving them each a distinct and equal vote for the purpose of defending themselves in the general councils.

Mr. WILSON's respect for Doctor JOHNSON, added to the importance of the subject, led him to attempt, unprepared
14

as he was, to solve the difficulty which had been started. It was asked, how the General Government and individuality of the particular States could be reconciled to each other,— and how the latter could be secured against the former? Might it not, on the other side, be asked, how the former was to be secured against the latter? It was generally admitted, that a jealousy and rivalship would be felt, between the general and particular Governments. As the plan now stood, though indeed contrary to his opinion, one branch of the General Government (the Senate, or second branch) was to be appointed by the State Legislatures. The State Legislatures, therefore, by this participation in the General Government, would have an opportunity of defending their rights. Ought not a reciprocal opportunity to be given to the General Government of defending itself, by having an appointment of some one constituent branch of the State Governments. If a security be necessary on one side, it would seem reasonable to demand it on the other. But taking the matter in a more general view, he saw no danger to the States, from the General Government. In case a combination should be made by the large ones, it would produce a general alarm among the rest, and the project would be frustrated. But there was no temptation to such a project. The States having in general a similar interest, in case of any propositions in the National Legislature to encroach on the State Legislatures, he conceived a general alarm would take place in the National Legislature itself; that it would communicate itself to the State Legislatures; and would finally spread among the people at large. The General Government will be as ready to preserve the rights of the States, as the latter are to preserve the rights of individuals,— all the members of the former having a common interest, as representatives of all the people of the latter, to leave the State Governments in possession of what the people wish them to retain. He could not discover, therefore, any danger whatever on the side from which it was apprehended.

On the contrary, he conceived, that, in spite of every precaution, the General Government would be in perpetual
danger of encroachments from the State Governments.

Mr. MADISON was of opinion, — in the first place, that
there was less danger of encroachment from the General
Government than from the State Governments; and in the
second place, that the mischiefs from encroachments would
be less fatal if made by the former, than if made by the
latter.

1. All the examples of other confederacies prove the
greater tendency, in such systems, to anarchy than to
tyranny; to a disobedience of the members, than usurpations of the Federal head. Our own experience had fully
illustrated this tendency. But it will be said, that the proposed change in the principles and form of the Union will
vary the tendency; that the General Government will have
real and greater powers, and will be derived, in one branch
at least, from the people, not from the Governments of the
States. To give full force to this objection, let it be supposed for a moment that indefinite power should be given to
the General Legislature, and the States reduced to corporations dependent on the General Legislature, — why should
it follow that the General Government would take from the
States any branch of their power, as far as its operation was
beneficial, and its continuance desirable to the people? In
some of the States, particularly in Connecticut, all the
townships are incorporated, and have a certain limited jurisdiction, — have the representatives of the people of the
townships in the Legislature of the State ever endeavoured
to despoil the townships of any part of their local authority?
As far as this local authority is convenient to the people,
they are attached to it; and their representatives, chosen by
and amenable to them, naturally respect their attachment
to this, as much as their attachment to any other right or
interest. The relation of a General Government to State
Governments is parallel.

2. Guards were more necessary against encroachments

of the State Governments on the General Government,
than of the latter on the former, The great objection
made against an abolition of the State Governments was,
that the General Government could not extend its care to
all the minute objects which fall under the cognizance of
the local jurisdictions. The objection as stated lay not
against the probable abuse of the general power, but against
the imperfect use that could be made of it throughout so
great an extent of country, and over so great a variety of
objects. As far as its operation would be practicable, it
could not in this view be improper; as far as it would be
impracticable, the convenience of the General Government
itself would concur with that of the people in the maintenance of subordinate governments. Were it practicable for
the General Government to extend its care to every requisite object without the co-operation of the State Governments, the people would not be less free as members of one
great Republic, than as members of thirteen small ones. A
citizen of Delaware was not more free than a citizen of
Virginia; nor would either be more free than a citizen of
America. Supposing, therefore, a tendency in the General
Government to absorb the State Governments, no *fatal*
consequence could result. Taking the reverse as the supposition, that a tendency should be left in the State Governments towards an independence of the General Government, and the gloomy consequences need not be pointed
out. The imagination of them must have suggested to the
States the experiment we are now making, to prevent the
calamity, and must have formed the chief motive with those
present to undertake the arduous task.

On the question for resolving, "that the Legislature
ought to consist of two branches," — Massachusetts, Connecticut, Pennsylvania, Virginia, North Carolina, South
Carolina, Georgia, aye — 7; New York, New Jersey, Delaware, no — 3; Maryland, divided.

The *third* Resolution of the Report being taken into
consideration—

General PINCKNEY moved, "that the first branch, instead of being elected by the people, should be elected in such manner as the Legislature of each State should direct." He urged, — first, that this liberty would give more satisfaction, as the Legislatures could then accommodate the mode to the convenience and opinions of the people; secondly, that it would avoid the undue influence of large counties, which would prevail if the elections were to be made in districts, as must be the mode intended by the report of the Committee; thirdly, that otherwise disputed elections must be referred to the General Legislature, which would be attended with intolerable expense and trouble to the distant parts of the Republic.

Mr. L. MARTIN seconded the motion.

Col. HAMILTON considered the motion as intended manifestly to transfer the election from the people to the State Legislatures, which would essentially vitiate the plan. It would increase that State influence which could not be too watchfully guarded against. All, too, must admit the possibility, in case the General Government should maintain itself, that the State Governments might gradually dwindle into nothing. The system, therefore, should not be engrafted on what might possibly fail.

Mr. MASON urged the necessity of retaining the election by the people. Whatever inconvenience may attend the democratic principle, it must actuate one part of the Government. It is the only security for the rights of the people.

Mr. SHERMAN would like an election by the Legislatures best, but is content with the plan as it stands.

Mr. RUTLEDGE could not admit the solidity of the distinction between a mediate and immediate election by the people. It was the same thing to act by one's self, and to act by another. An election by the Legislature would be more refined, than an election immediately by the people; and would be more likely to correspond with the sense of the whole community. If this Convention had been chosen by the people in districts, it is not to be supposed that such proper characters would have been preferred. The Delegates to Congress, he thought, had also been fitter men than would have been appointed by the people at large.

Mr. WILSON considered the election of the first branch by the people not only as the corner-stone, but as the foundation of the fabric; and that the difference between a mediate and immediate election was immense. The difference was particularly worthy of notice in this respect, that the Legislatures are actuated not merely by the sentiment of the people; but have an official sentiment opposed to that of the General Government, and perhaps to that of the people themselves.

Mr. KING enlarged on the same distinction. He supposed the Legislatures would constantly choose men subservient to their own views, as contrasted to the general interest; and that they might even devise modes of election that would be subversive of the end in view. He remarked several instances in which the views of a State might be at variance with those of the General Government; and mentioned particularly a competition between the National and State debts, for the most certain and productive funds.

General PINCKNEY was for making the State Governments a part of the general system. If they were to be abolished, or lose their agency, South Carolina and the other States would have but a small share of the benefits of Government.

On the question for General PINCKNEY's motion, to substitute " election to the first branch in such mode as the Legislatures should appoint," instead of its being " elected by the people,"— Connecticut, New Jersey, Delaware, South Carolina, aye — 4: Massachusetts, New York, Pennsylvania, Virginia, North Carolina, Georgia, no — 6; Maryland divided.

General PINCKNEY then moved, " that the first branch be elected *by the people* in such mode as the Legislatures should direct," but waived it on its being hinted that such a provision might be more properly tried in the detail of the plan.

On the question for the election of the first branch "by the *people*,"— Massachusetts, Connecticut, New York, Pennsylvania, Delaware, Virginia, North Carolina, South Carolina, Georgia, aye — 9; New Jersey, no —1; Maryland divided.

The election of the first branch "for the term of three years," being considered,—

Mr. RANDOLPH moved to strike out "three years," and insert "two years." He was sensible that annual elections were a source of great mischiefs in the States, yet it was the want of such checks against the popular intemperance as were now proposed, that rendered them so mischievous. He would have preferred annual to biennial, but for the extent of the United States, and the inconvenience which would result from them to the representatives of the extreme parts of the Empire. The people were attached to frequency of elections. All the Constitutions of the States, except that of South Carolina, had established annual elections.

Mr. DICKINSON. The idea of annual elections was borrowed from the ancient usage of England, a country much less extensive than ours. He supposed biennial would be inconvenient. He preferred triennial; and in order to prevent the inconvenience of an entire change of the whole number at the same moment, suggested a rotation, by an annual election of one-third.

Mr. ELLSWORTH was opposed to three years, supposing that even one year was preferable to two years. The people were fond of frequent elections, and might be safely indulged in one branch of the Legislature. He moved for " one year."

Mr. STRONG seconded and supported the motion.

Mr. WILSON, being for making the first branch an effectual representation of the people at large, preferred an annual election of it. This frequency was most familiar and pleasing to the people. It would not be more inconvenient to them than triennial elections, as the people in all the States have annual meetings with which the election of the national Representatives might be made to coincide. He did not conceive that it would be necessary for the National Legislature to sit constantly, perhaps not half, perhaps not one-fourth of the year.

Mr. MADISON was persuaded that annual elections would be extremely inconvenient, and apprehensive that biennial would be too much so ; he did not mean inconvenient to the electors, but to the Representatives. They would have to travel seven or eight hundred miles from the distant parts of the Union ; and would probably not be allowed even a reimbursement of their expenses. Besides, none of those who wished to be re-elected would remain at the seat of government, confiding that their absence would not affect them. The members of Congress had done this with few instances of disappointment. But as the choice was here to be made by the people themselves, who would be much less complaisant to individuals, and much more susceptible of impressions from the presence of a rival candidate, it must be supposed that the members from the most distant States would travel backwards and forwards at least as often as the elections should be repeated. Much was to be said, also, on the time requisite for new members, who would always form a large proportion, to acquire that knowledge of the affairs of the States in general, without which their trust could not be usefully discharged.

Mr. SHERMAN preferred annual elections, but would be content with biennial. He thought the Representatives ought to return home and mix with the people. By remaining at the seat of government, they would acquire the habits of the place, which might differ from those of their constituents.

Colonel MASON observed, that, the States being differently situated, such a rule ought to be formed as would put them as nearly as possible on a level. If elections were annual, the middle States would have a great advantage over the extreme ones. He wished them to be biennial, and the rather as in that case they would coincide with the periodical elections of South Carolina, as well of the other States.

Colonel HAMILTON urged the necessity of three years. There ought to be neither too much nor too little dependence on the popular sentiments. The checks in the other branches of the Government would be but feeble, and would need every auxiliary principle that could be interwoven. The British House of Commons were elected septennially, yet the democratic spirit of the Constitution had not ceased. Frequency of elections tended to make the people listless to them ; and to facilitate the success of little cabals. This evil was complained of in all the States. In Virginia it had been lately found necessary to force the attendance and voting of the people by severe regulations.

On the question for striking out "three years,"— Massachusetts, Connecticut, Pennsylvania, Virginia, North Carolina, South Carolina, Georgia, aye — 7 ; New York, Delaware, Maryland, no — 3 ; New Jersey divided.

The motion for "two years" was then inserted, *nem. con.*
Adjourned.

FRIDAY, JUNE 22D.

In Convention,— The clause in the third Resolution "to receive fixed stipends, to be paid out of the National Treasury," being considered,—

Mr. ELLSWORTH moved to substitute payment by the States, out of their own treasuries: observing, that the manners of different States were very different in the style of living, and in the profits accruing from the exercise of like talents. What would be deemed, therefore, a reasonable compensation in some States, in others would be very unpopular, and might impede the system of which it made a part.

Mr. WILLIAMSON favored the idea. He reminded the House of the prospect of new States to the westward. They would be too poor — would pay little into the common treasury — and would have a different interest from the old States. He did not think, therefore, that the latter ought to pay the expense of men that would be employed in thwarting their measures and interests.

Mr. GORHAM wished not to refer the matter to the State Legislatures, who were always paring down salaries in such a manner as to keep out of office men most capable of executing the functions of them. He thought, also, it would be wrong to fix the compensation by the Constitution, because we could not venture to make it as liberal as it ought to be, without exciting an enmity against the whole plan. Let the National Legislature provide for their own wages from time to time, as the State Legislatures do. He had not seen this part of their power abused, nor did he apprehend an abuse of it.

Mr. RANDOLPH said he feared we were going too far in consulting popular prejudices. Whatever respect might be due to them in lesser matters, or in cases where they formed the permanent character of the people, he thought it neither incumbent on, nor honorable for, the Convention, to sacrifice right and justice to that consideration. If the States were to pay the members of the National Legislature, a dependence would be created that would vitiate the whole system. The whole nation has an interest in the attendance and services of the members. The National Treasury therefore is the proper fund for supporting them.

Mr. KING urged the danger of creating a dependence on the States by leaving to them the payment of the members of the National Legislature. He supposed it would be best to be explicit as to the compensation to be allowed. A reserve on that point, or a reference to the National Legislature of the quantum, would excite greater opposition than any sum that would be actually necessary or proper.

Mr. SHERMAN contended for referring both the quantum and the payment of it to the State Legislatures.

Mr. WILSON was against *fixing* the compensation, as circumstances would change and call for a change of the amount. He thought it of great moment that the members of the National Government should be left as independent as possible of the State Governments in all respects.

Mr. MADISON concurred in the necessity of preserving the compensations for the National Government independent of the State Governments; but at the same time approved of *fixing* them by the Constitution, which might be done by taking a standard which would not vary with circumstances. He disliked particularly the policy, suggested by Mr. WILLIAMSON, of leaving the members from the poor States beyond the mountains to the precarious and parsimonious support of their constituents. If the Western States hereafter arising should be admitted into the Union, they ought to be considered as equals and as brethren. If their representatives were to be associated in the common councils, it was of common concern that such provisions should be made as would invite the most capable and respectable characters into the service.

Mr. HAMILTON apprehended inconvenience from *fixing* the wages. He was strenuous against making the national council dependent on the legislative rewards of the States. Those who pay are the masters of those who are paid. Payment by the States would be unequal, as the distant States would have to pay for the same term of attendance and more days in traveling to and from the seat of government. He expatiated emphatically on the difference between the feelings and views of the *people* and the *governments* of the States, arising from the personal interest and official inducements which must render the latter unfriendly to the General Government.

Mr. WILSON moved that the salaries of the first branch

" be ascertained by the National Legislature and be paid
out of the National Treasury."

Mr. MADISON thought the members of the Legislature too
much interested, to ascertain their own compensation.   It
would be indecent to put their hands into the public purse
for the sake of their own pockets.

On this question, " shall the salaries of the first branch
be ascertained by the national Legislature?" — New Jersey, Pennsylvania, aye — 2; Massachusetts, Connecticut,
Delaware, Maryland, Virginia, North Carolina, South Carolina, no — 7; New York, Georgia, divided.

On the question for striking out "National Treasury,"
as moved by Mr. ELLSWORTH, —

Mr. HAMILTON renewed his opposition to it.   He
pressed the distinction between the State Governments and
the people.   The former would be the rivals of the General
Government.   The State Legislatures ought not, therefore,
to be the paymasters of the latter.

Mr. ELLSWORTH.   If we are jealous of the State Governments, they will be so of us.   If on going home I tell
them, we gave the General Government such powers because
we could not trust you, will they adopt it?   And without
their approbation it is a nullity.

On the question, — Massachusetts,* Connecticut, North
Carolina, South Carolina, aye — 4; New Jersey, Pennsyl-
vania, Delaware, Maryland, Virginia, no — 5; New York,
Georgia, divided; so it passed in the negative.

On a question for substituting " adequate compensation " in place of "fixed stipends," it was agreed to, *nem.
con.*, the friends of the latter being willing that the practicability of *fixing* the compensation should be considered
hereafter in forming the details.

It was then moved by Mr. BUTLER, that a question be
taken on both points jointly, to wit, " adequate compensa-

---

* It appeared that Massachusetts concurred, not because they thought the State
Treasury ought to be substituted; but because they thought nothing should be said
on the subject, in which case it would silently devolve on the National Treasury to
support the National Legislature.

tion to be paid out of the National Treasury." It was objected to as out of order, the parts having been separately decided on. The President referred the question of order to the House, and it was determined to be in order, — Connecticut, New Jersey, Delaware, Maryland, North Carolina, South Carolina, aye — 6; New York, Pennsylvania, Virginia, Georgia, no — 4: Massachusetts, divided. The question on the sentence was then postponed by South Carolina, in right of the State.

Col. MASON moved to insert " twenty-five years of age as a qualification for the members of the first branch." He thought it absurd that a man to-day should not be permitted by the law to make a bargain for himself, and to-morrow should be authorized to manage the affairs of a great nation. It was the more extraordinary, as every man carried with him, in his own experience, a scale for measuring the deficiency of young politicians ; since he would, if interrogated, be obliged to declare that his political opinions at the age of twenty-one were too crude and erroneous to merit an influence on public measures. It had been said, that Congress had proved a good school for our young men. It might be so, for any thing he knew; but if it were, he chose that they should bear the expense of their own education.

Mr. WILSON was against abridging the rights of election in any shape. It was the same thing whether this were done by disqualifying the objects of choice, or the persons choosing. The motion tended to damp the efforts of genius and of laudable ambition. There was no more reason for incapacitating *youth* than *age*, where the requisite qualifications were found. Many instances might be mentioned of signal services, rendered in high stations, to the public, before the age of twenty-five. The present Mr. Pitt and Lord Bolingbroke were striking instances.

On the question for inserting " twenty-five years of age,"—Connecticut, New Jersey, Delaware, Maryland, Vir-

ginia, North Carolina, South Carolina, aye,— 7; Massachusetts, Pennsylvania, Georgia, no,— 3; New York, divided.

Mr. GORHAM moved to strike out the last member of the
third Resolution, concerning ineligibility of members of the
first branch to office during the term of their membership,
and for one year after. He considered it unnecessary and
injurious. It was true, abuses had been displayed in Great
Britain; but no one could say how far they might have
contributed to preserve the due influence of the Government,
nor what might have ensued in case the contrary theory had
been tried.

Mr. BUTLER opposed it. This precaution against intrigue was necessary. He appealed to the example of
Great Britain, where men get into Parliament that they
might get offices for themselves or their friends. This was
the source of the corruption that ruined their government.

Mr. KING thought we were refining too much. Such a
restriction on the members would discourage merit. It
would also give a pretext to the Executive for bad appointments, as he might always plead this as a bar to the choice
he wished to have made.

Mr. WILSON was against fettering elections, and discouraging merit. He suggested, also, the fatal consequence
in time of war, of rendering, perhaps, the best commanders
ineligible; appealed to our situation during the late war,
and indirectly leading to a recollection of the appointment
of the Commander-in-Chief out of Congress.

Colonel MASON was for shutting the door at all events
against corruption. He enlarged on the venality and
abuses, in this particular, in Great Britain; and alluded to
the multiplicity of foreign embassies by Congress. The
disqualification he regarded as a corner-stone in the fabric.

Colonel HAMILTON. There are inconveniences on both
sides. We must take man as we find him; and if we expect
him to serve the public, must interest his passions in doing
so. A reliance on pure patriotism had been the source of
many of our errors. He thought the remark of Mr. GOR-

HAM a just one. It was impossible to say what would be the effect in Great Britain of such a reform as had been urged. It was known that one of the ablest politicians (Mr. Hume) had pronounced all that influence on the side of the Crown which went under the name of *corruption*, an essential part of the weight which maintained the equilibrium of the Constitution.

On Mr. GORHAM'S motion for striking out "ineligibility," it was lost by an equal division of the votes,— Massachusetts, New Jersey, North Carolina, Georgia, aye — 4; Connecticut, Maryland, Virginia, South Carolina, no,— 4 New York, Pennsylvania, Delaware, divided.

Adjourned.

SATURDAY, JUNE 23D.

In Convention,—the third Resolution being resumed,— On the question, yesterday postponed by South Carolina, for agreeing to the whole sentence, "for allowing an adequate compensation, to be paid out of the *Treasury of the United States,*"—Massachusetts, New Jersey, Pennsylvania, Maryland, Virginia, aye — 5; Connecticut, New York, Delaware, North Carolina, South Carolina, no — 5; Georgia, divided. So the question was lost, and the sentence not inserted.

General PINCKNEY moves to strike out the ineligibility of members of the first branch to offices established "by a particular State." He argued from the inconvenience to which such a restriction would expose both the members of the first branch, and the States wishing for their services; and from the smallness of the object to be attained by the restriction. It would seem from the ideas of some, that we are erecting a kingdom to be divided against itself: he disapproved such a fetter on the Legislature.

Mr. SHERMAN seconds the motion. It would seem that we are erecting a kingdom at war with itself. The Legislature ought not to be fettered in such a case.

On the question,— Connecticut, New York, New Jersey, Maryland, Virginia, North Carolina, South Carolina, Georgia, aye — 8; Massachusetts, Pennsylvania, Delaware, no — 3.

Mr. MADISON renewed his motion, yesterday made and waived, to render the members of the first branch "ineligible during their term of service, and for one year after, to such offices only, as should be established, or the emolument augmented, by the Legislature of the United States during the time of their being members." He supposed that the unnecessary creation of offices, and increase of salaries, were the evils most experienced, and that if the door was shut against them, it might properly be left open for the appointment of members to other offices as an encouragement to the legislative service.

Mr. ALEXANDER MARTIN seconded the motion.

Mr. BUTLER. The amendment does not go far enough, and would be easily evaded.

Mr. RUTLEDGE was for preserving the Legislature as pure as possible, by shutting the door against appointments of its own members to office, which was one source of its corruption.

Mr. MASON. The motion of my colleague is but a partial remedy for the evil. He appealed to him as a witness of the shameful partiality of the Legislature of Virginia to its own members. He enlarged on the abuses and corruption in the British Parliament connected with the appointment of its members. He could not suppose that a sufficient number of citizens could not be found who would be ready, without the inducement of eligibility to offices, to undertake the Legislative service. Genius and virtue, it may be said, ought to be encouraged. Genius, for aught he knew, might; but that virtue should be encouraged by such a species of venality, was an idea that at least had the merit of being new.

Mr. KING remarked that we were refining too much in this business; and that the idea of preventing intrigue and solicitation of offices was chimerical. You say, that no member shall himself be eligible to any office. Will this restrain him from availing himself of the same means which would gain appointments for himself, to gain them for his son, his brother, or any other object of his partiality? We were losing, therefore, the advantages on one side, without avoiding the evils on the other.

Mr. WILSON supported the motion. The proper cure, he said, for corruption in the Legislature was to take from it the power of appointing to offices. One branch of corruption would, indeed, remain, that of creating unnecessary offices, or granting unnecessary salaries, and for that the amendment would be a proper remedy. He animadverted on the impropriety of stigmatizing with the name of venality the laudable ambition of rising into the honourable offices of the Government, — an ambition most likely to be felt in the early and most incorrupt period of life, and which all wise and free governments had deemed it sound policy to cherish, not to check. The members of the Legislature have, perhaps, the hardest and least profitable task of any who engage in the service of the State. Ought this merit to be made a disqualification ?

Mr. SHERMAN observed that the motion did not go far enough. It might be evaded by the creation of a new office, the translation to it of a person from another office, and the appointment of a member of the Legislature to the latter. A new embassy might be established to a new Court, and an ambassador taken from another, in order to *create* a vacancy for a favorite member. He admitted that inconveniences lay on both sides. He hoped there would be sufficient inducements to the public service without resorting to the prospect of desirable offices ; and on the whole was rather against the motion of Mr. MADISON.

Mr. GERRY thought, there was great weight in the objection of Mr. SHERMAN. He added, as another objection against admitting the eligibility of members in any case, that it would produce intrigues of ambitious men for dis-

15

placing proper officers, in order to create vacancies for themselves. In answer to Mr. KING, he observed, that, although members, if disqualified themselves, might still intrigue and cabal for their sons, brothers, &c., yet as their own interests would be dearer to them than those of their nearest connexions, it might be expected they would go greater lengths to promote them.

Mr. MADISON had been led to this motion, as a middle ground between an eligibility in all cases and an absolute disqualification. He admitted the probable abuses of an eligibility of the members to offices particularly within the gift of the Legislature. He had witnessed the partiality of such bodies to their own members, as had been remarked of the Virginia Assembly by his colleague (Colonel MASON). He appealed, however, to him in turn to vouch another fact not less notorious in Virginia, that the backwardness of the best citizens to engage in the Legislative service gave but too great success to unfit characters. The question was not to be viewed on one side only. The advantages and disadvantages on both ought to be fairly compared. The objects to be aimed at were to fill all offices with the fittest characters, and to draw the wisest and most worthy citizens into the legislative service. If, on one hand, public bodies were partial to their own members, on the other, they were as apt to be misled by taking characters on report, or the authority of patrons and dependents. All who had been concerned in the appointment of strangers, on those recommendations must be sensible of this truth. Nor would the partialities of such bodies be obviated by disqualifying their own members. Candidates for office would hover round the seat of government, or be found among the residents there, and practise all the means of courting the favor of the members. A great proportion of the appointments made by the States were evidently brought about in this way. In the General Government, the evil must be still greater, the characters of distant States being much less known throughout the United States, than those of the distant parts of the same State. The elections byCongress had generally turned on men living at the Seat of the Federal Government, or in its neighbourhood. As to the next object, the impulse to the legislative service was evinced by experience to be in general too feeble with those best qualified for it. This inconvenience would also be more felt in the National Government than in the State Governments, as the sacrifices required from the distant members would be much greater, and the pecuniary provisions, probably, more disproportionate. It would therefore be impolitic to add fresh objections to the legislative service by an absolute disqualification of its members. The point in question was, whether this would be an objection with the most capable citizens. Arguing from experience, he concluded that it would. The legislature of. Virginia would probably have been without many of its best members, if in that situation they had been ineligible to Congress, to the Government, and other honourable offices of the State.

Mr. BUTLER thought characters fit for office would never be unknown.

Colonel MASON. If the members of the Legislature are disqualified, still the honours of the State will induce those who aspire to them to enter that service, as the field in which they can best display and improve their talents, and lay the train for their subsequent advancement.

Mr. JENIFER remarked, that in Maryland the Senators, chosen for five years, could hold no other office; and that this circumstance gained them the greatest confidence of the people.

On the question for agreeing to the motion of Mr. MADISON, — Connecticut, New Jersey, aye — 2; New York, Pennsylvania, Delaware, Maryland, Virginia, North Carolina, South Carolina, Georgia, no — 8; Massachusetts, divided.

Mr. SHERMAN moved to insert the words, " and incapable of holding " after the words " ineligible to," which was agreed to without opposition.

The word "established," and the words "under the national government," were struck out of the third Resolution.

Mr. SPAIGHT called for a division of the question, in consequence of which it was so put as that it turned on the first member of it, on the ineligibility of members *during the term for which they were elected* — whereon the States were, Connecticut, New York, New Jersey, Delaware, Maryland, Virginia, North Carolina, South Carolina, aye — 8, Pennsylvania, Georgia, no — 2; Massachusetts, divided.

On the second member of the sentence, extending ineligibility of members to one year after the term for which they were elected, —

Colonel MASON thought this essential to guard against evasions by resignations, and stipulations for office to be fulfilled at the expiration of the legislative term.

Mr. GERRY had known such a case.

Mr. HAMILTON. Evasions could not be prevented, — as by proxies — by friends holding for a year, and then opening the way, &c.

Mr. RUTLEDGE admitted the possibility of evasions, but was for contracting them as far as possible. On the question, — New York, Delaware, Maryland, South Carolina, aye — 4; Massachusetts, Connecticut, New Jersey, Virginia, North Carolina, Georgia, no — 6; Pennsylvania, divided.

Adjourned.

MONDAY, JUNE 25TH.

In Convention, —The fourth Resolution being taken up,

Mr. PINCKNEY spoke as follows:

The efficacy of the system will depend on this article. In order to form a right judgment in the case, it will be proper to examine the situation of this country more accurately than it has yet been done.

The people of the United States are perhaps the most singular of any we are acquainted with. Among them there are fewer distinctions of fortune, and less of rank, than among the inhabitants of any other nation. Every freeman has a right to the same protection and security; and a very moderate share of property entitles them to the possession of all the honors and privileges the public can bestow. Hence, arises a greater equality than is to be found among the people of any other country; and an equality which is more likely to continue. I say, this equality is likely to continue; because in a new country, possessing immense tracts of uncultivated lands, where every temptation is offered to emigration, and where industry must be rewarded with competency, there will be few poor, and few dependent. Every member of the society almost will enjoy an equal power of arriving at the supreme offices, and consequently of directing the strength and sentiments of the whole community. None will be excluded by birth, and few by fortune, from voting for proper persons to fill the offices of government. The whole community will enjoy, in the fullest sense, that kind of political liberty which consists in the power, the members of the State reserve to themselves, of arriving at the public offices, or at least of having votes in the nomination of those who fill them.

If this state of things is true, and the prospect of its continuance probable, it is perhaps not politic to endeavour too close an imitation of a government calculated for a people whose situation is, and whose views ought to be, extremely different.

Much has been said of the Constitution of Great Britain. I will confess that I believe it to be the best constitution in existence; but, at the same time, I am confident it is one that will not or cannot be introduced into this country, for many centuries. If it were proper to go here into a historical dissertation on the British Constitution, it might easily be shown 'that the peculiar excellence, the distinguishing feature, of that government cannot possibly be

introduced into our system — that its balance between the
Crown and the people cannot be made a part of our Constitution,— that we neither have nor can have the members
to compose it, nor the rights, privileges and properties of
so distinct a class of citizens to guard,— that the materials
for forming this balance or check do not exist, nor is there
a necessity for having so permanent a part of our Legislative, until the Executive power is so constituted as to have
something fixed and dangerous in its principle. By this I
mean a sole, hereditary, though limited Executive.

That we cannot have a proper body for forming a
Legislative balance between the inordinate power of the
Executive and the people, is evident from a review of the
accidents and circumstances which gave rise to the peerage
of Great Britain. I believe it is well ascertained, that the
parts which compose the British Constitution arose immediately from the forests of Germany; but the antiquity of
the establishment of nobility is by no means clearly defined.
Some authors are of opinion that the dignity denoted by
the title of *dux* and *comes*, was derived from the old Roman,
to the German, Empire; while others are of opinion that
they existed among the Germans long before the Romans
were acquainted with them. The institution, however, of
nobility is immemorial among the nations who may properly
be termed the ancestors of Great Britain. At the time
they were summoned in England to become a part of the
national council, the circumstances which contributed to
make them a constituent part of that Constitution, must be
well known to all gentlemen who have had industry and
curiosity enough to investigate the subject. The nobles,
with their possessions and dependents, composed a body
permanent in their nature, and formidable in point of
power. They had a distinct interest both from the King
and the people,— an interest which could only be represented by themselves, and the guardianship of which could
not be safely intrusted to others. At the time they were
originally called to form a part of the national council,

necessity perhaps, as much as other causes induced the monarch to look up to them. It was necessary to demand the aid of his subjects in personal and pecuniary services. The power and possessions of the nobility would not permit taxation from any assembly of which they were not a part: and the blending of the deputies of the commons with them, and thus forming what they called their *parler-ment*, was perhaps as much the effect of chance as of any thing else. The commons were at that time completely subordinate to the nobles, whose consequence and influence seem to have been the only reasons for their superiority; a superiority so degrading to the commons, that in the first summons, we find the peers are called upon to *consult*, the commons to *consent*. From this time the peers have composed a part of the British Legislature; and notwithstanding their power and influence have diminished, and those of the commons have increased, yet still they have always formed an excellent balance against either the encroachments of the Crown or the people.

I have said that such a body cannot exist in this country for ages; and that until the situation of our people is exceedingly changed, no necessity will exist for so permanent a part of the Legislature. To illustrate this, I have remarked that the people of the United States are more equal in their circumstances than the people of any other country; that they have very few rich men among them — by rich men I mean those whose riches may have a dangerous influence, or such as are esteemed rich in Europe — perhaps there are not one hundred such on the continent; that it is not probable this number will be greatly increased; that the genius of the people, their mediocrity of situation, and the prospects which are afforded their industry, in a country which must be a new one for centuries, are unfavorable to the rapid distinction of ranks. The destruction of the right of primogeniture, and the equal division of the property of intestates, will also have an effect to preserve this mediocrity; for laws invariably affect the manners of a people. On the other hand, that vast extent of unpeopled territory, which opens to the frugal and industrious a sure road to competency and independence, will effectually prevent, for a considerable time, the increase of the poor or discontented, and be the means of preserving that equality of condition which so eminently distinguishes us.

If equality is, as I contend, the leading feature of the United States, where, then, are the riches and wealth whose representation and protection is the peculiar province of this permanent body? Are they in the hands of the few who may be called rich,— in the possession of less than a hundred citizens? Certainly not. They are in the great body of the people, among whom there are no men of wealth, and very few of real poverty. Is it probable that a change will be created, and that a new order of men will arise? If under the British government for a century no such change was produced, I think it may be fairly concluded it will not take place while even the semblance of republicanism remains. How is the change to be effected? Where are the sources from whence it is to flow? From the landed interest? No. That is too unproductive, and too much divided in most of the States. From the monied interest? If such exists at present, little is to be apprehended from that source. Is it to spring from commerce? I believe it would be the first instance in which a nobility sprang from merchants. Besides, sir, I apprehend that on this point the policy of the United States has been much mistaken. We have unwisely considered ourselves as the inhabitants of an old, instead of a new, country. We have adopted the maxims of a state full of people, and manufactures, and established in credit. We have deserted our true interest, and instead of applying closely to those improvements in domestic policy which would have ensured the future importance of our commerce, we have rashly and prematurely engaged in schemes as extensive as they are imprudent. This, however, is an error which daily corrects itself; and I have no doubt that a few more severe

trials will convince us, that very different commercial principles ought to govern the conduct of these States.

The people of this country are not only very different
from the inhabitants of any state we are acquainted with in
the modern world, but I assert that their situation is distinct from either the people of Greece or Rome, or of any
states we are acquainted with among the ancients. Can the
orders introduced by the institution of Solon, can they be
found in the United States? Can the military habits and
manners of Sparta be resembled to our habits and manners?
Are the distinction of patrician and plebeian known among
us? Can the Helvetic or Belgic confederacies, or can the
unwieldy, unmeaning body called the Germanic Empire, can
they be said to possess either the same, or a situation like
ours? I apprehend, not. They are perfectly different, in
their distinctions of rank, their constitutions, their manners
and their policy.

Our true situation appears to me to be this,— a new
extensive country, containing within itself the materials for
forming a government capable of extending to its citizens
all the blessings of civil and religious liberty — capable of
making them happy at home. This is the great end of
republican establishments. We mistake the object of our
Government, if we hope or wish that it is to make us respectable abroad. Conquest or superiority among other
powers is not, or ought not ever to be, the object of republican systems. If they are sufficiently active and energetic
to rescue us from contempt, and preserve our domestic happiness and security, it is all we can expect from them,— it
is more than almost any other government ensures to its
citizens.

I believe this observation will be found generally true,
— that no two people are so exactly alike in their situation
or circumstances, as to admit the exercise of the same government with equal benefit; that a system must be suited to
the habits and genius of the people it is to govern, and
must grow out of them.

The people of the United States may be divided into
three classes,— *professional men,* who must, from their particular pursuits, always have a considerable weight in the
government, while it remains popular,— *commercial men,*
who may or may not have weight, as a wise or injudicious
commercial policy is pursued.   If that commercial policy is
pursued which I conceive to be the true one, the merchants
of this country will not, or ought not, for a considerable
time, to have much weight in the political scale.   The third
is the *landed interest,* the owners and cultivators of the soil,
who are, and ought ever to be, the governing spring in the
system.   These three classes, however distinct in their pursuits, are individually equal in the political scale, and may
be easily proved to have but one interest.   The dependence
of each on the other is mutual.   The merchant depends on
the planter.   Both must, in private as well as public affairs,
be connected with the professional men; who in their turn
must in some measure depend on them.   Hence it is clear,
from this manifest connexion, and the equality which I
before stated exists, and must, for the reasons then assigned,
continue, that after all there is one, but one great and
equal body of citizens composing the inhabitants of this
country, among whom there are no distinctions of rank, and
very few or none of fortune.

For a people thus circumstanced are we, then, to form
a Government; and the question is, what sort of government is best suited to them?

Will it be the British Government? No. Why? Because
Great Britain contains three orders of people distinct in
their situation, their possessions, and their principles.
These orders, combined, form the great body of the nation;
and as in national expenses the wealth of the whole community must contribute, so ought each component part to
be duly and properly represented. No other combination
of power could form this due representation, but the one
that exists. Neither the peers or the people could represent the royalty; nor could the royalty and the people form

a proper representation for the peers. Each, therefore, must of necessity be represented by itself, or the sign of itself; and this accidental mixture has certainly formed a Government admirably well balanced.

But the United States contain but one order that can be assimilated to the British nation — this is the order of Commons. They will not, surely then, attempt to form a Government consisting of three branches two of which shall have nothing to represent. They will not have an Executive and Senate [hereditary], because the King and Lords of England are so. The same reasons do not exist, and therefore the same provisions are not necessary.

We must, as has been observed, suit our Government to the people it is to direct. These are, I believe, as active, intelligent and susceptible of good government as any people in the world. The confusion which has produced the present relaxed state is not owing to them. It is owing to the weakness and [defects] of a government incapable of combining the various interests it is intended to unite, and destitute of energy. All that we have to do, then, is to distribute the powers of government in such a manner, and for such limited periods, as, while it gives a proper degree of permanency to the magistrate, will reserve to the people the right of election they will not or ought not frequently to part with. I am of opinion that this may easily be done; and that, with some amendments, the propositions before the Committee will fully answer this end.

No position appears to me more true than this; that the General Government cannot effectually exist without reserving to the States the possession of their local rights. They are the instruments upon which the Union must frequently depend for the support and execution of their powers, however immediately operating upon the people, and not upon the States.

Much has been said about the propriety of abolishing the distinction of State Governments, and having but one general system.   Suffer me for a moment to examine this question.*

The mode of constituting the second branch being under consideration, the word "national" was struck out, and " United States " inserted.

Mr. GORHAM inclined to a compromise as to the rule of proportion.   He thought there was some weight in the ob· jections of the small States.   If Virginia should have six- teen votes, and Delaware with several .other States together sixteen, those from Virginia would be more likely to unite than the others, and would therefore have an undue influ- ence.   This remark was applicable not only to States, but to counties or other districts of the same State.   Accord- ingly the Constitution of Massachusetts, had provided that the representatives of the larger districts should not be in an exact ratio to their numbers; and experience, he thought, had shown the provision to be expedient.

Mr. READ.   The States have heretofore been. in a sort of partnership.   They ought to adjust their old affairs be- fore they opened a new account.   He brought into view the appropriation of the common interest in the western lands to the use of particular States.   Let justice be done on this head; let the fund be applied fairly and equally to the dis- charge of the general debt; and the smaller States, who had been injured, would listen then, perhaps, to those ideas of just representation which had been held out.

Mr. GORHAM could not see how the Convention could interpose in the case.   Errors, he allowed, had been com- mitted on the subject.   But Congress were now using their endeavours to rectify them.   The best remedy would be such a government as would have vigor enough to do jus- tice throughout.   This was certainly the best chance that could be afforded to the smaller States.

Mr. WILSON.   The question is, shall the members of the second branch be chosen by the Legislatures of the States? When he considered the amazing extent of country —

* The residue of this speech was not furnished, like the aoove, by Mr. Pinckney.

the immense population which is to fill it — the influence of the Government we are to form will have, not
only on the present generation of our people and their multiplied posterity, but on the whole globe,— he was lost
in the magnitude of the object.   The project of Henry IV.
and his statesmen, was but the picture in miniature of the
great portrait to be exhibited.   He was opposed to an election by the State Legislatures.   In explaining his reasons
it was necessary to observe the twofold relation in which
the people would stand,— first, as citizens of the General
Government; and secondly as citizens of their particular
State.   The General Government was meant for them in the
first capacity; the State Governments in the second.   Both
governments were derived from the people — both meant
for the people — both, therefore, ought to be regulated on
the same principles.   The same train of ideas which belonged to the relation of the citizens to their State Governments, were applicable to their relation to the General Government; and in forming the latter we ought to proceed by
abstracting as much as possible from the idea of the State
Governments.   With respect to the province and object of
the General Government they should be considered as having no existence.   The election of the second branch by the
Legislatures will introduce and cherish local interests and
local prejudices.   The General Government is not an assem-
blage of States, but of individuals, for certain political purposes; it is not meant for the States, but for the individuals
composing them; the *individuals*, therefore, not the *States*,
ought to be represented in it.   A proportion in this representation can be preserved in the second, as well as in the
first, branch; and the election can be made by electors
chosen by the people for that purpose.   He moved an
amendment to that effect; which was not seconded.

Mr. ELLSWORTH saw no reason for departing from the
mode contained in the Report.   Whoever chooses the member, he will be a citizen of the State he is to represent; and
will feel the same spirit, and act the same part, whether he

be appointed by the people or the Legislature. Every State has its particular views and prejudices, which will find their way into the general council, through whatever channel they may flow. Wisdom was one of the characteristics which it was in contemplation to give the second branch, — would not more of it issue from the Legislatures than from an immediate election by the people? He urged the necessity of maintaining the existence and agency of the States. Without their co-operation it would be impossible to support a republican government over so great an extent of country. An army could scarcely render it practicable. The largest States are the worst governed. Virginia is obliged to acknowledge her incapacity to extend her government to Kentucky. Massachusetts cannot keep the peace one hundred miles from her capital, and is now forming an army for its support. How long Pennsylvania may be free from a like situation, cannot be foreseen. If the principles and materials of our Government are not adequate to the extent of these single States, how can it be imagined that they can support a single government throughout the United States? The only chance of supporting a General Government lies in grafting it on those of the individual States.

Doctor JOHNSON urged the necessity of preserving the State Governments, which would be at the mercy of the General Government on Mr. WILSON's plan.

Mr. MADISON thought it would obviate difficulty if the present Resolution were postponed, and the eighth taken up, which is to fix the right of suffrage in the second branch.

Mr. WILLIAMSON professed himself a friend to such a system as would secure the existence of the State Governments. The happiness of the people depended on it. He was at a loss to give his vote as to the Senate until he knew the number of its members. In order to ascertain this, he moved to insert, after "second branch of the National Legislature," the words, "who shall bear such pro-

portion to the number of the first branch as one to ——— .'
He was not seconded.

Mr. MASON. It has been agreed on all hands that an
efficient government is necessary; that, to render it such, it
ought to have the faculty of self-defence; that to render its
different branches effectual, each of them ought to have the
same power of self-defence. He did not wonder that such
an agreement should have prevailed on these points. He
only wondered that there should be any disagreement about
the necessity of allowing the State Governments the same
self-defence. If they are to be preserved, as he conceived
to be essential, they certainly ought to have this power; and
the only mode left of giving it to them was by allowing
them to appoint the second branch of the National Legislature.

Mr. BUTLER, observing that we were put to difficulties
at every step by the uncertainty whether an equality or a
ratio of representation would prevail finally in the second
branch, moved to postpone the fourth Resolution, and to
proceed to the eighth Resolution on that point. Mr. MAD-
ISON seconded him.

On the question,— New York, Virginia, South Carolina,
Georgia, aye — 4; Massachusetts, Connecticut, New Jersey, Pennsylvania, Delaware, Maryland, North Carolina,
no — 7.

On a question to postpone the fourth, and take up the
seventh, Resolution, — Maryland, Virginia, North Carolina,
South Carolina, Georgia, aye — 5; Massachusetts, Connecticut, New York, New Jersey, Pennsylvania, Delaware, no
— 6.

On the question to agree, "that the members of the
second branch be chosen by the individual Legislatures,"
— Massachusetts, Connecticut, New York, New Jersey,
Delaware, Maryland, North Carolina, South Carolina,
Georgia, aye — 9; Pennsylvania, Virginia, no — 2.*

---

* It must be kept in view that the largest States, particularly Pennsylvania and
Virginia, always considered the choice of the second branch by the State Legislat-

On a question on the clause requiring the age of thirty years at least, — it was unanimously agreed to.

On a question to strike out the words, "sufficient to ensure their independence," after the word " term," — it was agreed to.

The clause, that the second branch hold their offices for a term of "seven years," being considered, —

Mr. GORHAM suggests a term of "four years," one fourth to be elected every year.

Mr. RANDOLPH supported the idea of rotation, as favorable to the wisdom and stability of the corps; which might possibly be always sitting, and aiding the Executive, and moves, after "seven years," to add, " to go out in fixed proportion," which was agreed to.

Mr. WILLIAMSON suggests " six years," as more convenient for rotation than seven years.

Mr. SHERMAN seconds him.

Mr. READ proposed that they should hold their offices "during good behaviour." Mr. R. MORRIS seconds him.

General PINCKNEY proposed " four years." A longer time would fix them at the seat of government. They would acquire an interest there, perhaps transfer their property, and lose sight of the States they represent. Under these circumstances, the distant States would labor under great disadvantages.

Mr. SHERMAN moved to strike out " seven years," in order to take questions on the several propositions.

On the question to strike out " seven," — Massachusetts, Connecticut, New York, New Jersey, North Carolina, South Carolina, Georgia, aye — 7; Pennsylvania, Delaware, Virginia, no — 3; Maryland divided.

On the question to insert " six years," which failed, five States being, aye ; five, no ; and one, divided,—Connecticut, Pennsylvania, Delaware, Virginia, North Carolina, aye —

---

ures as opposed to a proportional representation, to which they were attached as a fundamental principle of just government. The smaller States, who had opposite views, were reinforced by the members from the large States most anxious to secure the importance of the State Governments.

5 ; Massachusetts, New York, New Jersey, South Carolina, Georgia, no — 5 ; Maryland divided.

On a motion to adjourn, the votes were, five for, five against it ; and one divided,— Connecticut, New Jersey, Pennsylvania, Delaware, Virginia, aye — 5 ; Massachusetts, New York, North Carolina, South Carolina, Georgia, no — 5 ; Maryland divided.

On the question for "five years," it was lost, — Connecticut, Pennsylvania, Delaware, Virginia, North Carolina, aye — 5 ; Massachusetts, New York, New Jersey, South Carolina, Georgia, no — 5 ; Maryland divided.

Adjourned.

TUESDAY, JUNE 26TH.

In Convention, — The duration of the second branch being under consideration,—

Mr. GORHAM moved to fill the blank with "six years," one-third of the members to go out every second year.

Mr. WILSON seconded the motion.

General PINCKNEY opposed six years, in favor of four years. The States, he said, had different interests. Those of the Southern, and of South Carolina in particular, were different from the Northern. If the Senators should be appointed for a long term, they would settle in the State where they exercised their functions, and would in a little time be rather the representatives of that, than of the State appointing them.

Mr. READ moved that the term be nine years. This would admit of a very convenient rotation, one-third going out triennially. He would still prefer "during good behaviour ;" but being little supported in that idea, he was willing to take the longest term that could be obtained.

Mr. BROOM seconded the motion.

Mr. MADISON. In order to judge of the form to be given to this institution, it will be proper to take a view of the ends to be served by it. These were, — first, to protect

16

the people against their rulers, secondly, to protect the
people against the transient impressions into which they
themselves might be led. A people deliberating in a
temperate moment, and with the experience of other nations
before them, on the plan of government most likely to
secure their happiness, would first be aware, that those
charged with the public happiness might betray their trust.
An obvious precaution against this danger would be, to
divide the trust between different bodies of men, who might
watch and check each other. In this they would be governed by the same prudence which has prevailed in organizing the subordinate departments of government, where all
business liable to abuses is made to pass through separate
hands, the one being a check on the other. It would next
occur to such a people, that they themselves were liable to
temporary errors, through want of information as to their
true interest ; and that men chosen for a short term, and
employed but a small portion of that in public affairs, might
err from the same cause. This reflection would naturally
suggest, that the government be so constituted as that one
of its branches might have an opportunity of acquiring a
competent knowledge of the public interests. Another
reflection equally becoming a people on such an occasion,
would be, that they themselves, as well as a numerous body
of representatives, were liable to err, also, from fickleness
and passion. A necessary fence against this danger would
be, to select a portion of enlightened citizens, whose limited
number, and firmness, might seasonably interpose against
impetuous counsels. It ought, finally, to occur to a people
deliberating on a government for themselves, that as different interests necessarily result from the liberty meant to
be secured, the major interest might, under sudden impulses, be tempted to commit injustice on the minority. In
all civilized countries the people fall into different classes,
having a real or supposed difference of interests. There
will be creditors and debtors ; farmers, merchants, and
manufacturers. There will be, particularly, the distinction

of rich and poor. It was true, as had been observed (by
Mr. PINCKNEY), we had not among us those hereditary distinctions of rank which were a great source of the contests
in the ancient governments, as well as the modern States of
Europe ; nor those extremes of wealth or poverty, which
characterize the latter. We cannot, however, be regarded,
even at this time, as one homogeneous mass, in which every
thing that affects a part will affect in the same manner the
whole. In framing a system which we wish to last for
ages, we should not lose sight of the changes which ages
will produce. An increase of population will of necessity
increase the proportion of those who will labor under all the
hardships of life, and secretly sigh for a more equal distribution of its blessings. These may in time outnumber
those who are placed above the feelings of indigence. According to the equal laws of suffrage, the power will slide
into the hands of the former. No agrarian attempts have
yet been made in this country ; but symptoms of a levelling
spirit, as we have understood, have sufficiently appeared in
a certain quarter, to give notice of the future danger. How
is this danger to be guarded against, on the republican
principles? How is the danger, in all cases of interested
coalitions to oppress the minority, to be guarded against ?
Among other means, by the establishment of a body, in the
government, sufficiently respectable for its wisdom and
virtue to aid, on such emergencies, the preponderance of
justice, by throwing its weight into that scale. Such being
the objects of the second branch in the proposed Government, he thought a considerable duration ought to be given
to it. He did not conceive that the term of nine years
could threaten any real danger ; but, in pursuing his particular ideas on the subject, he should require that the long
term allowed to the second branch should not commence
till such a period of life as would render a perpetual disqualification to be re-elected, little inconvenient, either in a
public or private view. He observed, that as it was more
than probable we were now digesting a plan which in its

operation would decide for ever the fate of republican government, we ought, not only to provide every guard to liberty that its preservation could require, but be equally careful to supply the defects which our own experience had particularly pointed out.

Mr. SHERMAN. Government is instituted for those who live under it. It ought, therefore to be so constituted as not to be dangerous to their liberties. The more permanency it has, the worse, if it be a bad government. Frequent elections are necessary to preserve the good behaviour of rulers. They also tend to give permanency to the government, by preserving that good behaviour, because it ensures their re-election. In Connecticut elections have been very frequent, yet great stability and uniformity, both as to persons and measures, have been experienced from its original establishment to the present time; a period of more than a hundred and thirty years. He wished to have provision made for steadiness and wisdom, in the system to be adopted; but he thought six, or four, years would be sufficient. He should be content with either.

Mr READ wished it to be considered by the small States that it was their interest that we should become one people as much as possible; that State attachments should be extinguished as much as possible; that the Senate should be so constituted as to have the feelings of citizens of the whole.

Mr. HAMILTON. He did not mean to enter particularly into the subject. He concurred with Mr. MADISON in thinking we were now to decide forever the fate of republican government; and that if we did not give to that form due stability and wisdom, it would be disgraced and lost among ourselves, disgraced and lost to mankind forever. He acknowledged himself not to think favorably of republican government; but addressed his remarks to those who did think favorably of it, in order to prevail on them to tone their government as high as possible. He professed himself to be as zealous an advocate for liberty as any man whatever; and trusted he should be as willing a martyr to it, though he differed as to the form in which it was most eligible. He concurred also, in the general observations of Mr. MADISON on the subject, which might be supported by others if it were necessary. It was certainly true, that nothing like an equality of property existed; that an inequality would exist as long as liberty existed, and that it would unavoidably result from that very liberty itself. This inequality of property constituted the great and fundamental distinction in society. When the Tribunitial power had levelled the boundary between the *patricians* and *plebeians*, what followed? The distinction between rich and poor was substituted. He meant not, however, to enlarge on the subject. He rose principally to remark, that Mr. SHERMAN seemed not to recollect that one branch of the proposed Government was so formed as to render it particularly the guardians of the poorer orders of citizens; nor to have adverted to the true causes of the stability which had been exemplified in Connecticut. Under the British system, as well as the Federal, many of the great powers appertaining to government, particularly all those relating to foreign nations, were not in the hands of the government there. Their internal affairs, also, were extremely simple, owing to sundry causes, many of which were peculiar to that country. Of late the Government had entirely given way to the people, and had in fact suspended many of its ordinary functions, in order to prevent those turbulent scenes which had appeared elsewhere. He asks Mr. SHERMAN, whether the State, at this time, dare impose and collect a tax on the people? To these causes, and not to the frequency of elections, the effect, as far as it existed, ought to be chiefly ascribed.

Mr. GERRY wished we could be united in our ideas concerning a permanent Government. All aim at the same end, but there are great differences as to the means. One circumstance, he thought, should be carefully attended to. There was not a one-thousandth part of our fellow-citizens who were not against every approach towards monarchy, — will they ever agree to a plan which seems to make such an approach? The Convention ought to be extremely cautious ·in what they hold out to the people. Whatever plan may be proposed will be espoused with warmth by many, out of respect to the quarter it proceeds from, as well as from an approbation of the plan itself. And if the plan should be of such a nature as to rouse a violent opposition, it is easy to foresee that discord and confusion will ensue; and it is even possible that we may become a prey to foreign powers. He did not deny the position of Mr. MADISON, that the majority will generally violate justice when they have an interest in so doing; but did not think there was any such temptation in this country. Our situation was different from that of Great Britain; and the great body of lands yet to be parcelled out and settled would very much prolong the difference. Notwithstanding the symptoms of injustice which had marked many of our public councils, they had not proceeded so far as not to leave hopes that there would be a sufficient sense of justice and virtue for the purpose of government. He admitted the evils arising from a frequency of elections, and would agree to give the Senate a duration of four or five years. A longer term would defeat itself. It never would be adopted by the people.

Mr. WILSON did not mean to repeat what had fallen from others, but would add an observation or two which he believed had not yet been suggested. Every nation may be regarded in two relations, first, to its own citizens; secondly, to foreign nations. It is, therefore, not only liable to anarchy and tyranny within, but has wars to avoid and treaties to obtain from abroad. The Senate will probably be the depository of the powers concerning the latter objects. It ought therefore to be made respectable in the eyes of foreign nations. The true reason why Great Britain has not yet listened to a commercial treaty with us has been, because she had no confidence in the stability or efficacy of our Government. Nine years, with a rotation, will provide these desirable qualities; and give our Government an advantage in this respect over monarchy itself. In a monarchy, much must always depend on the temper of the man. In such a body, the personal character will be lost in the political. He would add another observation. The popular objection against appointing any public body for a long term, was, that it might, by gradual encroachments, prolong itself, first into a body for life, and finally become a hereditary one. It would be a satisfactory answer to this objection, that as one-third would go out triennially, there would be always three divisions holding their places for unequal times, and consequently acting under the influence of different views, and different impulses.

On the question for nine years, one-third to go out triennially,— Pennsylvania, Delaware, Virginia, aye — 3; Massachusetts, Connecticut, New York, New Jersey, Maryland, North Carolina, South Carolina, Georgia, no — 8.

On the question for six years, one-third to go out biennially, — Massachusetts, Connecticut, Pennsylvania, Delaware, Maryland, Virginia, North Carolina, aye — 7; New York, New Jersey, South Carolina, Georgia, no — 4.

The clause of the fourth Resolution, "to receive fixed stipends by which they may be compensated for their services" being considered,—

General PINCKNEY proposed, that no salary should be allowed As this (the Senatorial) branch was meant to represent the wealth of the country, it ought to be composed of persons of wealth; and if no allowance was to be made, the wealthy alone would undertake the service. He moved to strike out the clause.

Doctor FRANKLIN seconded the motion. He wished the Convention to stand fair with the people. There were in it a number of young men who would probably be of the Senate. If lucrative appointments should be recommended, we might be chargeable with having carved out places for ourselves.

On the question,— Massachusetts, Connecticut,* Pennsylvania, Maryland, South Carolina, aye — 5; New York, New Jersey, Delaware, Virginia, North Carolina, Georgia, no — 6.

Mr. WILLIAMSON moved to change the expression into these words, to wit, "to receive a compensation for the devotion of their time to the public service." The motion was seconded by Mr. ELLSWORTH, and agreed to by all the States except South Carolina. It seemed to be meant only to get rid of the word "fixed," and leave greater room for modifying the provision on this point.

Mr. ELLSWORTH moved to strike out, "to be paid out of the National Treasury," and insert, "to be paid by their respective States." If the Senate was meant to strengthen the Government, it ought to have the confidence of the States. The States will have an interest in keeping up a representation, and will make such provision for supporting the members as will ensure their attendance.

Mr. MADISON considered this as a departure from a fundamental principle, and subverting the end intended by allowing the Senate a duration of six years. They would, if this motion should be agreed to, hold their places during pleasure; during the pleasure of the State Legislatures. One great end of the institution was, that being a firm, wise and impartial body, it might not only give stability to the General Government, in its operations on individuals, but hold an even balance among different States. The motion would make the Senate, like Congress, the mere agents and advocates of State interests and views, instead of being the impartial umpires and guardians of justice and the general good. Congress had lately, by the establishment of a board with full powers to decide on the mutual claims between the United States and the individual States, fairly acknowledged themselves to be unfit for discharging this part of the business referred to them by the Confederation.

---

* Quere. Whether Connecticut should not be, no, and Delaware, aye ? J. M.

Mr. DAYTON considered the payment of the Senate by the States as fatal to their independence. He was decided for paying them out of the National Treasury.

On the question of payment of the Senate to be left to the States, as moved by Mr. ELLSWORTH, it passed in the negative,— Connecticut, New York, New Jersey, South Carolina, Georgia, aye — 5; Massachusetts, Pennsylvania, Delaware, Maryland, Virginia, North Carolina, no — 6.

Col. MASON. He did not rise to make any motion, but to hint an idea which seemed to be proper for consideration. One important object in constituting the Senate was, to secure the rights of property. To give them weight and firmness for this purpose, a considerable duration in office was thought necessary. But a longer term than six years would be of no avail in this respect, if needy persons should be appointed. He suggested, therefore, the propriety of annexing to the office a qualification of property. He thought this would be very practicable; as the rules of taxation would supply a scale for measuring the degree of wealth possessed by every man.

A question was then taken, whether the words " to be paid out of the National Treasury," should stand,— Massachusetts, Pennsylvania, Delaware, Maryland, Virginia, aye — 5; Connecticut, New York, New Jersey, North Carolina, South Carolina, Georgia, no — 6.

Mr. BUTLER moved to strike out the ineligibility of Senators to *State offices*.

Mr. WILLIAMSON seconded the motion.

Mr. WILSON remarked the additional dependence this would create in the Senators on the States. The longer the time, he observed, allotted to the officer the more complete will be the dependence, if it exists at all.

General PINCKNEY was for making the States, as much as could be conveniently done, a part of the General Government. If the Senate was to be appointed by the States, it ought, in pursuance of the same idea, to be paid by the States; and the States ought not to be barred from the opportunity of calling members of it into offices at home. Such a restriction would also discourage the ablest men from going into the Senate.

Mr. WILLIAMSON moved a Resolution, so penned as to admit of the two following questions,— first, whether the members of the Senate should be ineligible to, and incapable of holding, offices *under the United States;* secondly, whether, &c., under the *particular States.*

On the question to postpone, in order to consider Mr. WILLIAMSON's ˙ Resolution, — Connecticut, Pennsylvania, Delaware, Maryland, Virginia, North Carolina, South Carolina, Georgia, aye — 8; Massachusetts, New York, New Jersey, no — 3.

Mr. GERRY and Mr. MADISON move to add to Mr. WILLIAMSON's first question, "and for one year thereafter."

On this amendment,— Connecticut, New York, Delaware, Maryland, Virginia, North Carolina, South Carolina, aye — 7; Massachusetts, New Jersey, Pennsylvania, Georgia, no — 4.

On Mr. WILLIAMSON's first question as amended, viz., "ineligible and incapable &c. for one year &c."— agreed to unanimously.

On the second question as to ineligibility, &c. to *State offices,*— Massachusetts, Pennsylvania, Virginia, aye — 3; Connecticut, New York, New Jersey, Delaware, Maryland, North Carolina, South Carolina, Georgia, no — 8.

The fifth Resolution, "that each branch have the right of originating acts," was agreed to, *nem. con.*

Adjourned.

WEDNESDAY, JUNE 27TH.

In Convention,—Mr. RUTLEDGE moved to postpone the sixth Resolution, defining the powers of Congress, in order to take up the seventh and eighth, which involved the most fundamental points, the rules of suffrage in the two branches; which was agreed to, *nem. con.*

A question being proposed on the seventh Resolution, declaring that the suffrage in the first branch should be according to an equitable ratio,—

Mr. L. MARTIN contended, at great length, and with great eagerness, that the General Government was meant merely to preserve the State Governments, not to govern individuals. That its powers ought to be kept within narrow limits. That if too little power was given to it, more might be added; but that if too much, it could never be resumed. That individuals, as such, have little to do, but with their own States; that the General Government has no more to apprehend from the States composing the Union, while it pursues proper measures, than a government over individuals has to apprehend from its subjects. That to resort to the citizens at large for their sanction to a new government, will be throwing them back into a state of nature; that the dissolution of the State Governments is involved in the nature of the process; that the people have no right to do this, without the consent of those to whom they have delegated their power for State purposes. Through their tongues only they can speak, through their ears only can hear. That the States have shewn a good disposition to comply with the acts of Congress, weak, contemptibly weak, as that body has been; and have failed through inability alone to comply. That the heaviness of the private debts, and the waste of property during the war, were the chief causes of this inability,— that he did not conceive the instances mentioned by Mr. MADISON, of compacts between Virginia and Maryland, between Pennsylvania and New Jersey, or of troops raised by Massachusetts for defence against the rebels, to be violations of the Articles of Confederation. That an equal vote in each State was essential to the Federal idea, and was founded in justice and freedom, not merely in policy. That though the States may give up this right of sovereignty, yet they had not, and ought not. That the States, like individuals, were in a state of nature equally sovereign and free. In order to

prove that individuals in a state of nature are equally free
and independent, he read passages from Locke, Vattel,
Lord Somers, Priestley.   To prove that the case is the same
with states, till they surrender their equal sovereignty, he
read other passages in Locke and Vattel, and also Ruther-
ford.   That the States, being equal, cannot treat or confederate so as to give up an equality of votes, without
giving up their liberty.   That the propositions on the table
were a system of slavery for ten States.   That as Virginia,
Massachusetts and Pennsylvania have forty-two ninetieths
of the votes, they can do as they please, without a miraculous
union of the other ten.   That they will have nothing to do
but to gain over one of the ten, to make them complete
masters of the rest; that they can then appoint an Executive, and Judiciary, and Legislature for them, as they please.
That there was, and would continue, a national predilection
and partiality in men for their own States; that the states,
particularly the smaller, would never allow a negative to be
exercised over their laws: that no State, in ratifying the
Confederation, had objected to the equality of votes; that
the complaints at present ran not against this equality, but
the want of power.   That sixteen members from Virginia
would be more likely to act in concert, than a like number
formed of members from different States.   That instead of
a junction of the small States as a remedy, he thought a
division of the large States would be more eligible.   This
was the substance of a speech which was continued more
than three hours.   He was too much exhausted, he said, to
finish his remarks, and reminded the House that he should
to-morrow resume them.

Adjourned.

THURSDAY, JUNE 28TH.

In Convention, — Mr. L. MARTIN resumed his discourse,
contending that the General Government ought to be formed
for the States, not for individuals; that if the States

were to have votes in proportion to their numbers of people, it would be the same thing, whether their Representatives were chosen by the Legislatures or the people; the smaller States would be equally enslaved. That if the large States have the same interest with the smaller, as was urged, there could be no danger in giving them an equal vote; they would not injure themselves, and they could not injure the large ones, on that supposition, without injuring themselves; and if the interests were not the same, the inequality of suffrage would be dangerous to the smaller States. That it will be in vain to propose any plan offensive to the rulers of the States, whose influence over the people will certainly prevent their adopting it. That the large States were weak at present in proportion to their extent; and could only be made formidable to the small ones by the weight of their votes. That in case a dissolution of the Union should take place, the small States would have nothing to fear from their power; that if, in such a case, the three great States should league themselves together, the other ten could do so too; and that he had rather see partial confederacies take place, than the plan on the table. This was the substance of the residue of his discourse, which was delivered with much diffuseness, and considerable vehemence.

Mr. LANSING and Mr. DAYTON moved to strike out "not," so that the seventh article might read, "that the right of suffrage in the first branch ought to be according to the rule established by the Confederation."

Mr. DAYTON expressed great anxiety that the question might not be put till to-morrow, Governor LIVINGSTON being kept away by indisposition, and the representation of New Jersey thereby suspended.

Mr. WILLIAMSON thought, that, if any political truth could be grounded on mathematical demonstration, it was, that if the States were equally sovereign now, and parted with equal proportions of sovereignty, that they would remain equally sovereign. He could not comprehend how the smaller States would be injured in the case, and wished some gentleman would vouchsafe a solution of it. He observed that the small States, if they had a plurality of votes, would have an interest in throwing the burdens off their own shoulders on those of the large ones. He begged that the expected addition of new States from the westward might be taken into view. They would be small States; they would be poor States; they would be unable to pay in proportion to their numbers, their distance from market rendering the produce of their labor less valuable; they would consequently be tempted to combine for the purpose of laying burdens on commerce and consumption which would fall with greater weight on the old States..

Mr. MADISON said, he was much disposed to concur in any expedient, not inconsistent with fundamental principles, that could remove the difficulty concerning the rule of representation. But he could neither be convinced that the rule contended for was just, nor that it was necessary for the safety of the small States against the large States. That it was not just, had been conceded by Mr. BREARLY and Mr. PATTERSON themselves. The expedient proposed by them was a new partition of the territory of the United States. The fallacy of the reasoning drawn from the equality of sovereign states, in the formation of compacts, lay in confounding mere treaties, in which were specified certain duties to which the parties were to be bound, and certain rules by which their subjects were to be reciprocally governed in their intercourse, with a compact by which an authority was created paramount to the parties, and making laws for the government of them. If France, England and Spain were to enter into a treaty for the regulation of commerce, &c., with the Prince of Monacho, and four or five other of the smallest sovereigns of Europe, they would not hesitate to treat as equals, and to make the regulations perfectly reciprocal. Would the case be the same, if a Council were to be formed of deputies from each, with authority and discretion to raise money, levy troops, determine the value of coin, etc. ? Would thirty or forty millions of people submit their fortunes into the hands of a few thousands? If they did, it would only prove that they expected more from the terror of their superior force, than they feared from the selfishness of their feeble associates. Why are counties of the same States represented in proportion to their numbers? Is it because the representatives are chosen by the people themselves? So will be the Representatives in the National Legislature. Is it because the larger have more at stake than the smaller? The case will be the same with the larger and smaller States. Is it because the laws are to operate immediately on their persons and properties? The same is the case, in some degree, as the Articles of Confederation stand; the same will be the case, in a far greater degree, under the plan proposed to be substituted. In the cases of captures, of piracies, and of offences in a Federal army, the property and persons of individuals depend on the laws of Congress. By the plan proposed a complete power of taxation, the highest prerogative of supremacy, is proposed to be vested in the National Government. Many other powers are added which assimilate it to the government of individual States. The negative proposed on the State laws will make it an essential branch of the State Legislatures, and of course will require that it should be exercised by a body, established on like principles with the branches of those Legislatures. That it is not necessary to secure the small States against the large ones, he conceived to be equally obvious. Was a combination of the large ones dreaded? This must arise either from some interest common to Virginia, Massachusetts and Pennsylvania, and distinguishing them from the other States; or from the mere circumstance of similarity of size. Did any such common interest exist? In point of situation, they could not have been more effectually separated from each other, by the most jealous citizen of the most jealous States. In point of manners, religion, and the other circumstances which sometimes beget affection

between different communities, they were not more assimilated than the other States. In point of the staple productions, they were as dissimilar as any three other States in
the Union. The staple of Massachusetts was *fish*, of
Pennsylvania *flour*, of Virginia *tobacco*. Was a combination to be apprehended from the mere circumstance of
equality of size? Experience suggested no such danger.
The Journals of Congress did not present any peculiar
association of these States in the votes recorded. It had
never been seen that different counties in the same State,
conformable in extent, but disagreeing in other circumstances, betrayed a propensity to such combinations.
Experience rather taught a contrary lesson. Among individuals of superior eminence and weight in society, rivalships were much more frequent than coalitions. Among
independent nations, pre-eminent over their neighbours, the
same remark was verified. Carthage and Rome tore one
another to pieces, instead of uniting their forces to devour the
weaker nations of the earth. The Houses of Austria and
France were hostile as long as they remained the greatest
powers of Europe. England and France have succeeded to
the pre-eminence and to the enmity. To this principle we
owe perhaps our liberty: A coalition between those powers
would have been fatal to us. Among the principal members of the ancient and modern confederacies, we find
the same effect from the same cause. The contentions, not
the coalitions, of Sparta, Athens, and Thebes, proved fatal
to the smaller members of the Amphictyonic confederacy.
The contentions, not the combinations, of Russia and Austria, have distracted and oppressed the German Empire.
Were the large States formidable, *singly*, to their smaller
neighbours? On this supposition, the latter ought to wish
for such a General Government as will operate with equal
energy on the former as on themselves. The more lax the
band, the more liberty the larger will have to avail themselves of their superior force. Here again, experience was
an instructive monitor. What is the situation of the weak

compared with the strong, in those stages of civilization in
which the violence of individuals is least controlled by an
efficient government? The heroic period of ancient Greece,
the feudal licentiousness of the middle ages of Europe, the
existing condition of the American savages, answer this
question. What is the situation of the minor sovereigns
in the great society of independent nations, in which the more
powerful are under no control, but the nominal authority of
the law of nations? Is not the danger to the former exactly in proportion to their weakness? But there are cases
still more in point. What was the condition of the weaker
members of the Amphictyonic confederacy? Plutarch (see
Life of Themistocles) will inform us, that it happened but
too often, that the strongest cities corrupted and awed the
weaker, and that judgment went in favor of the more powerful party. What is the condition of the lesser States in
the German confederacy? We all know that they are exceedingly trampled upon, and that they owe their safety, as
far as they enjoy it, partly to their enlisting themselves
under the rival banners of the pre-eminent members, partly
to alliances with neighbouring princes, which the constitution of the Empire does not prohibit. What is the state of
things in the lax system of the Dutch confederacy? Holland contains about half the people, supplies about half the
money, and by her influence silently and indirectly governs
the whole republic. In a word, the two extremes before
us are, a perfect separation, and a perfect incorporation of
the thirteen States. In the first case, they would be independent nations, subject to no law but the law of nations.
In the last they would be mere counties of one entire republic, subject to one common law. In the first case, the
smaller States would have every thing to fear from the
larger. In the last they would have nothing to fear. The
true policy of the small States, therefore, lies in promoting
those principles, and that form of government, which will
most approximate the States to the condition of counties.
Another consideration may be added. If the General Gov-

ernment be feeble, the larger States, distrusting its continuance, and foreseeing that their importance and security
may depend on their own size and strength, will never submit to a partition.   Give to the General Government sufficient energy and permanency, and you remove the objection.
Gradual partitions of the large, and junctions of the small
States, will be facilitated, and time may effect that equalization which is wished for by the small States now, but can
never be accomplished at once.

Mr. WILSON.   The leading argument of those who contend for equality of votes among the States is, that the
States, as such, being equal, and being represented, not as
districts of individuals, but in their political and corporate
capacities, are entitled to an equality of suffrage.   According to this mode of reasoning, the representation of the boroughs in England, which has been allowed on all hands to
be the rotten part of the Constitution, is perfectly right and
proper.   They are, like the States, represented in their
corporate capacity; like the States, therefore, they are entitled to equal voices — Old Sarum to as many as London.
And instead of the injury supposed hitherto to be done to
London, the true ground of complaint lies with Old Sarum;
for London instead of two, which is her proper share, sends
four representatives to Parliament.

Mr. SHERMAN.   The question is, not what rights naturally belong to man, but how they may be most equally and
effectually guarded in society.   And if some give up more
than others, in order to obtain this end, there can be no
room for complaint.   To do otherwise, to require an equal
concession from all, if it would create danger to the rights
of some, would be sacrificing the end to the means.   The
rich man who enters into society along with the poor man
gives up more than the poor man, yet with an equal vote he
is equally safe.   Were he to have more votes than the poor
man, in proportion to his superior stake, the rights of the
poor man would immediately cease to be secure.   This con-

sideration prevailed when the Articles of Confederation were formed.

The determination of the question, for striking out the word " not," was put off till to-morrow, at the request of the Deputies from New York.

Doctor FRANKLIN. Mr. President, The small progress we have made after four or five weeks close attendance and continual reasonings with each other — our different sentiments on almost every question, several of the last producing as many noes as ayes — is, methinks, a melancholy proof of the imperfection of the human understanding. We indeed seem to feel our own want of political wisdom, since we have been running about in search of it. We have gone back to ancient history for models of government, and examined the different forms of those republics which, having been formed with seeds of their own dissolution, now no longer exist. And we have viewed modern states all round Europe, but find none of their constitutions suitable to our circumstances.

In this situation of this Assembly, groping as it were in the dark to find political truth, and scarce able to distinguish it when presented to us, how has it happened, Sir, that we have not hitherto once thought of humbly applying to the Father of lights, to illuminate our understandings? In the beginning of the contest with Great Britain, when we were sensible of danger, we had daily prayer in this room for the divine protection. Our prayers, Sir, were heard, and they were graciously answered. All of us who were engaged in the struggle must have observed frequent instances of a superintending Providence in our favor. To that kind Providence we owe this happy opportunity of consulting in peace on the means of establishing our future national felicity. And have we now forgotten that powerful friend? Or do we imagine that we no longer need his assistance? I have lived, Sir, a long time, and the longer I live, the more convincing proofs I see of this truth — *that God governs in the affairs of men.* And if a sparrow cannot fall to the ground without his notice, is it probable that an empire can rise without his aid? We have been assured, Sir, in the sacred writings, that " except the Lord build the house they labor in vain that build it." I firmly believe this; and I also believe that without his concurring aid we shall succeed in this political building no better than the builders of Babel. We shall be divided by our little partial local interests; our projects will be confounded; and we ourselves shall become a reproach and by-word down to future ages. And what is worse, mankind may hereafter, from this unfortunate instance, despair of establishing governments by human wisdom, and leave it to chance, war and conquest.

I therefore beg leave to move — that henceforth prayèrs imploring the assistance of Heaven, and its blessings on our deliberations, be held in this Assembly every morning before we proceed to business, and that one or more of the clergy of this city be requested to officiate in that service.

Mr. SHERMAN seconded the motion.

Mr. HAMILTON and several others expressed their apprehensions, that, however proper such a resolution might have been at the beginning of the Convention, it might at this late day, in the first place, bring on it some disagreeable animadversions; and in the second, lead the public to believe that the embarrassments and dissensions within the Convention had suggested this measure. It was answered, by Doctor FRANKLIN, Mr. SHERMAN, and others, that the past omission of a duty could not justify a further omission; that the rejection of such a proposition would expose the Convention to more unpleasant animadversions than the adoption of it; and that the alarm out of doors that might be excited for the state of things within would at least be as likely to do good as ill.

Mr. WILLIAMSON observed, that the true cause of the omission could not be mistaken. The Convention had no funds.

Mr. RANDOLPH proposed, in order to give a favorable

aspect to the measure, that a sermon be preached at the request of the Convention on the Fourth of July, the anniversary of Independence; and thenceforward prayers, &c., to be read in the Convention every morning. Doctor FRANKLIN seconded this motion. After several unsuccessful attempts for silently postponing this matter by adjourning, the adjournment was at length carried, without any vote on the motion.

FRIDAY, JUNE 29TH.

In Convention.—Doctor JOHNSON. The controversy must be endless whilst gentlemen differ in the grounds of their arguments; those on one side considering the States as districts of people composing one political society: those on the other, considering them as so many political societies. The fact is, that the States do exist as political societies, and a government is to be formed for them in their political capacity, as well as for the individuals composing them. Does it not seem to follow, that if the States, as such, are to exist, they must be armed with some power of self-defence? This is the idea of Colonel MASON, who appears to have looked to the bottom of this matter. Besides the aristocratic and other interests, which ought to have the means of defending themselves, the States have their interests as such, and are equally entitled to like means. On the whole he thought, that, as in some respects the States are to be considered in their political capacity, and in others as districts of individual citizens, the two ideas embraced on different sides, instead of being opposed to each other, ought to be combined; that in *one* branch the *people* ought to be represented, in the *other* the *States*.

Mr. GORHAM. The States, as now confederated, have no doubt a right to refuse to be consolidated, or to be formed into any new system. But he wished the small States, which seemed most ready to object, to consider which are to give up most, they or the larger ones. He conceived that a rupture of the Union would be an event unhappy for all; but surely the large States would be least unable to take care of themselves, and to make connections with one another. The weak, therefore, were most inter-ested in establishing some general system for maintaining order. If, among individuals composed partly of weak, and partly of strong, the former most need the protection of law and government, the case is exactly the same with weak and powerful States. What would be the situation of Delaware, (for these things he found must be spoken out, and it might as well be done at first as last), what would be the situation of Delaware in case of a separation of the States? Would she not be at the mercy of Pennsylvania? Would not her true interest lie in being consolidated with her: and ought she not now to wish for such a union with Pennsylvania, under one Government, as will put it out of the power of Pennsylvania to oppress her? Nothing can be more ideal than the danger apprehended by the States from their being formed into one nation. Massachusetts was originally three colonies, viz.; old Massachusetts, Ply-mouth, and the Province of Maine. These apprehensions existed then. An incorporation took place; all parties were safe and satisfied; and every distinction is now forgotten. The case was similar with Connecticut and New Haven.. The dread of union was reciprocal; the consequence of it equally salutary and satisfactory. In like manner, New Jersey has been made one society out of two parts. Should a separation of the States take place, the fate of New Jer-sey would be worst of all. She has no foreign commerce, and can have but little. Pennsylvania and New York will continue to levy taxes on her consumption. If she consults her interest, she would beg of all things to be annihilated. The apprehensions of the small States ought to be appeased by another reflection. Massachusetts will be divided. The Province of Maine is already considered as approaching the term of its annexation to it: and Pennsylvania will probably

not increase, considering the present state of her population, and other events that may happen.   On the whole, he
considered a union of the States as necessary to their happiness, and a firm General Government as necessary to their
union.   He should consider it his duty, if his colleagues
viewed the matter in the same light he did, to stay here as
long as any other State would remain with them, in order
to agree on some plan that could, with propriety, be recommended to the people.

Mr. ELLSWORTH did not despair.   He still trusted that
some good plan of government would be devised and
adopted.

Mr. READ.   He should have no objection to the system
if it were truly national, but it has too much of a federal
mixture in it.   The little States, he thought, had not much
to fear.   He suspected that the large States felt their want
of energy, and wished for a General Government to supply
the defect.   Massachusetts was evidently laboring under
her weakness, and he believed Delaware would not be in
much danger if in her neighbourhood.   Delaware had enjoyed tranquillity, and he flattered himself would continue
to do so.   He was not, however, so selfish as not to wish
for a good General Government.   In order to obtain one,
the whole States must be incorporated.   If the States remain, the representatives of the large ones will stick together, and carry every thing before them.   The Executive,
also, will be chosen under the influence of this partiality,
and will betray it in his administration.   These jealousies
are inseparable from the scheme of leaving the States in
existence.   They must be done away.   The ungranted lands,
also, which have been assumed by particular States, must
be given up.   He repeated his approbation of the plan of
Mr. HAMILTON, and wished it to be substituted for that on
the table.

Mr. MADISON agreed with Doctor JOHNSON, that the
mixed nature of the Government ought to be kept in view;
but thought too much stress was laid on the rank of the

States as political societies. There was a gradation, he observed, from the smallest corporation, with the most limited powers, to the largest empire, with the most perfect sovereignty. He pointed out the limitations on the sovereignty of the States, as now confederated. Their laws, in relation to the paramount law of the Confederacy, were analogous to that of bye-laws to the supreme law within a State. Under the proposed Government the powers of the States will be much farther reduced. According to the views of every member, the General Government will have powers far beyond those exercised by the British Parliament when the States were part of the British Empire. It will, in particular, have the power, without the consent of the State Legislatures, to levy money directly from the people themselves; and therefore, not to divest such *unequal* portions of the people as composed the several States of an *equal* voice, would subject the system to the reproaches and evils which have resulted from the vicious representation in Great Britain.

He entreated the gentlemen representing the small States to renounce a principle which was confessedly unjust; which could never be admitted; and which, if admitted, must infuse mortality into a Constitution which we wished to last forever. He prayed them to ponder well the consequences of suffering the Confederacy to go to pieces. It had been said that the want of energy in the large States would be a security to the small. It was forgotten that this want of energy proceeded from the supposed security of the States against all external danger. Let each State depend on itself for its security, and let apprehensions arise of danger from distant powers or from neighbouring States, and the languishing condition of all the States, large as well as small, would soon be transformed into vigorous and high-toned Governments. His great fear was, that their Governments would then have too much energy; that this might not only be formidable in the large to the small States, but fatal to the internal liberty of all. The same causes which have rendered the old world the theatre of incessant wars, and have banished liberty from the face of it, would soon produce the same effects here. The weakness and jealousy of the small States would quickly introduce some regular military force, against sudden danger from their powerful neighbours. The example would be followed by others, and would soon become universal. In time of actual war, great discretionary powers are constantly given to the Executive magistrate. Constant apprehension of war has the same tendency to render the head too large for the body. A standing military force, with an overgrown Executive, will not long be safe companions to liberty. The means of defence against foreign danger have been always the instruments of tyranny at home. Among the Romans it was a standing maxim, to excite a war whenever a revolt was apprehended. Throughout all Europe, the armies kept up under the pretext of defending, have enslaved, the people. It is, perhaps, questionable, whether the best concerted system of absolute power in Europe, could maintain itself, in a situation where no alarms of external danger could tame the people to the domestic yoke. The insular situation of Great Britain was the principal cause of her being an exception to the general fate of Europe. It has rendered less defence necessary, and admitted a kind of defence, which could not be used for the purpose of oppression. These consequences, he conceived, ought to be apprehended, whether the States should run into a total separation from each other, or should enter into partial confederacies. Either event would be truly deplorable; and those who might be accessory to either, could never be forgiven by their country, nor by themselves.

*Mr. HAMILTON observed, that individuals forming political societies modify their rights differently, with regard to suffrage. Examples of it are found in all the States. In all of them, some individuals are deprived of the right altogether, not having the requisite qualification

---

* From this date he was absent till the 13th of August.

of property. In some of the States, the right of suffrage is
allowed in some cases, and refused in others. To vote for
a member in one branch, a certain quantum of property; to
vote for a member in another branch of the Legislature, a
higher quantum of property, is required. In like manner,
States may modify their right of suffrage differently, the
larger exercising a larger, the smaller a smaller, share of it.
But as States are a collection of individual men, which
ought we to respect most, the rights of the people composing them, or of the artificial beings resulting from the com-
position? Nothing could be more preposterous or absurd
than to sacrifice the former to the latter. It has been said,
that if the smaller States renounce their *equality*, they renounce at the same time their *liberty*. The truth is, it is a
contest for power, not for liberty. Will the men composing
the small States be less free than those composing the
larger? The State of Delaware having forty thousand
souls will lose *power*, if she has one-tenth only of the votes
allowed to Pennsylvania having four hundred thousand; but
will the people of Delaware *be less free*, if each citizen has
an equal vote with each citizen of Pennsylvania? He admitted that common residence within the same State would
produce a certain degree of attachment; and that this principle might have a certain influence on public affairs. He
thought, however, that this might, by some precautions, be
in a great measure excluded; and that no material inconvenience could result from it; as there could not be any ground
for combination among the States whose influence was most
dreaded. The only considerable distinction of interests lay
between the carrying and non-carrying States, which di-
vides, instead of uniting, the largest States. No considerable inconvenience had been found from the division of
the State of New York into different districts of different
sizes.

Some of the consequences of a dissolution of the Union,
and the establishment of partial confederacies, had been
pointed out. He would add another of a most serious

nature.   Alliances will immediately be formed with different rival and hostile nations of Europe, who will foment
disturbances among ourselves, and make us parties to all
their own quarrels.   Foreign nations having American dominion are, and must be, jealous of us.   Their representatives betray the utmost anxiety for our fate, and for the result of this meeting, which must have an essential influence
on it.   It had been said, that respectability in the eyes of
foreign nations was not the object at which we aimed;
that the proper object of republican government was
domestic tranquillity and happiness.   This was an ideal
distinction.   No government could give us tranquillity
and happiness at home, which did not possess sufficient
stability and strength to make us respectable abroad.   This
was the critical moment for forming such a government.
We should run every risk in trusting to future amendments.   As yet we retain the habits of union.   We are
weak, and sensible of our weakness.   Henceforward, the
motives will become feebler, and the difficulties greater.   It
is a miracle that we are now here, exercising our tranquil
and free deliberations on the subject.   It would be madness
to trust to future miracles.   A thousand causes must obstruct a reproduction of them.

Mr. PIERCE considered the equality of votes under the
Confederation as the great source of the public difficulties.
The members of Congress were advocates for local advan-
tages.   State distinctions must be sacrificed, as far as the
general good required, but without destroying the States.
Though from a small State, he felt himself a citizen of the
United States.

Mr. GERRY urged, that we never were independent
States, were not such now, and never could be, even on the
principles of the Confederation.   The States, and the advocates for them, were intoxicated with the idea of their
sovereignty.   He was a member of Congress at the time the
Federal Articles were formed.   The injustice of allowing
each State an equal vote was long insisted on.   He voted

for it, but it was against his judgment, and under the
pressure of public danger, and the obstinacy of the lesser
States. The present Confederation he considered as dissolving. The fate of the Union will be decided by the
Convention. If they do not agree on something, few delegates will probably be appointed to Congress. If they do,
Congress will probably be kept up till the new system
should be adopted. He lamented that, instead of coming
here like a band of brothers, belonging to the same family,
we seem to have brought with us the spirit of political
negotiators.

Mr. L. MARTIN remarked, that the language, of the
States being *sovereign and independent*, was once familiar
and understood; though it seemed now so strange and
obscure. He read those passages in the Articles of Confederation which describe them in that language.

On the question, as moved by Mr LANSING, shall the
word " not " be struck out? — Connecticut, New York, New
Jersey, Delaware, aye — 4; Massachusetts, Pennsylvania,
Virginia, North Carolina, South Carolina, Georgia, no — 6;
Maryland, divided.

On the motion to agree to the clause as reported, " that
the rule of suffrage in the first branch ought not to be
according to that established by the Articles of the Confederation,"— Massachusetts, Pennsylvania, Virginia, North
Carolina, South Carolina, Georgia, aye — 6; Connecticut,
New York, New Jersey, Delaware, no — 4; Maryland,
divided.

Doctor JOHNSON and Mr. ELLSWORTH moved to postpone
the residue of the clause, and take up the eighth Resolution.

On the question,— Connecticut, New York, New Jersey,
Pennsylvania, Maryland, Virginia, North Carolina, South
Carolina, Georgia, aye — 9; Massachusetts, Delaware, no
— 2.

Mr. ELLSWORTH moved, " that the rule of suffrage in
the second branch be the same with that established by the
Articles of Confederation." He was not sorry on the whole,

he said, that the vote just passed had determined against this rule in the first branch. He hoped it would become a ground of compromise with regard to the second branch. We were partly national, partly federal. The proportional representation in the first branch was conformable to the national principle, and would secure the large States against the small. An equality of voices was conformable to the federal principle, and was necessary to secure the small States against the large. He trusted that on this middle ground a compromise would take place. He did not see that it could on any other, and if no compromise should take place, our meeting would not only be in vain, but worse than in vain. To the eastward, he was sure Massachusetts was the only State that would listen to a proposition for excluding the States, as equal political societies, from an equal voice in both branches. The others would risk every consequence rather than part with so dear a right. An attempt to deprive them of it was at once cutting the body of America in two, and, as he supposed would be the case, somewhere about this part of it. The large States he conceived would, notwithstanding the equality of votes, have an influence that would maintain their superiority. Holland, as had been admitted (by Mr. MADISON), had, notwithstanding a like equality in the Dutch confederacy, a prevailing influence in the public measures. The power of self-defence was essential to the small States. Nature had given it to the smallest insect of the creation. He could never admit that there was no danger of combinations among the large States. They will like individuals find out and avail themselves of the advantage to be gained by it. It was true the danger would be greater if they were contiguous, and had a more immediate and common interest. A defensive combination of the small States was rendered more difficult by their greater number. He would mention another consideration of great weight. The existing Confederation was founded on the equality of the States in the article of suffrage,— was it meant to pay no regard to this antecedent plighted faith. Let a strong Executive, a Judiciary, and Legislative power, be created, but let not too much be attempted, by which all may be lost. He was not in general a half-way man, yet he preferred doing half the good we could, rather than do nothing at all. The other half may be added when the necessity shall be more fully experienced.

Mr. BALDWIN could have wished that the powers of the general Legislature had been defined, before the mode of constituting it had been agitated. He should vote against the motion of Mr. ELLSWORTH, though he did not like the Resolution as it stood in the Report of the Committee of the Whole. He thought the second branch ought to be the representation of property, and that, in forming it, therefore, some reference ought to be had to the relative wealth of their constituents, and to the principles on which the Senate of Massachusetts was constituted. He concurred with those who thought it would be impossible for the General Legislature to extend its cares to the local matters of the States.

Adjourned.

SATURDAY, JUNE 30TH.

In Convention, — Mr. BREARLY moved that the President write to the Executive of New Hampshire, informing it that the business depending before the Convention was of such a nature as to require the immediate attendance of the Deputies of that State. In support of his motion, he observed that the difficulties of the subject, and the diversity of opinions called for all the assistance we could possibly obtain. (It was well understood that the object was to add New Hampshire to the number of States opposed to the doctrine of proportional representation, which it was presumed, from her relative size, she must be adverse to).

Mr. PATTERSON seconded the motion.

Mr. RUTLEDGE could see neither the necessity nor propriety of such a measure. They are not unapprized of the meeting, and can attend if they choose. Rhode Island might as well be urged to appoint and send deputies. Are we to suspend the business until the Deputies arrive ? If we proceed, he hoped all the great points would be adjusted before the letter could produce its effect.

Mr. KING said he had written more than once as a private correspondent, and the answer gave him every reason to expect that State would be represented very shortly, if it should be so at all. Circumstances of a personal nature had hitherto prevented it. A letter could have no effect.

Mr. WILSON wished to know, whether it would be consistent with the rule or reason of secrecy, to communicate to New Hampshire that the business was of such a nature as the motion described. It would spread a great alarm. Besides, he doubted the propriety of soliciting any State on the subject, the meeting being merely voluntary.

On motion of Mr. BREARLY,

New York, New Jersey, aye — 2 ; Massachusetts, Connecticut, Virginia, North Carolina, South Carolina, no — 5 ; Maryland, divided ; Pennsylvania, Delaware, Georgia, not on the floor.

The motion of Mr. ELLSWORTH being resumed, for allowing each State an equal vote in the second branch, —

Mr. WILSON did not expect such a motion after the establishment of the contrary principle in the first branch ; and considering the reasons which would oppose it, even if an equal vote had been allowed in the first branch. The gentleman from Connecticut (Mr. ELLSWORTH) had pronounced, that if the motion should not be acceded to, of all the States north of Pennsylvania one only would agree to any General Government. He entertained more favourable hopes of Connecticut and of the other Northern States. He hoped the alarms exceeded their cause, and that they would not abandon a country to which they were bound by so many strong and endearing ties. But should the deplored event happen, it would neither stagger his sentiments

nor his duty. If the minority of the people of America
refuse to coalesce with the majority on just and proper
principles ; if a separation must take place, it could never
happen on better grounds. The votes of yesterday against
the just principle of representation, were as twenty-two to
ninety, of the people of America. Taking the opinions to
be the same on this point, and he was sure, if there was any
room for change, it could not be on the side of the majority,
the question will be, shall less than one-fourth of the United
States withdraw themselves from the Union, or shall more
than three-fourths renounce the inherent, indisputable and
unalienable rights of men, in favor of the artificial system
of States ? If issue must be joined, it was on this point he
would choose to join it. The gentleman from Connecticut,
in supposing that the preponderance secured to the majority
in the first branch had removed the objections to an
equality of votes in the second branch for the security
of the minority, narrowed the case extremely. Such an
equality will enable the minority to control, in all cases
whatsoever, the sentiments and interests of the majority.
Seven States will control six : seven States, according to
the estimates that had been used, composed twenty-four
ninetieths of the whole people. It would be in the power,
then, of less than one-third to overrule two-thirds, whenever
a question should happen to divide the States in that manner. Can we forget for whom we are forming a Government ? Is it for *men*, or for the imaginary beings called
States ? Will our honest constituents be satisfied with
metaphysical distinctions ? Will they, ought they to, be
satisfied with being told, that the one-third compose the
greater number of States ? The rule of suffrage ought on
every principle to be the same in the second as in the first
branch. If the Government be not laid on this foundation,
it can be neither solid nor lasting. Any other principle
will be local, confined and temporary. This will expand
with the expansion, and grow with the growth of the United
States. Much has been said of an imaginary combination

of three States. Sometimes a danger of monarchy, sometimes of aristocracy, has been charged on it. No explanation, however, of the danger has been vouchsafed. It would
be easy to prove, both from reason and history, that rivalships would be more probable than coalitions ; and that
there are no coinciding interests that could produce the
latter. No answer has yet been given to the observations
of Mr. MADISON on this subject. Should the Executive
magistrate be taken from one of the large States, would not
the other two be thereby thrown into the scale with the
other States ? Whence, then, the danger of monarchy ?
Are the people of the three large States more aristocratic
than those of the small ones ? Whence, then, the danger
of aristocracy from their influence ? It is all a mere
illusion of names. We talk of States, till we forget what
they are composed of. Is a real and fair majority the
natural hot-bed of aristocracy? It is a part of the definition of this species of government, or rather of tyranny,
that the smaller number governs the greater. It is true
that a majority of States in the second branch cannot carry
a law against a majority of the people in the first. But
this removes half only of the objection. Bad governments
are of two sorts,— first, that which does too little; secondly,
that which does too much; that which fails through weakness, and that which destroys through oppression. Under
which of these evils do the United States at present groan?
Under the weakness and inefficiency of its government. To
remedy this weakness we have been sent to this Convention. If the motion should be agreed to, we shall leave
the United States fettered precisely as heretofore; with
the additional mortification of seeing the good purposes of
the fair representation of the people in the first branch,
defeated in the second. Twenty-four will still control
sixty-six. He lamented that such a disagreement should
prevail on the point of representation; as he did not foresee
that it would happen on the other point most contested,
the boundary between the general and the local authorities.

18

He thought the States necessary and valuable parts of a good system.

Mr. ELLSWORTH. The capital objection of Mr. WILSON, "that the minority will rule the majority," is not true. The power is given to the few to save them from being destroyed by the many. If an equality of votes had been given to them in both branches, the objection might have had weight. Is it a novel thing that the few should have a check on the many? Is it not the case in the British Constitution, the wisdom of which so many gentlemen have united in applauding? Have not the House of Lords, who form so small a proportion of the nation, a negative on the laws, as a necessary defence of their peculiar rights against the encroachments of the Commons? No instance of a confederacy has existed in which an equality of voices has not been exercised by the members of it. We are running from one extreme to another. We are razing the foundations of the building, when we need only repair the roof. No salutary measure has been lost for want of *a majority of the States* to favor it. If security be all that the great States wish for, the first branch secures them. The danger of combinations among them is not imaginary. Although no particular abuses could be foreseen by him, the possibility of them would be sufficient to alarm him. But he could easily conceive cases in which they might result from such combinations. Suppose, that, in pursuance of some commercial treaty or arrangement, three or four free ports and no more were to be established, would not combinations be formed in favor of Boston, Philadelphia, and some port of the Chesapeake? A like concert might be formed in the appointment of the great offices. He appealed again to the obligations of the Federal compact, which was still in force, and which had been entered into with so much solemnity; persuading himself that some regard would still be paid to the plighted faith under which each State, small as well as great, held an equal right of suffrage in the general councils. His remarks were not the result of partial or local views.   The State he represented (Connecticut) held a middle rank.

Mr. MADISON did justice to the able and close reasoning of Mr. ELLSWORTH, but must observe that it did not always accord with itself.   On another occasion, the large States were described by him as the aristocratic States, ready to oppress the small.   Now the small are the House of Lords, requiring a negative to defend them against the more numerous Commons.   Mr. ELLSWORTH had also erred in saying that no instance had existed in which confederated states had not retained to themselves a perfect equality of suffrage.   Passing over the German system, in which the King of Prussia has nine voices, he reminded Mr. ELLSWORTH of the Lycian confederacy, in which the component members had votes proportioned to their importance, and which Montesquieu recommends as the fittest model for that form of government.   Had the fact been as stated by Mr. ELLSWORTH, it would have been of little avail to him, or rather would have strengthened the arguments against him; the history and fate of the several confederacies, modern as well as ancient, demonstrating some radical vice in their structure.   In reply to the appeal of Mr. ELLSWORTH to the faith plighted in the existing federal compact, he remarked, that the party claiming from others an adherence to a common engagement, ought at least to be guiltless itself of a violation.   Of all the States, however, Connecticut was perhaps least able to urge this plea.   Besides the various omissions to perform the stipulated acts, from which no State was free, the Legislature of that State had, by a pretty recent vote, *positively refused* to pass a law for complying with the requisitions of Congress, and had transmitted a copy of the vote to Congress.   It was urged, he said, continually, that an equality of votes in the second branch was not only necessary to secure the small, but would be perfectly safe to the large ones; whose majority in the first branch was an effectual bulwark.   But notwithstanding this apparent defence, the majority of States might still injure the majority of the people. In the first place, they could *obstruct* the wishes and interests of the majority. Secondly, they could *extort* measures repugnant to the wishes and interest of the majority. Thirdly, they could *impose* measures adverse thereto; as the second branch will probably exercise some great powers, in which the first will not participate. He admitted that every peculiar interest, whether in any class of citizens, or any description of States, ought to be secured as far as possible. Wherever there is danger of attack, there ought to be given a constitutional power of defence. But he contended that the States were divided into different interests, not by their difference of size, but other circumstances; the most material of which resulted partly from climate, but principally from the effects of their having or not having slaves. These two causes concurred in forming the great division of interests in the United States. It did not lie between the large and small States. It lay between the Northern and Southern; and if any defensive power were necessary, it ought to be mutually given to these two interests. He was so strongly impressed with this important truth, that he had been casting about in his mind for some expedient that would answer the purpose. The one which had occurred was, that, instead of proportioning the votes of the States in both branches, to their respective numbers of inhabitants, computing the slaves in the ratio of five to three, they should be represented in one branch according to the number of free inhabitants only; and in the other according to the whole number, counting the slaves as free. By this arrangement the Southern scale would have the advantage in one House, and the Northern in the other. He had been restrained from proposing this expedient by two considerations; one was his unwillingness to urge any diversity of interests on an occasion where it is but too apt to arise of itself; the other was the inequality of powers that must be vested in the two branches, and which would destroy the equilibrium of interests.

Mr. ELLSWORTH assured the House, that, whatever might be thought of the Representatives of Connecticut, the State was entirely Federal in her disposition. He appealed to her great exertions during the war, in supplying both men and money. The muster-rolls would show she had more troops in the field than Virginia. If she had been delinquent, it had been from inability, and not more so than other States.

Mr. SHERMAN. Mr. MADISON animadverted on the delinquency of the States, when his object required him to prove that the constitution of Congress was faulty. Congress is not to blame for the faults of the States. Their measures have been right, and the only thing wanting has been a further power in Congress to render them effectual.

Mr. DAVIE was much embarrassed, and wished for explanations. The Report of the Committee, allowing the Legislatures to choose the Senate, and establishing a proportional representation in it, seemed to be impracticable. There will, according to this rule, be ninety members in the outset, and the number will increase as new States are added. It was impossible that so numerous a body could possess the activity and other qualities required in it. Were he to vote on the comparative merits of the Report, as it stood, and the amendment, he should be constrained to prefer the latter. The appointment of the Senate by electors, chosen by the people for that purpose, was, he conceived, liable to an insuperable difficulty. The larger counties or districts, thrown into a general district, would certainly prevail over the smaller counties or districts, and merit in the latter would be excluded altogether. The report, therefore, seemed to be right in referring the appointment to the Legislatures, whose agency in the general system did not appear to him objectionable, as it did to some others. The fact was, that the local prejudices and interests which could not be denied to exist, would find their way into the national councils, whether the Representatives should be chosen by the Legislatures, or by the people themselves. On the other hand,

if a proportional representation was attended with insuperable difficulties, the making the Senate the representative of
the States looked like bringing us back to Congress again,
and shutting out all the advantages expected from it.
Under this view of the subject, he could not vote for any
plan for the Senate yet proposed. He thought that, in
general, there were extremes on both sides. We were
partly federal, partly national, in our union; and he did not
see why the Government might not in some respects operate on the States, in others on the people.

Mr. WILSON admitted the question concerning the number of Senators to be embarrassing. If the smallest States
be allowed one, and the others in proportion, the Senate will
certainly be too numerous. He looked forward to the time
when the smallest States will contain a hundred thousand
souls at least. Let there be then one Senator in each, for
every hundred thousand souls, and let the States not having
that number of inhabitants be allowed one. He was willing himself to submit to this temporary concession to the
small States; and threw out the idea as a ground of compromise.

Doctor FRANKLIN. The diversity of opinions turns on
two points. If a proportional representation takes place,
the small States contend that their liberties will be in danger. If an equality of votes is to be put in its place, the
large States say their money will be in danger. When a
broad table is to be made, and the edges of planks do not
fit, the artist takes a little from both, and makes a good
joint. In like manner, here, both sides must part from
some of their demands, in order that they may join in some
accommodating proposition. He had prepared one which
he would read, that it might lie on the table for consideration. The proposition was in the words following:

"That the Legislatures of the several States shall
choose and send an equal number of delegates, namely,
———————, who are to compose the second branch of the
General Legislature.

" That in all cases or questions wherein the sovereignty of individual States may be affected, or whereby their authority over their own citizens may be diminished, or the authority of the General Government within the several States augmented, each State shall have equal suffrage.

" That in the appointment of all civil officers of the General Government, in the election of whom the second branch may by the constitution have part, each State ·shall have equal suffrage.

" That in fixing the salaries of such officers, and in all allowances for public services, and generally in all appropriations and dispositions of money to be drawn out of the general Treasury; and in all laws for supplying that Treasury, the Delegates of the several States shall have suffrage in proportion to the sums which their respective States do actually contribute to the Treasury."

Where a ship had many owners, this was the rule of deciding on her expedition. He had been one of the ministers from this country to France during the joint war, and would have been very glad if allowed to vote in distributing the money to carry it on.

Mr. KING observed, that the simple question was, whether each State should have an equal vote in the second branch; that it must be apparent to those gentlemen who liked neither the motion for this quality, nor the Report as it stood, that the Report was as susceptible of melioration as the motion; that a reform would be nugatory and nominal only, if we should make another Congress of the proposed Senate; that if the adherence to an equality of votes was fixed and unalterable, there could not be less obstinacy on the other side; and that we were in fact cut asunder already, and it was in vain to shut our eyes against it. That he was, however, filled with astonishment, that, if we were convinced that every *man* in America was secured in all his rights, we should be ready to sacrifice this substantial good to the phantom of *State* sovereignty. That his feelings were more harrowed and his fears more agitated for his country than he could express; that he conceived this to be the last opportunity of providing for its liberty and happiness: that he could not, therefore, but repeat his amazement, that when a just government, founded on a fair representation of the *people* of America, was within our reach, we should renounce the blessing, from an attachment to the ideal freedom and importance of *States*. That should this wonderful illusion continue to prevail, his mind was prepared for every event, rather than sit down under a Government founded on a vicious principle of representation, and which must be as short-lived as it would be unjust. He might prevail on himself to accede to some such expedient as had been hinted by Mr. WILSON; but he never could listen to an equality of votes as proposed in the motion.

Mr. DAYTON. When assertion is given for proof, and terror substituted for argument, he presumed they would have no effect, however eloquently spoken. It should have been shown that the evils we have experienced have proceeded from the equality now objected to; and that the seeds of dissolution for the State Governments are not sown in the General Government. He considered the system on the table as a novelty, an amphibious monster; and was persuaded that it never would be received by the people.

Mr. MARTIN would never confederate, if it could not be done on just principles.

Mr. MADISON would acquiesce in the concession hinted by Mr. WILSON, on condition that a due independence should be given to the Senate. The plan in its present shape makes the Senate absolutely dependent on the States. The Senate, therefore, is only another edition of Congress. He knew the faults of that body, and had used a bold language against it. Still he would preserve the State rights as carefully as the trial by jury.

Mr. BEDFORD contended, that there was no middle way between a perfect consolidation, and a mere confederacy of the States. The first is out of the question; and in the latter they must continue, if not perfectly, yet equally, sovereign. If political societies possess ambition, avarice, and all the other passions which render them formidable to each other, ought we not to view them in this light here? Will not the same motives operate in America as elsewhere? If any gentleman doubts it, let him look at the votes. Have they not been dictated by interest, by ambition? Are not the large States evidently seeking to aggrandize themselves at the expense of the small? They think, no doubt, that they have right on their side, but interest had blinded their eyes. Look at Georgia. Though a small State at present, she is actuated by the prospect of soon being a great one. South Carolina is actuated both by present interest, and future prospects. She hopes, too, to see the other States cut down to her own dimensions. North Carolina has the same motives of present and future interest. Virginia follows. Maryland is not on that side of the question. Pennsylvania has a direct and future interest. Massachusetts has a decided and palpable interest in the part she takes. Can it be expected that the small States will act from pure disinterestedness. Look at Great Britain. Is the representation there less unequal? But we shall be told again, that that is the rotten part of the Constitution. Have not the boroughs, however, held fast their constitutional rights? And are we to act with greater purity than the rest of mankind? An exact proportion in the representation is not preserved in any one of the States. Will it be said that an inequality of power will not result from an inequality of votes. Give the opportunity, an ambition will not fail to abuse it. The whole history of mankind proves it. The three large States have a common interest to bind them together in commerce. But whether a combination, as we supposed, or a competition, as others supposed, shall take place among them, in either case the small States must be ruined. We must, like Solon, make such a government as the people will approve. Will the smaller States ever agree to the proposed degradation of them? It is not true that the

people will not agree to enlarge the powers of the present
Congress. The language of the people has been, that
Congress ought to have the power of collecting an impost,
and of coercing the States where it may be necessary. On
the first point they have been explicit, and, in a manner,
unanimous in their declarations. And must they not agree
to this, and similar measures, if they ever mean to discharge their engagements? The little States are willing to
observe their engagements, but will meet the large ones on
no ground but that of the Confederation. We have been
told, with a dictatorial air, that this is the last moment for a
fair trial in favor of a good government. It will be the
last, indeed, if the propositions reported from the Committee go forth to the people. He was under no apprehensions. The large States dare not dissolve the Confederation. If they do, the small ones will find some foreign
ally, of more honour and good faith, who will take them by
the hand, and do them justice. He did not mean, by this,
to intimidate or alarm. It was a natural consequence, which
ought to be avoided by enlarging the Federal powers, not
annihilating the Federal system. This is what the people
expect. All agree in the necessity of a more efficient
government, and why not make such an one as they desire?

Mr. ELLSWORTH. Under a National Government, he
should participate in the national security, as remarked by
Mr. KING; but that was all. What he wanted was domestic happiness. The National Government could not descend
to the local objects on which this depended. It could only
embrace objects of a general nature. He turned his eyes,
therefore, for the preservation of his rights, to the State
Governments. From these alone he could derive the greatest happiness he expects in this life. His happiness depends
on their existence, as much as a new-born infant on its
mother for nourishment. If this reasoning was not satisfactory, he had nothing to add that could be so.

Mr. KING was for preserving the States in a subordinate
degree, and as far as they could be necessary for the pur-

poses stated by Mr. ELLSWORTH. He did not think a full
answer had been given to those who apprehended a dangerous encroachment on their jurisdictions. Expedients might be
devised, as he conceived, that would give them all the security the nature of things would admit of. In the establishment of societies, the Constitution was to the Legislature,
what the laws were to individuals. As the fundamental
rights of individuals are secured by express provisions in
the State Constitutions, why may not a like security be provided for the rights of States in the National Constitution?
The Articles of Union between England and Scotland furnish an example of such a provision, in favor of sundry
rights of Scotland. When that union was in agitation, the
same language of apprehension which has been heard from
the smaller States, was in the mouths of the Scotch patriots.
The articles, however, have not been violated, and the
Scotch have found an increase of prosperity and happiness.
He was aware that this will be called a mere *paper security.*
He thought it a sufficient answer to say, that if fundamental
articles of compact are no sufficient defence against physical power, neither will there be any safety against it, if
there be no compact. He could not sit down without taking some notice of the language of the honorable gentleman from Delaware (Mr. BEDFORD). It was not he that
had uttered a dictatorial language. This intemperance had
marked the honorable gentleman himself. It was not he
who, with a vehemence unprecedented in that House, had
declared himself ready to turn his hopes from our common
country, and court the protection of some foreign hand.
This, too, was the language of the honorable member himself. He was grieved that such a thought had entered his
heart. He was more grieved that such an expression had
dropped from his lips. The gentleman could only excuse
it to himself on the score of passion. For himself, whatever might be his distress, he would never court relief from
a foreign power.

Adjourned.

MONDAY, JULY 2D.

In Convention,—On the question for allowing each State one vote in the second branch, as moved by Mr. ELLSWORTH, it was lost, by an equal division of votes,—Connecticut, New York, New Jersey, Delaware, Maryland,* aye—5; Massachusetts, Pennsylvania, Virginia, North Carolina, South Carolina, no—5; Georgia, divided (Mr. Baldwin aye, Mr. Houston, no),

Mr. PINCKNEY thought an equality of votes in the second branch inadmissible. At the same time, candor obliged him to admit, that the large States would feel a partiality for their own citizens, and give them a preference in appointments: that they might also find some common points in their commercial interests, and promote treaties favorable to them. There is a real distinction between the Northern and Southern interests. North Carolina, South Carolina and Georgia, in their rice and indigo, had a peculiar interest which might be sacrificed. How, then, shall the larger States be prevented from administering the General Government as they please, without being themselves unduly subjected to the will of the smaller? By allowing them some, but not a full, proportion. He was extremely anxious that something should be done, considering this as the last appeal to a regular experiment. Congress have failed in almost every effort for an amendment of the Federal system. Nothing has prevented a dissolution of it, but the appointment of this Convention; and he could not express his alarms for the consequence of such an event. He read his motion to form the States into classes, with an apportionment of Senators among them (see Article 4, of his plan—May 29th, page 61).

General PINCKNEY was willing the motion might be considered. He did not entirely approve it. He liked better the motion of Doctor Franklin, (q. v. June 30, page 278).

---

* Mr. JENIFER not being present, Mr. MARTIN alone voted.

Some compromise seemed to be necessary, the States being exactly divided on the question for an equality of votes in the second branch.   He proposed that a Committee consisting of a member from each State should be appointed to devise and report some compromise.

Mr. L. MARTIN had no objection to a commitment, but no modifications whatever could reconcile the smaller States to the least diminution of their equal sovereignty.

Mr. SHERMAN.   We are now at full stop; and nobody, he supposed, meant that we should break up without doing something.   A committee he thought most likely to hit on some expedient.

Mr. GOUVERNEUR MORRIS* thought a Committee advisable, as the Convention had been equally divided.   He had a stronger reason also.   The mode of appointing the second branch tended, he was sure, to defeat the object of it. What is this object?   To check the precipitation, changeableness, and excesses of the first branch.   Every man of observation had seen in the democratic branches of the State Legislatures, precipitation — in Congress, changeableness — in every department, excesses against personal liberty, private property, and personal safety.   What qualities are necessary to constitute a check in this case?   *Abilities* and *virtue* are equally necessary in both branches. Something more, then, is now wanted.   In the first place, the checking branch must have a personal interest in checking the other branch.   One interest must be opposed to another interest.   Vices, as they exist, must be turned against each other.   In the second place, it must have great personal property; it must have the aristocratic spirit; it must love to lord it through pride.   Pride is, indeed, the great principle that actuates both the poor and the rich. It is this principle which in the former resists, in the latter abuses, authority.   In the third place it should be independent.   In religion the creature is apt to forget its Cre-

* He had just returned from New York, having left the Convention a few days after it commenced business.

ator. That it is otherwise in political affairs, the late debates here are an unhappy proof. The aristocratic body should
be as independent, and as firm, as the democratic. If the
members of it are to revert to a dependence on the democratic choice, the democratic scale will preponderate. All
the guards contrived by America have not restrained the
Senatorial branches of the Legislatures from a servile complaisance to the democratic. If the second branch is to be
dependent, we are better without it. To make it independent, it should be for life. It will then do wrong, it will be
said. He believed so; he hoped so. The rich will strive
to establish their dominion, and enslave the rest. They
always did. They always will. The proper security
against them is to form them into a separate interest. The
two forces will then control each other. Let the rich mix
with the poor, and in a commercial country they will establish an oligarchy. Take away commerce, and the democracy will triumph. Thus it has been all the world over.
So it will be among us. Reason tells us we are but men;
and we are not to expect any particular interference of
Heaven in our favor. By thus combining, and setting
apart, the aristocratic interest, the popular interest will be
combined against it. There will be a mutual check and
mutual security. In the fourth place, an independence for
life, involves the necessary permanency. If we change our
measures nobody will trust us, — and how avoid a change
of measures, but by avoiding a change of men? Ask any
man if he confides in Congress — if he confides in the State
of Pennsylvania — if he will lend his money, or enter into
contract? He will tell you, no. He sees no stability. He
can repose no confidence. If Great Britain were to explain
her refusal to treat with us, the same reasoning would be
employed. He disliked the exclusion of the second branch
from holding offices. It is dangerous. It is like the imprudent exclusion of the military officers, during the war,
from civil appointments. It deprives the Executive of the
principal source of influence. If danger be apprehended

from the Executive, what a left-handed way is this of obviating it! If the son, the brother, or the friend can be appointed, the danger may be even increased, as the disqualified father, &c. can then boast of a disinterestedness which he does not possess. Besides, shall the best, the most able, the most virtuous citizens not be permitted to hold offices? Who then are to hold them? He was also against paying the Senators. They will pay themselves, if they can. If they cannot, they will be rich, and can do without it. Of such the second branch ought to consist; and none but such can compose it, if they are not to be paid. He contended that the Executive should appoint the Senate, and fill up vacancies. This gets rid of the difficulty in the present question. You may begin with any ratio you please, it will come to the same thing. The members being independent, and for life, may be taken as well from one place as from another. It should be considered, too, how the scheme could be carried through the States. He hoped there was strength of mind enough in this House to look truth in the face. He did not hesitate, therefore, to say that loaves and fishes must bribe the demagogues. They must be made to expect higher offices under the General, than the State Governments. A Senate for life will be a noble bait. Without such captivating prospects, the popular leaders will oppose and defeat the plan. He perceived that the first branch was to be chosen by the people of the States, the second by those chosen by the people. Is not here a government by the States — a government by compact between Virginia in the first and second branch, Massachusetts in the first and second branch, &c.? This is going back to mere treaty. It is no government at all. It is altogether dependent on the States, and will act over again the part which Congress has acted. A firm government alone can protect our liberties. He fears the influence of the rich. They will have the same effect here as elsewhere, if we do not, by such a government, keep them within their proper spheres. We should remember that the people never act from reason alone. The rich will take the advantage of their passions, and make these the instruments for oppressing them. The result of the contest will be a violent aristocracy, or a more violent despotism. The schemes of the rich will be favoured by the extent of the country. The people in such distant parts cannot communicate and act in concert. They will be the dupes of those who have more knowledge and intercourse. The only security against encroachments, will be a select and sagacious body of men, instituted to watch against them on all sides. He meant only to hint these observations, without grounding any motion on them.

Mr. RANDOLPH favored the commitment, though he did not expect much benefit from the expedient. He animadverted on the warm and rash language of Mr. BEDFORD on Saturday; reminded the small States that if the large States should combine, some danger of which he did not deny, there would be a check in the revisionary power of the Executive; and intimated, that, in order to render this still more effectual, he would agree, that in the choice of an Executive each State should have an equal vote. He was persuaded that two such opposite bodies as Mr. MORRIS had planned could never long co-exist. Dissensions would arise, as has been seen even between the Senate and House of Delegates in Maryland; appeals would be made to the people; and in a little time commotions would be the result. He was far from thinking the large States could subsist of themselves, any more than the small; an avulsion would involve the whole in ruin; and he was determined to pursue such a scheme of government as would secure us against such a calamity.

Mr. STRONG was for the commitment; and hoped the mode of constituting both branches would be referred. If they should be established on different principles, contentions would prevail, and there would never be a concurrence in necessary measures.

Doctor WILLIAMSON. If we do not concede on both

sides, our business must soon be at end.   He approved of
the commitment, supposing that, as the Committee would
be a smaller body, a compromise would be pursued with
more coolness.

Mr. WILSON objected to the Committee, because it would
decide according to that very rule of voting, which was
opposed on one side.   Experience in Congress had also
proved the inutility of Committees consisting of members
from each State.

Mr. LANSING would not oppose the commitment, though
expecting little advantage from it.

Mr. MADISON opposed the commitment.   He had rarely
seen any other effect than delay from *such* committees in
Congress.   Any scheme of compromise that could be proposed in the Committee might as easily be proposed in the
House; and the report of the Committee, where it contained
merely the *opinion* of the Committee, would neither shorten
the discussion, nor influence the decision of the House.

Mr. GERRY was for the commitment.   Something must
be done, or we shall disappoint not only America, but the
whole world.   He suggested a consideration of the state we
should be thrown into by the failure of the Union.   We
should be without an umpire to decide controversies, and
must be at the mercy of events.   What, too, is to become
of our treaties — what of our foreign debts — what of our
domestic ?   We must make concessions on both sides.
Without these, the Constitutions of the several States would
never have been formed.

On the question for committing, generally, — Massachusetts, Connecticut, New York, Pennsylvania, Maryland,
Virginia, North Carolina, South Carolina, Georgia, aye —
9 ; New Jersey, Delaware, no — 2.

On the question for committing it " to a member from
each State," — Massachusetts, Connecticut, New York, New
Jersey, Delaware, Maryland, Virginia, North Carolina,
South Carolina, Georgia, aye — 10 ; Pennsylvania, no — 1.

The Committee, elected by ballot, were, Mr. GERRY, Mr.

19

ELLSWORTH, Mr. YATES, Mr. PATTERSON, Dr. FRANKLIN, Mr. BEDFORD, Mr. MARTIN, Mr. MASON, Mr. DAVY, Mr RUTLEDGE, Mr. BALDWIN.

That time might be given to the Committee, and to such as chose to attend to the celebrations on the anniversary of Independence the Convention adjourned till Thursday.

THURSDAY, JULY 5TH.

In Convention, — Mr. GERRY delivered in, from the Committee appointed on Monday last, the following Report :

"The Committee to whom was referred the eighth Resolution of the Report from the Committee of the Whole House, and so much of the seventh as has not been decided on, submit the following Report :

"That the subsequent propositions be recommended to the Convention on condition that both shall be generally adopted.

"1. That in the first branch of the Legislature each of the States now in the Union shall be allowed one member for every forty thousand inhabitants, of the description reported in the seventh Resolution of the Committee of the Whole House : that each State not containing that number shall be allowed one member : that all bills for raising or appropriating money, and for fixing the salaries of the officers of the Government of the United States, shall originate in the first branch of the Legislature, and shall not be altered or amended by the second branch ; and that no money shall be drawn from the public Treasury but in pursuance of appropriations to be originated in the first branch.

"2. That in the second branch, each State shall have an equal vote." *

_____

* This Report was founded on a motion in the Committee made by Doctor FRANKLIN. It was barely acquiesced in by the members from the States opposed to an equity of votes in the second branch, and was evidently considered by the members on the other side, as a gaining of their point. A motion was made by Mr SHERMAN, (who acted in the place of Mr. ELLSWORTH who was kept away by indisposi-

Mr. GORHAM observed, that, as the report consisted of propositions mutually conditional, he wished to hear some explanations touching the grounds on which the conditions were estimated.

Mr. GERRY. The Committee were of different opinions, as well as the Deputations from which the Committee were taken; and agreed to the Report merely in order that some ground of accommodation might be proposed. Those opposed to the equality of votes have only assented conditionally; and if the other side do not generally agree, will not be under any obligation to support the Report.

Mr. WILSON thought the Committee had exceeded their powers.

Mr. MARTIN was for taking the question on the whole Report.

Mr. WILSON was for a division of the question; otherwise it would be a leap in the dark.

Mr. MADISON could not regard the privilege of originating money bills as any concession on the side of the small States. Experience proved that it had no effect. If seven States in the upper branch wished a bill to be originated, they might surely find some member from some of the same States in the lower branch, who would originate it. The restriction as to amendments was of as little consequence. Amendments could be handed privately by the Senate to members in the other House. Bills could be negatived, that they might be sent up in the desired shape. If the Senate should yield to the obstinacy of the first branch, the use of that body as a check, would be lost. If the first branch should yield to that of the Senate, the privilege would be nugatory. Experience had also shown, both in Great Britain, and the States having a similar

tion), in the Committee, to the following effect, "that each State should have an equal vote in the second branch ; provided that no decision therein should prevail unless the majority of States concurring should also comprise a majority of the inhabitants of the United States." This motion was not much deliberated on, nor approved, in the Committee. A similar proviso had been proposed, in the debates on the Articles of Confederation, in 1777, to the articles giving certain powers to "nine States." See Journals of Congress for 1777, page 462.

regulation, that it was a source of frequent and obstinate altercations. These considerations had produced a rejection of a like motion on a former occasion, when judged by its own merits. It could not, therefore, be deemed any concession on the present, and left in force all the objections which had prevailed against allowing each State an equal voice. He conceived that the Convention was reduced to the alternative, of either departing from justice in order to conciliate the smaller States, and the minority of the people of the United States, or of displeasing these, by justly gratifying the larger States and the majority of the people. He could not himself hesitate as to the option he ought to make. The Convention, with justice and a majority of the people on their side, had nothing to fear. With injustice and the minority on their side, they had every thing to fear. It was in vain to purchase concord in the Convention on terms which would perpetuate discord among their constituents. The Convention ought to pursue a plan which would bear the test of examination, which would be espoused and supported by the enlightened and impartial part of America, and which they could themselves vindicate and urge. It should be considered, that, although at first many may judge of the system recommended by their opinion of the Convention, yet finally all will judge of the Convention by the system. The merits of the system alone can finally and effectually obtain the public suffrage. He was not apprehensive that the people of the small States would obstinately refuse to accede to a government founded on just principles, and promising them substantial protection. He could not suspect that Delaware would brave the consequences of seeking her fortunes apart from the other States, rather than submit to such a Government; much less could he suspect that she would pursue the rash policy, of courting foreign support, which the warmth of one of her Representatives (Mr. BEDFORD) had suggested; or if she should, that any foreign nation would be so rash as to hearken to the overture. As little could he suspect that the

people of New Jersey, notwithstanding the decided tone of
the gentleman from that State, would choose rather to stand
on their own legs, and bid defiance to events, than to
acquiesce under an establishment founded on principles the
justice of which they could not dispute, and absolutely
necessary to redeem them from the exactions levied on them
by the commerce of the neighbouring States. A review of
other States would prove that there was as little reason to
apprehend an inflexible opposition elsewhere. Harmony
in the Convention was, no doubt, much to be desired. Satisfaction to all the States, in the first instance, still more
so. But if the principal States comprehending a majority
of the people of the United States, should concur in a just
and judicious plan, he had the firmest hopes that all the
other States would by degrees accede to it.

Mr. BUTLER said, he could not let down his idea of the
people of America so far as to believe they would, from mere
respect to the Convention, adopt a plan evidently unjust.
He did not consider the privilege concerning money bills
as of any consequence. He urged, that the second branch
ought to represent the States according to their property.

Mr. GOUVERNEUR MORRIS thought the form as well as
the matter of the Report objectionable. It seemed, in the
first place, to render amendment impracticable. In the
next place, it seemed to involve a pledge to agree to the
second part, if the first should be agreed to. He conceived
the whole aspect of it to be wrong. He came here as a
Representative of America; he flattered himself he came
here in some degree as a Representative of the whole human race; for the whole human race will be affected by the
proceedings of this Convention. He wished gentlemen to
extend their views beyond the present moment of time;
beyond the narrow limits of place from which they derive
their political origin. If he were to believe some things
which he had heard, he should suppose that we were assembled to truck and bargain for our particular States. He
cannot descend to think that any gentlemen are really actu-

ated by these views.   We must look forward to the effects
of what we do.   These alone ought to guide us.   Much has
been said of the sentiments of the people.   They were unknown.   They could not be known.   All that we can infer
is, that, if the plan we recommend be reasonable and right,
all who have reasonable minds and sound intentions will
embrace it, notwithstanding what had been said by some
gentlemen.   Let us suppose that the larger States shall
agree, and that the smaller refuse; and let us trace the consequences.   The opponents of the system in the smaller
States will no doubt make a party, and a noise for a time,
but the ties of interest, of kindred, and of common habits,
which connect them with other States, will be too strong
to be easily broken.   In New Jersey, particularly, he was
sure a great many would follow the sentiments of Pennsylvania and New York.   This country must be united.   If
persuasion does not unite it, the sword will.   He begged
this consideration might have its due weight.   The scenes
of horror attending civil commotion cannot be described;
and the conclusion of them will be worse than the term of
their continuance.   The stronger party will then make
traitors of the weaker; and the gallows and halter will finish the work of the sword.   How far foreign powers would
be ready to take part in the confusions, he would not say.
Threats that they will be invited have, it seems, been
thrown out.   He drew the melancholy picture of foreign
intrusions, as exhibited in the history of Germany, and
urged it as a standing lesson to other nations.   He trusted
that the gentlemen who may have hazarded such expressions did not entertain them till they reached their own
lips.   But returning to the Report, he could not think it in
any respect calculated for the public good.   As the second
branch is now constituted, there will be constant disputes
and appeals to the States, which will undermine the General Government, and control and annihilate the first
branch.   Suppose that the Delegates from Massachusetts
and Rhode Island, in the upper house, disagree, and that

the former are outvoted. What results? They will immediately declare that their State will not abide by the decision, and make such representations as will produce that
effect. The same may happen as to Virginia and other
States. Of what avail, then, will be what is on paper?
State attachments, and State importance have been the bane
of this country. We cannot annihilate, but we may perhaps take out the teeth of, the serpents. He wished our
ideas to be enlarged to the true interest of man, instead of
being circumscribed within the narrow compass of a particular spot. And, after all, how little can be the motive
yielded by selfishness for such a policy? Who can say,
whether he himself, much less whether his children, will
the next year be an inhabitant of this or that State?

Mr. BEDFORD. He found that what he had said, as to
the small States being taken by the hand, had been mis-
understood, — and he rose to explain. He did not mean
that the small States would court the aid and interposition
of foreign powers. He meant that they would not consider the federal compact as dissolved until it should be so
by the acts of the large States. In this case, the consequence of the breach of faith on their part, and the readiness of the small States to fulfil their engagements, would
be that foreign nations having demands on this Country,
would find it their interest to take the small States by the
hand, in order to do themselves justice. This was what he
meant. But no man can forsee to what extremities the
small States may be driven by oppression. He observed,
also, in apology, that some allowance ought to be made, for
the habits of his profession, in which warmth was natural
and sometimes necessary. But is there not an apology in
what was said by (Mr. GOUVERNEUR MORRIS), that the
sword is to unite — by Mr. GORHAM, that Delaware must be
annexed to Pennsylvania, and New Jersey divided between
Pennsylvania and New York? To hear such language
without emotion, would be to renounce the feelings of a
man and the duty of a citizen. As to the propositions of

the Committee, the lesser States have thought it necessary
to have a security somewhere. This has been thought
necessary for the Executive magistrate of the proposed
government, who has a sort of negative on the laws; and is
it not of more importance that the States should be protected, than that the Executive branch of the Government
should be protected? In order to obtain this, the smaller
States have conceded as to the constitution of the first
branch, and as to money bills. If they be not gratified by
correspondent concessions, as to the second branch, is it to
be supposed they will ever accede to the plan? And
what will be the consequence, if nothing should be done?
The condition of the United States requires that something
should be immediately done. It will be better that a defective plan should be adopted, than that none should be
recommended. He saw no reason why defects might not be
supplied by meetings ten, fifteen or twenty years hence.

Mr. ELLSWORTH said, he had not attended the proceedings of the Committee, but was ready to accede to the compromise they had reported. Some compromise was necessary; and he saw none more convenient or reasonable.

Mr. WILLIAMSON hoped that the expressions of individuals would not be taken for the sense of their colleagues,
much less of their States, which was not and could not be
known. He hoped, also, that the meaning of those expressions would not be misconstrued or exaggerated. He did
not conceive that (Mr. GOUVERNEUR MORRIS) meant that
the sword ought to be drawn against the smaller States.
He only pointed out the probable consequences of anarchy
in the United States. A similar exposition ought to be given
of the expressions of (Mr. GORHAM). He was ready to
hear the Report discussed; but thought the propositions
contained in it the most objectionable of any he had yet
heard.

Mr. PATTERSON said that he had, when the report was
agreed to in the Committee, reserved to himself the right
of freely discussing it. He acknowledged that the warmth

complained of was improper; but he thought the sword and the gallows little calculated to produce conviction. He complained of the manner in. which Mr. MADISON and Mr. G. MORRIS had treated the small States.

Mr. GERRY. Though he had assented to the Report in the Committee, he had very material objections to it. We were, however, in a peculiar situation. We were neither the same nation, nor different nations. We ought not, therefore, to pursue the one or the other of these ideas too closely. If no compromise should take place, what will be the consequence. A secession he foresaw would take place; for some gentlemen seemed decided on it. Two different plans will be proposed, and the result no man could foresee. If we do not come to some agreement among ourselves, some foreign sword will probably do the work for us.

Mr. MASON. The Report was meant not as specific propositions to be adopted, but merely as a general ground of accommodation. There must be some accommodation on this point, or we shall make little further progress in the work. Accommodation was the object of the House in the appointment of the Committee, and of the Committee in the report they had. made. And, however liable the Report might be to objections, he thought it preferable to an appeal to the world by the different sides, as had been talked of by some gentlemen. It could not be more inconvenient to any gentleman to remain absent from his private affairs, than it was for him, but he would bury his bones in this city, rather than expose his country to the consequences of a dissolution of the Convention without any thing being done.

The first proposition in the Report for fixing the representation in the first branch, " one member for every forty thousand inhabitants," being taken up,—

Mr. GOUVERNEUR MORRIS objected to that scale of apportionment. He thought property ought to be taken into the estimate as well as the number of inhabitants. Life and liberty were generally said to be of more value than

property.   An accurate view of the matter would, nevertheless, prove that property was the main object of society.
The savage state was more favorable to liberty than the civilized; and sufficiently so to life.   It was preferred by all
men who had not acquired a taste for property; it was only
renounced for the sake of property which could only be
secured by the restraints of regular government.   These
ideas might appear to some new, but they were nevertheless just.   If property, then, was the main object of government, certainly it ought to be one measure of the influence due to those who were to be affected by the government.   He looked forward, also, to that range of new
States which would soon be formed in the West.   He
thought the rule of representation ought to be so fixed, as
to secure to the Atlantic States a prevalence in the national
councils.   The new States will know less of the public interest than these; will have an interest in many respects
different; in particular will be little scrupulous of involving the community in wars the burdens and operations of
which would fall chiefly on the maritime States.   Provision ought, therefore, to be made to prevent the maritime
States from being hereafter outvoted by them.   He thought
this might be easily done, by irrevocably fixing the number of representatives which the Atlantic States should respectively have, and the number which each new State will
have.   This would not be unjust, as the western settlers
would previously know the conditions on which they were
to possess their lands.   It would be politic, as it would
recommend the plan to the present, as well as future, interest of the States which must decide the fate of it.

Mr. RUTLEDGE.   The gentleman last up had spoken
some of his sentiments precisely.   Property was certainly
the principal object of society.   If numbers should be made
the rule of representation, the Atlantic States would be
subjected to the western.   He moved that the first proposition in the Report be postponed, in order to take up the
following, viz.: "that the suffrages of the several States be

regulated and proportioned according to the sums to be paid towards the general revenue by the inhabitants of each State respectively; that an apportionment of suffrages, according to the ratio aforesaid shall be made and regulated at the end of —— years from the first meeting of the Legislature of the United States, and at the end of every —— years; but that for the present, and until the period above mentioned, the suffrages shall be for New Hampshire ——, for Massachusetts ——, &c."

Col. MASON said, the case of new States was not unnoticed in the Committee; but it was thought, and he was himself decidedly of opinion, that if they made a part of the Union, they ought to be subject to no unfavorable discriminations.   Obvious considerations required it.

Mr. RANDOLPH concurred with Mr. MASON. -

On the question on Mr. RUTLEDGE's motion,— South Carolina, aye — 1; Massachusetts, Connecticut, New York, New Jersey, Pennsylvania, Delaware, Maryland, Virginia, North Carolina, no — 9; Georgia, not on the floor. Adjourned.

FRIDAY, JULY 6TH.

In Convention,— Mr. GOUVERNEUR MORRIS moved to commit so much of the Report as relates to "one member for every forty thousand inhabitants."   His view was, that they might absolutely fix the number for each State in the first instance; leaving the Legislature at liberty to provide for changes in the relative importance of the States, and for the case of new States.

Mr. WILSON seconded the motion; but with a view of leaving the Committee under no implied shackles.

Mr. GORHAM apprehended great inconvenience from fixing directly the number of Representatives to be allowed to each State.   He thought the number of inhabitants the true guide, though perhaps some departure might be expedient from the full proportion.   The States, also, would vary in their relative extent by separations of parts of the largest States. A part of Virginia is now on the point of a separation. In the province of Maine, a Convention is at this time deliberating on a separation from Massachusetts. In such events the number of Representatives ought certainly be reduced. He hoped to see all the States made small by proper divisions, instead of their becoming formidable as was apprehended to the small States. He conceived, that, let the government be modified as it might, there would be a constant tendency in the State Governments to encroach upon it; it was of importance, therefore, that the extent of the States should be reduced as much, and as fast, as possible. The stronger the government shall be made in the first instance, the more easily will these divisions be effected; as it will be of less consequence in the opinion of the States, whether they be of great or small extent.

Mr. GERRY did not think with his colleague, that the larger States ought to be cut up. This policy has been inculcated by the middling and small States, ungenerously and contrary to the spirit of the Confederation. Ambitious men will be apt to solicit needless divisions, till the States be reduced to the size of counties. If this policy should still actuate the small States, the large ones could not confederate safely with them ; but would be obliged to consult their safety by confederating only with one another. He favored the commitment, and thought that representation ought to be in the combined ratio of numbers of inhabitants and of wealth, and not of either singly.

Mr. KING wished the clause to be committed chiefly in order to detach it from the Report, with which it had no connection. He thought, also, that the ratio of representation proposed could not be safely fixed, since in a century and an half our computed increase of population would carry the number of Representatives to an enormous excess ; that the number of inhabitants was not the proper index of ability and wealth ; that property was the primary object of society ; and that, in fixing a ratio, this ought not to be excluded from the estimate. With regard to new States, he observed that there was something peculiar in the business, which had not been noticed. The United States were now admitted to be proprietors of the country North West of the Ohio. Congress, by one of their ordinances, have impolitically laid it out into ten States, and have made it a fundamental article of compact with those who may become settlers, that as soon as the number in any one State shall equal that of the smallest of the thirteen original States, it may claim admission into the Union. Delaware does not contain, it is computed, more than thirty-five thousand souls ; and for obvious reasons will not increase much for a considerable time. It is possible, then, that if this plan be persisted in by Congress, ten new votes may be added, without a greater addition of inhabitants than are represented by the single vote of Pennsylvania. The plan, as it respects one of the new States, is already irrevocable ; the sale of the lands having commenced, and the purchasers and settlers will immediately become entitled to all the privileges of the compact.

Mr. BUTLER agreed to the commitment, if the Committee were to be left at liberty. He was persuaded, that, the more the subject was examined, the less it would appear that the number of inhabitants would be a proper rule of proportion. If there were no other objection, the changeableness of the standard would be sufficient. He concurred with those who thought some balance was necessary between the old and the new States. He contended strenuously, that property was the only just measure of representation. This was the great object of government ; the great cause of war ; the great means of carrying it on.

Mr. PINCKNEY saw no good reason for committing. The value of land had been found, on full investigation, to be an impracticable rule. The contributions of revenue, including imports and exports, must be too changeable in their amount ; too difficult to be adjusted ; and too injurious to the non-commercial States. The number of inhabitants appeared to him the only just and practicable rule. He thought the blacks ought to stand on an equality with the whites ; but would agree to the ratio settled by Congress. He contended that Congress had no right, under the Articles of Confederation, to authorize the admission of new States, no such case having been provided for.

Mr. DAVY was for committing the clause, in order to get at the merits of the question arising on the Report. He seemed to think that wealth or property ought to be represented in the second branch; and numbers in the first branch.

On the motion for committing, as made by Mr. GOUVER-NEUR MORRIS, — Massachusetts, Connecticut, Pennsylvania, Virginia, North Carolina, South Carolina, Georgia, aye — 7; New York, New Jersey, Delaware, no — 3; Maryland, divided.

The members appointed by ballot were Mr. GOUVERNEUR MORRIS, Mr. GORHAM, Mr. RANDOLPH, Mr. RUTLEDGE, Mr. KING.

Mr. WILSON signified, that his view in agreeing to the commitment was, that the Committee might consider the propriety of adopting a scale similar to that established by the Constitution of Massachusetts, which would give an advantage to the small States without substantially departing from the rule of proportion.

Mr. WILSON and Mr. MASON moved to postpone the clause relating to money bills, in order to take up the clause relating to an equality of votes in the second branch.

On the question of postponement, — New York, New Jersey, Pennsylvania, Delaware, Maryland, Virginia, South Carolina, Georgia, aye — 8; Massachusetts, Connecticut, North Carolina, no — 3.

The clause relating to equality of votes being under consideration, —

Doctor FRANKLIN observed, that this question could not be properly put by itself, the Committee having reported several propositions as mutual conditions of each other. He could not vote for it if separately taken; but should vote for the whole together.

Colonel MASON perceived the difficulty, and suggested a reference of the rest of the Report to the Committee just appointed, that the whole might be brought into one view.

Mr. RANDOLPH disliked the reference to that Committee, as it consisted of members from States opposed to the wishes of the small States, and could not, therefore, be acceptable to the latter.

Mr. MARTIN and Mr. JENIFER moved to postpone the clause till the Committee last appointed should report.

Mr. MADISON observed, that if the uncommitted part of the Report was connected with the part just committed, it ought also to be committed; if not connected, it need not be postponed till report should be made.

On the question for postponing, moved by Mr. MARTIN and Mr. JENIFER, — Connecticut, New Jersey, Delaware, Maryland, Virginia, Georgia, aye — 6; Pennsylvania, North Carolina, South Carolina, no — 3; Massachusetts, New York, divided.

The first clause, relating to the originating of money bills, was then resumed.

Mr. GOUVERNEUR MORRIS was opposed to a restriction of this right in either branch, considered merely in itself, and as unconnected with the point of representation in the second branch. It will disable the second branch from proposing its own money plans, and give the people an opportunity of judging, by comparison, of the merits of those proposed by the first branch.

Mr. WILSON could see nothing like a concession here, on the part of the smaller States. If both branches were to say *yes* or *no*, it was of little consequence which should say *yes* or *no* first, which last. If either was, indiscriminately, to have the right of originating, the reverse of the Report would, he thought, be most proper ; since it was a maxim, that the least numerous body was the fittest for deliberation — the most numerous, for decision. He ob-

served that this discrimination had been transcribed from
the British into several American Constitutions.   But he
was persuaded that, on examination of the American experiments, it would be found to be a ' trifle light as air.'   Nor
could he ever discover the advantage of it in the parliamentary history of Great Britain.   He hoped, if there was any
advantage in the privilege, that it would be pointed out.

Mr. WILLIAMSON thought that if the privilege were not
common to both branches, it ought rather to be confined to
the second, as the bills in that case would be more narrowly
watched, than if they originated with the branch having
most of the popular confidence.

Mr. MASON. The consideration which weighed with
the Committee was, that the first branch would be the immediate representatives of the people ; the second would
not.   Should the latter have the power of giving away the
people's money, they might soon forget the source from
whence they received it.   We might soon have an aristocracy.   He had been much concerned at the principles
which had been advanced by some gentlemen, but had the
satisfaction to find they did not generally prevail.   He was
a friend to proportional representation in both branches ;
but supposed that some points must be yielded for the sake
of accommodation.

Mr. WILSON.   If he had proposed that the second branch
should have an independent disposal of public money, the
observations of Colonel MASON would have been a satisfactory answer.   But nothing could be farther from what
he had said.   His question was, how is the power of the
first branch increased, or that of the second diminished, by
giving the proposed privilege to the former ?   Where is
the difference, in which branch it begins, if both must concur, in the end ?

Mr. GERRY would not say that the concession was a
sufficient one on the part of the small States.   But he
could not but regard it in the light of a concession.   It
would make it a constitutional principle, that the second

branch were not possessed of the confidence of the people in money matters, which would lessen their weight and influence. In the next place, if the second branch were dispossessed of the privilege, they would be deprived of the opportunity which their continuance in office three times as long as the first branch would give them, of making three successive essays in favor of a particular point.

Mr. PINCKNEY thought it evident that the concession was wholly on one side, that of the large States; the privilege of originating money bills being of no account.

Mr. GOUVERNEUR MORRIS had waited to hear the good effects of the restriction. As to the alarm sounded, of an aristocracy, his creed was that there never was, nor ever will be, a civilized society without an aristocracy. His endeavour was, to keep it as much as possible from doing mischief. The restriction, if it has any real operation, will deprive us of the services of the second branch in digesting and proposing money bills, of which it will be more capable than the first branch. It will take away the responsibility of the second branch, the great security for good behaviour. It will always leave a plea, as to an obnoxious money bill, that it was disliked, but could not be constitutionally amended, nor safely rejected. It will be a dangerous source of disputes between the two Houses. We should either take the British Constitution altogether, or make one for ourselves. The Executive there has dissolved two Houses, as the only cure for such disputes. Will our Executive be able to apply such a remedy? Every law, directly or indirectly, takes money out of the pockets of the people. Again, what use may be made of such a privilege in case of great emergency? Suppose an enemy at the door, and money instantly and absolutely necessary for repelling him, — may not the popular branch avail itself of this duresse, to extort concessions from the Senate, destructive of the Constitution itself? He illustrated this danger by the example of the Long Parliament's expe-

20

dients for subverting the House of Lords; concluding, on the whole, that the restriction would be either useless or pernicious.

Doctor FRANKLIN did not mean to go into a justification of the Report; but as it had been asked what would be the use of restraining the second branch from meddling with money bills, he could not but remark, that it was always of importance that the people should know who had disposed of their money, and how it had been disposed of. It was a maxim, that those who feel, can best judge. This end would, he thought, be best attained, if money affairs were to be confined to the immediate representatives of the people. This was his inducement to concur in the Report. As to the danger or difficulty that might arise from a negative in the second branch, where the people would not be proportionally represented, it might easily be got over by declaring that there should be no such negative; or, if that will not do, by declaring that there be no such branch at all.

Mr. MARTIN said, that it was understood in the Committee, that the difficulties and disputes which had been apprehended should be guarded against in the detailing of the plan.

Mr. WILSON. The difficulties and disputes will increase with the attempts to define and obviate them. Queen Ann was obliged to dissolve her Parliament in order to terminate one of these obstinate disputes between the two houses. Had it not been for the mediation of the Crown, no one can say what the result would have been. The point is still *sub judice* in England. He approved of the principles laid down by the Honourable President* (Doctor FRANKLIN) his colleague, as to the expediency of keeping the people informed of their money affairs. But thought they would know as much, and be as well satisfied, in one way as in the other.

General PINCKNEY was astonished that this point should

---

* He was at that time President of the State of Pennsylvania.

have been considered as a concession. He remarked, that the restriction as to money bills had been rejected on the merits singly considered, by eight* States against three; and that the very States which now called it a concession were then against it, as nugatory or improper in itself.

On the question whether the clause relating to money bills in the Report of the Committee consisting of a member from each State, should stand as part of the Report,— Connecticut, New Jersey, Delaware, Maryland, North Carolina, aye — 5; Pennsylvania, Virginia, South Carolina, no — 3; Massachusetts, New York, Georgia, divided.

A question was then raised, whether the question was carried in the affirmative; there being but five ayes, out of eleven States present. For the words of the Rule, see May 28th.

On this question,— Massachusetts, Connecticut, New Jersey, Pennsylvania, Delaware, Maryland, North Carolina, South Carolina, Georgia, aye — 9; New York, Virginia, no — 2.

(In several preceding instances like votes had *sub silentio* been entered as decided in the affirmative.)

Adjourned.

SATURDAY, JULY 7TH.

In Convention,—The question, shall the clause "allowing each State one vote in the second branch, stand as part of the Report," being taken up,—

Mr. GERRY. This is the critical question. He had rather agree to it than have no accommodation. A Government short of a proper national plan, if generally acceptable, would be preferable to a proper one which, if it could be carried at all, would operate on discontented States. He thought it would be best to suspend this question till the Committee appointed yesterday should make report.

Mr. SHERMAN supposed that it was the wish of every one that some General Government should be established.

An equal vote in the second branch would, he thought, be
most likely to give it the necessary vigor. The small States
have more vigor in their Governments than the large ones;
the more influence therefore the large ones have, the weaker
will be the Government.   In the large States it will be most
difficult to collect the real and fair sense of the people.
Fallacy and undue influence will be practised with most
success; and improper men will most easily get into office.
If they vote by States in the second branch, and each State
has an equal vote, there must be always a majority of
States, as well as a majority of the people, on the side of
public measures, and the Government will have decision
and efficacy.   If this be not the case in the second branch,
there may be a majority of States against public measures;
and the difficulty of compelling them to abide by the public
determination will render the Government feebler than it
has ever yet been.

Mr. WILSON was not deficient in a conciliating temper,
but firmness was sometimes a duty of higher obligation.
Conciliation was also misapplied in this instance.   It was
pursued here rather among the representatives, than among
the constituents; and it would be of little consequence if
not established among the latter; and there could be little
hope of its being established among them, if the foundation should not be laid in justice and right.

On the question, shall the words stand as part of the
Report? — Connecticut, New York, New Jersey, Delaware,
Maryland, North Carolina, aye — 6; Pennsylvania, Virginia,
South Carolina, no — 3; Massachusetts, Georgia, divided.*

Mr. GERRY thought it would be proper to proceed to
enumerate and define the powers to be vested in the General
Government, before a question on the Report should be
taken as to the rule of representation in the second branch.

Mr. MADISON observed that it would be impossible to
say what powers could be safely and properly vested in the

---

* Several votes were given here in the affirmative, or were divided, because
another final question was to be taken on the whole Report.

Government, before it was known in what manner the States were to be represented in it. He was apprehensive that if a just representation were not the basis of the Government, it would happen, as it did when the Articles of Confederation were depending, that every effectual prerogative would be withdrawn or withheld, and the new Government would be rendered as impotent and as short-lived as the old.

Mr. PATTERSON would not decide whether the privilege concerning money bills were a valuable consideration or not; but he considered the mode and rule of representation in the first branch as fully so; and that after the establishment of that point, the small States would never be able to defend themselves without an equality of votes in the second branch. There was no other ground of accommodation. His resolution was fixed. He would meet the large States on that ground, and no other. For himself, he should vote against the Report, because it yielded too much.

Mr. GOUVERNEUR MORRIS. He had no resolution unalterably fixed except to do what should finally appear to him right. He was against the Report because it maintained the improper constitution of the second branch. It made it another Congress, a mere whisp of straw. It had been said (by Mr. GERRY), that the new Government would be partly national, partly federal ; that it ought in the first quality to protect individuals; in the second, the State. But in what quality was it to protect the aggregate interest of the whole? Among the many provisions which had been urged, he had seen none for supporting the dignity and splendor of the American Empire. It had been one of our greatest misfortunes that the great objects of the nation had been sacrificed constantly to local views; in like manner as the general interest of States had been sacrificed to those of the counties. What is to be the check in the Senate? None; unless it be to keep the majority of the people from injuring particular States. But particular States ought to be injured for the sake of a majority of the people, in case their conduct should deserve it. Suppose they should insist on claims evidently unjust, and pursue them in a manner detrimental to the whole body: suppose they should give themselves up to foreign influence: Ought they to be protected in such cases? They were originally nothing more than colonial corporations. On the Declaration of Independence, a Government was to be formed. The small States aware of the necessity of preventing anarchy, and taking advantage of the moment, extorted from the large ones an equality of votes. Standing now on that ground, they demand, under the new system, greater rights, as men, than their fellow-citizens of the large States. The proper answer to them is, that the same necessity of which they formerly took advantage does not now exist; and that the large States are at liberty now to consider what is right, rather than what may be expedient. We must have an efficient Government, and if there be an efficiency in the local Governments, the former is impossible. Germany alone proves it. Notwithstanding their common Diet, notwithstanding the great prerogatives of the Emperor, as head of the Empire, and his vast resources, as sovereign of his particular dominions, no union is maintained; foreign influence disturbs every internal operation, and there is no energy whatever in the general government. Whence does this proceed? From the energy of the local authorities; from its being considered of more consequence to support the Prince of Hesse, than the happiness of the people of Germany. Do gentlemen wish this to be the case here? Good God, Sir, is it possible they can so delude themselves? What if all the Charters and Constitutions of the States were thrown into the fire, and all their demagogues into the ocean — what would it be to the happiness of America? And will not this be the case here, if we pursue the train in which the business lies? We shall establish an Aulic Council, without an Emperor to execute its decrees. The same circumstances which unite the people here unite them in Germany. They have there a common language, a common law, common usages and manners, and a common interest in being united; yet their local jurisdictions destroy every tie. The case was the same in the Grecian states. The United Netherlands are at this time torn in factions. With these examples before our eyes, shall we form establishments which must necessarily produce the same effects? It is of no consequence from what districts the second branch shall be drawn, if it be so constituted as to yield an asylum against these evils. As it is now constituted, he must be against its being drawn from the States in equal portions; but shall be ready to join in devising such an amendment of the plan as will be most likely to secure our liberty and happiness.

Mr. SHERMAN and Mr. ELLSWORTH moved to postpone the question on the Report from the Committee of a member from each State, in order to wait for the Report from the Committee of five last appointed,— Massachusetts, Connecticut, New Jersey, Pennsylvania, Delaware, Maryland, aye —6 ; New York, Virginia, North Carolina, South Carolina, Georgia, no — 5.

Adjourned.

MONDAY, JULY 9TH.

In Convention,— Mr. DANIEL CARROLL, from Maryland, took his seat.

Mr. GOUVERNEUR MORRIS delivered a Report from the Committee of five members, to whom was committed the clause in the Report of the Committee consisting of a member from each State, stating the proper ratio of representatives in the first branch to be as one to every forty thousand inhabitants, as follows, viz : .

" The Committee to whom was referred the first clause of the first proposition reported from the Grand Committee, beg leave to report :

" That in the first meeting of the Legislature the first branch thereof consist of fifty-six members, of which number New Hampshire shall have 2, Massachusetts 7,

Rhode Island 1, Connecticut 4, New York 5, New Jersey 3, Pennsylvania 8, Delaware 1, Maryland 4, Virginia 9, North Carolina 5, South Carolina 5, Georgia 2.

" But as the present situation of the States may probably alter, as well in point of wealth as in the number of their inhabitants, that the Legislature be authorized from time to time to augment the number of Representatives. And in case any of the States shall hereafter be divided, or any two or more States united, or any new States created within the limits of the United States, the Legislature shall possess authority to regulate the number of Representatives in any of the foregoing cases, upon the principles of their wealth and number of inhabitants."

Mr. SHERMAN wished to know, on what principles or calculations the Report was founded. It did not appear to correspond with any rule of numbers, or of any requisition hitherto adopted by Congress.

Mr. GORHAM. Some provision of this sort was necessary in the outset. The number of blacks and whites, with some regard to supposed wealth, was the general guide. Fractions could not be observed. The Legislature is to make alterations from time to time, as justice and propriety may require. Two objections prevailed against the rule of one member for every forty thousand inhabitants. The first was, that the representation would soon be too numerous, the second that the Western States, who may have a different interest, might, if admitted on that principle, by degrees outvote the Atlantic. Both these objections are removed. The number will be small in the first instance, and may be continued so. And the Atlantic States, having the Government in their own hands, may take care of their own interest, by dealing out the right of representation in safe proportions to the Western States. These were the views of the Committee.

Mr. L. MARTIN wished to know whether the Committee were guided in the ratio by the wealth, or number of inhabitants, of the States, or both ; noting its variations from former apportionments by Congress.

Mr. Gouverneur Morris and Mr. Rutledge moved to postpone the first paragraph, relating to the number of members to be allowed to each State in the first instance and to take up the second paragraph, authorizing the Legislature to alter the number from time to time according to wealth and inhabitants. The motion was agreed to, *nem. con.*

On the question on the second paragraph, taken without any debate,— Massachusetts, Connecticut, Pennsylvania, Delaware, Maryland, Virginia, North Carolina, South Carolina, Georgia, aye — 9 ; New York, New Jersey, no — 2.

Mr. Sherman moved to refer the first part, apportioning the representatives, to a Committee of a member from each State.

Mr. Gouverneur Morris seconded the motion ; observing that this was the only case in which such committees were useful.

Mr. Williamson thought it would be necessary to return to the rule of numbers, but that the Western States stood on different footing. If their property should be rated as high as that of the Atlantic States, then their representation ought to hold a like proportion. Otherwise, if their property was not to be equally rated.

Mr. Gouverneur Morris. The Report is little more than a guess. Wealth was not altogether disregarded by the Committee. Where it was apparently in favor of one State whose numbers were superior to the numbers of another, by a fraction only, a member extraordinary was allowed to the former ; and so *vice versa*. The Committee meant little more than to bring the matter to a point for the consideration of the House.

Mr. Read asked, why Georgia was allowed two members, when her number of inhabitants had stood below that of Delaware ?

Mr. Gouverneur Morris. Such is the rapidity of the

population of that State, that before the plan takes effect, it will probably be entitled to two Representatives.

Mr. RANDOLPH disliked the Report of the Committee, but had been unwilling to object to it. He was apprehensive that, as the number was not to be changed, till the National Legislature should please, a pretext would never be wanting to postpone alterations, and keep the power in the hands of those possessed of it. He was in favor of the commitment to a member from each State.

Mr. PATTERSON considered the proposed estimate for the future according to the combined rules of numbers and wealth, as too vague. For this reason New Jersey was against it. He could regard negro slaves in no light but as property. They are no free agents, have no personal liberty, no faculty of acquiring property, but on the contrary are themselves property, and like other property entirely at the will of the master. Has a man in Virginia a number of votes in proportion to the number of his slaves ? and if negroes are not represented in the States to which they belong, why should they be represented in the General Government. What is the true principle of representation ? It is an expedient by which an assembly of certain individuals, chosen by the people, is substituted in place of the inconvenient meeting of the people themselves. If such a meeting of the people was actually to take place, would the slaves vote ? They would not. Why then should they be represented ? He was also against such an indirect encouragement of the slave trade ; observing that Congress, in their Act relating to the change of the eighth Article of Confederation, had been ashamed to use the term "slaves," and had substituted a description.

Mr. MADISON reminded Mr. PATTERSON that his doctrine of representation, which was in its principle the genuine one, must forever silence the pretensions of the small States to an equality of votes with the large ones. They ought to vote in the same proportion in which their citizens would do, if the people of all the States were collectively met. He suggested as a proper ground of compromise, that in the first branch the States should be represented according to their number of free inhabitants; and in the second, which had for one of its primary objects the guardianship of property, according to the whole number, including slaves.

Mr. BUTLER urged warmly the justice and necessity of regarding wealth in the apportionment of representation.

Mr. KING had always expected, that, as the Southern States are the richest, they would not league themselves with the Northern, unless some respect were paid to their superior wealth. If the latter expect those preferential distinctions in commerce, and other advantages which they will derive from the connexion, they must not expect to receive them without allowing some advantages in return. Eleven out of thirteen of the States had agreed to consider slaves in the apportionment of taxation; and taxation and representation ought to go together.

On the question for committing the first paragraph of the Report to a member from each State, — Massachusetts, Connecticut, New Jersey, Pennsylvania, Delaware, Maryland, Virginia, North Carolina, Georgia, aye — 9; New York, South Carolina, no — 2.

The Committee appointed were Messrs. KING, SHERMAN, YATES, BREARLY, GOUVERNEUR MORRIS, READ, CARROLL, MADISON, WILLIAMSON, RUTLEDGE, HOUSTON.

Adjourned.

TUESDAY, JULY 10TH.

In Convention,—Mr. KING reported, from the Committee yesterday appointed, " that the States at the first meeting of the General Legislature, should be represented by sixty-five members, in the following proportions, to wit:— New Hampshire, by 3; Massachusetts, 8; Rhode Island, 1; Connecticut, 5; New York, 6; New Jersey, 4; Pennsylvania,

8; Delaware, 1; Maryland, 6; Virginia, 10; North Carolina, 5; South Carolina, 5; Georgia, 3."

Mr. RUTLEDGE moved that New Hampshire be reduced from three to two members. Her numbers did not entitle her to three, and it was a poor State.

General PINCKNEY seconds the motion.

Mr. KING. New Hampshire has probably more than 120,000 inhabitants, and has an extensive country of tolerable fertility. Its inhabitants may therefore be expected to increase fast. He remarked that the four Eastern States, having 800,000 souls, have one - third fewer representatives than the four Southern States, having not more than 700,-000 souls, rating the blacks as five for three. The Eastern people will advert to these circumstances, and be dissatisfied. He believed them to be very desirous of uniting with their Southern brethren, but did not think it prudent to rely so far on that disposition, as to subject them to any gross inequality. He was fully convinced that the question concerning a difference of interests did not lie where it had hitherto been discussed, between the great and small States; but between the Southern and Eastern. For this reason he had been ready to yield something, in the proportion of representatives, for the security of the Southern. No principle would justify the giving them a majority. They were brought as near an equality as was possible. He was not averse to giving them a still greater security, but did not see how it could be done.

General PINCKNEY. The Report before it was committed was more favorable to the Southern States than as it now stands. If they are to form so considerable a minority, and the regulation of trade is to be given to the General Government, they will be nothing more than overseers for the Northern States. He did not expect the Southern States to be raised to a majority of representatives; but wished them to have something like an equality. At present, by the alterations of the Committee in favor of the Northern States, they are removed further from it than they were before. One member indeed had been added to Virginia, which he was glad of, as he considered her as a Southern State. He was glad also that the members of Georgia were increased.

Mr. WILLIAMSON was not for reducing New Hampshire from three to two, but for reducing some others. The Southern interest must be extremely endangered by the present arrangement. The Northern States are to have a majority in the first instance, and the means of perpetuating it.

Mr. DAYTON observed, that the line between Northern and Southern interest had been improperly drawn; that Pennsylvania was the dividing State, there being six on each side of her.

General PINCKNEY urged the reduction; dwelt on the superior wealth of the Southern States, and insisted on its having its due weight in the Government.

Mr. GOUVERNEUR MORRIS regretted the turn of the debate. The States, he found, had many representatives on the floor. Few, he feared, were to be deemed the Representatives of America. He thought the Southern States have, by the Report, more than their share of representation. Property ought to have its weight, but not all the weight. If the Southern States are to supply money, the Northern States are to spill their blood. Besides, the probable revenue to be expected from the Southern States has been greatly overrated. He was against reducing New Hampshire.

Mr. RANDOLPH was opposed to a reduction of New Hampshire, not because she had a full title to three members; but because it was in his contemplation, first, to make it the duty, instead of leaving it to the discretion, of the Legislature to regulate the representation by a periodical census; secondly, to require more than a bare majority of votes in the Legislature, in certain cases, and particularly in commercial cases.

On the question for reducing New Hampshire from

three to two Representatives, it passed in the negative,—
North Carolina,* South Carolina, aye — 2; Massachusetts,
Connecticut, New Jersey, Pennsylvania, Delaware, Mary-
land, Virginia, Georgia,* no — 8.

General PINCKNEY and Mr. ALEXANDER MARTIN moved
that six Representatives, instead of five, be allowed to North
Carolina.

On the question it passed in the negative,— North Carolina, South Carolina, Georgia, aye — 3; Massachusetts,
Connecticut, New Jersey, Pennsylvania, Delaware, Maryland, Virginia, no — 7.

General PINCKNEY and Mr. BUTLER made the same motion in favor of South Carolina.

On the question, it passed in the negative,— Delaware,
North Carolina, South Carolina, Georgia, aye — 4; Massachusetts, Connecticut, New York, New Jersey, Pennsylvania, Maryland, Virginia, no — 7.

General PINCKNEY and Mr. HOUSTON moved that Georgia be allowed four instead of three Representatives; urging the unexampled celerity of its population.

On the question, it passed in the negative,— Virginia,
North Carolina, South Carolina, Georgia, aye — 4; Massachusetts, Connecticut, New York, New Jersey, Pennsylvania, Delaware, Maryland, no — 7.

.Mr. MADISON moved that the number allowed to each
State be doubled. A *majority* of a *Quorum* of sixty-five
members was too small a number to represent the whole inhabitants of the United States. They would not possess
enough of the confidence of the people, and would be too
sparsely taken from the people, to bring with them all the
local information which would be frequently wanted.
Double the number will not be too great, even with the
future additions from the new States. The additional expense
was too inconsiderable to be regarded in so important a
case. And as far as the augmentation might be unpopular

---

* In the printed Journal, North Carolina, no; Georgia, aye.

on that score, the objection was overbalanced by its effect on the hopes of a greater number of the popular candidates.

Mr. ELLSWORTH urged the objection of expense; and that the greater the number, the more slowly would the business proceed; and the less probably be decided as it ought, at last. He thought the number of representatives too great in most of the State Legislatures; and that a large number was less necessary in the General Legislature, than in those of the States; as its business would relate to a few great national objects only.

Mr. SHERMAN would have preferred fifty to sixty-five. The great distance they will have to travel will render their attendance precarious, and will make it difficult to prevail on a sufficient number of fit men to undertake the service. He observed that the expected increase from new States also deserved consideration.

Mr. GERRY was for increasing the number beyond sixty-five. The larger the number, the less the danger of their being corrupted. The people are accustomed to, and fond of, a numerous representation; and will consider their rights as better secured by it. The danger of excess in the number may be guarded against by fixing a point within which the number shall always be kept.

Colonel MASON admitted, that the objection drawn from the consideration of expense had weight both in itself, and as the people might be affected by it. But he thought it outweighed by the objections against the smallness of the number. Thirty-eight will, he supposes, as being a majority of sixty-five, form a quorum. Twenty will be a majority of thirty-eight. This was certainly too small a number to make laws for America. They would neither bring with them all the necessary information relative to various local interests, nor possess the necessary confidence of the people. After doubling the number, the laws might still be made by so few as almost to be objectionable on that account.

Mr. READ was in favor of the motion. Two of the

States (Delaware and Rhode Island) would have but a single member if the aggregate number should remain at sixty-five; and in case of accident to either of these, one State would have no Representative present to give explanations or informations of its interests or wishes. The people would not place their confidence in so small a number. He hoped the objects of the General Government would be much more numerous than seemed to be expected by some gentlemen, and that they would become more and more so. As to the new States, the highest number of Representatives for the whole might be limited, and all danger of excess thereby prevented. Mr. RUTLEDGE opposed the motion. The Representatives were too numerous in all the States. The full-number allotted to the States may be expected to attend, and the lowest possible quorum should not therefore be considered. The interests of their constituents will urge their attendance too strongly for it to be omitted: and he supposed the General Legislature would not sit more than six or eight weeks in the year.

On the question for doubling the number, it passed in the negative, — Delaware, Virginia, aye — 2; Massachusetts, Connecticut,. New York, New Jersey, Pennsylvania, Maryland, North Carolina, South Carolina, Georgia, no — 9.

On the question for agreeing to the apportionment of Representatives, as amended by the last Committee, it passed in the affirmative, — Massachusetts, Connecticut, New York, New Jersey, Pennsylvania, Delaware, Maryland, Virginia, North Carolina, aye — 9; South Carolina, Georgia, no — 2.

Mr. BROOM gave notice to the House, that he had concurred with a reserve to himself of an intention to claim for his State an equal voice in the second branch ; which he thought could not be denied after this concession of the the small States as to the first branch.

Mr. RANDOLPH moved, as an amendment to the Report of the Committee of five, " that in order to ascertain the alterations in the population and wealth of the several

States, the Legislature should be required to cause a census and estimate to be taken within one year after its first meeting ; and every —— years thereafter ; and that the Legislature arrange the representation accordingly."

Mr. GOUVERNEUR MORRIS opposed it, as fettering the Legislature too much. Advantage may be taken of it in time of war or the apprehension of it, by new States to extort particular favors. If the mode was to be fixed for taking a census, it might certainly be extremely inconvenient : if unfixed, the Legislature may use such a mode as will defeat the object ; and perpetuate the inequality. He was always against such shackles on the Legislature. They had been found very pernicious in most of the State Constitutions. He dwelt much on the danger of throwing such a preponderance into the western scale ; suggesting that in time the western people would outnumber the Atlantic States. He wished therefore to put it in the power of the latter to keep a majority of votes in their own hands. It was objected, he said, that, if the Legislature are left at liberty, they will never re-adjust the representation. He admitted that this was possible, but he did not think it probable, unless the reasons against a revision of it were very urgent ; and in this case, it ought not to be done.

It was moved to postpone the proposition of Mr. RANDOLPH, in order to take up the following, viz : " that the Committee of eleven, to whom was referred the Report of the Committee of five on the subject of Representation, be requested to furnish the Convention with the principles on which they grounded the report ;" which was disagreed to,— South Carolina alone voting in the affirmative.

Adjourned.

WEDNESDAY, JULY 11TH.

In Convention,— Mr. RANDOLPH's motion, requiring the Legislature to take a periodical census for the purpose of redressing inequalities in the representation was resumed.

21

Mr. SHERMAN was against shackling the Legislature too much. We ought to choose wise and good men, and then confide in them.

Mr. MASON. The greater the difficulty we find in fixing a proper rule of representation, the more unwilling ought we be to throw the task from ourselves on the General Legislature. He did not object to the conjectural ratio which was to prevail in the outset ; but considered a revision from time to time, according to some permanent and precise standard, as essential to the fair representation required in the first branch. According to the present population of America, the northern part of it had a right to preponderate, and he could not deny it. But he wished it not to preponderate hereafter, when the reason no longer continued. From the nature of man, we may be sure that those who have power in their hands will not give it up, while they can retain it. On the contrary, we know that they will always, when they can, rather increase it. If the Southern States, therefore, should have three-fourths of the people of America within their limits, the Northern will hold fast the majority of Representatives. One-fourth will govern the three-fourths. The Southern States will complain, but they may complain from generation to generation without redress. Unless some principle, therefore, which will do justice to them hereafter, shall be inserted in the Constitution, disagreeable as the declaration was to him, he must declare he could neither vote for the system here, nor support it in his State. Strong objections had been drawn from the danger to the Atlantic interests from new Western States. Ought we to sacrifice what we know to be right in itself, lest it should prove favourable to States which are not yet in existence ? If the Western States are to be admitted into the Union, as they arise, they must, he would repeat, be treated as equals, and subjected to no degrading discriminations. They will have the same pride, and other passions, which we have ; and will either not unite with, or will speedily revolt from, the Union, if they are not in all

respects placed on an equal footing with their brethren.   It
has been said, they will be poor, and unable to make equal
contributions to the general treasury.   He did not know
but that, in time, they would be both more numerous and
more wealthy, than their Atlantic brethren.   The extent
and fertility of their soil made this probable; and though
Spain might for a time deprive them of the natural outlet
for their productions, yet she will, because she must, finally
yield to their demands.   He urged that numbers of inhabitants, though not always a precise standard of wealth, was
sufficiently so for every substantial purpose.

Mr. WILLIAMSON was for making it a duty of the Legislature to do what was right, and not leaving it at liberty to
do or not to do it.   He moved that Mr. RANDOLPH's propositions be postponed, in order to consider the following,
" that in order to ascertain the alterations that may happen
in the population and wealth of the States, a census shall be
taken of the free white inhabitants, and three-fifths of those
of other descriptions on the first year after this government
shall have been adopted, and every ———— year thereafter;
and that the representation be regulated accordingly."

Mr. RANDOLPH agreed that Mr. WILLIAMSON's proposition should stand in place of his.   He observed that the
ratio fixed for the first meeting was a mere conjecture; that
it placed the power in the hands of that part of America
which could not always be entitled to it; that this power
would not be voluntarily renounced; and that it was consequently the duty of the Convention to secure its renuncia-
tion, when justice might so require, by some constitutional
provisions.   If equality between great and small States be
inadmissible, because in that case unequal numbers of constituents would be represented by equal numbers of votes,
was it not equally inadmissible, that a larger and more
populous district of America should hereafter have less
representation than a smaller and less populous district? If
a fair representation of the people be not secured, the injustice of the Government will shake it to its foundations.

What relates to suffrage, is justly stated by the celebrated Montesquieu as a fundamental article in Republican Governments. If the danger suggested by Mr. GOUVERNEUR MORRIS be real, of advantage being taken of the Legislature in pressing moments, it was an additional reason for tying their hands in such a manner, that they could not sacrifice their trust to momentary considerations. Congress have pledged the public faith to new States, that they shall be admitted on equal terms. They never would, nor ought to, accede on any other. The census must be taken under the direction of the General Legislature. The States will be too much interested, to take an impartial one for themselves.

. Mr. BUTLER and General PINCKNEY insisted that blacks be included in the rule of representation *equally* with the whites; and for that purpose moved that the words "three-fifths " be struck out.

Mr. GERRY thought that three-fifths of them was, to say the least, the full proportion that could be admitted.

Mr. GORHAM. This ratio was fixed by Congress as a rule of taxation. Then, it was urged, by the Delegates representing the States having slaves, that the blacks were still more inferior to freemen. At present, when the ratio of representation is to be established, we are assured that they are equal to freemen. The arguments on the former occasion had convinced him, that three-fifths was pretty near the just proportion, and he should vote according to the same opinion now.

Mr. BUTLER insisted that the labor of a slave in South Carolina was as productive and valuable, as that of a freeman in Massachusetts; that as wealth was the great means of defence and utility to the nation, they were equally valuable to it with freemen; and that consequently an equal representation ought to be allowed for them in a government which was instituted principally for the protection of property, and was itself to be supported by property.

Mr. MASON could not agree to the motion, notwithstand-

ing it was favourable to Virginia, because he thought it unjust.   It was certain that the slaves were valuable, as they
raised the value of land, increased the exports and imports,
and of course the revenue, would supply the means of feed-
ing and supporting an army, and might in cases of emergency become themselves soldiers.   As in these important
respects they were useful to the community at large, they
ought not to be excluded from the estimate of representation.   He could not, however, regard them as equal to freemen, and could not vote for them as such.   He added, as
worthy of remark, that the Southern States have this peculiar species of property, over and above the other species of
property common to all the States.

Mr. WILLIAMSON reminded Mr. GORHAM that if the
Southern States contended for the inferiority of blacks to
whites when taxation was in view, the Eastern States, on
the same occasion, contended for their equality.   He did
not, however, either then or now, concur in either extreme,
but approved of the ratio of three - fifths.

On Mr. BUTLER's motion, for considering blacks as
equal to whites in the apportionment of representation, —
Delaware, South Carolina, Georgia, aye — 3; Massachusetts,
Connecticut, New Jersey, Pennsylvania, Maryland, Virginia,
North Carolina, no — 7; New York, not on the floor.

Mr. GOUVERNEUR MORRIS said he had several objections
to the proposition of Mr. WILLIAMSON.   In the first place,
it fettered the Legislature too much.   In the second place,
it would exclude some States altogether who would not
have a sufficient number to entitle them to a single representation.   In the third place, it will not consist with the
resolution passed on Saturday last, authorizing the Legislature to adjust the representation from time to time on the
principles of population and wealth; nor with the principles of equity.   If slaves were to be considered as inhabitants, not as wealth, then the said Resolution would not be
pursued; if as wealth, then why is no other wealth but
slaves included?   These objections may perhaps be removed

by amendments. His great objection was, that the number
of inhabitants was not a proper standard of wealth. The
amazing difference between the comparative numbers and
wealth of different countries rendered all reasoning superfluous on the subject. Numbers might with greater propriety be deemed a measure of strength, than of wealth;
yet the late defence made by Great Britain, against her
numerous enemies proved, in the clearest manner, that it is
entirely fallacious even in this respect.

Mr. KING thought there was great force in the objections
of Mr. GOUVERNEUR MORRIS. He would, however, accede
to the proposition for the sake of doing something.

Mr. RUTLEDGE contended for the admission of wealth
in the estimate by which representation should be regulated. The Western States will not be able to contribute in
proportion to their numbers; they should not therefore be
represented in that proportion. The Atlantic States will
not concur in such a plan. He moved that, " at the end of
—— years after the first meeting of the Legislature, and
of every —— years thereafter, the Legislature shall proportion the representation according to the principles of
wealth and population."

Mr. SHERMAN thought the number of people alone the
best rule for measuring wealth as well as representation;
and that if the Legislature were to be governed by wealth,
they would be obliged to estimate it by numbers. He was
at first for leaving the matter wholly to the discretion of
the Legislature; but he had been convinced by the observation of (Mr. RANDOLPH and Mr. MASON), that the *periods*
and the *rule,* of revising the representation, ought to be
fixed by the Constitution.

Mr. READ thought, the Legislature ought not to be too
much shackled. It would make the Constitution like
religious creeds, embarrassing to those bound to conform
to them, and more likely to produce dissatisfaction and
schism, than harmony and union.

Mr. MASON objected to Mr. RUTLEDGE's motion, as requiring of the Legislature something too indefinite and impracticable, and leaving them a pretext for doing nothing.

Mr. WILSON had himself no objection to leaving the Legislature entirely at liberty, but considered wealth as an impracticable rule.

Mr. GORHAM. If the Convention, who are comparatively so little biassed by local views, are so much perplexed, how can it be expected that the Legislature hereafter, under the full bias of those views will be able to settle a standard? He was convinced, by the arguments of others and his own reflections, that the Convention ought to fix some standard or other.

Mr. GOUVERNEUR MORRIS. The argument of others and his own reflections had led him to a very different conclusion. If we cannot agree on a rule that will be just at this time, how can we expect to find one that will be just in all times to come? Surely those who come after us will judge better of things present, than we can of things future. He could not persuade himself that numbers would be a just rule at any time. The remarks of (Mr. MASON) relative to the Western country had not changed his opinion on that head. Among other objections, it must be apparent, they would not be able to furnish men equally enlightened, to share in the administration of our common interests. The busy haunts of men, not the remote wilderness, was the proper school of political talents. If the western people get the power into their hands, they will ruin the Atlantic interests. The back members are always most averse to the best measures. He mentioned the case of Pennsylvania formerly. The lower part of the State had the power in the first instance. They kept it in their own hands, and the country was the better for it. Another objection with him, against admitting the blacks into the census, was, that the people of Pennsylvania would revolt at the idea of being put on a footing with slaves. They would reject any plan that was to have such an effect. Two objections had been raised against leaving the adjustment of the representation, from time to time, to the discretion of the Legislature. The first was, they would be unwilling to revise it at all. The second, that, by referring to *wealth*, they would be bound by a rule which, if willing, they would be unable to execute. The first objection distrusts their fidelity. But if their duty, their honor, and their oaths, will not bind them, let us not put into their hands our liberty, and all our other great interests; let us have no government at all. In the second place, if these ties will bind them, we need not distrust the practicability of the rule. It was followed in part by the Committee in the apportionment of Representatives yesterday reported to the House. The best course that could be taken would be to leave the interests of the people to the representatives of the people.

Mr. MADISON was not a little surprised to hear this implicit confidence urged by a member who, on all occasions, had inculcated so strongly the political depravity of men, and the necessity of checking one vice and interest by opposing to them another vice and interest. If the representatives of the people would be bound by the ties he had mentioned, what need was there of a Senate? What of a revisionary power? But his reasoning was not only inconsistent with his former reasoning, but with itself. At the same time that he recommended this implicit confidence to the Southern States in the Northern majority, he was still more zealous in exhorting all to a jealousy of a western majority. To reconcile the gentleman with himself, it must be imagined that he determined the human character by the points of the compass. The truth was, that all men having power ought to be distrusted, to a certain degree. The case of Pennsylvania had been mentioned, where it was admitted that those who were possessed of the power in the original settlement never admitted the new settlements to a due share of it. England was a still more striking example. The power there had long been in the hands of the boroughs — of the minority — who had opposed_and defeated every reform which had been attempted. Virginia was, in a less degree, another example. With regard to the Western States, he was clear and firm in opinion, that no unfavourable distinctions were admissible, either in point of justice or policy. He thought also, that the hope of contributions to the Treasury from them had been much underrated. Future contributions, it seemed to be understood on all hands, would be principally levied on imports and exports. The extent and fertility of the Western soil would for a long time give to agriculture a preference over manufactures. Trials would be repeated till some articles could be raised from it, that would bear a transportation to places where they could be exchanged for imported manufactures. Whenever the Mississippi should be opened to them, which would of necessity be the case as soon as their population would subject them to any considerable share of the public burden, imposts on their trade could be collected with less expense, and greater certainty, than on that of the Atlantic States. In the mean time, as their supplies must pass through the *Atlantic States*, their contributions would be levied in the same manner with those of the Atlantic States. He could not agree that any substantial objection lay against fixing numbers for the perpetual standard of representation. It was said, that representation and taxation were to go together; that taxation and wealth ought to go together; that population and wealth were not measures of each other. He admitted that in different climates, under different forms of government, and in different stages of civilization, the inference was perfectly just. He would admit that in no situation numbers of inhabitants were an accurate measure of wealth. He contended, however, that in the United States it was sufficiently so for the object in contemplation. Although their climate varied considerably, yet as the governments, the laws, and the manners of all, were nearly the same, and the intercourse between different parts perfectly free, population, industry, arts, and the value of labor, would constantly tend to equalize themselves. The value of labor might be considered as the principal criterion of wealth and ability to support taxes; and this would find its level in different places, where the intercourse should be easy and free, with as much certainty as the value of money or any other thing. Whereever labor would yield most, people would resort; till the competition should destroy the inequality. Hence it is that the people are constantly swarming from the more, to the less, populous places — from Europe to America — from the Northern and middle parts of the United States to the Southern and Western. They go where land is cheaper, because there labor is dearer. If it be true that the same quantity of produce raised on the banks of the Ohio is of less value than on the Delaware, it is also true that the same labor will raise twice or thrice the quantity in the former, that it will raise in the latter situation.

Colonel MASON agreed with Mr. G. MORRIS, that we ought to leave the interests of the people to the representatives of the people ; but the objection was, that the Legislature would cease to be the representatives of the people. It would continue so no longer than the States now containing a majority of the people should retain that majority. As soon as the southern and western population should predominate, which must happen in a few years, the power would be in the hands of the minority, and would never be yielded to the majority, unless provided for by the Constitution.

On the question for postponing Mr. WILLIAMSON's motion, in order to consider that of Mr. RUTLEDGE, it passed in the negative,— Massachusetts, Pennsylvania, Delaware, South Carolina, Georgia, aye — 5 ; Connecticut, New Jersey, Maryland, Virginia, North Carolina, no — 5.

On the question on the first clause of Mr. WILLIAMSON's motion, as to taking a census of the *free* inhabitants, it passed in the affirmative,— Massachusetts, Connecticut,

New Jersey, Pennsylvania, Virginia, North Carolina, aye —
6 ; Delaware, Maryland, South Carolina, Georgia, no — 4.

The next clause as to three-fifths of the negroes being
considered,—

Mr. KING, being much opposed to fixing numbers as
the rule of representation, was particularly so on account
of the blacks. He thought the admission of them along
with whites at all, would excite great discontent among
the States having no slaves. He had never said, as to any
particular point, that he would in no event acquiesce in and
support it ; but he would say that if in any case such a
declaration was to be made by him, it would be in this.
He remarked that in the temporary allotment of representatives made by the Committee, the Southern States had
received more than the number of their white and three-
fifths of their black inhabitants entitled them to.

Mr. SHERMAN. South Carolina had no more beyond
her proportion than New York and New Hampshire ; nor
either of them more than was necessary in order to avoid
fractions, or reducing them below their proportion.
Georgia had more ; but the rapid growth of that State
seemed to justify it. In general the allotment might not
be just, but considering all circumstances he was satisfied
with it.

Mr. GORHAM supported the propriety of establishing
numbers as the rule. He said that in Massachusetts estimates had been taken in the different towns, and that
persons had been curious enough to compare these estimates with the respective numbers of people; and it had
been found, even including Boston, that the most exact
proportion prevailed between numbers and property. He
was aware that there might be some weight in what had
fallen from his colleague, as to the umbrage which might be
taken by the people of the Eastern States. But he recollected that when the proposition of Congress for changing
the eighth Article of the Confederation was before the
Legislature of Massachusetts, the only difficulty then was,

to satisfy them that the negroes ought not to have been counted equally with the whites, instead of being counted in the ratio of three-fifths only.*

Mr. WILSON did not well see, on what principle the admission of blacks in the proportion of three-fifths could be explained. Are they admitted as citizens — then why are they not admitted on an equality with white citizens? Are they admitted as property — then why is not other property admitted into the computation? These were difficulties, however, which he thought must be overruled by the necessity of compromise. He had some apprehensions also, from the tendency of the blending of the blacks with the whites, to give disgust to the people of Pennsylvania, as had been intimated by his colleague (Mr. GOUVERNEUR MORRIS). But he differed from him in thinking numbers of inhabitants so incorrect a measure of wealth. He had seen the western settlements of Pennsylvania, and on a comparison of them with the city of Philadelphia could discover little other difference, than that property was more unequally divided here than there. Taking the same number in the aggregate, in the two situations, he believed there would be little difference in their wealth and ability to contribute to the public wants.

Mr. GOUVERNEUR MORRIS was compelled to declare himself reduced to the dilemma of doing injustice to the Southern States, or to human nature; and he must therefore do it to the former. For he could never agree to give such encouragement to the slave trade, as would be given by allowing them a representation for their negroes; and he did not believe those States would ever confederate on terms that would deprive them of that trade.

On the question for agreeing to include three-fifths of the blacks,— Connecticut, Virginia, North Carolina, Georgia, aye — 4; Massachusetts, New Jersey, Pennsylvania, Delaware, Maryland,† South Carolina, no — 6.

---

* They were then to have been a rule of taxation only.

† Mr. Carroll said, in explanation of the vote of Maryland, that he wished the

On the question as to taking the census "the first year after the meeting of the Legislature,"— Massachusetts, New Jersey, Pennsylvania, Delaware, Virginia, North Carolina, South Carolina, aye — 7; Connecticut, Maryland, Georgia, no — 3.

On filling the blank for the periodical census with fifteen years,— agreed to, *nem. con.*

Mr. MADISON moved to add, after "fifteen years," the words "at least," that the Legislature might anticipate when circumstances were likely to render a particular year inconvenient.

On this motion, for adding "at least," it passed in the negative, the States being equally divided,— Massachusetts, Virginia, North Carolina, South Carolina, Georgia, aye — 5; Connecticut, New Jersey, Pennsylvania, Delaware, Maryland, no — 5.

A change in the phraseology of the other clause, so as to read, "and the Legislature shall alter or augment the representation accordingly," was agreed to, *nem. con.*

On the question on the whole resolution of Mr. WILLIAMSON, as amended,— Massachusetts, Connecticut, New Jersey, Delaware Maryland, Virginia, North Carolina, South Carolina, Georgia, no — 9; so it was rejected unanimously.

Adjourned.

THURSDAY, JULY 12TH.

In Convention,— Mr. GOUVERNEUR MORRIS moved to add to the clause empowering the Legislature to vary the representation according to the principles of wealth and numbers of inhabitants, a proviso, "that taxation shall be in proportion to representation."

Mr. BUTLER contended again, that representation should be according to the full number of inhabitants, including

---

phraseology to be so altered as to obviate, if possible, the danger which had been expressed of giving umbrage to the Eastern and Middle States.

all the blacks; admitting the justice of Mr. GOUVERNEUR MORRIS's motion.

Mr. MASON also admitted the justice of the principle, but was afraid embarrassments might be occasioned to the Legislature by it. It might drive the Legislature to the plan of requisitions.

Mr. GOUVERNEUR MORRIS admitted that some objections lay against his motion, but supposed they would be removed by restraining the rule to *direct* taxation. With regard to indirect taxes on *exports* and imports, and on consumption, the rule would be inapplicable. Notwithstanding what had been said to the contrary, he was persuaded that the imports and consumption were pretty nearly equal throughout the Union.

General PINCKNEY liked the idea. He thought it so just that it could not be objected to; but foresaw, that, if the revision of the census was left to the discretion of the Legislature, it would never be carried into execution. The rule must be fixed, and the execution of it enforced, by the Constitution. He was alarmed at what was said* yesterday, concerning the negroes. He was now again alarmed at what had been thrown out concerning the taxing of exports. South Carolina has in one year exported to the amount of £600,000 sterling, all which was the fruit of the labor of her blacks. Will she be represented in proportion to this amount? She will not. Neither ought she then to be subject to a tax on it. He hoped a clause would be inserted in the system, restraining the Legislature from taxing exports.

Mr. WILSON approved the principle, but could not see how it could be carried into execution; unless restrained to direct taxation.

Mr. GOUVERNEUR MORRIS having so varied his motion by inserting the word "direct," it passed *nem. con.*, as follows: "provided always that direct taxation ought to be proportioned to representation."

---

* By Mr. GOUVERNEUR MORRIS.

Mr. DAVIE said it was high time now to speak out. He saw that it was meant by some gentlemen to deprive the Southern States of any share of representation for their blacks. He was sure that North Carolina would never confederate on any terms that did not rate them at least as three - fifths. If the Eastern States meant, therefore, to exclude them altogether, the business was at an end.

Doctor JOHNSON thought that wealth and population were the true, equitable rules of representation; but he conceived that these two principles resolved themselves into one, population being the best measure of wealth. He concluded, therefore, that the number of people ought to be established as the rule, and that all descriptions, including blacks *equally* with the whites, ought to fall within the computation. As various opinions had been expressed on the subject, he would move that a committee might be appointed to take them into consideration, and report them.

Mr. GOUVERNEUR MORRIS. It had been said that it is high time to speak out. As one member, he would candidly do so. He came here to form a compact for the good of America. He was ready to do so with all the States. He hoped, and believed, that all would enter into such a compact. If they would not, he was ready to join with any States that would. But as the compact was to be voluntary, it is in vain for the Eastern States to insist on what the Southern States will never agree to. It is equally vain for the latter to require, what the other States can never admit; and he verily believed the people of Pennsylvania will never agree to a representation of negroes. What can be desired by these States more than has been already proposed — that the Legislature shall from time to time regulate representation according to population and wealth?

General PINCKNEY desired that the rule of wealth should be ascertained, and not left to the pleasure of the Legislature; and that property in slaves should not be exposed to danger, under a government instituted for the protection of property.

The first clause in the Report of the first Grand Committee was postponed.

Mr. ELLSWORTH, in order to carry into effect the principle established, moved to add to the last clause adopted by the House the words following, " and that the rule of contribution by direct taxation, for the support of the Government of the United States, shall be the number of white inhabitants, and three-fifths of every other description in the several States, until some other rule that shall more accurately ascertain the wealth of the several States can be devised and adopted by the Legislature."

Mr. BUTLER seconded the motion, in order that it might be committed.

Mr. RANDOLPH was not satisfied with the motion. The danger will be revived, that the ingenuity of the Legislature may evade or pervert the rule, so as to perpetuate the power where it shall be lodged in the first instance. He proposed, in lieu of Mr. ELLSWORTH's motion, " that in order to ascertain the alterations in representation that may be required, from time to time, by changes in the relative circumstances of the States, a census shall be taken within two years from the first meeting of the General Legislature of the United States, and once within the term of every —— years afterwards, of all the inhabitants, in the manner and according to the ratio recommended by Congress, in their Resolution of the eighteenth day of April, 1783, (rating the blacks at three - fifths of their number); and that the Legislature of the United States shall arrange the representation accordingly." He urged strenuously that express security ought to be provided for including slaves in the ratio of representation. He lamented that such a species of property existed. But as it did exist, the holders of it would require this security. It was perceived that the design was entertained by some of excluding slaves altogether; the Legislature therefore ought not to be left at liberty.

Mr. ELLSWORTH withdraws his motion, and seconds that of Mr. RANDOLPH.

Mr. WILSON observed, that less umbrage would perhaps be taken against an admission of the slaves into the rule of representation, if it should be so expressed as to make them indirectly only an ingredient in the rule, by saying that they should enter into the rule of taxation; and as representation was to be according to taxation, the end would be equally attained. He accordingly moved, and was seconded, so to alter the last clause adopted by the House, that, together with the amendment proposed, the whole should read as follows: " provided always that the representation ought to be proportioned according to direct taxation; and in order to ascertain the alterations in the direct taxation which may be required from time to time by the changes in the relative circumstances of the States, *Resolved,* that a census be taken within two years from the first meeting of the Legislature of the United States, and once within the term of every —— years afterwards, of all the inhabitants of the United States, in the manner and according to the ratio recommended by Congress in their Resolution of the eighteenth day of April, 1783; and that the Legislature of the United States shall proportion the direct taxation accordingly."

Mr. KING. Although this amendment varies the aspect somewhat, he had still two powerful objections against tying down the Legislature to the rule of numbers, — first, they were at this time an uncertain index of the relative wealth of the States; secondly, if they were a just index at this time, it cannot be supposed always to continue so. He was far from wishing to retain any unjust advantage whatever in one part of the Republic. If justice was not the basis of the connection, it could not be of long duration. He must be short-sighted indeed who does not foresee, that, whenever the Southern States shall be more numerous than the Northern, they can and will hold a language that will awe them into justice. If they threaten to separate now in case

22

injury shall be done them, will their threats be less urgent
or effectual when force shall back their demands.   Even in
the intervening period, there will be no point of time at
which they will not be able to say, do us justice or we will
separate.   He urged the necessity of placing confidence to
a certain degree in every government, and did not conceive
that the proposed confidence, as to a periodical re-adjust-
ment of the representation, exceeded that degree.

Mr. PINCKNEY moved to amend Mr. RANDOLPH'S motion,
so as to make "blacks equal to the whites in the ratio of
representation."   This he urged was nothing more than
justice.   The blacks are the laborers, the peasants, of
the Southern States.   They are as productive of pecuniary
resources as those of the Northern States.   They add
equally to the wealth, and, considering money as the sinew
of war, to the strength, of the nation.   It will also be politic
with regard to the Northern States, as taxation is to keep
pace with representation.

General PINCKNEY moves to insert six years instead of
two, as the period, computing from the first meeting of the
Legislature, within which the first census should be taken.
On this question for inserting six years, instead of "two,"
in the proposition of Mr. WILSON, it passed in the affirma-
tive,— Connecticut, New Jersey, Pennsylvania, Maryland,
South Carolina, aye — 5 ; Massachusetts, Virginia, North
Carolina, Georgia, no — 4 ; Delaware, divided.

On the question for filling the blank for the periodical
census with twenty years, it passed in the negative,— Connecticut, New Jersey, Pennsylvania, aye — 3 ; Massachu·
setts, Delaware, Maryland, Virginia, North Carolina, South
Carolina, Georgia, no — 7.

On the question for ten years, it passed in the affirmative,— Massachusetts, Pennsylvania, Delaware, Maryland,
Virginia, North Carolina, South Carolina, Georgia, aye —
8 ; Connecticut, New Jersey, no — 2.

On Mr. PINCKNEY'S motion, for rating blacks as equal
to whites, instead of as three-fifths,— South Carolina,

Georgia, aye — 2 ; Massachusetts, Connecticut (Doctor JOHNSON, aye), New Jersey, Pennsylvania (three against two), Delaware, Maryland, Virginia, North Carolina, no — 8.

Mr. RANDOLPH'S proposition, as varied by Mr WILSON, being read for taking the question on the whole, —

Mr. GERRY urged that the principle of it could not be carried into execution, as the States were not to be taxed as States. With regard to taxes on imposts, he conceived they would be no more productive where there were no slaves, than where there were ; the consumption being greater.

Mr ELLSWORTH. In case of a poll-tax there would be no difficulty. But there would probably be none. The sum allotted to a State may be levied without difficulty, according to the plan used by the State in raising its own supplies.

On the question on the whole proposition, as proportioning representation to direct taxation, and both to the white and three-fifths of the black inhabitants, and requiring a census within six years, and within every ten years afterwards, — Connecticut, Pennsylvania, Maryland, Virginia, North Carolina, Georgia, aye — 6 ; New Jersey, Delaware, no — 2 ; Massachusetts, South Carolina, divided.

Adjourned.

FRIDAY, JULY 13TH.

In Convention, — It being moved to postpone the clause in the Report of the Committee of Eleven as to the originating of money bills in the *first* branch, in order to take up the following, "that in the second branch each State shall have an equal voice," —

Mr. GERRY moved to add, as an amendment to the last clause agreed to by the house, " that from the first meeting of the Legislature of the United States till a census shall be taken, all moneys to be raised for supplying the public Treasury by direct taxation shall be assessed on the inhabitants of the several States according to the number of their Representatives respectively in the first branch." He said this would be as just before as after the census, according to the general principle that taxation and representation ought to go together.

Mr. WILLIAMSON feared that New Hampshire will have reason to complain. Three members were allotted to her as a liberal allowance, for this reason among others, that she might not suppose any advantage to have been taken of her absence. As she was still absent, and had no opportunity of deciding whether she would choose to retain the number on the condition of her being taxed in proportion to it, he thought the number ought to be reduced from three to two, before the question was taken on Mr. GERRY's motion.

Mr. READ could not approve of the proposition. He had observed, he said, in the Committee a backwardness in some of the members from the large States, to take their full proportion of Representatives. He did not then see the motive. He now suspects it was to avoid their due share of taxation. He had no objection to a just and accurate adjustment of representation and taxation to each other.

Mr. GOUVERNEUR MORRIS and Mr. MADISON answered, that the charge itself involved an acquittal; since, notwithstanding the augmentation of the number of members allotted to Massachusetts and Virginia, the motion for proportioning the burdens thereto was made by a member from the former State, and was approved by Mr. MADISON, from the latter, who was on the Committee. Mr. GOUVERNEUR MORRIS said, that he thought Pennsylvania had her due share in eight members; and he could not in candour ask for more. Mr. MADISON said, that having always conceived that the difference of interest in the United States lay not between the large and small, but the Northern and Southern States, and finding that the number of members allotted to the Northern States was greatly superior, he should have preferred an addition of two members to the

Southern States, to wit, one to North and one to South Carolina, rather than of one member to Virginia. He liked the present motion, because it tended to moderate the views both of the opponents and advocates for rating very high the negroes.

Mr. ELLSWORTH hoped the proposition would be withdrawn. It entered too much into detail. The general principle was already sufficiently settled. As fractions cannot be regarded in apportioning the number of Representatives, the rule will be unjust, until an actual census shall be made. After that, taxation may be precisely proportioned, according to the principle established, to the *number of inhabitants.*

Mr. WILSON hoped the motion would not be withdrawn. If it should, it will be made from another quarter. The rule will be as reasonable and just before, as after, a census. As to fractional numbers, the census will not destroy, but ascertain them. And they will have the same effect after, as before, the census; for as he understands the rule, it is to be adjusted not to the number of *inhabitants*, but of *Representatives.*

Mr. SHERMAN opposed the motion. He thought the Legislature ought to be left at liberty; in which case they would probably conform to the principles observed by Congress.

Mr. MASON did not know that Virginia would be a loser by the proposed regulation, but had some scruple as to the justice of it. He doubted much whether the conjectural rule which was to precede the census would be as just as it would be rendered by an actual census.

Mr. ELLSWORTH and Mr. SHERMAN moved to postpone the motion of Mr. GERRY.

On the question, it passed in the negative,— Connecticut, New Jersey, Delaware, Maryland, aye —4; Massachusetts, Pennsylvania, Virginia, North Carolina, South Carolina, Georgia, no — 6.

On the question on Mr GERRY's motion, it passed in the

negative, the States being equally divided,— Massachusetts, *Pennsylvania*, North Carolina, South Carolina, Georgia, aye — 5; Connecticut, New Jersey, Delaware, Maryland, *Virginia*, no — 5.

Mr. GERRY finding that the loss of the question had proceeded from an objection, with some, to the proposed assessment of direct taxes on the *inhabitants* of the States, which might restrain the Legislature to a poll-tax, moved his proposition again, but so varied as to authorize the assessment on the *States*, which leaves the mode to the Legislature, viz: "that from the first meeting of the Legislature of the United States, until a census shall be taken, all moneys for supplying the public Treasury by direct taxation shall be raised from the said several States, according to the number of their Representatives respectively in the first branch."

On this varied question it passed in the affirmative,— Massachusetts, *Virginia*, North Carolina, South Carolina, Georgia, aye — 5; Connecticut, New Jersey, Delaware, Maryland, no — 4; *Pennsylvania*, divided.

On the motion of Mr. RANDOLPH, the vote of Monday last, authorizing the Legislature to adjust, from time to time, the representation upon the principles of *wealth* and numbers of inhabitants, was reconsidered by common consent, in order to strike out *wealth* and adjust the resolution to that requiring periodical revisions according to the number of whites and three-fifths of the blacks. The motion was in the words following:—" But as the present situation of the States may probably alter in the number of their inhabitants, that the Legislature of the United States be authorized, from time to time, to apportion the number of Representatives; and in case any of the States shall hereafter be divided, or any two or more States united, or new States created within the limits of the United States, the Legislature of the United States shall possess authority to regulate the number of Representatives in any of the foregoing cases, upon the principle of their number of inhabitants, according to the provisions hereafter mentioned."

Mr. GOUVERNEUR MORRIS opposed the alteration, as leaving still an incoherence. If negroes were to be viewed as inhabitants, and the revision was to proceed on the principle of numbers of inhabitants, they ought to be added in their entire number, and not in the proportion of three-fifths. If as property, the word wealth was right; and striking it out would produce the very inconsistency which it was meant to get rid of. The train of business, and the late turn which it had taken, had led him, he said, into deep meditation on it, and he would candidly state the result. A distinction had been set up, and urged, between the Northern and Southern States. He had hitherto considered this doctrine as heretical. He still thought the distinction groundless. He sees, however, that it is persisted in; and the Southern gentlemen will not be satisfied unless they see the way open to their gaining a majority in the public councils. The consequence of such a transfer of power from the maritime to the interior and landed interest, will, he foresees, be such an oppression to commerce, that he shall be obliged to vote for the vicious principle of equality in the second branch, in order to provide some defence for the Northern States against it. But to come more to the point, either this distinction is fictitious or real; if fictitious, let it be dismissed, and let us proceed with due confidence. If it be real, instead of attempting to blend incompatible things, let us at once take a friendly leave of each other. There can be no end of demands for security, if every particular interest is to be entitled to it. The Eastern States may claim it for their fishery, and for other objects, as the Southern States claim it for their peculiar objects. In this struggle between the two ends of the Union, what part ought the Middle States, in point of policy, to take? To join their Eastern brethren, according to his ideas. If the Southern States get the power into their hands, and be joined, as they will be, with the interior country, they will inevitably bring on a war with Spain for the Mississippi. This language is already held. The

interior country, having no property nor interest exposed on the sea, will be little affected by such a war. He
wished to know what security the Northern and Middle
States will have against this danger. It has been said that
North Carolina, South Carolina, and Georgia only, will in
a little time have a majority of the people of America.
They must in that case include the great exterior country,
and everything was to be apprehended from their getting
the power into their hands.

Mr. BUTLER. The security the Southern States want is
that their negroes may not be taken from them, which some
gentlemen within or without doors have a very good mind
to do. It was not supposed that North Carolina, South
Carolina and Georgia would have more people than all the
other States, but many more relatively to the other States,
than they now have. The people and strength of America
are evidently bearing southwardly, and south westwardly.

Mr. WILSON. If a general declaration would satisfy
any gentleman, he had no indisposition to declare his sentiments. Conceiving that all men, wherever placed, have
equal rights, and are equally entitled to confidence, he
viewed without apprehension the period when a few States
should contain the superior number of people. The majority of people, wherever found, ought in all questions, to
govern the minority. If the interior country should acquire
this majority, it will not only have the right, but will avail
itself of it, whether we will or no. This jealousy misled
the policy of Great Britain with regard to America. The
fatal maxims espoused by her were, that the Colonies were
growing too fast, and that their growth must be stinted in
time. What were the consequences ? First, enmity on
our part, then actual separation. Like consequences will
result on the part of the interior settlements, if like jealousy
and policy be pursued on ours. Further, if numbers be not
a proper rule, why is not some better rule pointed out ?
No one has yet ventured to attempt it. Congress have
never been able to discover a better. No State, as far as

he had heard, had suggested any other. In 1783, after elaborate discussion of a measure of wealth, all were satisfied then, as they now are, that the rule of numbers does not differ much from the combined rule of numbers and wealth. Again, he could not agree that property was the sole or primary object of government and society. The cultivation and improvement of the human mind was the most noble object. With respect to this object, as well as to other *personal* rights, numbers were surely the natural and precise measure of representation. And with respect to property, they could not vary much from the precise measure. In no point of view, however, could the establishment of numbers, as the rule of representation in the first branch, vary his opinion as to the impropriety of letting a vicious principle into the second branch.

On the question to strike out *wealth*, and to make the change as moved by Mr. RANDOLPH, it passed in the affirmative,—Massachusetts, Connecticut, New Jersey, Pennsylvania, Maryland, Virginia, North Carolina, South Carolina, Georgia, aye — 9 ; Delaware, divided.

Mr. READ moved to insert, after the word "divided," "or enlarged by addition of territory ;" which was agreed to, *nem con.* *

Adjourned.

SATURDAY, JULY 14th.

In Convention,—Mr. L. MARTIN called for the question on the whole Report, including the parts relating to the origination of money bills, and the equality of votes in the second branch.

Mr. GERRY wished, before the question should be put, that the attention of the House might be turned to the dangers apprehended from Western States. He was for admitting them on liberal terms, but not for putting ourselves into their hands. They will, if they acquire power, like all

---

* His object probably was to provide for such cases as an enlargement of Delaware by annexing to it the peninsula on the East side of the Chesapeake.

men, abuse it.   They will oppress commerce, and drain our wealth into the Western country. To guard against these consequences, he thought it necessary to limit the number of new States to be admitted into the Union, in such a manner that they should never be able to outnumber the Atlantic States.   He accordingly moved, " that in order to secure the liberties of the States already confederated, the number of Representatives in the first branch, of the States which shall hereafter be established, shall never exceed in number, the Representatives from such of the States as shall accede to this Confederation."

Mr. KING seconded the motion.

Mr. SHERMAN thought there was no probability that the number of future States would exceed that of the existing States.   If the event should ever happen, it was too remote to be taken into consideration at this time.   Besides, we are providing for our posterity, for our children and our grand children, who would be as likely to be citizens of new western States, as of the old States.   On this consideration alone, we ought to make no such discrimination as was proposed by the motion.

Mr. GERRY.   If some of our children should remove, others will stay behind, and he thought incumbent on us to provide for their interests.   There was a rage of emigration from the Eastern States to the western country, and he did not wish those remaining behind to be at the mercy of the emigrants.   Besides, foreigners are resorting to that country, and it is uncertain what turn things may take there.

On the question for agreeing to the motion of Mr. GERRY, it passed in the negative,— Massachusetts, Connecticut, Delaware, Maryland, aye — 4; New Jersey, Virginia, North Carolina, South Carolina, Georgia, no — 5; Pennsylvania, divided.

Mr. RUTLEDGE proposed to reconsider the two propositions touching the originating of money bills in the first, and the equality of votes in the second, branch.

Mr. SHERMAN was for the question on the whole at once. It was, he said, a conciliatory plan; it had been considered in all its parts; a great deal of time had been spent upon it; and if any part should now be altered, it would be necessary to go over the whole ground again.

Mr. L. MARTIN urged the question on the whole. He did not like many parts of it. He did not like having two branches, nor the inequality of votes in the first branch. He was willing, however, to make trial of the plan, rather than do nothing.

Mr. WILSON traced the progress of the report through its several stages; remarking, that when on the question concerning an equality of votes, the House was divided, our constituents, had they voted as their Representatives did, would have stood as two-thirds against the equality, and one-third only in favor of it. This fact would ere long be known, and it would appear that this fundamental point has been carried by one-third against two-thirds. What hopes will our constituents entertain when they find that the essential principles of justice have been violated in the outset of the Government? As to the privilege of originating money bills, it was not considered by any as of much moment, and by many as improper in itself. He hoped both clauses would be reconsidered. The equality of votes was a point of such critical importance, that every opportunity ought to be allowed for discussing and collecting the mind of the Convention upon it.

Mr. L. MARTIN denies that there were two-thirds against the equality of votes. The States that please to call themselves large, are the weakest in the Union. Look at Massachusetts — look at Virginia — are they efficient States? He was for letting a separation take place, if they desired it. He had rather there should be two confederacies, than one founded on any other principle than an equality of votes in the second branch at least.

Mr. WILSON was not surprised that those who say that a minority does more than a majority, should say the mi-

nority is stronger than the majority.   He supposed the next
assertion will be, that they are richer also; though he hardly
expected it would be persisted in, when the States shall be
called on for taxes and troops.

Mr. GERRY also animadverted on Mr. L. MARTIN's remarks on the weakness of Massachusetts.   He favored the
reconsideration, with a view, not of destroying the equality
of votes, but of providing that the States should vote *per
capita*, which, he said, would prevent the delays and inconveniences that had been experienced in Congress, and would
give a national aspect and spirit to the management of business.   He did not approve of a reconsideration of the
clause relating to money bills.   It was of great consequence.   It was the corner stone of the accommodation.   If
any member of the Convention had the exclusive privilege
of making propositions, would any one say that it would
give him no advantage over other members?   The Report
was not altogether to his mind; but he would agree to it as
it stood, rather than throw it out altogether.

The reconsideration being tacitly agreed to, —

Mr. PINCKNEY moved, that, instead of an equality of
votes, the States should be represented in the second
branch as follows: New Hampshire by two members;
Massachusetts, four; Rhode Island, one; Connecticut,
three; New York, three; New Jersey, two; Pennsylvania,
four; Delaware, one; Maryland, three; Virginia, five; North
Carolina, three; South Carolina, three: Georgia, two; making in the whole, thirty-six.

Mr. WILSON seconds the motion.

Mr. DAYTON.   The smaller States can never give up
their equality.   For himself, he would in no event yield
that security for their rights.

Mr. SHERMAN urged the equality of votes, not so much
as a security for the small States, as for the State Governments, which could not be preserved unless they were represented, and had a negative in the General Government.
He had no objection to the members in the second branch

voting *per capita*, as had been suggested by (Mr. GERRY.)

Mr. MADISON concurred in this motion of Mr. PINCKNEY, as a reasonable compromise.

Mr. GERRY said, he should like the motion, but could see no hope of success. An accommodation must take place, and it was apparent from what had been seen, that it could not do so on the ground of the motion. He was utterly against a partial confederacy, leaving other States to accede or not accede, as had been intimated.

Mr. KING said, it was always with regret that he differed from his colleagues, but it was his duty to differ from (Mr. GERRY) on this occasion. He considered the proposed Government as substantially and formally a General and National Government over the people of America. There never will be a case in which it will act as a Federal Government, on the States and not on the individual citizens. And is it not a clear principle, that in a free government, those who are to be the objects of a government, ought to influence the operations of it? What reason can be assigned, why the same rule of representation should not prevail in the second, as in the first, branch? He could conceive none. On the contrary, every view of the subject that presented itself seemed to require it. Two objections had been raised against it, drawn, first, from the terms of the existing compact; secondly, from a supposed danger to the smaller States. As to the first objection, he thought it inapplicable. According to the existing Confederation, the rule by which the public burdens is to be apportioned is *fixed*, and must be pursued. In the proposed Government, it cannot be fixed, because indirect taxation is to be substituted. The Legislature, therefore, will have full discretion to impose taxes in such modes and proportions as they may judge expedient. As to the second objection, he thought it of as little weight. The General Government can never wish to intrude on the State Governments. There could be no temptation. None had been pointed out. In order to prevent the interference of measures which seemed most likely to happen, he would have no objection to throwing all the State debts into the Federal debt, making one aggregate debt of about $70,000,000, and leaving it to be discharged by the General Government. According to the idea of securing the State Governments, there ought to be three distinct legislative branches. The second was admitted to be necessary, and was actually meant, to check the first branch, to give more wisdom, system and stability to the Government; and ought clearly, as it was to operate on the people, to be proportioned to them. For the third purpose of securing the States, there ought then to be a third branch, representing the States as such, and guarding, by equal votes, their rights and dignities. He would not pretend to be as thoroughly acquainted with his immediate constituents as his colleagues, but it was his firm belief that Massachusetts would never be prevailed on to yield to an equality of votes. In New York, (he was sorry to be obliged to say anything relative to that State in the absence of its representatives, but the occasion required it,) in New York he had seen that the most powerful argument used by the considerate opponents to the grant of the Impost to Congress, was pointed against the vicious constitution of Congress with regard to representation and suffrage. He was sure that no government would last that was not founded on just principles. He preferred the doing of nothing, to an allowance of an equal vote to all the States. It would be better, he thought, to submit to a little more confusion and convulsion, than to submit to such an evil. It was difficult to say what the views of different gentlemen might be. Perhaps there might be some who thought no Government co-extensive with the United States could be established with a hope of its answering the purpose. Perhaps there might be other fixed opinions incompatible with the object we are pursuing. If there were, he thought it but candid, that gentlemen should speak out, that we might understand one another.

Mr. STRONG. The Convention had been much divided

in opinion. In order to avoid the consequences of it, an accommodation had been proposed. A committee had been appointed; and though some of the members of it were averse to an equality of votes, a report had been made in favor of it. It is agreed, on all hands, that Congress are nearly at an end. If no accommodation takes place, the Union itself must soon be dissolved. It has been suggested that if we cannot come to any general agreement, the principal States may form and recommend a scheme of government. But will the small States, in that case, ever accede to it? Is it probable that the large States themselves will, under such circumstances, embrace and ratify it? He thought the small States had made a considerable concession, in the article of money bills, and that they might naturally expect some concessions on the other side. From this view of the matter, he was compelled to give his vote for the Report taken altogether.

Mr. MADISON expressed his apprehensions that if the proper foundation of government was destroyed, by substituting an equality in place of a proportional representation, no proper superstructure would be raised. If the small States really wish for a government armed with the powers necessary to secure their liberties, and to enforce obedience on the larger members as well as themselves, he could not help thinking them extremely mistaken in the means. He reminded them of the consequences of laying the *existing Confederation* on improper principles. All the principal parties to its compilation joined immediately in mutilating and fettering the Government, in such a manner that it has disappointed every hope placed on it. He appealed to the doctrine and arguments used by themselves, on a former occasion. It had been very properly observed (by Mr. PATTERSON), that representation was an expedient by which the meeting of the people themselves was rendered unnecessary; and that the representatives ought therefore to bear a proportion to the votes which their constituents, if convened, would respectively have. Was not this remark as applicable to one branch of the representation as to the other?   But it had been said that the Government would, in its operation, be partly federal, partly national; that although in the latter respect the representatives of the people ought to be in proportion to the people, yet in the former, it ought to be according to the number of States. If there was any solidity in this distinction, he was ready to abide by it; if there was none, it ought to be abandoned. In all cases where the General Government is to act on the people, let the people be represented, and the votes be proportional.   In all cases where the Government is to act on the States as such, in like manner as Congress now acts on them, let the States be represented and the votes be equal. This was the true ground of compromise, if there was any ground at all.   But he denied that there was any ground. He called for a single instance in which the General Government was not to operate on the people individually. The practicability of making laws, with coercive sanctions, for the States as political bodies, had been exploded on all hands.   He observed that the people of the large States would, in some way or other, secure to themselves a weight proportioned to the importance accruing from their superior numbers.   If they could not effect it by a proportional representation in the Government, they would probably accede to no government which did not, in a great measure, depend for its efficacy on their voluntary co-operation; in which case they would indirectly secure their object.   The existing Confederacy proved that where the acts of the General Government were to be executed by the particular Governments, the latter had a weight in proportion to their importance.   No one would say, that, either in Congress or out of Congress, Delaware had equal weight with Pennsylvania. If the latter was to supply ten times as much money as the former, and no compulsion could be used, it was of ten times more importance, that she should voluntarily furnish the supply.   In the Dutch Confederacy the votes of the **provinces were equal.   But Holland, which supplies about** half the money, governed the whole Republic.   He enumerated the objections against an equality of votes in the second branch, notwithstanding the proportional representation in the first.   1. The minority could negative the will of the majority of the people.   2. They could extort measures, by making them a condition of their assent to other necessary measures.   3. They could obtrude measures on the majority, by virtue of the peculiar powers which would be vested in the Senate.   4. The evil, instead of being cured by time, would increase with every new State that should be admitted, as they must all be admitted on the principle of equality.   5. The perpetuity it would give to the preponderance of the Northern against the Southern scale, was a serious consideration.   It seemed now to be pretty well understood, that the real difference of interests lay, not between the large and small, but between the Northern and Southern States.   The institution of slavery, and its consequences, formed the line of discrimination.   There were five States on the Southern, eight on the Northern side of this line.   Should a proportional representation take place, it was true, the Northern would still outnumber the other; but not in the same degree, at this time; and every day would tend towards an equilibrium.

Mr. WILSON would add a few words only.   If equality in the second branch was an error that time would correct, he should be less anxious to exclude it, being sensible that perfection was unattainable in any plan ; but being a fundamental and a perpetual error it ought by all means to be avoided.   A vice in the representation, like an error in the first concoction, must be followed by disease, convulsions, and finally death itself.   The justice of the general principle of proportional representation has not, in argument at least, been yet contradicted.   But it is said that a departure from it, so far as to give the States an equal vote in one branch of the Legislature, is essential to their preservation.   He had considered this position maturely, but could not see its application.   That the States ought to be

23

preserved, he admitted. But does it follow, that an equality
of votes is necessary for the purpose ? Is there any reason
to suppose that, if their preservation should depend more
on the large than on the small States, the security of
the States against the general government, would be
diminished ? Are the large States less attached to
their existence, more likely to commit suicide, than the
small ? An equal vote, then, is not necessary, as far
as he can conceive, and is liable, among other objections,
to this insuperable one,— the great fault of the existing
Confederacy is its inactivity. It has never been a complaint against Congress that they governed over much.
The complaint has been, that they have governed too little.
To remedy this defect we were sent here. Shall we effect
the cure by establishing an equality of votes, as is proposed ? No : this very equality carries us directly to
Congress,— to the system which is our duty to rectify.
The small States cannot indeed act, by virtue of this equality, but they may control the government, as they have done
in Congress. This very measure is here prosecuted by a
minority of the people of America. Is then, the object of
the Convention likely to be accomplished in this way ?
Will not our constituents say, we sent you to form an efficient government, and you have given us one, more complex,
indeed, but having all the weakness of the former government. He was anxious for uniting all the States under one
government. He knew there were some respectable men
who preferred three Confederacies, united by offensive and
defensive alliances. Many things may be plausibly said,
some things may be justly said, in favor of such a project.
He could not, however, concur in it himself ; but he
thought nothing so pernicious as bad first principles.

Mr. ELLSWORTH asked two questions,— one of Mr.
WILSON, whether he had ever seen a good measure fail in
Congress for want of a majority of States in its favor ? He
had himself never known such an instance. The other of
Mr. MADISON, whether a negative lodged with the majority

of the States, even the smallest, could be more dangerous than the qualified negative proposed to be lodged in a single Executive Magistrate, who must be taken from some one State ?

Mr. Sherman signified that his expectation was that the General Legislature would in some cases act on the *federal principle*, of requiring quotas. But he thought it ought to be empowered to carry their own plans into execution, if the States should fail to supply their respective quotas.

On the question for agreeing to Mr. Pinckney's motion, for allowing New Hampshire two; Massachusetts four, &c., it passed in the negative, —Pennsylvania, Maryland, Virginia, South Carolina, aye — 4; Massachusetts, (Mr. King, aye, Mr. Gorham absent), Connecticut, New Jersey, Delaware, North Carolina, Georgia, no — 6.

Adjourned.

Monday, July 16th.

In Convention, — On the question for agreeing to the whole Report, as amended, and including the equality of votes in the second branch, it passed in the affirmative, — Connecticut, New Jersey, Delaware, Maryland, North Carolina, (Mr. Spaight, no) aye — 5; Pennsylvania, Virginia, South Carolina, Georgia, no — 4; Massachusetts, divided, (Mr. Gerry, Mr. Strong, aye; Mr. King, Mr. Gorham, no).

The whole thus passed is in the words following, viz.

" *Resolved*, that in the original formation of the Legislature of the United States, the first branch thereof shall consist of sixty-five members, of which number New Hampshire shall send, 3; Massachusetts, 8; Rhode Island, 1; Connecticut, 5; New York, 6; New Jersey, 4; Pennsylvania, 8; Delaware, 1; Maryland, 6; Virginia, 10; North Carolina, 5; South Carolina, 5; Georgia, 3. But as the present situation of the States may probably alter in the number of their inhabitants, the Legislature of the United States shall be authorized, from time to time, to apportion the number of Representatives, and in case any of the States shall hereafter be divided, or enlarged by addition of territory, or any two or more States united, or any new States created within the limits of the United States, the Legislature of the United States shall possess authority to regulate the number of Representatives in any of the foregoing cases, upon the principle of their number of inhabitants, according to the provisions hereafter mentioned: provided always, that representation ought to be proportioned according to direct taxation. And in order to ascertain the alteration in the direct taxation, which may be required from time to time by the changes in the relative circumstances of the States —

"*Resolved,* that a census be taken within six years from the first meeting of the Legislature of the United States, and once within the term of every ten years afterwards, of all the inhabitants of the United States, in the manner and according to the ratio recommended by Congress in their Resolution of the eighteenth day of April, 1783; and that the Legislature of the United States shall proportion the direct taxation accordingly.

"*Resolved,* that all bills for raising or appropriating money, and for fixing the salaries of officers of the Government of the United States, shall originate in the first branch of the Legislature of the United States; and shall not be altered or amended in the second branch; and that no money shall be drawn from the public Treasury, but in pursuance of appropriations to be originated in the first branch.

"*Resolved,* that in the second branch of the Legislature of the United States, each State shall have an equal vote."

The sixth Resolution in the Report from the Committee of the Whole House, which had been postponed, in order to consider the seventh and eighth Resolutions, was now resumed, (see the Resolution.)

"That the National Legislature ought to possess the

legislative rights vested in Congress by the Confederation," was agreed to, *nem. con.*

" And moreover to legislate in all cases to which the separate States are incompetent ; or in which the harmony of the United States may be interrupted by the exercise of individual legislation," being read for a question,—

Mr. BUTLER calls for some explanation of the extent of this power ; particularly of the word *incompetent.* The vagueness of the terms rendered it impossible for any precise judgment to be formed.

Mr. GORHAM. The vagueness of the terms constitutes the propriety of them. We are now establishing general principles, to be extended hereafter into details, which will be precise and explicit.

Mr. RUTLEDGE urged the objection started by Mr. BUTLER ; and moved that a clause should be committed, to the end that a specification of the powers comprised in the general terms, might be reported.

On the question for commitment, the votes were equally divided,—Connecticut, Maryland, Virginia, South Carolina, Georgia, aye — 5 ; Massachusetts, New Jersey, Pennsylvania, Delaware, North Carolina, no — 5. So it was lost.

Mr. RANDOLPH. The vote of this morning (involving an equality of suffrage in the second branch) had embarrassed the business extremely. All the powers given in the Report from the Committee of the Whole were founded on the supposition that a proportional representation was to prevail in both branches of the Legislature. When he came here this morning, his purpose was to have offered some propositions that might, if possible, have united a great majority of votes, and particularly might provide against the danger suspected on the part of the smaller States, by enumerating the cases in which it might lie, and allowing an equality of votes in such cases. But finding from the preceding vote, that they persist in demanding an equal vote in all cases ; that they have succeeded in obtaining it ; and that New York, if present, would probably be on the same side ; he could not but think we were unprepared to discuss this subject further. It will probably be in vain to come to any final decision, with a bare majority on either side. For these reasons he wished the Convention to adjourn, that the large States might consider the steps proper to be taken, in the present solemn crisis of the business ; and that the small States might also deliberate on the means of conciliation.

Mr. PATTERSON thought with Mr. RANDOLPH, that it was high time for the Convention to adjourn ; that the rule of secrecy ought to be rescinded ; and that our constituents should be consulted. No conciliation could be admissible on the part of the smaller States, on any other ground than that of an equality of votes in the second branch. If Mr. RANDOLPH would reduce to form his motion for an adjournment *sine die*, he would second it with all his heart.

General PINCKNEY wished to know of Mr. RANDOLPH, whether he meant an adjournment *sine die*, or only an adjournment for the day. If the former was meant, it differed much from his idea. He could not think of going to South Carolina and returning again to this place. Besides it was chimerical, to suppose that the States, if consulted, would ever accord separately and beforehand.

Mr. RANDOLPH had never entertained an idea of an adjournment *sine die ;* and was sorry that his meaning had been so readily and strangely misinterpreted. He had in view merely an adjournment till to-morrow, in order that some conciliatory experiment might, if possible, be devised; and that in case the smaller States should continue to hold back, the larger might then take such measures — he would not say what — as might be necessary.

Mr. PATTERSON seconded the adjournment till to-morrow, as an opportunity seemed to be wished by the larger States to deliberate further on conciliatory expedients.

On the question for adjourning till to-morrow, the States were equally divided,— New Jersey, Pennsylvania, Maryland, Virginia, North Carolina, aye — 5; Massachusetts, Connecticut, Delaware, South Carolina, Georgia, no — 5; so it was lost.

Mr. Broom thought it his duty to declare his opinion against an adjournment *sine die*, as had been urged by Mr. Patterson. Such a measure, he thought, would be fatal. Something must be done by the Convention, though it should be by a bare majority.

Mr. Gerry observed that Massachusetts was opposed to an adjournment, because they saw no new ground of compromise. But as it seemed to be the opinion of so many States that a trial should be made, the State would now concur in the adjournment.

Mr. Rutledge could see no need of an adjournment, because he could see no chance of a compromise. The little States were fixed. They had repeatedly and solemnly declared themselves to be so. All that the large States, then, had to do was, to decide whether they would yield or not. For his part, he conceived, that, although we could not do what we thought best in itself, we ought to do something. Had we not better keep the Government up a little longer, hoping that another convention will supply our omissions, than abandon every thing to hazard? Our constituents will be very little satisfied with us if we take the latter course.

Mr. Randolph and Mr. King renewed the motion to adjourn till to-morrow.

On the question,— Massachusetts, New Jersey, Pennsylvania, Maryland, Virginia, North Carolina, South Carolina, aye — 7; Connecticut, Delaware, no — 2; Georgia, divided.

Adjourned.

[On the morning following, before the hour of the Convention, a number of the members from the larger

States, by common agreement, met for the purpose of consulting on the proper steps to be taken in consequence of the vote in favor of an equal representation in the second branch, and the apparent inflexibility of the smaller States on that point. Several members from the latter States also attended. The time was wasted in vague conversation on the subject, without any specific proposition or agreement. It appeared, indeed, that the opinions of the members who disliked the equality of votes differed much as to the importance of that point; and as to the policy of risking a failure of any general act of the Convention by inflexibly opposing it. Several of them — supposing that no good government could or would be built on that foundation; and that, as a division of the Convention into two opinions was unavoidable, it would be better that the side comprising the principal States, and a majority of the people of America, should propose a scheme of government to the States, than that a scheme should be proposed on the other side — would have concurred in a firm opposition to the smaller States, and in a separate recommendation, if eventually necessary. Others seemed inclined to yield to the smaller States, and to concur in such an act, however imperfect and exceptionable, as might be agreed on by the Convention as a body, though decided by a bare majority of States and by a minority of the people of the United States. It is probable that the result of this consultation satisfied the smaller States, that they had nothing to apprehend from a union of the larger in any plan whatever against the equality of votes in the second branch.]

TUESDAY, JULY 17TH.

In Convention,—Mr. GOUVERNEUR MORRIS moved to reconsider the whole Resolution agreed to yesterday concerning the constitution of the two branches of the Legislature. His object was to bring the House to a consideration, in the abstract, of the powers necessary to be vested in the General

Government. It had been said, Let us know how the government is to be modelled, and then we can determine what powers can be properly given to it. He thought the most eligible course was, first to determine on the necessary powers, and then so to modify the Government, as that it might be justly and properly enabled to administer them. He feared, if we proceeded to a consideration of the powers, whilst the vote of yesterday, including an equality of the States in the second branch, remained in force, a reference to it, either mental or expressed, would mix itself with the merits of every question concerning the powers. This motion was not seconded. [It was probably approved by several members who either despaired of success, or were apprehensive that the attempt would inflame the jealousies of the smaller States.]

The sixth Resolution in the Report of the Committee of the Whole, relating to the powers, which had been postponed in order to consider the seventh and eighth, relating to the constitution, of the National Legislature, was now resumed.

Mr. SHERMAN observed, that it would be difficult to draw the line between the powers of the General Legislature, and those to be left with the States; that he did not like the definition contained in the Resolution; and proposed, in its place, to the words "individual legislation," inclusive, to insert "to make laws binding on the people of the United States in all cases which may concern the common interests of the Union; but not to interfere with the government of the individual States in any matters of internal police which respect the government of such States only, and wherein the general welfare of the United States is not concerned."

Mr. WILSON seconded the amendment, as better expressing the general principle.

Mr. GOUVERNEUR MORRIS opposed it. The internal police, as it would be called and understood by the States, ought to be infringed in many cases, as in the case of paper-money, and other tricks by which citizens of other States may be affected.

Mr. SHERMAN, in explanation of his idea, read an enumeration of powers, including the power of levying taxes on trade, but not the power of *direct taxation*.

Mr. GOUVERNEUR MORRIS remarked the omission, and inferred, that, for the deficiencies of taxes on consumption, it must have been the meaning of Mr. SHERMAN that the General Government should recur to quotas and requisitions, which are subversive of the idea of government.

Mr. SHERMAN acknowledged that his enumeration did not include direct taxation. Some provision, he supposed, must be made for supplying the deficiency of other taxation, but he had not formed any.

On the question on Mr. SHERMAN's motion, it passed in the negative, — Connecticut, Maryland, aye — 2; Massachusetts, New Jersey, Pennsylvania, Delaware, Virginia, North Carolina, South Carolina, Georgia, no — 8.

Mr. BEDFORD moved that the second member of the sixth Resolution be so altered as to read, " and moreover to legislate in all cases for the general interests of the Union, and also in those to which the States are severally incompetent, or in which the harmony of the United States may be interrupted by the exercise of individual legislation."

Mr. GOUVERNEUR MORRIS seconds the motion.

Mr. RANDOLPH. This is a formidable idea, indeed. It involves the power of violating all the laws and Constitutions of the States, and of intermeddling with their police. The last member of the sentence is also superfluous, being included in the first.

Mr. BEDFORD. It is not more extensive or formidable than the clause as it stands: *no State* being *separately* competent to legislate for the *general interest* of the Union.

On the question for agreeing to Mr. BEDFORD's motion, it passed in the affirmative, — Massachusetts, New Jersey, Pennsylvania, Delaware, Maryland, North Carolina, aye — 6; Connecticut, Virginia, South Carolina, Georgia, no — 4.

On the sentence as amended, it passed in the affirmative, — Massachusetts, Connecticut, New Jersey, Pennsylvania, Delaware, Maryland, Virginia, North Carolina, aye — 8; South Carolina, Georgia, no — 2.

The next clause, "To negative all laws passed by the several States contravening, in the opinion of the National Legislature, the Articles of Union, or any treaties subsisting under the authority of the Union," was then taken up.

Mr. GOUVERNEUR MORRIS opposed this power as likely to be terrible to the States, and not necessary if sufficient Legislative authority should be given to the General Government.

Mr. SHERMAN thought it unnecessary; as the Courts of the States would not consider as valid any law contravening the authority of the Union, and which the Legislature would wish to be negatived.

Mr. L. MARTIN considered the power as improper and inadmissible. Shall all the laws of the States be sent up to the General Legislature before they shall be permitted to operate?

Mr. MADISON considered the negative on the laws of the States as essential to the efficacy and security of the General Government. The necessity of a General Government proceeds from the propensity of the States to pursue their particular interests in opposition to the general interest. This propensity will continue to disturb the system unless effectually controlled. Nothing short of a negative on their laws will control it. They will pass laws which will accomplish their injurious objects before they can be repealed by the General Legislature, or set aside by the National tribunals. Confidence cannot be put in the state tribunals as guardians of the National authority and interests. In all the States these are more or less dependent on the Legislatures. In Georgia they are appointed annually by the Legislature. In Rhode Island the Judges who refused to execute an unconstitutional law were displaced, and others substituted, by the Legislature, who would be the willing instruments of the wicked, and arbitrary plans of their masters. A power of negativing the improper laws of the States is at once the most mild and certain means of preserving the harmony of the system. Its utility is sufficiently displayed in the British system. Nothing could maintain the harmony and subordination of the various parts of the Empire, but the prerogative by which the Crown stifles in the birth every act of every part tending to discord or encroachment. It is true. the prerogative is sometimes misapplied, through ignorance or partiality to one particular part of the Empire; but we have not the same reason to fear such misapplications in our system. As to the sending all laws up to the National Legislature, that might be rendered unnecessary by some emanation of the power into the States, so far at least as to give a temporary effect to laws of immediate necessity.

Mr. Gouverneur Morris was more and more opposed to the negative. The proposal of it would disgust all the States. A law that ought to be negatived, will be set aside in the Judiciary department; and if that security should fail, may be repealed by a National law.

Mr. Sherman. Such a power involves a wrong principle, to wit, that a law of a State contrary to the Articles of the Union would, if not negatived, be valid and operative.

Mr. Pinckney urged the necessity of the negative.

On the question for agreeing to the power of negativing laws of States, &c. it passed in the negative, — Massachusetts, Virginia, North Carolina, aye — 3; Connecticut, New Jersey, Pennsylvania, Delaware, Maryland, South Carolina, Georgia, no — 7.

Mr. L. Martin moved the following resolution, " That the Legislative acts of the United States made by virtue and in pursuance of the Articles of Union, and all treaties made and ratified under the authority of the United States, shall be the supreme law of the respective States, as far as those acts or treaties shall relate to the said States, or their citizens and inhabitants; and that the Judiciaries of the several States shall be bound thereby in their decisions, anything in the respective laws of the individual States to the contrary notwithstanding;" which was agreed to, *nem. con.*

The ninth Resolution being taken up, the first clause, " That a National Executive be instituted, to consist of a single person," was agreed to, *nem. con.*

The next clause, " To be chosen by the National Legislature," being considered, —

Mr. GOUVERNEUR MORRIS was pointedly against his being so chosen. He will be the mere creature of the Legislature, if appointed and impeachable by that body. He ought to be elected by the people at large, by the freeholders of the country. That difficulties attend this mode, he admits. But they have been found superable in New York and in Connecticut, and would, he believed, be found so in the case of an Executive for the United States. If the people should elect, they will never fail to prefer some man of distinguished character, or services; some man, if he might so speak, of continental reputation. If the Legislature elect, it will be the work of intrigue, of cabal, and of faction; it will be like the election of a pope by a conclave of cardinals; real merit will rarely be the title to the appointment. He moved to strike out " National Legislature," and insert " citizens of the United States."

Mr. SHERMAN thought that the sense of the nation would be better expressed by the Legislature, than by the people at large. The latter will never be sufficiently informed of characters, and besides will never give a majority of votes to any one man. They will generally vote for some man in their own State, and the largest State will have the best chance for the appointment. If the choice be made by the Legislature, a majority of voices may be made necessary to constitute an election.

Mr. WILSON. Two arguments have been urged against an election of the Executive magistrate by the people. The first is, the example of Poland, where an election of the supreme magistrate is attended with the most dangerous commotions. The cases, he observed, were totally dissimilar. The Polish nobles have resources and dependants which enable them to appear in force, and to threaten the Republic as well as each other. In the next place, the electors all assemble at one place; which would not be the case with us. The second argument is, that a majority of the people would never concur. It might be answered, that the concurrence of a majority of the people is not a necessary principle of election, nor required as such in any of the States. But allowing the objection all its force, it may be obviated by the expedient used in Massachusetts, where the Legislature, by a majority of voices, decide in case a majority of the people do not concur in favor of one of the candidates. This would restrain the choice to a good nomination at least, and prevent in a great degree intrigue and cabal. A particular objection with him against an absolute election by the Legislature was, that the Executive in that case would be too dependent to stand the mediator between the intrigues and sinister views of the Representatives and the general liberties and interests of the people.

Mr. PINCKNEY did not expect this question would again have been brought forward; an election by the people being liable to the most obvious and striking objections. They will be led by a few active and designing men. The most populous States, by combining in favor of the same individual, will be able to carry their points. The national Legislature being most immediately interested in the laws made by themselves, will be most attentive to the choice of a fit man to carry them properly into execution.

Mr. GOUVERNEUR MORRIS. It is said, that in case of an election by the people the populous States will combine and elect whom they please. Just the reverse. The people of such States cannot combine. If there be any combination, it must be among their Representatives in the Legislature. It is said, the people will be led by a few designing men.

This might happen in a small district. It can never happen throughout the continent. In the election of a Governor of New York, it sometimes is the case in particular spots, that the activity and intrigues of little partizans are successful; but the general voice of the State is never influenced by such artifices. It is said, the multitude will be uninformed. It is true they would be uninformed of what passed in the Legislative conclave, if the election were to be made there; but they will not be uninformed of those great and illustrious characters which have merited their esteem and confidence. If the Executive be chosen by the national Legislature, he will not be independent of it; and if not independent, usurpation and tyranny on the part of the Legislature will be the consequence. This was the case in England in the last century. It has been the case in Holland, where their Senates have engrossed all power. It has been the case everywhere. He was surprised that an election by the people at large should ever have been likened to the Polish election of the first Magistrate. An election by the Legislature will bear a real likeness to the election by the Diet of Poland. The great must be the electors in both cases, and the corruption and cabal which are known to characterize the one would soon find their way into the other. Appointments made by numerous bodies are always worse than those made by single responsible individuals or by the people at large.

Col. Mason. It is curious to remark the different language held at different times. At one moment we are told that the Legislature is entitled to thorough confidence, and to indefinite power. At another, that it will be governed by intrigue and corruption, and cannot be trusted at all. But not to dwell on this inconsistency, he would observe that a government which is to last ought at least to be practicable. Would this be the case if the proposed election should be left to the people at large? He conceived it would be as unnatural to refer the choice of a proper character for Chief Magistrate to the people, as it would, to refer a trial of colors to a blind man. The extent of the country renders it impossible, that the people can have the requisite capacity to judge of the respective pretensions of the candidates.

Mr. WILSON could not see the contrariety stated by Col. MASON. The Legislature might deserve confidence in some respects, and distrust in others. In acts which were to affect them and their constituents precisely alike, confidence was due; in others, jealousy was warranted. The appointment to great offices, where the Legislature might feel many motives not common to the public, confidence was surely misplaced. This branch of business, it was notorious, was the most corruptly managed, of any that had been committed to legislative bodies.

Mr. WILLIAMSON conceived that there was the same difference between an election in this case, by the people and by the Legislature, as between an appointment by lot and by choice. There are at present distinguished characters, who are known perhaps to almost every man. This will not always be the case. The people will be sure to vote for some man in their own State; and the largest State will be sure to succeed. This will not be Virginia, however. Her slaves will have no suffrage. As the salary of the Executive will be fixed and he will not be eligible a second time, there will not be such a dependence on the Legislature as has been imagined.

On the question on an election by the people instead of the Legislature, it passed in the negative,— Pennsylvania, aye — 1; Massachusetts, Connecticut, New Jersey, Delaware, Maryland, Virginia, North Carolina, South Carolina, Georgia, no — 9.

Mr. L. MARTIN moved that the Executive be chosen by Electors appointed by the several Legislatures of the individual States.

Mr. BROOM seconds.

On the question it passed in the negative,— Delaware, Maryland, aye — 2; Massachusetts, Connecticut, New Jersey, Pennsylvania, Virginia, North Carolina, South Carolina, Georgia, no — 8.

On the question on the words, "to be chosen by the National Legislature," it passed unanimously in the affirmative.

"For the term of seven years,"— postponed, *nem. con.,* on motion of Mr. HOUSTON and Mr. GOUVERNEUR MORRIS.

"To carry into execution the national laws,"— agreed to, *nem. con.*

"To appoint to offices in cases not otherwise provided for,"— agreed to *nem. con.*

"To be ineligible a second time,"— Mr. HOUSTON moved to strike out this clause.

Mr. SHERMAN seconds the motion.

Mr. GOUVERNEUR MORRIS espoused the motion. The ineligibility proposed by the clause as it stood, tended to destroy the great motive to good behaviour, the hope of being rewarded by a re-appointment. It was saying to him, make hay while the sun shines.

On the question for striking out, as moved by Mr. HOUSTON, it passed in the affirmative,— Massachusetts, Connecticut, New Jersey, Pennsylvania, Maryland, Georgia, aye — 6 ; Delaware, Virginia, North Carolina, South Carolina, no — 4.

The clause, "for the term of seven years," being resumed,—

Mr. BROOM was for a shorter term, since the Executive Magistrate was now to be re-eligible. Had he remained ineligible a second time, he should have preferred a longer term.

Doctor M'CLURG* moved to strike out seven years, and insert "during good behaviour." By striking out the words declaring him not re-eligible, he was put into a situation that would keep him dependent forever on the

---

*The probable object of this motion was merely to enforce the argument against the re-eligibility of the Executive magistrate, by holding out a tenure during good behaviour as the alternative for keeping him independent of the Legislature.

24

Legislature ; and he conceived the independence of the Executive to be equally essential with that of the Judiciary department.

Mr. GOUVERNEUR MORRIS seconded the motion. He expressed great pleasure in hearing it. This was the way to get a good Government. His fear that so valuable an ingredient would not be attained had led him to take the part he had done. He was indifferent how the Executive should be chosen, provided he held his place by this tenure.

Mr. BROOM highly approved the motion. It obviated all his difficulties.

Mr. SHERMAN considered such a tenure as by no means safe or admissible. As the Executive Magistrate is now re-eligible, he will be on good behaviour as far as will be necessary. If he behaves well, he will be continued ; if otherwise, displaced, on a succeeding election.

Mr. MADISON.* If it be essential to the preservation of liberty that the Legislative, Executive, and Judiciary powers be separate, it is essential to a maintenance of the separation, that they should be independent of each other. The Executive could not be independent of the Legislature, if dependent on the pleasure of that branch for a re-appointment. Why was it determined that the Judges should not hold their places by such a tenure ? Because they might be tempted to cultivate the Legislature, by an undue complaisance, and thus render the Legislature the virtual expositor, as well as the maker of the laws. In like manner, a dependence of the Executive on the Legislature would render it the executor as well as the maker of laws ; and then, according to the observation of Montesquieu, tyrannical laws may be made that they may be executed in a tyrannical manner. There was an analogy between the Executive and Judiciary departments in several respects.

---

* The view here taken of the subject was meant to aid in parrying the animadversions likely to fall on the motion of Doctor McClurg, for whom J. M. had a particular regard. The Doctor, though possessing talents of the highest order, was modest and unaccustomed to exert them in public debate.

The latter executed the laws in certain cases as the former did in others. The former expounded and applied them for certain purposes, as the latter did for others. The difference between them seemed to consist chiefly in two circumstances,— first, the collective interest and security were much more in the power belonging to the Executive, than to the Judiciary, department ; secondly, in the administration of the former, much greater latitude is left to opinion and discretion, than in the administration of the latter. But if the second consideration proves that it will be more difficult to establish a rule sufficiently precise for trying the Executive, than the Judges, and forms an objection to the same tenure of office, both considerations prove that it might be more dangerous to suffer a union between the Executive and Legislative powers, than between the Judiciary and Legislative powers. He conceived it to be absolutely necessary to a well constituted Republic, that the two first should be kept distinct and independent of each other. Whether the plan proposed by the motion was a proper one, was another question ; as it depended on the practicability of instituting a tribunal for impeachments as certain and as adequate in the one case, as in the other. On the other hand, respect for the mover entitled his proposition to a fair hearing and discussion, until a less objectionable expedient should be applied for guarding against a dangerous union of the Legislative and Executive departments.

Colonel MASON. This motion was made some time ago, and negatived by a very large majority. He trusted that it would be again negatived. It would be impossible to define the misbehaviour in such a manner as to subject it to a proper trial; and perhaps still more impossible to compel so high an offender, holding his office by such a tenure, to submit to a trial. He considered an Executive during good behaviour as a softer name only for an Executive for life, And that the next would be an easy step to hereditary monarchy. If the motion should finally succeed, he might himself live to see such a revolution. If he did not, it was probable his children or grand children would. He trusted there were few men in that House who wished for it. No State, he was sure, had so far revolted from republican principles, as to have the least bias in its favor.

Mr. MADISON was not apprehensive of being thought to favor any step towards monarchy. The real object with him was to prevent its introduction. Experience had proved a tendency in our government to throw all power into the Legislative vortex. The Executives of the States are in general little more than cyphers; the Legislatures omnipotent. If no effectual check be devised for restraining the instability and encroachments of the latter, a revolution of some kind or other would be inevitable. The preservation of republican government therefore required some expedient for the purpose, but required evidently, at the same time, that, in devising it, the genuine principles of that form should be kept in view.

Mr. GOUVERNEUR MORRIS was as little a friend to monarchy as any gentleman. He concurred in the opinion that the way to keep out monarchical government was to establish such a Republican government as would make the people happy, and prevent a desire of change.

Doct. McCLURG was not so much afraid of the shadow of monarchy, as to be unwilling to approach it; nor so wedded to republican government, as not to be sensible of the tyrannies that had been and may be exercised under that form. It was an essential object with him to make the Executive independent of the Legislature; and the only mode left for effecting it, after the vote destroying his ineligibility a second time, was to appoint him during good behaviour.

On the question for inserting "during good behaviour," in place of "seven years [with a re-eligibility]," it passed in the negative,— New Jersey, Pennsylvania, Delaware,

Virginia, aye — 4; Massachusetts, Connecticut, Maryland, North Carolina, South Carolina, Georgia, no — 6.*

On the motion to strike out " seven years," it passed in the negative, — Massachusetts, Pennsylvania, Delaware, North Carolina, aye — 4; Connecticut, New Jersey, Maryland, Virginia, South Carolina, Georgia, no — 6.†

It was now unanimously agreed that the vote which had struck out the words " to be ineligible a second time," should be reconsidered to-morrow.

Adjourned.

WEDNESDAY, JULY 18TH.

In Convention,— On motion of Mr. L. MARTIN to fix to-morrow for reconsidering the vote concerning the ineligibility of the Executive a second time, it passed in the affirmative,— Massachusetts, Connecticut, Pennsylvania, Delaware, Maryland, Virginia, North Carolina, South Carolina, aye — 8; New Jersey, Georgia, absent.

The residue of the ninth Resolution, concerning the Executive, was postponed till to-morrow.

The tenth Resolution, " that the Executive shall have a right to negative legislative acts not afterwards passed by two-thirds of each branch," was passed, *nem. con.*

The eleventh Resolution, " that a National Judiciary shall be established to consist of one supreme tribunal," agreed to *nem. con.*

On the clause, " The judges of which to be appointed by the second branch of the National Legislature,"—

---

* This vote is not to be considered as any certain index of opinion, as a number in the affirmative probably had it chiefly in view to alarm those attached to a dependence of the Executive on the Legislature, and thereby facilitate some final arrangement of a contrary tendency. The avowed friends of an Executive "during good behaviour" were not more than three or four, nor is it certain they would have adhered to such a tenure.

An independence of the three great departments of each other, as far as possible, and the responsibility of all to the will of the community, seemed to be generally admitted as the true basis of a well constructed Government.

† There was no debate on this motion. The apparent object of many in the affirmative was to secure the re-eligibility by shortening the term, and of many in the negative to embarrass the plan of referring the appointment and dependence of the Executive to the Legislature.

Mr. GORHAM would prefer an appointment by the second branch to an appointment by the whole Legislature; but he thought even that branch too numerous, and too little personally responsible, to ensure a good choice. He suggested that the Judges be appointed by the Executive with the advice and consent of the second branch, in the mode prescribed by the Constitution of Massachusetts. This mode had been long practised in that country, and was found to answer perfectly well.

Mr. WILSON would still prefer an appointment by the Executive; but if that could not be attained, would prefer, in the next place, the mode suggested by Mr. GORHAM. He thought it his duty, however, to move in the first instance, "that the Judges be appointed by the Executive."

Mr. GOUVERNEUR MORRIS seconded the motion.

Mr. L. MARTIN was strenuous for an appointment by the second branch. Being taken from all the States, it would be best informed of characters, and most capable of making a fit choice.

Mr. SHERMAN concurred in the observations of Mr. MARTIN, adding that the Judges ought to be diffused, which would be more likely to be attended to by the second branch, than by the Executive.

Mr. MASON. The mode of appointing the Judges may depend in some degree on the mode of trying impeachments of the Executive. If the Judges were to form a tribunal for that purpose, they surely ought not to be appointed by the Executive. There were insuperable objections besides against referring the appointment to the Executive. He mentioned, as one, that as the seat of government must be in some one State; and as the Executive would remain in office for a considerable time, for four, five, or six years at least, he would insensibly form local and personal attachments within the particular State that would deprive equal merit elsewhere of an equal chance of promotion.

Mr. GORHAM. As the Executive will be responsible, in

point of character at least, for a judicious and faithful discharge of his trust, he will be careful to look through all the States for proper characters. The Senators will be as likely to form their attachments at the seat of government where they reside, as the Executive. If they cannot get the man of the particular State to which they may respectively belong, they will be indifferent to the rest. Public bodies feel no personal responsibility, and give full play to intrigue and cabal. Rhode Island is a full illustration of the insensibility to character produced by a participation of numbers in dishonourable measures, and of the length to which a public body may carry wickedness and cabal.

Mr. GOUVERNEUR MORRIS supposed it would be improper for an impeachment of the Executive to be tried before the Judges. The latter would in such case be drawn into intrigues with the Legislature, and an impartial trial would be frustrated. As they would be much about the seat of government, they might even be previously consulted, and arangements might be made for a prosecution of the Executive. He thought, therefore, that no argument could be drawn from the probability of such a plan of impeachments against the motion before the House.

Mr. MADISON suggested, that the Judges might oe appointed by the Executive, with the concurrence of one-third at least of the second branch. This would unite the advantage of responsibility in the Executive, with the security afforded in the second branch against any incautious or corrupt nomination by the Executive.

Mr. SHERMAN was clearly for an election by the Senate. It would be composed of men nearly equal to the Executive, and would of course have on the whole more wisdom. They would bring into their deliberations a more diffusive knowledge of characters. It would be less easy for candidates to intrigue with them, than with the Executive Magistrate. For these reasons he thought there would be a better security for a proper choice in the Senate, than in the Executive.

Mr. RANDOLPH. It is true that when the appointment of the Judges was vested in the second branch an equality of votes had not been given to it. Yet he had rather leave the appointment there than give it to the Executive. He thought the advantage of personal responsibility might be gained in the Senate, by requiring the respective votes of the members to be entered on the Journal. He thought, too, that the hope of receiving appointments would be more diffusive, if they depended on the Senate, the members of which would be diffusively known, than if they depended on a single man, who could not be personally known to a very great extent; and consequently, that opposition to the system would be so far weakened.

Mr. BEDFORD thought, there were solid reasons against leaving the appointment to the Executive. He must trust more to information than the Senate. It would put it in his power to gain over the larger States by gratifying them with a preference of their citizens. The responsibility of the Executive, so much talked of, was chimerical. He could not be punished for mistakes.

Mr. GORHAM remarked, that the Senate could have no better information than the Executive. They must like him trust to information from the members belonging to the particular State where the candidate resided. The Executive would certainly be more answerable for a good appointment, as the whole blame of a bad one would fall on him alone. He did not mean that he would be answerable under any other penalty than that of public censure, which with honourable minds was a sufficient one.

On the question for referring the appointment of the Judges to the Executive, instead of the second branch, — Massachusetts, Pennsylvania, aye — 2; Connecticut, Delaware, Maryland, Virginia, North Carolina South Carolina, no — 6; Georgia, absent.

Mr. GORHAM moved, "that the Judges be nominated and appointed by the Executive, by and with the advice and consent of the second branch; and every such nomination

shall be made at least —— days prior to such appointment."
This mode, he said, had been ratified by the experience of
a hundred and forty years in Massachusetts. If the appointment should be left to either branch of the Legislature, it will be a mere piece of jobbing.

Mr. Gouverneur Morris seconded and supported the
motion.

Mr. Sherman thought it less objectionable than an absolute appointment by the Executive; but disliked it, as too
much fettering the Senate.

On the question on Mr. Gorham's motion, — Massachusetts, Pennsylvania, Maryland, Virginia, aye — 4; Connecticut, Delaware, North Carolina, South Carolina, no — 4;
Georgia, absent.

Mr. Madison moved, "that the Judges should be
nominated by the Executive, and such nomination should
become an appointment if not disagreed to within ——
days by two-thirds of the second branch."

Mr. Gouverneur Morris seconded the motion.

By common consent the consideration of it was postponed till to-morrow.

"To hold their offices during good behaviour, and to
receive fixed salaries,"— agreed to, *nem. con.*

"In which [salaries of Judges] no increase or diminution shall be made so as to affect the persons actually in
office at the time."

Mr. Gouverneur Morris moved to strike out "or
increase." He thought the Legislature ought to be at
liberty to increase salaries, as circumstances might require ;
and that this would not create any improper dependence in
the Judges.

Doctor Franklin was in favor of the motion. Money
may not only become plentier ; but the business of the
Department may increase, as the country becomes more
populous.

Mr. Madison. The dependence will be less if the
increase alone should be permitted ; but it will be improper

even so far to permit a dependence.   Whenever an increase
is wished by the Judges, or may be in agitation in the
Legislature, an undue complaisance in the former may be
felt towards the latter.   If at such a crisis there should be
in court suits to which leading members of the Legislature may be parties, the Judges will be in a situation which
ought not to be suffered, if it can be prevented.   The
variations in the value of money may be guarded against
by taking for a standard wheat or some other thing of permanent value.   The increase of business will be provided
for by an increase of the number who are to do it.   An
increase of salaries may easily be so contrived as not to
affect persons in office.

Mr. GOUVERNEUR MORRIS.   The value of money may
not only alter, but the state of society may alter.   In this
event, the same quantity of wheat, the same value, would
not be the same compensation.   The amount of salaries
must always be regulated by the manners and the style
of living in a country.   The increase of business cannot be
provided for in the supreme tribunal, in the way that has
been mentioned.   All the business of a certain description,
whether more or less, must be done in that single tribunal.
Additional labor alone in the Judges can provide for additional business.   Additional compensation, therefore ought
not to be prohibited.

On the question for striking out, " or increase,"— Massachusetts, Connecticut, Pennsylvania, Delaware, Maryland,
South Carolina, aye — 6 ; Virginia, North Carolina, no —
2 ; Georgia, absent.

The whole clause, as amended, was then agreed to,
nem. con.

The twelfth Resolution, " that the National Legislature
be empowered to appoint inferior tribunals," being taken
up,—

Mr. BUTLER could see no necessity for such tribunals.
The State tribunals might do the business.

Mr. L. MARTIN concurred.   They will create jealousies

and oppositions in the State tribunals, with the jurisdiction of which they will interfere.

Mr. GORHAM. There are in the States already Federal Courts, with jurisdiction for trial of piracies, &c. committed on the seas. No complaints have been made by the States or the courts of the States. Inferior tribunals are essential to render the authority of the National Legislature effectual.

Mr. RANDOLPH observed, that the courts of the States cannot be trusted with the administration of the National laws. The objects of jurisdiction are such as will often place the general and local policy at variance.

Mr. GOUVERNEUR MORRIS urged also the necessity of such a provision.

Mr. SHERMAN was willing to give the power to the Legislature, but wished them to make use of the State tribunals, whenever it could be done with safety to the general interest.

Col. MASON thought many circumstances might arise, not now to be foreseen, which might render such a power absolutely necessary.

On the question for agreeing to the twelfth Resolution, empowering the National Legislature to appoint inferior tribunals,— it was agreed to, *nem. con.*

The clause of "Impeachments of national officers," was struck out, on motion for the purpose.

The thirteenth Resolution, " The jurisdiction of the National Judiciary, &c." being then taken up, several criticisms having been made on the definition, it was proposed by Mr. MADISON so to alter it as to read thus; "that the jurisdiction shall extend to all cases arising under the national laws; and to such other questions as may involve the national peace and harmony," which was agreed to, *nem. con.*

The fourteenth Resolution, providing for the admission of new States, was agreed to, *nem. con.*

The fifteenth Resolution, " that provision ought to be

made for the continuance of Congress, &c. and for the completion of their engagements," being considered,-

Mr. GOUVERNEUR MORRIS thought the assumption of their engagements might as well be omitted; and that Congress ought not to be continued till all the States should adopt the reform; since it may become expedient to give effect to it whenever a certain number of States shall adopt it.

Mr. MADISON. The clause can mean nothing more than that provision ought to be made for preventing an interregnum; which must exist, in the interval between the adoption of the new Government and the commencement of its operation, if the old Government should cease on the first of these events.

Mr. WILSON did not entirely approve of the manner in which the clause relating to the engagements of Congress was expressed; but he thought some provision on the subject would be proper in order to prevent any suspicion that the obligations of the Confederacy might be dissolved along with the Government under which they were contracted.

On the question on the first part, relating to the continuance of Congress,— Virginia, North Carolina, South Carolina,* aye — 3; Massachusetts, Connecticut, Pennsylvania, Delaware, Maryland, Georgia, no — 6. The second part, as to the completion of their engagements, was disagreed to, *nem. con.*

The sixteenth Resolution, " That a republican Constitution and its existing laws ought to be guaranteed to each State by the United States " being considered,—

Mr. GOUVERNEUR MORRIS thought the Resolution very objectionable. He should be very unwilling that such laws as exist in Rhode Island should be guaranteed.

Mr. WILSON. The object is merely to secure the States against dangerous commotions, insurrections and rebellions.

Col. MASON. If the General Government should have no right to suppress rebellions against particular States, it will be in a bad situation indeed. As rebellions against

---

* In the printed Journal, South Carolina, no.

itself originate in and against individual States, it must remain a passive spectator of its own subversion.

Mr. RANDOLPH. The Resolution has two objects,— first, to secure a republican government; secondly, to suppress domestic commotions. He urged the necessity of both these provisions.

Mr. MADISON moved to substitute, "that the constitutional authority of the States shall be guaranteed to them respectively against domestic as well as foreign violence."

Doctor McCLURG seconded the motion.

Mr. HOUSTON was afraid of perpetuating the existing Constitutions of the States. That of Georgia was a very bad one, and he hoped would be revised and amended. It may also be difficult for the General Government to decide between contending parties, each of which claim the sanction of the Constitution.

Mr. L. MARTIN was for leaving the States to suppress rebellions themselves.

Mr. GORHAM thought it strange that a rebellion should be known to exist in the Empire, and the General Government should be restrained from interposing to subdue it. At this rate an enterprising citizen might erect the standard of monarchy in a particular State, might gather together partizans from all quarters, might extend his views from State to State, and threaten to establish a tyranny over the whole, and the General Government be compelled to remain an inactive witness of its own destruction. With regard to different parties in a State, as long as they confine their disputes to words, they will be harmless to the General Government and to each other. If they appeal to the sword, it will then be necessary for the General Government, however difficult it may be, to decide on the merits of their contest, to interpose and put an end to it.

Mr. CARROLL. Some such provision is essential. Every State ought to wish for it. It has been doubted whether it is a *casus fœderis* at present; and no room ought to be left for such a doubt hereafter.

Mr. RANDOLPH moved to add, as an amendment to the motion, "and that no State be at liberty to form any other than a republican government."

Mr. MADISON seconded the motion.

Mr. RUTLEDGE thought it unnecessary to insert any guarantee. No doubt could be entertained but that Congress had the authority, if they had the means, to co-operate with any State in subduing a rebellion. It was and would be involved in the nature of the thing.

Mr. WILSON moved, as a better expression of the idea, "that a republican form of Government shall be guaranteed to each State; and that each State shall be protected against foreign and domestic violence."

This seeming to be well received, Mr. MADISON and Mr. RANDOLPH withdrew their propositions, and on the question for agreeing to Mr. WILSON's motion, it passed, *nem. con.*

Adjourned.

THURSDAY, JULY 19TH.

In Convention, — On re-consideration of the vote rendering the Executive re-eligible a second time, Mr. MARTIN moved to re-instate the words, "to be ineligible a second time."

Mr. GOUVERNEUR MORRIS. It is necessary to take into one view all that relates to the establishment of the Executive; on the due formation of which must depend the efficacy and utility of the union among the present and future States. It has been a maxim in political science, that republican government is not adapted to a large extent of country, because the energy of the executive magistracy cannot reach the extreme parts of it. Our country is an extensive one. We must either then renounce the blessings of the Union, or provide an Executive with sufficient vigor to pervade every part of it. This subject was of so much importance that he hoped to be indulged in an extensive view of it. One great object of the Executive is, to control the Legislature. The Legislature will continually seek to aggrandize and perpetuate themselves; and will seize those critical moments produced by war, invasion, or convulsion, for that purpose. It is necessary, then, that the Executive magistrate should be the guardian of the people, even of the lower classes, against legislative tyranny; against the great and the wealthy, who in the course of things will necessarily compose the legislative body. Wealth tends to corrupt the mind; — to nourish its love of power; and to stimulate it to oppression. History proves this to be the spirit of the opulent. The check provided in the second branch was not meant as a check on legislative usurpations of power, but on the abuse of lawful powers, on the propensity of the first branch to legislate too much, to run into projects of paper-money, and similar expedients. It is no check on legislative tyranny. On the contrary it may favor it; and if the first branch can be seduced, may find the means of success. The Executive, therefore, ought to be so constituted, as to be the great protector of the mass of the people. It is the duty of the Executive to appoint the officers, and to command the forces, of the Republic; to appoint, first, ministerial officers for the administration of public affairs; secondly, officers for the dispensation of justice. Who will be the best judges whether these appointments be well made? The people at large, who will know, will see, will feel, the effects of them. Again, who can judge so well of the discharge of military duties for the protection and security of the people, as the people themselves, who are to be protected and secured? He finds, too, that the Executive is not to be re-eligible. What effect will this have? In the first place, it will destroy the great incitement to merit, public esteem, by taking away the hope of being rewarded with a re-appointment. It may give a dangerous turn to one of the strongest passions in the human breast. The love of fame is the great spring to noble and illustrious actions. Shut the civil road to glory, and he may be compelled to

seek it by the sword. In the second place, it will tempt
him to make the most of the short space of time allotted
him, to accumulate wealth and provide for his friends. In
the third place, it will produce violations of the very Constitution it is meant to secure. In moments of pressing
danger, the tried abilities and established character of a
favorite magistrate will prevail over respect for the forms
of the Constitution. The Executive is also to be impeachable. This is a dangerous part of the plan. It will hold
him in such dependence, that he will be no check on the
Legislature, will not be a firm guardian of the people and
of the public interest. He will be the tool of a faction, of
some leading demagogue in the Legislature. These then,
are the faults of the Executive establishment, as now proposed. Can no better establishment be devised? If he is
to be the guardian of the people, let him be appointed by
the people. If he is to be a check on the Legislature, let
him not be impeachable. Let him be of short duration,
that he may with propriety be re-eligible. It has been
said that the candidates for this office will not be known to
the people. If they be known to the Legislature, they
must have such a notoriety and eminence of character,
that they cannot possibly be unknown to the people at large.
It cannot be possible that a man shall have sufficiently distinguished himself to merit this high trust, without having
his character proclaimed by fame throughout the Empire.
As to the danger from an unimpeachable magistrate, he
could not regard it as formidable. There must be certain
great officers of state, a minister of finance, of war, of
foreign affairs, &c. These, he presumes, will exercise
their functions in subordination to the Executive, and will
be amenable, by impeachment, to the public justice.
Without these ministers, the Executive can do nothing of
consequence. He suggested a biennial election of the
Executive, at the time of electing the first branch; and the
Executive to hold over, so as to prevent any interregnum in
the administration. An election by the people at large,

throughout so great an extent of country, could not be
influenced by those little combinations and those momentary lies, which often decide popular elections within a
narrow sphere. It will probably be objected, that the election will be influenced by the members of the Legislature,
particularly of the first branch; and that it will be nearly
the same thing with an election by the Legislature itself.
It could not be denied that such an influence would exist.
But it might be answered, that as the Legislature or the
candidates for it, would be divided the enmity of one part
would counteract the friendship of another; that if the
administration of the Executive were good, it would be unpopular to oppose his re-election; if bad, it ought to be
opposed, and a re-appointment prevented; and lastly, that
in every view this indirect dependence on the favor of the
Legislature could not be so mischievous as a direct dependence for his appointment. He saw no alternative for making
the Executive independent of the Legislature, but either
to give him his office for life, or make him eligible by the
people. Again, it might be objected, that two years would
be too short a duration. But he believes that as long as he
should behave himself well he would be continued in his
place. The extent of the country would secure his re-election against the factions and discontents of particular
States. It deserved consideration, also, that such an
ingredient in the plan would render it extremely palatable
to the people. These were the general ideas which
occurred to him on the subject, and which led him to wish
and move that the whole constitution of the Executive
might undergo re-consideration.

Mr. RANDOLPH urged the motion of Mr. L. MARTIN for
restoring the words making the Executive ineligible a second time. If he ought to be independent, he should not be
left under a temptation to court a re-appointment. If he
should be re-appointable by the Legislature, he will be no
check on it. His revisionary power will be of no avail.
He had always thought and contended, as he still did, that

25

the danger apprehended by the little States was chimerical;
but those who thought otherwise ought to be peculiarly
anxious for the motion. If the Executive be appointed, as
has been determined, by the Legislature, he will probably be appointed, either by joint ballot of both houses, or
be nominated by the first and appointed by the second
branch. In either case the large States will preponderate.
If he is to court the same influence for his re-appointment,
will he not make his revisionary power, and all the other
functions of his administration, subservient to the views of
the large States? Besides, is there not great reason to
apprehend, that, in case he should be re-eligible, a false
complaisance in the Legislature might lead them to continue
an unfit man in office, in preference to a fit one? It has
been said, that a constitutional bar to re-appointment, will
inspire unconstitutional endeavours to perpetuate himself.
It may be answered, that his endeavours can have no effect
unless the people be corrupt to such a degree as to render
all precautions hopeless; to which may be added, that this
argument supposes him to be more powerful and dangerous, than other arguments which have been used admit, and
consequently calls for stronger fetters on his authority.
He thought an election by the Legislature, with an incapacity to be elected a second time, would be more acceptable to the people than the plan suggested by Mr. GOUVER-
NEUR MORRIS.

Mr. KING did not like the ineligibility. He thought
there was great force in the remarks of Mr. SHERMAN, that
he who has proved himself most fit for an office, ought not
to be excluded by the Constitution from holding it. He
would therefore prefer any other reasonable plan that could
be substituted. He was much disposed to think, that in
such cases the people at large would choose wisely. There
was indeed some difficulty arising from the improbability of
a general concurrence of the people in favor of any one
man. On the whole, he was of opinion that an appointment

by electors chosen by the people for the purpose would be liable to fewest objections.

Mr. PATTERSON's ideas nearly coincided, he said, with those of Mr. KING. He proposed that the Executive should be appointed by electors, to be chosen by the States in a ratio that would allow one elector to the smallest, and three to the largest, States.

Mr. WILSON. It seems to be the unanimous sense that the Executive should not be appointed by the Legislature, unless he be rendered ineligible a second time: he perceived with pleasure that the idea was gaining ground of an election, mediately or immediately, by the people.

Mr. MADISON. If it be a fundamental principle of free government that the Legislative, Executive and Judiciary powers should be *separately* exercised, it is equally so that they be *independently* exercised. There is the same, and perhaps greater, reason why the Executive should be independent of the Legislature, than why the Judiciary should. A coalition of the two former powers, would be more immediately and certainly dangerous to public liberty. It is essential, then, that the appointment of the Executive should either be drawn from some source, or held by some tenure, that will give him a free agency with regard to the Legislature. This could not be, if he was to be appointable, from time to time, by the Legislature. It was not clear that an appointment in the first instance, even with an ineligibility afterwards, would not establish an improper connection between the two Departments. Certain it was, that the appointment would be attended with intrigues and contentions, that ought not to be unnecessarily admitted. He was disposed, for these reasons, to refer the appointment to some other source. The people at large was, in his opinion, the fittest in itself. It would be as likely as any that could be devised, to produce an Executive Magistrate of distinguished character. The people generally could only know and vote for some citizen whose merits had rendered him an object of general attention and esteem. There was one difficulty, however, of a serious nature, attending an immediate choice by the people. The right of suffrage was much more diffusive in the Northern than the Southern States; and the latter could have no influence in the election, on the score of the negroes. The substitution of Electors obviated this difficulty, and seemed on the whole to be liable to fewest objections.

Mr. GERRY. If the Executive is to be elected by the Legislature, he certainly ought not to be re-eligible. This would make him absolutely dependent. He was against a popular election. The people are uninformed, and would be misled by a few designing men. He urged the expediency of an appointment of the Executive, by Electors to be chosen by the State Executives. The people of the States will then choose the first branch; the Legislatures of the States, the second branch of the National Legislature; and the Executives of the States, the National Executive. This he thought would form a strong attachment in the States to the National system. The popular mode of electing the Chief Magistrate would certainly be the worst of all. If he should be so elected, and should do his duty, he will be turned out for it, like Governor Bowdoin in Massachusetts, and President Sullivan in New Hampshire.

On the question on Mr. GOUVERNEUR MORRIS's motion, to reconsider generally the constitution of the Executive, — Massachusetts, Connecticut, New Jersey, and all the others, aye.

Mr. ELLSWORTH moved to strike out the appointment by the National Legislature, and to insert, "to be chosen by Electors, appointed by the Legislatures of the States in the following ratio; to wit: one for each State not exceeding two hundred thousand inhabitants; two for each above that number and not exceeding three hundred thousand; and three for each State exceeding three hundred thousand."

Mr. BROOM seconded the motion.

Mr. RUTLEDGE was opposed to all the modes, except the

appointment by the National Legislature. He will be sufficiently independent, if he be not re-eligible.

Mr. GERRY preferred the motion of Mr. ELLSWORTH to an appointment by the National Legislature, or by the people; though not to an appointment by the State Executives. He moved that the Electors proposed by Mr. ELLSWORTH should be twenty-five in number, and allotted in the following proportion: to New Hampshire, one; to Massachusetts, three; to Rhode Island, one; to Connecticut, two; to New York, two; to New Jersey, two; to Pennsylvania, three; to Delaware, one; to Maryland, two; to Virginia, three; to North Carolina, two; to South Carolina two; to Georgia, one.

The question, as moved by Mr. ELLSWORTH, being divided, on the first part "Shall the National Executive be appointed by Electors?" — Connecticut, New Jersey, Pennsylvania, Delaware, Maryland, Virginia, aye — 6; North Carolina, South Carolina, Georgia, no — 3; Massachusetts, divided.

On the second part, "Shall the Electors be chosen by the State Legislatures?" — Massachusetts, Connecticut, New Jersey, Pennsylvania, Delaware, Maryland, North Carolina, Georgia, aye — 8; Virginia, South Carolina no — 2.

The part relating to the ratio in which the States should choose Electors was postponed, *nem. con.*

Mr. L. MARTIN moved that the Executive be ineligible a second time,

Mr. WILLIAMSON seconds the motion. He had no great confidence in electors to be chosen for the special purpose. They would not be the most respectable citizens; but persons not occupied in the high offices of government. They would be liable to undue influence, which might the more readily be practised, as some of them will probably be in appointment six or eight months before the object of it comes on.

Mr. ELLSWORTH supposed any persons might be appointed Electors, except, solely, members of the National Legislature.

On the question, "Shall he be ineligible a second time?" — North Carolina, South Carolina, aye — 2; Massachusetts, Connecticut, New Jersey, Pennsylvania, Delaware, Maryland, Virginia, Georgia, no — 8.

On the question, "Shall the Executive continue for seven years?" It passed in the negative, — * Connecticut, South Carolina, Georgia, aye — 3 ; * New Jersey, Pennsylvania, Delaware, Maryland, Virginia, no — 5 ; Massachusetts, North Carolina, divided.

Mr. KING was afraid we should shorten the term too much.

Mr. GOUVERNEUR MORRIS was for a short term, in order to avoid impeachments, which would be otherwise necessary.

Mr. BUTLER was against the frequency of the elections. Georgia and South Carolina were too distant to send electors often.

Mr. ELLSWORTH was for six years. If the elections be too frequent, the Executive will not be firm enough. There must be duties which will make him unpopular for the moment. There will be *outs* as well as *ins*. His administration, therefore, will be attacked and misrepresented.

Mr. WILLIAMSON was for six years. The expense will be considerable, and ought not to be unnecessarily repeated. If the elections are too frequent, the best men will not undertake the service, and those of an inferior character will be liable to be corrupted.

On the question of six years, — Massachusetts, Connecticut, New Jersey, Pennsylvania, Maryland, Virginia, North Carolina, South Carolina, Georgia, aye — 9 ; Delaware, no.

Adjourned.

---

* In the printed Journal, Connecticut, no; New Jersey, aye.

FRIDAY, JULY 20TH.

In Convention,— The proposed ratio of Electors for appointing the Executive, to wit : one for each State whose inhabitants do not exceed two hundred thousand, &c., being taken up,—

Mr. MADISON observed that this would make, in time, all or nearly all the States equal, since there were few that would not in time contain the number of inhabitants entitling them to three Electors ; that this ratio ought either to be made temporary, or so varied as that it would adjust itself to the growing population of the States.

Mr. GERRY moved that *in the first instance* the Electors should be allotted to the States in the following ratio : to New Hampshire, one ; Massachusetts, three ; Rhode Island, one ; Connecticut two ; New York, two ; New Jersey, two ; Pennsylvania, three ; Delaware, one ; Maryland, two ; Virginia, three ; North Carolina, two ; South Carolina, two ; Georgia, one.

On the question to postpone in order to take up this motion of Mr. GERRY, it passed in the affirmative,—Massachusetts, Pennsylvania, Virginia, North Carolina, South Carolina, Georgia, aye — 6 ; Connecticut, New Jersey, Delaware, Maryland, no — 4.

Mr. ELLSWORTH moved that two Electors be allotted to New Hampshire. Some rule ought to be pursued ; and New Hampshire has more than a hundred thousand inhabitants. He thought it would be proper also to allot two to Georgia.

Mr. BROOM and Mr. MARTIN moved to postpone Mr. GERRY's allotment of Electors, leaving a fit ratio to be reported by the Committee to be appointed for detailing the Resolutions.

On this motion, — New Jersey, Delaware, Maryland, aye, — 3; Massachusetts, Connecticut, Pennsylvania, Virginia, North Carolina, South Carolina, Georgia, no — 7.

Mr. HOUSTON seconded the motion of Mr. ELLSWORTH to add another Elector to New Hampshire and Georgia.

On the question, — Connecticut, South Carolina, Georgia, aye — 3; Massachusetts, New Jersey, Pennsylvania, Delaware, Maryland, Virginia, North Carolina, no — 7.

Mr. WILLIAMSON moved as an amendment to Mr. GERRY's allotment of Electors, in the first instance, that in future elections of the National Executive the number of Electors to be appointed by the several States shall be regulated by their respective numbers of representatives in the first branch, pursuing as nearly as may be, the present proportions.

On the question on Mr. GERRY's ratio of Electors, — Massachusetts, Connecticut, Pennsylvania, Virginia, North Carolina, South Carolina, aye — 6: New Jersey, Delaware, Maryland, Georgia, no — 4.

On the clause, "to be removable on impeachment and conviction for malpractice or neglect of duty," (see the ninth Resolution),—

Mr. PINCKNEY and Mr. GOUVERNEUR MORRIS moved to strike out this part of the Resolution. Mr. PINCKNEY observed, he ought not to be impeachable whilst in office.

Mr. DAVIE. If he be not impeachable whilst in office, he will spare no efforts or means whatever to get himself re-elected. He considered this as an essential security for the good behaviour of the Executive.

Mr. WILSON concurred in the necessity of making the Executive impeachable whilst in office.

Mr. GOUVERNEUR MORRIS. He could do no criminal act without coadjutors, who may be punished. In case he should be re-elected, that will be a sufficient proof of his innocence. Besides, who is to impeach? Is the impeachment to suspend his functions? If it is not, the mischief will go on. If it is, the impeachment will be nearly equivalent to a displacement; and will render the Executive dependent on those who are to impeach.

Colonel MASON. No point is of more importance than

that the right of impeachment should be continued. Shall any man be above justice? Above all, shall that man be above it who can commit the most extensive injustice? When great crimes were committed, he was for punishing the principal as well as the coadjutors. There had been much debate and difficulty as to the mode of choosing the Executive. He approved of that which had been adopted at first, namely, of referring the appointment to the National Legislature. One objection against Electors was the danger of their being corrupted by the candidates, and this furnished a peculiar reason in favor of impeachments whilst in office. Shall the man who has practised corruption, and by that means procured his appointment in the first instance, be suffered to escape punishment by repeating his guilt?

Doctor FRANKLIN was for retaining the clause as favourable to the Executive. History furnishes one example only of a First Magistrate being formally brought to public justice. Every body cried out against this as unconstitutional. What was the practice before this, in cases where the Chief Magistrate rendered himself obnoxious? Why, recourse was had to assassination, in which he was not only deprived of his life, but of the opportunity of vindicating his character. It would be the best way, therefore, to provide in the Constitution for the regular punishment of the Executive, where his misconduct should deserve it, and for his honorable acquittal, where he should be unjustly accused.

Mr. GOUVERNEUR MORRIS admits corruption, and some few other offences, to be such as ought to be impeachable; but thought the cases ought to be enumerated and defined.

Mr. MADISON thought it indispensable that some provision should be made for defending the community against the incapacity, negligence, or perfidy of the Chief Magistrate. The limitation of the period of his service was not a sufficient security. He might lose his capacity after his appointment. He might pervert his administration into a scheme of peculation or oppression. He might betray his

trust to foreign powers. The case of the Executive magistracy was very distinguishable from that of the Legislature,
or any other public body, holding offices of limited duration.
It could not be presumed that all, or even the majority, of
the members of an Assembly would either lose their capacity for discharging, or be bribed to betray, their trust.
Besides, the restraints of their personal integrity and honor,
the difficulty of acting in concert for purposes of corruption
was a security to the public. And if one or a few members
only should be seduced, the soundness of the remaining
members would maintain the integrity and fidelity of the
body. In the case of the Executive magistracy, which was
to be administered by a single man, loss of capacity or corruption was more within the compass of probable events,
and either of them might be fatal to the Republic.

Mr. PINCKNEY did not see the necessity of impeachments.
He was sure they ought not to issue from the Legislature,
who would in that case hold them as a rod over the Executive, and by that means effectually destroy his independence. His revisionary power in particular would be rendered altogether insignificant.

Mr. GERRY urged the necessity of impeachments. A
good magistrate will not fear them. A bad one ought to
be kept in fear of them. He hoped the maxim would never
be adopted here that the chief magistrate could do no
wrong.

Mr. KING expressed his apprehensions that an extreme
caution in favor of liberty, might enervate the government
we were forming. He wished the House to recur to the
primitive axiom, that the three great departments of government should be separate and independent; that the Executive and Judiciary should be so as well as the Legislative;
that the Executive should be so equally with the Judiciary.
Would this be the case if the Executive should be impeachable? It had been said, that the Judiciary would be impeachable. But it should have been remembered, at the
same time, that the Judiciary hold their places not for a

limited time, but during good behaviour. It is necessary, therefore, that a form should be established for trying misbehaviour. Was the Executive to hold his place during good behaviour? The Executive was to hold his place for a limited time, like the members of the Legislature. Like them, particularly the Senate, whose members would continue in appointment the same term of six years, he would periodically be tried for his behaviour by his electors, who would continue or discontinue him in trust according to the manner in which he had discharged it. Like them, therefore, he ought to be subject to no intermediate trial, by impeachment. He ought not to be impeachable unless he held his office during good behaviour, a tenure which would be most agreeable to him, provided an independent and effectual forum could be devised. But under no circumstances ought he to be impeachable by the Legislature. This would be destructive of his independence, and of the principles of the Constitution. He relied on the vigor of the Executive, as a great security for the public liberties.

Mr. RANDOLPH. The propriety of impeachments was a favorite principle with him. Guilt, wherever found, ought to be punished. The Executive will have great opportunities of abusing his power; particularly in time of war, when the military force, and in some respects the public money, will be in his hands. Should no regular punishment be provided, it will be irregularly inflicted by tumults and insurrections. He is aware of the necessity of proceeding with a cautious hand, and of excluding as much as possible the influence of the Legislature from the business. He suggested for consideration an idea which had fallen (from Colonel HAMILTON), of composing a forum out of the Judges belonging to the States; and even of requiring some preliminary inquest, whether just ground of impeachment existed.

Doctor FRANKLIN mentioned the case of the Prince of Orange, during the late war. An arrangement was made between France and Holland, by which their two fleets were

to unite at a certain time and place. The Dutch fleet did
not appear. Every body began to wonder at it. At length
it was suspected that the Stadtholder was at the bottom of
the matter. This suspicion prevailed more and more. Yet
as he could not be impeached, and no regular examination
took place, he remained in his office; and strengthening his
own party, as the party opposed to him became formidable,
he gave birth to the most violent animosities and contentions. Had he been impeachable, a regular and peaceable
inquiry would have taken place, and he would, if guilty,
have been duly punished,—if innocent, restored to the confidence of the public.

Mr. KING remarked, that the case of the Stadtholder
was not applicable. He held his place for life, and was not
periodically elected. In the former case, impeachments are
proper to secure good behaviour. In the latter, they are
unnecessary; the periodical responsibility to the Electors
being an equivalent security.

Mr. WILSON observed, that if the idea were to be pursued,
the Senators who are to hold their places during the same
term with the Executive, ought to be subject to impeachment and removal.

Mr. PINCKNEY apprehended that some gentlemen
reasoned on a supposition that the Executive was to have
powers which would not be committed to him. He presumed
that his powers would be so circumscribed as to render
impeachments unnecessary.

Mr. GOUVERNEUR MORRIS's opinion had been changed
by the arguments used in the discussion. He was now
sensible of the necessity of impeachments, if the Executive
was to continue for any length of time in office. Our
Executive was not like a magistrate having a life interest,
much less, like one having an hereditary interest, in his office.
He may be bribed by a greater interest to betray his trust;
and no one would say that we ought to expose ourselves to
the danger of seeing the First Magistrate in foreign pay,
without being able to guard against it by displacing him.

One would think the King of England well secured against bribery. He has, as it were, a fee simple in the whole Kingdom. Yet Charles II. was bribed by Louis XIV. The Executive ought, therefore, to be impeachable for treachery. Corrupting his Electors, and incapacity, were other causes of impeachment. For the latter he should be punished, not as a man, but as an officer, and punished only by degradation from his office. This Magistrate is not the King, but the prime minister. The people are the King. When we make him amenable to justice, however, we should take care to provide some mode that will not make him dependent on the Legislature.

It was moved and seconded to postpone the question of impeachments, &c.? which was negatived,—Massachusetts and South Carolina, only, being aye.

On the question, Shall the Executive be removable on impeachments, &c.?—Connecticut, New Jersey, Pennsylvania, Delaware, Maryland, Virginia, North Carolina, Georgia, aye—8; Massachusetts, South Carolina, no—2.

"The Executive to receive fixed compensation,"—agreed to, *nem. con.*

"To be paid out of the National Treasury,"—agreed to, New Jersey only in the negative.

Mr. GERRY and Mr. GOUVERNEUR MORRIS moved, "that the Electors of the Executive shall not be members of the National Legislature, nor officers of the United States, nor shall the Electors themselves be eligible to the supreme magistracy." Agreed to, *nem. con.*

Doctor MCCLURG asked, whether it would not be necessary, before a committee for detailing the Constitution should be appointed, to determine on the means by which the Executive is to carry the laws into effect, and to resist combinations against them. Is he to have a military force for the purpose, or to have the command of the Militia, the only existing force that can be applied to that use? As the Resolutions now stand, the Committee will have no determinate directions on this great point.

Mr. WILSON thought that some additional directions to the Committee would be necessary.

Mr. KING. The Committee are to provide for the end. Their discretionary power to provide for the means is involved, according to an established axiom.

Adjourned.

SATURDAY, JULY 21ST.

In Convention,— Mr. WILLIAMSON moved, "that the Electors of the Executive should be paid out of the National Treasury for the service to be performed by them." Justice required this, as it was a national service they were to render. The motion was agreed to, *nem. con.*

Mr. WILSON moved, as an amendment to the tenth Resolution, "that the Supreme National Judiciary should be associated with the Executive in the revisionary power." This proposition had been before made and failed; but he was so confirmed by reflection in the opinion of its utility, that he thought it incumbent on him to make another effort. The judiciary ought to have an opportunity of remonstrating against projected encroachments on the people as well as on themselves. It had been said, that the Judges, as expositors of the laws, would have an opportunity of defending their constitutional rights. There was weight in this observation; but this power of the Judges did not go far enough. Laws may be unjust, may be unwise, may be dangerous, may be destructive; and yet may not be so unconstitutional as to justify the Judges in refusing to give them effect. Let them have a share in the revisionary power, and they will have an opportunity of taking notice of those characters of a law, and of counteracting, by the weight of their opinions, the improper views of the Legislature.— Mr. MADISON seconded the motion.

Mr. GORHAM did not see the advantage of employing the Judges in this way. As Judges they are not to be presumed to possess any peculiar knowledge of the mere policy of public measures. Nor can it be necessary as a security for their constitutional rights. The Judges in England have no such additional provision for their defence, yet their jurisdiction is not invaded. He thought it would be best to let the Executive alone be responsible, and at most to authorize him to call on the Judges for their opinions.

Mr. ELLSWORTH approved heartily of the motion. The aid of the Judges will give more wisdom and firmness to the Executive. They will possess a systematic and accurate knowledge of the laws, which the Executive cannot be expected always to possess. The Law of Nations also will frequently come into question. Of this the Judges alone will have competent information.

Mr. MADISON considered the object of the motion as of great importance to the meditated Constitution. It would be useful to the Judiciary Department by giving it an additional opportunity of defending itself against Legislative encroachments. It would be useful to the Executive, by inspiring additional confidence and firmness in exerting the revisionary power. It would be useful to the Legislature, by the valuable assistance it would give in preserving a consistency, conciseness, perspicuity, and technical propriety in the laws, qualities peculiarly necessary, and yet shamefully wanting in our Republican codes. It would, moreover, be useful to the community at large, as an additional check against a pursuit of those unwise and unjust measures which constituted so great a portion of our calamities. If any solid objection could be urged against the motion, it must be on the supposition that it tended to give too much strength, either to the Executive, or Judiciary. He did not think there was the least ground for this apprehension. It was much more to be apprehended, that, notwithstanding this co-operation of the two departments, the Legislature would still be an overmatch for them. Experience in all the States had evinced a powerful tendency in the Legislature to absorb all power into its vortex. This was the real source of danger to the American Constitutions; and suggested the necessity of giving every defensive authority to the other departments that was consistent with republican principles.

Mr. MASON said, he had always been a friend to this provision. It would give a confidence to the Executive, which he would not otherwise have, and without which the revisionary power would be of little avail.

Mr. GERRY did not expect to see this point, which had undergone full discussion, again revived. The object he conceived of the revisionary power was merely to secure the Executive department against Legislative encroachment. The Executive, therefore, who will best know and be ready to defend his rights, ought alone to have the defence of them. The motion was liable to strong objections. It was combining and mixing together the Legislative and the other departments. It was establishing an improper coalition between the Executive and Judiciary departments. It was making statesmen of the Judges, and setting them up as the guardians of the rights of the people. He relied, for his part, on the Representatives of the people, as the guardians of their rights and interests. It was making the expositors of the laws the legislators, which ought never to be done. A better expedient for correcting the laws would be to appoint, as had been done in Pennsylvania, a person or persons of proper skill, to draw bills for the Legislature.

Mr. STRONG thought, with Mr. GERRY, that the power of making, ought to be kept distinct from that of expounding, the laws. No maxim was better established. The Judges in exercising the function of expositors might be influenced by the part they had taken in passing the laws.

Mr. GOUVERNEUR MORRIS. Some check being necessary on the Legislature, the question is, in what hands it should be lodged ? On one side, it was contended, that the Executive alone ought to exercise it. He did not think that an Executive appointed for six years, and impeachable whilst in office, would be a very effectual check. On the other side, it was urged, that he ought to be reinforced by the Judiciary department. Against this it was objected, that expositors of laws ought to have no hand in making them, and arguments in favor of this had been drawn from England. What weight was due to them might be easily determined by an attention to facts. The truth was, that the Judges in England had a great share in the legislation. They are consulted in difficult and doubtful cases. They may be, and some of them are, members of the Legislature. They are, or may be, members of the Privy Council ; and can there advise the Executive, as they will do with us if the motion succeeds. The influence the English Judges may have, in the latter capacity, in strengthening the Executive check, cannot be ascertained, as the King, by his influence, in a manner dictates the laws. There is one difference in the two cases, however, which disconcerts all reasoning from the British to our proposed Constitution. The British Executive has so great an interest in his prerogatives, and such power for means of defending them, that he will never yield any part of them. The interest of our Executive is so inconsiderable and so transitory, and his means of defending it so feeble, that there is the justest ground to fear his want of firmness in resisting encroachments. He was extremely apprehensive that the auxiliary firmness and weight of the Judiciary would not supply the deficiency. He concurred in thinking the public liberty in greater danger from Legislative usurpations, than from any other source. It had been said that the Legislature ought to be relied on, as the proper guardians of liberty. The answer was short and conclusive. Either bad laws will be pushed, or not. On the latter supposition, no check will be wanted. On the former, a strong check will be necessary. And this is the proper supposition. Emissions of paper-money, largesses to the people, a remission of debts, and similar measures, will at some times be popular, and will be pushed for that reason. At other times, such measures will coincide with the

26

interests of the Legislature themselves, and that will be a reason not less cogent for pushing them. It may be thought that the people will not be deluded and misled in the latter case. But experience teaches another lesson. The press is indeed a great means of diminishing the evil; yet it is found to be unable to prevent it altogether.

Mr. L. MARTIN considered the association of the Judges with the Executive, as a dangerous innovation; as well as one that could not produce the particular advantage expected from it. A knowledge of mankind, and of Legislative affairs, cannot be presumed to belong in a higher degree to the Judges than to the Legislature. And as to the constitutionality of laws, that point will come before the Judges in their official character. In this character they have a negative on the laws. Join them with the Executive in the revision, and they will have a double negative. It is necessary that the Supreme Judiciary should have the confidence of the people. This will soon be lost, if they are employed in the task of remonstrating against popular measures of the Legislature. Besides, in what mode and proportion are they to vote in the Council of Revision?

Mr. MADISON could not discover in the proposed association of the Judges with the Executive, in the revisionary check on the Legislature, any violation of the maxim which requires the great departments of power to be kept separate and distinct. On the contrary, he thought it an auxiliary precaution, in favor of the maxim. If a constitutional discrimination of the departments on paper were a sufficient security to each against encroachments of the others, all further provisions would indeed be superfluous. But experience had taught us a distrust of that security; and that it is necessary to introduce such a balance of powers and interests as will guarantee the provisions on paper. Instead, therefore, of contenting ourselves with laying down the theory in the Constitution, that each department ought to be separate and distinct, it was proposed to add a defensive power to each, which should maintain the theory in practice. In so doing, we did not blend the departments together. We erected effectual barriers for keeping them separate. The most regular example of this theory was in the British Constitution. Yet it was not only the practice there to admit the Judges to a seat in the Legislature, and in the Executive Councils, and submit to their previous examination all laws of a certain description, but it was a part of their Constitution that the Executive might negative any law whatever; a part of *their* Constitution which had been universally regarded as calculated for the preservation of the whole. The objection against a union of the Judiciary and Executive branches, in the revision of the laws, had either no foundation, or was not carried far enough. If such a union was an improper mixture of powers, or such a Judiciary check on the laws was inconsistent with the theory of a free constitution, it was equally so to admit the Executive to any participation in the making of laws; and the revisionary plan ought to be discarded altogether.

Colonel MASON observed, that the defence of the Executive was not the sole object of the revisionary power. He expected even greater advantages from it. Notwithstanding the precautions taken in the constitution of the Legislature, it would still so much resemble that of the individual States, that it must be expected frequently to pass unjust and pernicious laws. This restraining power was therefore essentially necessary. It would have the effect, not only of hindering the final passage of such laws, but would discourage demagogues from attempting to get them passed. It has been said (by Mr. L. MARTIN), that if the Judges were joined in this check on the laws, they would have a double negative, since in their expository capacity of Judges they would have one negative. He would reply, that in this capacity they could impede, in one case only, the operation of laws. They could declare an unconstitutional law void. But with regard to every law, however unjust, oppressive or pernicious, that did not come plainly under this description, they would be under the necessity, as Judges, to give it a free course. He wished the further use to be made of the Judges of giving aid in preventing every improper law. Their aid will be the more valuable, as they are in the habit and practice of considering laws in their true principles, and in all their consequences.

Mr. WILSON. The separation of the departments does not require that they should have separate objects; but that they should act separately, though on the same objects. It is necessary that the two branches of the Legislature should be separate and distinct, yet they are both to act precisely on the same object.

Mr. GERRY had rather give the Executive an absolute negative for its own defence, than thus to blend together the Judiciary and Executive departments. It will bind them together in an offensive and defensive alliance against the Legislature, and render the latter unwilling to enter into a contest with them.

Mr. GOUVERNEUR MORRIS was surprised that any defensive provision for securing the effectual separation of the departments should be considered as an improper mixture of them. Suppose that the three powers were to be vested in three persons, by compact among themselves; that one was to have the power of making, another of executing, and a third of judging, the laws. Would it not be very natural for the two latter, after having settled the partition on paper, to observe, and would not candor oblige the former to admit, that, as a security against legislative acts of the former, which might easily be so framed as to undermine the powers of the two others, the two others ought to be armed with a veto for their own defence; or at least to have an opportunity of stating their objections against acts of encroachment? And would any one pretend, that such a right tended to blend and confound powers that ought to be separately exercised? As well might it be said that if three neighbours had three distinct farms, a right in each to defend his farm against his neighbours, tended to blend the farms together.

Mr. GORHAM. All agree that a check on the Legislature is necessary. But there are two objections against admitting the Judges to share in it, which no observations on the other side seem to obviate. The first is, that the Judges ought to carry into the exposition of the laws no prepossessions with regard to them; the second, that, as the Judges will outnumber the Executive, the revisionary check would be thrown entirely out of the Executive hands, and, instead of enabling him to defend himself, would enable the Judges to sacrifice him.

Mr. WILSON. The proposition is certainly not liable to all the objections which have been urged against it. According to Mr. GERRY, it will unite the Executive and Judiciary in an offensive and defensive alliance against the Legislature. According to Mr. GORHAM, it will lead to a subversion of the Executive by the Judiciary influence. To the first gentleman the answer was obvious: that the joint weight of the two Departments was necessary to balance the single weight of the Legislature. To the first objection stated by the other gentleman it might be answered, that, supposing the prepossession to mix itself with the exposition, the evil would be over-balanced by the advantages promised by the expedient. To the second objection, that such a rule of voting might be provided, in the detail, as would guard against it.

Mr. RUTLEDGE thought the Judges of all men the most unfit to be concerned in the Revisionary Council. The Judges ought never to give their opinion on a law, till it comes before them. He thought it equally unnecessary. The Executive could advise with the officers of state, as of War, Finance, &c., and avail himself of their information and opinions.

On the question on Mr. WILSON's motion for joining the Judiciary in the revision of laws, it passed in the negative,— Connecticut, Maryland, Virginia, aye — 3; Massachusetts, Delaware, North Carolina, South Carolina, no — 4; Pennsylvania, Georgia, divided; New Jersey, not present.

The tenth Resolution, giving the Executive a qualified vote, requiring two-thirds of each branch of the Legislature. to overrule it, was then agreed to, *nem. con.*

The motion made by Mr. MADISON, on the eighteenth of July, and then postponed, " that the Judges should be nominated by the Executive, and such nominations become appointments unless disagreed to by two-thirds of the second branch of the Legislature," was now resumed

Mr. MADISON stated as his reasons for the motion: first, that it secured the responsibility of the Executive, who would in general be more capable and likely to select fit characters than the Legislature, or even the second branch of it, who might hide their selfish motives under the number concerned in the appointment. Secondly, that in case of any flagrant partiality or error in the nomination, it might be fairly presumed that two-thirds of the second branch would join in putting a negative on it. Thirdly, that as the second branch was very differently constituted, when the appointment of the Judges was formerly referred to it, and was now to be composed of equal votes from all the States, the principle of compromise which had prevailed in other instances required in this that there should be a concurrence of two authorities, in one of which the people, in the other the States, should be represented. The executive magistrate would be considered as a national officer, acting for and equally sympathizing with every part of the United States. If the second branch alone should have this power, the Judges might be appointed by a minority of the people, though by a majority of the States; which could not be justified on any principle, as their proceedings were to relate to the people rather than to the States; and as it would, moreover, throw the appointments entirely into the hands of the Northern States, a perpetual ground of jealousy and discontent would be furnished to the Southern States.

Mr. PINCKNEY was for placing the appointment in the second branch exclusively. The Executive will possess neither the requisite knowledge of characters, nor confidence of the people, for so high a trust.

Mr. RANDOLPH would have preferred the mode of appointment proposed formerly by Mr. GORHAM, as adopted in the Constitution of Massachusetts, but thought the motion depending so great an improvement of the clause as it stands, that he anxiously wished it success.   He laid great stress on the responsibility of the Executive, as a security for fit appointments.   Appointments by the Legislatures have generally resulted from cabal, from personal regard, or some other consideration than a title derived from the proper qualifications.   The same inconveniences will proportionally prevail, if the appointments be referred to either branch of the Legislature, or to any other authority administered by a number of individuals.

Mr. ELLSWORTH would prefer a negative in the Executive on a nomination by the second branch, the negative to be overruled by a concurrence of two-thirds of the second branch, to the mode proposed by the motion, but preferred an absolute appointment by the second branch to either.   The Executive will be regarded by the people with a jealous eye.   Every power for augmenting unnecessarily his influence will be disliked.   As he will be stationary, it was not to be supposed he could have a better knowledge of characters.   He will be more open to caresses and intrigues than the Senate.   The right to supersede his nomination will be ideal only.   A nomination under such circumstances will be equivalent to an appointment.

Mr. GOUVERNEUR MORRIS supported the motion.   First, the States, in their corporate capacity, will frequently have an interest staked on the determination of the Judges.   As in the Senate the States are to vote, the Judges ought not to be appointed by the Senate.   Next to the impropriety of being judge in one's own cause, is the appointment of the Judge.   Secondly, it had been said, the Executive would be uninformed of characters.   The reverse was the truth.   The Senate will be so.   They must take the character of candidates from the flattering pictures drawn by their friends. The Executive, in the necessary intercourse with every part of the United States required by the nature of his administration, will or may have the best possible information. Thirdly, it had been said that a jealousy would be entertained of the Executive. If the Executive can be safely trusted with the command of the army, there cannot surely be any reasonable ground of jealousy in the present case. He added, that if the objections against an appointment of the Executive by the Legislature had the weight that had been allowed, there must be some weight in the objection to an appointment of the Judges by the Legislature, or by any part of it.

Mr. GERRY. The appointment of the Judges, like every other part of the Constitution, should be so modeled as to give satisfaction both to the people and to the States. The mode under consideration will give satisfaction to neither. He could not conceive that the Executive could be as well informed of characters throughout the Union, as the Senate. It appeared to him, also, a strong objection, that two-thirds of the Senate were required to reject a nomination of the Executive. The Senate would be constituted in the same manner as Congress, and the appointments of Congress have been generally good.

Mr. MADISON observed, that he was not anxious that two-thirds should be necessary, to disagree to a nomination. He had given this form to his motion, chiefly to vary it the more clearly from one which had just been rejected. He was content to obviate the objection last made, and accordingly so varied the motion as to let a majority reject.

Col. MASON found it his duty to differ from his colleagues in their opinions and reasonings on this subject. Notwithstanding the form of the proposition, by which the appointment seemed to be divided between the Executive and the Senate, the appointment was substantially vested in the former alone. The false complaisance which usually prevails in such cases will prevent a disagreement to the

first nominations. He considered the appointment by the
Executive as a dangerous prerogative. It might even give
him an influence over the Judiciary Department itself. He
did not think the difference of interest between the Northern and Southern States could be properly brought into
this argument. It would operate, and require some precautions in the case of regulating navigation, commerce
and imposts; but he could not see that it had any connection with the Judiciary department.

On the question, the motion being now, " that the Executive should nominate, and such nominations should become
appointments unless disagreed to by the Senate," Massachusetts, Pennsylvania, Virginia, aye — 3; Connecticut,
Delaware, Maryland, North Carolina, South Carolina,
Georgia, no — 6.

On the question for agreeing to the clause as it stands,
by which the Judges are to be appointed by the second
branch, — Connecticut, Delaware, Maryland, North Carolina, South Carolina, Georgia, aye — 6; Massachusetts,
Pennsylvania, Virginia, no — 3; so it passed in the affirmative.

Adjourned.

Monday, June 23d.

In Convention, — Mr. John Langdon and Mr. Nicholas
Gillman, from New Hampshire, took their seats.

The seventeenth Resolution, that provision ought to be
made for future amendments of the Articles of the Union,
was agreed to, *nem. con.*

The eighteenth Resolution, requiring the Legislative,
Executive and Judiciary of the States to be bound by oath
to support the Articles of Union, was taken into consideration.

Mr. Williamson suggests, that a reciprocal oath should
be required from the National officers, to support the Governments of the States.

Mr. GERRY moved to insert, as an amendment, that the oath of the officers of the National Government also should extend to the support of the National Government, which was agreed to, *nem. con.*

Mr. WILSON said, he was never fond of oaths, considering them as a left-handed security only. A good government did not need them, and a bad one could not or ought not to be supported. He was afraid they might too much trammel the members of the existing government, in case future alterations should be necessary; and prove an obstacle to the seventeenth Resolution, just agreed to.

Mr. GORHAM did not know that oaths would be of much use; but could see no inconsistency between them and the seventeenth Resolution, or any regular amendment of the Constitution. The oath could only require fidelity to the existing Constitution. A constitutional alteration of the Constitution could never be regarded as a breach of the Constitution, or of any oath to support it.

Mr. GERRY thought, with Mr. GORHAM, there could be no shadow of inconsistency in the case. Nor could he see any other harm that could result from the Resolution. On the other side, he thought one good effect would be produced by it. Hitherto the officers of the two Governments had considered them as distinct from, and not as parts of, the general system, and had, in all cases of interference given a preference to the State Governments. The proposed oath will cure that error.

The Resolution (the eighteenth) was agreed to, *nem. con.*

The nineteenth Resolution, referring the new Constitution to Assemblies to be chosen by the people, for the express purpose of ratifying it, was next taken into consideration.

Mr. ELLSWORTH moved that it be referred to the Legislatures of the States for ratification. Mr. PATTERSON seconded the motion.

Colonel MASON considered a reference of the plan to the authority of the people, as one of the most important and essential of the Resolutions. The Legislatures have no

power to ratify it. They are the mere creatures of the
State Constitutions, and cannot be greater than their
creators.   And he knew of no power in any of the Constitutions — he knew there was no power in some of them —
that could be competent to this object. Whither, then,
must we resort ? To the people, with whom all power
remains that has not been given up in the constitutions
derived from them. It was of great moment, he observed,
that this doctrine should be cherished, as the basis of free
government. Another strong reason was, that admitting
the Legislatures to have a competent authority, it would be
wrong to refer the plan to them, because succeeding Legislatures, having equal authority, could undo the acts of
their predecessors ; and the National Government would
stand in each State on the weak and tottering foundation
of an act of Assembly. There was a remaining consideration, of some weight. In some of the States, the governments were not derived from the clear and undisputed
authority of the people. This was the case in Virginia.
Some of the best and wisest citizens considered the Constitution as established by an assumed authority. A National
Constitution derived from such a source would be exposed
to the severest criticisms.

Mr. RANDOLPH. One idea has pervaded all our proceedings, to wit, that opposition as well from the States as
from individuals, will be made to the system to be proposed.
Will it not then be highly imprudent to furnish any unnecessary pretext, by the mode of ratifying it ? Added to
other objections against a ratification by the Legislative
authority only, it may be remarked, that there have been
instances in which the authority of the common law has
been set up in particular States against that of the Confederation, which has had no higher sanction than Legislative
ratification. Whose opposition will be most likely to be
excited against the system ? That of the local demagogues
who will be degraded by it, from the importance they now
hold. These will spare no efforts to impede that progress

in the popular mind, which will be necessary to the adoption of the plan ; and which every member will find to have taken place in his own, if he will compare his present opinions with those he brought with him into the Convention. It is of great importance, therefore, that the consideration of this subject should be transferred from the Legislatures, where this class of men have their full influence, to a field in which their efforts can be less mischievous. It is moreover worthy of consideration, that some of the States are averse to any change in their Constitution, and will not take the requisite steps, unless expressly called upon, to refer the question to the people.

Mr. GERRY. The arguments of Colonel MASON and Mr. RANDOLPH prove too much. They prove an unconstitutionality in the present Federal system, and even in some of the State Governments. Inferences drawn from such a source must be inadmissible. Both the State Governments and the Federal Government have been too long acquiesced in, to be now shaken. He considered the Confederation to be paramount to any State Constitution. The last Article of it, authorizing alterations, must consequently be so as well as the others; and every thing done in pursuance of the article, must have the same high authority with the article. Great confusion, he was confident, would result from a recurrence to the people. They would never agree on any thing. He could not see any ground to suppose, that the people will do what their rulers will not. The rulers will either conform to, or influence the sense of the people.

Mr. GORHAM was against referring the plan to the Legislatures. 1. Men chosen by the people for the particular purpose will discuss the subject more candidly than members of the Legislature, who are to lose the power which is to be given up to the General Government. 2. Some of the Legislatures are composed of several branches. It will consequently be more difficult, in these cases, to get the plan through the Legislatures, than through a Convention.

3. In the States many of the ablest men are excluded from the Legislatures, but may be elected into a Convention. Among these may be ranked many of the clergy, who are generally friends to good government. Their services were found to be valuable in the formation and establishment of the Constitution of Massachusetts. 4. The Legislatures will be interrupted with a variety of little business; by artfully pressing which, designing men will find means to delay from year to year, if not to frustrate altogether, the national system. 5. If the last Article of the confederation is to be pursued, the unanimous concurrence of the States will be necessary. But will any one say that all the States are to suffer themselves to be ruined, if Rhode Island should persist in her opposition to general measures? Some other States might also tread in her steps. The present advantage, which New York seems to be so much attached to, of taxing her neighbours by the regulation of her trade, makes it very probable that she will be of the number. It would, therefore, deserve serious consideration, whether provision ought not to be made for giving effect to the system, without waiting for the unanimous concurrence of the States.

Mr. ELLSWORTH. If there be any Legislatures who should find themselves incompetent to the ratification, he should be content to let them advise with their constituents and pursue such a mode as would be competent. He thought more was to be expected from the Legislatures, than from the people. The prevailing wish of the people in the Eastern States is, to get rid of the public debt; and the idea of strengthening the National Government carries with it that of strengthening the public debt. It was said by Colonel MASON,—in the first place, that the Legislatures have no authority in this case; and in the second, that their successors, having equal authority, could rescind their acts. As to the second point he could not admit it to be well founded. An act to which the States, by their Legislatures, make themselves parties, becomes a compact from which no

one of the parties can recede of itself. As to the first
point, he observed that a new set of ideas seemed to have
crept in since the Articles of Confederation were established.
Conventions of the people, or with power derived expressly
from the people, were not then thought of. The Legislatures were considered as competent. Their ratification has
been acquiesced in without complaint. To whom have
Congress applied on subsequent occasions for further
powers? To the Legislatures, not to the people. The fact
is, that we exist at present, and we need not inquire how,
as a federal society, united by a charter, one article of which
is, that alterations therein may be made by the Legislative
authority of the States. It has been said, that if the Confederation is to be observed, the States must *unanimously*
concur in the proposed innovations. He would answer,
that if such were the urgency and necessity of our situation
as to warrant a new compact among a part of the States,
founded on the consent of the people; the same pleas would
be equally valid, in favor of a partial compact, founded on
the consent of the Legislatures.

Mr. WILLIAMSON thought the Resolution (the nineteenth) so expressed, as that it might be submitted either
to the Legislatures or to Conventions recommended by the
Legislatures. He observed that some Legislatures were
evidently unauthorized to ratify the system. He thought,
too, that Conventions were to be preferred, as more likely
to be composed of the ablest men in the States.

Mr. GOUVERNEUR MORRIS considered the inference of
Mr. ELLSWORTH from the plea of necessity, as applied to
the establishment of a new system, on the consent of the
people of a part of the States, in favor of a like establishment, on the consent of a part of the Legislatures, as a *non-
sequitur*. If the Confederation is to be pursued, no alteration can be made without the unanimous consent of the
Legislatures. Legislative alterations not conformable to
the Federal compact would clearly not be valid. The
Judges would consider them as null and void. Whereas,

in case of an appeal to the people of the United States, the supreme authority, the Federal compact may be altered by a *majority of them*, in like manner as the Constitution of a particular State may be altered by a majority of the people of the State. The amendment moved by Mr. ELLSWORTH erroneously supposes, that we are proceeding on the basis of the Confederation. This Convention is unknown to the Confederation.

Mr. KING thought with Mr. ELLSWORTH that the Legislatures had a competent authority, the acquiescence of the people of America in the Confederation being equivalent to a formal ratification by the people. He thought with Mr. ELLSWORTH, also, that the plea of necessity was as valid in the one case, as the other. At the same time, he preferred a reference to the authority of the people expressly delegated to Conventions, as the most certain means of obviating all disputes and doubts concerning the legitimacy of the new Constitution, as well as the most likely means of drawing forth the best men in the States to decide on it. He remarked that among other objections, made in the State of New York to granting powers to Congress, one had been, that such powers as would operate within the States could not be reconciled to the Constitution, and therefore were not grantable by the Legislative authority. He considered it as of some consequence, also, to get rid of the scruples which some members of the State Legislatures might derive from their oaths to support and maintain the existing Constitutions.

Mr. MADISON thought it clear that the Legislatures were incompetent to the proposed changes. These changes would make essential inroads on the State Constitutions; and it would be a novel and dangerous doctrine, that a Legislature could change the Constitution under which it held its existence. There might indeed be some Constitutions within the Union, which had given a power to the Legislature to concur in alterations of the Federal compact. But there were certainly some which had not; and in the case of these, a ratification must of necessity be obtained from the people. He considered the difference between a system founded on the Legislatures only, and one founded on the people, to be the true difference between a *league* or *treaty*, and a *Constitution.* The former, in point of *moral obligation*, might be as inviolable as the latter. In point of *political operation*, there were two important distinctions in favor of the latter. First, a law violating a treaty ratified by a pre-existing law might be respected by the Judges as a law, though an unwise or perfidious one. A law violating a Constitution established by the people themselves, would be considered by the Judges as null and void. Secondly, the doctrine laid down by the law of nations in the case of treaties is, that a breach of any one article by any of the parties frees the other parties from their engagements. In the case of a union of people under one constitution, the nature of the pact has always been understood to exclude such an interpretation. Comparing the two modes, in point of expediency, he thought all the considerations which recommended this Convention, in preference to Congress, for proposing the reform, were in favor of State Conventions, in preference to the Legislatures for examining and adopting it.

On the question on Mr. ELLSWORTH's motion to refer the plan to the Legislatures of the States, — Connecticut, Delaware, Maryland, aye — 3; New Hampshire, Massachusetts, Pennsylvania, Virginia, North Carolina, South Carolina, Georgia, no — 7.

Mr. GOUVERNEUR MORRIS moved, that the reference of the plan be made to one General Convention, chosen and authorized by the people, to consider, *amend*, and establish the same. Not seconded.

On the question for agreeing to the nineteenth Resolution, touching the mode of ratification as reported from the Committee of the Whole, viz., to refer the Constitution, after the approbation of Congress, to assemblies chosen by the people, — New Hampshire, Massachusetts, Connecticut,

Pennsylvania, Maryland, Virginia, North Carolina, South Carolina, Georgia, aye — 9; Delaware, no — 1.

Mr. GOUVERNEUR MORRIS and Mr. KING moved, that the representation in the second branch consist of —— members from each State, who shall vote *per capita*.

Mr. ELLSWORTH said he had always approved of voting in that mode.

Mr. GOUVERNEUR MORRIS moved to fill the blank with *three*. He wished the Senate to be a pretty numerous body. If two members only should be allowed to each State, and a majority be made a quorum, the power would be lodged in fourteen members, which was too small a number for such a trust.

Mr. GORHAM preferred two to three members for the blank. A small number was most convenient for deciding on peace and war, &c., which he expected would be vested in the second branch. The number of States will also increase. Kentucky, Vermont, the Province of Maine and Franklin, will probably soon be added to the present number. He presumed also that some of the largest States would be divided. The strength of the General Government will be, not in the largeness, but the smallness, of the States.

Col. MASON thought *three* from each State, including new States, would make the second branch too numerous. Besides other objections, the additional expense ought always to form one, where it was not absolutely necessary.

Mr. WILLIAMSON. If the number be too great, the distant States will not be on an equal footing with the nearer States. The latter can more easily send and support their ablest citizens. He approved of the voting *per capita*.

On the question for filling the blank with "*three*," — Pennsylvania, aye — 1; New Hampshire, Massachusetts, Connecticut, Delaware, Virginia, North Carolina, South Carolina, Georgia, no — 8.

On the question for filling it with "*two*," — agreed to, *nem. con.*

27

Mr. L. MARTIN was opposed to voting *per capita*, as departing from the idea of the *States* being represented in the second branch.

Mr. CARROLL was not struck with any particular objection against the mode; but he did not wish so hastily to make so material an innovation.

On the question on the whole motion, viz.: " the second branch to consist of two members from each State, and to vote *per capita*," — New Hampshire, Massachusetts, Connecticut, Pennsylvania, Delaware, Virginia, North Carolina, South Carolina, Georgia, aye — 9; Maryland, no — 1.

Mr. HOUSTON and Mr. SPAIGHT moved, "that the appointment of the Executive by Electors chosen by the Legislatures of the States," be reconsidered. Mr. HOUSTON urged the extreme inconveniency and the considerable expense of drawing together men from all the States for the single purpose of electing the chief magistrate.

On the question, which was put without debate, — New Hampshire, Massachusetts, Connecticut, Delaware, North Carolina, South Carolina, Georgia, aye — 7; Pennsylvania, Maryland, Virginia, no — 3.

Ordered, that tomorrow be assigned for the reconsideration; — Connecticut and Pennsylvania, no; all the rest, aye.

Mr. GERRY moved, that the proceedings of the Convention for the establishment of a National Government (except the part relating to the Executive) be referred to a Committee to prepare and report a Constitution conformable thereto.

General PINCKNEY reminded the Convention, that if the Committee should fail to insert some security to the Southern State against an emancipation of slaves, and taxes on exports, he should be bound by duty to his State to vote against their report.

The appointment of a Committee, as moved by Mr. GERRY, was agreed to, *nem. con.*

On the question, Shall the Committee consist of ten

members, one from each State present? — all the States were *no*, except Delaware, *aye*.

Shall it consist of seven members? — New Hampshire, Massachusetts, Connecticut, Maryland, South Carolina, aye — 5; Pennsylvania, Delaware Virginia, North Carolina, Georgia, no — 5.

The question being lost by an equal division of votes, it was agreed, *nem. con.*, that the Committee should consist of five members to be appointed tomorrow.

Adjourned.

TUESDAY, JULY 24TH.

In Convention, — The appointment of the Executive by Electors being reconsidered,—

Mr. HOUSTON moved that he be appointed by the National Legislature, instead of " Electors appointed by the State Legislatures," according to the last decision of the mode. He dwelt chiefly on the improbability that capable men would undertake the service of Electors from the more distant States.

Mr. SPAIGHT seconded the motion.

Mr. GERRY opposed it. He thought there was no ground to apprehend the danger urged by Mr. HOUSTON. The election of the Executive Magistrate will be considered as of vast importance, and will create great earnestness. The best men, the Governors of the States, will not hold it derogatory from their character to be the Electors. If the motion should be agreed to, it will be necessary to make the Executive ineligible a second time, in order to render him independent of the Legislature; which was an idea extremely repugnant to his way of thinking.

Mr. STRONG supposed that there would be no necessity, if the Executive should be appointed by the Legislature, to make him ineligible a second time, as new Elections of the Legislature will have intervened; and he will not depend for his second appointment on the same set of men that his first was received from. It had been suggested that *gratitude* for his past appointment would produce the same effect as dependence for his future appointment. He thought very differently. Besides, this objection would lie against the Electors, who would be objects of gratitude as well as the Legislature. It was of great importance not to make the government too complex, which would be the case if a new set of men, like the Electors, should be introduced into it. He thought, also, that the first characters in the States would not feel sufficient motives to undertake the office of Electors.

Mr. WILLIAMSON was for going back to the original ground, to elect the Executive for seven years, and render him ineligible a second time. The proposed Electors would certainly not be men of the first, nor even of the second, grade in the States. These would all prefer a seat in the Senate, or the other branch of the Legislature. He did not like the unity in the Executive. He had wished the Executive power to be lodged in three men, taken from three districts, into which the States should be divided. As the Executive is to have a kind of veto on the laws, and there is an essential difference of interest between the Northern and Southern States, particularly in the carrying trade, the power will be dangerous, if the Executive is to be taken from part of the Union, to the part from which he is not taken. The case is different here from what it is in England; where there is a sameness of interests throughout the kingdom. Another objection against a single magistrate is, that he will be an elective king, and will feel the spirit of one. He will spare no pains to keep himself in for life, and will then lay a train for the succession of his children. It was pretty certain he thought, that we should at some time or other have a king; but he wished no precaution to be omitted that might postpone the event as long as possible. Ineligibility a second time appeared to him to be the best precaution. With this precaution he had no objection to a longer term than seven years. He would go as far as ten or twelve years.

Mr. GERRY moved that the Legislatures of the States should vote by ballot for the Executive, in the same proportions as it had been proposed they should choose Electors; and that in case a majority of the votes should not centre on the same person, the first branch of the National Legislature should choose two out of the four candidates having most votes; and out of these two the second branch should choose the Executive.

Mr. KING seconded the motion; and on the question to postpone, in order to take it into consideration, the *noes* were so predominant, that the States were not counted.

On the question on Mr. HOUSTON's motion, that the Executive be appointed by the National Legislature,— New Hampshire, Massachusetts, New Jersey, Delaware, North Carolina, South Carolina, Georgia, aye — 7; Connecticut, Pennsylvania, Maryland, Virginia, no — 4.

Mr. L. MARTIN and Mr. GERRY moved to re-instate the ineligibility of the Executive a second time.

Mr. ELLSWORTH. With many this appears a natural consequence of his being elected by the Legislature. It was not the case with him. The Executive he thought should be re-elected if his conduct proved him worthy of it. And he will be more likely to render himself worthy of it if he be rewardable with it. The most eminent characters, also, will be more willing to accept the trust under this condition, than if they foresee a necessary degradation at a fixed period.

Mr. GERRY. That the Executive should be independent of the Legislature, is a clear point. The longer the duration of his appointment, the more will his dependence be diminished. It will be better, then, for him to continue ten, fifteen, or even twenty years, and be ineligible afterwards.

Mr. KING was for making him re-eligible. This is too great an advantage to be given up, for the small effect it will have on his dependence, if impeachments are to lie. He considered these as rendering the tenure during pleasure.

Mr. L. MARTIN, suspended his motion as to the ineligibility, moved, "that the appointment of the Executive shall continue for eleven years."

Mr. GERRY suggested fifteen years.

Mr. KING twenty years.* This is the medium life of princes.

Mr. DAVIE eight years.

Mr. WILSON. The difficulties and perplexities into which the House is thrown, proceed from the election by the Legislature, which he was sorry had been re-instated. The inconvenience of this mode was such, that he would agree to almost any length of time in order to get rid of the dependence which must result from it. He was persuaded that the longest term would not be equivalent to a proper mode of election, unless indeed it should be during good behaviour. It seemed to be supposed that at a certain advance of life a continuance in office would cease to be agreeable to the officer, as well as desirable to the public. Experience had shown in a variety of instances, that both a capacity and inclination for public service existed in very advanced stages. He mentioned the instance of a Doge of Venice who was elected after he was eighty years of age. The Popes have generally been elected at very advanced periods, and yet in no case had a more steady or a better concerted policy been pursued than in the Court of Rome. If the Executive should come into office at thirty-five years of age, which he presumes may happen, and his continuance should be fixed at fifteen years, at the age of fifty, in the very prime of life, and with all the aid of experience, he must be cast aside like a useless hulk. What an irreparable loss would the British jurisprudence have sustained, had the age of fifty been fixed there as the ultimate limit of capacity or readiness to serve the public. The great

---

* This might possibly be meant as a caricature of the previous motions, in order to defeat the object of them.

luminary Lord Mansfield, held his seat for thirty years after his arrival at that age. Notwithstanding what had been done, he could not but hope that a better mode of election would yet be adopted ; and one that would be more agreeable to the general sense of the House. That time might be given for further deliberation, he would move that the present question be postponed till to-morrow.

Mr. BROOM seconded the motion to postpone.

Mr. GERRY. We seem to be entirely at a loss on this head. He would suggest whether it would not be advisable to refer the clause relating to the Executive to the committee of detail to be appointed. Perhaps they will be able to hit on something that may unite the various opinions which have been thrown out.

Mr. WILSON. As the great difficulty seems to spring from the mode of election, he would suggest a mode which had not been mentioned. It was, that the Executive be elected for six years by a small number, not more than fifteen of the National Legislature, to be drawn from it, not by ballot, but by lot, and who should retire immediately and make the election without separating. By this mode intrigue would be avoided in the first instance, and the dependence would be diminished. This was not, he said, a digested idea, and might be liable to strong objections.

Mr. GOUVERNEUR MORRIS. Of all possible modes of appointment that by Legislature is the worst. If the Legislature is to appoint, and to impeach, or to influence the impeachment, the Executive will be the mere creature of.it. He had been opposed to the impeachment, but was now convinced that impeachments must be provided for, if the appointment was to be of any duration. No man would say, that an Executive known to be in the pay of an enemy should not be removable in some way or other. He had been charged heretofore (by Col. MASON), with inconsistency in pleading for confidence in the Legislature on some occasions, and urging a distrust on others. The charge was not well founded. The Legislature is worthy of un-

bounded confidence in some respects, and liable to equal
distrust in others.   When their interest coincides precisely
with that of their constituents, as happens in many of their
acts, no abuse of trust is to be apprehended.   When a
strong personal interest happens to be opposed to the general interest, the Legislature cannot be too much distrusted.
In all public bodies there are two parties.   The Executive
will necessarily be more connected with one than with the
other.   There will be a personal interest, therefore, in one
of the parties, to oppose, as well as in the other to support,
him.   Much had been said of the intrigues that will be
practised by the Executive to get into office.   Nothing had
been said on the other side, of the intrigues to get him out of
office.   Some leader of a party will always covet his seat,
will perplex his administration, will cabal with the Legislature, till he succeeds in supplanting him.   This was the way
in which the King of England was got out, he meant the
real king, the Minister. · This was the way in which Pitt
(Lord Chatham) forced himself into place.   Fox was for
pushing the matter still further.   If he had carried his
India bill, which he was very near doing, he would have
made the Minister the king in form almost, as well as in
substance.   Our President will be the British Minister, yet
we are about to make him appointable by the Legislature.
Something has been said of the danger of monarchy.   If a
good government should not now be formed, if a good
organization of the Executive should not be provided, he
doubted whether we should not have something worse than
a limited monarchy.   In order to get rid of the dependence
of the Executive upon the Legislature, the expedient of
making him ineligible a second time had been devised. This
was as much as to say, we should give him the benefit of
experience, and then deprive ourselves of the use of it. But
make him ineligible a second time — and prolong his duration even to fifteen years — will he, by any wonderful interposition of Providence at that period, cease to be a man ?
No ; he will be unwilling to quit his exaltation ; the road

to his object through the Constitution will be shut ; he will be in possession of the sword ; a civil war will ensue, and the commander of the victorious army, on which ever side, will be the despot of America. This consideration renders him particularly anxious that the Executive should be properly constituted. The vice here would not, as in some other parts of the system, be curable. It is the most difficult of all, rightly to balance the Executive. Make him too weak — the Legislature will usurp his power. Make him too strong — he will usurp on the Legislature. He preferred a short period, a re-eligibility, but a different mode of election. A long period would prevent an adoption of the plan. It ought to do so. He should himself be afraid to trust it. He was not prepared to decide on Mr. WILSON's mode of election just hinted by him. He thought it deserved consideration. It would be better that chance should decide than intrigue.

On the question to postpone the consideration of the resolution on the subject of the Executive,— Connecticut, Pennsylvania, Maryland, Virginia, aye — 4; New Hampshire, Massachusetts, New Jersey, North Carolina, South Carolina, Georgia, no — 6; Delaware, divided.

Mr. WILSON then moved, that the Executive be chosen every ——— years by ——— Electors, to be taken by lot from the National Legislature, who shall proceed immediately to the choice of the Executive, and not separate until it be made.

Mr. CARROLL seconds the motion.

Mr. GERRY. This is committing too much to chance. If the lot should fall on a set of unworthy men, an unworthy Executive must be saddled on the country. He thought it had been demonstrated that no possible mode of electing by the Legislature could be a good one.

Mr. KING. The lot might fall on a majority from the same State, which would ensure the election of a man from that State. We ought to be governed by reason, not by chance. As nobody seemed to be satisfied, he wished the matter to be postponed.

Mr. WILSON did not move this as the best mode. His opinion remained unshaken, that we ought to resort to the people for the election. He seconded the postponement.

Mr. GOUVERNEUR MORRIS observed, that the chances were almost infinite against a majority of Electors from the same State.

On a question whether the last motion was in order, it was determined in the affirmative,— ayes, 7; noes, 4.

On the question of postponement, it was agreed to, *nem. con.*

Mr. CARROLL took occasion to observe, that he considered the clause declaring that direct taxation on the States should be in proportion to representation, previous to the obtaining an actual census, as very objectionable; and that he reserved to himself the right of opposing it, if the report of the Committee of detail should leave it in the plan.

Mr. GOUVERNEUR MORRIS hoped the Committee would strike out the whole of the clause proportioning direct taxation to representation. He had only meant it as a bridge* to assist us over a certain gulf; having passed the gulf, the bridge may be removed. He thought the principle laid down with so much strictness liable to strong objections.

On a ballot for a committee to report a Constitution conformable to the Resolutions passed by the Convention, the members chosen were:—

Mr. RUTLEDGE, Mr. RANDOLPH, Mr. GORHAM, Mr. ELLSWORTH, Mr. WILSON.

On motion to discharge the Committee of the Whole from the propositions submitted to the Convention by Mr. C. PINCKNEY as the basis of a Constitution, and to refer

---

* The object was to lessen the eagerness, on one side, for, and the opposition, on the other, to the share of representation claimed by the Southern States on account of the negroes.

them to the Committee of Detail just appointed, it was agreed to, *nem. con.*

A like motion was then made and agreed to, *nem. con.*, with respect to the propositions of Mr. PATTERSON.

Adjourned.

WEDNESDAY, JULY 25TH.

In Convention,— The clause relating to the Executive being again under consideration,—

Mr. ELLSWORTH moved, " that the Executive be appointed by the Legislature, except when the magistrate last chosen shall have continued in office the whole term for which he was chosen, and be re-eligible; in which case the choice shall be by Electors appointed by the Legislatures of the States for that purpose." By this means a deserving magistrate may be re-elected without *making him dependent on the Legislature.*

Mr. GERRY repeated his remark, that an election at all by the National Legislature was radically and incurably wrong; and moved, " that the Executive be appointed by the Governors and Presidents of the States, with advice of their Councils, and where there are no Councils, by Electors chosen by the Legislatures. The Executives to vote in the following proportions, viz: ——."

Mr. MADISON. There are objections against every mode that has been, or perhaps can be, proposed. The election must be made, either by some existing authority under the National or State Constitutions, — or by some special authority derived from the people, — or by the people themselves. The two existing authorities under the National Constitution would be the Legislative and Judiciary. The latter he presumed was out of the question. The former was, in his judgment, liable to insuperable objections. Besides the general influence of that mode on the independence of the Executive, in the first place, the election of the chief magistrate would agitate and divide the Legislature so much, that the public interest would materially suffer by it. Public bodies are always apt to be thrown into contentions, but into more violent ones by such occasions than by any others. In the second place, the candidate would intrigue with the Legislature; would derive his appointment from the predominant faction, and be apt to render his administration subservient to its views. In the third place, the ministers of foreign powers would have, and would make use of, the opportunity to mix their intrigues and influence with the election. Limited as the powers of the Executive are, it will be an object of great moment with the great rival powers of Europe who have American possessions, to have at the head of our government a man attached to their respective politics and interests. No pains, nor perhaps expense, will be spared, to gain from the Legislature an appointment favourable to their wishes. Germany and Poland are witnesses of this danger. In the former, the election of the Head of the Empire, till it became in a manner hereditary, interested all Europe, and was much influenced by foreign interference. In the latter, although the elective magistrate has very little real power, his election has at all times produced the most eager interference of foreign princes, and has in fact at length slid entirely into foreign hands. The existing authorities in the States are the Legislative, Executive and Judiciary. The appointment of the National Executive by the first was objectionable in many points of view, some of which had been already mentioned. He would mention one which of itself would decide his opinion. The Legislatures of the States had betrayed a strong propensity to a variety of pernicious measures. One object of the National Legislature was to control this propensity. One object of the National Executive, so far as it would have a negative on the laws, was to control the National Legislature, so far as it might be infected with a similar propensity. Refer the appointment of the National Executive to the State Legislatures, and this controlling purpose may be defeated. The Legislatures can and will act with some kind of regular plan, and will promote the appointment of a man who will not oppose himself to a favorite object. Should a majority of the Legislatures, at the time of election, have the same object, or different objects of the same kind, the National Executive would be rendered subservient to them. An appointment by the State Executives was liable, among other objections, to this insuperable one, that being standing bodies, they could and would be courted, and intrigued with by the candidates, by their partizans, and by the ministers of foreign powers. The State Judiciaries had not been, and he presumed would not be, proposed as a proper source of appointment. The option before us, then, lay between an appointment by Electors chosen by the people, and an immediate appointment by the people. He thought the former mode free from many of the objections which had been urged against it, and greatly preferable to an appointment by the National Legislature. As the Electors would be chosen for the occasion, would meet at once, and proceed immediately to an appointment, there would be very little opportunity for cabal, or corruption: as a further precaution, it might be required that they should meet at some place distinct from the seat of government; and even that no person within a certain distance of the place at the time, should be eligible. This mode, however, had been rejected so recently, and by so great a majority, that it probably would not be proposed anew. The remaining mode was an election by the people, or rather by the qualified part of them at large. With all its imperfections, he liked this best. He would not repeat either the general arguments for, or the objections against, this mode. He would only take notice of two difficulties, which he admitted to have weight. The first arose from the disposition in the people to prefer a citizen of their own State, and the disadvantage this would throw on the smaller States. Great as this objection might be, he did not think it equal to such as lay against every other mode which had been proposed. He thought, too, that some expedient might be hit upon that would obviate it. The second difficulty arose from the disproportion of qualified voters in the Northern and Southern States, and the disadvantages which this mode would throw on the latter. The answer to this objection was — in the first place, that this disproportion would be continually decreasing under the influence of the republican laws introduced in the Southern States, and the more rapid increase of their population; in the second place, that local considerations must give way to the general interest. As an individual from the Southern States, he was willing to make the sacrifice.

Mr. ELLSWORTH. The objection drawn from the different sizes of the States is unanswerable. The citizens of the largest States would invariably prefer the candidate within the State; and the largest States would invariably have the man.

On the question on Mr. ELLSWORTH's motion, as above, — New Hampshire, Connecticut, Pennsylvania, Maryland, aye — 4; Massachusetts, New Jersey, Delaware, Virginia, North Carolina, South Carolina, Georgia, no — 7.

Mr. PINCKNEY moved, "that the election by the Legislature be qualified with a proviso, that no person be eligible for more than six years in any twelve years." He thought this would have all the advantage, and at the same time avoid in some degree the inconvenience, of an absolute ineligibility a second time.

Col. MASON approved the idea. It had the sanction of experience in the instance of Congress, and some of the Executives of the States. It rendered the Executive as effectually independent, as an ineligibility after his first election; and opened the way, at the same time, for the advantage of his future services. He preferred on the whole the election by the National Legislature; though candor obliged him to admit, that there was great danger of foreign influence, as had been suggested. This was the most serious objection, with him, that had been urged.

Mr. BUTLER. The two great evils to be avoided are, cabal at home, and influence from abroad. It will be difficult to avoid either, if the election be made by the National Legislature. On the other hand the Government should not be made so complex and unwieldy as to disgust the States. This would be the case if the election should be referred to the people. He liked best an election by Electors chosen by the Legislatures of the States. He was against a re-eligibility at all events. He was also against a ratio of votes in the States. An equality should prevail in this case. The reasons for departing from it do not hold in the case of the Executive, as in that of the Legislature.

Mr. GERRY approved of Mr. PINCKNEY'S motion, as lessening the evil.

Mr. GOUVERNEUR MORRIS was against a rotation in every case. It formed a political school, in which we were always governed by the scholars, and not by the masters. The evils to be guarded against in this case are,— first, the undue influence of the Legislature; secondly, instability of councils; thirdly, misconduct in office. To guard against the first, we run into the second evil. We adopt a rotation which produces instability of councils. To avoid Scylla we fall into Charybdis. A change of men is ever followed by a change of measures. We see this fully exemplified in the vicissitudes among ourselves, particularly in the State of Pennsylvania. The self-sufficiency of a victorious party scorns to tread in the paths of their predecessors. Rehoboam will not imitate Solomon. Secondly, the rotation in office will not prevent intrigue and dependence on the Legislature. The man in office will look forward to the period at which he will become re-eligible. The distance of the period, the improbability of such a protraction of his life, will be no obstacle. Such is the nature of man — formed by his benevolent Author, no doubt, for wise ends — that although he knows his existence to be limited to a span, he takes his measures as if he were to live forever. But taking another supposition, the inefficacy of the expedient will be manifest. If the magistrate does not look forward to his re-election to the Executive, he will be pretty sure to keep in view the opportunity of his going into the Legislature itself. He will have little objection then to an extension of power on a theatre where he expects to act a distinguished part; and will be very unwilling to take any step that may endanger his popularity with the Legislature, on his influence over which the figure he is to make will depend. Finally, to avoid the third evil, impeachments will be essential; and hence an additional reason against an election by the Legislature. He considered an election by the people as the best, by the Legislature as the worst, mode. Putting both these aside, he could not but favor the idea of Mr. WILSON, of introducing a mixture of lot. It will diminish, if not destroy, both cabal and dependence.

Mr. WILLIAMSON was sensible that strong objections lay against an election of the Executive by the Legislature, and that it opened a door for foreign influence. The principal objection against an election by the people seemed to be, the disadvantage under which it would place the smaller States. He suggested as a cure for this difficulty, that each man should vote for three candidates; one of them, he observed, would be probably of his own State, the other two of some other States; and as probably of a small as a large one.

Mr. GOUVERNEUR MORRIS liked the idea; suggesting as an amendment, that each man should vote for two persons, one of whom at least should not be of his own State.

Mr. MADISON also thought something valuable might be made of the suggestion, with the proposed amendment of it. The second best man in this case would probably be the first in fact. The only objection which occurred was, that each citizen, after having given his vote for his favorite fellow citizen, would throw away his second on some obscure citizen of another State, in order to ensure the object of his first choice. But it could hardly be supposed that the citizens of many States would be so sanguine of having their favorite elected, as not to give their second vote with sincerity to the next object of their choice. It might, moreover, be provided, in favor of the smaller States, that the Executive should not be eligible more than —— times in —— years from the same State.

Mr. GERRY. A popular election in this case is radically vicious. The ignorance of the people would put it in the power of some one set of men dispersed through the Union, and acting in concert, to delude them into any appointment. He observed that such a society of men existed in the Order of the Cincinnati. They are respectable, united and influential. They will, in fact, elect the Chief Magistrate in every instance, if the election be referred to the people. His respect for the characters composing this Society, could not blind him to the danger and impropriety of throwing such a power into their hands.

Mr. DICKINSON. As far as he could judge from the discussions which had taken place during his attendance, insuperable objections lay against an election of the Executive by the National Legislature; as also by the Legislatures or Executives of the States. He had long leaned towards an election by the people, which he regarded as the best and purest source. Objections he was aware lay against this mode, but not so great, he thought, as against the other modes. The greatest difficulty, in the opinion of the House, seemed to arise from the partiality of the States to their respective citizens. But might not this very partiality be turned to a useful purpose? Let the people of each State choose its best citizen. The people will know the most eminent characters of their own States; and the people of different States will feel an emulation in selecting those of whom they will have the greatest reason to be proud. Out of the thirteen names thus selected, an Executive Magistrate may be chosen either by the National Legislature, or by Electors appointed by it.

On a question which was moved, for postponing Mr. PINCKNEY'S motion, in order to make way for some such

28

proposition as had been hinted by Mr. WILLIAMSON and others, it passed in the negative, — Connecticut, New Jersey, Pennsylvania, Maryland, Virginia aye — 5; New Hampshire, Massachusetts, Delaware, North Carolina, South Carolina, Georgia, no — 6.

On Mr. PINCKNEY'S motion, that no person shall serve in the Executive more than six years in twelve years, it passed in the negative, — New Hampshire, Massachusetts, North Carolina, South Carolina, Georgia, — 5; Connecticut, New Jersey, Pennsylvania, Delaware, Maryland, Virginia, no — 6.

On a motion that the members of the Committee be furnished with copies of the proceedings, it was so determined, South Carolina alone being in the negative.

It was then moved, that the members of the House might take copies of the Resolutions which had been agreed to; which passed in the negative,— Connecticut, New Jersey, Delaware, Virginia, North Carolina, aye — 5; New Hampshire, Massachusetts, Pennsylvania, Maryland, South Carolina, Georgia, no — 6.

Mr. GERRY and Mr. BUTLER moved to refer the resolution relating to the Executive (except the clause making it consist of a single person) to the Committee of detail.

Mr. WILSON hoped that so important a branch of the system would not be committed, until a general principle should be fixed by a vote of the House.

Mr. LANGDON was for the commitment.

Adjourned.

———

THURSDAY, JULY 26TH.

In Convention, — Mr. MASON. In every stage of the question relative to the Executive, the difficulty of the subject and the diversity of the opinions concerning it, have appeared. Nor have any of the modes of constituting that Department been satisfactory. First, it has been proposed that the election should be made by the people at large;

that is, that an act which ought to be performed by those who know most of eminent characters and qualifications, should be performed by those who know least; secondly, that the election should be made by the Legislatures of the States; thirdly, by the Executives of the States. Against these modes, also, strong objections have been urged. Fourthly, it has been proposed that the election should be made by Electors chosen by the people for that purpose. This was at first agreed to; but on further consideration has been rejected. Fifthly, since which, the mode of Mr. WILLIAMSON, requiring each freeholder to vote for several candidates, has been proposed. This seemed, like many other propositions, to carry a plausible face, but on closer inspection is liable to fatal objections. A popular election in any form, as Mr. GERRY has observed, would throw the appointment into the hands of the Cincinnati, a society for the members of which he had a great respect, but which he never wished to have a preponderating influence in the government. Sixthly, another expedient was proposed by Mr. DICKINSON, which is liable to so palpable and material an inconvenience, that he had little doubt of its being by this time rejected by himself. It would exclude every man who happened not to be popular within his own State; though the causes of his local unpopularity might be of such a nature, as to recommend him to the states at large. Seventhly, among other expedients, a lottery has been introduced. But as the tickets do not appear to be in much demand, it will probably not be carried on, and nothing therefore need be said on that subject. After reviewing all these various modes, he was led to conclude, that an election by the National Legislature, as originally proposed, was the best. If it was liable to objections, it was liable to fewer than any other. He conceived, at the same time, that a second election ought to be absolutely prohibited. Having for his primary object — for the polar star of his political conduct — the preservation of the rights of the people, he held it as an essential point, as the very palladium of civil liberty, that the great officers of state, and particularly the Executive, should at fixed periods return to that mass from which they were at first taken, in order that they may feel and respect those rights and interests which are again to be personally valuable to them. He concluded with moving, that the constitution of the Executive, as reported by the Committee of the Whole, be reinstated, viz. "that the Executive be appointed for seven years, and be ineligible a second time."

Mr. DAVIE seconded the motion.

Doctor FRANKLIN. It seems to have been imagined by some, that the returning to the mass of the people was degrading the magistrate. This he thought was contrary to republican principles. In free governments the rulers are the servants, and the people their superiors and sovereigns. For the former, therefore, to return among the latter, was not to *degrade*, but to *promote*, them. And it would be imposing an unreasonable burden on them, to keep them always in a state of servitude, and not allow them to become again one of the masters.

On the question on Col. MASON's motion, as above, it passed in the affirmative,—

New Hampshire, New Jersey, Maryland, Virginia, North Carolina, South Carolina, Georgia, aye — 7; Connecticut, Pennsylvania, Delaware, no — 3; Massachusetts, not on the floor.

Mr. GOUVERNEUR MORRIS was now against the whole paragraph. In answer to Col. MASON's position, that a periodical return of the great officers of the state into the mass of the people was the palladium of civil liberty, he would observe, that on the same principle the Judiciary ought to be periodically degraded; certain it was, that the Legislature ought, on every principle, yet no one had proposed, or conceived that the members of it should not be re-eligible. In answer to Doctor FRANKLIN, that a return into the mass of the people would be a promotion, instead of a degradation, he had no doubt that our Executive, like most others, would have too much patriotism to shrink from the burthen of his office, and too much modesty not to be willing to decline the promotion.

On the question on the whole Resolution, as amended, in the words following: "that a National Executive be instituted, to consist of a single person, to be chosen by the National Legislature, for the term of seven years, to be ineligible a second time, with power to carry into execution the national laws, to appoint to offices in cases not otherwise provided for, to be removable on impeachment and conviction of mal-practice or neglect of duty, to receive a fixed compensation for the devotion of his time to the public service, to be paid out of the national Treasury,"— it passed in the affirmative,—

New Hampshire, Connecticut, New Jersey, North Carolina, South Carolina, Georgia, aye — 6 ; Pennsylvania, Delaware, Maryland, no — 3 ; Massachusetts, not on the floor ; Virginia, divided — Mr. BLAIR and Col. MASON, aye ; General WASHINGTON and Mr. MADISON, no. Mr. RANDOLPH happened to be out of the House.

Mr. MASON moved, "that the Committee of Detail be instructed to receive a clause requiring certain qualifications of landed property, and citizenship of the United States, in members of the National Legislature ; and disqualifying persons having unsettled accounts with, or being indebted to, the United States, from being members of the National Legislature." He observed that persons of the latter descriptions had frequently got into the State Legislatures, in order to promote laws that might shelter their delinquencies ; and that this evil had crept into Congress, if report was to be regarded.

Mr. PINCKNEY seconded the motion.

Mr. GOUVERNEUR MORRIS. If qualifications are proper, he would prefer them in the electors, rather than the elected. As to debtors of the United States, they are but few. As to persons having unsettled accounts, he believed them to be pretty many. He thought, however, that such a discrimination to be both odious and useless, and in many instances, unjust and cruel. The delay of settlement had been more the fault of the public, than of the individuals. What will be done with those patriotic citizens who have lent money, or services, or property, to their country, without having been yet able to obtain a liquidation of their claims ? Are they to be excluded ?

Mr. GORHAM was for leaving to the Legislature the providing against such abuses as had been mentioned.

Col. MASON mentioned the parliamentary qualifications adopted in the reign of Queen Anne, which he said had met with universal approbation.

Mr. MADISON had witnessed the zeal of men having accounts with the public, to get into the Legislatures for sinister purposes. He thought, however, that if any precaution were taken for excluding them, the one proposed by Col. MASON ought to be re-modelled. It might be well to limit the exclusion to persons who had received money from the public, and had not accounted for it.

Mr. GOUVERNEUR MORRIS. It was a precept of great antiquity, as well as of high authority, that we should not be righteous overmuch. He thought we ought to be equally on our guard against being wise overmuch. The proposed regulation would enable the Government to exclude particular persons from office as long as they pleased. He mentioned the case of the Commander-in-Chief's presenting his account for secret services, which, he said, was so moderate that every one was astonished at it ; and so simple that no doubt could arise on it. Yet, had the Auditor been disposed to delay the settlement, how easily he might have effected it, and how cruel would it be in such a case to keep a distinguished and meritorious citizen under a temporary disability and disfranchisement. He mentioned this case, merely to illustrate the objectionable nature of the proposition. He was opposed to such minutious regulations in a Constitution. The parliamentary qualifications quoted by Col. MASON had been disregarded

in practice ; and were but a scheme of the landed against
the monied interest.

Mr. PINCKNEY and General PINCKNEY moved to insert,
by way of amendment, the words "Judiciary and Executive," so as to extend the qualifications to those Departments; which was agreed to, *nem. con.*

Mr. GERRY thought the inconvenience of excluding a
few worthy individuals, who might be public debtors, or
have unsettled accounts, ought not to be put in the scale
against the public advantages of the regulation, and that
the motion did not go far enough.

Mr. KING observed, that there might be great danger
in requiring landed property as a qualification; since it
might exclude the monied interest, whose aids may be
essential in particular emergencies to the public safety.

Mr. DICKINSON was against any recital of qualifications
in the Constitution.   It was impossible to make a complete
one; and a partial one would, by implication, tie up the
hands of the Legislature from supplying the omissions.
The best defence lay in the freeholders who were to elect
the Legislature.   Whilst this resource should remain pure,
the public interest would be safe.   If it ever should be
corrupt, no little expedients would repel the danger.   He
doubted the policy of interweaving into a republican Constitution a veneration for wealth.   He had always understood that a veneration for poverty and virtue were the
objects of republican encouragement.   It seemed improper
that any man of merit should be subjected to disabilities
in a republic, where merit was understood to form the great
·title to public trust, honors, and rewards.

Mr. GERRY.   If property be one object of government,
provisions to secure it cannot be improper.

Mr. MADISON moved to strike out the word "*landed*,"
before the word "qualifications."   If the proposition
should be agreed to, he wished the Committee to be at
liberty to report the best criterion they could devise.
Landed possessions were no certain evidence of real wealth.

Many enjoyed them to a great extent who were more in debt than they were worth. The unjust laws of the States had proceeded more from this class of men, than any others. It had often happened that men who had acquired landed property on credit got into the Legislatures with a view of promoting an unjust protection against their creditors. In the next place, if a small quantity of land should be made the standard, it would be no security; if a large one, it would exclude the proper representatives of those classes of citizens, who were not landholders. It was politic as well as just, that the interests and rights of every class should be duly represented and understood in the public councils. It was a provision every where established, that the country should be divided into districts, and representatives taken from each, in order that the Legislative assembly might equally understand and sympathize with the rights of the people in every part of the community. It was not less proper, that every class of citizens should have an opportunity of making their rights be felt and understood in the public councils. The three principal classes into which our citizens were divisible, were the landed, the commercial, and the manufacturing. The second and third class bear, as yet, a small proportion to the first. The proportion, however, will daily increase. We see in the populous countries of Europe now, what we shall be hereafter. These classes understand much less of each other's interests and affairs, than men of the same class inhabiting different districts. It is particularly requisite, therefore, that the interests of one or two of them, should not be left entirely to the care or impartiality of the third. This must be the case, if landed qualifications should be required; few of the mercantile, and scarcely any of the manufacturing, class, choosing, whilst they continue in business, to turn any part of their stock into landed property. For these reasons he wished, if it were possible, that some other criterion than the mere possession of land should be devised. He concurred with Mr. GOUVERNEUR

MORRIS in thinking that qualifications in the electors would be much more effectual than in the elected. The former would discriminate between real and ostensible property in the latter; but he was aware of the difficulty of forming any uniform standard that would suit the different circumstances and opinions prevailing in the different States.

Mr. GOUVERNEUR MORRIS seconded the motion.

On the question for striking out "landed,"— New Hampshire, Massachusetts, Connecticut, New Jersey, Pennsylvania, Delaware, Virginia, North Carolina, South Carolina, Georgia, aye — 10; Maryland, no — 1.

On the question on the first part of Colonel MASON's proposition, as to "qualification of property and citizenship," as so amended,— New Hampshire, Massachusetts, New Jersey, Maryland, Virginia, North Carolina, South Carolina, Georgia, aye — 8; Connecticut, Pennsylvania, Delaware, no — 3.

The second part, for disqualifying debtors, and persons having unsettled accounts, being under consideration,—

Mr. CARROLL moved to strike out, "having unsettled accounts."

Mr. GORHAM seconded the motion; observing, that it would put the commercial and manufacturing part of the people on a worse footing than others, as they would be most likely to have dealings with the public.

Mr. L. MARTIN. If these words should be struck out, and the remaining words concerning debtors retained, it will be the interest of the latter class to keep their accounts unsettled as long as possible.

Mr. WILSON was for striking them out. They put too much power in the hands of the auditors, who might combine with rivals in delaying settlements, in order to prolong the disqualifications of particular men. We should consider that we are providing a Constitution for future generations, and not merely for the peculiar circumstances of the moment. The time has been, and will again be, when the public safety may depend on the voluntary aids

of individuals, which will necessarily open accounts with
the public; and when such accounts will be a characteristic
of patriotism.   Besides, a partial enumeration of cases will
disable the Legislature from disqualifying odious and dangerous characters.

Mr. LANGDON was for striking out the whole clause, for
the reasons given by Mr. WILSON.   So many exclusions, he
thought, too, would render the system unacceptable to the
people.

Mr. GERRY.   If the arguments used to-day were to prevail, we might have a Legislature composed of public debtors, pensioners, placemen, and contractors.   He thought
the proposed disqualifications would be pleasing to the people.   They will be considered as a security against unnecessary or undue burdens being imposed on them.   He
moved to add " pensioners " to the disqualified characters;
which was negatived,— Massachusetts, Maryland, Georgia,
aye— 3; New Hampshire, Connecticut, New Jersey, Pennsylvania, Delaware, Virginia, South Carolina, no — 7; North
Carolina, divided.

Mr. GOUVERNEUR MORRIS.   The last clause, relating to
public debtors, will exclude every importing merchant.
Revenue will be drawn, it is foreseen, as much as possible
from trade.   Duties, of course, will be bonded; and the
merchants will remain debtors to the public.   He repeated
that it had not been so much the fault of individuals, as of
the public, that transactions between them, had not been
more generally liquidated and adjusted.   At all events, to
draw from our short and scanty experience rules that are to
operate through succeeding ages does not savor much of
real wisdom.

On the question for striking out, " persons having unsettled accounts with the United States,"— New Hampshire,
Massachusetts, Connecticut, Pennsylvania, Delaware, Maryland, Virginia, North Carolina, South Carolina, aye — 9;
New Jersey, Georgia, no — 2.

Mr. ELLSWORTH was for disagreeing to the remainder of

the clause disqualifying public debtors; and for leaving to the wisdom of the Legislature, and the virtue of the citizens, the task of providing against such evils. Is the smallest as well as the largest debtor to be excluded? Then every arrear of taxes will disqualify. Besides, how is it to be known to the people, when they elect, who are, or are not, public debtors. The exclusion of pensioners and placemen in England is founded on a consideration not existing here. As persons of that sort are dependent on the crown, they tend to increase its influence.

Mr. PINCKNEY said he was at first a friend to the proposition, for the sake of the clause relating to qualifications of property; but he disliked the exclusion of public debtors; it went too far. It would exclude persons who had purchased confiscated property, or should purchase western territory of the public; and might be some obstacle to the sale of the latter.

On the question for agreeing to the clause disqualifying public debtors,—

North Carolina, Georgia, aye — 2; New Hampshire, Massachusetts, Connecticut, New Jersey, Pennsylvania, Delaware, Maryland, Virginia, South Carolina, no — 9.

Colonel MASON observed that it would be proper, as he thought, that some provision should be made in the Constitution against choosing for the seat of the General Government the city or place at which the seat of any State Government might be fixed. There were two objections against having them at the same place, which, without mentioning others, required some precaution on the subject. The first was, that it tended to produce disputes concerning jurisdiction. The second and principal one was, that the intermixture of the two Legislatures tended to give a provincial tincture to the national deliberations. He moved that the Committee be instructed to receive a clause to prevent the seat of the National Government being in the same city or town with the seat of the Government of any State longer than until the necessary public buildings could be erected.

Mr. ALEXANDER MARTIN seconded the motion.

Mr. GOUVERNEUR MORRIS did not dislike the idea, but was apprehensive that such a clause might make enemies of Philadelphia and New York, which had expectations of becoming the seat of the General Government.

Mr. LANGDON approved the idea also; but suggested the case of a State moving its seat of government to the national seat after the erection of the public buildings.

Mr. GORHAM. The precaution may be evaded by the National Legislature, by delaying to erect the public buildings.

Mr. GERRY conceived it to be the general sense of America, that neither the seat of a State Government, nor any large commercial city should be the seat of the General Government.

Mr. WILLIAMSON liked the idea; but knowing how much the passions of men were agitated by this matter, was apprehensive of turning them against the system. He apprehended, also, that an evasion might be practised in the way hinted by Mr. GORHAM.

Mr. PINCKNEY thought the seat of a State Government ought to be avoided; but that a large town, or its vicinity, would be proper for the seat of the General Government.

Col. MASON did not mean to press the motion at this time, nor to excite any hostile passions against the system. He was content to withdraw the motion for the present.

Mr. BUTLER was for fixing, by the Constitution, the place, and a central one, for the seat of the National Government.

The proceedings since Monday last were unanimously referred to the Committee of Detail; and the Convention then unanimously adjourned till Monday, August 6th, that the Committee of Detail might have time to prepare and report the Constitution. The whole Resolutions, as referred, are as follows:

1. *Resolved*, That the Goverment of the United States ought to consist of a supreme Legislative, Judiciary, and Executive.

2. *Resolved,* That the Legislature consist of two branches.

3. *Resolved,* That the members of the first branch of the Legislature ought to be elected by the people of the several States for the term of two years; to be paid out of the public treasury; to receive an adequate compensation for their services; to be of the age of twenty-five years at least; to be ineligible to, and incapable of holding, any office under the authority of the United States (except those peculiarly belonging to the functions of the first branch) during the term of service of the first branch.

4. *Resolved,* That the members of the second branch of the Legislature of the United States ought to be chosen by the individual Legislatures; to be of the age of thirty years at least; to hold their offices for six years, one-third to go out biennally; to receive a compensation for the devotion of their time to the public service; to be ineligible to, and and incapable of holding, any office under the authority of the United States (except those peculiarly belonging to the functions of the second branch) during the term for which they are elected, and for one year thereafter.

5. *Resolved,* That each branch ought to possess the right of originating acts.

6. *Resolved,* That the National Legislature ought to possess the legislative rights vested in Congress by the Confederation; and, moreover, to legislate in all cases for the general interests of the Union, and also in those to which the States are separately incompetent, or in which the harmony of the United States may be interrupted by the exercise of individual legislation.

7. *Resolved,* That the legislative acts of the United States, made by virtue and in pursuance of the Articles of Union, and all treaties made and ratified under the authority of the United States, shall be the supreme law of the respective States, as far as those acts or treaties shall relate to the said States, or their citizens and inhabitants; and that the Judiciaries of the several States shall be bound thereby

in their decisions, any thing in the respective laws of the individual States to the contrary notwithstanding.

8. *Resolved*, That in the original formation of the Legislature of the United States, the first branch thereof shall consist of sixty-five members; of which number,

New Hampshire shall send . . .	three,
Massachusetts	eight,
Rhode Island	one,
Connecticut	five,
New York	six,
New Jersey	four,
Pennsylvania	eight,
Delaware	one,
Maryland	six,
Virginia	ten,
North Carolina	five,
South Carolina	five,
Georgia	three.

But as the present situation of the states, may probably alter in the number of their inhabitants, the Legislature of the United States shall be authorized, from time to time, to apportion the number of representatives; and in case any of the States shall hereafter be divided, or enlarged by addition of territory, or any two or more States united, or any new States created within the limits of the United States, the Legislature of the United States shall possess authority to regulate the number of representatives, in any of the foregoing cases, upon the principle of their number of inhabitants, according to the provisions hereafter mentioned, namely — Provided always, that representation ought to be proportioned to direct taxation. And in order to ascertain the alteration in the direct taxation, which may be required from time to time, by the changes in the relative circumstances of the States,—

9. *Resolved*, That a census be taken within six years from the first meeting of the Legislature of the United States, and once within the term of every ten years after-

wards, of all the inhabitants of the United States, in the manner and according to the ratio recommended by Congress in their resolution of the eighteenth of April, 1783 ; and that the Legislature of the United States shall proportion the direct taxation accordingly.

10. *Resolved*, That all bills for raising or appropriating money, and for fixing the salaries of the officers of the Government of the United States, shall originate in the first branch of the Legislature of the United States, and shall not be altered or amended by the second branch ; and that no money shall be drawn from the public treasury, but in pursuance of appropriations to be originated by the first branch.

11. *Resolved*, That in the second branch of the Legislature of the United States, each State shall have an equal vote.

12. *Resolved*, That a National Executive be instituted, to consist of a single person ; to be chosen by the National Legislature, for the term of seven years ; to be ineligible a second time ; with power to carry into execution the national laws ; to appoint to offices in cases not otherwise provided for ; to be removable on impeachment, and conviction of malpractice or neglect of duty ; to receive a fixed compensation for the devotion of his time to the public service, to be paid out of the public treasury.

13. *Resolved*, That the National Executive shall have a right to negative any legislative act ; which shall not be afterwards passed, unless by two-third parts of each branch of the National Legislature.

14. *Resolved*, That a National Judiciary be established, to consist of one supreme tribunal, the Judges of which shall be appointed by the second branch of the national Legislature ; to hold their offices during good behaviour ; to receive punctually at stated times, a fixed compensation for their services, in which no diminution shall be made so as to affect the persons actually in office at the time of such diminution.

15. *Resolved*, That the National Legislature be empowered to appoint inferior tribunals.

16. *Resolved*, That the jurisdiction of the National Judiciary shall extend to cases arising under laws passed by the General Legislature ; and to such other questions as involve the national peace and harmony.

17. *Resolved*, That provision ought to be made for the admission of States lawfully arising within the limits of the United States, whether from a voluntary junction of government and territory, or otherwise, with the consent of a number of voices in the National Legislature less than the whole.

18. *Resolved*, That a republican form of government shall be guaranteed to each State; and that each State shall be protected against foreign and domestic violence.

19. *Resolved*, That provision ought to be made for the amendment of the Articles of Union, whensoever it shall seem necessary.

20. *Resolved*, That the Legislative, Executive and Judiciary powers, within the several States, and of the National Government, ought to be bound, by oath, to support the Articles of Union.

21. *Resolved*, That the amendments which shall be offered to the Confederation by the Convention ought, at a proper time or times, after the approbation of Congress, to be submitted to an assembly, or assemblies, of representatives, recommended by the several Legislatures, to be expressly chosen by the people to consider and decide thereon.

22. *Resolved*, That the representation in the second branch of the Legislature of the United States shall consist of two members from each State, who shall vote *per capita*.

23. *Resolved*, That it be an instruction to the Committee to whom were referred the proceedings of the Convention for the establishment of a National Government, to receive a clause, or clauses, requiring certain qualifications of property and citizenship in the United States, for

the Executive, the Judiciary, and the members of both branches of the Legislature of the United States.

With the above Resolutions were referred the propositions offered by Mr. C. PINCKNEY on the twenty-ninth of May, and by Mr. PATTERSON on the fifteenth of June.

Adjourned.

MONDAY, AUGUST 6TH.

In Convention, — Mr. JOHN FRANCIS MERCER, from Maryland, took his seat.

Mr. RUTLEDGE delivered in the Report of the Committee of Detail, as follows — a printed copy being at the same time furnished to each member:

We the people of the States of New Hampshire, Massachusetts, Rhode Island and Providence Plantations, Connecticut, New York, New Jersey Pennsylvania, Delaware, Maryland, Virginia, North Carolina, South Carolina, and Georgia, do ordain, declare, and establish the following Constitution for the government of ourselves and our posterity.

ARTICLE I.

The style of the Government shall be, "The United States of America."

ARTICLE II.

The Government shall consist of supreme Legislative, Executive, and Judicial powers.

ARTICLE III.

The legislative power shall be vested in a Congress, to consist of two separate and distinct bodies of men, a House of Representatives and a Senate; each of which shall in all cases have a negative on the other. The Legislature shall meet on the first Monday in December in every year.

ARTICLE IV.

Sect. 1. The members of the House of Representatives shall be chosen every second year, by the people of the

29

several States comprehended within this Union. The qualifications of the electors shall be the same from time to time, as those of the electors in the several States, of the most numerous branch of their own Legislatures.

Sect. 2. Every member of the House of Representatives shall be of the age of twenty-five years at least; shall have been a citizen in the United States for at least three years before his election; and shall be, at the time of his election, a resident of the State in which he shall be chosen.

Sect. 3. The House of Representatives shall, at its first formation, and until the number of citizens and inhabitants shall be taken in the manner hereinafter described, consist of sixty-five members, of whom three shall be chosen in New Hampshire, eight in Massachusetts, one in Rhode Island and Providence Plantations, five in Connecticut, six in New York, four in New Jersey, eight in Pennsylvania, one in Delaware, six in Maryland, ten in Virginia, five in North Carolina, five in South Carolina, and three in Georgia.

Sect. 4. As the proportions of numbers in different States will alter from time to time; as some of the States may hereafter be divided; as others may be enlarged by addition of territory; as two or more States may be united; as new States will be erected within the limits of the United States, the Legislature shall, in each of these cases, regulate the number of Representatives by the number of inhabitants, according to the provisions hereinafter made, at the rate of one for every forty thousand.

Sect. 5. All bills for raising or appropriating money, and for fixing the salaries of the officers of government, shall originate in the House of Representatives, and shall not be altered or amended by the Senate. No money shall be drawn from the public treasury, but in pursuance of appropriations that shall originate in the House of Representatives.

Sect. 6. The House of Representatives shall have the

sole power of impeachment. It shall choose its Speaker and other officers.

Sect. 7. Vacancies in the House of Representatives shall be supplied by writs of election from the Executive authority of the State in the representation from which they shall happen.

ARTICLE V.

Sect. 1. The Senate of the United States shall be chosen by the Legislatures of the several States. Each Legislature shall choose two members. Vacancies may be supplied by the Executive until the next meeting of the Legislature. Each member shall have one vote.

Sect. 2. The Senators shall be chosen for six years; but immediately after the first election, they shall be divided, by lot, into three classes, as nearly as may be, numbered one, two, and three. The seats of the members of the first class shall be vacated at the expiration of the second year; of the second class at the expiration of the fourth year; of the third class at the expiration of the sixth year; so that a third part of the members may be chosen every second year.

Sect. 3. Every member of the Senate shall be of the age of thirty years at least; shall have been a citizen in the United States for at least four years before his election; and shall be, at the time of his election, a resident of the State for which he shall be chosen.

Sect. 4. The Senate shall choose its own President and other officers.

ARTICLE VI.

Sect. 1 The times, and places, and manner of holding the elections of the members of each House, shall be prescribed by the Legislature of each State; but their provisions concerning them may, at any time, be altered by the Legislature of the United States.

Sect. 2. The Legislature of the United States shall have authority to establish such uniform qualifications of the members of each House, with regard to property, as to the said Legislature shall seem expedient.

Sect. 3. In each House a majority of the members shall constitute a quorum to do business; but a smaller number may adjourn from day to day.

Sect. 4. Each House shall be the judge of the elections, returns and qualifications, of its own members.

Sect. 5. Freedom of speech and debate in the Legislature shall not be impeached or questioned in any court or place out of the Legislature; and the members of each House shall, in all cases, except treason, felony, and breach of the peace, be privileged from arrest during their attendance at Congress, and in going to and returning from it.

Sect. 6. Each House may determine the rules of its proceedings; may punish its members for disorderly behaviour; and may expel a member.

Sect. 7. The House of Representatives, and the Senate, when it shall be acting in a legislative capacity, shall keep a journal of their proceedings; and shall, from time to time, publish them; and the yeas and nays of the members of each House, on any question, shall, at the desire of one fifth part of the members present, be entered on the Journal.

Sect. 8. Neither House, without the consent of the other, shall adjourn for more than three days, nor to any other place than that at which the two Houses are sitting. But this regulation shall not extend to the Senate when it shall exercise the powers mentioned in the ——— Article.

Sect. 9. The members of each House shall be ineligible to, and incapable of holding, any office under the authority of the United States, during the time for which they shall respectively be elected: and the members of the Senate shall be ineligible to, and incapable of holding, any such office for one year afterwards.

Sect. 10. The members of each House shall receive a compensation for their services, to be ascertained and paid by the State in which they shall be chosen.

Sect. 11. The enacting style of the laws of the United States shall be, "Be it enacted, and it is hereby enacted, by the House of Representatives, and by the Senate of the United States, in Congress assembled."

Sect. 12. Each House shall possess the right of originating bills, except in the cases before mentioned.

Sect. 13. Every bill, which shall have passed the House of Representatives and the Senate, shall, before it becomes a law, be presented to the President of the United States for his revision. If, upon such revision, he approve of it, he shall signify his approbation by signing it. But if, upon such revision, it shall appear to him improper for being passed into a law, he shall return it, together with his objections against it, to that House in which it shall have originated ; who shall enter the objections at large on their Journal, and proceed to reconsider the bill. But if, after such reconsideration, two-thirds of that House shall, notwithstanding the objections of the President, agree to pass it, it shall, together with his objections, be sent to the other House, by which it shall likewise be re-considered, and if approved by two-thirds of the other House also, it shall become a law. But in all such cases, the votes of both Houses shall be determined by Yeas and Nays ; and the names of the persons voting for or against the bill, shall be entered on the Journal of each House respectively. If any bill shall not be returned by the President within seven days after it shall have been presented to him, it shall be a law, unless the Legislature, by their adjournment, prevent its return ; in which case it shall not be a law.

ARTICLE VII.

Sect. 1. The Legislature of the United States shall have the power to lay and collect taxes, duties, imposts and excises ;

To regulate commerce with foreign nations, and among the several States ;

To establish an uniform rule of naturalization throughout the United States ;

To coin money ;

To regulate the value of foreign coin ;

To fix the standard of weights and measures ;

To establish post-offices ;

To borrow money, and emit bills on the credit of the United States ;

To appoint a Treasurer by ballot ;

To constitute tribunals inferior to the Supreme Court ;

To make rules concerning captures on land and water ;

To declare the law and punishment of piracies and felonies committed on the high seas, and the punishment of counterfeiting the coin of the United States, and of offences against the law of nations ;

To subdue a rebellion in any State, on the application of its Legislature ;

To make war;

To raise armies;

To build and equip fleets;

To call forth the aid of the militia, in order to execute the laws of the Union, enforce treaties, suppress insurrections, and repel invasions;

And to make all laws that shall be necessary and proper for carrying into execution the foregoing powers, and all other powers vested by this Constitution in the Government of the United States, or in any department or office thereof.

Sect. 2. Treason against the United States shall consist only in levying war against the United States, or any of them; and in adhering to the enemies of the United States, or any of them. The Legislature of the United States shall have power to declare the punishment of treason. No person shall be convicted of treason, unless on the testimony of two witnesses. No attainder of treason shall work corruption of blood, nor forfeiture, except during the life of the person attainted.

Sect. 3. The proportions of direct taxation shall be

regulated by the whole number of white and other free citizens and inhabitants of every age, sex and condition, including those bound to servitude for a term of years, and three-fifths of all other persons not comprehended in the foregoing description, (except Indians not paying taxes); which number shall, within six years after the first meeting of the Legislature, and within the term of every ten years afterwards, be taken in such a manner as the said Legislature shall direct.

Sect. 4. No tax or duty shall be laid by the Legislature on articles exported from any State; nor on the migration or importation of such persons as the several States shall think proper to admit; nor shall such migration or importation be prohibited.

Sect. 5. No capitation tax shall be laid, unless in proportion to the census herein before directed to be taken.

Sect. 6. No navigation act shall be passed without the assent of two-thirds of the members present in each House.

Sect. 7. The United States shall not grant any title of nobility.

ARTICLE VIII.

The acts of the Legislature of the United States made in pursuance of this Constitution, and all treaties made under the authority of the United States, shall be the supreme law of the several States, and of their citizens and inhabitants; and the Judges in the several States shall be bound thereby in their decisions, any thing in the Constitutions or laws of the several States to the contrary notwithstanding.

ARTICLE IX.

Sect. 1. The Senate of the United States shall have power to make treaties, and to appoint ambassadors, and Judges of the Supreme Court.

Sect. 2. In all disputes and controversies now subsisting, or that may hereafter subsist, between two or more States, respecting jurisdiction or territory, the Senate shall possess the following powers: — Whenever the Legislature, or the Executive authority, or lawful agent of any State, in controversy with another, shall by memorial to the Senate, state the matter in question, and apply for a hearing, notice of such memorial and application shall be given, by order of the Senate, to the Legislature, or the Executive authority, of the other State in controversy. The Senate shall also assign a day for the appearance of the parties, by their agents, before that House. The agents shall be directed to appoint, by joint consent, commissioners or judges to constitute a court for hearing and determining the matter in question. But if the agents cannot agree, the Senate shall name three persons out of each of the several States; and from the list of such persons, each party shall alternately strike out one, until the number shall be reduced to thirteen; and from that number, not less than seven, nor more than nine names, as the Senate shall direct, shall, in their presence, be drawn out by lot; and the persons whose names shall be so drawn, or any five of them, shall be commissioners or judges to hear and finally determine the controversy; provided a majority of the judges who shall hear the cause agree in the determination. If either party shall neglect to attend at the day assigned, without showing sufficient reasons for not attending, or being present shall refuse to strike, the Senate shall proceed to nominate three persons out of each State, and the Clerk of the Senate shall strike in behalf of the party absent or refusing. If any of the parties shall refuse to submit to the authority of such court, or shall not appear to prosecute or defend their claim or cause, the court shall nevertheless proceed to pronounce judgment. The judgment shall be final and conclusive. The proceedings shall be transmitted to the President of the Senate, and shall be lodged among the public records for the security of the parties concerned. Every commissioner shall, before he sit in judgment, take an oath to be administered by one of the judges of the Supreme or Superior Court of the State where the cause shall be tried, "well and truly to hear and determine the matter in question, according to the best of his judgment, without favor, affection, or hope of reward."

Sect. 3. All controversies concerning lands claimed under different grants of two or more States, whose jurisdictions, as they respect such lands, shall have been decided or adjusted subsequently to such grants, or any of them, shall, on application to the Senate, be finally determined, as near as may be, in the same manner as is before prescribed for deciding controversies between different States.

ARTICLE X.

Sect. 1. The Executive power of the United States shall be vested in a single person. His style shall be, "The President of the United States of America," and his title shall be, "His Excellency." He shall be elected by ballot by the Legislature. He shall hold his office during the term of seven years; but shall not be elected a second time.

Sect. 2. He shall, from time to time, give information to the Legislature of the state of the Union. He may recommend to their consideration such measures as he shall judge necessary, and expedient. He may convene them on extraordinary occasions. In case of disagreement between the two Houses, with regard to the time of adjournment, he may adjourn them to such time as he thinks proper. He shall take care that the laws of the United States be duly and faithfully executed. He shall commission all the officers of the United States; and shall appoint officers in all cases not otherwise provided for by this Constitution. He shall receive Ambassadors, and may correspond with the supreme executives of the several States. He shall have power to grant reprieves and pardons, but his pardon shall not be pleadable in bar of an impeachment. He shall be Commander-in-chief of the army and navy of the United States, and of the militia of the several States. He shall, at stated times, receive for his services a compensation, which shall neither be increased nor diminished during his continuance in office. Before he shall enter on the duties of his department, he shall take the following oath or affirmation, "I —— solemnly swear, (or affirm) that I will faithfully execute the office of President of the United States of America." He shall be removed from his office on impeachment by the House of Representatives, and conviction in the Supreme Court, of treason, bribery, or corruption. In case of his removal, as aforesaid, death, resignation, or disability to discharge the powers and duties of his office, the President of the Senate shall exercise those powers and duties, until another President of the United States be chosen, or until the disability of the President be removed.

ARTICLE XI.

Sect. 1. The Judicial power of the United States shall be vested in one Supreme Court, and in such inferior courts, as shall, when necessary, from time to time, be constituted by the Legislature of the United States.

Sect. 2. The Judges of the Supreme Court, and of the inferior courts, shall hold their offices during good behaviour. They shall, at stated times, receive for their services a compensation, which shall not be diminished during their continuance in office.

Sect. 3. The jurisdiction of the Supreme Court shall extend to all cases arising under laws passed by the Legislature of the United States; to all cases affecting ambassadors, other public ministers and consuls ; to the trial of impeachments of officers of the United States; to all cases of admiralty and maritime jurisdiction; to controversies between two or more States, (except such as shall regard territory or jurisdiction); between a state and citizens of another State; between citizens of different States; and between a state, or the citizens thereof, and foreign states, citizens or subjects. In cases of impeachment, cases affecting ambassadors, other public ministers and consuls, and those in which a State shall be party, this jurisdiction shall be original.   In all the other cases beforementioned, it shall be appellate, with such exceptions, and under such regulations, as the Legislature shall make. The Legislature may assign any part of the jurisdiction above mentioned (except the trial of the President of the United States) in the manner, and under the limitations which it shall think proper, to such inferior courts, as it shall constitute from time to time.

Sect. 4. The trial of all criminal offences (except in cases of impeachment) shall be in the State where they shall be committed; and shall be by jury.

Sect. 5. Judgment, in cases of impeachment, shall not extend further than to removal from office, and disqualification to hold and enjoy any office of honor, trust or profit, under the United States. But the party convicted shall nevertheless be liable and subject to indictment, trial, judgment and punishment according to law.

ARTICLE XII.

No State shall coin money; nor grant letters of marque and reprisal; nor enter into any treaty, alliance or confederation; nor grant any title of nobility.

ARTICLE XIII.

No State, without the consent of the Legislature of the United States, shall emit bills of credit, or make anything but specie a tender in payment of debts; nor lay imposts or duties on imports; nor keep troops or ships of war in time of peace; nor enter into any agreement or compact with another State, or with any foreign power; nor engage in any war, unless it shall be actually invaded by enemies, or the danger of invasion be so imminent as not to admit of a delay until the Legislature of the United States can be consulted.

ARTICLE XIV.

The citizens of each State shall be entitled to all privileges and immunities of citizens in the several States.

ARTICLE XV.

Any person charged with treason, felony or high misdemeanour in any State, who shall flee from justice, and shall be found in any other State, shall, on demand of the Executive power of the State from which he fled, be delivered up and removed to the State having jurisdiction of the offence.

ARTICLE XVI.

Full faith shall be given in each State to the acts of the Legislatures, and to the records and judicial proceedings of the courts and magistrates, of every other State.

ARTICLE XVII.

New States lawfully constituted or established within the limits of the United States may be admitted, by the Legislature, into this government; but to such admission the consent of two-thirds of the members present in each House shall be necessary. If a new State shall arise within the limits of any of the present States, the consent of the Legislatures of such States shall be also necessary to its admission. If the admission be consented to, the new States shall be admitted on the same terms with the original States. But the Legislature may make conditions with the new States, concerning the public debt which shall be then subsisting.

ARTICLE XVIII.

The United States shall guarantee to each State a republican form of government; and shall protect each State against foreign invasions, and, on the application of its Legislature, against domestic violence.

Article XIX.

On the application of the Legislatures of two-thirds of the States in the Union, for an amendment of this Constitution, the Legislature of the United States shall call a convention for that purpose.

Article XX.

The members of the Legislatures, and the Executive and Judicial officers of the United States, and of the several States, shall be bound by oath to support this Constitution.

Article XXI.

The ratification of the Conventions of ——— States shall be sufficient for organizing this Constitution.

Article XXII.

This Constitution shall be laid before the United States in Congress assembled, for their approbation; and it is the opinion of this Convention, that it should be afterwards submitted to a Convention chosen in each State, under the recommendation of its Legislature, in order to receive the ratification of such Convention.

Article XXIII.

To introduce this government, it is the opinion of this Convention, that each assenting Convention should notify its assent and ratification to the United States in Congress assembled; that Congress, after receiving the assent and ratification of the Conventions of ——— States, should appoint and publish a day, as early as may be, and appoint a place, for commencing proceedings under this Constitution; that after such publication, the Legislatures of the several States should elect members of the Senate and direct the election of members of the House of Representatives; and that the members of the Legislature should meet at the time and place assigned by Congress, and should, as soon as may be after their meeting, choose the President of the United States, and proceed to execute this Constitution.

A motion was made to adjourn till Wednesday, in order to give leisure to examine the Report; which passed in the negative, — Pennsylvania, Maryland, Virginia, aye — 3; New Hampshire, Massachusetts, Connecticut, North Carolina, South Carolina, no — 5.

The House then adjourned till to-morrow at eleven o'clock.

TUESDAY, AUGUST 7TH, 1787.

In Convention, — The Report of the Committee of Detail being taken up, —

Mr. PINCKNEY moved that it be referred to a Committee of the Whole. This was strongly opposed by Mr. GORHAM and several others, as likely to produce unnecessary delay; and was negatived, — Delaware, Maryland, and Virginia, only being in the affirmative.

The preamble of the Report was agreed to, *nem. con.* So were Articles 1 and 2.

Article 3 being considered, — Col. MASON doubted the propriety of giving each branch a negative on the other "in all cases." There were some cases in which it was, he supposed, not intended to be given, as in the case of balloting for appointments.

Mr. G. MORRIS moved to insert "legislative acts," instead of "all cases." Mr. WILLIAMSON seconds him.

Mr. SHERMAN. This will restrain the operation of the clause too much. It will particularly exclude a mutual negative in the case of ballots, which he hoped would take place.

Mr. GORHAM contended, that elections ought to be made by *joint ballot.* If separate ballots should be made for the

President, and the two branches should be each attached to a favorite, great delay, contention and confusion may ensue. These inconveniences have been felt in Massachusetts, in the election of officers of little importance compared with the Executive of the United States. The only objection against a joint ballot is, that it may deprive the Senate of their due weight; but this ought not to prevail over the respect due to the public tranquillity and welfare.

Mr. WILSON was for a joint ballot in several cases at least; particularly in the choice of a President; and was therefore for the amendment. Disputes between the two Houses, during and concerning the vacancy of the Executive, might have dangerous consequences.

Col. MASON thought the amendment of Mr. GOUVERNEUR MORRIS extended too far. Treaties are in a subsequent part declared to be laws; they will therefore be subjected to a negative, although they are to be made, as proposed, by the Senate alone. He proposed that the mutual negative should be restrained to " cases requiring the distinct assent " of the two Houses. Mr. GOUVERNEUR MORRIS thought this but a repetition of the same thing; the mutual negative and distinct assent being equivalent expressions. Treaties he thought were not laws.

Mr. MADISON moved to strike out the words, " each of which shall in all cases have a negative on the other;" the idea being sufficiently expressed in the preceding member of the Article, " vesting the Legislative power " in " distinct bodies," especially as the respective powers, and mode of exercising them, were fully delineated in a subsequent Article.

General PINCKNEY seconded the motion.

On the question for inserting " legislative acts," as moved by Mr. GOUVERNEUR MORRIS, it passed in the negative, the votes being equally divided, — New Hampshire, Massachusetts, Connecticut, Pennsylvania, North Carolina, aye — 5; Delaware, Maryland, Virginia, South Carolina, Georgia no — 5.

On the question for agreeing to Mr. MADISON's motion to strike out, &c. — New Hampshire, Massachusetts, Pennsylvania, Delaware, Virginia, South Carolina, Georgia, aye — 7; Connecticut, Maryland, North Carolina, no — 3.

Mr. MADISON wished to know the reasons of the Committee for fixing by the Constitution the time of meeting for the Legislature; and suggested, that it be required only that one meeting at least should be held every year, leaving the time to be fixed or varied by law.

Mr. GOUVERNEUR MORRIS moved to strike out the sentence. It was improper to tie down the Legislature to a particular time, or even to require a meeting every year. The public business might not require it. Mr. PINCKNEY concurred with Mr. MADISON.

Mr. GORHAM. If the time be not fixed by the Constitution, disputes will arise in the Legislature; and the States will be at a loss to adjust thereto the times of their elections. In the New England States, the annual time of meeting had been long fixed by their charters and constitutions, and no inconvenience had resulted. He thought it necessary that there should be one meeting at least every year, as a check on the Executive department.

Mr. ELLSWORTH was against striking out the words. The Legislature will not know, till they are met, whether the public interest required their meeting or not. He could see no impropriety in fixing the day, as the Convention could judge of it as well as the Legislature.

Mr. WILSON thought, on the whole, it would be best to fix the day.

Mr. KING could not think there would be a necessity for a meeting every year. A great vice in our system was that of legislating too much. The most numerous objects of legislation belong to the States. Those of the National Legislature were but few. The chief of them were commerce and revenue. When these should be once settled, alterations would be rarely necessary and easily made.

Mr. MADISON thought, if the time of meeting should be

fixed by a law, it would be sufficiently fixed, and there would be no difficulty then, as had been suggested, on the part of the States in adjusting their elections to it. One consideration appeared to him to militate strongly against fixing a time by the Constitution. It might happen that the Legislature might be called together by the public exigencies and finish their session but a short time before the annual period. In this case it would be extremely inconvenient to re-assemble so quickly, and without the least necessity. He thought one annual meeting ought to be required; but did not wish to make two unavoidable.

Colonel MASON thought the objections against fixing the time insuperable; but that an annual meeting ought to be required as essential to the preservation of the Constitution. The extent of the country will supply business. And if it should not the Legislature, besides *legislative*, is to have *inquisitorial* powers, which cannot safely be long kept in a state of suspension.

Mr. SHERMAN was decided for fixing the time, as well as for frequent meetings of the legislative body. Disputes and difficulties will arise between the two Houses, and between both and the States, if the time be changeable. Frequent meetings of parliament were required at the Revolution in England, as an essential safeguard of liberty. So also are annual meetings in most of the American charters and constitutions. There will be business enough to require it. The western country, and the great extent and varying state of our affairs in general, will supply objects.

Mr. RANDOLPH was against fixing any day irrevocably; but as there was no provision made any where in the Constitution for regulating the periods of meeting, and some precise time must be fixed, until the Legislature shall make provision, he could not agree to strike out the words altogether. Instead of which he moved to add the words following: "unless a different day shall be appointed by law."

Mr. MADISON seconded the motion; and on the question,
— Massachusetts, Pennsylvania, Delaware, Maryland, Vir-

ginia, North Carolina, South Carolina, Georgia, aye — 8; New Hampshire, Connecticut, no — 2.

Mr. GOUVERNEUR MORRIS moved to strike out "December," and insert "May." It might frequently happen that our measures ought to be influenced by those in Europe, which were generally planned during the winter, and of which intelligence would arrive in the spring.

Mr. MADISON seconded the motion. He preferred May to December, because the latter would require the travelling to and from the seat of government in the most inconvenient seasons of the year.

Mr. WILSON. The winter is the most convenient season for business.

Mr. ELLSWORTH. The summer will interfere too much with private business, that of almost all the probable members of the Legislature being more or less connected with agriculture.

Mr. RANDOLPH. The time is of no great moment now, as the Legislature can vary it. On looking into the Constitutions of the States, he found that the times of their elections, with which ·the elections of the National Representatives would no doubt be made to coincide, would suit better with December than May, and it was advisable to render our innovations as little incommodious as possible.

On the question for "May" instead of "December," — South Carolina, Georgia aye — 2; New Hampshire, Massachusetts, Connecticut, Pennsylvania, Delaware, Maryland, Virginia, North Carolina, no — 8.

Mr. REED moved to insert after the word, "Senate," the words, "subject to the negative to be hereafter provided." His object was to give an absolute negative to the Executive. He considered this as so essential to the Constitution, to the preservation of liberty, and to the public welfare, that his duty compelled him to make the motion.

Mr. GOUVERNEUR MORRIS seconded him; and on the question, —

Delaware, aye — 1; New Hampshire, Massachusetts,

Connecticut, Pennsylvania, Maryland, Virginia, North Carolina, South Carolina, Georgia, no — 9.

Mr. RUTLEDGE. Although it is agreed on all hands that an annual meeting of the Legislature should be made necessary, yet that point seems not to be free from doubt as the clause stands. On this suggestion, "once at least in every year," were inserted, *nem. con.*

Article 3, with the foregoing alterations, was agreed to, *nem. con.*, and is as follows: "The Legislative power shall be vested in a Congress to consist of two separate and distinct bodies of men, a House of Representatives and a Senate. The Legislature shall meet at least once in every year; and such meeting shall be on the first Monday in December, unless a different day shall be appointed by law."

Article 4, Sect. 1, was taken up.

Mr. GOUVERNEUR MORRIS moved to strike out the last member of the section, beginning with the words, "qualifications of Electors," in order that some other provision might be substituted which would restrain the right of suffrage to freeholders.

Mr. FITZSIMONS seconded the motion.

Mr. WILLIAMSON was opposed to it.

Mr. WILSON. This part of the Report was well considered by the Committee, and he did not think it could be changed for the better. It was difficult to form any uniform rule of qualifications, for all the States. Unnecessary innovations, he thought, too, should be avoided. It would be very hard and disagreeable for the same persons, at the same time, to vote for representatives in the State Legislature, and to be excluded from a vote for those in the National Legislature.

Mr. GOUVERNEUR MORRIS. Such a hardship would be neither great nor novel. The people are accustomed to it, and not dissatisfied with it, in several of the States. In some, the qualifications are different for the choice of the Governor and of the Representatives; in others, for different houses of the Legislature. Another objection against the clause, as it stands, is, that it makes the qualifications of the National Legislature depend on the will of the States, which he thought not proper.

Mr. ELLSWORTH thought the qualifications of the electors stood on the most proper footing. The right of suffrage was a tender point, and strongly guarded by most of the State Constitutions. The people will not readily subscribe to the National Constitution, if it should subject them to be disfranchised. The States are the best judges of the circumstances and temper of their own people.

Colonel MASON. The force of habit is certainly not attended to by those gentlemen who wish for innovations on this point. Eight or nine States have extended the right of suffrage beyond the freeholders. What will the people there say, if they should be disfranchised? A power to alter the qualifications, would be a dangerous power in the hands of the Legislature.

Mr. BUTLER. There is no right of which the people are more jealous than that of suffrage. Abridgments of it tend to the same revolution as in Holland, where they have at length thrown all power into the hands of the Senates, who fill up vacancies themselves, and form a rank aristocracy.

Mr. DICKINSON had a very different idea of the tendency of vesting the right of suffrage in the freeholders of the country. He considered them as the best guardians of liberty; and the restriction of the right to them as a necessary defence against the dangerous influence of those multitudes without property and without principle, with which our country, like all others, will in time abound. As to the unpopularity of the innovation, it was, in his opinion, chimerical. The great mass of our citizens is composed at this time of freeholders, and will be pleased with it.

Mr. ELLSWORTH. How shall the freehold be defined? Ought not every man who pays a tax, to vote for the representative who is to levy and dispose of his money? Shall the wealthy merchants and manufacturers, who will bear a full share of the public burthens, be not allowed a voice in the imposition of them? Taxation and representation ought to go together.

Mr. GOUVERNEUR MORRIS. He had long learned not to be the dupe of words. The sound of aristocracy, therefore, had no effect upon him. It was the thing, not the name, to which he was opposed; and one of his principal objections to the Constitution, as it is now before us, is, that it threatens the country with an aristocracy. The aristocracy will grow out of the House of Representatives. Give the votes to people who have no property and they will sell them to the rich, who will be able to buy them. We should not confine our attention to the present moment. The time is not distant when this country will abound with mechanics and manufacturers, who will receive their bread from their employers. Will such men be the secure and faithful guardians of liberty? Will they be the impregnable barrier against aristocracy? He was as little duped by the association of the words, "taxation and representation." The man who does not give his vote freely, is not represented. It is the man who dictates the vote. Children do not vote. Why? Because they want prudence; because they have no will of their own. The ignorant and the dependent can be as little trusted with the public interest. He did not conceive the difficulty of defining " freeholders" to be insuperable. Still less than the restriction could be unpopular. Nine-tenths of the people are at present freeholders, and these will certainly be pleased with it. As to merchants &c., if they have wealth, and value the right, they can acquire it. If not, they don't deserve it.

Col. MASON. We all feel too strongly the remains of ancient prejudices, and view things too much through a British medium. A freehold is the qualification in England, and hence it is imagined to be the only proper one. The true idea, in his opinion, was, that every man having evidence of attachment to, and permanent common interest with, the society, ought to share in all its rights and privileges. Was this qualification restrained to freeholders? Does no other kind of property but land evidence a common interest in the proprietor? Does nothing besides property mark a permanent attachment? Ought the merchant, the monied man, the parent of a number of children whose fortunes are to be pursued in his own country, to be viewed as suspicious characters, and unworthy to be trusted with the common rights of their fellow citizens?

Mr. MADISON. The right of suffrage is certainly one of the fundamental articles of republican government, and ought not to be left to be regulated by the Legislature. A gradual abridgment of this right has been the mode in which aristocracies have been built on the ruins of popular forms. Whether the constitutional qualification ought to be a freehold, would with him depend much on the probable reception such a change would meet with in the States, where the right was now exercised by every description of people. In several of the States a freehold was now the qualification. Viewing the subject in its merits alone, the freeholders of the country would be the safest depositories of republican liberty. In future times, a great majority of the people will not only be without landed, but any other sort of property. These will either combine, under the influence of their common situation — in which case the rights of property and the public liberty will not be secure in their hands — or, what is more probable, they will become the tools of opulence and ambition ; in which case, there will be equal danger on another side. The example of England has been misconceived (by Col. MASON). A very small proportion of the Representatives are there chosen by freeholders. The greatest part are chosen by the cities and boroughs, in many of which the qualification of suffrage is as low as it is in any one of the United States ; and it was in the boroughs and cities, rather than the counties, that bribery most prevailed, and the influence of the Crown on elections was most dangerously exerted.

Doctor FRANKLIN. It is of great consequence that we should not depress the virtue and public spirit of our common people ; of which they displayed a great deal during the war, and which contributed principally to the favourable issue of it. He related the honourable refusal of the American seamen, who were carried in great numbers into the British prisons during the war to redeem themselves from misery, or to seek their fortunes, by entering on board the ships of the enemies to their country ; contrasting their patriotism with a contemporary instance, in which the British seamen made prisoners by the Americans readily entered on the ships of the latter, on being promised a share of the prizes that might be made out of their own country. This proceeded, he said, from the different manner in which the common people were treated in America and Great Britain. He did not think that the elected had any right, in any case, to narrow the privileges of the electors. He quoted, as arbitrary, the British statute setting forth the danger of tumultuous meetings, and, under that pretext, narrowing the right of suffrage to persons having freeholds of a certain value ; observing that this statute was soon followed by another, under the succeeding parliament, subjecting the people who had no votes to peculiar labors and hardships. He was persuaded, also, that such a restriction as was proposed would give great uneasiness in the populous States. The sons of a substantial farmer, not being themselves freeholders, would not be pleased at being disfranchised, and there are a great many persons of that description.

Mr. MERCER. The Constitution is objectionable in many points, but in none more than the present. He objected to the footing on which the qualification was put, but particularly to the *mode of election* by the people. The people cannot know and judge of the characters of candidates. The worst possible choice will be made. He quoted the case of the Senate in Virginia, as an example in point. The people in towns can unite their votes in favor of one favorite; and by that means always prevail over the people of the country; who being dispersed will scatter their votes among a variety of candidates.

Mr. RUTLEDGE thought the idea of restraining the right of suffrage to the freeholders a very unadvised one. It would create division among the people; and make enemies of all those who should be excluded.

On the question for striking out, as moved by Mr. GOU-VERNEUR MORRIS, from the word " qualifications" to the end of the third article,— Delaware, aye — 1; New Hampshire, Massachusetts, Connecticut, Pennsylvania, Virginia, North Carolina, South Carolina, no — 7; Maryland, divided; Georgia, not present.

Adjourned.

WEDNESDAY, AUGUST 8TH.

In Convention,—Article 4, sect. 1, being under consideration,—

Mr. MERCER expressed his dislike of the whole plan, and his opinion that it never could succeed.

Mr. GORHAM. He had never seen any inconvenience from allowing such as were not freeholders to vote, though it had long been tried. The elections in Philadelphia, New York, and Boston, where the merchants and mechanics vote, are at least as good as those made by freeholders only. The case in England was not accurately stated yesterday (by Mr. MADISON). The cities and large towns are not the seat of Crown influence and corruption. These prevail in the boroughs, and not on account of the right which those who are not freeholders have to vote, but of the smallness of the number who vote. The people have been long accustomed to this right in various parts of America, and will never allow it to be abridged. We must consult their rooted prejudices if we expect their concurrence in our propositions.

Mr. MERCER did not object so much to an election by the people at large, including such as were not freeholders, as to their being left to make their choice without any

guidance. He hinted that candidates ought to be nominated by the State Legislatures.

On the question for agreeing to Article 4, Sect. 1, it
passed, *nem. con.*

Article 4, Sect. 2, was then taken up.

Colonel MASON was for opening a wide door for emigrants; but did not choose to let foreigners and adven-
turers make laws for us and govern us. Citizenship for
three years was not enough for ensuring that local knowledge which ought to be possessed by the representative.
This was the principal ground of his objection to so short a
term. It might also happen, that a rich foreign nation, for
example Great Britain, might send over her tools, who
might bribe their way into the Legislature for insidious
purposes. He moved that " seven " years, instead of
" three," be inserted.

Mr. GOUVERNEUR MORRIS seconded the motion; and on
the question, all the States agreed to it, except Connecticut.

Mr. SHERMAN moved to strike out the word " resident "
and insert " inhabitant," as less liable to misconstruction.

Mr. MADISON seconded the motion. Both were vague,
but the latter least so in common acceptation, and would
not exclude persons absent occasionally for a considerable
time on public or private business. Great disputes had
been raised in Virginia concerning the meaning of residence
as a qualification of representatives, which were determined
more according to the affection or dislike to the man in
question than to any fixed interpretation of the word.

Mr. WILSON preferred " inhabitant."

Mr. GOUVERNEUR MORRIS was opposed to both, and for
requiring nothing more than a freehold. He quoted great
disputes in New York occasioned by these terms, which
were decided by the arbitrary will of the majority. Such a
regulation is not necessary. People rarely choose a non-
resident. It is improper, as in the first branch, *the people
at large*, not the *States*, are represented.

Mr. RUTLEDGE urged and moved, that a residence of

seven years should be required in the State wherein the member should be elected. An emigrant from New England to South Carolina or Georgia would know little of its affairs, and could not be supposed to acquire a thorough knowledge in less time.

Mr. READ reminded him that we were now forming a *national government*, and such a regulation would correspond little with the idea that we were one people.

Mr. WILSON enforced the same consideration.

Mr. MADISON suggested the case of new States in the west, which could have, perhaps, no representation on that plan.

Mr. MERCER. Such a regulation would present a greater alienship than existed under the old federal system. It would interweave local prejudices and State distinctions, in the very Constitution which is meant to cure them. He mentioned instances of violent disputes raised in Maryland concerning the term "residence."

Mr. ELLSWORTH thought seven years of residence was by far too long a term; but that some fixed term of previous residence would be proper. He thought one year would be sufficient, but seemed to have no objection to three years.

Mr. DICKINSON proposed that it should read "inhabitant actually resident for —— years." This would render the meaning less indeterminate.

Mr. WILSON. If a short term should be inserted in the blank, so strict an expression might be construed to exclude the members of the Legislature, who could not be said to be actual residents in their States, whilst at the seat of the General Government.

Mr. MERCER. It would certainly exclude men, who had once been inhabitants, and returning from residence elsewhere to resettle in their original State, although a want of the necessary knowledge could not in such cases be presumed.

Mr. MASON thought seven years too long, but would

never agree to part with the principle. It is a valuable principle. He thought it a defect in the plan, that the Representatives would be too few to bring with them all the local knowledge necessary. If residence be not required, rich men of neighbouring States may employ with success the means of corruption in some particular district, and thereby get into the public councils after having failed in their own States. This is the practice in the boroughs of England.

On the question for postponing in order to consider Mr. DICKINSON's motion, —

Maryland, South Carolina, Georgia, aye — 3; New Hampshire, Massachusetts, Connecticut, New Jersey, Pennsylvania, Delaware, Virginia, North Carolina, no — 8.

On the question for inserting "inhabitant," in place of " resident," — agreed to, *nem. con.*

Mr. ELLSWORTH and Col. MASON moved to insert "one year " for previous inhabitancy.

Mr. WILLIAMSON liked the Report as it stood. He thought resident a good enough term. He was against requiring any period of previous residence. New residents, if elected, will be most zealous to conform to the will of their constituents, as their conduct will be watched with a more jealous eye.

Mr. BUTLER and Mr. RUTLEDGE moved " three years, " instead of " one year," for previous inhabitancy.

On the question for " three years,"—

South Carolina, Georgia, aye — 2; New Hampshire, Massachusetts, Connecticut, New Jersey, Pennsylvania, Delaware, Maryland, Virginia, North Carolina, no — 9,

On the question for " one year," —

New Jersey, North Carolina, South Carolina, Georgia, aye — 4; New Hampshire, Massachusetts, Connecticut, Pennsylvania, Delaware, Virginia, no — 6; Maryland, divided.

Article 4, Sect. 2, as amended in manner preceding, was agreed to, *nem. con.*

Article 4, Sect. 3, was then taken up.

General PINCKNEY and Mr. PINCKNEY moved that the number of Representatives allotted to South Carolina be " six."

On the question, —

Delaware, North Carolina, South Carolina, Georgia, aye — 4; New Hampshire, Massachusetts, Connecticut, New Jersey, Pennsylvania, Maryland, Virginia, no — 7.

The third section of Article 4, was then agreed to.

Article 4, Sect. 4, was then taken up.

Mr. WILLIAMSON moved to strike out, " according to the provisions hereinafter made," and to insert the words, "according to the rule hereafter to be provided for direct taxation."—See Art. 7, Sect. 3.

On the question for agreeing to Mr. WILLIAMSON'S amendment, —

New Hampshire, Massachusetts, Connecticut, Pennsylvania, Maryland, Virginia, North Carolina, South Carolina, Georgia, aye — 9; New Jersey, Delaware, no — 2.

Mr. KING wished to know what influence the vote just passed was meant to have on the succeeding part of the Report, concerning the admission of slaves into the rule of representation. He could not reconcile his mind to the Article, if it was to prevent objections to the latter part. The admission of slaves was a most grating circumstance to his mind, and he believed would be so to a great part of the people of America. He had not made a strenuous opposition to it heretofore, because he had hoped that this concession would have produced a readiness, which had not been manifested, to strengthen the General Government, and to mark a full confidence in it. The Report under consideration had, by the tenor of it, put an end to all those hopes. In two great points the hands of the Legislature were absolutely tied. The importation of slaves could not be prohibited. Exports could not be taxed. Is this reasonable? What are the great objects of the general system? First, defence against foreign invasion; secondly, against internal sedition. Shall all the States, then, be bound to defend each, and shall each be at liberty to introduce a weakness which will render defence more difficult? Shall one part of the United States be bound to defend another part and that other part be at liberty, not only to increase its own danger, but to withhold the compensation for the burden? If slaves are to be imported, shall not the exports produced by their labor supply a revenue the better to enable the General Government to defend their masters? There was so much inequality and unreasonableness in all this, that the people of the Northern States could never be reconciled to it. No candid man could undertake to justify it to them. He had hoped that some accommodation would have taken place on this subject; that at least a time would have been limited for the importation of slaves. He never could agree to let them be imported without limitation, and then be represented in the National Legislature. Indeed, he could so little persuade himself of the rectitude of such a practice, that he was not sure he could assent to it under any circumstances. At all events, either slaves should not be represented, or exports should be taxable.

Mr. SHERMAN regarded the slave trade as iniquitous; but the point of representation having been settled after much difficulty and deliberation, he did not think himself bound to make opposition; especially as the present Article, as amended, did not preclude any arrangement whatever on that point, in another place of the Report.

Mr. MADISON objected to one for every forty thousand inhabitants as a perpetual rule. The future increase of population, if the Union should be permanent will render the number of Representatives excessive.

Mr. GORHAM. It is not to be supposed that the Government will last so long as to produce this effect. Can it be supposed that this vast country, including the western territory, will, one hundred and fifty years hence, remain one nation?

Mr. ELLSWORTH. If the Government should continue

so long, alterations may be made in the Constitution in the manner proposed in a subsequent article.

Mr. SHERMAN and Mr. MADISON moved to insert the words, " not exceeding," before the words, " one for every forty thousand," which was agreed to, *nem. con.*

Mr. GOUVERNEUR MORRIS moved to insert " free " before the word " inhabitants." Much, he said, would depend on this point. He never would concur in upholding domestic slavery. It was a nefarious institution. It was the curse of Heaven on the States where it prevailed. Compare the free regions of the Middle States, where a rich and noble cultivation marks the prosperity and happiness of the people, with the misery and poverty which overspread the barren wastes of Virginia, Maryland, and the other States having slaves. Travel through the whole continent, and you behold the prospect continually varying with the appearance and disappearance of slavery. The moment you leave the Eastern States, and enter New York, the effects of the institution become visible. Passing through the Jerseys and entering Pennsylvania, every criterion of superior improvement witnesses the change. Proceed southwardly, and every step you take, through the great regions of slaves, presents a desert, increasing with the increasing proportion of these wretched beings. Upon what principle is it that the slaves shall be computed in the representation? Are they men? Then make them citizens, and let them vote. Are they property? Why, then, is no other property included? The houses in this city (Philadelphia) are worth more than all the wretched slaves who cover the rice swamps of South Carolina. The admission of slaves into the representation, when fairly explained, comes to this, that the inhabitant of Georgia and South Carolina who goes to the coast of Africa, and, in defiance of the most sacred laws of humanity, tears away his fellow creatures from their dearest connections, and damns them to the most cruel bondage, shall have more votes in a government instituted for protection of the rights of mankind, than the citizen of Pennsylvania or New Jersey, who views with a laudable horror so nefarious a practice. He would add, that domestic slavery is the most prominent feature in the aristocratic countenance of the proposed Constitution. The vassalage of the poor has ever been the favourite offspring of aristocracy. And what is the proposed compensation to the Northern States, for a sacrifice of every principle of right, of every impulse of humanity? They are to bind themselves to march their militia for the defence of the Southern States, for their defence against those very slaves of whom they complain. They must supply vessels and seamen, in case of foreign attack. The Legislature will have indefinite power to tax them by excises, and duties on imports; both of which will fall heavier on them than on the Southern inhabitants; for the Bohea tea used by a Northern freeman will pay more tax than the whole consumption of the miserable slave, which consists of nothing more than his physical subsistence and the rag that covers his nakedness. On the other side the Southern States are not to be restrained from importing fresh supplies of wretched Africans, at once to increase the danger of attack, and the difficulty of defence; nay, they are to be encouraged to it, by an assurance of having their votes in the National Government increased in proportion; and are, at the same time, to have their exports and their slaves exempt from all contributions for the public service. Let it not be said, that direct taxation is to be proportioned to representation. It is idle to suppose that the General Government can stretch its hand directly into the pockets of the people, scattered over so vast a country. They can only do it through the medium of exports, imports and excises. For what, then, are all the sacrifices to be made? He would sooner submit himself to a tax for paying for all the negroes in the United States, than saddle posterity with such a Constitution.

Mr. DAYTON seconded the motion. He did it, he said,

that his sentiments on the subject might appear, whatever might be the fate of the amendment.

Mr. SHERMAN did not regard the admission of the negroes into the ratio of representation, as liable to such insuperable objections. It was the freemen of the Southern States who were, in fact, to be represented according to the taxes paid by them, and the negroes are only included in the estimate of the taxes. This was his idea of the matter.

Mr. PINCKNEY considered the fisheries, and the Western frontier, as more burthensome to the United States than the slaves. He thought this could be demonstrated, if the occasion were a proper one.

Mr. WILSON thought the motion premature. An agreement to the clause would be no bar to the object of it.

On the question, on the motion to insert "free" before "inhabitants,"— New Jersey, aye — 1 ; New Hampshire, Massachusetts, Connecticut, Pennsylvania, Delaware, Maryland, Virginia, North Carolina, South Carolina, Georgia, no — 10.

On the suggestion of Mr. DICKINSON, the words, "provided that each State shall have one representative at least," were added, nem. con.

Article 4, Sect. 4, as amended, was agreed to, nem, con.
Article 4, Sect. 5, was then taken up.

Mr. PINCKNEY moved to strike out Sect. 5, as giving no peculiar advantage to the House of Representatives, and as clogging the Government. If the Senate can be trusted with the many great powers proposed, it surely may be trusted with that of originating money bills.

Mr. GORHAM was against allowing the Senate to originate, but was for allowing it only to amend.

Mr. GOUVERNEUR MORRIS. It is particularly proper that the Senate should have the right of originating money bills. They will sit constantly, will consist of a smaller number, and will be able to prepare such bills with due correctness ; and so as to prevent delay of business in the other House.

Col. MASON was unwilling to travel over this ground again. To strike out the section, was to unhinge the compromise of which it made a part. The duration of the Senate made it improper. He does not object to that duration. On the contrary, he approved of it. But joined with the smallness of the number, it was an argument against adding this to the other great powers vested in that body. His idea of an aristocracy was, that it was the government of the few over the many. An aristocratic body, like the screw in mechanics, working its way by slow degrees, and holding fast whatever it gains, should ever be suspected of an encroaching tendency. The purse-strings should never be put into its hands.

Mr. MERCER considered the exclusive power of originating money bills as so great an advantage, that it rendered the equality of votes in the Senate ideal and of no consequence.

Mr. BUTLER was for adhering to the principle which had been settled.

Mr. WILSON was opposed to it on its merits, without regard to the compromise.

Mr. ELLSWORTH did not think the clause of any consequence; but as it was thought of consequence by some members from the larger States, he was willing it should stand.

Mr. MADISON was for striking it out; considering it as of no advantage to the large States, as fettering the Government, and as a source of injurious altercations between the two Houses.

On the question for striking out "Article 4, Sect. 5,"— New Jersey, Pennsylvania, Delaware, Maryland, Virginia, South Carolina, Georgia, aye — 7; New Hampshire, Massachusetts, Connecticut, North Carolina, no — 4.

Adjourned.

31

Thursday, August 9th.

In Convention,—Article 4, Sect. 6, was taken up.

Mr. RANDOLPH expressed his dissatisfaction at the disagreement yesterday to Sect. 5, concerning money bills, as endangering the success of the plan, and extremely objectionable in itself; and gave notice that he should move for a reconsideration of the vote.

Mr. WILLIAMSON said he had formed a like intention.

Mr. WILSON gave notice that he should move to reconsider the vote requiring seven instead of three years of citizenship, as a qualification of candidates for the House of Representatives.

Article 4, Sections 6 and 7, were agreed to, *nem. con.*

Article 5, Sect. 1, was then taken up.

Mr. WILSON objected to vacancies in the Senate being supplied by the Executives of the States. It was unnecessary, as the Legislatures will meet so frequently. It removes the appointment too far from the people, the Executives in most of the States being elected by the Legislatures. As he had always thought the appointment of the Executive by the Legislative department wrong, so it was still more so that the Executive should elect into the Legislative department.

Mr. RANDOLPH thought it necessary in order to prevent inconvenient chasms in the Senate. In some States the Legislatures meet but once a year. As the Senate will have more power and consist of a smaller number than the other House, vacancies there will be of more consequence. The Executives might be safely trusted, he thought, with the appointment for so short a time.

Mr. ELLSWORTH. It is only said that the Executive *may* supply vacancies. When the Legislative meeting happens to be near, the power will not be exerted. As there will be but two members from a State, vacancies may be of great moment.

Mr. WILLIAMSON. Senators may resign or not accept. This provision is therefore absolutely necessary.

On the question for striking out, "vacancies shall be supplied by the Executives," — Pennsylvania, aye — 1; New Hampshire, Massachusetts, Connecticut, New Jersey, Virginia, North Carolina, South Carolina, Georgia, no — 8; Maryland, divided.

Mr. WILLIAMSON moved to insert, after "vacancies shall be supplied by the Executives," the words, "unless other provision shall be made by the Legislature" (of the State).

Mr. ELLSWORTH. He was willing to trust the Legislature, or the Executive of a State, but not to give the former a discretion to refer appointments for the Senate to whom they pleased.

On the question on Mr. WILLIAMSON'S motion, — Maryland, North Carolina, South Carolina, Georgia, aye, 4; New Hampshire, Massachusetts, Connecticut, New Jersey, Pennsylvania, Virginia, no — 6.

Mr. MADISON, in order to prevent doubts whether resignations could be made by Senators, or whether they could refuse to accept, moved to strike out the words after "vacancies," and insert the words, "happening by refusals to accept, resignations, or otherwise, may be supplied by the Legislature of the State in the representation of which such vacancies shall happen, or by the Executive thereof until the next meeting of the Legislature."

Mr. GOUVERNEUR MORRIS. This is absolutely necessary; otherwise, as members chosen into the Senate are disqualified from being appointed to any office by Sect. 9, of this Article, it will be in the power of a Legislature, by appointing a man a Senator against his consent to deprive the United States of his services.

The motion of Mr. MADISON was agreed to, *nem. con.*

Mr. RANDOLPH called for a division of the Section, so as to leave a distinct question on the last words, "each member shall have one vote." He wished this last sentence to be postponed until the reconsideration should have taken place on Article 4, Sect. 5, concerning money bills. If that section should be re-instated, his plan would be to vary the representation in the Senate.

Mr. STRONG concurred in Mr. RANDOLPH'S ideas on this point.

Mr. READ did not consider the section as to money-bills of any advantage to the larger States, and had voted for striking it out as being viewed in the same light by the larger States. If it was considered by them as of any value, and as a condition of the equality of votes in the Senate, he had no objection to its being re-instated.

Mr. WILSON, Mr. ELLSWORTH, and Mr. MADISON, urged, that it was of no advantage to the larger States; and that it might be a dangerous source of contention between the two Houses. All the principal powers of the National Legislature had some relation to money.

Doctor FRANKLIN considered the two clauses, the originating of money bills, and the equality of votes in the Senate, as essentially connected by the compromise which had been agreed to.

Colonel MASON said this was not the time for discussing this point. When the originating of money bills shall be reconsidered, he thought it could be demonstrated, that it was of essential importance to restrain the right to the House of Representatives, the immediate choice of the people.

Mr. WILLIAMSON. The State of North Carolina had agreed to an equality in the Senate merely in consideration that money bills should be confined to the other House: and he was surprised to see the smaller States forsaking the condition on which they had received their equality.

On the question on the first section, down to the last sentence, — New Hampshire, Connecticut, New Jersey, Delaware, Maryland, Virginia, Georgia aye — 7; Massachusetts, Pennsylvania,* North Carolina, no — 3; South Carolina, divided.

Mr. RANDOLPH moved that the last sentence "each member shall have one vote," be postponed.

It was observed that this could not be necessary; as in case the sanction as to originating money bills should not be reinstated, and a revision of the Constitution should ensue, it would still be proper that the members should vote *per capita*. A postponement of the preceding sentence, allowing to each State two members, would have been more proper.

Mr. MASON did not mean to propose a change of this mode of voting *per capita*, in any event. But as there might be other modes proposed, he saw no impropriety in postponing the sentence. Each State may have two members, and yet may have unequal votes. He said that unless the exclusive right of originating money bills should be restored to the House of Representatives, he should — not from obstinacy, but duty and conscience — oppose throughout the equality of representation in the Senate.

Mr. GOUVERNEUR MORRIS. Such declarations were he supposed, addressed to the smaller States, in order to alarm them for their equality in the Senate, and induce them, against their judgments, to concur in restoring the section concerning money bills. He would declare in his turn, that as he saw no prospect of amending the Constitution of the Senate, and considered the section relating to money bills as intrinsically bad, he would adhere to the section establishing the equality, at all events.

Mr. WILSON. It seems to have been supposed by some that the section concerning money bills is desirable to the large States. The fact was, that two of those States (Pennsylvania and Virginia) had uniformly voted against it, without reference to any other part of the system.

Mr. RANDOLPH urged, as Col. MASON had done, that the

---

*In the printed Journal, Pennsylvania, aye.

sentence under consideration was connected with that relating to money bills, and might possibly be affected by the result of the motion for reconsidering the latter. That the postponement was therefore not improper.

On the question for postponing, "each member shall have one vote,"—

Virginia, North Carolina, aye — 2; Massachusetts, Connecticut, New Jersey, Pennsylvania, Delaware, Maryland, South Carolina, Georgia, no — 8; New Hampshire, divided.

The words were then agreed to as part of the section.

Mr. RANDOLPH then gave notice that he should move to reconsider this whole Article 5, Sect. 1, as connected with the Article 4, Sect. 5, as to which he had already given such notice.

Article 5, Sect. 2, was then taken up.

Mr. GOUVERNEUR MORRIS moved to insert, after the words, "immediately after," the following: "they shall be assembled in consequence of," which was agreed to, *nem. con.*, as was then the whole section.

Article 5, Sect. 3, was then taken up.

Mr. GOUVERNEUR MORRIS moved to insert fourteen instead of four years citizenship, as a qualification for Senators; urging the danger of admitting strangers into our public councils.

Mr. PINCKNEY seconded him.

Mr. ELLSWORTH was opposed to the motion, as discouraging meritorious aliens from emigrating to this country.

Mr. PINCKNEY. As the Senate is to have the power of making treaties and managing our foreign affairs, there is peculiar danger and impropriety in opening its door to those who have foreign attachments. He quoted the jealousy of the Athenians on this subject, who made it death for any stranger to intrude his voice into their legislative proceedings.

Col. MASON highly approved of the policy of the motion. Were it not that many, not natives of this country, had acquired great credit during the Revolution, he should be for restraining the eligibility into the Senate, to natives.

Mr. MADISON was not averse to some restrictions on this subject, but could never agree to the proposed amendment. He thought any restriction, however, in the *Constitution* unnecessary and improper;— unnecessary, because the National Legislature is to have the right of regulating naturalization, and can by virtue thereof fix different periods of residence, as conditions of enjoying different privileges of citizenship;— improper, because it will give a tincture of illiberality to the Constitution; because it will put out of the power of the national Legislature, even by special acts of naturalization, to confer the full rank of citizens on meritorious strangers; and because it will discourage the most desirable class of people from emigrating to the United States. Should the proposed Constitution have the intended effect of giving stability and reputation to our Governments, great numbers of respectable Europeans, men who loved liberty, and wished to partake its blessings, will be ready to transfer their fortunes hither. All such would feel the mortification of being marked with suspicious incapacitations, though they should not covet the public honors. He was not apprehensive that any dangerous number of strangers would be appointed by the State Legislatures, if they were left at liberty to do so; nor that foreign powers would make use of strangers, as instruments for their purposes. Their bribes would be expended on men whose circumstances would rather stifle than excite jealousy and watchfulness in the public.

Mr. BUTLER was decidedly opposed to the admission of foreigners without a long residence in the country. They bring with them, not only attachments to other countries, but ideas of government so distinct from ours, that in every point of view they are dangerous. He acknowledged that if he himself had been called into public life within a short time after his coming to America, his foreign habits, opinions, and attachments, would have rendered him an improper agent in public affairs. He mentioned the great strictness observed in Great Britain on this subject.

Doctor FRANKLIN was not against a reasonable time, but should be very sorry to see any thing like illiberality inserted in the Constitution. The people in Europe are friendly to this country. Even in the country with which we have been lately at war, we have now, and had during the war, a great many friends, not only among the people at large, but in both Houses of Parliament. In every other country in Europe, all the people are our friends. We found in the course of the Revolution, that many strangers served us faithfully, and that many natives took part against their country. When foreigners after looking about for some other country in which they can obtain more happiness, give a preference to ours, it is a proof of attachment which ought to excite our confidence and affection.

Mr. RANDOLPH did not know but it might be problematical whether emigrations to this country were on the whole useful or not: but he could never agree to the motion for disabling them, for fourteen years, to participate in the public honors. He reminded the Convention of the language held by our patriots during the Revolution, and the principles laid down in all our American Constitutions. Many foreigners may have fixed their fortunes among us, under the faith of these invitations. All persons under this description, with all others who would be affected by such a regulation, would enlist themselves under the banners of hostility to the proposed system. He would go as far as seven years, but no further.

Mr. WILSON said he rose with feelings which were perhaps peculiar ; mentioning the circumstance of his not being a native, and the possibility, if the ideas of some gentlemen should be pursued, of his being incapacitated from holding a place under the very Constitution which he had shared in the trust of making. He remarked the illiberal complexion which the motion would give to the system, and the effect which a good system would have in inviting meritorious foreigners among us, and the discouragement and mortification they must feel from the degrading discrimination now proposed. He had himself experienced this mortification. On his removal into Maryland, he found himself, from defect of residence, under certain legal incapacities which never ceased to produce chagrin, though he assuredly did not desire, and would not have accepted, the offices to which they related. To be appointed to a place may be matter of indifference. To be incapable of being appointed, is a circumstance grating and mortifying.

Mr. GOUVERNEUR MORRIS. The lesson we are taught is, that we should be governed as much by our reason, and as little by our feelings, as possible. What is the language of reason on this subject? That we should not be polite at the expense of prudence. There was a moderation in all things. It is said that some tribes of Indians carried their hospitality so far as to offer to strangers their wives and daughters. Was this a proper model for us? He would admit them to his house, he would invite them to his table, would provide for them comfortable lodgings, but would not carry the complaisance so far as to bed them with his wife. He would let them worship at the same altar, but did not choose to make priests of them. He ran over the privileges which emigrants would enjoy among us, though they should be deprived of that of being eligible to the great offices of government; observing that they exceeded the privileges allowed to foreigners in any part of the world; and that as every society, from a great nation down to a club, had the right of declaring the conditions on which new members should be admitted, there could be no room for complaint. As to those philosophical gentlemen, those citizens of the world, as they called themselves, he owned, he did not wish to see any of them in our public councils. He would not trust them. The men who can shake off their attachments to their own country, can never love any other. These attachments are the wholesome prejudices which uphold all governments. Admit a Frenchman into your Senate, and he will study to increase the commerce of France : an Englishman and he will feel an equal bias in favor of that of England. It has been said, that the Legislatures will not choose foreigners, at least improper ones. There was no knowing what Legislatures would do. Some appointments made by them proved that every thing ought to be apprehended from the cabals practised on such occasions. He mentioned the case of a foreigner who left this State in disgrace, and worked himself into an appointment from another to Congress.

On the question, on the motion of Mr. GOUVERNEUR MORRIS, to insert fourteen in place of four years,—

New Hampshire, New Jersey, South Carolina, Georgia, aye — 4 ; Massachusetts, Connecticut, Pennsylvania, Delaware, Maryland, Virginia, North Carolina, no — 7.

On the question for thirteen years, moved by Mr. GOUVERNEUR MORRIS, it was negatived, as above.

On ten years, moved by General PINCKNEY, the votes were the same.

Doctor FRANKLIN reminded the Convention, that it did not follow, from an omission to insert the restriction in the Constitution, that the persons in question would be actually chosen into the Legislature.

Mr. RUTLEDGE. Seven years of citizenship have been required for the House of Representatives. Surely a longer time is requisite for the Senate which will have more power.

Mr. WILLIAMSON. It is more necessary to guard the Senate in this case, than the other House. Bribery and cabal can be more easily practised in the choice of the Senate which is to be made by the Legislatures composed of a few men, than of the House of Representatives who will be chosen by the people.

Mr. RANDOLPH will agree to nine years, with the expectation that it will be reduced to seven, if Mr. WILSON'S motion to reconsider the vote fixing seven years for the

House of Representatives should produce a reduction of that period.

On the question for nine years, —

New Hampshire, New Jersey, Delaware, Virginia, South Carolina, Georgia, aye — 6; Massachusetts, Connecticut, Pennsylvania, Maryland, no — 4; North Carolina, divided.

The term "resident" was struck out, and "inhabitant" inserted, *nem. con.*

Article 5, Sect. 3, as amended, was then agreed to, *nem. con.*

Article 5, Sect. 4, was agreed to, *nem. con.*

Article 6, Sect. 1, was then taken up.

Mr. MADISON and Mr. GOUVERNEUR MORRIS moved to strike out, "each House," and to insert, "the House of Representatives," the right of the Legislatures to regulate the times and places, &c., in the election of Senators, being involved in the right of appointing them; which was disagreed to.

A division of the question being called for, it was taken on the first part down to, "but their provisions concerning," &c.

The first part was agreed to *nem. con.*

Mr. PINCKNEY and Mr. RUTLEDGE moved to strike out the remaining part, viz., "but their provisions concerning them may at any time be altered by the Legislature of the United States." The States, they contended, could and must be relied on in such cases.

Mr. GORHAM. It would be as improper to take this power from the National Legislature, as to restrain the British Parliament from regulating the circumstances of elections, leaving this business to the counties themselves.

Mr. MADISON. The necessity of a General Government supposes that the State Legislatures will sometimes fail or refuse to consult the common interest at the expense of their local convenience or prejudices. The policy of referring the appointment of the House of Representatives to the people, and not to the Legislatures of the States, supposes that the result will be somewhat influenced by the mode. This view of the question seems to decide that the Legislatures of the States ought not to have the uncontrolled right of regulating the times, places, and manner, of holding elections. These were words of great latitude. It was impossible to foresee all the abuses that might be made of the discretionary power. Whether the electors should vote by ballot, or *viva voce;* should assemble at this place or that place; should be divided into districts, or all meet at one place; should all vote for all the Representatives, or all in a district vote for a number allotted to the district, — these and many other points would depend on the Legislatures, and might materially affect the appointments. Whenever the State Legislatures had a favourite measure to carry, they would take care so to mould their regulations as to favour the candidates they wished to succeed. Besides, the inequality of the representation in the Legislatures of particular States would produce a like inequality in their representation in the National Legislature, as it was presumable that the counties having the power in the former case, would secure it to themselves in the latter. What danger could there be in giving a controlling power to the National Legislature? Of whom was it to consist? First, of a Senate to be chosen by the State Legislatures. If the latter, therefore could be trusted, their representatives could not be dangerous. Secondly, of Representatives elected by the same people who elect the State Legislatures. Surely, then, if confidence is due to the latter, it must be due to the former. It seemed as improper in principle, though it might be less inconvenient in practice, to give to the State Legislatures this great authority over the election of the representatives of the people in the General Legislature, as it would be to give to the latter a like power over the election of their representatives in the State Legislature.

Mr. KING. If this power be not given to the National Legislature, their right of judging of the returns of their members may be frustrated.   No probability has been suggested of its being abused by them.   Although this scheme of erecting the General Government on the authority of the State Legislatures has been fatal to the Federal establishment, it would seem as if many gentlemen still foster the dangerous idea.

Mr. GOUVERNEUR MORRIS observed, that the States might make false returns, and then make no provisions for new elections.

Mr. SHERMAN did not know but it might be best to retain the clause, though he had himself sufficient confidence in the State Legislatures.

The motion of Mr. PINCKNEY and Mr. RUTLEDGE did not prevail.

The word "respectively" was inserted after the word "State."

On the motion of Mr. READ, the word "their" was struck out, and "regulations in such cases," inserted in place of "provisions concerning them," — the clause then reading: "but regulations, in each of the foregoing cases, may, at any time, be made or altered by the Legislature of the United States."   This was meant to give the National Legislature a power not only to alter the provisions of the States, but to make regulations, in case the States should fail or refuse altogether.   Article 6, Sect. 1, as thus amended, was agreed to, *nem. con.*

Adjourned.

FRIDAY, AUGUST 10TH.

In Convention, — Article 6, Sect. 2, was taken up.

Mr. PINCKNEY.   The Committee, as he had conceived, were instructed to report the proper qualifications of property for the members of the National Legislature; instead of which they have referred the task to the National Legislature itself.   Should it be left on this footing, the first Legislature will meet without any particular qualifications of property; and if it should happen to consist of rich men they might fix such qualifications as may be too favourable to the rich; if of poor men, an opposite extreme might be run into. He was opposed to the establishment of an undue aristocratic influence in the Constitution, but he thought it essential that the members of the Legislature, the Executive, and the Judges, should be possessed of competent property to make them independent and respectable. It was prudent, when such great powers were to be trusted, to connect the tie of property with that of reputation in securing a faithful administration. The Legislature would have the fate of the nation put into their hands. The president would also have a very great influence on it. The Judges would not only have important causes between citizen and citizen, but also where foreigners are concerned. They will even be the umpires between the United States, and individual States; as well as between one State and another. Were he to fix the quantum of property which should be required, he should not think of less than one hundred thousand dollars for the President, half of that sum for each of the Judges, and in like proportion for the members of the National Legislature. He would, however, leave the sums blank. His motion was, that the President of the United States, the Judges, and members of the Legislature, should be required to swear that they were respectively possessed of a clear unincumbered estate, to the amount of ——— in the case of the President, &c., &c.

Mr. RUTLEDGE seconded the motion; observing, that the Committee had reported no qualifications, because they could not agree on any among themselves, being embarrassed by the danger, on one side of displeasing the people, by making them high, and on the other, of rendering them nugatory, by making them low.

Mr. ELLSWORTH. The different circumstances of different parts of the United States, and the probable difference between the present and future circumstances of the whole, render it improper to have either *uniform* or *fixed* qualifications. Make them so high as to be useful in the Southern States, and they will be inapplicable to the Eastern States. Suit them to the latter, and they will serve no purpose, in the former. In like manner, what may be accommodated to the existing state of things among us, may be very inconvenient in some future state of them. He thought for these reasons, that it was better to leave this matter to the Legislative discretion, than to attempt a provision for it in the Constitution.

Doctor FRANKLIN expressed his dislike to everything that tended to debase the spirit of the common people. If honesty was often the companion of wealth, and if poverty was exposed to peculiar temptation, it was not less true that the possession of property increased the desire of more property. Some of the greatest rogues he was ever acquainted with were the richest rogues. We should remember the character which the Scripture requires in rulers, that they should be men hating covetousness. This Constitution will be much read and attended to in Europe; and if it should betray a great partiality to the rich, will not only hurt us in the esteem of the most liberal and enlightened men there, but discourage the common people from removing to this country.

The motion of Mr. PINCKNEY was rejected by so general a *no*, that the States were not called.

Mr. MADISON was opposed to the section, as vesting an improper and dangerous power in the Legislature. The qualifications of electors and elected were fundamental articles in a republican government, and ought to be fixed by the Constitution. If the Legislature could regulate those of either, it can by degrees subvert the Constitution. A Republic may be converted into an aristocracy or oligarchy, as well by limiting the number capable of being elected, as the number authorized to elect. In all cases where the representatives of the people will have a personal interest distinct from that of their constituents, there was the same reason for being jealous of them, as there was for relying on them with full confidence, when they had a common interest. This was one of the former cases. It was as improper as to allow them to fix their own wages, or their own privileges. It was a power, also, which might be made subservient to the views of one faction against another. Qualifications founded on artificial distinctions, may be devised by the stronger in order to keep out partizans of a weaker faction.

Mr. ELLSWORTH admitted that the power was not unexceptionable; but he could not view it as dangerous. Such a power with regard to the electors would be dangerous, because it would be much more liable to abuse.

Mr. GOUVERNEUR MORRIS moved to strike out " with regard to property," in order to leave the Legislature entirely at large.

Mr. WILLIAMSON. This would surely never be admitted. Should a majority of the Legislature be composed of any particular description of men, of lawyers for example, which is no improbable supposition, the future elections might be secured to their own body.

Mr. MADISON observed that the British Parliament possessed the power of regulating the qualifications, both of the electors and the elected; and the abuse they had made of it was a lesson worthy of our attention. They had made the changes, in both cases, subservient to their own views, or to the views of political or religious parties.

On the question on the motion to strike out, " with regard to property,"— Connecticut, New Jersey, Pennsylvania, Georgia, aye — 4; New Hampshire, Massachusetts, Delaware,* Maryland, Virginia, North Carolina, South Carolina, no — 7.

Mr. RUTLEDGE was opposed to leaving the power to the Legislature. He proposed that the qualifications should be the same as for members of the State Legislatures.

Mr. WILSON thought it would be best, on the whole, to

* In the printed Journal, Delaware did not vote.

let the section go out. A uniform rule would probably never be fixed by the Legislature; and this particular power would constructively exclude every other power of regulating qualifications.

On the question for agreeing to Article 6, Sect. 2,— New Hampshire, Massachusetts, Georgia, aye — 3; Connecticut, New Jersey, Pennsylvania, Maryland, Virginia, North Carolina, South Carolina, no — 7.

On motion of Mr. WILSON to reconsider Article 4, Sect. 2, so as to restore "three," in place of "seven," years of citizenship, as a qualification for being elected into the House of Representatives,— Connecticut, Pennsylvania, Delaware, Maryland, Virginia, North Carolina, aye — 6; New Hampshire, Massachusetts, New Jersey, South Carolina, Georgia, no — 5.

Monday next was then assigned for the reconsideration; all the States being aye, except Massachusetts and Georgia.

Article 6. Sect. 3, was then taken up.

MR. GORHAM contended that less than a majority in each House should be made a quorum; otherwise great delay might happen in business, and great inconvenience from the future increase of numbers.

Mr. MERCER was also for less than a majority. So great a number will put it in the power of a few, by seceding at a critical moment, to introduce convulsions, and endanger the Government. Examples of secession have already happened in some of the States. He was for leaving it to the Legislature to fix the quorum, as in Great Britain, where the requisite number is small and no inconvenience has been experienced.

Col. MASON. This is a valuable and necessary part of the plan. In this extended country, embracing so great a diversity of interests, it would be dangerous to the distant parts, to allow a small number of members of the two Houses to make laws. The central States could always take care to be on the spot; and by meeting earlier than the distant ones, or wearying their patience, and outstaying

32

them, could carry such measures as they pleased. He admitted that inconveniences might spring from the secession of a small number; but he had also known good produced by an apprehension of it. He had known a paper emission prevented by that cause in Virginia. He thought the Constitution, as now moulded, was founded on sound principles, and was disposed to put into it extensive powers. At the same time, he wished to guard against abuses as much as possible. If the Legislature should be able to reduce the number at all, it might reduce it as low as it pleased, and the United States might be governed by a junto. A majority of the number which had been agreed on, was so few that he feared it would be made an objection against the plan.

Mr. KING admitted there might be some danger of giving an advantage to the central States, but was of opinion that the public inconvenience, on the other side, was more to be dreaded.

Mr. GOUVERNEUR MORRIS moved to fix the quorum at thirty-three members in the House of Representatives, and fourteen in the Senate. This is a majority of the present number, and will be a bar to the Legislature. Fix the number low, and they will generally attend, knowing that the advantage may be taken of their absence. The secession of a small number ought not to be suffered to break a quorum. Such events in the States may have been of little consequence. In the national councils they may be fatal. Besides other mischief, if a few can break up a quorum, they may seize a moment, when a particular part of the continent may be in need of immediate aid, to extort, by threatening a secession, some unjust and selfish measure.

Mr. MERCER seconded the motion.

Mr. KING said he had just prepared a motion which, instead of fixing the numbers proposed by Mr. GOUVERNEUR MORRIS as quorums, made those the lowest numbers, leaving the Legislature at liberty to increase them or not. He thought the future increase of members would render a majority of the whole extremely cumbersome.

Mr. MERCER agreed to substitute Mr. KING's motion in place of Mr. MORRIS'S.

Mr. ELLSWORTH was opposed to it. It would be a pleasing ground of confidence to the people, that no law or burthen could be imposed on them by a few men. He reminded the movers that the Constitution proposed to give such a discretion, with regard to the number of Representatives, that a very inconvenient number was not to be apprehended. The inconvenience of secessions may be guarded against, by giving to each House an authority to require the attendance of absent members.

Mr. WILSON concurred in the sentiments of Mr. ELLSWORTH.

Mr. GERRY seemed to think that some further precaution than merely fixing the quorum, might be necessary. He observed, that as seventeen would be a majority of a quorum of thirty-three, and eight of fourteen, questions might by possibility be carried in the House of Representatives by two large States, and in the Senate by the same States with the aid of two small ones. He proposed that the number for a quorum in the House of Representatives, should not exceed fifty, nor be less than thirty-three; leaving the intermediate discretion to the Legislature.

Mr. KING. As the quorum could not be altered, without the concurrence of the President, by less than two-thirds of each House, he thought there could be no danger in trusting the Legislature.

Mr. CARROLL. This would be no security against the continuance of the quorums at thirty-three, and fourteen, when they ought to be increased.

On the question of Mr. KING's motion, that not less than thirty-three in the House of Representatives, nor less than fourteen in the Senate should constitute a quorum, which may be increased by a law, on additions to the members in either House,—

Massachusetts, Delaware, aye — 2; New Hampshire, Connecticut, New Jersey, Pennsylvania, Maryland, Virginia, North Carolina, South Carolina, Georgia, no — 9.

Mr. RANDOLPH and Mr. MADISON moved to add to the end of Article 6, Sect. 3, "and may be authorized to compel the attendance of absent members, in such manner, and under such penalties, as each House may provide." Agreed to by all except Pennsylvania, which was divided.

Article 6, Sect. 3, was agreed to as amended, *nem. con.*

Sections 4 and 5, of Article 6, were then agreed to, *nem. con.*

Mr. MADISON observed that the right of expulsion (Article 6, Sect. 6) was too important to be exercised by a bare majority of a quorum; and, in emergencies of faction, might be dangerously abused. He moved that, "with the concurrence of two-thirds," might be inserted between "may" and "expel."

Mr. RANDOLPH and Mr. MASON approved the idea.

Mr. GOUVERNEUR MORRIS. This power may be safely trusted to a majority. To require more may produce abuses on the side of the minority. A few men, from factious motives, may keep in a member who ought to be expelled.

Mr. CARROLL thought that the concurrence of two-thirds, at least, ought to be required.

On the question requiring two-thirds, in cases of expelling a member, — ten States were in the affirmative; Pennsylvania, divided.

Article 6, Sect. 6, as thus amended, was then agreed to, *nem. con.*

Article 6, Sect. 7, was then taken up.

Mr. GOUVERNEUR MORRIS urged, that if the Yeas and Nays were proper at all, any individual ought to be authorized to call for them; and moved an amendment to that effect. The small States may otherwise be under a disadvantage, and find it difficult to get a concurrence of one-fifth.

Mr. RANDOLPH seconded the motion.

Mr. SHERMAN had rather strike out the Yeas and Nays altogether. They have never done any good, and have done much mischief. They are not proper, as the reasons governing the voter never appear along with them.

Mr. ELLSWORTH was of the same opinion.

Colonel MASON liked the section as it stood. It was a middle way between two extremes.

Mr. GORHAM was opposed to the motion for allowing a single member to call the Yeas and Nays, and recited the abuses of it in Massachusetts; first, in stuffing the Journals with them on frivolous occasions; secondly, in misleading the people, who never know the reasons determining the votes.

The motion for allowing a single member to call the Yeas and Nays, was disagreed to, *nem. con.*

Mr. CARROLL and Mr. RANDOLPH moved to strike out the words, " each House," and to insert the words, " the House of Representatives," in Sect. 7, Article 6; and to add to the section the words, " and any member of the Senate shall be at liberty to enter his dissent."

Mr. GOUVERNEUR MORRIS and Mr. WILSON observed, that if the minority were to have a right to enter their votes and reasons, the other side would have a right to complain if it were not extended to them: and to allow it to both, would fill the Journals, like the records of a court, with replications, rejoinders, &c.

On the question on Mr. CARROLL's motion to allow a member to enter his dissent,— Maryland, Virginia, South Carolina, aye — 3; New Hampshire, Massachusetts, Connecticut, New Jersey, Pennsylvania, Delaware, North Carolina, Georgia, no — 8.

Mr. GERRY moved to strike out the words, " when it shall be acting in its legislative capacity," in order to extend the provision to the Senate when exercising its peculiar authorities ; and to insert, " except such parts thereof as in their judgment require secrecy," after the words " publish them." — (It was thought by others that provision should be made with respect to these, when that part came under consideration which proposed to vest those additional authorities in the Senate.)

On this question for striking out the words, "when acting in its legislative capacity," Massachusetts, Delaware, Maryland, Virginia, North Carolina, Georgia, aye — 7 ; Connecticut, New Jersey, Pennsylvania, no — 3 ; New Hampshire, divided.

Adjourned.

SATURDAY, AUGUST 11TH.

In Convention,—Mr. MADISON and Mr. RUTLEDGE moved, "that each House shall keep a Journal of its proceedings, and shall publish the same from time to time ; except such part of the proceedings of the Senate, when acting not in its legislative capacity, as may be judged by that House to require secrecy."

Mr. MERCER. This implies that other powers than legislative will be given to the Senate, which he hoped would not be given.

Mr. MADISON and Mr. RUTLEDGE's motion was disagreed to, by all the States except Virginia.

Mr. GERRY and Mr. SHERMAN moved to insert, after the words, "publish them," the following, "except such as relate to treaties and military operations." Their object was to give each House a discretion in such cases. On this question,— Massachusetts, Connecticut, aye — 2 ; New Hampshire, New Jersey, Pennsylvania, Delaware, Virginia, North Carolina, South Carolina, Georgia, no — 8.

Mr. ELLSWORTH. As the clause is objectionable in so many shapes, it may as well be struck out altogether. The Legislature will not fail to publish their proceedings from time to time. The people will call for it, if it should be improperly omitted.

Mr. WILSON thought the expunging of the clause would be very improper. The people have a right to know what their agents are doing or have done, and it should not be in the option of the Legislature to conceal their proceedings. Besides, as this is a clause in the existing confederation, the not retaining it would furnish the adversaries of the reform with a pretext by which weak and suspicious minds may be easily misled.

Mr. MASON thought it would give a just alarm to the people, to make a conclave of their Legislature.

Mr. SHERMAN thought the Legislature might be trusted in this case, if in any.

On the question on the first part of the section, down to "*publish them*," inclusive,— it was agreed to, *nem. con.*

On the question on the words to follow, to wit, "except such parts thereof as may in their judgment require secrecy,"— Massachusetts, Connecticut, New Jersey, Virginia, North Carolina, Georgia, aye — 6 ; Pennsylvania, Delaware, Maryland, South Carolina, no — 4 ; New Hampshire, divided.

The remaining part, as to Yeas and Nays, was agreed to, *nem. con.*

Article 6, Sect. 8, was then taken up.

Mr. KING remarked that the section authorized the two Houses to adjourn to a new place. He thought this inconvenient. The mutability of place had dishonored the Federal Government, and would require as strong a cure as we could devise. He thought a law at least should be made necessary to a removal of the seat of government.

Mr. MADISON viewed the subject in the same light, and joined with Mr. King in a motion requiring a law.

Mr. GOUVERNEUR MORRIS proposed the additional alteration by inserting the words, "during the session, &c."

Mr. SPAIGHT. This will fix the seat of government at New York. The present Congress will convene them there in the first instance, and they will never be able to remove; especially if the President should be a Northern man.

Mr. GOUVERNEUR MORRIS. Such a distrust is inconsistent with all government.

Mr. MADISON supposed that a central place for the seat of government was so just, and would be so much insisted on by the House of Representatives, that though a law should be made requisite for the purpose, it could and would be obtained. The necessity of a central residence of the Government would be much greater under the new than old Government. The members of the new Government would be more numerous. They would be taken more from the interior parts of the States; they would not, like members of the present Congress, come so often from the distant States by water. As the powers and objects of the new Government would be far greater than heretofore, more private individuals would have business calling them to the seat of it; and it was more necessary that the Government should be in that position from which it could contemplate with the most equal eye, and sympathize most equally with every part of the nation. These considerations, he supposed, would extort a removal, even if a law were made necessary. But in order to quiet suspicions, both within and without doors, it might not be amiss to authorize the two Houses, by a concurrent vote, to adjourn at their first meeting to the most proper place, and to require thereafter the sanction of a law to their removal.

The motion was accordingly moulded into the following form: " the Legislature shall at their first assembling determine on a place at which their future sessions shall be held; neither House shall afterwards, during the session of the House of Representatives, without the consent of the other, adjourn for more than three days; nor shall they adjourn to any other place than such as shall have been fixed by law."

Mr. GERRY thought it would be wrong to let the President check the will of the two Houses on this subject at all.

Mr. WILLIAMSON supported the ideas of Mr. SPAIGHT.

Mr. CARROLL was actuated by the same apprehensions.

Mr. MERCER. It will serve no purpose to require the

two Houses at their first meeting to fix on a place. They will never agree.

After some further expressions from others denoting an apprehension that the seat of government might be continued at an improper place, if a law should be made necessary to a removal, and after the motion above stated, with another for re-committing the section, had been negatived, the section was left in the shape in which it was reported, as to this point. The words, "during the session of the Legislature," were prefixed to the eighth section; and the last sentence, "but this regulation shall not extend to the Senate when it shall exercise the powers mentioned in the —— Article," struck out. The eighth section, as amended, was then agreed to.

Mr. RANDOLPH moved, according to notice, to reconsider Article 4, Sect. 5, concerning money bills, which had been struck out. He argued,—first, that he had not wished for this privilege, whilst a proportional representation in the Senate was in contemplation; but since an equality had been fixed in that House, the large States would require this compensation at least. Secondly, that it would make the plan more acceptable to the people, because they will consider the Senate as the more aristocratic body, and will expect that the usual guards against its influence will be provided according to the example of Great Britain. Thirdly, the privilege will give some advantage to the House of Representatives, if it extends to the originating only; but still more, if it restrains the Senate from amending. Fourthly, he called on the smaller States to concur in the measure, as the condition by which alone the compromise had entitled them to an equality in the Senate. He signified that he should propose, instead of the original section, a clause specifying that the bills in question should be for the purpose of revenue, in order to repel the objection against the extent of the words, "*raising money*," which might happen incidentally; and that the Senate should not so amend or alter as to increase or diminish the sum; in order to obviate the inconveniences urged against a restriction of the Senate to a simple affirmation or negative.

Mr. WILLIAMSON seconded the motion.

Mr. PINCKNEY was sorry to oppose the opportunity gentlemen asked to have the question again opened for discussion, but as he considered it a mere waste of time he could not bring himself to consent to it. He said that, notwithstanding what had been said as to the compromise, he always considered this section as making no part of it. The rule of representation in the first branch was the true condition of that in the second branch. Several others spoke for and against the reconsideration, but without going into the merits.

On the question to reconsider,—

New Hampshire, Massachusetts, Connecticut, New Jersey,* Pennsylvania, Delaware, Virginia, North Carolina, Georgia, aye — 9 ; Maryland, no — 1 ; South Carolina, divided.

Monday was then assigned for the reconsideration.

Adjourned.

MONDAY, AUGUST 13TH.

In Convention,—Article 4, Sect. 2, being reconsidered,—

Mr. WILSON and Mr. RANDOLPH moved to strike out " seven years," and insert " four years," as the requisite term of citizenship to qualify for the House of Representatives. Mr. WILSON said it was very proper the electors should govern themselves by this consideration; but unnecessary and improper that the Constitution should chain them down to it.

Mr. GERRY wished that in future the eligibility might be confined to natives. Foreign powers will intermeddle in our affairs, and spare no expense to influence them. Persons having foreign attachments will be sent among us and insinuated into our councils, in order to be made in-

----

* In the printed Journal, New Jersey, no.

struments for their purposes.   Every one knows the vast
sums laid out in Europe for secret services.   He was not
singular in these ideas.   A great many of the most influential men in Massachusetts reasoned in the same manner.

Mr. WILLIAMSON moved to insert nine years instead of
seven.   He wished this country to acquire as fast as possible national habits.   Wealthy emigrants do more harm
by their luxurious examples, than good by the money they
bring with them.

Colonel HAMILTON was in general against embarrassing
the Government with minute restrictions.   There was, on
one side, the possible danger that had been suggested.   On
the other side, the advantage of encouraging foreigners was
obvious and admitted.   Persons in Europe of moderate fortunes will be fond of coming here, where they will be on a
level with the first citizens.   He moved that the section be
so altered as to require merely " citizenship and inhabitancy."   The right of determining the rule of naturalization
will then leave a discretion to the Legislature on this subject, which will answer every purpose.

Mr. MADISON seconded the motion.   He wished to
maintain the character of liberality which had been professed in all the Constitutions and publications of America.
He wished to invite foreigners of merit and republican principles among us.   America was indebted to emigration for
her settlement and prosperity.   That part of America which
had encouraged them most, had advanced most rapidly in
population, agriculture and the arts.   There was a possible
danger, he admitted, that men with foreign predilections
might obtain appointments; but it was by no means probable that it would happen in any dangerous degree.   For
the same reason that they would be attached to their native
country, our own people would prefer natives of this country
to them.   Experience proved this to be the case.   Instances
were rare of a foreigner being elected by the people within
any short space after his coming among us.   If bribery was
to be practised by foreign powers, it would not be attempted

among the electors, but among the elected, and among natives having full confidence of the people, not among strangers who would be regarded with a jealous eye.

Mr. WILSON cited Pennsylvania as a proof of the advantage of encouraging emigrations. It was perhaps the youngest settlement (except Georgia) on the Atlantic; yet it was at least among the foremost in population and prosperity. He remarked that almost all the general officers of the Pennsylvania line of the late army were foreigners; and no complaint had ever been made against their fidelity or merit. Three of her Deputies to the Convention (Mr. R. MORRIS, Mr. FITZSIMONS, and himself) were also not natives. He had no objection to Colonel HAMILTON's motion, and would withdraw the one made by himself.

Mr. BUTLER was strenuous against admitting foreigners into our public councils.

On the question on Colonel HAMILTON's motion, —

Connecticut, Pennsylvania, Maryland, Virginia, aye — 4; New Hampshire, Massachusetts, New Jersey, Delaware, North Carolina, South Carolina, Georgia, no — 7.

On the question on Mr. WILLIAMSON's motion, to insert " nine years " instead of " seven," —

New Hampshire, South Carolina, Georgia, aye — 3; Massachusetts, Connecticut, New Jersey, Pennsylvania, Delaware, Maryland Virginia, North Carolina, no — 8.

Mr. WILSON renewed the motion for four years instead of seven; and on the question, —

Connecticut, Maryland, Virginia, aye — 3; New Hampshire, Massachusetts, New Jersey, Pennsylvania, Delaware, North Carolina, South Carolina, Georgia, no — 8.

Mr. GOUVERNEUR MORRIS moved to add to the end of the section (Article 4, Sect. 2,) a proviso that the limitation of seven years should not affect the rights of any person now a citizen.

Mr. MERCER seconded the motion. It was necessary, he said, to prevent a disfranchisement of persons who had be- ·come citizens, under the faith and according to the laws and

Constitution, from their actual level in all respects with natives.

Mr. RUTLEDGE. It might as well be said that all qualifications are disfranchisements, and that to require the age of twenty-five years was a disfranchisement. The policy of the precaution was as great with regard to foreigners now citizens, as to those who are to be naturalized in future.

Mr. SHERMAN. The United States have not invited foreigners, nor pledged their faith that they should enjoy equal privileges with native citizens. The individual States alone have done this. The former therefore are at liberty to make any discriminations they may judge requisite.

Mr. GORHAM. When foreigners are naturalized, it would seem as if they stand on an equal footing with natives. He doubted, then, the propriety of giving a retrospective force to the restriction.

Mr. MADISON animadverted on the peculiarity of the doctrine of Mr. SHERMAN. It was subtilty by which every national engagement might be evaded. By parity of reason, whenever our public debts or foreign treaties become inconvenient, nothing more would be necessary to relieve us from them, than to re-model the Constitution. It was said that the *United States*, as such, have not pledged their faith to the naturalized foreigners, and therefore are not bound. Be it so, and that the States alone are bound. Who are to form the new constitution by which the condition of that class of citizens is to be made worse than the other class? Are not the States the agents? Will they not be the members of it? Did they not appoint this Convention? Are not they to ratify its proceedings? Will not the new Constitution be their act? If the new Constitution, then, violates the faith pledged to any description of people, will not the makers of it, will not the States, be the violators? To justify the doctrine, it must be said that the States can get rid of the obligation by revising the Constitution, though they could not do it by repealing the law under which foreigners held their privileges. He considered this a matter of real importance. It would expose us to the reproaches of all those who should be affected by it, reproaches which would soon be echoed from the other side of the Atlantic; and would unnecessarily enlist among the adversaries of the reform a very considerable body of citizens. We should moreover reduce every State to the dilemma of rejecting it, or of violating the faith pledged to a part of its citizens.

Mr. GOUVERNEUR MORRIS considered the case of persons under twenty-five years of age as very different from that of foreigners. No faith could be pleaded by the former in bar of the regulation. No assurance had ever been given that persons under that age should be in all cases on a level with those above it. But with regard to foreigners among us, the faith had been pledged that they should enjoy the privileges of citizens. If the restriction as to age had been confined to natives, and had left foreigners under twenty-five years of age eligible in this case, the discrimination would have been an equal injustice on the other side.

Mr. PINCKNEY remarked that the laws of the States had varied much the terms of naturalization in different parts of America; and contended that the United States could not be bound to respect them on such an occasion as the present. It was a sort of recurrence to first principles.

Col. MASON was struck, not, like Mr. MADISON, with the *peculiarity*, but the *propriety*, of the doctrine of Mr. SHERMAN. The States have formed different qualifications themselves for enjoying different rights of citizenship. Greater caution would be necessary in the outset of the Government than afterwards. All the great objects would then be provided for. Every thing would be then set in motion. If persons among us attached to Great Britain should work themselves into our councils, a turn might be given to our affairs, and particularly to our commercial regulations, which might have pernicious consequences. The great houses of British merchants would spare no pains to insinuate the instruments of their views into the Government.

Mr. WILSON read the clause in the Constitution of Pennsylvania giving to foreigners, after two years' residence, all the rights whatsoever of citizens; combined it with the Article of Confederation making the citizens of one State citizens of all, inferred the obligation Pennsylvania was under to maintain the faith thus pledged to her citizens of foreign birth, and the just complaint which her failure would authorize. He observed, likewise, that the princes and states of Europe would avail themselves of such breach of faith, to deter their subjects from emigrating to the United States.

Mr. MERCER enforced the same idea of a breach of faith.

Mr. BALDWIN could not enter into the force of the arguments against extending the disqualification to foreigners now citizens. The discrimination of the place of birth was not more objectionable than that of age, which all had concurred in the propriety of.

On the question on the proviso of Mr. GOUVERNEUR MORRIS in favor of foreigners now citizens,—Connecticut, New Jersey, Pennsylvania, Maryland, Virginia, aye — 5; New Hampshire, Massachusetts, Delaware, North Carolina, South Carolina, Georgia, no — 6.

Mr. CARROLL moved to insert " five " years, instead of " seven " in Article 4, Sect. 2,— Connecticut, Maryland, Virginia, aye — 3 ; New Hampshire, Massachusetts, New Jersey, Delaware, North Carolina, South Carolina, Georgia, no — 7 ; Pennsylvania, divided.

The Section (Article 4, Sect. 2,) as formerly amended, was then agreed to, *nem. con.*

Mr. WILSON moved that, in Article 5, Sect. 3, nine years be reduced to seven ; which was disagreed to, and the Article 5, Sect. 3, confirmed by the following vote,— New Hampshire, Massachusetts, New Jersey, Delaware, Virginia, North Carolina, South Carolina, Georgia, aye — 8 ; Connecticut, Pennsylvania, Maryland, no — 3.

Article 4, Sect. 5, being reconsidered,—

Mr. RANDOLPH moved that the clause be altered so as

to read : " Bills for raising money for the *purpose of revenue*, or for appropriating the same, shall originate in the House of Representatives ; and shall not be so amended or altered by the Senate as to increase or diminish the sum to be raised, or change the mode of levying it, or the object of its appropriation." He would not repeat his reasons, but barely reminded the members from the smaller States of the compromise by which the larger States were entitled to this privilege.

Colonel MASON. This amendment removes all the objections urged against the section, as it stood at first. By specifying *purposes of revenue*, it obviated the objection that the section extended to all bills under which money might incidentally arise. By authorizing amendments in the Senate, it got rid of the objections that the Senate could not correct errors of any sort, and that it would introduce into the House of Representatives the practice of tacking foreign matter to money bills. These objections being removed, the arguments in favor of the proposed restraint on the Senate ought to have their full force. First, the Senate did not represent the *people*, but the *States*, in their political character. It was improper therefore that it should tax the people. The reason was the same against their doing it, as it had been against Congress doing it. Secondly, nor was it in any respect necessary, in order to cure the evils of our republican system. He admitted that, notwithstanding the superiority of the republican form over every other, it had its evils. The chief ones were, the danger of the majority oppressing the minority, and the mischievous influence of demagogues. The general government of itself will cure them. As the States will not concur at the same time in their unjust and oppressive plans, the General Government will be able to check and defeat them, whether they result from the wickedness of the majority, or from the misguidance of demagogues. Again the Senate is not, like the House of Representatives, chosen frequently and obliged to return frequently among the people. They are to be chosen by the States for six years — will probably settle themselves at the seat of government — will pursue schemes for their own aggrandisement — will be able, by wearying out the House of Representatives, and taking advantage of their impatience at the close of a long session, to extort measures for that purpose. If they should be paid, as he expected would be yet determined and wished to be so, out of the national treasury, they will, particularly, extort an increase of their wages. A bare negative was a very different thing, from that of originating bills. The practice in England was in point. The House of Lords does not represent nor tax the people, because not elected by the people. If the Senate can originate, they will in the recess of the Legislative sessions, hatch their mischievous projects, for their own purposes, and have their money bills cut and dried (to use a common phrase) for the meeting of the House of Representatives. He compared the case to Poyning's law, and signified that the House of Representatives might be rendered by degrees, like the parliament of Paris, the mere depositary of the decrees of the Senate. As to the compromise, so much had passed on that subject that he would say nothing about it. He did not mean, by what he had said, to oppose the permanency of the Senate. On the contrary, he had no repugnance to an increase of it, nor to allowing it a negative, though the Senate was not, by its present constitution, entitled to it. But in all events, he would contend that the purse strings should be in the hands of the representatives of the people.

Mr. WILSON was himself directly opposed to the equality of votes granted to the Senate, by its present constitution. At the same time he wished not to multiply the vices of the system. He did not mean to enlarge on a subject which had been so much canvassed, but would remark, as an insuperable objection against the proposed restriction of money bills to the House of Representatives, that it would be a source of perpetual contentions, where there was no

33

mediator to decide them. The President here could not, like the Executive Magistrate in England, interpose by a prorogation, or dissolution. This restriction had been found pregnant with altercation in every State where the constitution had established it. The House of Representatives will insert other things in money bills, and by making them conditions of each other destroy the deliberate liberty of the Senate. He stated the case of a preamble to a money bill sent up by the House of Commons in the reign of Queen Anne, to the House of Lords, in which the conduct of the misplaced Ministry, who were to be impeached before the Lords, was condemned; the Commons thus extorting a premature judgment without any hearing of the parties to be tried; and the House of Lords being thus reduced to the poor and disgraceful expedient of opposing, to the authority of a law, a protest on their Journals against its being drawn into precedent. If there was anything like Poyning's law in the present case, it was in the attempt to vest the exclusive right of originating in the House of Representatives, and so far he was against it. He should be equally so if the right were to be exclusively vested in the Senate. With regard to the purse-strings, it was to be observed that the purse was to have two strings, one of which was in the hands of the House of Representatives, the other in those of the Senate. Both Houses must concur in untying, and of what importance could it be, which untied first, which last. He could not conceive it to be any objection to the Senate's preparing the bills, that they would have leisure for that purpose, and would be in the habits of business. War, commerce and revenue were the great objects of the General Government. All of them are connected with money. The restriction in favor of the House of Representatives would exclude the Senate from originating any important bills whatever.

Mr. GERRY considered this as a part of the plan that would be much scrutinized. Taxation and representation are strongly associated in the minds of the people; and they

will not agree that any but their immediate representatives
shall meddle with their purses. In short, the acceptance
of the plan will inevitably fail, if the Senate be not restrained from originating money bills.

Mr. GOUVERNEUR MORRIS. All the arguments suppose
the right to originate and to tax, to be exclusively vested in
the Senate. The effects commented on, may be produced
by a negative only in the Senate. They can tire out the
other House, and extort their concurrence in favorite measures, as well by withholding their negative, as by adhering
to a bill introduced by themselves.

Mr. MADISON thought, if the substitute offered by Mr.
RANDOLPH for the original section is to be adopted, it would
be proper to allow the Senate at least so to amend as to
diminish the sums to be raised. Why should they be restrained from checking the extravagance of the other
House? One of the greatest evils incident to republican government was the spirit of contention and faction. The proposed substitute, which in some respects lessened the objections against the section, had a contrary
effect with respect to this particular. It laid a foundation
for new difficulties and disputes between the two Houses.
The word *revenue* was ambiguous. In many acts, particularly in the regulation of trade, the object would be two-
fold. The raising of revenue would be one of them. How
could it be determined which was the primary or predominant one; or whether it was necessary that revenue should
be the sole object, in exclusion even of other incidental
effects? When the contest was first opened with Great
Britain, their power to regulate trade was admitted, — their
power to raise revenue rejected. An accurate investigation
of the subject afterwards proved that no line could be drawn
between the two cases. The words *amend or alter* form an
equal source of doubt and altercation. When an obnoxious
paragraph shall be sent down from the Senate to the House
of Representatives, it will be called an origination under the
name of an amendment. The Senate may actually couch

extraneous matter under that name. In these cases, the question will turn on the *degree* of connection between the matter and object of the bill, and the altercation or amendment offered to it. Can there be a more fruitful source of dispute, or a kind of dispute more difficult to be settled? His apprehensions on this point were not conjectural. Disputes had actually flowed from this source in Virginia, where the Senate can originate no bill. The words, "so as to *increase or diminish* the sum to be raised," were liable to the same objections. In levying indirect taxes, which it seemed to be understood were to form the principal revenue of the new Government, the sum to be raised, would be increased or diminished by a variety of collateral circumstances influencing the consumption, in general, — the consumption of foreign or of domestic articles, — of this or that particular species of articles, — and even by the mode of collection which may be closely connected with the productiveness of a tax. The friends of this section had argued its necessity from the permanency of the Senate. He could not see how this argument applied. The Senate was not more permanent now than in the form it bore in the original propositions of Mr. RANDOLPH, and at the time when no objection whatever was hinted against its originating money bills. Or if in consequence of a loss of the present question, a proportional vote in the Senate should be reinstated, as has been urged as the indemnification, the permanency of the Senate will remain the same. If the right to originate be vested exclusively in the House of Representatives, either the Senate must yield, against its judgment, to that House, — in which case the utility of the check will be lost, — or the Senate will be inflexible, and the House of Representatives must adapt its money bill to the views of the Senate; in which case the exclusive right will be of no avail. As to the compromise of which so much had been said, he would make a single observation. There were five States which had opposed the equality of votes in the Senate, viz: Massachusetts, Pennsylvania, Virginia, North Carolina, and South Carolina. As a compensation for the sacrifice extorted from them on this head, the exclusive origination of money bills in the other House had been tendered. Of the five States a majority, viz: Pennsylvania, Virginia, and South Carolina, have uniformly voted against the proposed compensation, on its own merits, as rendering the plan of government still more objectionable. Massachusetts has been divided. North Carolina alone has set a value on the compensation, and voted on that principle. What obligation, then, can the small States be under to concur, against their judgments, in reinstating the section?

Mr. DICKINSON. Experience must be our only guide. Reason may mislead us. It was not reason that discovered the singular and admirable mechanism of the English constitution. It was not reason that discovered, or ever could have discovered, the odd, and, in the eyes of those who are governed by reason, the absurd mode of trial by jury. Accidents probably produced these discoveries, and experience has given a sanction to them. This is, then, our guide. And has not experience verified the utility of restraining money bills to the immediate representatives of the people? Whence the effect may have proceeded, he could not say; whether from the respect with which this privilege inspired the other branches of government, to the House of Commons, or from the turn of thinking it gave to the people at large with regard to their rights; but the effect was visible and could not be doubted. Shall we oppose, to this long experience, the short experience of eleven years which we had ourselves on this subject? As to disputes, they could not be avoided any way. If both Houses should originate, each would have a different bill to which it would be attached, and for which it would contend. He observed that all the prejudices of the people would be offended by refusing this exclusive privilege to the House of Representatives, and these prejudices should never be disregarded by us when no essential purpose was to be served.

When this plan goes forth, it will be attacked by the popular leaders. Aristocracy will be the watchword, the Shibboleth, among its adversaries. Eight States have inserted in their Constitutions the exclusive right of originating money bills in favor of the popular branch of the Legislature. Most of them, however, allowed the other branch to amend. This, he thought, would be proper for us to do.

Mr. RANDOLPH regarded this point as of such consequence, that, as he valued the peace of this country, he would press the adoption of it. We had numerous and monstrous difficulties to combat. Surely we ought not to increase them. When the people behold in the Senate the countenance of an aristocracy, and in the President the form at least of a little monarch, will not their alarms be sufficiently raised without taking from their immediate representatives a right which has been so long appropriated to them? The Executive will have more influence over the Senate, than over the House of Representatives. Allow the Senate to originate in this case, and that influence will be sure to mix itself in their deliberations and plans. The declaration of war, he conceived, ought not to be in the Senate, composed of twenty-six men only, but rather in the other House. In the other House ought to be placed the origination of the means of war. As to commercial regulations which may involve revenue, the difficulty may be avoided by restraining the definition to bills for the *mere* or *sole* purpose of raising revenue. The Senate will be more likely to be corrupt than the House of Representatives, and should therefore have less to do with money matters. His principal object, however, was to prevent popular objections against the plan, and to secure its adoption.

Mr. RUTLEDGE. The friends of this motion are not consistent in their reasoning. They tell us that we ought to be guided by the long experience of Great Britain, and not our own experience of eleven years; and yet they themselves propose to depart from it. The *House of Commons* not only have the exclusive right of originating, but the

Lords are not allowed to alter or amend a money bill. Will not the people say that this restriction is but a mere tub to the whale? They cannot but see that it is of no real consequence; and will be more likely to be displeased with it as an attempt to bubble them than to impute it to a watchfulness over their rights. For his part, he would prefer giving the exclusive right to the Senate, if it was to be given exclusively at all. The Senate being more conversant in business, and having more leisure, will digest the bills much better, and as they are to have no effect, till examined and approved by the House of Representatives, there can be no possible danger. These clauses in the Constitutions of the States had been put in through a blind adherence to the British model. If the work was to be done over now, they would be omitted. The experiment in South Carolina, where the Senate cannot originate or amend money bills, has shown that it answers no good purpose; and produces the very bad one of continually dividing and heating the two Houses. Sometimes, indeed, if the matter of the amendment of the Senate is pleasing to the other House, they wink at the encroachment; if it be displeasing, then the Constitution is appealed to. Every session is distracted by altercations on this subject. The practice now becoming frequent is for the Senate not to make formal amendments, but to send down a schedule of the alterations which will procure the bill their assent.

Mr. CARROLL. The most ingenious men in Maryland are puzzled to define the case of money-bills, or explain the Constitution on that point; though it seemed to be worded with all possible plainness and precision. It is a source of continual difficulty and squabble between the two Houses.

Mr. McHENRY mentioned an instance of extraordinary subterfuge, to get rid of the apparent force of the Constitution.

On the question on the first part of the motion, as to the exclusive originating of money-bills in the House of Representatives,—

New Hampshire, Massachusetts, Virginia, (Mr. BLAIR and MADISON, no; Mr. RANDOLPH, Colonel MASON, and General WASHINGTON,* aye;) North Carolina, aye — 4; Connecticut, New Jersey, Pennsylvania, Delaware Maryland, South Carolina, Georgia, no — 7.

On the question on originating by the House of Representatives, and *amending* by the Senate. as reported, Article 4, Sect. 5,—

New Hampshire, Massachusetts, Virginia,† North Carolina, aye — 4; Connecticut, New Jersey, Pennsylvania, Delaware, Maryland, South Carolina, Georgia, no — 7.

On the question on the last clause of Article 4, Sect. 5, viz., "No money shall be drawn from the public treasury, but in pursuance of *appropriations* that shall originate in the House of Representatives," it passed in the negative,— Massachusetts, aye — 1; New Hampshire, Connecticut, New Jersey, Pennsylvania, Delaware, Maryland, Virginia, North Carolina, South Carolina, Georgia, no — 10.

Adjourned.

TUESDAY, AUGUST 14TH.

In Convention,— Article 6, Sect. 9, was taken up.

Mr. PINCKNEY argued that the making the members ineligible to offices was *degrading* to them, and the more improper as their election into the Legislature implied that they had the confidence of the people; that it was *inconvenient*, because the Senate might be supposed to contain the fittest men. He hoped to see that body become a school of public ministers, a nursery of statesmen. That it was *impolitic*, because the Legislature would cease to be a magnet to the first talents and abilities. He moved to postpone the section, in order to take up the following proposition, viz.,

---

* He disapproved, and till now voted against, the exclusive privilege. He gave up his judgment, he said, because it was not of very material weight with him, and was made an essential point with others, who, if disappointed, might be less cordial in other points of real weight.

† In the printed Journal, Virginia, no.

" the members of each House shall be incapable of holding any office under the United States, for which they, or any others for their benefit, receive any salary, fees, or emoluments of any kind; and the acceptance of such office shall vacate their seats respectively."

General MIFFLIN seconded the motion.

Colonel MASON ironically proposed to strike out the whole section, as a more effectual expedient for encouraging that exotic corruption which might not otherwise thrive so well in the American soil; for completing that aristocracy which was probably in the contemplation of some among us; and for inviting into the legislative service those generous and benevolent characters, who will do justice to each other's merit, by carving out offices and rewards for it. In the present state of American morals and manners, few friends, it may be thought, will be lost to the plan, by the opportunity of giving premiums to a mercenary and depraved ambition.

Mr. MERCER. It is a first principle in political science, that whenever the rights of property are secured, an aristocracy will grow out of it. Elective governments also necessarily become aristocratic, because the rulers being few can and will draw emoluments for themselves from the many. The governments of America will become aristocracies. They are so already. The public measures are calculated for the benefit of the governors, not of the people. The people are dissatisfied, and complain. They change their rulers, and the public measures are changed, but it is only a change of one scheme of emolument to the rulers, for another. The people gain nothing by it, but an addition of instability and uncertainty to their other evils. Governments can only be maintained by *force* or *influence*. The Executive has not *force* — deprive him of *influence*, by rendering the members of the Legislature ineligible to Executive offices, and he becomes a mere phantom of authority. The aristocratic part will not even let him in for a share of the plunder. The Legislature must and will be composed of

wealth and abilities, and the people will be governed by a
junto.   The Executive ought to have a Council, being members of both Houses.   Without such an influence the war
will be between the aristocracy and the people.   He wished
it to be between the aristocracy and the Executive.   Nothing else can protect the people against those speculating
Legislatures, which are now plundering them throughout
the United States.

Mr. GERRY read a resolution of the Legislature of Massachusetts, passed before the act of Congress recommending the Convention, in which her deputies were instructed
not to depart from the rotation established in the fifth Article of the Confederation; nor to agree, in any case, to give
to the members of Congress a capacity to hold offices under
the government.   This, he said, was repealed in consequence of the act of Congress, with which the State
thought it proper to comply in an unqualified manner.
The sense of the State, however, was still the same.   He
could not think with Mr. PINCKNEY, that the disqualification
was degrading.   Confidence is the road to tyranny.   As to
ministers and ambassadors, few of them were necessary.
It is the opinion of a great many that they ought to be dis-
continued on our part, that none may be sent among us;
and that source of influence shut up.   If the Senate were
to appoint ambassadors, as seemed to be intended, they will
multiply embassies for their own sakes.   He was not so
fond of those productions, as to wish to establish nurseries
for them.   If they are once appointed, the House of Representatives will be obliged to provide salaries for them,
whether they approve of the measures or not.   If men will
not serve in the Legislature without a prospect of such
offices, our situation is deplorable indeed.   If our best citizens are actuated by such mercenary views, we had better
choose a single despot at once.   It will be more easy to
satisfy the rapacity of one than of many.   According to the
idea of one gentleman (Mr. MERCER), our government, it
seems, is to be a government of plunder.   In that case, it

certainly would be prudent to have but one, rather than many to be employed in it. We cannot be too circumspect in the formation of this system. It will be examined on all sides, and with a very suspicious eye. The people, who have been so lately in arms against Great Britain for their liberties, will not easily give them up. He lamented the evils existing, at present, under our governments; but imputed them to the faults of those in office, not to the people. The misdeeds of the former will produce a critical attention to the opportunities afforded by the new system to like or greater abuses. As it now stands, it is as complete an aristocracy as ever was framed. If great powers should be given to the Senate, we shall be governed in reality by a junto, as has been apprehended. He remarked that it would be very differently constituted from Congress. In the first place, there will be but two Deputies from each State; in Congress there may be seven, and are generally, five. In the second place, they are chosen for six years; those of Congress annually. In the third place, they are not subject to recall; those of Congress are. And finally, in Congress *nine* States are necessary for all great purposes; here eight *persons* will suffice. Is it to be presumed that the people will ever agree to such a system? He moved to render the members of the House of Representatives, as well as of the Senate, ineligible, not only during, but for one year after the expiration of their terms. If it should be thought that this will injure the Legislature, by keeping out of it men of abilities, who are willing to serve in other offices it may be required as a qualification for other offices, that the candidates shall have served a certain time in the Legislature.

Mr. GOUVERNEUR MORRIS. Exclude the officers of the Army and Navy, and you form a band having a different interest from, and opposed to, the civil power. You stimulate them to despise and reproach those "talking Lords who dare not face the foe." Let this spirit be roused at the end of a war, before your troops shall have laid down their arms, and though the civil authority be "entrenched in parchment to the teeth," they will cut their way to it. He was against rendering the members of the Legislature ineligible to offices. He was for rendering them eligible again, after having vacated their seats by accepting office. Why should we not avail ourselves of their services if the people choose to give them their confidence? There can be little danger of corruption, either among the people, or the Legislatures, who are to be the electors. If they say, we see their merits — we honor the men — we choose to renew our confidence in them; have they not a right to give them a preference — and can they be properly abridged of it?

Mr. WILLIAMSON introduced his opposition to the motion, by referring to the question concerning "money bills." That clause, he said, was dead. Its ghost, he was afraid, would, notwithstanding, haunt us. It had been a matter of conscience with him, to insist on it, as long as there was hope of retaining it. He had swallowed the vote of rejection with reluctance. He could not digest it. All that was said, on the other side, was, that the restriction was not *convenient.* We have now got a House of Lords which is to originate money bills. To avoid another *inconvenience,* we are to have a whole Legislature, at liberty to cut out offices for one another. He thought a self-denying ordinance for ourselves, would be more proper. Bad as the Constitution has been made by expunging the restriction on the Senate concerning money bills, he did not wish to make it worse, by expunging the present section. He had scarcely seen a single corrupt measure in the Legislature of North Carolina, which could not be traced up to office hunting.

Mr. SHERMAN. The Constitution should lay as few temptations as possible in the way of those in power. Men of abilities will increase as the country grows more populous, and as the means of education are more diffused.

Mr. PINCKNEY. No State has rendered the members of

the Legislature ineligible to offices. In South Carolina the Judges are eligible into the Legislature. It cannot be supposed, then, that the motion will be offensive to the people. If the State Constitution should be revised, he believed restrictions of this sort would be rather diminished than multiplied.

Mr. WILSON could not approve of the section as it stood, and could not give up his judgment to any supposed objections that might arise among the people. He considered himself as acting and responsible for the welfare of millions, not immediately represented in this House. He had also asked himself the serious question, what he should say to his constituents, in case they should call upon him to tell them, why he sacrificed his own judgment in a case where they authorized him to exercise it? Were he to own to them that he sacrificed it in order to flatter their prejudices, he should dread the retort — did you suppose the people of Pennsylvania had not good sense enough to receive a good government? Under this impression, he should certainly follow his own judgment, which disapproved of the section. He would remark, in addition to the objections urged against it, that as one branch of the Legislature was to be appointed by the Legislatures of the States, the other by the people of the States; as both are to be paid by the States, and to be appointable to State offices; nothing seemed to be wanting to prostrate the National Legislature, but to render its members ineligible to national offices, and by that means take away its power of attracting those talents which were necessary to give weight to the Government, and to render it useful to the people. He was far from thinking the ambition which aspired to offices of dignity and trust an ignoble or culpable one. He was sure it was not politic to regard it in that light, or to withhold from it the prospect of those rewards which might engage it in the career of public service. He observed that the State of Pennsylvania, which had gone as far as any State into the policy of fettering power, had not rendered the members of the Legislature ineligible to offices of government.

Mr. ELLSWORTH did not think the mere postponement of the reward would be any material discouragement of merit. Ambitious minds will serve two years, or seven years in the Legislature, for the sake of qualifying themselves for other offices. This he thought a sufficient security for obtaining the services of the ablest men in the Legislature ; although, whilst members, they should be ineligible to public offices. Besides, merit will be most encouraged, when most impartially rewarded. If rewards are to circulate only within the Legislature, merit out of it will be discouraged.

Mr. MERCER was extremely anxious on this point. What led to the appointment of this Convention ? The corruption and mutability of the legislative councils of the States. If the plan does not remedy these, it will not recommend itself ; and we shall not be able in our private capacities to support and enforce it: nor will the best part of our citizens exert themselves for the purpose. It is a great mistake to suppose that the paper we are to propose, will govern the United States. It is the men whom it will bring into the Government, and interest in maintaining it, that are to govern them. The paper will only mark out the mode and the form. Men are the substance and must do the business. All government must be by force or influence. It is not the King of France, but 200,000 janissaries of power, that govern that kingdom. There will be no such force here ; influence, then, must be substituted ; and he would ask, whether this could be done, if the members of the Legislature should be ineligible to offices of State ; whether such a disqualification would not determine all the most influential men to stay at home. and prefer appointments within their respective States.

Mr. WILSON was by no means satisfied with the answer given by Mr. ELLSWORTH to the argument as to the discouragement of merit. The members must either go a second time into the Legislature, and disqualify themselves; or say to their constituents, we served you before only from the mercenary view of qualifying ourselves for offices, and having answered this purpose, we do not choose to be again elected.

Mr. GOUVERNEUR MORRIS put the case of a war, and the citizen most capable of conducting it happening to be a member of the Legislature. What might have been the consequence of such a regulation at the commencement, or even in the course, of the late contest for our liberties?

On the question for postponing, in order to take up Mr. PINCKNEY's motion, it was lost,— New Hampshire, Pennsylvania, Delaware, Maryland, Virginia, aye — 5; Massachusetts, Connecticut, New Jersey, North Carolina, South Carolina, no — 5; Georgia, divided.

Mr. GOUVERNEUR MORRIS moved to insert, after "office," "except offices in the Army or Navy: but, in that case, their offices shall be vacated."

Mr. BROOM seconds him.

Mr. RANDOLPH had been, and should continue, uniformly opposed to the striking out of the clause, as opening a door for influence and corruption. No arguments had made any impression on him, but those which related to the case of war, and a coëxisting incapacity of the fittest commanders to be employed. He admitted great weight in these, and would agree to the exception proposed by Mr. GOUVERNEUR MORRIS.

Mr. BUTLER and Mr. PINCKNEY urged a general postponement of Article 6, Sect. 9, till it should be seen what powers would be vested in the Senate, when it would be more easy to judge of the expediency of allowing the officers of State to be chosen out of that body.

A general postponement was agreed to, *nem. con.*

Article 6, Sect. 10, was then taken up,—"that members be paid by their respective States."

Mr. ELLSWORTH said, that in reflecting on this subject, he had been satisfied, that too much dependence on the

States would be produced by this mode of payment. He moved to strike it out, and insert, "that they should be paid out of the treasury of the United States an allowance not exceeding ——— dollars per day, or the present value thereof.

Mr. GOUVERNEUR MORRIS remarked that if the members were to be paid by the States, it would throw an unequal burthen on the distant States, which would be unjust, as the Legislature was to be a national assembly. He moved that the payment be out of the national treasury; leaving the quantum to the discretion of the National Legislature. There could be no reason to fear that they would overpay themselves.

Mr. BUTLER contended for payment by the States; particularly in the case of the Senate, who will be so long out of their respective States that they will lose sight of their constituents, unless dependent on them for their support.

Mr. LANGDON was against payment by the States. There would be some difficulty in fixing the sum, but it would be unjust to oblige the distant States to bear the expense of their members in travelling to and from the seat of government.

Mr. MADISON. If the House of Representatives is to be chosen *biennially*, and the Senate to be *constantly* dependent on the Legislatures, which are chosen *annually*, he could not see any chance for that stability in the General Government the want of which was a principal evil in the State Governments. His fear was, that the organization of the Government supposing the Senate to be really independent for six years, would not effect our purpose. It was nothing more than a combination of the peculiarities of two of the State Governments, which separately had been found insufficient. The Senate was formed on the model of that of Maryland. The revisionary check on that of New York. What the effect of a union of these provisions might be, could not be foreseen. The enlargement of the sphere of the Government was, indeed a circumstance which he thought would be favourable, as he had on several occasions undertaken to show. He was, however, for fixing at least two extremes not to be exceeded by the National Legislature in the payment of themselves.

Mr. GERRY. There are difficulties on both sides. The observation of Mr. BUTLER has weight in it. On the other side, the State Legislatures may turn out the Senators by reducing their salaries. Such things have been practiced.

Col MASON. It has not yet been noticed, that the clause as it now stands makes the House of Representatives also dependent on the State Legislatures: so that both Houses will be made the instruments of the politics of the States, whatever they may be.

Mr. BROOM could see no danger in trusting the General Legislature with the payment of themselves. The State Legislatures had this power, and no complaint had been made of it.

Mr. SHERMAN was not afraid that the Legislature would make their own wages too high, but too low; so that men ever so fit could not serve unless they were at the same time rich. He thought the best plan would be, to fix a moderate allowance to be paid out of the national treasury, and let the States make such additions as they might judge fit. He moved that five dollars per day be the sum, any further emoluments to be added by the States.

Mr. CARROLL had been much surprised at seeing this clause in the Report. The dependence of both Houses on the State Legislatures is complete; especially as the members of the former are eligible to State offices. The States can now say: If you do not comply with our wishes, we will starve you; if you do, we will reward you. The new Government in this form was nothing more than a second edition of Congress, in two volumes instead of one, and perhaps with very few amendments.

Mr. DICKINSON took it for granted that all were convinced of the necessity of making the General Government independent of the prejudices, passions, and improper views

34

of the State Legislatures. The contrary of this was effected
by the section as it stands. On the other hand, there were
objections against taking a permanent standard, as wheat,
which had been suggested on a former occasion; as well as
against leaving the matter to the pleasure of the National
Legislature. He proposed that an act should be passed,
every twelve years, by the National Legislature settling the
quantum of their wages. If the General Government
should be left dependent on the State Legislatures, it would
be happy for us if we had never met in this room.

Mr. ELLSWORTH was not unwilling himself to trust the
Legislature with authority to regulate their own wages,
but well knew that an unlimited discretion for that purpose
would produce strong, though perhaps not insuperable
objections. He thought changes in the value of money
provided for by his motion in the words, "or the present
value thereof."

Mr. L. MARTIN. As the Senate is to represent the
States, the members of it ought to be paid by the States.

Mr. CARROLL. The Senate was to represent and manage
the affairs of the whole and not to be the advocates of
State interests. They ought then not to be dependent on,
nor paid by the States.

On the question for paying the members of the legislature out of the national treasury,— New Hampshire, Connecticut, New Jersey, Pennsylvania, Delaware, Maryland,
Virginia, North Carolina, Georgia, aye — 9; Massachusetts,
South Carolina, no — 2.

Mr. ELLSWORTH moved that the pay be fixed at five dollars, or the present value thereof, per day, during their
attendance, and for every thirty miles in travelling to and
from Congress.

Mr. STRONG preferred four dollars, leaving the States at
liberty to make additions.

On the question for fixing the pay at five dollars,—
— Connecticut, Virginia, aye — 2; New Hampshire, Mas-

sachusetts, New Jersey, Pennsylvania, Delaware, Maryland, North Carolina, South Carolina, Georgia no — 9.

Mr. DICKINSON proposed that the wages of the members of both Houses should be required to be the same.

Mr. BROOM seconded him.

Mr. GORHAM. This would be unreasonable. The Senate will be detained longer from home, will be obliged to remove their families, and in time of war perhaps to sit constantly. Their allowance should certainly be higher. The members of the Senates in the States are allowed more than those of the other House.

Mr. DICKINSON withdrew his motion.

It was moved and agreed, to amend the section by adding, "to be ascertained by law."

The section (Article 6, Section 10,) as amended, was then agreed to, *nem. con.*

Adjourned.

————

WEDNESDAY, AUGUST 15TH.

In Convention,—Article, 6, Section 11, was agreed to, *nem. con.*

Article 6, Section 12, was then taken up.

Mr. STRONG moved to amend the article so as to read, "Each House shall possess the right of originating all bills, except bills for raising money for the purposes of revenue, or for appropriating the same, and for fixing the salaries of the officers of the Government, which shall originate in the House of Representatives; but the Senate may propose or concur with amendments as in other cases."

Colonel MASON seconds the motion. He was extremely earnest to take this power from the Senate, who he said, could already sell the whole country by means of treaties.

Mr. GORHAM urged the amendment as of great importance. The Senate will first acquire the habit of preparing money-bills, and then the practice will grow into an exclusive right of preparing them.

Mr. GOUVERNEUR MORRIS opposed it, as unnecessary and inconvenient.

Mr. WILLIAMSON. Some think this restriction on the Senate essential to liberty ; others think it of no importance. Why should not the former be indulged ? He was for an efficient and stable government ; but many would not strengthen the Senate, if not restricted in the case of money-bills. The friends of the Senate, would therefore, lose more than they would gain, by refusing to gratify the other side. He moved to postpone the subject, till the powers of the Senate should be gone over.

Mr. RUTLEDGE seconds the motion.

Mr. MERCER should hereafter be against returning to a reconsideration of this section. He contended (alluding to Mr. MASON's observations) that the Senate ought not to have the power of treaties. This power belonged to the Executive department ; adding, that treaties would not be final, so as to alter the laws of the land, till ratified by legislative authority. This was the case of treaties in Great Britain ; particularly the late treaty of commerce with France.

Colonel MASON did not say that a treaty would repeal a law ; but that the Senate, by means of treaties, might alienate territory, &c., without legislative sanction. The cessions of the British Islands in the West Indies, by treaty alone, were an example. If Spain should possess herself of Georgia, therefore, the Senate might by treaty dismember the Union. He wished the motion to be decided now, that the friends of it might know how to conduct themselves.

On the question for postponing Sect. 12, it passed in the affirmative,—

New Hampshire, Massachusetts, Virginia, North Carolina, South Carolina, Georgia, aye — 6 ; Connecticut, New Jersey, Pennsylvania, Delaware, Maryland, no — 5.

Mr. MADISON moved the following amendment of Article 6, Sect. 13 : " Every bill which shall have passed the two

Houses shall, before it become a law, be severally presented
to the President of the United States, and to the Judges of
the Supreme Court, for the revision of each. If, upon
such revision, they shall approve of it, they shall respectively signify their approbation by signing it ; but if, upon
such revision, it shall appear improper to either, or both,
to be passed into a law, it shall be returned, with the objections against it, to that House in which it shall have
originated, who shall enter the objections at large on their
Journal, and proceed to reconsider the bill : but if, after
such reconsideration, two-thirds of that House, when either
the President, or a majority of the judges shall object, or
three-fourths, where both shall object, shall agree to pass
it, it shall, together with the objections, be sent to the
other House ; by which it shall likewise be reconsidered,
and, if approved by two-thirds, or three-fourths of the
other House, as the case may be, it shall become a law."

Mr. WILSON seconds the motion.

Mr. PINCKNEY opposed the interference of the Judges in
the legislative business: it will involve them in parties,
and give a previous tincture to their opinions.

Mr. MERCER heartily approved the motion. It is an
axiom that the Judiciary ought to be separate from the
Legislative; but equally so that it ought to be independent
of that department. The true policy of the axiom is, that
legislative usurpation and oppression may be obviated. He
disapproved of the doctrine, that the Judges, as expositors
of the Constitution, should have authority to declare a law
void. He thought laws ought to be well and cautiously
made, and then to be uncontrollable.

Mr. GERRY. This motion comes to the same thing with
what has been already negatived.

On the question on the motion of Mr. MADISON, —

Delaware, Maryland, Virginia, aye — 3; New Hampshire, Massachusetts, Connecticut, New Jersey, Pennsylvania, North Carolina, South Carolina, Georgia, no — 8.

Mr. GOUVERNEUR MORRIS regretted that something like

the proposed check could not be agreed to. He dwelt on the importance of public credit, and the difficulty of supporting it without some strong barrier against the instability of legislative assemblies. He suggested the idea of requiring three-fourths of each House to *repeal* laws where the President should not concur. He had no great reliance on the revisionary power, as the Executive was now to be constituted (elected by Congress). The Legislature will contrive to soften down the President. He recited the history of paper emissions, and the perseverance of the legislative assemblies in repeating them, with all the distressing effects of such measures before their eyes. Were the National Legislature formed, and a war was now to break out, this ruinous expedient would again be resorted to, if not guarded against. The requiring three-fourths to repeal would, though not a complete remedy, prevent the hasty passage of laws, and the frequency of those repeals which destroy faith in the public, and which are among our greatest calamities.

Mr. DICKINSON was strongly impressed with the remark of Mr. MERCER, as to the power of the Judges to set aside the law. He thought no such power ought to exist. He was, at the same time, at a loss what expedient to substitute. The Justiciary of Arragon, he observed, became by degrees the law-giver.

Mr. GOUVERNEUR MORRIS suggested the expedient of an absolute negative in the Executive. He could not agree that the Judiciary, which was part of the Executive, should be bound to say, that a direct violation of the Constitution was law. A control over the Legislature might have its inconveniences. But view the danger on the other side. The most virtuous citizens will often, as members of a Legislative body, concur in measures which afterwards, in their private capacity, they will be ashamed of. Encroachments of the popular branch of the Government ought to be guarded against. The Ephori at Sparta became in the end absolute. The Report of the Council of Censors in Pennsylvania points out the many invasions of the Legislative department on the Executive, numerous as the latter[*] is, within the short term of seven years; and in a State where a strong party is opposed to the Constitution, and watching every occasion of turning the public resentments against it. If the Executive be overturned by the popular branch, as happened in England, the tyranny of one man will ensue. In Rome, where the aristocracy overturned the throne, the consequence was different. He enlarged on the tendency of the Legislative authority to usurp on the Executive, and wished the section to be postponed, in order to consider of some more effectual check than requiring two-thirds only to overrule the negative of the Executive.

Mr. SHERMAN. Can one man be trusted better than all the others, if they all agree? This was neither wise nor safe. He disapproved of judges meddling in politics and parties. We have gone far enough in forming the negative, as it now stands.

Mr. CARROLL. When the negative to be overruled by two-thirds only was agreed to, the *quorum* was not fixed. He remarked that as a majority was now to be the quorum, seventeen in the larger, and eight in the smaller, house, might carry points. The advantage that might be taken of this seemed to call for greater impediments to improper laws. He thought the controlling power, however, of the Executive, could not be well decided, till it was seen how the formation of that department would be finally regulated. He wished the consideration of the matter to be postponed.

Mr. GORHAM saw no end to these difficulties and postponements. Some could not agree to the form of government, before the powers were defined. Others could not agree to the powers till it was seen how the government was to be formed. He thought a majority as large a quorum as was necessary. It was the quorum almost every where fixed in the United States.

---

[*]The Executive consisted at that time of about twenty members.

Mr. WILSON, after viewing the subject with all the coolness and attention possible, was most apprehensive of a dissolution of the Government from the Legislature swallowing up all the other powers. He remarked, that the prejudices against the Executive resulted from a misapplication of the adage, that the parliament was the palladium of liberty. Where the Executive was really formidable, *king* and *tyrant* were naturally associated in the minds of people; not *legislature* and *tyranny*. But where the Executive was not formidable, the two last were most properly associated. After the destruction of the King in Great Britain, a more pure and unmixed tyranny sprang up, in the Parliament than had been exercised by the monarch. He insisted that we had not guarded against the danger on this side, by a sufficient self-defensive power, either to the Executive or Judiciary Department.

Mr. RUTLEDGE, was strenuous against postponing; and complained much of the tediousness of the proceedings.

Mr. ELLSWORTH held the same language. We grow more and more sceptical as we proceed. If we do not decide soon, we shall be unable to come to any decision.

The question for postponement passed in the negative, — Delaware and Maryland only being in the affirmative

Mr. WILLIAMSON moved to change, " two-thirds of each House," into " three-fourths," as requisite to overrule the dissent of the President. He saw no danger in this, and preferred giving the power to the President alone, to admitting the Judges into the business of legislation.

Mr. WILSON seconds the motion; referring to and repeating the ideas of Mr. CARROLL.

On this motion for three-fourths instead of two-thirds; it passed in the affirmative,— Connecticut, Delaware, Maryland, Virginia, North Carolina, South Carolina, aye — 6; New Hampshire, Massachusetts, New Jersey, Georgia, no — 4; Pennsylvania, divided.

Mr. MADISON, observing that if the negative of the President was confined to *bills*, it would be evaded by acts under the form and name of Resolutions, votes, etc., proposed that " or resolve," should be added after " *bill*," in the beginning of section 13, with an exception as to votes of adjournment, &c. After a short and rather confused conversation on the subject, the question was put and rejected, the votes being as follows,—Massachusetts, Delaware, North Carolina, aye — 3; New Hampshire, Connecticut, New Jersey, Pennsylvania, Maryland, Virginia, South Carolina, Georgia, no —8.

"Ten days (Sundays excepted)," instead of "*seven*," were allowed to the President for returning bills with his objections,—New Hampshire and Massachusetts only voting against it.

The thirteenth Section of Article 6, as amended was then agreed to.

Adjourned.

THURSDAY, AUGUST 16TH.

In Convention,—MR. RANDOLPH, having thrown into a new form the motion putting votes, resolutions, &c. on a footing with bills, renewed it as follows — " Every order, resolution, or vote, to which the concurrence of the Senate and House of Representatives may be necessary (except on a question of adjournment, and in the cases hereinafter mentioned) shall be presented to the President for his revision; and before the same shall have force, shall be approved by him, or, being disapproved by him, shall be repassed by the Senate and House of Representatives, according to the rules and limitations prescribed in the case of a bill."

MR. SHERMAN thought it unnecessary, except as to votes taking money out of the treasury, which might be provided for in another place.

On the question as moved by MR. RANDOLPH, it was agreed to,— New Hampshire, Connecticut, Pennsylvania, Delaware, Maryland, Virginia, North Carolina, South Carolina, Georgia, aye — 9; New Jersey, no — 1; Massachusetts, not present.

The amendment was made a fourteenth section of Article 6.

Article 7, Sect. 1, was then taken up.

Mr. L. MARTIN asked, what was meant by the Committee of Detail in the expression, — "*duties*," and "*imposts*." If the meaning were the same, the former was unnecessary; if different, the matter ought to be made clear.

Mr. WILSON. *Duties* are applicable to many objects to which the word *imposts* does not relate. The latter are appropriated to commerce, the former extend to a variety of objects, as stamp duties, &c.

Mr. CARROLL reminded the Convention of the great difference of interests among the States; and doubts the propriety, in that point of view, of letting a majority be a quorum.

Mr. MASON urged the necessity of connecting with the powers of levying taxes, duties, &c., the prohibition in Article 6, Sect. 4, "that no tax shall be laid on exports." He was unwilling to trust to its being done in a future article. He hoped the Northern States did not mean to deny the Southern this security. It would hereafter be as desirable to the former, when the latter should become the most populous. He professed his jealousy for the productions of the Southern, or, as he called them, the staple, States. He moved to insert the following amendment: "provided, that no tax, duty, or imposition, shall be laid by the Legislature of the United States on articles exported from any State."

Mr. SHERMAN had no objection to the proviso here, other than that it would derange the parts of the Report as made by the Committee, to take them in such an order.

Mr. RUTLEDGE. It being of no consequence in what order points are decided, he should vote for the clause as it stood, but on condition that the subsequent parts relating to negroes should also be agreed to.

Mr. GOUVERNEUR MORRIS considered such a proviso as inadmissible any where. It was so radically objectionable, that it might cost the whole system the support of some members. He contended that it would not in some cases be equitable to tax imports without taxing exports; and that taxes on exports would be often the most easy and proper of the two.

Mr. MADISON. First, the power of laying taxes on exports is proper in itself; and as the States cannot with propriety exercise it separately, it ought to be vested in them collectively. Secondly, it might with particular advantage be exercised with regard to articles in which America was not rivalled in foreign markets, as tobacco, &c. The contract between the French Farmers-General and Mr. MORRIS, stipulating that, if taxes should be laid in America on the export of tobacco, they should be paid by the Farmers, showed that it was understood by them, that the price would be thereby raised in America, and consequently the taxes be paid by the European consumer. Thirdly, it would be unjust to the States whose produce was exported by their neighbours, to leave it subject to be taxed by the latter. This was a grievance which had already filled New Hampshire, Connecticut, New Jersey, Delaware, and North Carolina with loud complaints, as it related to imports, and they would be equally authorized by taxes by the States on exports. Fourthly, the Southern States, being most in danger and most needing naval protection, could the less complain, if the burthen should be somewhat heaviest on them. And finally, we are not providing for the present moment only; and time will equalize the situation of the States in this matter. He was, for these reasons, against the motion.

Mr. WILLIAMSON considered the clause proposed against taxes on exports, as reasonable and necessary.

Mr. ELLSWORTH was against taxing exports; but thought the prohibition stood in the most proper place, and was against deranging the order reported by the Committee.

Mr. WILSON was decidedly against prohibiting general taxes on exports. He dwelt on the injustice and impolicy of leaving New Jersey, Connecticut, &c., any longer subject to the exactions of their commercial neighbours.

Mr. GERRY thought the Legislature could not be trusted with such a power. It might ruin the country. It might be exercised partially, raising one and depressing another part of it.

Mr. GOUVERNEUR MORRIS. However the Legislative power may be formed, it will, if disposed, be able to ruin the country. He considered the taxing of exports to be in many cases highly politic. Virginia has found her account in taxing tobacco. All countries having peculiar articles tax the exportation of them, — as France her wines and brandies. A tax here on lumber would fall on the West Indies, and punish their restrictions on our trade. The same is true of live stock, and in some degree of flour. In case of a dearth in the West Indies, we may extort what we please. Taxes on exports are a necessary source of revenue. For a long time the people of America will not have money to pay direct taxes. Seize and sell their effects, and you push them into revolts.

Mr. MERCER was strenuous against giving Congress power to tax exports. Such taxes are impolitic, as encouraging the raising of articles not meant for exportation, The States had now a right where their situation permitted, to tax both the imports and the exports of their uncommercial neighbours. It was enough for them to sacrifice one half of it. It had been said the Southern States had most need of naval protection. The reverse was the case. Were it not for promoting the carrying trade of the Northern States, the Southern States could let the trade go into foreign bottoms, where it would not need our protection. Virginia, by taxing her tobacco, had given an advantage to that of Maryland.

Mr. SHERMAN. To examine and compare the States in relation to imports and exports, will be opening a boundless field. He thought the matter had been adjusted, and that imports were to be subject, and exports not, to be taxed. He thought it wrong to tax exports, except it might be such articles as ought not to be exported. The complexity of the business in America would render an equal tax on exports impracticable. The oppression of the uncommercial States was guarded against by the power to regulate trade between the States. As to compelling foreigners, that might be done by regulating trade in general. The Government would not be trusted with such a power. Objections are most likely to be excited by considerations relating to taxes and money. A power to tax exports would shipwreck the whole.

Mr. CARROLL was surprised that any objection should be made to an exception of exports from the power of taxation.

It was finally agreed, that the question concerning exports should lie over for the place in which the exception stood in the Report,— Maryland alone voting against it.

Article 7, Section 1, clause first, was then agreed to — Mr. GERRY alone answering, no.

The clause for regulating commerce with foreign nations, &c., was agreed to, *nem. con.*

The several clauses,— for coining money — for regulating foreign coin — for fixing the standard of weights and measures,— were agreed to, *nem. con.*

On the clause, "To establish post offices,"—

Mr. GERRY moved to add, "and post-roads."

Mr. MERCER seconded ; and on the question,

Massachusetts, Delaware, Maryland, Virginia, South Carolina, Georgia, aye — 6 ; New Hampshire, Connecticut, New Jersey, Pennsylvania, North Carolina, no — 5.

Mr. GOUVERNEUR MORRIS moved to strike out, "and emit bills on the credit of the United States." If the United States had credit, such bills would be unnecessary ; if they had not, unjust and useless.

Mr. BUTLER seconds the motion.

Mr. MADISON. Will it not be sufficient to prohibit the making them a *tender* ? This will remove the temptation to emit them with unjust views. And promissory notes, in that shape, may in some emergencies be best.

Mr. GOUVERNEUR MORRIS. Striking out the words will leave room still for notes of a *responsible* minister, which will do all the good without the mischief. The moneyed interest will oppose the plan of government, if paper emissions be not prohibited.

Mr. GORHAM was for striking out without inserting any prohibition. If the words stand, they may suggest and lead to the measure.

Mr. MASON had doubts on the subject. Congress, he thought, would not have the power, unless it were expressed. Though he had a mortal hatred to paper-money, yet as he could not foresee all emergencies, he was unwilling to tie the hands of the Legislature. He observed that the late war could not have been carried on, had such a prohibition existed.

Mr. GORHAM. The power, as far as it will be necessary, or safe, is involved in that of borrowing.

Mr. MERCER was a friend to paper-money, though in the present state and temper of America, he should neither propose nor approve of such a measure. He was consequently opposed to a prohibition of it altogether. It will stamp suspicion on the Government, to deny it a discretion on this point. It was impolitic, also, to excite the opposition of all those who were friends to paper-money. The people of property would be sure to be on the side of the plan, and it was impolitic to purchase their further attachment with the loss of the opposite class of citizens.

Mr. ELLSWORTH thought this a favourable moment, to shut and bar the door against paper-money. The mischiefs of the various experiments which had been made were now fresh in the public mind, and had excited the disgust of all the respectable part of America. By withholding the power from the new Government, more friends of influence would be gained to it than by almost anything else. Paper-money can in no case be necessary. Give the Government credit, and other resources will offer. The power may do harm, never good.

Mr. RANDOLPH, notwithstanding his antipathy to paper-money, could not agree to strike out the words, as he could not foresee all the occasions that might arise.

Mr. WILSON. It will have a most salutary influence on the credit of the United States, to remove the possibility of paper-money. This expedient can never succeed whilst its mischiefs are remembered. And as long as it can be resorted to, it will be a bar to other resources.

Mr. BUTLER remarked, that paper was a legal tender in no country in Europe. He was urgent for disarming the government of such a power.

Mr. MASON was still averse to tying the hands of the Legislature *altogether*. If there was no example in Europe, as just remarked, it might be observed, on the other side, that there was none in which the Government was restrained on this head.

Mr. READ thought the words, if not struck out, would be as alarming as the mark of theBeast in Revelation.

Mr. LANGDON had rather reject the whole plan, than retain the three words, " and emit bills."

On the motion for striking out,—

New Hampshire, Massachusetts, Connecticut, Pennsylvania, Delaware, Virginia,* North Carolina, South Carolina, Georgia, aye — 9; New Jersey, Maryland, no — 2.

The clause for borrowing money was agreed to, *nem. con.*

Adjourned.

---

* This vote in the affirmative by Virginia was occasioned by the acquiescence of Mr. MADISON, who became satisfied that striking out the words would not disable the Government from the use of public notes, as far as they could be safe and proper; and would only cut off the pretext for a *paper-currency* and particularly for making the bills *a tender*, either for public or private debts.

FRIDAY, AUGUST 17TH.

In Convention,—Article 7, Sect. 1, was resumed.

On the clause, " to appoint a Treasurer by ballot,"—

Mr. GORHAM moved to insert "joint" before ballot, as more convenient, as well as reasonable, than to require the separate concurrence of the Senate.

Mr. PINCKNEY seconds the motion.

Mr. SHERMAN opposed it, as favoring the larger States.

Mr. READ moved to strike out the clause, leaving the appointment of a Treasurer, as of other officers, to the Executive. The Legislature was an improper body for appointments. Those of the State Legislatures were a proof of it. The Executive being responsible, would make a good choice.

Mr. MERCER seconds the motion of Mr. READ.

On the motion for inserting the word " joint " before " ballot,"—New Hampshire, Massachusetts, Pennsylvania, Virginia, North Carolina, South Carolina, Georgia, aye — 7; Connecticut, New Jersey, Maryland, no — 3.

Col. MASON, in opposition to Mr. READ's motion, desired it might be considered, to whom the money would belong; if to the people, the Legislature, representing the people, ought to appoint the keepers of it.

On striking out the clause, as amended, by inserting " joint,"—Pennsylvania, Delaware, Maryland, South Carolina, aye — 4; New Hampshire, Massachusetts, Connecticut, Virginia, North Carolina, Georgia, no —6.

The clause, " to constitute inferior tribunals," was agreed to *nem. con.;* as also the clause, " to make rules as to captures on land and water."

The clause, "to declare the law and punishment of piracies and felonies, &c. &c." being considered —

Mr. MADISON moved to strike out, "and punishment, &c." after the words "to declare the law."

Mr. MASON doubts the safety of it, considering the

strict rule of construction in criminal cases. He doubted also the propriety of taking the power in all these cases, wholly from the States.

Mr. GOUVERNEUR MORRIS thought it would be necessary to extend the authority further, so as to provide for the punishment of counterfeiting in general. Bills of exchange, for example, might be forged in one State, and carried into another.

It was suggested by some other member, that *foreign* paper might be counterfeited by citizens; and that it might be politic to provide by national authority for the punishment of it.

Mr. RANDOLPH did not conceive that expunging "the punishment" would be a constructive exclusion of the power. He doubted only the efficacy of the word "declare."

Mr. WILSON was in favor of the motion. Strictness was not necessary in giving authority to enact penal laws though necessary in enacting and expounding them.

On the question for striking out " and punishment," as moved by Mr. MADISON, — Massachusetts, Pennsylvania, Delaware, Virginia, North Carolina, South Carolina, Georgia, aye — 7; New Hampshire, Connecticut, Maryland, no — 3.

Mr. GOUVERNEUR MORRIS moved to strike out " declare the law," and insert " punish," before " piracies;" and on the question,— New Hampshire, Massachusetts, Pennsylvania, Delaware, Maryland, South Carolina, Georgia, aye — 7; Connecticut, Virginia, North Carolina, no — 3.

Mr. MADISON and Mr. RANDOLPH moved to insert "define and," before " punish."

Mr. WILSON thought " felonies " sufficiently defined by common law.

Mr. DICKINSON concurred with Mr. WILSON.

Mr. MERCER was in favor of the amendment.

Mr. MADISON. Felony at common law is vague. It is also defective. One defect is supplied by Statute of Anne,

35

as to running away with vessels, which at common law was a breach of trust only. Besides, no foreign law should be a standard, further than it is expressly adopted. If the laws of the States were to prevail on this subject, the citizens of different States would be subject to different punishments for the same offence at sea. There would be neither uniformity nor stability in the law. The proper remedy for all these difficulties was, to vest the power proposed by the term " define," in the National Legislature.

Mr. GOUVERNEUR MORRIS would prefer *designate* to *define*, the latter being, as he conceived, limited to the pre-existing meaning.

It was said by others to be applicable to the creating of offences also, and therefore suited the case both of felonies and piracies.

The motion of Mr. MADISON and Mr. RANDOLPH was agreed to.

Mr. ELLSWORTH enlarged the motion, so as to read, " to define and punish piracies and felonies committed on the high seas, counterfeiting the securities and current coin of the United States, and offences against the laws of nations," which was agreed to, *nem. con.*

The clause, "to subdue a rebellion in any State, on the application of its Legislature," was next considered.

Mr. PINCKNEY moved to strike out, " on the application of its Legislature."

Mr. GOUVERNEUR MORRIS seconds.

Mr. L. MARTIN opposed it, as giving a dangerous and unnecessary power. The consent of the State ought to precede the introduction of any extraneous force whatever.

Mr. MERCER supported the opposition of Mr. MARTIN.

Mr. ELLSWORTH proposed to add, after "legislature," " or Executive."

Mr. GOUVERNEUR MORRIS. The Executive may possibly be at the head of the rebellion. The General Government should enforce obedience in all cases where it may be necessary.

Mr. ELLSWORTH. In many cases the General Government ought not to be able to interpose, unless called upon. He was willing to vary his motion, so as to read, "or without it, when the Legislature cannot meet."

Mr. GERRY was against letting loose the myrmidons of the United States on a State, without its own consent. The States will be the best judges in such cases. More blood would have been spilt in Massachusetts, in the late insurrection, if the general authority had intermeddled.

Mr. LANGDON was for striking out, as moved by Mr. PINCKNEY. The apprehension of the National force will have a salutary effect, in preventing insurrections.

Mr. RANDOLPH. If the National Legislature is to judge whether the State Legislature can or cannot meet, that amendment would make the clause as objectionable as the motion of Mr. PINCKNEY.

Mr. GOUVERNEUR MORRIS. We are acting a very strange part. We first form a strong man to protect us, and at the same time wish to tie his hands behind him. The Legislature may surely be trusted with such a power to preserve the public tranquillity.

On the motion to add, " or without it [application] when the Legislature cannot meet," it was agreed to,—

New Hampshire, Connecticut, Virginia, South Carolina, Georgia, aye — 5; Massachusetts, Delaware, Maryland, no 3; Pennsylvania, North Carolina, divided.

Mr. MADISON and Mr. DICKINSON moved to insert, as explanatory, after " State," " against the Government thereof." There might be a rebellion against the United States. The motion was agreed to, *nem. con.*

On the clause as amended,—

New Hampshire, Connecticut, Virginia, Georgia, aye — 4; Delaware, Maryland, North Carolina, South Carolina, no — 4; Massachusetts,* Pennsylvania, absent. So it was lost.

On the clause, " to make war,"—

---

* In the printed Journal, Massachusetts, no.

Mr. PINCKNEY opposed the vesting this power in the Legislature. Its proceedings were too slow. It would meet but once a year. The House of Representatives would be too numerous for such deliberations. The Senate would be the best depository, being more acquainted with foreign affairs, and most capable of proper resolutions. If the States are equally represented in the Senate, so as to give no advantage to the large States, the power will, notwithstanding, be safe, as the small have their all at stake in such cases as well as the large States. It would be singular for one authority to make war, and another peace.

Mr. BUTLER. The objections against the Legislature lie in a great degree against the Senate. He was for vesting the power in the President, who will have all the requisite qualities, and will not make war but when the nation will support it.

Mr. MADISON and Mr. GERRY moved to insert "*declare*," striking out "*make*" war; leaving to the Executive the power to repel sudden attacks.

Mr. SHERMAN thought it stood very well. The Executive should be able to repel, and not to commence, war. "Make" is better than declare, the latter narrowing the power too much.

Mr. GERRY never expected to hear, in a republic, a motion to empower the Executive alone to declare war.

Mr. ELLSWORTH. There is a material difference between the cases of making *war* and making *peace*. It should be more easy to get out of war, than in to it. War also is a simple and overt declaration, peace attended with intricate and secret negotiations.

Mr. MASON was against giving the power of war to the Executive, because not safely to be trusted with it; or to the Senate, because not so constructed as to be entitled to it. He was for clogging, rather than facilitating war; but for facilitating peace. He preferred "*declare*" to "*make*."

On the motion to insert "*declare*" in place of "*make*" it was agreed to,—

Connecticut,* Pennsylvania, Delaware, Maryland, Virginia, North Carolina, South Carolina, Georgia, aye — 8; New Hampshire, no — 1; Massachusetts, absent.

Mr. PINCKNEY'S motion to strike out the whole clause, was disagreed to, without call of States.

Mr. BUTLER moved to give the Legislature the power of peace, as they were to have that of war.

Mr. GERRY seconds him. Eight Senators may possibly exercise the power, if vested in that body; and fourteen, if all should be present; and may consequently give up part of the United States. The Senate are more liable to be corrupted by an enemy, than the whole Legislature.

On the motion for adding " and peace," after " war,"— it was unanimously negatived.

Adjourned.

SATURDAY, AUGUST 18TH.

In Convention,— Mr. MADISON submitted, in order to be referred to the Committee on Detail, the following powers, as proper to be added to those of the General Legislature:

" To dispose of the unappropriated lands of the United States.

" To institute temporary governments for new States arising therein.

" To regulate affairs with the Indians, as well within as without the limits of the United States.

" To exercise exclusively legislative authority at the seat of the General Government, and over a district around the same not exceeding ———— square miles; the consent of the Legislature of the State or States, comprising the same, being first obtained.

" To grant charters of corporations in cases where the

---

* Connecticut voted in the negative; but on the remark by Mr. King, that " *make*" war might be understood to " conduct " it, which was an Executive function, Mr. Ellsworth gave up his objection, and the vote was changed to *aye*.

public good may require them, and the authority of a single
State may be incompetent.

"To secure to literary authors their copy-rights for a
limited time.

"To establish a university.

"To encourage by premiums and provisions the advancement of useful knowledge and discoveries.

"To authorize the Executive to procure, and hold for
the use of the United States, landed property for the erection of forts, magazines, and other necessary buildings."

These propositions were referred to the Committee of
Detail which had prepared the Report; and at the same
time the following, which were moved by Mr. PINCKNEY—
in both cases unanimously:

"To fix and permanently establish the seat of government of the United States, in which they shall possess the
exclusive right of soil and jurisdiction.

"To establish seminaries for the promotion of literature
and the arts and sciences.

"To grant charters of incorporation.

"To grant patents for useful inventions.

"To secure to authors exclusive rights for a certain
time.

"To establish public institutions, rewards, and immunities for the promotion of agriculture, commerce, trades,
and manufactures.

"That funds which shall be appropriated for the payment of public creditors, shall not during the time of such
appropriation, be diverted or applied to any other purpose,
and that the Committee prepare a clause or clauses for
restraining the Legislature of the United States from
establishing a perpetual revenue.

"To secure the payment of the public debt.

"To secure all creditors under the new Constitution
from a violation of the public faith when pledged by the
authority of the Legislature.

"To grant letters of marque and reprisal.

"To regulate stages on the post-roads."

Mr. MASON introduced the subject of regulating the militia. He thought such a power necessary to be given to the General Government. He hoped there would be no standing army in time of peace, unless it might be for a few garrisons. The militia ought, therefore, to be more effectually prepared for the public defence. Thirteen States will never concur in any one system, if the disciplining of the militia be left in their hands. If they will give up the power over the whole, they probably will over a part as a select militia. He moved, as an addition to the propositions just referred to the Committee of Detail, and to be referred in like manner, "a power to regulate the militia."

Mr. GERRY remarked, that some provision ought to be made in favor of public securities, and something inserted concerning letters of marque, which he thought not included in the power of war. He proposed that these subjects should also go to a Committee.

Mr. RUTLEDGE moved to refer a clause, "that funds appropriated to public creditors should not be diverted to other purposes."

Mr. MASON was much attached to the principle, but was afraid such a fetter might be dangerous in time of war. He suggested the necessity of preventing the danger of perpetual revenue, which must of necessity subvert the liberty of any country. If it be objected to on the principle of Mr. RUTLEDGE's motion, that public credit may require perpetual provisions, that case might be excepted; it being declared that in other cases no taxes should be laid for a longer term than ——— years. He considered the caution observed in Great Britain on this point, as the palladium of public liberty.

Mr. RUTLEDGE's motion was referred. He then moved that a Grand Committee be appointed to consider the necessity and expediency of the United States assuming all the State debts. A regular settlement between the Union and the several States would never take place. The assumption would be just, as the State debts were contracted in the common defence. It was necessary, as the taxes on imports, the only sure source of revenue, were to be given up to the Union. It was politic, as by disburthening the people of the State debts, it would conciliate them to the plan.

Mr. KING and Mr. PINCKNEY seconded the motion.

Col. MASON interposed a motion, that the Committee prepare a clause for restraining perpetual revenue, which was agreed to, *nem. con.*

MR. SHERMAN thought it would be better to authorize the Legislature to assume the State debts, than to say positively it should be done. He considered the measure as just, and that it would have a good effect to say something about the matter.

Mr. ELLSWORTH differed from Mr. SHERMAN. As far as the State debts ought in equity to be assumed, he conceived that they might and would be so.

Mr. PINCKNEY observed that a great part of the State debts were of such a nature that, although in point of policy and true equity they ought to be, yet would they not be, viewed in the light of Federal expenditures.

Mr. KING thought the matter of more consequence than Mr. ELLSWORTH seemed to do; and that it was well worthy of commitment. Besides the considerations of justice and policy which had been mentioned, it might be remarked, that the State creditors, an active and formidable party, would otherwise be opposed to a plan which transferred to the Union the best resources of the States, without transferring the State debts at the same time. The State creditors had generally been the strongest foes to the impost plan. The State debts probably were of greater amount, than the Federal. He would not say that it was practicable to consolidate the debts, but he thought it would be prudent to have the subject considered by a Committee.

On Mr. RUTLEDGE's motion, that a committee be appointed

to consider of the assumption, &c., it was agreed to,— Massachusetts, Connecticut, Virginia, North Carolina, South Carolina, Georgia, aye — 6; New Hampshire, New Jersey, Delaware, Maryland, no — 4; Pennsylvania, divided.

Mr. GERRY's motion to provide for public securities, for stages on post roads, and for letters of marque and reprisal, was committed, *nem. con.*

Mr. KING suggested that all unlocated lands of particular States ought to be given up if State debts were to be assumed. Mr. WILLIAMSON concurred in the idea.

A Grand Committee was appointed consisting of Mr. LANGDON, Mr. KING, Mr. SHERMAN, Mr. LIVINGSTON, Mr. CLYMER, Mr. DICKINSON, Mr. McHENRY, Mr. MASON, Mr. WILLIAMSON, Mr. C. C. PINCKNEY, and Mr. BALDWIN.

Mr. RUTLEDGE remarked on the length of the session, the probable impatience of the public, and the extreme anxiety of many members of the Convention to bring the business to an end; concluding with a motion that the Convention meet henceforward, precisely at ten o'clock, A. M.; and that, precisely at four o'clock, P. M., the President adjourn the House without motion for the purpose; and that no motion to adjourn sooner be allowed.

On this question — New Hampshire, Massachusetts, Connecticut, New Jersey, Delaware, Virginia, North Carolina, South Carolina, Georgia, aye — 9; Pennsylvania, Maryland, no — 2.

Mr. ELLSWORTH observed that a Council had not yet been provided for the President. He conceived there ought to be one. His proposition was, that it should be composed of the President of the Senate, the Chief Justice, and the Ministers as they might be established for the departments of foreign and domestic affairs, war, finance and marine; who should advise but not conclude the President.

Mr. PINCKNEY wished the proposition to lie over, as notice had been given for a like purpose by Mr. GOUVERNEUR MORRIS, who was not then on the floor. His own idea was, that the President should be authorized to call for advice, or not, as he might choose. Give him an able Council, and it will thwart him; a weak one, and he will shelter himself under their sanction.

Mr. GERRY was against letting the heads of the Departments, particularly of finance, have any thing to do in business connected with legislation. He mentioned the Chief Justice also, as particularly exceptionable. These men will also be so taken up with other matters, as to neglect their own proper duties.

Mr. DICKINSON urged that the great appointments should be made by the Legislature, in which case they might properly be consulted by the Executive, but not if made by the Executive himself.

This subject by general consent lay over; and the House proceeded to the clause, " to raise armies."

Mr. GORHAM moved to add, " and support," after " raise." Agreed to, *nem. con.*; and then the clause was agreed to, *nem. con.*, as amended.

Mr. GERRY took notice that there was no check here against standing armies in time of peace. The existing Congress is so constructed that it cannot of itself maintain an army. This would not be the case under the new system. The people were jealous on this head, and great opposition to the plan would spring from such an omission. He suspected that preparations of force were now making against it. [He seemed to allude to the activity of the Governor of New York at this crisis in disciplining the militia of that State.] He thought an army dangerous in time of peace, and could never consent to a power to keep up an indefinite number. He proposed that there should not be kept up in time of peace more than ———— thousand troops. His idea was, that the blank should be filled with two or three thousand.

Instead of " to build and equip fleets," " to provide and maintain a Navy," was agreed to, *nem. con.*, as a more convenient definition of the power.

A clause, " to make rules for the government and regulation of the land and naval forces," was added from the existing Articles of Confederation.

Mr. L. MARTIN and Mr. GERRY now regularly moved, " provided that in time of peace the army shall not consist of more than ———— thousand men."

General PINCKNEY asked, whether no troops were ever to be raised until an attack should be made on us?

Mr. GERRY. If there be no restriction, a few States may establish a military government.

Mr. WILLIAMSON reminded him of Mr. MASON's motion for limiting the appropriation of revenue as the best guard in this case.

Mr. LANGDON saw no room for Mr. GERRY's distrust of the representatives of the people.

Mr. DAYTON. Preparations for war are generally made in time of peace; and a standing force of some sort may, for ought we know, become unavoidable. He should object to no restrictions consistent with these ideas.

The motion of Mr. MARTIN and Mr. GERRY was disagreed to, *nem. con.*

Mr. MASON moved, as an additional power, "to make laws for the regulation and discipline of the militia of the several States, reserving to the States the appointment of the officers." He considered uniformity as necessary in the regulation of the militia, throughout the Union.

General PINCKNEY mentioned a case, during the war, in which a dissimilarity in the militia of different States had produced the most serious mischiefs. Uniformity was essential. The States would never keep up a proper discipline of the militia.

Mr. ELLSWORTH was for going as far, in submitting the militia to the General Government, as might be necessary; but thought the motion of Mr. MASON went too far. He moved, "that the militia should have the same arms and exercise, and be under rules established by the General Goverment when in actual service of the United States; and when States neglect to provide regulations for militia, it should be regulated and established by the Legislature of the United States." The whole authority over the militia ought by no means to be taken away from the States, whose consequence would pine away to nothing after such a sacrifice of power. He thought the general authority could not sufficiently pervade the Union for such a purpose, nor could it accommodate itself to the local genius of the people. It must be vain to ask the States to give the militia out of their hands.

Mr. SHERMAN seconds the motion.

Mr. DICKINSON. We are come now to a most important matter — that of the sword. His opinion was, that the States never would, nor ought to, give up all authority over the militia. He proposed to restrain the general power to one-fourth part at a time, which by rotation would discipline the whole militia.

Mr. BUTLER urged the necessity of submitting the whole militia to the general authority, which had the care of the general defence.

Mr. MASON had suggested the idea of a select militia. He was led to think that would be, in fact, as much as the General Government could advantageously be charged with. He was afraid of creating insuperable objections to the plan. He withdrew his original motion, and moved a power to make laws for regulating and disciplining the militia, not exceeding one-tenth part in any one year, and reserving the appointment of officers to the States.

General PINCKNEY renewed Mr. MASON's original motion. For a part to be under the General and a part under the State Governments, would be an incurable evil. He saw no room for such distrust of the General Government.

Mr. LANGDON seconds General PINCKNEY's renewal. He saw no more reason to be afraid of the General Government, than of the State Governments. He was more apprehensive of the confusion of the different authorities on this subject, than of either.

Mr. MADISON thought the regulation of the militia

naturally appertaining to the authority charged with the public defence. It did not seem, in its nature, to be divisible between two distinct authorities. If the States would trust the General Government with a power over the public treasury, they would, from the same consideration of necessity, grant it the direction of the public force. Those who had a full view of the public situation, would, from a sense of the danger, guard against it. The States would not be separately impressed with the general situation, nor have the due confidence in the concurrent exertions of each other.

Mr. ELLSWORTH considered the idea of a select militia as impracticable ; and if it were not, it would be followed by ruinous declension of the great body of the militia. The States would never submit to the same militia laws. Three or four shillings as a penalty will enforce obedience better in New England, than forty lashes in some other places.

Mr. PINCKNEY thought the power such an one as could not be abused, and that the States would see the necessity of surrendering it. He had, however, but a scanty faith in militia. There must be also a real military force. This alone can effectually answer the purpose. The United States had been making an experiment without it, and we see the consequence in their rapid approaches toward anarchy.*

Mr. SHERMAN took notice that the States might want their militia for defence against invasions and insurrections, and for enforcing obedience to their laws. They will not give up this point. In giving up that of taxation, they retain a concurrent power of raising money for their own use.

Mr. GERRY thought this the last point remaining to be surrendered. If it be agreed to by the Convention, the plan will have as black a mark as was set on Cain. He had no such confidence in the General Government as some

---

* This had reference to the disorders, particularly, that had occurred in Massachusetts, which had called for the interposition of the Federal troops.

gentlemen possessed, and believed it would be found that the States have not.

Col. MASON thought. there was great weight in the remarks of Mr. SHERMAN, and moved an exception to his motion, " of such part of the militia as might be required by the States for their own use."

Mr. READ doubted the propriety of leaving the appointment of the militia officers to the States. In some States, they are elected by the Legislatures ; in others, by the people themselves. He thought at least an appointment by the State Executives ought to be insisted on.

On the question for committing to the Grand Committee last appointed, the latter motion of Col. MASON, and the original one revived by General PINCKNEY,—

New Hampshire, Massachusetts, Pennsylvania, Delaware, Virginia, North Carolina, South Carolina, Georgia, aye — 8 ; Connecticut, New Jersey, no — 2 ; Maryland, divided.

Adjourned.

MONDAY, AUGUST 20TH.

In Convention,— Mr. PINCKNEY submitted to the House, in order to be referred to the Committee of Detail, the following propositions:

" Each House shall be the judge of its own privileges, and shall have authority to punish by imprisonment every person violating the same, or who, in the place where the Legislature may be sitting and during the time of its session, shall threaten any of its members for any thing said or done in the House; or who shall assault any of them therefor; or who shall assault or arrest any witness or other person ordered to attend either of the Houses, in his way going or returning; or who shall rescue any person arrested by their order.

" Each branch of the Legislature, as well as the Supreme Executive, shall have authority to require the opinions of the Supreme Judicial Court upon important questions of law, and upon solemn occasions.

The privileges and benefit of the writ of Habeas Corpus shall be enjoyed in this Government, in the most expeditious and ample manner; and shall not be suspended by the Legislature, except upon the most urgent and pressing occasions, and for a limited time not exceeding —— months.

" The liberty of the press shall be inviolably preserved.

" No troops shall be kept up in time of peace, but by consent of the Legislature.

" The military shall always be subordinate to the civil power; and no grants of money shall be made by the Legislature for supporting military land forces, for more than one year at a time.

" No soldier shall be quartered in any house, in time of peace, without consent of the owner.

"No person holding the office of President of the United States, a Judge of their Supreme Court, Secretary for the department of Foreign affairs, of Finance, of Marine, of War, or of —— shall be capable of holding at the same time any other office of trust or emolument, under the United States, or an individual State.

" No religious test or qualification shall ever be annexed to any oath of office, under the authority of the United States.

" The United States shall be forever considered as one body corporate and politic in law, and entitled to all the rights, privileges and immunities, which to bodies corporate do or ought to appertain.

" The Legislature of the United States shall have the power of making the Great Seal, which shall be kept by the President of the United States, or in his absence by the President of the Senate, to be used by them as the occasion may require. It shall be called the Great Seal of the United States, and shall be affixed to all laws.

"All commissions and writs shall run in the name of the United States.

"The jurisdiction of the Supreme Court shall be extended to all controversies between the United States and an individual State; or the United States and the citizens of an individual State."

These propositions were referred to the Committee of Detail, without debate or consideration of them by the House.

Mr. GOUVERNEUR MORRIS, seconded by Mr. PINCKNEY, submitted the following propositions, which were, in like manner, referred to the Committee of Detail:

"To assist the President in conducting the public affairs, there shall be a Council of State composed of the following officers:

"1. The Chief Justice of the Supreme Court, who shall from time to time recommend such alterations of and additions to the laws of the United States, as may in his opinion be necessary to the due administration of justice; and such as may promote useful learning and inculcate sound morality throughout the Union. He shall be President of the Council, in the absence of the President.

"2. The Secretary of Domestic affairs, who shall be appointed by the President, and hold his office during pleasure. It shall be his duty to attend to matters of general police, the state of agriculture and manufactures, the opening of roads and navigations, and the facilitating communications through the United States; and he shall from time to time recommend such measures and establishments as may tend to promote those objects.

"3. The Secretary of Commerce and Finance, who shall also be appointed by the President during pleasure. It shall be his duty to superintend all matters relating to the public finances, to prepare and report plans of revenue and for the regulation of expenditures, and also to recommend such things as may, in his judgment, promote the commercial interests of the United States.

"4. The Secretary of Foreign Affairs, who shall also be appointed by the President during pleasure. It shall be his duty to correspond with all foreign ministers, prepare plans of treaties, and consider such as may be transmitted from abroad; and generally to attend to the interests of the United States in their connections with foreign powers.

"5. The Secretary of War, who shall also be appointed by the President during pleasure. It shall be his duty to superintend every thing relating to the War department, such as the raising and equipping of troops, the care of military stores, public fortifications, arsenals, and the like; also in time of war to prepare and recommend plans of offence and defence.

"6. The Secretary of the Marine, who shall also be appointed during pleasure. It shall be his duty to superintend every thing relating to the Marine department, the public ships, dock-yards, naval stores and arsenals; also in the time of war to prepare and recommend plans of offence and defence.

"The President shall also appoint a Secretary of State, to hold his office during pleasure; who shall be Secretary to the Council of State, and also public Secretary to the President. It shall be his duty to prepare all public dispatches from the President which he shall countersign. The President may from time to time submit any matter to the discussion of the Council of State, and he may require the written opinions of any one or more of the members. But he shall in all cases exercise his own judgment, and either conform to such opinions, or not, as he may think proper; and every officer above mentioned shall be responsible for his opinion, on the affairs relating to his particular department.

"Each of the officers above mentioned shall be liable to impeachment and removal from office, for neglect of duty, malversation or corruption."

Mr. GERRY moved, "that the Committee be instructed to report proper qualifications for the President, and a mode of trying the Supreme Judges in cases of impeachment."

The clause, "to call forth the aid of the militia, &c.,"

36

was postponed till report should be made as to the power over the militia, referred yesterday to the Grand Committee of eleven.

Mr. MASON moved to enable Congress "to enact sumptuary laws." No government can be maintained unless the manners be made consonant to it. Such a discretionary power may do good, and can do no harm. A proper regulation of exercises and of trade, may do a great deal; but it is best to have an express provision. It was objected to sumptuary laws, that they were contrary to nature. This was a vulgar error. The love of distinction, it is true, is natural; but the object of sumptuary laws is not to extinguish this principle, but to give it a proper direction,

Mr. ELLSWORTH. The best remedy is to enforce taxes and debts. As far as the regulation of eating and drinking can be reasonable it is provided for in the power of taxation.

Mr. GOUVERNEUR MORRIS argued that sumptuary laws tended to create a landed nobility, by fixing in the great landholders, and their posterity their present possessions.

Mr. GERRY. The law of necessity is the best sumptuary law.

On the motion of Mr. MASON as to " sumptuary laws,"—

Delaware, Maryland, Georgia, aye — 3; New Hampshire, Massachusetts, Connecticut, New Jersey, Pennsylvania, Virginia, North Carolina, South Carolina, no — 8.

On the clause, "and to make all laws necessary and proper for carrying into execution the foregoing powers and all other powers vested, by this Constitution, in the Government of the United States, or any department or officer thereof,"—

Mr. MADISON and Mr. PINCKNEY moved to insert, between "laws" and "necessary," "and establish all offices;" it appearing to them liable to cavil, that the latter was not included in the former.

Mr. GOUVERNEUR MORRIS, Mr. WILSON, Mr. RUTLEDGE,

and Mr. ELLSWORTH, urged that the amendment could not be necessary.

On the motion for inserting " and establish all offices,"—

Massachusetts, Maryland, aye — 2; New Hampshire, Connecticut, New Jersey, Pennsylvania, Delaware, Virginia, North Carolina, South Carolina, Georgia, no — 9.

The clause as reported was then agreed to, *nem. con.*

Article 7, Sect. 2, concerning treason, was then taken up.

Mr. MADISON thought the definition too narrow. It did not appear to go as far as the statute of Edward III. He did not see why more latitude might not be left to the Legislature. It would be as safe as in the hands of State Legislatures; and it was inconvenient to bar a discretion which experience might enlighten, and which might be applied to good purposes as well as be abused.

Mr. MASON was for pursuing the statute of Edward III.

Mr. GOUVERNEUR MORRIS was for giving to the Union an exclusive right to declare what should be treason. In case of a contest between the United States and a particular State, the people of the latter must, under the disjunctive terms of the clause, be traitors to one or other authority.

Mr. RANDOLPH thought the clause defective in adopting the words, " in adhering," only. The British statute adds, "giving them aid and comfort," which had a more extensive meaning.

Mr. ELLSWORTH considered the definition as the same in fact with that of the statute.

Mr. GOUVERNEUR MORRIS. "Adhering' does not go so far as "giving aid and comfort," or the latter words may be restrictive of " adhering." In either case the statute is not pursued.

Mr. WILSON held "giving aid and comfort" to be explanatory, not operative words; and that it was better to omit them.

Mr. DICKINSON thought the addition of "giving aid and comfort" unnecessary and improper; being too vague and

extending too far. He wished to know what was meant by
the " testimony of two witnesses;" whether they were to be
witnesses to the same overt act, or to different overt acts.
He thought also, that proof of an overt act ought to be expressed as essential in the case.

Doctor JOHNSON considered "giving aid and comfort"
as explanatory of "adhering," and that something should
be inserted in the definition concerning overt acts. He
contended that treason could not be both against the United
States, and individual States; being an offense against the
sovereignty, which can be but one in the same community.

Mr. MADISON remarked that "and," before "in adhering," should be changed into "or;" otherwise both offences,
viz. of "levying war," and of "adhering to the enemy,"
might be necessary to constitute treason. He added, that,
as the definition here was of treason against *the United
States*, it would seem that the individual States would be
left in possession of a concurrent power, so far as to define
and punish treason particularly against themselves, which
might involve double punishment.

It was moved that the whole clause be recommitted,
which was lost, the votes being equally divided, —

New Jersey, Pennsylvania, Maryland, Virginia, Georgia, aye — 5; New Hampshire, Massachusetts, Connecticut,
Delaware, South Carolina, no — 5; North Carolina, divided.

Mr. WILSON and Doctor JOHNSON moved that " or any of
them," after "United States," be struck out, in order to remove the embarrassment; which was agreed to, *nem. con.*

Mr. MADISON. This has not removed the embarrassment. The same act might be treason against the United
States, as here defined; and against a particular State,
according to its laws.

Mr. ELLSWORTH. There can be no danger to the general
authority from this; as the laws of the United States are to
be apparent.

Doctor JOHNSON was still of opinion there could be no
treason against a particular State. It could not, even at

present, as the Confederation now stands; the sovereignty being in the Union; much less can it be under the proposed system.

Col. MASON. The United States will have a qualified sovereignty only. The individual States will retain a part of the sovereignty. An act may be treason against a particular State, which is not so against the United States. He cited the rebellion of Bacon in Virginia, as an illustration of the doctrine.

Doctor JOHNSON. That case would amount to treason against the sovereign, the supreme sovereign, the United States.

Mr. KING observed, that the controversy relating to treason, might be of less magnitude than was supposed; as the Legislature might punish capitally under other names than treason.

Mr. GOUVERNEUR MORRIS and Mr. RANDOLPH wished to substitute the words of the British statute, and moved to postpone Article 7, Section 2, in order to consider the following substitute: " Whereas it is essential to the preservation of liberty to define precisely and exclusively what shall constitute the crime of treason, it is therefore ordained, declared and established, that if a man do levy war against the United States, within their territories, or be adherent to the enemies of the United States within the said territories, giving them aid and comfort within their territories or elsewhere, and thereof be provably attainted of open deed, by the people of his condition, he shall be adjudged guilty of treason."

On this question, —

New Jersey, Virginia, aye, 2; Massachusetts, Connecticut, Pennsylvania, Delaware, Maryland, North Carolina, South Carolina, Georgia, no — 8.

It was then moved to strike out "against the United States" after "treason," so as to define treason generally; and on this question, —

Massachusetts, Connecticut, New Jersey, Pennsylvania,

Delaware, Maryland, South Carolina, Georgia, aye — 8; Virginia, North Carolina, no — 2.

It was then moved to insert, after "two witnesses," the words, "to the same overt act."

Doctor FRANKLIN wished this amendment to take place. Prosecutions for treason were generally virulent; and perjury too easily made use of against innocence.

Mr. WILSON. Much may be said on both sides. Treason may sometimes be practiced in such a manner as to render proof extremely difficult — as in a traitorous correspondence with an enemy.

On the question, as to "same overt act," — New Hampshire, Massachusetts, Connecticut, Pennsylvania, Delaware, Maryland, South Carolina, Georgia, aye — 8; New Jersey, Virginia, North Carolina, no — 3.

Mr. KING moved to insert, before the word "power," the word, "sole," giving the United States the exclusive right to declare the punishment of treason.

Mr. BROOM seconds the motion.

Mr. WILSON. In cases of a general nature, treason can only be against the United States ; and in such they should have the sole right to declare the punishment ; yet in many cases it may be otherwise. The subject was, however, intricate, and he distrusted his present judgment on it.

Mr. KING. This amendment results from the vote defining treason generally, by striking out, "against the United States," which excludes any treason against particular States. These may, however, punish offences, as high misdemeanours.

On the question for inserting the word "sole," it passed in the negative,— New Hampshire, Massachusetts, Pennsylvania, Delaware, South Carolina, aye — 5 ; Connecticut, New Jersey, Maryland, Virginia, North Carolina, Georgia, no — 6.

Mr. WILSON. The clause is ambiguous now. "Sole" ought either to have been inserted, or "against the United States," to be re-instated.

Mr. KING. No line can be drawn between levying war and adhering to the enemy against the United States, and against an individual State. Treason against the latter must be so against the former.

Mr. SHERMAN. Resistance against the laws of the United States, as distinguished from resistance against the laws of a particular State, forms the line.

Mr. ELLSWORTH. The United States are sovereign on one side of the line, dividing the jurisdictions — the States on the other. Each ought to have power to defend their respective sovereignties.

Mr. DICKINSON. War or insurrection against a member of the Union must be so against the whole body ; but the Constitution should be made clear on this point.

The clause was reconsidered, *nem. con. ;* and then Mr. WILSON and Mr. ELLSWORTH moved to reinstate, "against the United States," after "treason ;" on which question,— Connecticut, New Jersey, Maryland, Virginia, North Carolina, Georgia, aye — 6 ; New Hampshire, Massachusetts, Pennsylvania, Delaware, South Carolina, no — 5.

Mr. MADISON was not satisfied with the footing on which the clause now stood. As treason against the United States involves treason against particular States, and *vice-versa,* the same act may be twice tried, and punished by the different authorities.

Mr. GOUVERNEUR MORRIS viewed the matter in the same light.

It was moved and seconded to amend the sentence to read : "Treason against the United States shall consist only in levying war against them, or in adhering to their enemies ;" which was agreed to.

Col. MASON moved to insert the words, "giving them aid and comfort," as restrictive of "adhering to their enemies, &c." The latter, he thought, would be otherwise too indefinite. This motion was agreed to,— Connecticut, Delaware and Georgia only being in the negative.

Mr. L. MARTIN moved to insert after conviction, &c.,

"or on confession in open court;" and on the question (the negative States thinking the words superfluous,) it was agreed to,— New Hampshire, Connecticut, New Jersey, Pennsylvania, Delaware, Maryland, Virginia, aye — 7 ; Massachusetts, South Carolina, Georgia, no — 3 ; North Carolina, divided.

Article 7, Sect. 2, as amended, was then agreed to, *nem. con.*

Article 7, Sect. 3, was taken up. The words "white and others," were struck out, *nem. con.*, as superfluous.

Mr. ELLSWORTH moved to require the first census to be taken within "three," instead of "six," years, from the first meeting of the Legislature; and on the question,— New Hampshire, Massachusetts, Connecticut, New Jersey, Pennsylvania, Delaware, Maryland, Virginia, North Carolina, aye — 9; South Carolina, Georgia, no — 2.

Mr. KING asked, what was the precise meaning of *direct* taxation? No one answered.

Mr. GERRY moved to add to Article 7, Sect. 3, the following clause: "That from the first meeting of the Legislature of the United States until a census shall be taken, all moneys for supplying the public treasury by direct taxation shall be raised from the several States according to the number of their Representatives respectively in the first branch."

Mr. LANGDON. This would bear unreasonably hard on New Hampshire, and he must be against it.

Mr. CARROLL opposed it. The number of Representatives did not admit of a proportion exact enough for a rule of taxation.

Before any question, the House
Adjourned.

_____

TUESDAY, AUGUST 21ST.

In Convention,— Governor LIVINGSTON, from the Committee of eleven to whom was referred the propositions respecting the debts of the several States, and also the militia, entered on the eighteenth inst., delivered the following report:

"The Legislature of the United States shall have power to fulfil the engagements which have been entered into by Congress, and to discharge, as well the debts of the United States, as the debts incurred by the several States, during the late war, for the common defence and general welfare.

"To make laws for organizing, arming, and disciplining the militia, and for governing such part of them as may be employed in the service of the United States; reserving to the States, respectively, the appointment of the officers, and the authority of training the militia, according to the discipline prescribed by the United States."

Mr. GERRY considered giving the power only, without adopting the obligation, as destroying the security now enjoyed by the public creditors of the United States. He enlarged on the merit of this class of citizens, and the solemn faith which had been pledged under the existing Confederation. If their situation should be changed, as here proposed, great opposition would be excited against the plan. He urged, also, that as the States had made different degrees of exertion to sink their respective debts, those who had done most would be alarmed, if they were now to be saddled with a share of the debts of States which had done least.

Mr. SHERMAN. It means neither more nor less than the Confederation, as it relates to this subject.

Mr. ELLSWORTH moved that the Report delivered in by Governor LIVINGSTON should lie on the table; which was agreed to, *nem. con.*

Article 7, Section 3, was then resumed.

Mr. DICKINSON moved to postpone this, in order to reconsider Article 4, Section 4, and to *limit* the number of Representatives to be allowed to the large States. Unless this were done, the small States would be reduced to entire insignificance, and encouragement given to the importation of slaves.

Mr. SHERMAN would agree to such a re-consideration; but did not see the necessity of postponing the section before the House. Mr. DICKINSON withdrew his motion.

Article 7, Section 3, was then agreed to, — ten ayes; Delaware alone, no.

Mr. SHERMAN moved to add to Section 3, the following clause: "and all accounts of supplies furnished, services performed, and moneys advanced, by the several States to the United States, or by the United States to the several States, shall be adjusted by the same rule."

Mr. GOUVERNEUR MORRIS seconds the motion.

Mr. GORHAM thought it wrong to insert this in the Constitution. The Legislature will no doubt do what is right. The present Congress have such a power, and are now exercising it.

Mr. SHERMAN. Unless some rule be expressly given, none will exist under the new system.

Mr. ELLSWORTH. Though the contracts of Congress will be binding, there will be no rule for executing them on the States; and one ought to be provided.

Mr. SHERMAN withdrew his motion, to make way for one of Mr. WILLIAMSON, to add to Section 3, — "By this rule the several quotas of the States shall be determined, in settling the expenses of the late war."

Mr. CARROLL brought into view the difficulty that might arise on this subject, from the establishment of the Constitution as intended, without the *unanimous* consent of the States.

Mr. WILLIAMSON's motion was postponed, *nem. con.*

Article 6, Section 12, which had been postponed on the fifteenth of August, was now called for by Colonel MASON, who wished to know how the proposed amendment, as to money bills, would be decided, before he agreed to any further points.

Mr. GERRY's motion of yesterday, "that previous to a census direct taxation be proportioned on the States according to the number of Representatives," was taken up. He observed, that the principal acts of Government would probably take place within that period; and it was but reasonable that the States should pay in proportion to their share in them.

Mr. ELLSWORTH thought such a rule unjust. There was a great difference between the number of Representatives, and the number of inhabitants, as a rule in this case.

Even if the former were proportioned as nearly as possible to the latter, it would be a very inaccurate rule. A State might have one Representative only, that had inhabitants enough for one and a half, or more, if fractions could be applied, and so forth. He proposed to amend the motion by adding the words, "subject to a final liquidation by the foregoing rule, when a census shall have been taken."

Mr. MADISON. The last appointment of Congress, on which the number of Representatives was founded, was conjectural and meant only as a temporary rule, till a census should be established.

Mr. READ. The requisitions of Congress had been accommodated to the impoverishment produced by the war; and to other local and temporary circumstances.

Mr. WILLIAMSON opposed Mr. GERRY's motion.

Mr. LANGDON was not here when New Hampshire was allowed three members. It was more than her share; he did not wish for them.

Mr. BUTLER contended warmly for Mr. GERRY's motion, as founded in reason and equity.

Mr. ELLSWORTH's proviso to Mr. GERRY's motion was agreed to, *nem. con.*

Mr. KING thought the power of taxation given to the Legislature rendered the motion of Mr. GERRY altogether unnecessary.

On Mr. GERRY's motion, as amended,—

Massachusetts, South Carolina, aye —2; New Hampshire, Connecticut, New Jersey, Pennsylvania, Delaware, Maryland, Virginia, Georgia, no — 8; North Carolina, divided.

On a question, "Shall Article 6, Sect. 12, with the amendment to it, proposed and entered on the fifteenth inst., as called for by Colonel MASON, be now taken up?" it passed in the negative —

[New Hampshire, Connecticut, Virginia, Maryland, North Carolina, aye — 5; Massachusetts, New Jersey, Pennsylvania, Delaware, South Carolina, Georgia, no — 6.

Mr. L. MARTIN. The power of taxation is most likely to be criticised by the public. Direct taxation should not be used but in cases of absolute necessity; and then the States will be the best judges of the mode. He therefore moved the following addition to Article 7, Sect. 3: " and whenever the Legislature of the United States shall find it necessary that revenue should be raised by direct taxation, having apportioned the same according to the above rule on the several States, requisitions shall be made of the respective States to pay into the Continental Treasury their respective quotas, within a time in the said requisitions specified; and in case of any of the States failing to comply with such requisitions, then, and then only to devise and pass acts directing the mode, and authorizing the collection of the same."

Mr. McHENRY seconded the motion; there was no debate, and on the question, —

New Jersey, aye — 1; New Hampshire, Connecticut, Pennsylvania, Delaware, Virginia, North Carolina, South Carolina, Georgia, no — 8; Maryland, divided, (JENIFER and CARROLL, no.)

Article 7, Section 4, was then taken up.

Mr. LANGDON. By this section the States are left at liberty to tax exports. New Hampshire, therefore, with other non-exporting States, will be subject to be taxed by the States exporting its produce. This could not be admitted. It seems to be feared that the Northern States will oppress the trade of the Southern. This may be guarded against, by requiring the concurrence of two-thirds, or three fourths of the Legislature, in such cases.

Mr. ELLSWORTH. It is best as it stands. The power of regulating trade between the States will protect them against each other. Should this not be the case, the attempts of one to tax the produce of another, passing through its hands, will force a direct exportation and defeat themselves. There are solid reasons against Congress taxing exports. First, it will discourage industry, as taxes on imports discourage luxury. Secondly, the produce of different States is such as to prevent uniformity in such taxes. There are indeed but a few articles that could be taxed at all; as tobacco, rice, and indigo; and a tax on these alone would be partial and unjust. Thirdly, the taxing of exports would engender incurable jealousies.

Mr. WILLIAMSON. Though North Carolina has been taxed by Virginia by a duty on twelve thousand hogsheads of her tobacco through Virginia, yet he would never agree to this power. Should it take place, it would destroy the last hope of the adoption of the plan.

Mr. GOUVERNEUR MORRIS. These local considerations ought not to impede the general interest. There is great weight in the argument, that the exporting States will tax the produce of their uncommercial neighbours. The power of regulating the trade between Pennsylvania and New Jersey will never prevent the former from taxing the latter. Nor will such a tax force a direct exportation from New Jersey. The advantages possessed by a large trading city outweigh the disadvantage of a moderate duty; and will retain the trade in that channel. If no tax can be laid on exports, an embargo cannot be laid, though in time of war such a measure may be of critical importance. Tobacco, lumber and live stock, are three objects belonging to different States of which great advantage might be made by a power to tax exports. To these may be added ginseng and masts for ships, by which a tax might be thrown on other nations. The idea of supplying the West Indies with lumber from Nova Scotia, is one of the many follies of Lord Sheffield's pamphlet. The state of the country, also, will change, and render duties on exports, as skins, beaver and other peculiar raw materials, politic in the view of encouraging American manufactures.

Mr. BUTLER was strenuously opposed to a power over exports, as unjust and alarming to the staple States.

Mr. LANGDON suggested a prohibition on the States from taxing the produce of other States exported from their harbours.

Mr. DICKINSON. The power of taxing exports may be inconvenient at present; but it must be of dangerous consequence to prohibit it with respect to all articles, and for ever. He thought it would be better to except particular articles from the power.

Mr. SHERMAN. It is best to prohibit the National Legislature in all cases. The States will never give up all power over trade. An enumeration of particular articles would be difficult, invidious, and improper.

Mr. MADISON. As we ought to be governed by national and permanent views, it is a sufficient argument for giving the power over exports, that a tax, though it may not be expedient at present, may be so hereafter. A proper regulation of exports may, and probably will, be necessary hereafter and for the same purposes as the regulation of imports, viz., for revenue, domestic manufactures, and procuring equitable regulations from other nations. An embargo may be of absolute necessity, and can be alone effectuated by the general authority. The regulation of trade between State and State cannot effect more than indirectly to hinder a State from taxing its own exports, by authorizing its citizens to carry their commodities freely into a neighbouring State, which might decline taxing exports, in order to draw into its channel the trade of its neighbours. As to the fear of disproportionate burthens on the non-exporting States, it might be remarked that it was agreed, on all hands, that the revenue would principally be drawn from trade, and as only a given revenue would be needed, it was not material whether all should be drawn wholly from imports, or half from those and half from exports. The imports and exports must be pretty nearly equal in every State, and, relatively, the same among the different States.

Mr. ELLSWORTH did not conceive an embargo by the Congress interdicted by this section.

Mr. McHENRY conceived that power to be included in the power of war.

Mr. WILSON. Pennsylvania exports the produce of Maryland, New Jersey, Delaware, and will by and by, when the river Delaware is opened, export for New York. In favoring the general power over exports, therefore, he opposed the particular interest of his State. He remarked that the power had been attacked by reasoning which could only have held good, in case the General Government had been *compelled*, instead of *authorized*, to lay duties on exports. To deny this power is to take from the common Government half the regulation of trade. It was his opinion, that a power over exports might be more effectual, than that over imports, in obtaining beneficial treaties of commerce.

Mr. GERRY was strenuously opposed to the power over exports. It might be made use of to compel the States to comply with the will of the General Government, and to grant it any new powers which might be demanded. We have given it more power already than we know how will be exercised. It will enable the General Government to oppress the States, as much as Ireland is oppressed by Great Britain.

Mr. FITZSIMONS would be against a tax on exports to be laid immediately; but was for giving a power of laying the tax when a proper time may call for it. This would certainly be the case when America should become a manufacturing country. He illustrated his argument by the duties in Great Britain on wool, &c.

Col. MASON. If he were for reducing the States to mere corporations, as seemed to be the tendency of some arguments, he should be for subjecting their exports as well as imports to a power of general taxation. He went on a principle often advanced and in which he concurred, that a majority, when interested, will oppress the minority. This maxim had been verified by our own Legislature [of Virginia]. If we compare the States in this point of view, the eight Northern States have an interest different from the five Southern States; and have, in one branch of the Legislature, thirty-six votes, against twenty-nine, and in the other in the proportion of eight against five. The Southern States had therefore ground for their suspicions. The case of exports was not the same with that of imports. The latter were the same throughout the States; the former very different. As to tobacco, other nations do raise it, and are capable of raising it, as well as Virginia, &c. The impolicy of taxing that article had been demonstrated by the experiment of Virginia.

Mr. CLYMER remarked, that every State might reason with regard to its particular productions in the same manner as the Southern States. The Middle States may apprehend an oppression of their wheat, flour, provisions, &c.; and with more reason, as these articles were exposed to a competition in foreign markets not incident to tobacco, rice, &c. They may apprehend also combinations against them, between the Eastern and Southern States, as much as the latter can apprehend them between the Eastern and middle. He moved, as a qualification of the power of taxing exports, that it should be restrained to regulations of trade, by inserting, after the word "duty," Article 7, Section 4, the words, "for the purpose of revenue."

On the question on Mr. CLYMER's motion,—

New Jersey, Pennsylvania, Delaware, aye — 3 ; New Hampshire, Massachusetts, Connecticut, Maryland, Virginia, North Carolina, South Carolina, Georgia, no — 8.

Mr. MADISON, in order to require two-thirds of each House to tax exports, as a lesser evil than a total prohibition, moved to insert the words, "unless by consent of two-thirds of the Legislature."

Mr. WILSON seconds; and on this question it passed in the negative,—

New Hampshire, Massachusetts, New Jersey, Pennsylvania, Delaware, aye — 5; Connecticut, Maryland, Virginia, (Colonel MASON, Mr. RANDOLPH, Mr. BLAIR, no; General WASHINGTON, Mr. MADISON, aye,) North Carolina, South Carolina, Georgia, no — 6.

On the question on Article 7, Section 4, as far as to " no tax shall be laid on exports," it passed in the affirmative,—

Massachusetts, Connecticut, Maryland, Virginia, (General WASHINGTON and Mr. MADISON, no,) North Carolina, South Carolina, Georgia, aye — 7; New Hampshire, New Jersey, Pennsylvania, Delaware, no — 4.

Mr. L. MARTIN proposed to vary Article 7, Section 4, so as to allow a prohibition or tax on the importation of slaves. In the first place, as five slaves are to be counted as three freemen, in the apportionment of Representatives, such a clause would leave an encouragement to this traffic. In the second place, slaves weakened one part of the Union, which the other parts were bound to protect; the privilege of importing them was therefore unreasonable. And in the third place, it was inconsistent with the principles of the Revolution, and dishonourable to the American character, to have such a feature in the Constitution.

Mr. RUTLEDGE did not see how the importation of slaves could be encouraged by this section. He was not apprehensive of insurrections, and would readily exempt the other States from the obligation to protect the Southern against them. Religion and humanity had nothing to do with this question. Interest alone is the governing principle with nations. The true question at present is, whether the Southern States shall or shall not be parties to the Union. If the Northern States consult their interest, they will not oppose the increase of slaves, which will increase the commodities of which they will become the carriers.

Mr. ELLSWORTH was for leaving the clause as it stands.

37

Let every State import what it pleases. The morality or wisdom of slavery are considerations belonging to the States themselves. What enriches a part enriches the whole, and the States are the best judges of their particular interest. The old Confederation had not meddled with this point; and he did not see any greater necessity for bringing it within the policy of the new one.

Mr. PINCKNEY. South Carolina can never receive the plan if it prohibits the slave-trade. In every proposed extension of the powers of Congress, that State has expressly and watchfully excepted that of meddling with the importation of negroes. If the States be all left at liberty on this subject, South Carolina may perhaps, by degrees, do of herself what is wished, as Virginia and Maryland already have done.

Adjourned.

WEDNESDAY, AUGUST 22d.

In Convention.—Article 7, Section 4, was resumed.

Mr. SHERMAN was for leaving the clause as it stands. He disapproved of the slave trade; yet as the States were now possessed of the right to import slaves, as the public good did not require it to be taken from them, and as it was expedient to have as few objections as possible to the proposed scheme of government, he thought it best to leave the matter as we find it. He observed that the abolition of slavery seemed to be going on in the United States, and that the good sense of the several States would probably by degrees complete it. He urged on the Convention the necessity of despatching its business.

Col. MASON. This infernal traffic originated in the avarice of British merchants. The British Government constantly checked the attempts of Virginia to put a stop to it. The present question concerns not the importing States alone, but the whole Union. The evil of having slaves was experienced during the late war. Had slaves

been treated as they might have been by the enemy, they
would have proved dangerous instruments in their hands.
But their folly dealt by the slaves as it did by the tories.
He mentioned the dangerous insurrections of the slaves in
Greece and Sicily ; and the instructions given by Cromwell
to the commissioners sent to Virginia, to arm the servants
and slaves, in case other means of obtaining its submission
should fail.   Maryland and Virginia he said had already
prohibited the importation of slaves expressly.   North Carolina had done the same in substance.   All this would be
in vain, if South Carolina and Georgia be at liberty to
import.   The Western people are already calling out for
slaves for their new lands ; and will fill that country with
slaves, if they can be got through South Carolina and
Georgia.   Slavery discourages arts and manufactures.
The poor despise labor when performed by slaves.
They prevent the emigration of whites, who really
enrich and strengthen a country.   They produce the most
pernicious effect on manners.   Every master of slaves is
born a petty tyrant.   They bring the judgment of Heaven
on a country.   As nations cannot be rewarded or punished
in the next world, they must be in this.   By an inevitable
chain of causes and effects, Providence punishes national
sins by national calamities.   He lamented that some of our
Eastern brethren had, from a lust of gain, embarked in this
nefarious traffic.   As to the States being in possession of
the right to import, this was the case with many other
rights, now to be properly given up.   He held it essential
in every point of view, that the General Government should
have power to prevent the increase of slavery.

Mr. ELLSWORTH, as he had never owned a slave, could
not judge of the effects of slavery on character.   He said,
however, that if it was to be considered in a moral light,
we ought to go further and free those already in the country.   As slaves also multiply so fast in Virginia and Maryland that it is cheaper to raise than import them, whilst in
the sickly rice swamps foreign supplies are necessary, if we

go no further than is urged, we shall be unjust towards South Carolina and Georgia. Let us not intermeddle. As population increases, poor laborers will be so plenty as to render slaves useless. Slavery, in time, will not be a speck in our country. Provision is already made in Connecticut for abolishing it. And the abolition has already taken place in Massachusetts. As to the danger of insurrections from foreign influence, that will become a motive to kind treatment of the slaves.

Mr. PINCKNEY. If slavery be wrong, it is justified by the example of all the world. He cited the case of Greece, Rome and other ancient States, the sanction given by France, England, Holland and other modern states. In all ages one half of mankind have been slaves. If the Southern States were let alone, they will probably of themselves stop importations. He would himself, as a citizen of South Carolina, vote for it. An attempt to take away the right, as proposed, will produce serious objections to the Constitution, which he wished to see adopted.

General PINCKNEY declared it to be his firm opinion that if himself and all his colleagues were to sign the Constitution and use their personal influence, it would be of no avail towards obtaining the assent of their constituents. South Carolina and Georgia cannot do without slaves. As to Virginia, she will gain by stopping the importations. Her slaves will rise in value, and she has more than she wants. It would be unequal, to require South Carolina and Georgia to confederate on such unequal terms. He said the Royal assent, before the Revolution, had never been refused to South Carolina, as to Virginia. He contended that the importation of slaves would be for the interest of the whole Union. The more slaves the more produce to employ the carrying trade; the more consumption also; and the more of this, the more revenue for the common treasury. He admitted it to be reasonable that slaves should be dutied like other imports, but should consider a rejection of the clause as an exclusion of South Carolina from the Union.

Mr. BALDWIN had conceived national objects alone to be before the Convention ; not such as, like the present, were of a local nature. Georgia was decided on this point. That State has always hitherto supposed a General Government to be the pursuit of the central states, who wished to have a vortex for every thing ; that her distance would preclude her, from equal advantage ; and that she could not prudently purchase it by yielding national powers. From this it might be understood, in what light she would view an attempt to abridge one of her favorite prerogatives. If left to herself, she may probably put a stop to the evil. As one ground for this conjecture, he took notice of the sect of ———— ; which he said was a respectable class of people, who carried their ethics beyond the mere *equality of men*, extending their humanity to the claims of the whole animal creation.

Mr. WILSON observed that if South Carolina and Georgia were themselves disposed to get rid of the importation of slaves in a short time, as had been suggested, they would never refuse to unite because the importation might be prohibited. As the section now stands, all articles imported are to be taxed. Slaves alone are exempt. This is in fact a bounty on that article.

Mr. GERRY thought we had nothing to do with the conduct of the States as to slaves, but ought to be careful not to give any sanction to it.

Mr. DICKINSON considered it as inadmissible, on every principle of honor and safety, that the importation of slaves should be authorized to the States by the Constitution. The true question was, whether the national happiness would be promoted or impeded by the importation ; and this question ought to be left to the National Government, not to the States particularly interested. If England and France permit slavery, slaves are, at the same time, excluded from both those kingdoms. Greece and Rome were made unhappy by their slaves. He could not believe that the Southern States would refuse to confederate on the account apprehended ; especially as the power was not likely to be immediately exercised by the General Government.

Mr. WILLIAMSON stated the law of North Carolina on the subject, to-wit, that it did not directly prohibit the importation of slaves. It imposed a duty of £5 on each slave imported from Africa ; £10 on each from elsewhere ; and £50 on each from a State licensing manumission. He thought the Southern States could not be members of the Union, if the clause should be rejected ; and that it was wrong to force any thing down not absolutely necessary, and which any State must disagree to.

Mr. KING thought the subject should be considered in a political light only. If two States will not agree to the Constitution, as stated on one side, he could affirm with equal belief, on the other, that great and equal opposition would be experienced from the other States. He remarked on the exemption of slaves from duty, whilst every other import was subjected to it, as an inequality that could not fail to strike the commercial sagacity of the Northern and Middle States.

Mr. LANGDON was strenuous for giving the power to the General Government. He could not, with a good conscience, leave it with the States, who could then go on with the traffic, without being restrained by the opinions here given, that they will themselves cease to import slaves.

General PINCKNEY thought himself bound to declare candidly, that he did not think South Carolina would stop her importations of slaves, in any short time; but only stop them occasionally as she now does. He moved to commit the clause, that slaves might be made liable to an equal tax with other imports; which he thought right, and which would remove one difficulty that had been started.

Mr. RUTLEDGE. If the Convention thinks that North Carolina, South Carolina, and Georgia, will ever agree to the plan, unless their right to import slaves be untouched, the expectation is vain. The people of those States will never be such fools, as to give up so important an interest. He was strenuous against striking out the section, and seconded the motion of General PINCKNEY for a commitment.

Mr. GOUVERNEUR MORRIS wished the whole subject to be committed, including the clauses relating to taxes on exports and to a navigation act. These things may form a bargain among the Northern and Southern States.

Mr. BUTLER declared that he never would agree to the power taxing exports.

Mr. SHERMAN said it was better to let the Southern States import slaves, than to part with them, if they made that a *sine qua non*. He was opposed to a tax on slaves imported, as making the matter worse, because it implied they were *property*. He acknowledged that if the power of prohibiting the importation should be given to the General Government, that it would be exercised. He thought it would be its duty to exercise the power.

Mr. READ was for the commitment, provided the clause concerning taxes on exports should also be committed.

Mr. SHERMAN observed that that clause had been agreed to, and therefore could not be committed.

Mr. RANDOLPH was for committing, in order that some middle ground might, if possible, be found. He could never agree to the clause as it stands. He would sooner risk the Constitution. He dwelt on the dilemma to which the Convention was exposed. By agreeing to the clause, it would revolt the Quakers, the Methodists, and many others in States having no slaves. On the other hand, two States might be lost to the Union. Let us then, he said, try the chance of a commitment.

On the question for committing the remaining part of Sections 4 and 5, of Article 7,— Connecticut, New Jersey, Maryland, Virginia, North Carolina, South Carolina, Georgia, aye — 7; New Hampshire, Pennsylvania, Delaware, no — 3; Massachusetts absent.

Mr. PINCKNEY and Mr. LANGDON moved to commit Section 6, as to a navigation act by two thirds of each House.

Mr. GORHAM did not see the propriety of it. Is it meant to require a greater proportion of votes? He desired it to be remembered, that the Eastern States had no motive to union but a commercial one. They were able to protect themselves. They were not afraid of external danger, and did not need the aid of the Southern States.

Mr. WILSON wished for a commitment, in order to reduce the proportion of votes required.

Mr. ELLSWORTH was for taking the plan as it is. This widening of opinions had a threatening aspect. If we do not agree on this middle and moderate ground, he was afraid we should lose two States, with such others as may be disposed to stand aloof; should fly into a variety of shapes and directions, and most probably into several confederations,— and not without bloodshed.

On the question for committing Section 6, as to a navigation act, to a member from each State,— New Hampshire, Massachusetts, Pennsylvania, Delaware, Maryland, Virginia, North Carolina, South Carolina, Georgia, aye — 9; Connecticut, New Jersey, no — 2.

The committee appointed were, Messrs. LANGDON, KING, JOHNSON, LIVINGSTON, CLYMER, DICKINSON, L. MARTIN, MADISON, WILLIAMSON, C. C. PINCKNEY, and BALDWIN.

To this Committee were referred also the two clauses above mentioned of the fourth and fifth Sections of Article 7.

Mr. RUTLEDGE from the Committee to whom were referred, on the eighteenth and twentieth instant, the propositions of Mr. MADISON and Mr. PINCKNEY, made the report following:

"The Committee report, that, in their opinion, the following additions should be made to the report now before the Convention, namely:

"At the end of the first clause of the first section of the seventh article, add, 'for payment of the debts and necessary expenses of the United States ; provided, that no law of raising any branch of revenue, except what may be specially appropriated for the payment of interest on debts or loans, shall continue in force for more than —————— years.'

"At the end of the second clause, second section, seventh article, add, ' and with Indians, within the limits of any State, not subject to the laws thereof.'

"At the end of the sixteenth clause, of the second section, seventh article, add, ' and to provide, as may become necessary, from time to time, for the well managing and securing the common property and general interests and welfare of the United States in such manner as shall not interfere with the government of individual States, in matters which respect only their internal police, or for which their individual authority may be competent.'

"At the end of the first section, tenth article, add, ' he shall be of the age of thirty-five years, and a citizen of the United States, and shall have been an inhabitant thereof for twenty-one years.'

"After the second section, of the tenth article, insert the following as a third section : ' The President of the United States shall have a Privy Council, which shall consist of the President of the Senate, the Speaker of the House of Representatives, the Chief Justice of the Supreme Court, and the principal officer in the respective departments of foreign affairs, domestic affairs, war, marine, and finance, as such departments of office shall from time to time be established ; whose duty it shall be, to advise him in matters respecting the execution of his office, which he shall think proper to lay before them : but their advice shall not conclude him, nor affect his responsibility for the measures which he shall adopt.'

"At the end of the second section of the eleventh article, add, ' the Judges of the Supreme Court shall be triable by the Senate, on impeachment by the House of Representatives '

"Between the fourth and fifth lines of the third section

of the eleventh article, after the word 'controversies' insert, "between the United States and an individual State, or the United States and an individual person.'"

A motion to rescind the order of the House, respecting the hours of meeting and adjourning, was negatived,— Massachusetts, Pennsylvania, Delaware, Maryland, aye — 4; New Hampshire, Connecticut, New Jersey, Virginia, North Carolina, South Carolina, Georgia, no — 7.

Mr. GERRY and Mr. McHENRY moved to insert, after the second Section, Article 7, the clause following, to wit:

"The Legislature shall pass no bill of attainder, nor any *ex post facto* law. " *

Mr. GERRY urged the necessity of this prohibition, which he said was greater in the National than the State Legislature; because the number of members in the former being fewer, they were on that account the more to be feared.

Mr. GOUVERNEUR MORRIS thought the precaution as to *ex post facto* laws unnecessary; but essential as to bills of attainder.

Mr. ELLSWORTH contended that there was no lawyer, no civilian, who would not say, that *ex post facto* laws were void of themselves. It cannot, then, be necessary to prohibit them.

Mr. WILSON was against inserting any thing in the Constitution, as to *ex post facto* laws. It will bring reflections on the Constitution, and proclaim that we are ignorant of the first principles of legislation, or are constituting a government that will be so.

The question being divided, the first part of the motion relating to bills of attainder was agreed to, *nem. con.*

On the second part relating to *ex post facto* laws, —

Mr. CARROLL remarked, that experience overruled all other calculations. It had proved that, in whatever light

---

* The proceedings on this motion, involving the two questions on attainders and ex post facto laws, are not so fully stated in the printed Journal.

they might be viewed by civilians or others, the State Legislatures had passed them, and they had taken effect.

Mr. WILSON. If these prohibitions in the State Constitutions have no effect, it will be useless to insert them in this Constitution. Besides, both sides will agree to the principle, but will differ as to its application,

Mr. WILLIAMSON. Such a prohibitory clause is in the Constitution of North Carolina; and though it had been violated, it has done good there, and may do good here, because the Judges can take hold of it.

Doctor JOHNSON thought the clause unnecessary, and implying an improper suspicion of the National Legislature.

Mr. RUTLEDGE was in favor of the clause.

On the question for inserting the prohibition of *ex post facto* laws,—

New Hampshire, Massachusetts, Delaware, Maryland, Virginia, South Carolina, Georgia, aye — 7; Connecticut, New Jersey, Pennsylvania, no — 3; North Carolina, divided.

The Report of the Committee of five made by Mr. RUTLEDGE, was taken up, and then postponed, that each member might furnish himself with a copy.

The Report of the Committee of eleven, delivered in and entered on the Journal of the twenty-first instant, was then taken up; and the first clause, containing the words, "The Legislature of the United States *shall have power* to fulfil the engagements which have been entered into bv Congress," being under consideration,—

Mr. ELLSWORTH argued that they were unnecessary. The United States heretofore entered into engagements by Congress, who were their agents. They will hereafter be bound to fulfil them by their new agents.

Mr. RANDOLPH thought such a provision necessary; for though the United States will be bound, the new Government will have no authority in the case, unless it be given to them.

Mr. MADISON thought it necessary to give the authority,

in order to prevent misconstruction. He mentioned the
attempt made by the debtors to British subjects, to show
that contracts under the old Government were dissolved by
the Revolution, which destroyed the political identity of
the society.

Mr. GERRY thought it essential that some explicit provision should be made on this subject; so that no pretext
might remain for getting rid of the public engagements.

Mr. GOUVERNEUR MORRIS moved, by way of amendment,
to substitute, " The Legislature *shall* discharge the debts,
and fulfil the engagements of the United States."

It was moved to vary the amendment, by striking out
"discharge the debts," and to insert "liquidate the
claims;" which being negatived, the amendment moved by
Mr. GOUVERNEUR MORRIS was agreed to,— all the States
being in the affirmative.

It was moved and seconded, to strike the following
words out of the second clause of the Report: "and the
authority of training the militia according to the discipline
prescribed by the United States." Before a question was
taken, the House

Adjourned.

THURSDAY, AUGUST 23D.

In Convention.— The Report of the Committee of
eleven, made the twenty-first of August, being taken up,
and the following clause being under consideration, to wit:

"To make laws for organizing, arming and disciplining
the militia, and for governing such parts of them as may be
employed in the service of the United States; reserving to
the States, respectively, the appointment of the officers, and
authority of training the militia according to the discipline
prescribed,"—

Mr. SHERMAN moved to strike out the last member
"and authority of training," &c. He thought it unnecessary. The States will have this authority of course, if not
given up.

Mr. ELLSWORTH doubted the propriety of striking out the sentence. The reason assigned applies as well to the other reservation of the appointment to offices. He remarked at the same time, that the term discipline was of vast extent, and might be so expounded as to include all power on the subject.

Mr. KING, by way of explanation, said that by *organizing*, the Committee meant, proportioning the officers and men — by *arming*, specifying the kind, size and calibre of arms — and by *disciplining*, prescribing the manual exercise, evolutions, &c.

Mr. SHERMAN withdrew his motion.

Mr. GERRY. This power in the United States, as explained, is making the States drill-sergeants. He had as lief let the citizens of Massachusetts be disarmed, as to take the command from the States, and subject them to the General Legislature. It would be regarded as a system of despotism.

Mr. MADISON observed, that "*arming*," as explained, did not extend to furnishing arms; nor the term "*disciplining*," to penalties, and courts martial for enforcing them.

Mr. KING added to his former explanation, that *arming* meant not only to provide for uniformity of arms, but included the authority to regulate the modes of furnishing, either by the militia themselves, the State Governments, or the National Treasury; that *laws* for disciplining must involve penalties, and every thing necessary for enforcing penalties.

Mr. DAYTON moved to postpone the paragraph, in order to take up the following proposition: "To establish an uniform and general system of discipline for the militia of these States, and to make laws for organizing, arming, disciplining and governing *such part of them as may be employed in the service of the United States;* reserving to the States, respectively, the appointment of the officers, and all authority over the militia not herein given to the General Government."

On the question to postpone, in favour of this proposition, it passed in the negative, — New Jersey, Maryland, Georgia, aye—3; New Hampshire, Massachusetts, Connecticut, Pennsylvania, Delaware, Virginia, North Carolina, South Carolina, no —8.

Mr. ELLSWORTH and Mr. SHERMAN moved to postpone the second clause, in favour of the following: "To establish an uniformity of arms, exercise and organization for the militia, and to provide for the government of them when called into the service of the United States."

The object of this proposition was to refer the plan for the militia to the General Government, but to leave the execution of it to the State Governments.

Mr. LANGDON said he could not understand the jealousy expressed by some gentlemen. The General and State Governments were not enemies to each other, but different institutions for the good of the people of America. As one of the people, he could say, the National Government is mine, the State Government is mine. In transferring power from one to the other, I only take out of my left hand what it cannot so well use, and put it into my right hand where it can be better used.

Mr. GERRY thought it was rather taking out of the right hand, and putting it into the left. Will any man say that liberty will be as safe in the hands of eighty or an hundred men taken from the whole continent, as in the hands of two or three hundred taken from a single State?

Mr. DAYTON was against so absolute a uniformity. In some States there ought to be a greater proportion of cavalry than in others. In some places rifles would be most proper, in others muskets, &c.

General PINCKNEY preferred the clause reported by the Committee, extending the meaning of it to the case of fines, &c.

Mr. MADISON. The primary object is to secure an effectual discipline of the militia. This will no more be done, if left to the States separately, than the requisitions have been hitherto paid by them. The States neglect their militia now, and the more they are consolidated into one nation, the less each will rely on its own interior provisions for its safety, and the less prepare its militia for that purpose; in like manner as the militia of a State would have been still more neglected than it has been, if each county had been independently charged with the care of its militia. The discipline of the militia is evidently a *national* concern, and ought to be provided for in the *national* Constitution.

Mr. L. MARTIN was confident that the States would never give up the power over the militia; and that, if they were to do so, the militia would be less attended to by the General than by the State Governments.

Mr. RANDOLPH asked, what danger there could be, that the militia could be brought into the field, and made to commit suicide on themselves. This is a power that cannot, from its nature, be abused; unless, indeed, the whole mass should be corrupted. He was for trammelling the General Government whenever there was danger, but here there could be none. He urged this as an essential point; observing that the militia were every where neglected by the State Legislatures, the members of which courted popularity too much to enforce a proper discipline. Leaving the appointment of officers to the States protects the people against every apprehension that could produce murmur.

On the question on Mr. ELLSWORTH's motion,— Connecticut, aye; the other ten States, no.

A motion was then made to recommit the second clause; which was negatived.

On the question to agree to the first part of the clause, namely, "To make laws for organizing, arming and disciplining the militia, and for governing such part of them as may be employed in the service of the United States,"—

New Hampshire, Massachusetts, New Jersey, Pennsylvania, Delaware, Virginia, North Carolina, South Carolina, Georgia, aye — 9; Connecticut, Maryland, no — 2.

Mr. MADISON moved to amend the next part of the clause so as to read, "reserving to the States, respectively, the appointment of the officers, *under the rank of general officers.*"

Mr. SHERMAN considered this as absolutely inadmissible. He said that if the people should be so far asleep as to allow the most influential officers of the militia to be appointed by the General Government, every man of discernment would rouse them by sounding the alarm to them.

Mr. GERRY. Let us at once destroy the State Governments, have an Executive for life or hereditary, and a proper Senate; and then there would be some consistency in giving full powers to the General Government: but as the States, are not to be abolished, he wondered at the attempts that were made to give powers inconsistent with their existence. He warned the Convention against pushing the experiment too far. Some people will support a plan of vigorous government at every risk. Others, of a more democratic cast, will oppose it with equal determination; and a civil war may be produced by the conflict.

Mr. MADISON. As the greatest danger is that of disunion of the States, it is necessary to guard against it by sufficient powers to the common government; and as the greatest danger to liberty is from large standing armies, it is best to prevent them by an effectual provision for a good militia.

On the question to agree to Mr. MADISON's motion, — New Hampshire, South Carolina, Georgia,* aye — 3; Massachusetts, Connecticut, New Jersey, Pennsylvania, Delaware, Maryland, Virginia, North Carolina, no — 8.

On the question to agree to the "reserving to the States the appointment of the officers" — it was agreed to *nem. con.*

On the question on the clause, " and the authority of

---

* In the printed Journal, Georgia, no.

training the militia according to the discipline prescribed by the United States," —

New Hampshire, Massachusetts, Connecticut, New Jersey, Pennsylvania, Maryland, North Carolina, aye — 7; Delaware Virginia, South Carolina, Georgia, no — 4.

On the question to agree to Article 7, Section 7, as reported, it passed, *nem. con.*

Mr. PINCKNEY urged the necessity of preserving foreign ministers, and other officers of the United States, independent of external influence; and moved to insert after Article 7, Section 7, the clause following: "No person holding any office of trust or profit under the United States shall, without the consent of the Legislature, accept of any present, emolument, office or title of any kind whatever, from any king, prince or foreign State;" which passed, *nem. con.*

Mr. RUTLEDGE moved to amend Article 8; to read as follows : "This Constitution, and the laws of the United States made in pursuance thereof, and all the treaties made under the authority of the United States, shall be the supreme law of the several States and of their citizens and inhabitants; and the Judges of the several States shall be bound thereby in their decisions, any thing in the Constitutions or laws of the several States to the contrary notwithstanding;" which was agreed to, *nem. con.*

Article 9, being next for consideration,—

Mr. GOUVERNEUR MORRIS argued against the appointment of officers by the Senate. He considered the body as too numerous for that purpose; as subject to cabal; and as devoid of responsibility. If Judges were to be tried by the Senate, according to a late Report of a Committee, it was particularly wrong to let the Senate have the filling of vacancies which its own decrees were to create.

Mr. WILSON was of the same opinion, and for like reasons.

Article 9, being waived, and Article 7, Section 1, being resumed,—

Mr. GOUVERNEUR MORRIS moved to strike the following

38

words out of the eighteenth clause, "enforce treaties," as being superfluous, since treaties were to be "laws,"— which was agreed to, *nem. con.*

Mr. GOUVERNEUR MORRIS moved to alter the first part of the eighteenth clause, so as to read, "to provide for calling forth the militia, to execute the laws of the Union, suppress insurrections, and repel invasions," — which was agreed to, *nem. con.*

On the question then to agree to the eighteenth clause of Article 7, Sect. 1, as amended, it passed in the affirmative, *nem. con.*

Mr. CHARLES PINCKNEY moved to add, as an additional power, to be vested in the Legislature of the United States, "to negative all laws passed by the several States interfering, in the opinion of the Legislature, with the general interests and harmony of the Union; provided that two-thirds of the members of each House assent to the same." This principle, he observed, had formerly been agreed to. He considered the precaution as essentially necessary. The objection drawn from the predominance of the large States had been removed by the equality established in the Senate.

Mr. BROOM seconded the proposition.

Mr. SHERMAN thought it unnecessary; the laws of the General Government being supreme and paramount to the State laws, according to the plan as it now stands.

Mr. MADISON proposed that it should be committed. He had been from the beginning a friend to the principle; but thought the modification might be made better.

Mr. MASON wished to know how the power was to be exercised. Are all laws whatever to be brought up? Is no road nor bridge to be established without the sanction of the General Legislature? Is this to sit constantly in order to receive and revise the State laws? He did not mean, by these remarks, to condemn the expedient; but he was apprehensive that great objections would lie against it.

Mr. WILLIAMSON thought it unnecessary; and having

been already decided, a revival of the question was waste of time.

Mr. WILSON considered this as the key-stone wanted to complete the wide arch of government we are raising. The power of self-defence had been urged as necessary for the State Governments. It was equally necessary for the General Government. The firmness of Judges is not of itself sufficient. Something further is requisite. It will be better to prevent the passage of an improper law, than to declare it void when passed.

Mr. RUTLEDGE. If nothing else, this alone would damn, and ought to damn, the Constitution. Will any State ever agree to be bound hand and foot in this manner? It is worse than making mere corporations of them, whose by-laws would not be subject to this shackle.

Mr ELLSWORTH observed, that the power contended for would require, either that all laws of the State Legislatures should, previously to their taking effect, be transmitted to the General Legislature, or be repealable by the latter; or that the State Executives should be appointed by the General Government, and have a control over the State laws. If the last was meditated, let it be declared.

Mr. PINCKNEY declared, that he thought the State Executives ought to be so appointed, with such a control; and that it would be so provided if another Convention should take place.

Mr. GOUVERNEUR MORRIS did not see the utility or practicability of the proposition of Mr. PINCKNEY, but wished it to be referred to the consideration of a Committee.

Mr. LANGDON was in favor of the proposition. He considered it as resolvable into the question, whether the extent of the National Constitution was to be judged of by the General or the State Governments.

On the question for commitment, it passed in the negative,—

New Hampshire, Pennsylvania, Delaware, Maryland,

Virginia, aye — 5; Massachusetts, Connecticut, New Jersey, North Carolina, South Carolina, Georgia, no — 6.

Mr. PINCKNEY then withdrew his proposition.

The first clause of Article 7, Sect. 1, being so amended as to read, "The Legislature *shall* fulfil the engagements and discharge the debts of the United States; and shall have the power to lay and collect taxes, duties, imposts, and excises," was agreed to.

Mr. BUTLER expressed his dissatisfaction, lest it should compel payment, as well to the blood-suckers who had speculated on the distresses of others, as to those who had fought and bled for their country. He would be ready, he said, to-morrow, to vote for a discrimination between those classes of people; and gave notice that he would move for a re-consideration.

Article 9, Sect. 1, being resumed, to wit: "The Senate of the United States shall have power to make treaties, and to appoint Ambassadors, and Judges of the Supreme Court"—

Mr. MADISON observed, that the Senate represented the States alone; and that for this as well as other obvious reasons, it was proper that the President should be an agent in treaties.

Mr. GOUVERNEUR MORRIS did not know that he should agree to refer the making of treaties to the Senate at all, but for the present would move to add, as an amendment to the section, after "treaties," the following: "but no treaty shall be binding on the United States which is not ratified by law."

Mr. MADISON suggested the inconvenience of requiring a legal *ratification* of treaties of alliance, for the purposes of war, &c. &c. &c.

Mr. GORHAM. Many other disadvantages must be experienced, if treaties of peace and all negotiations are to be previously ratified ; and if not previously, the ministers would be at a loss how to proceed. What would be the case in Great Britain, if the King were to proceed in this

manner ? American ministers must go abroad not instructed by the same authority (as will be the case with
other ministers) which is to ratify their proceedings.

Mr. GOUVERNEUR MORRIS. As to treaties of alliance,
they will oblige foreign powers to send their ministers
here, the very thing we should wish for. Such treaties
could not be otherwise made, if his amendment should
succeed. In general he was not solicitous to multiply and
facilitate treaties. He wished none to be made with Great
Britain, till she should be at war. Then a good bargain
might be made with her. So with other foreign powers.
The more difficulty in making treaties, the more value will
be set on them.

Mr. WILSON. In the most important treaties, the King
of Great Britain, being obliged to resort to Parliament for
the execution of them, is under the same fetters as the
amendment of Mr. MORRIS's will impose on the Senate. It
was refused yesterday to permit even the Legislature to lay
duties on exports. Under the clause without the amendment, the Senate alone can make a treaty requiring all the
rice of South Carolina to be sent to some one particular port.

Mr. DICKINSON concurred in the amendment, as most
safe and proper, though he was sensible it was unfavourable
to the little States, which would otherwise have an *equal*
share in making treaties.

Doctor JOHNSON thought there was something of
solecism in saying, that the acts of a minister with pleni-
potentiary powers from one body should depend for ratification on another body. The example of the King of
Great Britain was not parallel. Full and complete power
was vested in him. If the Parliament should fail to provide the necessary means of execution, the treaty would be
violated.

Mr. GORHAM, in answer to Mr. GOUVERNEUR MORRIS,
said, that negotiations on the spot were not to be desired
by us ; especially if the whole Legislature is to have
any thing to do with treaties. It will be generally in-

fluenced by two or three men, who will be corrupted by the
ambassadors here. In such a government as ours, it is
necessary to guard against the Government itself being
seduced.

Mr. RANDOLPH, ooserving that almost every speaker had
made objections to the clause as it stood, moved in order to
a further consideration of the subject, that the motion of
Mr. GOUVERNEUR MORRIS should be postponed ; and on this
question, it was lost, the States being equally divided,

New Jersey, Pennsylvania, Delaware, Maryland, Virginia, aye — 5 ; Massachusetts, Connecticut, North Carolina, South Carolina, Georgia, no — 5.

On Mr. GOUVERNEUR MORRIS' motion,—

Pennsylvania, aye — 1 ; Massachusetts, Connecticut,
New Jersey, Delaware, Maryland, Virginia, South Carolina,
Georgia, no — 8 ; North Carolina, divided.

The several clauses of Article 9, Sect. 1, were then
separately postponed, after inserting, "and other public
ministers," next after "ambassadors."

Mr. MADISON hinted for consideration whether a distinction might not be made between different sorts of
treaties; allowing the President and Senate to make treaties
eventual, and of alliance for limited terms, and requiring
the concurrence of the whole Legislature in other treaties.

The first Section of Article 9, was finally referred *nem.
con.*, to the Committee of five, and the House then

Adjourned.

———

FRIDAY, AUGUST 24TH.

In Convention,— Governor LIVINGSTON, from the Committee of eleven, to whom were referred the two remaining
clauses of the fourth Section, and the fifth and sixth Sections, of the seventh Article, delivered in the following
Report:

"Strike out so much of the fourth Section as was
referred to the Committee, and insert, 'The migration or

importation of such persons as the several States, now existing, shall think proper to admit, shall not be prohibited by the Legislature prior to the year 1800; but a tax or duty may be imposed on such migration or importation, at a rate not exceeding the average of the duties laid on imports.'

" The fifth Section to remain as in the Report.

" The sixth Section to be stricken out."

Mr. BUTLER, according to notice, moved that the first clause of Article 7, Sect. 1, as to the discharge of debts, be re-considered to-morrow.   He dwelt on the division of opinion concerning the domestic debts, and the different pretensions of the different classes of holders.

General PINCKNEY seconded him.

Mr. RANDOLPH wished for a re-consideration, in order to better the expression, and to provide for the case of the State debts as is done by Congress.

On the question for re-considering,—

Massachusetts, Connecticut, New Jersey, Delaware, Virginia, South Carolina, Georgia, aye — 7; New Hampshire, Maryland, no — 2; Pennsylvania, North Carolina, absent.

And to-morrow assigned for the re-consideration.

The second and third Sections of Article 9, being taken up,—

Mr. RUTLEDGE said, this provision for deciding controversies between the States was necessary under the Confederation, but will be rendered unnecessary by the National Judiciary now to be established; and moved to strike it out.

Doctor JOHNSON seconded the motion.

Mr. SHERMAN concurred.   So did Mr. DAYTON.

Mr. WILLIAMSON was for postponing instead of striking out, in order to consider whether this might not be a good provision, in cases where the Judiciary were interested, or too closely connected with the parties.

Mr. GORHAM had doubts as to striking out.   The Judges might be connected with the States being parties.   He was inclined to think the mode proposed in the clause would be more satisfactory than to refer such cases to the Judiciary.

On the question for postponing the second and third sections, it passed in the negative,—

New Hampshire, North Carolina, Georgia, aye — 3 ; Massachusetts, Connecticut, New Jersey, Delaware, Maryland, Virginia, South Carolina, no — 7 ; Pennsylvania, absent.

Mr. WILSON urged the striking out, the Judiciary being a better provision.

The question for striking out the second and third Sections of Article 9,—

Hew Hampshire, Connecticut New Jersey, Delaware, Maryland, Virginia, South Carolina, aye — 8 : North Carolina, Georgia, no — 2 ; Pennsylvania, absent.

Article 10, Sect. 1. " The Executive power of the United States shall be vested in a single person. His style shall be " The President of the United States of America," and his title shall be " His Excellency." He shall be elected by ballot by the Legislature. He shall hold his office during the term of seven years ; but shall not be elected a second time."

On the question for vesting the power in a *single* *person*,—it was agreed to, *nem. con.* So also on the *style* and *title*.

Mr. RUTLEDGE moved to insert, " joint," before the word " ballot," as the most convenient mode of electing.

Mr. SHERMAN objected to it, as depriving the *States*, represented in the *Senate*, of the negative intended them in that House.

Mr. GORHAM said it was wrong to be considering, at every turn, who the Senate would represent. The public good was the true object to be kept in view. Great delay and confusion would ensue, if the two Houses should vote separately, each having a negative on the choice of the other.

Mr. DAYTON. It might be well for those not to consider how the Senate was constituted, whose interest it was to keep it out of sight. If the amendment should be agreed to, a joint ballot would in fact give the appointment to one House. He could never agree to the clause with such an amendment. There could be no doubt of the two Houses separately concurring in the same person for President. The importance and necessity of the case would ensure a concurrence.

Mr. CARROLL moved to strike out, "by the Legislature," and insert "by the people." Mr. WILSON seconded him ; and on the question,—

Pennsylvania, Delaware, aye — 2 ; New Hampshire, Massachusetts, Connecticut, New Jersey, Maryland, Virginia, North Carolina, South Carolina, Georgia, no — 9.

Mr. BREARLY was opposed to inserting the word, " joint." The argument that the small States should not put their hands into the pockets of the large ones did not apply in this case.

Mr. WILSON urged the reasonableness of giving the larger States a larger share of the appointment, and the danger of delay from a disagreement of the two Houses. He remarked also, that the Senate had peculiar powers balancing the advantage given by a joint ballot in this case to the other branch of the Legislature.

Mr. LANGDON. This general officer ought to be elected by the joint and general voice. In New Hampshire the mode of separate votes by the two Houses was productive of great difficulties. The negative of the Senate would hurt the feelings of the man elected by the votes of the other branch. He was for inserting "joint," though unfavorable to New Hampshire as a small State.

Mr. WILSON remarked, that as the President of the Senate was to be the President of the United States, that body, in cases of vacancy, might have an interest in throwing dilatory obstacles in the way, if its separate concurrence should be required.

Mr. MADISON. If the amendment be agreed to, the rule

of voting will give to the largest State, compared with the
smallest, an influence as four to one only, although the
population is as ten to one. This surely cannot be unreasonable, as the President is to act for the *people*, not for
the *States*. The President of the *Senate* also is to be
occasionally President of the United States, and by his
negative alone can make three-fourths of the other branch
necessary to the passage of a law. This is another advantage enjoyed by the Senate.

On the question for inserting "joint," it passed in the
affirmative,—

New Hampshire, Massachusetts, Pennsylvania, Delaware,
Virginia, North Carolina, South Carolina, aye — 7; Connecticut, New Jersey, Maryland, Georgia, no — 4.

Mr. DAYTON then moved to insert, after the word
"Legislature," the words, "each State having one vote."

Mr. BREARLY seconded him; and on the question, it
passed in the negative,— Connecticut, New Jersey, Delaware, Maryland, Georgia, aye — 5; New Hampshire, Massachusetts, Pennsylvania, Virginia, North Carolina, South
Carolina, no — 6.

Mr. PINCKNEY moved to insert, after the word "Legislature," the words, "to which election a majority of the
votes of the members present shall be required."

And on this question, it passed in the affirmative,—
New Hampshire, Massachusetts, Connecticut, Pennsylvania,
Delaware, Maryland, Virginia, North Carolina, South
Carolina, Georgia, aye — 10; New Jersey, no —1.

Mr. READ moved, that, "in case the number for the two
highest in votes should be equal, then the President of the
Senate shall have an additional casting vote," which was
disagreed to by a general negative.

Mr. GOUVERNEUR MORRIS opposed the election of the
President by the Legislature. He dwelt on the danger of
rendering the Executive uninterested in maintaining the
rights of his station, as leading to legislative tyranny. If
the Legislature have the Executive dependent on them,

they can perpetuate and support their usurpations by the influence of the tax-gatherers and other officers, by fleets, armies, &c.   Cabal and corruption are attached to that mode of election. So is ineligibility a second time.   Hence the Executive is interested in courting popularity in the Legislature, by sacrificing his Executive rights; and then he can go into that body after the expiration of his Executive office, and enjoy there the fruits of his policy.   To these considerations he added, that rivals would be continually intriguing to oust the President from his place. To guard against all these evils, he moved that the President "shall be chosen by Electors to be chosen by the people of the several States."

Mr. CARROLL seconded him; and on the question, it passed in the negative, — Connecticut, New Jersey, Pennsylvania, Delaware, Virginia, aye — 5; New Hampshire, Massachusetts, Maryland, North Carolina, South Carolina, Georgia, no — 6.

Mr. DAYTON moved to postpone the consideration of the two last clauses of Article 10, Sect. 1, which was disagreed to without a count of the States.

Mr. BROOM moved to refer the two clauses to a committee, of a member from each State; and on the question, it failed, the States being equally divided, —

New Jersey, Pennsylvania, Delaware, Maryland, Virginia, aye — 5; New Hampshire, Massachusetts, North Carolina, South Carolina, Georgia, no — 5; Connecticut, divided.

On the question taken on the first part of Mr. GOUVERNEUR MORRIS' motion, to wit: "shall be chosen by electors," as an abstract question, it failed, the States being equally divided, —

New Jersey, Pennsylvania, Delaware, Virginia, aye — 4; New Hampshire, North Carolina, South Carolina, Georgia, no — 4; Connecticut, Maryland, divided; Massachusetts, absent.

The consideration of the remaining clauses of Article 10, Sect. 1, was then postponed till to-morrow, at the instance of the Deputies of New Jersey.

Article 10, Sect. 2, being taken up, the word "information" was transferred, and inserted after "Legislature."

On motion of Mr. GOUVERNEUR MORRIS, "he may," was struck out and "and" inserted before "recommend," in the second clause of Article 10, Sect. 2, in order to make it the *duty* of the President to recommend, and thence prevent umbrage or cavil at his doing it.

Mr. SHERMAN objected to the sentence, "and shall appoint officers in all cases not otherwise provided for in this Constitution." He admitted it to be proper that many officers in the Executive department should be so appointed; but contended that many ought not,— as general officers in the army, in time of peace, &c. Herein lay the corruption in Great Britain. If the Executive can model the army, he may set up an absolute government; taking advantage of the close of a war, and an army commanded by his creatures. James II. was not obeyed by his officers, because they had been appointed by his predecessors, not by himself. He moved to insert, "or by law," after the word "constitution."

On motion of Mr. MADISON, "officers" was struck out, and "to offices" inserted, in order to obviate doubts that he might appoint officers without a previous creation of the offices by the Legislature.

On the question for inserting, "or by law," as moved by Mr. SHERMAN,— Connecticut, aye — 1; New Hampshire, Massachusetts, New Jersey, Pennsylvania, Delaware, Maryland, Virginia, South Carolina, Georgia, no — 9; North Carolina, absent.

Mr. DICKINSON moved to strike out the words, "and shall appoint to offices in all cases not otherwise provided for by this Constitution;" and insert, "and shall appoint to all offices established by this Constitution, except in cases herein otherwise provided for; and to all offices which may hereafter be created by law."

Mr. RANDOLPH observed, that the power of appointments was a formidable one both in the Executive and Legislative hands; and suggested whether the Legislature should not be left at liberty to refer appointments, in some cases, to some State authority.

Mr. DICKINSON'S motion passed in the affirmative,—

Connecticut, New Jersey, Pennsylvania, Maryland, Virginia, Georgia, aye — 6; New Hampshire, Massachusetts, Delaware, South Carolina, no — 4; North Carolina, absent.

Mr. DICKINSON then moved to annex to his last amendment, "except where by law the appointment shall be vested in the Legislatures or Executives of the several States."

Mr. RANDOLPH seconded the motion.

Mr. WILSON. If this be agreed to, it will soon be a standing instruction to the State Legislatures to pass no law creating offices, unless the appointment be referred to them.

Mr. SHERMAN objected to " Legislatures," in the motion, which was struck out by consent of the movers.

Mr. GOUVERNEUR MORRIS. This would be putting it in the power of the States to say, " you shall be viceroys, but we will be viceroys over you."

The motion was negatived without a count of the States.

Ordered unanimously, that the order respecting the adjournment at four o'clock be repealed, and that in future the House assemble at ten o'clock, and adjourn at three.

Adjourned.

SATURDAY, AUGUST 25TH.

In Convention,—The first clause of Article 7, Sect. 1, being reconsidered,—

Colonel MASON objected to the term " *shall* " fulfil the engagements and discharge the debts, &c., as too strong. It may be impossible to comply with it. The creditors

should be kept in the same plight. They will in one
respect be necessarily and properly in a better. The Government will be more able to pay them. The use of the
term *shall* will beget speculations, and increase the pesti-
lential practice of stock-jobbing. There was a great distinction between original creditors and those who purchased
fraudulently of the ignorant and distressed. He did not
mean to include those who have bought stock in the open
market. He was sensible of the difficulty of drawing the
line in this case, but he did not wish to preclude the attempt.
Even fair purchasers, at four, five, six, eight for one, did
not stand on the same footing with the first holders, supposing them not to be blamable. The interest they received,
even in paper, is equal to their purchase money. What he
particularly wished was, to leave the door open for buying
up the securities, which he thought would be precluded by
the term " shall," as requiring *nominal payment*, and which
was not inconsistent with his ideas of public faith. He was
afraid, also, the word " *shall* " might extend to all the old
continental paper.

Mr. LANGDON wished to do no more, than leave the
creditors *in statu quo.*

Mr. GERRY said, that, for himself, he had no interest in
the question, being not possessed of more of the securities
than would, by the interest, pay his taxes. He would
observe, however, that as the public had received the value
of the literal amount, they ought to pay that value to some-
body. The frauds on *the soldiers* ought to have been foreseen. These poor and ignorant people, could not but part
with their securities. There are other creditors, who will
part with any thing, rather than be cheated of the capital
of their advances. The interest of the States, he observed,
was different on this point; some having more, others less,
than their proportion of the paper. Hence the idea of a
scale for reducing its value had arisen. If the public faith
would admit, of which he was not clear, he would not
object to a revision of the debt, so far as to compel restitu-

tion to the ignorant and distressed, who have been defrauded. As to stock-jobbers, he saw no reason for the censures thrown on them. They keep up the value of the paper. Without them there would be no market.

Mr. BUTLER said he meant neither to increase nor diminish the security of the creditors.

Mr. RANDOLPH moved to postpone the clause, in favor of the following: "All debts contracted, and engagements entered into, by or under the authority of Congress, shall be as valid against the United States under this Constitution, as under the Confederation."

Doctor JOHNSON. The debts are debts of the United States, of the great body of America. Changing the Government cannot change the obligation of the United States, which devolves of course on the new Government. Nothing was, in his opinion, necessary to be said. If any thing, it should be a mere declaration, as moved by Mr. RANDOLPH.

Mr. GOUVERNEUR MORRIS said, he never had become a public creditor, that he might urge with more propriety the compliance with public faith. He had always done so, and always would, and preferred the term "shall," as the most explicit. As to buying up the debt, the term "shall" was not inconsistent with it, if provision be first made for paying the interest; if not, such an expedient was a mere evasion. He was content to say nothing, as the new Government would be bound of course; but would prefer the clause with the term "shall," because it would create many friends to the plan.

On Mr. RANDOLPH's motion,—

New Hampshire, Massachusetts, Connecticut, New Jersey, Delaware, Maryland, Virginia, North Carolina, South Carolina, Georgia, aye — 10; Pennsylvania, no — 1.

Mr. SHERMAN thought it necessary to connect with the clause for laying taxes, duties, &c., an express provision for the object of the old debts, &c.; and moved to add to the first clause of Article 7, Sect. 1: "for the payment of said debts, and for the defraying the expenses that shall be incurred for the common defence and general welfare."

The proposition, as being unnecessary, was disagreed to, — Connecticut alone being in the affirmative.

The Report of the Committee of eleven (see Friday, the twenty-fourth), being taken up,—

General PINCKNEY moved to strike out the words, "the year eighteen hundred," as the year limiting the importation of slaves ; and to insert the words, "the year eighteen hundred and eight."

Mr GORHAM seconded the motion.

Mr. MADISON. Twenty years will produce all the mischief that can be apprehended from the liberty to import slaves. So long a term will be more dishonourable to the American character, than to say nothing about it in the Constitution.

On the motion, which passed in the affirmative,—New Hampshire, Massachusetts, Connecticut, Maryland, North Carolina, South Carolina, Georgia, aye — 7 ; New Jersey, Pennsylvania, Delaware, Virginia, no — 4.

Mr. GOUVERNEUR MORRIS was for making the clause read at once, "the importation of slaves into North Carolina, South Carolina, and Georgia, shall not be prohibited, &c." This he said, would be most fair, and would avoid the ambiguity by which, under the power with regard to naturalization, the liberty reserved to the States might be defeated. He wished it to be known, also, that this part of the Constitution was a compliance with those States. If the change of language, however, should be objected to, by the members from those States, he should not urge it.

Colonel MASON was not against using the term "slaves," but against naming North Carolina, South Carolina, and Georgia, lest it should give offence. to the people of those States.

Mr. SHERMAN liked a description better than the terms proposed, which had been declined by the old Congress. and were not pleasing to some people.

Mr. CLYMER concurred with Mr. SHERMAN.

Mr. WILLIAMSON said, that both in opinion and practice he was against slavery ; but thought it more in favor of humanity, from a view of all circumstances, to let in South Carolina, and Georgia on those terms, than to exclude them from the Union.

Mr. GOUVERNEUR MORRIS withdrew his motion.

Mr. DICKINSON wished the clause to be confined to the States which had not themselves prohibited the importation of slaves ; and for that purpose moved to amend the clause, so as to read: "The importation of slaves into such of the States as shall permit the same, shall not be prohibited by the Legislature of the United States, until the year 1808 ;" which was disagreed to, *nem. con.**

The first part of the Report was then agreed to, amended as follows : "The migration or importation of such persons as the several States now existing shall think proper to admit, shall not be prohibited by the Legislature prior to the year 1808,"—

New Hampshire, Massachusetts, Connecticut, Maryland, North Carolina, South Carolina, Georgia, aye — 7; New Jersey, Pennsylvania, Delaware, Virginia, no — 4.

Mr. BALDWIN, in order to restrain and more explicitly define, "the average duty," moved to strike out of the second part the words, "average of the duties laid on imports," and insert " common impost on articles not enumerated;" which was agreed to, *nem. con.*

Mr. SHERMAN was against this second part, as acknowledging men to be property, by taxing them as such under the character of slaves.

Mr. KING and Mr. LANGDON considered this as the price of the first part.

General PINCKNEY admitted that it was so.

Colonel MASON. Not to tax, will be equivalent to a bounty on, the importation of slaves.

---

* In the printed Journals, Connecticut, Virginia, and Georgia, voted in the affirmative.

39

Mr. GORHAM thought that Mr. SHERMAN should consider the duty, not as implying that slaves are property, but as a discouragement to the importation of them.

Mr. GOUVERNEUR MORRIS remarked, that, as the clause now stands, it implies that the Legislature may tax freemen imported.

Mr. SHERMAN, in answer to Mr. GORHAM, observed, that the smallness of the duty showed revenue to be the object, not the discouragement of the importation.

Mr. MADISON thought it wrong to admit in the Constitution the idea that there could be property in men. The reason of duties did not hold, as slaves are not, like merchandise consumed, &c.

Colonel MASON, in answer to Mr. GOUVERNEUR MORRIS. The provision, as it stands, was necessary for the case of convicts, in order to prevent the introduction of them.

It was finally agreed, *nem. con.*, to make the clause read: "but a tax or duty may be imposed on such importation, not exceeding ten dollars for each person;" and then the second part, as amended, was agreed to.

Article 7, Sect. 5, was agreed to, *nem. con.*, as reported.

Article 7, Sect. 6, in the Report was postponed.

On motion of Mr. MADISON, seconded by Mr. GOUVERNEUR MORRIS, Article 8 was reconsidered; and after the words, "all treaties made," were inserted, *nem. con.*, the words, "or which shall be made." This insertion was meant to obviate all doubt concerning the force of treaties pre-existing, by making the words, "all treaties made," to refer to them, as the words inserted would refer to future treaties.

Mr. CARROLL and Mr. L. MARTIN expressed their apprehensions, and the probable apprehensions of their constituents, that under the power of regulating trade the General Legislature might favor the ports of particular States, by requiring vessels destined to or from other States to enter and clear thereat; as vessels belonging or bound to Baltimore, to enter and clear at Norfolk, &c. They moved the following proposition:

"The Legislature of the United States shall not oblige vessels belonging to citizens thereof, or to foreigners, to enter or pay duties or imposts in any other State than in that to which they may be bound, or to clear out in any other than the State in which their cargoes may be laden on board; nor shall any privilege or immunity be granted to any vessel on entering or clearing out, or paying duties or imposts in one State in preference to another."

Mr. GORHAM thought such a precaution unnecessary; and that the revenue might be defeated, if vessels could run up long rivers, through the jurisdiction of different States, without being required to enter, with the opportunity of landing and selling their cargoes by the way.

Mr. McHENRY and Gen. PINCKNEY made the following propositions:

"Should it be judged expedient by the Legislature of the United States, that one or more ports for collecting duties or imposts, other than those ports of entrance and clearance already established by the respective States, should be established, the Legislature of the United States shall signify the same to the Executives of the respective States, ascertaining the number of such ports judged necessary, to be laid by the said Executives before the Legislatures of the States at their next session; and the Legislature of the United States shall not have the power of fixing or establishing the particular ports for collecting duties or imposts in any State, except the Legislature of such State shall neglect to fix and establish the same during their first session to be held after such notification by the Legislature of the United States to the Executive of such State.

"All duties, imposts and excise, prohibitions or restraints, laid or made by the Legislature of the United States, shall be uniform and equal throughout the United States."

These several propositions were referred, *nem. con.*, to a

committee composed of a member from each State. The Committee appointed by ballot, were, Mr. LANGDON, Mr. GORHAM, Mr. SHERMAN, Mr. DAYTON, Mr. FITZSIMONS, Mr. READ, Mr. CARROLL, Mr. MASON, Mr. WILLIAMSON, Mr. BUTLER, Mr. FEW.

On the question now taken on Mr. DICKINSON'S motion of yesterday, allowing appointments to offices to be referred by the General Legislature to "the Executives of the several States," as a further amendment to Article 10, Sect. 2, the votes were,— Connecticut, Virginia, Georgia, aye — 3; New Hampshire, Massachusetts, Pennsylvania, Delaware, North Carolina, South Carolina, no — 6; Maryland, divided.

In amendment of the same section, the words, "other public Ministers," were inserted after "ambassadors."

Mr. GOUVERNEUR MORRIS moved to strike out of the section, "and may correspond with the supreme Executives of the several States," as unnecessary, and implying that he could not correspond with others.

Mr. BROOM seconded him.

On the question,— New Hampshire, Massachusetts, Connecticut, Pennsylvania, Delaware, Virginia, North Carolina, South Carolina, Georgia, aye — 9; Maryland, no — 1.

The clause, "Shall receive ambassadors and other public Ministers," was agreed to, *nem. con.*

Mr. SHERMAN moved to amend the "power to grant reprieves and pardons," so as to read, "to grant reprieves until the ensuing session of the Senate, and pardons with consent of the Senate."

On the question,— Connecticut, aye,— 1 ; New Hampshire, Massachusetts, Pennsylvania, Maryland, Virginia, North Carolina, South Carolina, Georgia, no — 8.

The words, "except in cases of impeachment," were inserted, *nem. con.*, after "pardons."

On the question to agree to, "but his pardon shall not be pleadable in bar," it passed in the negative,— New

Hampshire, Maryland, North Carolina, South Carolina, aye,—4; Massachusetts, Connecticut, Pennsylvania, Delaware, Virginia, Georgia, no—6.

Adjourned.

MONDAY, AUGUST 27TH.

In Convention,— Article 10, Section 2, being resumed,—

Mr. L. MARTIN moved to insert the words, "after conviction," after the words, "reprieves and pardons."

Mr. WILSON objected, that pardon before conviction might be necessary, in order to obtain the testimony of accomplices. He stated the case of forgeries, in which this might particularly happen.

Mr. L. MARTIN withdrew his motion.

Mr. SHERMAN moved to amend the clause giving the Executive the command of the militia, so as to read: "and of the militia of the several States, *when called into the actual service of the United States*;" and on the question,—

New Hampshire, Connecticut, Pennsylvania, Maryland, Virginia, Georgia, aye—6; Delaware, South Carolina, no—2; Massachusetts, New Jersey, North Carolina, absent.

The clause for removing the President, on impeachment by the House of Representatives, and conviction in the Supreme Court, of treason, bribery, or corruption, was postponed, *nem. con.,* at the instance of Mr. GOUVERNEUR MORRIS; who thought the tribunal an improper one, particularly, if the first Judge was to be of the Privy Council.

Mr. GOUVERNEUR MORRIS objected also to the President of the Senate being provisional successor to the President, and suggested a designation of the Chief Justice.

Mr. MADISON adds, as a ground of objection, that the Senate might retard the appointment of a President, in order to carry points whilst the revisionary power was in the President of their own body; but suggested that the executive powers during a vacancy be administered by the persons composing the Council to the President.

Mr. WILLIAMSON suggested that the Legislature ought to have power to provide for occasional successors; and moved that the last clause of Article 10, Sect. 2, relating to a provisional successor to the President, be postponed.

Mr. DICKINSON seconded the postponement, remarking that it was too vague. What is the extent of the term "disability," and who is to be the judge of it.

The postponement was agreed to, *nem. con.*

Col. MASON and Mr. MADISON moved to add to the oath to be taken by the Supreme Executive, " and will, to the best of my judgment and power, preserve, protect, and defend, the Constitution of the United States."

Mr. WILSON thought the general provision for oaths of office, in a subsequent place, rendered the amendment unnecessary.

On the question,—

New Hampshire, Connecticut, Pennsylvania, Maryland, Virginia, South Carolina, Georgia, aye — 7 ; Delaware, no — 1 ; Massachusetts, New Jersey, North Carolina, absent.

Article 11, being next taken up,—

Doctor JOHNSON suggested that the judicial power ought to extend to equity as well as law ; and moved to insert the words, "both in law and equity," after the words, "United States," in the first line of the first section.

Mr. READ objected to vesting these powers in the same court.

On the question,—

New Hampshire, Connecticut, Pennsylvania, Virginia, South Carolina, Georgia, aye — 6 ; Delaware, Maryland, no — 2 ; Massachusetts, New Jersey, North Carolina, absent.

On the question to agree to Article 11, Sect. 1, as amended, the States were the same as on the preceding question.

Mr. DICKINSON moved an amendment to Article 11, Sect. 2, after the words, "good behaviour," the words "provided that they may be removed by the Executive on the application by the Senate and House of Representatives."

Mr. GERRY seconded the motion.

Mr. GOUVERNEUR MORRIS thought it a contradiction in terms, during good behaviour, and yet be removeable without a trial. Besides, it was fundamentally wrong to subject judges to so arbitrary an authority.

Mr. SHERMAN saw no contradiction or impropriety, if this were made a part of the constitutional regulation of the Judiciary establishment. He observed that a like provision was contained in the British statutes.

Mr. RUTLEDGE. If the Supreme Court is to judge between the United States and particular States, this alone is an insuperable objection to the motion.

Mr. WILSON considered such a provision in the British Government as less dangerous than here ; the House of Lords and House of Commons being less likely to concur on the same occasions. Chief Justice Holt, he remarked, had *successively* offended, by his independent conduct, both Houses of Parliament. Had this happened at the same time, he would have been ousted. The .Judges would be in a bad situation, if made to depend on any gust of faction which might prevail in the two branches of our Government.

Mr. RANDOLPH opposed the motion, as weakening too much the independence of the Judges.

Mr. DICKINSON was not apprehensive that the Legislature, composed of different branches, constructed on such different principles, would improperly unite for the purpose of displacing a Judge.

On the question for agreeing to Mr. DICKINSON's motion, it was negatived,— Connecticut, aye; all the other States present, no.

On the question on Article 11, Section 2, as reported, Delaware and Maryland only, no.

Mr. MADISON and Mr. McHENRY moved to re-instate the words, "increased or," before the word "diminished," in Article 11, Section 2.

Mr. GOUVERNEUR MORRIS opposed it, for reasons urged by him on a former occasion.

Colonel MASON contended strenuously for the motion. There was no weight, he said, in the argument drawn from changes in the value of the metals, because this might be provided for by an increase of salaries, so made as not to affect persons in office; — and this was the only argument on which much stress seemed to have been laid.

General PINCKNEY. The importance of the Judiciary will require men of the first talents: large salaries will therefore be necessary, larger than the United States can afford in the first instance. He was not satisfied with the expedient mentioned by Col. MASON. He did not think it would have a good effect, or a good appearance, for new Judges to come in with higher salaries than the old ones.

Mr. GOUVERNEUR MORRIS said the expedient might be evaded, and therefore amounted to nothing. Judges might resign, and then be re-appointed to increased salaries.—

On the question,—

Virginia, aye — 1; New Hampshire, Connecticut, Pennsylvania, Delaware, South Carolina, no — 5; Maryland, divided; Massachusetts, New Jersey, North Carolina, Georgia, absent.

Mr. RANDOLPH and Mr. MADISON then moved to add the following words to Article 11, Section 2: "nor increased by any act of the Legislature which shall operate before the expiration of three years after the passing thereof."

On the question,— Maryland, Virginia, aye — 2; New Hampshire, Connecticut, Pennsylvania, Delaware, South Carolina, no — 5; Massachusetts, New Jersey, North Carolina, Georgia, absent.

Article 11, Section 3, being taken up, the following clause was postponed, viz: "to the trial of impeachments of officers of the United States;" by which the jurisdiction of the Supreme Court was extended to such cases.

Mr. MADISON and Mr. GOUVERNEUR MORRIS moved to insert, after the word "controversies," the words, "to which the United States shall be a party;" which was agreed to, *nem. con.*

Doctor JOHNSON moved to insert the words, " this Constitution and the," before the word " laws."

Mr. MADISON doubted whether it was not going too far, to extend the jurisdiction of the Court generally to cases arising under the Constitution, and whether it ought not to be limited to cases of a judiciary nature. The right of expounding the Constitution, in cases not of this nature, ought not to be given to that department.

The motion of Doctor JOHNSON was agreed to, *nem. con.*, it being generally supposed, that the jurisdiction given was constructively limited to cases of a judiciary nature.

On motion of Mr. RUTLEDGE, the words " passed by the Legislature," were struck out ; and after the words, " United States," were inserted, *nem. con.*, the words " and treaties made or which shall be made under their authority," conformably to a preceding amendment in another place.

The clause, " in cases of impeachment," was postponed.

Mr. GOUVERNEUR MORRIS wished to know what was meant by the words : "In all the cases before mentioned it [jurisdiction] shall be appellate, with such exceptions, &c."—whether it extended to matters of fact as well as law — and to cases of common law, as well as civil law.

Mr. WILSON. The Committee, he believed, meant facts as well as law, and common as well as civil law. The jurisdiction of the Federal court of appeals had, he said, been so construed.

Mr. DICKINSON moved to add, after the word " appellate," the words, "both as to law and fact ;" which was agreed to, *nem. con.*

Mr. MADISON and Mr. GOUVERNEUR MORRIS moved to strike out the beginning of the third section, " The jurisdiction of the Supreme Court," and to insert the words, " the Judicial power," which was agreed to, *nem. con.*

The following motion was disagreed to, to wit, to insert,

"In all the other cases before mentioned, the judicialpower shall be exercised in such manner as the Legislature shall direct."

Delaware, Virginia, aye — 2 ; New Hampshire, Connecticut, Pennsylvania, Maryland, South Carolina, Georgia, no — 6.

On the question for striking out the last sentence of the third Section, "The Legislature may assign, &c." it passed, *nem. con.*

Mr. SHERMAN moved to insert, after the words, "between citizens of different States," the words, "between citizens of the same State claiming lands under grants of different States," — according to the provision in the 9th Article of the Confederation ; which was agreed to, *nem. con.*

Adjourned.

_____

TUESDAY, AUGUST 28TH.

In Convention, — Mr. SHERMAN, from the Committee to whom were referred several propositions on the twenty-fifth instant, made the following report ; which was ordered to lie on the table :

"That there be inserted, after the fourth clause of the 7th Section : 'Nor shall any regulation of commerce or revenue give preference to the ports of one State over those of another, or oblige vessels bound to or from any State to enter, clear or pay duties in another ; and all tonnage, duties, imposts, and excises laid by the Legislature, shall be uniform throughout the United States.'"

Article 11, Section 3, being considered, — it was moved to strike out the words, "it shall be appellate," and to insert the words, "the Supreme Court shall have appellate jurisdiction," — in order to prevent uncertainty whether "it" referred to the *Supreme Court,* or to the *Judicial power.*

On the question, — New Hampshire, Massachusetts,

Connecticut, Pennsylvania, Delaware, Virginia, North Carolina, South Carolina, Georgia, aye — 9; Maryland, no — 1; New Jersey, absent.

Section 4 was so amended, *nem. con.*, as to read: "The trial of all crimes (except in cases of impeachment) shall be by jury; and such trial shall be held in the State where the said crimes shall have been committed; but when not committed within any State, then the trial shall be at such place or places as the Legislature may direct." The object of this amendment was, to provide for trial by jury of offences committed out of any State.

Mr. PINCKNEY, urging the propriety of securing the benefit of the Habeas Corpus in the most ample manner, moved, that it should not be suspended but on the most urgent occasions, and then only for a limited time not exceeding twelve months.

Mr. RUTLEDGE was for declaring the Habeas Corpus inviolate. He did not conceive that a suspension could ever be necessary, at the same time, through all the States.

Mr. GOUVERNEUR MORRIS moved, that, "The privilege of the writ of Habeas Corpus shall not be suspended, unless where, in cases of rebellion or invasion, the public safety may require it."

Mr. WILSON doubted whether in any case a suspension could be necessary, as the discretion now exists with Judges, in most important cases, to keep in gaol or admit to bail.

The first part of Mr. GOUVERNEUR MORRIS's motion, to the word "unless," was agreed to, *nem. con.* On the remaining part, — New Hampshire, Massachusetts, Connecticut, Pennsylvania, Delaware, Maryland, Virginia, aye — 7; North Carolina, South Carolina, Georgia, no — 3.

The fifth Section of Article 11, was agreed to, *nem. con.**

Article 12 being then taken up, —

Mr. WILSON and Mr. SHERMAN moved to insert, after the words, "coin money," the words, "nor emit bills of

---

* The vote on this section, as stated in the printed Journal, is not unanimous: the statement here is probably the right one.

credit, nor make any thing but gold and silver coin a tender
in payment of debts;" making these prohibitions absolute,
instead of making the measures allowable, as in the thirteenth Article, *with the consent of the Legislature of the
United States.*

Mr. GORHAM thought the purpose would be as well
secured by the provision of Article 13, which makes the
consent of the General Legislature necessary; and that in
that mode no opposition would be excited ; whereas an
absolute prohibition of paper-money would rouse the most
desperate opposition from its partisans.

Mr. SHERMAN thought this a favourable crisis for crushing paper-money. If the consent of the Legislature could
authorize emissions of it, the friends of paper-money would
make every exertion to get into the Legislature in order to
license it.

The question being divided,—on the first part: "nor
emit bills of credit,"—

New Hampshire, Massachusetts, Connecticut, Pennsylvania, Delaware, North Carolina, South Carolina, Georgia,
aye — 8; Virginia, no — 1; Maryland, divided.

The remaining part of Mr. WILSON's, and SHERMAN's
motion was agreed to, *nem. con.*

Mr. KING moved to add, in the words used in the ordinance of Congress establishing new States, a prohibition
on the States to interfere in private contracts.

Mr. GOUVERNEUR MORRIS. This would be going too far.
There are a thousand laws relating to bringing actions,
limitations of actions, &c., which affect contracts. The
judicial power of the United States will be a protection in
cases within their jurisdiction; and within the State itself
a majority must rule, whatever may be the mischief done
among themselves.

Mr. SHERMAN. Why then prohibit bills of credit?

Mr. WILSON was in favor of Mr. KING's motion.

Mr. MADISON admitted that inconveniences might arise
from such a prohibition; but thought on the whole it would

be overbalanced by the utility of it. He conceived, however, that a negative on the State laws could alone secure the effect. Evasions might and would be devised by the ingenuity of the Legislatures.

Col. MASON. This is carrying the restraint too far. Cases will happen that cannot be foreseen, where some kind of interference will be proper and essential. He mentioned the case of limiting the period for bringing actions on open account — that of bonds after a certain lapse of time — asking, whether it was proper to tie the hands of the States from making provision in such cases.

Mr. WILSON. The answer to these objections is, that retrospective *interferences* only are to be prohibited.

Mr. MADISON. Is not that already done by the prohibition of *ex post facto* laws, which will oblige the Judges to declare interferences null and void.

Mr. RUTLEDGE moved, instead of Mr. KING's motion, to insert, "nor pass bills of attainder, nor retrospective* laws."

On which motion,—New Hampshire, New Jersey, Pennsylvania, Delaware, North Carolina, South Carolina, Georgia, aye — 7; Connecticut, Maryland, Virginia, no — 3.

Mr. MADISON moved to insert, after the word "reprisal," (Article 12,) the words, "nor lay embargoes." He urged that such acts by the States would be unnecessary, impolitic, and unjust.

Mr. SHERMAN thought the States ought to retain this power, in order to prevent suffering and injury to their poor.

Col. MASON thought the amendment would be not only improper but dangerous, as the General Legislature would not sit constantly, and therefore could not interpose at the necessary moments. He enforced his objection by appealing to the necessity of sudden embargoes, during the war, to prevent exports, particularly in the case of a blockade.

Mr. GOUVERNEUR MORRIS considered the provision as

---

* In the printed Journal, " *ex post facto.*"

unnecessary; the power of regulating trade between State and State, already vested in the General Legislature, being sufficient.

On the question, —

Massachusetts, Delaware, South Carolina, aye — 3; New Hampshire, Connecticut, New Jersey, Pennsylvania, Maryland, Virginia, North Carolina, Georgia, no — 8.

Mr. MADISON moved, that the words, "nor lay imposts or duties on imports," be transferred from Article 13, where the consent of the General Legislature may license the act, into Article 12, which will make the prohibition on the States absolute. He observed, that as the States interested in this power, by which they could tax the imports of their neighbours passing through their markets, were a majority, they could give the consent of the Legislature to the injury of New Jersey, North Carolina, &c.

Mr. WILLIAMSON seconded the motion.

Mr. SHERMAN thought the power might safely be left to the Legislature of the United States.

Col. MASON observed, that particular States might wish to encourage, by impost duties, certain manufactures, for which they enjoyed natural advantages, as Virginia, the manufacture of hemp, &c.

Mr MADISON. The encouragement of manufactures in that mode requires duties, not only on imports directly from foreign countries, but from the other States in the Union, which would revive all the mischiefs experienced from the want of a general Government over commerce.

On the question, —

New Hampshire, New Jersey, Delaware, North Carolina, aye — 4; Massachusetts, Connecticut, Pennsylvania, Maryland, Virginia, South Carolina, Georgia, no — 7.

Article 12, as amended, was then agreed to, *nem. con.*

Article 13, was then taken up.

Mr. KING moved to insert, after the word "imports," the words, "or exports," so as to prohibit the States from taxing either; and on this question, it passed in the affirmative, —

New Hampshire, Massachusetts, New Jersey, Pennsylvania, Delaware, North Carolina, aye — 6; Connecticut, Maryland, Virginia, South Carolina, Georgia, no — 5.

Mr. SHERMAN moved to add, after the word "exports," the words, "nor with such consent, but for the use of the United States;" so as to carry the proceeds of all State duties on imports or exports, into the common treasury.

Mr. MADISON liked the motion, as preventing all State imposts; but lamented the complexity we were giving to the commercial system.

Mr. GOUVERNEUR MORRIS thought the regulation necessary, to prevent the Atlantic States from endeavouring to tax the Western States, and promote their interest by opposing the navigation of the Mississippi, which would drive the Western people into the arms of Great Britain.

Mr. CLYMER thought the encouragement of the Western country was suicide on the part of the old States. If the States have such different interests that they cannot be left to regulate their own manufactures, without encountering the interests of other States, it is a proof that they are not fit to compose one nation.

Mr. KING was afraid that the regulation moved by Mr. SHERMAN would too much interfere with the policy of States respecting their manufactures, which may be necessary. Revenue, he reminded the House, was the object of the General Legislature.

On Mr. SHERMAN's motion, —

New Hampshire, Connecticut, New Jersey, Pennsylvania, Delaware, Virginia, North Carolina, South Carolina, Georgia, aye — 9; Massachusetts, Maryland, no — 2.

Article 13, was then agreed to, as amended.

Article 14, was then taken up.

General PINCKNEY was not satisfied with it. He seemed to wish some provision should be included in favour of property in slaves.

On the question on Article 14, —

New Hampshire, Massachusetts, Connecticut, New Jersey, Pennsylvania, Delaware, Maryland, Virginia, North Carolina, aye — 9; South Carolina, no — 1; Georgia, divided.

Article 15, being then taken up, the words, "high misdemeanour," were struck out, and the words, "other crime," inserted, in order to comprehend all proper cases; it being doubtful whether "high misdemeanour" had not a technical meaning too limited.

Mr. Butler and Mr. Pinckney moved to require "fugitive slaves and servants to be delivered up like criminals."

Mr. Wilson. This would oblige the Executive of the State to do it, at the public expense.

Mr. Sherman saw no more propriety in the public seizing and surrendering a slave or servant, than a horse.

Mr. Butler withdrew his proposition, in order that some particular provision might be made, apart from this article.

Article 15, as amended, was then agreed to, *nem con.*
Adjourned.

WEDNESDAY, AUGUST 29TH.

In Convention,— Article 16, being taken up, —

Mr. Williamson moved to substitute, in place of it, the words of the Articles of Confederation on the same subject. He did not understand precisely the meaning of the article.

Mr. Wilson and Doctor Johnson supposed the meaning to be, that judgments in one State should be the ground of actions in other States; and that acts of the Legislatures should be included, for the sake of acts of insolvency, &c.

Mr. Pinckney moved to commit Article 16, with the following proposition: "To establish uniform laws upon the subject of bankruptcies, and respecting the damages arising on the protest of foreign bills of exchange."

Mr. GORHAM was for agreeing to the article, and committing the proposition.

Mr. MADISON was for committing both. He wished the Legislature might be authorized to provide for the *execution* of judgments in other States, under such regulations as might be expedient. He thought that this might be safely done, and was justified by the nature of the Union.

Mr. RANDOLPH said there was no instance of one nation executing judgments of the courts of another nation. He moved the following proposition:

"Whenever the act of any State, whether legislative, executive, or judiciary, shall be attested and exemplified under the seal thereof, such attestation and exemplification shall be deemed in other States as full proof of the existence of that act; and its operation shall be binding in every other State, in all cases to which it may relate, and which are within the cognizance and jurisdiction of the State wherein the said act was done."

On the question for committing Article 16, with Mr. PINCKNEY'S motion,—

Connecticut, New Jersey, Pennsylvania, Delaware, Maryland, Virginia, North Carolina, South Carolina, Georgia, aye — 9; New Hampshire, Massachusetts, no — 2.

The motion of Mr. RANDOLPH was also committed, *nem. con.*

Mr. GOUVERNEUR MORRIS moved to commit also the following proposition on the same subject:

"Full faith ought to be given in each State to the public acts, records, and judicial proceedings, of every other State; and the Legislature shall, by general laws, determine the proof and effect of such acts, records, and proceedings;" and it was committed, *nem. con.*

The Committee appointed for these references were, Mr. RUTLEDGE, Mr. RANDOLPH, Mr. GORHAM, Mr. WILSON, and Mr. JOHNSON.

Mr. DICKINSON mentioned to the House, that on examining Blackstone's Commentaries, he found that the term "*ex*

40

post facto " related to criminal cases only; that they would
not consequently restrain the States from retrospective laws
in civil cases; and that some further provision for this purpose would be requisite.

Article 7, Section 6, by the Committee of eleven reported
to be struck out (see the twenty-fourth inst) being now
taken up,—

Mr. PINCKNEY moved to postpone the Report, in favor
of the following proposition: " That no act of the Legislature
for the purpose of regulating the commerce of the United
States with foreign powers, among the several States shall
be passed without the assent of two-thirds of the members
of each House." He remarked that there were five distinct
commercial interests. 1. The fisheries and West India
trade, which belonged to the New England States. 2. The
interest of New York lay in a free trade. 3. Wheat and
flour the staples of the two Middle States (New Jersey and
Pennsylvania). 4. Tobacco, the staple of Maryland and
Virginia, and partly of North Carolina. 5. Rice and indigo, the staples of South Carolina and Georgia. These different interests would be a source of oppressive regulations,
if no check to a bare majority should be provided. States
pursue their interests with less scruple than individuals.
The power of regulating commerce was a pure concession
on the part of the Southern States. They did not need the
protection of the Northern States at present.

Mr. MARTIN seconded the motion.

General PINCKNEY said it was the true interest of the
Southern States to have no regulation of commerce; but
considering the loss brought on the commerce of the
Eastern States by the Revolution, their liberal conduct
towards the views* of South Carolina, and the interest the
weak Southern States had in being united with the strong

---

* He meant the permission to import slaves. An understanding on the two subjects of *navigation* and *slavery*, had taken place between those parts of the Union,
which explains the vote on the motion depending, as well as the language of General
Pinckney and others.

Eastern States, he thought it proper that no fetters should be imposed on the power of making commercial regulations, and that his constituents, though prejudiced against the Eastern States, would be reconciled to this liberality. He had, himself, he said, prejudices against the Eastern States before he came here, but would acknowledge that he had found them as liberal and candid as any men whatever.

Mr. CLYMER. The diversity of commercial interests, of necessity, creates difficulties which ought not to be increased by unnecessary restrictions. The Northern and Middle States will be ruined, if not enabled to defend themselves against foreign regulations.

Mr. SHERMAN, alluding to Mr. PINCKNEY's enumeration of particular interests, as requiring a security against abuse of the power, observed, that the diversity was of itself a security; adding, that to require more than a majority to decide a question was always embarrassing, as had been experienced in cases requiring the votes of nine States in Congress.

Mr. PINCKNEY replied, that his enumeration meant the five minute interests. It still left the two great divisions, of Northern and Southern interests.

Mr. GOUVERNEUR MORRIS opposed the object of the motion, as highly injurious. Preferences to American ships will multiply them, till they can carry the Southern produce cheaper than it is now carried. A navy was essential to security, particularly of the Southern States; and can only be had by a navigation act encouraging American bottoms and seamen. In those points of view, then, alone, it is the interest of the Southern States that navigation acts should be facilitated. Shipping, he said, was the worst and most precarious kind of property, and stood in need of public patronage,

Mr. WILLIAMSON was in favor of making two-thirds, instead of a majority, requisite, as more satisfactory to the Southern people. No useful measure, he believed, had been lost in Congress for want of nine votes. As to the weakness of the Southern States, he was not alarmed on that account. The sickliness of their climate for invaders would prevent their being made an object. He acknowledged that he did not think the motion requiring two-thirds necessary in itself; because if a majority of the Northern States should push their regulations too far, the Southern States would build ships for themselves; but he knew the Southern people were apprehensive on this subject, and would be pleased with the precaution.

Mr. SPAIGHT was against the motion. The Southern States could at any time save themselves from oppression, by building ships for their own use.

Mr. BUTLER differed from those who considered the rejection of the motion as no concession on the part of the Southern States. He considered the interest of these and of the Eastern States to be as different as the interests of Russia and Turkey. Being, notwithstanding, desirous of conciliating the affections of the Eastern States, he should vote against requiring two-thirds instead of a majority.

Col. MASON. If the Government is to be lasting it must be founded in the confidence and affections of the people ; and must be so constructed as to obtain these. The *majority* will be governed by their interests. The Southern States are the *minority* in both Houses. Is it to be expected that they will deliver themselves bound, hand and foot, to the Eastern States, and enable them to exclaim, in the words of Cromwell, on a certain occasion — " the Lord hath delivered them into our hands ? "

Mr. WILSON took notice of the several objections, and remarked, that if every peculiar interest was to be secured, *unanimity* ought to be required. The majority, he said, would be no more governed by interest than the minority. It was surely better to let the latter be bound hand and foot, than the former. Great inconveniences had, he contended, been experienced in Congress from the Article of Confederation requiring nine votes in certain cases.

Mr. MADISON went into a pretty full view of the subject.

He observed that the disadvantage to the Southern States from a navigation act lay chiefly in a temporary rise of freight, attended, however, with an increase of Southern as well as Northern shipping — with the emigration of Northern seamen and merchants to the Southern States — and with a removal of the existing and injurious retaliations among the States on each other. The power of foreign nations to obstruct our retaliating measures on them, by a corrupt influence, would also be less, if a majority should be made competent, than if two-thirds of each House should be required to legislative acts in this case. An abuse of the power would be qualified with all these good effects. But he thought an abuse was rendered improbable by the provision of two branches — by the independence of the Senate — by the negative of the Executive -- by the interest of Connecticut and New Jersey, which were agricultural, not commercial States — by the interior interest, which was also agricultural in the most commercial States — and by the accession of Western States, which would be altogether agricultural. He added, that the Southern States would derive an essential advantage, in the general security afforded by the increase of our maritime strength. He stated the vulnerable situation of them all, and of Virginia in particular. The increase of the coasting trade, and of seamen, would also be favorable to the Southern States, by increasing the consumption of their produce. If the wealth of the Eastern should in a still greater proportion be augmented, that wealth would contribute the more to the public wants, and be otherwise a national benefit.

Mr. RUTLEDGE was against the motion of his colleague. It did not follow from a grant of the power to regulate trade, that it would be abused. At the worst, a navigation act could bear hard a little while only on the Southern States. As we are laying the foundation for a great empire, we ought to take a permanent view of the subject, and not look at the present moment only. He reminded the House of the necessity of securing the West India trade to this country. That was the great object, and a navigation act was necessary for obtaining it.

Mr. RANDOLPH said that there were features so odious in the Constitution, as it now stands, that he doubted whether he should be able to agree to it. A rejection of the motion would complete the deformity of the system. He took notice of the argument in favor of giving the power over trade to a majority, drawn from the opportunity foreign powers would have of obstructing retaliatory measures, if two-thirds were made requisite. He did not think there was weight in that consideration. The difference between a majority and two-thirds, did not afford room for such an opportunity. Foreign influence would also be more likely to be exerted on the President, who could require three-fourths by his negative. He did not mean, however, to enter into the merits. What he had in view was merely to pave the way for a declaration, which he might be hereafter obliged to make; if an accumulation of obnoxious ingredients should take place, that he could not give his assent to the plan.

Mr. GORHAM. If the Government is to be so fettered as to be unable to relieve the Eastern States, what motive can they have to join in it, and thereby tie their own hands from measures which they could otherwise take for themselves? The Eastern States were not led to strengthen the Union by fear for their own safety. He deprecated the consequences of disunion; but if it should take place, it was the Southern part of the Continent that had most reason to dread them. He urged the improbability of a combination against the interest of the Southern States, the different situations of the Northern and Middle States being a security against it. It was, moreover, certain, that foreign ships would never be altogether excluded, especially those of nations in treaty with us.

On the question to postpone, in order to take up Mr. PINCKNEY's motion,—

Maryland, Virginia, North Carolina, Georgia, aye — 4;

New Hampshire, Massachusetts, Connecticut, New Jersey, Pennsylvania, Delaware, South Carolina, no — 7.

The Report of the Committee for striking out Section 6, requiring two-thirds of each House to pass a navigation act, was then agreed to, *nem. con.*

Mr. BUTLER moved to insert after Article 15, " If any person bound to service or labor in any of the United States, shall escape into another State, he or she shall not be discharged from such service or labor, in consequence of any regulations subsisting in the State to which they escape, but shall be delivered up to the person justly claiming their service or labor,"— which was agreed to, *nem. con.*

Article 17, being then taken up,—

Mr. GOUVERNEUR MORRIS moved to strike out the two last sentences, to wit: " If the admission be consented to, the new States shall be admitted on the same terms with the original States. But the Legislature may make conditions with the new States, concerning the public debt which shall be then subsisting." He did not wish to bind down the Legislature to admit Western States on the terms here stated.

Mr. MADISON opposed the motion; insisting that the Western States neither would, nor ought to submit to a union which degraded them from an equal rank with the other States.

Col. MASON. If it were possible by just means to prevent emigrations to the Western country, it might be good policy. But go the people will, as they find it for their interest; and the best policy is to treat them with that equality which will make them friends not enemies.

Mr. GOUVERNEUR MORRIS did not mean to discourage the growth of the Western country. He knew that to be impossible. He did not wish, however, to throw the power into their hands.

Mr. SHERMAN was against the motion, and for fixing an equality of privileges by the Constitution.

Mr. LANGDON was in favor of the motion. He did not know but circumstances might arise, which would render it inconvenient to admit new States on terms of equality.

Mr. WILLIAMSON was for leaving the Legislature free. The existing *small* States enjoy an equality now, and for *that* reason are admitted to it in the Senate. This reason is not applicable to new Western States.

On Mr. GOUVERNEUR MORRIS'S motion, for striking out,—

New Hampshire, Massachusetts, Connecticut, New Jersey, Pennsylvania, Delaware, North Carolina, South Carolina, Georgia, aye — 9; Maryland, Virginia, no — 2.

Mr. L. MARTIN and Mr. GOUVERNEUR MORRIS moved to strike out of Article 17, " but to such admission the consent of two-thirds of the members present shall be necessary." Before any question was taken on this motion,—

Mr. GOUVERNEUR MORRIS moved the following proposition, as a substitute for the seventeenth Article:

" New States may be admitted by the Legislature into the Union; but no new States shall be erected within the limits of any of the present States, without the consent of the Legislature of such State, as well as of the General Legislature."

The first part, to " Union," inclusive, was agreed to, *nem. con.*

Mr. L. MARTIN opposed the latter part. Nothing, he said, would so alarm the limited States, as to make the consent of the large States, claiming the Western lands, necessary to the establishment of new States within their limits. It is proposed to guarantee the States. Shall Vermont be reduced by force, in favor of the States claiming it? Frankland and the Western county of Virginia were in a like situation.

On Mr. GOUVERNEUR MORRIS'S motion, to substitute, &c., it was agreed to,—

Massachusetts, Pennsylvania, Virginia, North Carolina,

South Carolina, Georgia, aye — 6; New Hampshire, Connecticut, New Jersey, Delaware, Maryland, no — 5.

Article 17, being before the House, as amended,—

Mr. SHERMAN was against it. He thought it unnecessary. The Union cannot dismember a State without its consent.

Mr. LANGDON thought there was great weight in the argument of Mr. LUTHER MARTIN; and that the proposition substituted by Mr. GOUVERNEUR MORRIS would excite a dangerous opposition to the plan.

Mr. GOUVERNEUR MORRIS thought, on the contrary, that the small States would be pleased with the regulation, as it holds up the idea of dismembering the large States.

Mr. BUTLER. If new States were to be erected without the consent of the dismembered States, nothing but confusion would ensue. Whenever taxes should press on the people, demagogues would set up their schemes of new States.

Doctor JOHNSON agreed in general with the ideas of Mr. SHERMAN; but was afraid that, as the clause stood, Vermont would be subjected to New York, contrary to the faith pledged by Congress. He was of opinion that Vermont ought to be compelled to come into the Union.

Mr. LANGDON said his objections were connected with the case of Vermont. If they are not taken in, and remain exempt from taxes, it would prove of great injury to New Hampshire and the other neighbouring States.

Mr. DICKINSON hoped the article would not be agreed to. He dwelt on the impropriety of requiring the small States to secure the large ones in their extensive claims of territory.

Mr. WILSON. When the *majority* of a State wish to divide they can do so. The aim of those in opposition to the article, he perceived, was that the General Government should abet the *minority*, and by that means divide a State against its own consent.

Mr. GOUVERNEUR MORRIS. If the forced division of the

States is the object of the new system, and is to be pointed against one or two States, he expected the gentlemen from these would pretty quickly leave us.

Adjourned.

THURSDAY, AUGUST 30TH.

In Convention,—Article 17, being resumed, for a question on it, as amended by Mr. GOUVERNEUR MORRIS's substitute,—

Mr. CARROLL moved to strike out so much of the Article as requires the consent of the State to its being divided. He was aware that the object of this pre-requisite might be to prevent domestic disturbances; but such was our situation with regard to the Crown lands, and the sentiments of Maryland on that subject, that he perceived we should again be at sea, if no guard was provided for the right of the United States to the back lands. He suggested, that it might be proper to provide, that nothing in the Constitution should affect the right of the United States to lands ceded by Great Britain in the treaty of peace; and proposed a commitment to a member from each State. He assured the House, that this was a point of a most serious nature. It was desirable, above all things, that the act of the Convention might be agreed to unanimously. But should this point be disregarded, he believed that all risks would be run by a considerable minority, sooner than give their concurrence.

Mr. L. MARTIN seconded the motion for a commitment.

Mr. RUTLEDGE. Is it to be supposed that the States are to be cut up without their own consent? The case of Vermont will probably be particularly provided for. There could be no room to fear that Virginia or North Carolina would call on the United States to maintain their government over the mountains.

Mr. WILLIAMSON said that North Carolina was well disposed to give up her western lands; but attempts at compulsion were not the policy of the United States. He was for doing nothing in the Constitution, in the present case; and for leaving the whole matter *in statu quo.*

Mr. WILSON was against the commitment. Unanimity was of great importance, but not to be purchased by the majority's yielding to the minority. He should have no objection to leaving the case of the new States as heretofore. He knew nothing that would give greater or juster alarm than the doctrine, that a political society is to be torn asunder without its own consent.

On Mr. CARROLL's motion for commitment,—

New Jersey, Delaware, Maryland, aye — 3; New Hampshire, Massachusetts, Connecticut, Pennsylvania, Virginia, North Carolina, South Carolina, Georgia, no — 8.

Mr. SHERMAN moved to postpone the substitute for Article 17, agreed to yesterday, in order to take up the following amendment:

"The Legislature shall have power to admit other States into the Union; and new States to be formed by the division or junction of States now in the Union with the consent of the Legislature of such States." [The first part was meant for the case of Vermont, to secure its admission.]

On the question, it passed in the negative,—

New Hampshire, Massachusetts, Connecticut, Pennsylvania, South Carolina, aye — 5; New Jersey, Delaware, Maryland, Virginia, North Carolina, Georgia, no — 6.

Doctor JOHNSON moved to insert the words, "hereafter formed, or," after the words, "shall be," in the substitute for Article 17, [the more clearly to save Vermont, as being already formed into a State, from a dependence on the consent of New York for her admission.] The motion was agreed to,—Delaware and Maryland only, dissenting.

Mr. GOUVERNEUR MORRIS moved to strike out the word "limits," in the substitute, and insert the word "jurisdiction." [This also was meant to guard the case of Vermont; the jurisdiction of New York not extending over

Vermont, which was in the exercise of sovereignty, though Vermont was within the asserted limits of New York.]

On this question,—

New Hampshire, Massachusetts, Connecticut, Pennsylvania, Delaware, Maryland, Virginia, aye — 7; New Jersey, North Carolina, South Carolina, Georgia, no — 4.

Mr. L. MARTIN, urged the unreasonableness of forcing and guaranteeing the people of Virginia beyond the mountains, the Western people of North Carolina and Georgia, and the people of Maine, to continue under the States now governing them, without the consent of those States to their separation. Even if they should become the *majority*, the majority of *counties*, as in Virginia, may still hold fast the dominion over them. Again the majority may place the seat of government entirely among themselves, and for their own convenience; and still keep the injured parts of the States in subjection, under the guarantee of the General government against domestic violence. He wished Mr. WILSON had thought a little sooner of the value of *political* bodies. In the beginning, when the rights of the small States were in question, they were phantoms, ideal beings. Now when the great States were to be affected, political societies were of a sacred nature. He repeated and enlarged on the unreasonableness of requiring the small States to guarantee the Western claims of the large ones. It was said yesterday, by Mr. GOUVERNEUR MORRIS, that if the large States were to be split to pieces without their consent, their Representatives here would take their leave. If the small States are to be required to guarantee them in this manner, it will be found that the Representatives of other States will, with equal firmness, take their leave of the Constitution on the table.

It was moved by Mr. L. MARTIN to postpone the substituted article, in order to take up the following: "The Legislature of the United States shall have power to erect new States within, as well as without the territory claimed by the several States, or either of them; and admit the same into the Union: provided that nothing in this Constitution shall be construed to affect the claim of the United States to vacant lands ceded to them by the late treaty of peace;" which passed in the negative,— New Jersey, Delaware, and Maryland, only, aye.

On the question to agree to Mr. GOUVERNEUR MORRIS's substituted article, as amended, in the words following: "New States may be admitted by the Legislature into the Union; but no new State shall be hereafter formed or erected within the jurisdiction of any of the present States, without the consent of the Legislature of such State, as well as of the general Legislature,—New Hampshire, Massachusetts, Connecticut, Pennsylvania, Virginia, North Carolina, South Carolina, Georgia, aye — 8; New Jersey, Delaware, Maryland, no — 3.

Mr. DICKINSON moved to add the following clause to the last:

" Nor shall any State be formed by the junction of two or more States, or parts thereof, without the consent of the Legislature of such States, as well as of the Legislature of the United States;" which was agreed to without a count of the votes.

Mr. CARROLL moved to add: "Provided, nevertheless, that nothing in this Constitution shall be construed to affect the claim of the United States to vacant lands ceded to them by the treaty of peace." This, he said, might be understood as relating to lands not claimed by any particular States, but he had in view also some of the claims of particular States.

Mr. WILSON was against the motion. There was nothing in the Constitution affecting, one way or the other, the claims of the United States; and it was best to insert nothing, leaving every thing on that litigated subject *in statu quo.*

Mr. MADISON considered the claim of the United States as in fact favoured by the jurisdiction of the Judicial power of the United States over controversies to which they should be parties. He thought it best, on the whole, to be silent on the subject. He did not view the proviso of Mr. CARROLL as dangerous; but to make it neutral and fair, it ought to go further, and declare that the claims of particular States also should not be affected.

Mr. SHERMAN thought the proviso harmless, especially with the addition suggested by Mr. MADISON in favour of the claims of particular States.

Mr. BALDWIN did not wish any undue advantage to be given to Georgia. He thought the proviso proper with the addition proposed. It should be remembered that if Georgia has gained much by the cession in the treaty of peace, she was in danger during the war of a *Uti possedetis.*

Mr. RUTLEDGE thought it wrong to insert a proviso, where there was nothing which it could restrain, or on which it could operate.

Mr. CARROLL withdrew his motion and moved the following:

"Nothing in this Constitution shall be construed to alter the claims of the United States, or of the individual States, to the Western territory; but all such claims shall be examined into, and decided upon, by the Supreme Court of the United States."

Mr. GOUVERNEUR MORRIS moved to postpone this, in order to take up the following:

"The Legislature shall have power to dispose of, and make all needful rules and regulations respecting, the territory or other property belonging. to the United States; and nothing in this Constitution contained, shall be so construed as to prejudice any claims, either of the United States or of any particular State." The postponement agreed to, *nem. con.*

Mr. L. MARTIN moved to amend the proposition of Mr. GOUVERNEUR MORRIS, by adding: "But all such claims may be examined into, and decided upon, by the Supreme Court of the United States."

Mr. GOUVERNEUR MORRIS. This is unnecessary, as all

suits to which the United States are parties are already to be decided by the Supreme Court.

Mr. L. MARTIN. It is proper, in order to remove all doubts on this point.

On the question on Mr. L. MARTIN'S amendatory motion, —

New Jersey, Maryland, aye — 2 ; New Hampshire, Massachusetts, Connecticut, Pennsylvania, Delaware, Virginia, no — 6. States not further called, the negatives being sufficient, and the point being given up.

The motion of Mr. GOUVERNEUR MORRIS was then agreed to, Maryland alone dissenting.

Article 18, being taken up, the word "foreign" was struck out, *nem. con.* as superfluous being implied in the term "invasion."

Mr. DICKINSON moved to strike out, "on the application of its Legislature, against." He thought it of essential importance to the tranquillity of the United States, that they should in all cases suppress domestic violence, which may proceed from the State Legislature itself, or from disputes between the two branches where such exist.

Mr. DAYTON mentioned the conduct of Rhode Island as showing the necessity of giving latitude to the power of the United States on this subject.

On the question, —

New Jersey, Pennsylvania, Delaware, aye -- 3; New Hampshire, Massachusetts, Connecticut, Maryland, Virginia, North Carolina, South Carolina, Georgia, no — 8.

On a question for striking out "domestic violence," and inserting "insurrections," it passed in the negative, —

New Jersey, Virginia, North Carolina, South Carolina, Georgia, aye -- 5; New Hampshire, Massachusetts, Connecticut, Pennsylvania, Delaware, Maryland, no — 6.

Mr. DICKINSON moved to insert the words, " or Executive," after the words, " application of its Legislature." The occasion itself, he remarked, might hinder the Legislature from meeting.

On this question,—

New Hampshire, Connecticut, New Jersey Pennsylvania, Delaware, North Carolina, South Carolina, Georgia, aye 8; Massachusetts, Virginia, no — 2; Maryland, divided.

Mr. L. MARTIN moved to subjoin to the last amendment the words, "in the recess of the Legislature." On which question, Maryland only, aye.

On the question on the last clause, as amended,—

New Hampshire, Massachusetts, Connecticut, New Jersey, Pennsylvania, Virginia, North Carolina, South Carolina, Georgia, aye — 9; Delaware, Maryland, no — 2.

Article 19, was then taken up.

Mr. GOUVERNEUR MORRIS suggested, that the Legislature should be left at liberty to call a Convention whenever they pleased.

The Article was agreed to, *nem. con.*

Article 20 was then taken up. The words "or affirmation," were added, after "oath."

Mr. PINCKNEY moved to add to the Article: "but no religious test shall ever be required as a qualification to any office or public trust under the authority of the United States."

Mr. SHERMAN thought it unnecessary, the prevailing liberality being a sufficient security against such tests.

Mr. GOUVERNEUR MORRIS and General PINCKNEY approved the motion.

The motion was agreed to, *nem. con.*, and then the whole article,— North Carolina only, no; and Maryland, divided.

Article 21, being then taken up: "The ratifications of the Conventions of —— States shall be sufficient for organizing this Constitution."

Mr. WILSON proposed to fill the blank with "seven," that being a majority of the whole number, and sufficient for the commencement of the plan.

Mr. CARROLL moved to postpone the Article, in order to take up the Report of the Committee of eleven (see the twenty-eighth of August) and on the question,—

New Jersey, Delaware, Maryland, aye — 3; New Hampshire, Massachusetts, Connecticut, Pennsylvania, Virginia,
North Carolina, South Carolina, Georgia, no — 8.

Mr. GOUVERNEUR MORRIS thought the blank ought to be
filled in a two-fold way, so as to provide for the event of the
ratifying States being contiguous, which would render a
smaller number sufficient ; and the event of their being
dispersed, which would require a greater number for the
introduction of the Government.

Mr. SHERMAN observed that the States being now confederated by articles which require unanimity in changes,
he thought the ratification, in this case, of ten States at
least ought to be made necessary.

Mr. RANDOLPH was for filling the blank with "nine,"
that being a respectable majority of the whole, and being a
number made familiar by the constitution of the existing
Congress.

Mr. WILSON mentioned "eight," as preferable.

Mr. DICKINSON asked, whether the concurrence of Congress is to be essential to the establishment of the system
— whether the refusing States in the Confederacy could
be deserted — and whether Congress could concur in contravening the system under which they acted ?

Mr. MADISON remarked, that if the blank should be
filled with "seven," "eight," or "nine," the Constitution
as it stands might be put in force over the whole of the
people, though less than a majority of them should
ratify it.

Mr. WILSON. As the Constitution stands, the States
only which ratify can be bound. We must, he said, in this
case, go to the original powers of society. The house on
fire must be extinguished, without a scrupulous regard to
ordinary rights.

Mr. BUTLER was in favor of "nine." He revolted at
the idea that one or two States should restrain the rest
from consulting their safety.

Mr. CARROLL moved to fill the blank with, "the thir-
41

teen ;" unanimity being necessary to dissolve the existing Confederacy, which had been unanimously established.

Mr. KING thought this amendment necessary ; otherwise, as the Constitution now stands, it will operate on the whole, though ratified by a part only.

Adjourned.

FRIDAY, AUGUST 31ST.

In Convention,— Mr. KING moved to add, to the end of Article 21, the words, "between the said States ; " so as to confine the operation of the Government to the States ratifying it.

On the question, nine States voted in the affirmative ; Maryland, no ; Delaware, absent.

Mr. MADISON proposed to fill the blank in the Article with, "any seven or more States entitled to thirty-three members at least in the House of Representatives according to the allotment made in the third Section of Article 4."- This, he said, would require the concurrence of a majority of both the States and the people.

Mr. SHERMAN doubted the propriety of authorizing less than all the States to execute the Constitution, considering the nature of the existing Confederation.   Perhaps all the States may concur, and on that supposition it is needless to hold out a breach of faith.

Mr. CLYMER and Mr. CARROLL moved to postpone the consideration of Article 21, in order to take up the Reports of Committees not yet acted on.   On this question the States were equally divided,— New Hampshire, Pennsylvania, Delaware, Maryland, Georgia, aye — 5; Massachusetts, New Jersey, Virginia, North Carolina, South Carolina, no — 5; Connecticut, divided.

Mr. GOUVERNEUR MORRIS moved to strike out, " conventions of the," after " ratifications; " leaving the States to pursue their own modes of ratification.

Mr. CARROLL mentioned the mode of altering the Constitution of Maryland pointed out therein, and that no other mode could be pursued in that State.

Mr. KING thought that striking out "conventions," as the requisite mode, was equivalent to giving up the business altogether. Conventions alone, which will avoid all the obstacles from the complicated formation of the Legislatures, will succeed; and if not positively required by the plan, its enemies will oppose that mode.

Mr. GOUVERNEUR MORRIS said, he meant to facilitate the adoption of the plan, by leaving the modes approved by the several State Constitutions to be followed.

Mr. MADISON considered it best to require Conventions; among other reasons for this, that the powers given to the General Government being taken from the State Governments, the Legislatures would be more disinclined than Conventions composed in part at least of other men; and if disinclined, they could devise modes apparently promoting, but really thwarting, the ratification. The difficulty in Maryland was no greater than in other States, where no mode of change was pointed out by the Constitution, and all officers were under oath to support it. The people were, in fact, the fountain of all power, and by resorting to them, all difficulties were got over. They could alter constitutions as they pleased. It was a principle in the Bills of Rights, that first principles might be resorted to.

Mr. McHENRY said, that the officers of government in Maryland were under oath to support the mode of alteration prescribed by the Constitution.

Mr. GORHAM urged the expediency of "Conventions;" also Mr. PINCKNEY, for reasons formerly urged on a discussion of this question.

Mr. L. MARTIN insisted on a reference to the State Legislatures. He urged the danger of commotions from a resort to the people and to first principles; in which the Government might be on one side, and the people on the other. He was apprehensive of no such consequences, however, in Maryland, whether the Legislature or the people should be appealed to. Both of them would be generally against the Constitution. He repeated also the peculiarity in the Maryland Constitution.

Mr. KING observed, that the Constitution of Massachusetts was made unalterable till the year 1790; yet this was no difficulty with him. The State must have contemplated a recurrence to first principles, before they sent deputies to this Convention.

Mr. SHERMAN moved to postpone Article 21, and to take up Article 22; on which question,—

Connecticut, Pennsylvania, Delaware, Maryland, Virginia, aye—5; New Hampshire, Massachusetts, New Jersey, North Carolina, South Carolina, Georgia, no—6.

On Mr. GOUVERNEUR MORRIS's motion, to strike out "Conventions of the," it was negatived, —

Connecticut, Pennsylvania, Maryland, Georgia, aye — 4; New Hampshire, Massachusetts, New Jersey, Delaware, Virginia, South Carolina, no — 6.

On the question for filling the blank in Article 21, with "thirteen," moved by Mr. CARROLL and Mr. L. MARTIN,— all the States were no, except Maryland.

Mr. SHERMAN and Mr. DAYTON moved to fill the blank with "ten."

Mr. WILSON supported the motion of Mr. MADISON, requiring a majority both of the people and of States.

Mr. CLYMER was also in favor of it.

Colonel MASON was for preserving ideas familiar to the people. Nine States had been required in all great cases under the Confederation, and that number was on that account preferable.

On the question for "ten,"—

Connecticut, New Jersey, Maryland, Georgia, aye — 4; New Hampshire, Massachusetts, Pennsylvania, Delaware, Virginia, North Carolina, South Carolina, no — 7.

On the question for "nine,"—

New Hampshire, Massachusetts, Connecticut, New Jersey, Pennsylvania, Delaware, Maryland, Georgia, aye — 8; Virginia, North Carolina, South Carolina, no — 3.

Article 21, as amended, was then agreed to by all the States, Maryland excepted, and Mr. JENIFER being, aye.

Article 22, was then taken up, to wit: "This Constitution shall be laid before the United States in Congress assembled, for their approbation; and it is the opinion of this Convention that it should be afterwards submitted to a Convention chosen in each State, under the recommendation of its Legislature, in order to receive the ratification of such Convention."

Mr. GOUVERNEUR MORRIS and Mr. PINCKNEY moved to strike out the words, "for their approbation."

On this question,—

New Hampshire, Connecticut, New Jersey,* Pennsylvania, Delaware, Virginia, North Carolina, South Carolina, aye — 8; Massachusetts, Maryland, Georgia, no — 3.

Mr. GOUVERNEUR MORRIS and Mr. PINCKNEY then moved, to amend the Article so as to read:

"This Constitution shall be laid before the United States in Congress assembled; and it is the opinion of this Convention that it should afterwards be submitted to a Convention chosen in each State, in order to receive the ratification of such Convention; to which end the several Legislatures ought to provide for the calling Conventions within their respective States as speedily as circumstances will permit."

Mr. GOUVERNEUR MORRIS said his object was to impress in stronger terms the necessity of calling Conventions, in order to prevent enemies to the plan from giving it the go by. When it first appears, with the sanction of this Convention, the people will be favorable to it. By degrees, the State officers, and those interested in the State Governments, will intrigue, and turn the popular current against it.

---

* In the printed Journal, New Jersey, no.

Mr. L. MARTIN believed Mr. MORRIS to be right, that after a while the people would be against it; but for a different reason from that alleged. He believed they would not ratify it, unless hurried into it by surprise.

Mr. GERRY enlarged on the idea of Mr. L. MARTIN, in which he concurred; represented the system as full of vices; and dwelt on the impropriety of destroying the existing Confederation, without the unanimous consent of the parties to it.

On the question on Mr. GOUVERNEUR MORRIS's and Mr. PINCKNEY's motion,—

New Hampshire Massachusetts, Pennsylvania, Delaware, aye — 4; Connecticut, New Jersey, Maryland, Virginia, North Carolina, South Carolina, Georgia, no — 7.

Mr. GERRY moved to postpone Article 22.

Colonel MASON seconded the motion declaring that he would sooner chop off his right hand, than put it to the Constitution as it now stands. He wished to see some points, not yet decided, brought to a decision, before being compelled to give a final opinion on this Article. Should these points be improperly settled, his wish would then be to bring the whole subject before another General Convention.

Mr. GOUVERNEUR MORRIS was ready for a postponement. He had long wished for another Convention, that will have the firmness to provide a vigorous Government, which we are afraid to do.

Mr. RANDOLPH stated his idea to be, in case the final form of the Constitution should not permit him to accede to it, that the State Conventions should be at liberty to propose amendments, to be submitted to another General Convention, which may reject or incorporate them as may be judged proper.

On the question for postponing,—

New Jersey, Maryland, North Carolina, aye — 3; New Hampshire, Massachusetts, Connecticut, Pennsylvania, Delaware, Virginia, South Carolina, Georgia, no — 8.

On the question on Article 22, ten States, aye; Maryland, no.

Article 23, being taken up, as far as the words, "assigned by Congress," inclusive, was agreed to, *nem. con.*, the blank having been first filled with the word "nine," as of course.

On the motion for postponing the residue of the clause, "concerning the choice of the President, &c."—

Massachusetts, Delaware, Virginia, North Carolina, aye — 4; New Hampshire, Connecticut, New Jersey, Pennsylvania, Maryland, South Carolina, Georgia, no — 7.

Mr. GOUVERNEUR MORRIS then moved to strike out the words, "choose the President of the United States, and;" this point, of choosing the President, not being yet finally determined; and on this question,—

Massachusetts, Connecticut, New Jersey, Pennsylvania, Delaware, Virginia, North Carolina, South Carolina,* Georgia, aye — 9; New Hampshire, no — 1; Maryland, divided.

Article 23, as amended, was then agreed to, *nem. con.*

The report of the Grand Committee of eleven, made by Mr. SHERMAN, was then taken up (see the twenty-eighth of August).

On the question to agree to the following clause, to be inserted after Article 7, Sect. 4, " nor shall any regulation of commerce or revenue give preference to the ports of one State over those of another,"— agreed to, *nem. con.*

On the clause, " or oblige vessels bound to or from any State to enter, clear, or pay duties, in another,"—

Mr. MADISON thought the restriction would be inconvenient; as in the river Delaware, if a vessel cannot be required to make entry below the jurisdiction of Pennsylvania.

Mr. FITZSIMONS admitted that it might be inconvenient, but thought it would be a greater inconvenience, to re-

---

* In the printed Journal, South Carolina, no.

quire vessels bound to Philadelphia to enter below the jurisdiction of the State.

Mr. GORHAM and Mr. LANGDON contended, that the Government would be so fettered by this clause, as to defeat the good purpose of the plan. They mentioned the situation of the trade of Massachusetts and New Hampshire, the case of Sandy Hook, which is in the State of New Jersey, but where precautions against smuggling into New York ought to be established by the General Government.

Mr. McHENRY said, the clause would not screen a vessel from being obliged to take an officer on board, as a security for due entry, &c.

Mr. CARROLL was anxious that the clause should be agreed to. He assured the House, that this was a tender point in Maryland.

Mr. JENIFER urged the necessity of the clause in the same point of view.

On the question for agreeing to it,—

Connecticut, New Jersey, Pennsylvania, Delaware, Maryland, Virginia, North Carolina, Georgia, aye — 8; New Hampshire, South Carolina, no — 2.

The word "tonnage," was struck out, *nem con.*, as comprehended in " duties."

On the question on the clause of the Report, "and all duties, imposts and excises, laid by the Legislature, shall be uniform throughout the United States," it was agreed to, *nem. con.**

On motion of Mr. SHERMAN, it was agreed to refer such parts of the Constitution as have been postponed, and such parts of Reports as have not been acted on, to a Committee of a member from each State; the Committee, appointed by ballot, being, Mr. GILMAN, Mr. KING, Mr. SHERMAN, Mr. BREARLY, Mr. GOUVERNEUR MORRIS, Mr. DICKINSON, Mr. CARROLL, Mr. MADISON, Mr. WILLIAMSON, Mr. BUTLER, and Mr. BALDWIN.

Adjourned.

---

* In the printed Journal, New Hampshire and South Carolina entered in the negative.

Saturday, September 1st.

In Convention,—Mr. Brearly, from the Committee of eleven to which were referred yesterday the postponed part of the Constitution, and parts of Reports not acted upon, made the following partial report :

"That in lieu of Article 6, Sect. 9, the words following be inserted, viz : 'The members of each House shall be ineligible to any civil office under the authority of the United States, during the time for which they shall respectively be elected ; and no person holding an office under the United States shall be a member of either House during his continuance in office.' "

Mr. Rutledge, from the Committee to whom were referred sundry propositions, (see twenty-ninth of August) together with Article 16, reported that the following additions be made to the Report, viz :

" After the word ' States,' in the last line on the margin of the third page (see the printed Report,) add, ' to establish uniform laws on the subject of bankruptcies.'

" And insert the following as Article 16, viz : ' Full faith and credit ought to be given in each State to the public acts, records, and judicial proceedings of every other State ; and the Legislature shall, by general laws, prescribe the manner in which such acts, records, and proceedings shall be proved, and the effect which judgments obtained in one State, shall have in another.' "

After receiving these Reports, the House
Adjourned.

Monday, September 3d.

In Convention,— Mr. Gouverneur Morris moved to amend the Report concerning the respect to be paid to acts, records, &c. of one State in other States (see the first of September) by striking out, " judgments obtained in one State shall have in another ; " and to insert the word " thereof," after the word " effect."

Col. MASON favored the motion, particularly if the "effect" was to be restrained to judgments and judicial proceedings.

Mr. WILSON remarked, that if the Legislature were not allowed to *declare the effect*, the provision would amount to nothing more than what now takes place among all independent nations.

Doctor JOHNSON thought the amendment, as worded, would authorize the General Legislature to declare the effect of Legislative acts of one State in another State.

Mr. RANDOLPH considered it as strengthening the general objection against the plan, that its definition of the powers of the Government was so loose as to give it opportunities of usurping all the State powers. He was for not going further than the Report, which enables the Legislature to provide for the effect of *judgments*.

On the amendment, as moved by Mr. GOUVERNEUR MORRIS,—

Massachusetts, Connecticut, New Jersey, Pennsylvania, North Carolina, South Carolina, aye — 6 ; Maryland, Virginia, Georgia, no — 3.

On motion of Mr. MADISON, the words, "ought to," were struck out, and "shall" inserted; and "shall," between "Legislature" and "by general laws," struck out, and "may" inserted, *nem. con.*

On the question to agree to the Report as amended, viz: "Full faith and credit shall be given in each State to the public acts, records and judicial proceedings of every other State, and the Legislature may, by general laws, prescribe the manner in which such acts, records and proceedings shall be proved, and the effect thereof,"— it was agreed to without a count of the States.

The clause in the Report, "To establish uniform laws on the subject of bankruptcies," being taken up, —

Mr. SHERMAN observed, that bankruptcies were in some cases punishable with death, by the laws of England; and he did not choose to grant a power by which that might be done here.

Mr. GOUVERNEUR MORRIS said, this was an extensive and delicate subject. He would agree to it because he saw no danger of abuse of the power by the Legislature of the United States.

On the question to agree to the clause, Connecticut alone was in the negative.

Mr. PINCKNEY moved to postpone the Report of the Committee of eleven (see the first of September) in order to take up the following:

"The members of each House shall be incapable of holding any office under the United States for which they, or any other for their benefit, receive any salary, fees or emoluments of any kind; and the acceptance of such office shall vacate their seats respectively."

He was strenuously opposed to an ineligibility of members to office, and therefore wished to restrain the proposition to a mere incompatibility. He considered the eligibility of members of the Legislature to the honourable offices of Government, as resembling the policy of the Romans, in making the temple of Virtue the road to the temple of Fame.

On this question,—

Pennsylvania, North Carolina, aye — 2; New Hampshire, Massachusetts, Connecticut, New Jersey, Maryland, Virginia, South Carolina, Georgia, no — 8.

Mr. KING moved to insert the word "created," before the word "during," in the Report of the Committee. This, he said, would exclude the members of the first legislature under the Constitution, as most of the offices would then be created.

Mr. WILLIAMSON seconded the motion. He did not see why members of the Legislature should be ineligible to *vacancies* happening during the term of their election.

Mr. SHERMAN was for entirely incapacitating members of the Legislature. He thought their eligibility to offices would give too much influence to the Executive. He said the incapacity ought at least to be extended to cases where salaries should be *increased*, as well as *created*, during the term of the member. He mentioned also the expedient by which the restriction could be evaded, to wit; an existing officer might be translated to an office created, and a member of the Legislature be then put into the office vacated.

Mr. GOUVERNEUR MORRIS contended that the eligibility of members to office would lessen the influence of the Executive. If they cannot be appointed themselves, the Executive will appoint their relations and friends, retaining the service and votes of the members for his purposes in the Legislature. Whereas the appointment of the members deprives him of such an advantage.

Mr. GERRY thought the eligibility of members would have the effect of opening batteries against good officers, in order to drive them out and make way for members of the Legislature.

Mr. GORHAM was in favor of the amendment. Without it, we go further than has been done in any of the States, or indeed any other country. The experience of the State Governments, where there was no such ineligibility, proved that it was not necessary; on the contrary, that the eligibility was among the inducements for fit men to enter into the Legislative service.

Mr. RANDOLPH was inflexibly fixed against inviting men into the Legislature by the prospect of being appointed to offices.

Mr. BALDWIN remarked that the example of the States was not applicable. The Legislatures there are so numerous, that an exclusion of their members would not leave proper men for offices. The case would be otherwise in the General Government.

Colonel MASON. Instead of excluding merit, the ineligibility will keep out corruption, by excluding office-hunters.

Mr. WILSON considered the exclusion of members of the Legislature as increasing the influence of the Executive, as observed by Mr. GOUVERNEUR MORRIS; at the same time that it would diminish the general energy of the Government. He said that the legal disqualification for office would be odious to those who did not wish for office, but did not wish either to be marked by so degrading a distinction.

Mr. PINCKNEY. The first Legislature will be composed of the ablest men to be found. The States will select such to put the Government into operation. Should the report of the Committee, or even the amendment be agreed to, the great offices, even those of the Judiciary department, which are to continue for life, must be filled, while those most capable of filling them will be under a disqualification.

On the question on Mr. KING's motion,—

New Hampshire, Massachusetts, Pennsylvania, Virginia, North Carolina, aye — 5; Connecticut, New Jersey, Maryland, South Carolina, Georgia, no — 5.

The amendment being thus lost, by the equal division of the States, Mr. WILLIAMSON moved to insert the words " created, or the emoluments whereof shall have been increased," before the word "during," in the Report of the Committee.

Mr. KING seconded the motion, and on the question,—

New Hampshire, Massachusetts, Pennsylvania, Virginia, North Carolina, aye — 5; Connecticut, New Jersey, Maryland, South Carolina, no — 4; Georgia, divided.

The last clause, rendering a seat in the Legislature, and an office, incompatible, was agreed to, *nem. con.*

The Report, as amended and agreed to, is as follows:—

" The members of each House shall be ineligible to any civil office under the authority of the United States, created, or the emoluments whereof shall have been increased, during the time for which they shall respectively be elected. And no person holding any office under the United States shall be a member of either House during his continuance in office."

Adjourned.

TUESDAY, SEPTEMBER 4TH.

In Convention, — Mr. BREARLY, from the Committee of Eleven made a further partial Report as follows:

"The Committee of eleven, to whom sundry resolutions, &c., were referred on the thirty-first of August, report, that in their opinion the following additions and alterations should be made to the Report before the Convention, viz:*

"1. The first clause of Article 7, Section 1, to read as follows: 'The Legislature shall have power to lay and collect taxes, duties, imposts and excises, to pay the debts and provide for the common defence and general welfare of the United States.'

"2. At the end of the second clause of Article 7, Section 1, add, 'and with the Indian tribes.'

"3. In the place of the 9th Article, Section 1, to be inserted: 'The Senate of the United States shall have power to try all impeachments; but no person shall be convicted without the concurrence of two-thirds of the members present.'

"4. After the word 'Excellency,' in Section 1, Article 10, to be inserted: 'He shall hold his office during the term of four years, and together with the Vice President, chosen for the same term, be elected in the following manner, viz: Each State shall appoint, in such manner as its Legislature may direct, a number of Electors equal to the whole number of Senators and members of the House of Representatives to which the State may be entitled in the Legislature. The Electors shall meet in their respective States, and vote by ballot for two persons, of whom one at least shall not be an inhabitant of the same State with themselves; and they shall make a list of all the persons voted for, and of the number of votes for each, which list they shall sign and certify, and transmit sealed to the seat

---

*This is an exact copy. The variations in that in the printed Journal, are occasioned by its incorporation of subsequent amendments. This remark is applicable to other cases.

of the General Government, directed to the President of the Senate. The President of the Senate shall in that House open all the certificates, and the votes shall be then and there counted. The person having the greatest number of votes shall be the President, if such number be a majority of that of the Electors; and if there be more than one who have such a majority, and have an equal number of votes, then the Senate shall immediately choose by ballot one of them for President; but if no person have a majority, then from the five highest on the list, the Senate shall choose by ballot the President; and in every case after the choice of the President, the person having the greatest number of votes shall be Vice President; but if there should remain two or more who have equal votes, the Senate shall choose from them the Vice President. The Legislature may determine the time of choosing and assembling the Electors, and the manner of certifying and transmitting their votes.'

" 5. Section 2. ' No person except a natural born citizen, or a citizen of the United States at the time of the adoption of this Constitution, shall be eligible to the office of President; nor shall any person be elected to that office, who shall be under the age of thirty-five years, and who has not been, in the whole, at least fourteen years a resident within the United States.'

" 6. Section 3. ' The Vice President shall be *ex officio* President of the Senate; except when they sit to try the impeachment of the President; in which case the Chief Justice shall preside; and excepting also when he shall exercise the powers and duties of President; in which case, and in case of his absence, the Senate shall choose a president *pro tempore*. The Vice President, when acting as President of the Senate, shall not have a vote unless the House be equally divided.'

" 7. Section 4. ' The President, by and with the advice and consent of the Senate, shall have power to make treaties; and he shall nominate, and, by and with the advice and consent of the Senate, shall appoint ambassadors, and other public ministers, Judges of the Supreme Court, and all other officers of the United States whose appointments are not otherwise herein provided for. But no treaty shall be made without the consent of two-thirds of the members present.'

"8. After the words, 'into the service of the United States,' in Section 2, Article 10, add 'and may require the opinion in writing of the principal officer in each of the Executive Departments, upon any subject relating to the duties of their respective offices.'

"9. The latter part of Section 2, Article 10, to read as follows: 'He shall be removed from his office on impeachment by the House of Representatives, and conviction by the Senate, for treason or bribery; and in case of his removal as aforesaid, death, absence, resignation or inability to discharge the powers or duties of his office, the Vice President shall exercise those powers and duties, until another President be chosen, or until the inability of the President be removed.'"

The first clause of the Report was agreed to, *nem. con.*

The second clause was also agreed to, *nem. con.*

The third clause was postponed, in order to decide previously on the mode of electing the President.

The fourth clause was accordingly taken up.

Mr. Gorham disapproved of making the next highest after the President the Vice President, without referring the decision to the Senate in case the next highest should have less than a majority of votes. As the regulation stands, a very obscure man with very few votes may arrive at that appointment.

Mr. Sherman said the object of this clause of the Report of the Committee was to get rid of the ineligibility which was attached to the mode of election by the Legislature, and to render the Executive independent of the Legislature. As the choice of the President was to be made out of the five highest, obscure characters were sufficiently guarded against in that case; and he had no objection to requiring the Vice President to be chosen in like manner, where the choice was not decided by a majority in the first instance.

Mr. MADISON was apprehensive that by requiring both the President and Vice President to be chosen out of the highest candidates, the attention of the electors would be turned too much to making candidates, instead of giving their votes in order to a definitive choice. Should this turn be given to the business, the election would in fact be consigned to the Senate altogether. It would have the effect, at the same time, he observed, of giving the nomination of the candidates to the largest States.

Mr. GOUVERNEUR MORRIS concurred in, and enforced the remarks of Mr. MADISON.

Mr. RANDOLPH and Mr. PINCKNEY wished for a particular explanation, and discussion, of the reasons for changing the mode of electing the Executive.

Mr. GOUVERNEUR MORRIS said, he would give the reasons of the Committee, and his own. The first was the danger of intrigue and faction, if the appointment should be made by the Legislature. The next was the inconvenience of an ineligibility required by that mode in order to lessen its evils. The third was the difficulty of establishing a court of impeachments, other than the Senate, which would not be so proper for the trial, nor the other branch, for the impeachment of the President, if appointed by the Legislature. In the fourth place, nobody had appeared to be satisfied with an appointment by the Legislature. In the fifth place, many were anxious even for an immediate choice by the people. And finally, the sixth reason was the indispensable necessity of making the Executive independent of the Legislature. As the electors would vote at the same time, throughout the United States, and at so great a distance from each other, the great evil of cabal was avoided. It would be impossible, also, to corrupt them. A conclusive reason for making the Senate, instead of the Supreme

42

Court, the judge of impeachments, was, that the latter was to try the President, after the trial of the impeachment.

Col. MASON confessed that the plan of the Committee had removed some capital objections, particularly the danger of cabal and corruption. It was liable, however, to this strong objection, that nineteen times in twenty the President would be chosen by the Senate, an improper body for the purpose.

Mr. BUTLER thought the mode not free from objections; but much more so than an election by the Legislature, where, as in elective monarchies cabal faction and violence would be sure to prevail.

Mr. PINCKNEY stated as objections to the mode,— first, that it threw the whole appointment in fact, into the hands of the Senate. Secondly, the electors will be strangers to the several candidates, and of course unable to decide on their comparative merits. Thirdly, it makes the Executive re-eligible, which will endanger the public liberty. Fourthly, it makes the same body of men which will, in fact, elect the President, his judges in case of an impeachment.

Mr. WILLIAMSON had great doubts whether the advantage of re-eligibility, would balance the objection to such a dependence of the President on the Senate for his re-appoint-. ment. He thought, at least, the Senate ought to be restrained to the *two* highest on the list.

Mr. GOUVERNEUR MORRIS said, the principal advantage aimed at was, that of taking away the opportunity for cabal. The President may be made, if thought necessary, ineligible, on this as well as on any other mode of election. Other inconveniences may be no less redressed on this plan than any other.

Mr. BALDWIN thought the plan not so objectionable, when well considered, as at first view. The increasing intercourse among the people of the States would render important characters less and less unknown; and the Senate would, consequently be less and less likely to have the eventual appointment thrown into their hands.

Mr. WILSON. This subject has greatly divided the House, and will also divide the people out of doors. It is in truth the most difficult of all on which we have had to decide. He had never made up an opinion on it entirely to his own satisfaction. He thought the plan, on the whole, a valuable improvement on the former. It gets rid of one great evil, that of cabal and corruption; and continental characters, will multiply as we more and more coalesce, so as to enable the Electors in every part of the Union to know and judge of them. It clears the way also for a discussion of the question of re-eligibility, on its own merits, which the former mode of election seemed to forbid. He thought it might be better, however, to refer the eventual appointment to the Legislature than to the Senate, and to confine it to a smaller number than five of the candidates. The eventual election by the Legislature would not open cabal anew, as it would be restrained to certain designated objects of choice; and as these must have had the previous sanction of a number of the States; and if the election be made as it ought, as soon as the votes of the Electors are opened, and it is known that no one has a majority of the whole, there can be little danger of corruption. Another reason for preferring the Legislature to the Senate in this business was, that the House of Representatives will be so often changed as to be free from the influence, and faction, to which the permanence of the Senate may subject that branch.

Mr. RANDOLPH, preferred the former mode of constituting the Executive; but if the change was to be made, he wished to know why the eventual election was referred to the *Senate*, and not to the *Legislature?* He saw no necessity for this, and many objections to it. He was apprehensive, also, that the advantage of the eventual appointment, would fall into the hands of the States near the seat of government.

Mr. GOUVERNEUR MORRIS said the *Senate* was preferred because fewer could then say to the President, you owe your appointment to us. He thought the President would not depend so much on the Senate for his re-appointment, as on his general good conduct.

The further consideration of the Report was postponed, that each member might take a copy of the remainder of it.

The following motion was referred to the Committee of Eleven, to wit, to prepare and report a plan for defraying the expenses of the Convention.

* Mr. PINCKNEY moved a clause declaring, that each House should be judge of the privileges of its own members.

Mr. GOUVERNEUR MORRIS seconded the motion.

Mr. RANDOLPH and Mr. MADISON expressed doubts as to the propriety of giving such a power, and wished for a postponement.

Mr. GOUVERNEUR MORRIS thought it so plain a case, that no postponement could be necessary.

Mr. WILSON thought the power involved, and the express insertion of it needless. It might beget doubts as to the power of other public bodies, as courts, &c. Every court is the judge of its own privileges.

Mr. MADISON distinguished between the power of judging of privileges previously and duly established, and the effect of the motion, which would give a discretion to each House as to the extent of its own privileges. He suggested that it would be better to make provision for ascertaining by *law* the privileges of each House, than to allow each House to decide for itself. He suggested also the necessity of considering what privileges ought to be allowed to the Executive.

Adjourned.

_____

WEDNESDAY, SEPTEMBER 5TH.

In Convention,— Mr. BREARLY, from the Committee of Eleven, made a further Report, as follows :

" 1. To add to the clause, ' to declare war,' the words, ' and grant letters of marque and reprisal.'

---

* This motion is not contained in the printed Journal.

"2. To add to the clause, 'to raise and support armies,' the words, 'but no appropriation of money to that use shall be for a longer term than two years.'

"3. Instead of Sect. 12, Article 6, say : 'All bills for raising revenue shall originate in the House of Representatives, and shall be subject to alterations and amendments by the Senate : no money shall be drawn from the Treasury, but in consequence of appropriations made by law.'·

"4. Immediately before the last clause of Section 1, Article 7, insert 'To exercise exclusive legislation on all cases whatsoever over such district (not exceeding ten miles square) as may, by cession of particular States and the acceptance of the Legislature, become the seat of the government of the United States ; and to exercise like authority over all places purchased for the erection of forts, magazines, arsenals, dock-yards, and other needful buildings.'

"5. 'To promote the progress of science and the useful arts, by securing for limited times to authors and inventors, the exclusive right to their respective writings and discoveries.'"

This report being taken up, the first clause was agreed to, *nem. con.*

To the second clause Mr. GERRY objected, that it admitted of appropriations to an army for two years, instead of one; for which he could not conceive a reason; that it implied there was to be a standing army, which he inveighed against, as dangerous to liberty — as unnecessary even for so great an extent of country as this — and if necessary, some restriction on the number and duration ought to be provided. Nor was this a proper time for such an innovation. The people would not bear it.

Mr. SHERMAN remarked, that the appropriations were permitted only, not required to be for two years. As the Legislature is to be biennally elected, it would be inconvenient to require appropriations to be for one year, as there might be no session within the time necessary to renew them. He should himself, he said, like a reasonable restriction on the number and continuance of an army in time of peace.

The second clause was then agreed to, *nem. con.*

The third clause Mr. GOUVERNEUR MORRIS moved to postpone. It had been agreed to in the Committee on the ground of compromise; and he should feel himself at liberty to dissent from it, if on the whole he should not be satisfied with certain other parts to be settled.

Mr. PINCKNEY seconded the motion.

Mr. SHERMAN was for giving immediate ease to those who looked on this clause as of great moment, and for trusting to their concurrence in other proper measures.

On the question for postponing, —

New Hampshire, Connecticut, New Jersey, Pennsylvania, Delaware, Maryland, North Carolina, South Carolina, Georgia, aye — 9; Massachusetts, Virginia, no — 2.

So much of the fourth clause as related to the seat of government was agreed to, *nem. con.*

On the residue, to wit, " to exercise like authority over all places purchased for forts, &c."

Mr. GERRY contended that this power might be made use of to enslave any particular State by buying up its territory, and that the strong holds proposed would be a means of awing the State into an undue obedience to the General Government.

Mr. KING thought himself, the provision unnecessary, the power being already involved; but would move to insert, after the word " purchased," the words, " by the consent of the Legislature of the State." This would certainly make the power safe.

Mr. GOUVERNEUR MORRIS seconded the motion, which was agreed to, *nem. con.;* as was the residue of the clause as amended.

The fifth clause was agreed to, *nem. con.*

The following Resolution and order being reported from the Committee of Eleven, to wit:

Resolved, that the United States in Congress be requested to allow, and cause to be paid, to the Secretary and officers of this Convention, such sums, in proportion to their respective times of service as are allowed to the Secretary and similar officers of Congress.

" Ordered, that the Secretary make out and transmit to the Treasury office of the United States, an account for the said services and for the incidental expenses of this Convention."

The resolution and order were separately agreed to, *nem. con.*

Mr. GERRY gave notice that he should move to reconsider Articles 19, 20, 21, 22.

Mr. WILLIAMSON gave like notice as to the Article fixing the number of Representatives, which he thought too small. He wished, also, to allow Rhode Island more than one, as due to her probable number of people, and as proper to stifle any pretext arising from her absence on the occasion.

The report made yesterday as to the appointment of the Executive being then taken up, —

Mr. PINCKNEY renewed his opposition to the mode; arguing, first, that the electors will not have sufficient knowledge of the fittest men and will be swayed by an attachment to the eminent men of their respective States. Hence, secondly, the dispersion of the votes would leave the appointment with the Senate, and as the President's re-appointment will thus depend on the Senate, he will be the mere creature of that body. Thirdly, he will combine with the Senate against the House of Representatives. Fourthly, this change in the mode of election was meant to get rid of the ineligibility of the President a second time, whereby he will become fixed for life under the auspices of the Senate.

Mr. GERRY did not object to this plan of constituting the Executive in itself, but should be governed in his final vote by the powers that may be given to the President.

Mr. RUTLEDGE was much opposed to the plan reported

by the Committee. It would throw the whole power into the Senate. He was also against a re-eligibility. He moved to postpone the Report under consideration, and take up the original plan of appointment by the Legislature, to wit: "He shall be elected by joint ballot by the Legislature, to which election a majority of the votes of the members present shall be required. He shall hold his office during the term of seven years; but shall not be elected a second time."

On this motion to postpone, —

North Carolina, South Carolina, aye — 2; Massachusetts, Connecticut, New Jersey, Pennsylvania, Delaware, Maryland, Virginia, Georgia, no — 8; New Hampshire, divided.

Colonel MASON admitted that there were objections to an appointment by the Legislature, as originally planned. He had not yet made up his mind, but would state his objections to the mode proposed by the Committee. First, it puts the appointment, in fact, into the hands of the Senate; as it will rarely happen that a majority of the whole vote will fall on any one candidate; and as the existing President will always be one of the five highest, his re-appointment will of course depend on the Senate. Secondly, considering the powers of the President and those of the Senate, if a coalition should be established between these two branches, they will be able to subvert the Constitution. The great objection with him would be removed by depriving the Senate of the eventual election. He accordingly moved to strike out the words, "if such number be a majority of that of the Electors."

Mr. WILLIAMSON seconded the motion. He could not agree to the clause without some such modification. He preferred making the highest, though not having a majority of the votes, President, to a reference of the matter to the Senate. Referring the appointment to the Senate lays a certain foundation for corruption and aristocracy.

Mr. GOUVERNEUR MORRIS thought the point of less

consequence than it was supposed on both sides. It is probable that a majority of the votes will fall on the same man; as each Elector is to give two votes, more than one-fourth will give a majority. Besides, as one vote is to be given to a man out of the State, and as this vote will not be thrown away, half the votes will fall on characters eminent and generally known. Again, if the President shall have given satisfaction, the votes will turn on him of course; and a majority of them will re-appoint him, without resort to the Senate. If he should be disliked, all disliking him would take care to unite their votes, so as to ensure his being supplanted.

Colonel MASON. Those who think there is no danger of there not being a majority for the same person in the first instance, ought to give up the point to those who think otherwise.

Mr. SHERMAN reminded the opponents of the new mode proposed, that if the small States had the advantage in the Senate's deciding among the five highest candidates, the large States would have in fact the nomination of these candidates.

On the motion of Colonel MASON,—

Maryland,* North Carolina, aye; the other nine States, no.

Mr. WILSON moved to strike out " Senate," and insert the word " Legislature."

Mr. MADISON considered it a primary object, to render an eventual resort to any part of the Legislature improbable. He was apprehensive that the proposed alteration would turn the attention of the large States too much to the appointment of candidates, instead of aiming at an effectual appointment of the officer; as the large States would predominate in the Legislature, which would have the final choice out of the candidates. Whereas, if the Senate, in which the small States predominate, should have the final

---

* In the printed Journal, Maryland, no.

choice, the concerted effort of the large States would be to make the appointment in the first instance conclusive.

Mr. RANDOLPH. We have, in some revolutions of this plan, made a bold stroke for monarchy. We are now doing the same for an aristocracy. He dwelt on the tendency of such an influence in the Senate over the election of the President, in addition to its other powers, to convert that body into a real and dangerous aristocracy.

Mr. DICKINSON was in favor of giving the eventual election to the Legislature, instead of the Senate. It was too much influence to be superadded to that body.

On the question moved by Mr. WILSON,—

Pennsylvania, Virginia, South Carolina, aye — 3; Massachusetts, Connecticut, New Jersey, Delaware, Maryland, North Carolina, Georgia, no — 7; New Hampshire, divided.

Mr. MADISON and Mr. WILLIAMSON moved to strike out the word "majority," and insert " one-third;" so that the eventual power might not be exercised if less than a majority, but not less than one-third, of the Electors should vote for the same person.

Mr. GERRY objected, that this would put it in the power of three or four States to put in whom they pleased.

Mr. WILLIAMSON There are seven States which do not contain one-third of the people. If the Senate are to appoint, less than one-sixth of the people will have the power.

On the question, —

Virginia, North Carolina, aye; the other nine States, no.

Mr. GERRY suggested, that the eventual election should be made by six Senators and seven Representatives, chosen by joint ballot of both Houses.

Mr. KING observed, that the influence of the small States in the Senate was somewhat balanced by the influence of the large States in bringing forward the candidates,* and also by the concurrence of the small States in

*This explains the compromise alluded to by Mr. Gouverneur Morris. Col. Mason, Mr. Gerry, and other members from large States set great value on this privilege of originating money bills. Of this the members from the small States, with

the Committee in the clause vesting the exclusive origination of money bills in the House of Representatives.

Col. MASON moved to strike out the word "five," and insert the word "three," as the highest candidates for the Senate to choose out of.

Mr. GERRY seconded the motion.

Mr. SHERMAN would sooner give up the plan. He would prefer seven or thirteen.

On the question moved by Col. MASON and Mr. GERRY, — Virginia, North Carolina, aye; nine States, no.

Mr. SPAIGHT and Mr. RUTLEDGE moved to strike out "five," and insert "thirteen;" to which all the States disagreed, except North Carolina and South Carolina.

Mr. MADISON and Mr. WILLIAMSON moved to insert, after "Electors," the words, "who shall have balloted;" so that the non-voting Electors, not being counted, might not increase the number necessary as a majority of the whole to decide the choice without the agency of the Senate.

On this question,— Pennsylvania, Maryland, Virginia, North Carolina, aye — 4; New Hampshire, Massachusetts, Connecticut, New Jersey, Delaware, South Carolina, Georgia, no — 7.

Mr. DICKINSON moved, in order to remove ambiguity from the intention of the clause, as explained by the vote, to add, after the words, "if such number be a majority of the whole number of the Electors," the word "appointed."

On this motion,— New Hampshire, Massachusetts, Connecticut New Jersey, Pennsylvania, Delaware, Maryland, South Carolina, Georgia, aye — 9; Virginia, North Carolina, no — 2.

Col. MASON. As the mode of appointment is now regulated, he could not forbear expressing his opinion that it is utterly inadmissible. He would prefer the Government of Prussia to one which will put all power into the hands of

---

some from the large States who wished a high mounted Government, endeavoured to avail themselves, by making that privilege the price of arrangements in the Constitution favorable to the small States, and to the elevation of the Government.

seven or eight men, and fix an aristocracy worse than absolute monarchy.

The words, "and of their giving their votes," being
inserted, on motion for that purpose, after the words, "The
Legislature may determine the time of choosing and
assembling the Electors," —

The House adjourned.

THURSDAY, SEPTEMBER 6TH.

In Convention, — Mr. KING and Mr. GERRY moved to
insert in the fourth clause of the Report (see the 4th of
Sept, page 654), after the words, " may be entitled in the
Legislature," the words following: "But no person shall be
appointed an Elector who is a member of the Legislature
of the United States, or who holds any office of profit or
trust under the United States;" which passed, *nem. con.*

Mr. GERRY proposed, as the President was to be elected
by the Senate out of the five highest candidates, that if he
should not at the end of his term be re-elected by a
majority of the Electors, and no other candidate should
have a majority, the eventual election should be made by
the Legislature. This, he said, would relieve the President
from his particular dependence on the Senate, for his continuance in office.

Mr. KING liked the idea, as calculated to satisfy particular members, and promote unanimity; and as likely to
operate but seldom.

Mr. READ opposed it; remarking, that if individual
members were to be indulged, alterations would be necessary to satisfy most of them.

Mr. WILLIAMSON espoused it, as a reasonable precaution
against the undue influence of the Senate.

Mr. SHERMAN liked the arrangement as it stood, though
he should not be averse to some amendments. He thought,
he said, that if the Legislature were to have the eventual

appointment, instead of the Senate, it ought to vote in the case by the States, — in favour of the small States, as the large States would have so great an advantage in nominating the candidates.

Mr. GOUVERNEUR MORRIS thought favourably of Mr. GERRY's proposition. It would free the President from being tempted, in naming to offices, to conform to the will of the Senate, and thereby virtually give the appointments to office to the Senate.

Mr. WILSON said, that he had weighed everything carefully the Report of the Committee for re-modelling the constitution of the Executive; and on combining it with other parts of the plan, he was obliged to consider the whole as having a dangerous tendency to aristocracy; as throwing a dangerous power into the hands of the Senate. They will have, in fact, the appointment of the President, and through his dependence on them, the virtual appointment to offices; among others, the officers of the Judiciary department. They are to make treaties; and they are to try all impeachments. In allowing them thus to make the Executive and Judiciary appointments, to be the court of impeachments, and to make treaties which are to be laws of the land, the Legislative, Executive and Judiciary powers are all blended in one branch of the Government. The power of making treaties involves the case of subsidies, and here, as an additional evil, foreign influence is to be dreaded. According to the plan as it now stands, the President will not be the man of the people, as he ought to be; but the minion of the Senate. He cannot even appoint a tide-waiter without the Senate. He had always thought the Senate too numerous a body for making appointments to office. The Senate will, moreover, in all probability, be in constant session. They will have high salaries. And with all those powers, and the President in their interest, they will depress the other branch of Legislature, and aggrandize themselves in proportion. Add to all this, that the Senate, sitting in conclave, can by holding up to their respective States various and improbable candidates, contrive so to scatter their votes, as to bring the appointment of the President ultimately before themselves. Upon the whole, he thought the new mode of appointing the President, with some amendments, a valuable improvement; but he could never agree to purchase it at the price of the ensuing parts of the Report, nor befriend a system of which they made a part.

Mr. GOUVERNEUR MORRIS expressed his wonder at the observations of Mr. WILSON, so far as they preferred the plan in the printed Report, to the new modification of it before the House; and entered into a comparative view of the two, with an eye to the nature of Mr. WILSON'S objections to the last. By the first, the Senate, he observed, had a voice in appointing the President out of all of the citizens of the United States; by this they were limited to five candidates, previously nominated to them, with a probability of being barred altogether by the successful ballot of Electors. Here surely was no increase of power. They are now to appoint Judges, nominated to them by the President. Before, they had the appointment without any agency whatever of the President. Here again was surely no additional power. If they are to make treaties, as the plan now stands, the power was the same in the printed plan. If they are to try impeachments, the Judges must have been triable by them before. Wherein, then, lay the dangerous tendency of the innovations to establish an aristocracy in the Senate? As to the appointment of officers, the weight of sentiment in the House was opposed to the exercise of it by the President alone; though it was not the case with himself. If the Senate would act as was suspected, in misleading the States into a fallacious disposition of their votes for a President, they would, if the appointment were withdrawn wholly from them, make such representations in their several States where they have influence, as would favor the object of their partiality.

Mr. WILLIAMSON, replying to Mr. MORRIS, observed,

that the aristocratic complexion proceeds from the change in the mode of appointing the President, which makes him dependent on the Senate.

Mr. CLYMER said, that the aristocratic part, to which he could never accede, was that, in the printed plan, which gave the Senate the power of appointing to offices.

Mr. HAMILTON said, that he had been restrained from entering into the discussions, by his dislike of the scheme of government in general; but as he meant to support the plan to be recommended, as better than nothing, he wished in this place to offer a few remarks. He liked the new modification, on the whole, better than that in the printed Report. In this, the President was a monster, elected for seven years, and ineligible afterwards; having great powers in appointments to office; and continually tempted, by this constitutional disqualification, to abuse them in order to subvert the Government. Although he should be made re-eligible, still, if appointed by the Legislature, he would be tempted to make use of corrupt influence to be continued in office. It seemed peculiarly desirable, therefore, that some other mode of election should be devised. Considering the different views of different States, and the different districts, Northern, Middle, and Southern, he concurred with those who thought that the votes would not be concentered, and that the appointment would consequently, in the present mode devolve on the Senate. The nomination to offices will give great weight to the President. Here, then, is a mutual connexion and influence, that will perpetuate the President, and aggrandize both him and the Senate. What is to be the remedy? He saw none better than to let the highest number of ballots, whether a majority or not, appoint the President. What was the objection to this? Merely that too small a number might appoint. But as the plan stands, the Senate may take the candidate having the smallest number of votes, and make him President.

Mr. SPAIGHT and Mr. WILLIAMSON moved to insert

"seven," instead of "four" years, for the term of the President.*

On this motion,—

New Hampshire, Virginia, North Carolina. aye — 3; Massachusetts, Connecticut, New Jersey, Pennsylvania, Delaware, Maryland, South Carolina, Georgia, no — 8;

Mr. SPAIGHT and Mr. WILLIAMSON then moved to insert "six," instead of "four."

On which motion,—

North Carolina, South Carolina, aye —2; New Hampshire, Massachusetts, Connecticut, New Jersey, Pennsylvania, Delaware, Maryland, Virginia, Georgia, no — 9.

On the term "four," all the States were aye, except North Carolina, no.

On the question on the fourth clause in the Report, for appointing the President by Electors, down to the words, "entitled in the Legislature," inclusive,—

New Hampshire, Massachusetts, Connecticut, New Jersey, Pennsylvania, Delaware, Maryland, Virginia, Georgia, aye — 9; North Carolina, South Carolina, no — 2.

It was moved that the Electors meet at the seat of the General Government; which passed in the negative,—North Carolina only being, aye.

It was then moved to insert the words, "under the seal of the State," after the word "transmit," in the fourth clause of the Report; which was disagreed to; as was another motion to insert the words, "and who shall have given their votes," after the word "appointed," in the fourth clause of the Report, as added yesterday on motion of Mr. DICKINSON.

On several motions, the words, "in presence of the Senate and House of Representatives," were inserted after the word "counted;" and the word "immediately," before the word "choose;" and the words, "of the electors," after the word "votes."

---

* An ineligibility would have followed (though it would seem from the vote, not in the opinion of all) this prolongation of the term.

Mr. Spaight said, if the election by Electors is to be crammed down, he would prefer their meeting altogether, and deciding finally without any reference to the Senate; and moved, "that the Electors meet at the seat of the General Government."

Mr. Williamson seconded the motion; on which all the States were in the negative, except North Carolina.

On motion, the words, "But the election shall be on the same day throughout the United States," were added, after the words, "transmitting their votes."

New Hampshire, Connecticut, Pennsylvania, Maryland, Virginia, North Carolina, South Carolina, Georgia, aye — 8; Massachusetts, New Jersey, Delaware, no — 3.

On the question on the sentence in the fourth clause, "if such number be a majority of that of the Electors appointed,"—

New Hampshire, Massachusetts, Connecticut, New Jersey, Delaware, Maryland, South Carolina, Georgia, aye — 8; Pennsylvania, Virginia, North Carolina, no — 3.

On a question on the clause referring the eventual appointment of the President to the Senate,—

New Hampshire, Massachusetts, Connecticut, New Jersey, Pennsylvania, Delaware, Virginia, aye — 7; North Carolina, no. Here the call ceased.

Mr. Madison made a motion requiring two-thirds at least of the Senate to be present at the choice of a President.

Mr. Pinckney seconded the motion.

Mr. Gorham thought it a wrong principle to require more than a majority in any case. In the present, it might prevent for a long time any choice of a President.

On the question moved by Mr. Madison and Mr. Pinckney,—

New Hampshire, Maryland, Virginia, North Carolina, South Carolina, Georgia, aye — 6; Connecticut, New Jersey, Pennsylvania, Delaware, no — 4; Massachusetts, absent.

Mr. Williamson suggested, as better than an eventual

43

choice by the Senate, that this choice should be made by the Legislature, voting *by States* and not *per capita.*

Mr. SHERMAN suggested, "the House of Representatives," as preferable to "the Legislature;" and moved accordingly, to strike out the words, "The Senate shall immediately choose, &c.," and insert: "The House of Representatives shall immediately choose by ballot one of them for President, the members from each State having one vote."

Col. MASON liked the latter mode best, as lessening the aristocratic influence of the Senate.

On motion of Mr. SHERMAN,—

New Hampshire, Massachusetts, Connecticut, New Jersey, Pennsylvania, Maryland, Virginia, North Carolina, South Carolina, Georgia, aye — 10 ; Delaware, no — 1.

Mr. GOUVERNEUR MORRIS suggested the idea of providing that, in all cases, the President in office should not be one of the five candidates ; but be only re-eligible in case a majority of the Electors should vote for him. [This was another expedient for rendering the President independent of the Legislative body for his continuance in office.]

Mr. MADISON remarked that as a majority of members would make a quorum in the House of Representatives, it would follow from the amendment of Mr. SHERMAN, giving the election to a majority of States, that the President might be elected by two States only, Virginia and Pennsylvania, which have eighteen members, if these States alone should be present.

On a motion, that the eventual election of President, in case of an equality of the votes of the Electors, be referred to the House of Representatives,—

New Hampshire, Massachusetts, Pennsylvania, Virginia, North Carolina, South Carolina, Georgia, aye — 7 ; New Jersey, Delaware, Maryland, no — 3.

Mr. KING moved to add to the amendment of Mr. SHERMAN, "But a quorum for this purpose shall consist of a member or members from two-thirds of the States, and also a majority of the whole number of the House of Representatives."

Col. MASON liked it, as obviating the remark of Mr. MADISON.

The motion, as far as "States," inclusive, was agreed to. On the residue, to wit, "and also a majority of the whole number of the House of Representatives," it passed in the negative, —

Massachusetts, Connecticut, Pennsylvania, Virginia, North Carolina, aye — 5 ; New Hampshire, New Jersey, Delaware, Maryland, South Carolina, Georgia, no — 6.

The Report relating to the appointment of the Executive stands, as amended, as follows :

" He shall hold his office during the term of four years ; and, together with the Vice President, chosen for the same term, be elected in the following manner :

" Each State shall appoint, in such manner as its Legislature may direct, a number of electors equal to the whole number of Senators and members of the House of Representatives, to which the State may be entitled in the Legislature.

" But no person shall be appointed an elector who is a member of the Legislature of the United States, or who holds any office of profit or trust under the United States.

" The electors shall meet in their respective States, and vote by ballot, for two persons, of whom one at least shall not be an inhabitant of the same State with themselves ; and they shall make a list of all the persons voted for, and of the number of votes of each ; which list they shall sign and certify, and transmit sealed to the seat of the General Government, directed to the President of the Senate.

" The President of the Senate shall, in the presence of the Senate and House of Representatives, open all the certificates, and the votes shall then be counted.

" The person having the greatest number of votes shall be the President, if such number be a majority of the whole number of electors appointed; and if there be more than one who have such majority, and have an equal number of votes, then the House of Representatives shall immediately choose by ballot one of them for President; the representation from each State having one vote. But if no person have a majority, then from the five highest on the list the House of Representatives shall, in like manner, choose by ballot the President. In the choice of a President by the House of Representatives, a quorum shall consist of a member or members from two–thirds of the States [* and the concurrence of a majority of all the States shall be necessary to such choice]. And in every case after the choice of the President, the person having the greatest number of votes of the electors shall be the Vice President. But if there should remain two or more who have equal votes, the Senate shall choose from them the Vice President.

"The Legislature may determine the time of choosing the electors, and of their giving their votes; and the manner of certifying and transmitting their votes; but the election shall be on the same day throughout the United States."

Adjourned.

Friday, September 7th.

In Convention,— The mode of constituting the Executive being resumed,—

Mr. RANDOLPH moved to insert, in the first section of the Report made yesterday, the following:

"The Legislature may declare by law what officer of the United States shall act as President, in case of the death, resignation or disability of the President and Vice President; and such officer shall act accordingly, until the time of electing a President shall arrive."

----

* This clause was not inserted on this day. but on the seventh of September. See Page 678.

Mr. MADISON observed that this, as worded, would prevent a supply of the vacancy by an intermediate election of the President, and moved to substitute, " until such disability be removed, or a President shall be elected."*

Mr. GOUVERNEUR MORRIS seconded the motion, which was agreed to.

It seemed to be an objection to the provision, with some that, according to the process established for choosing the Executive, there would be difficulty in effecting it at other than the fixed periods; with others, that the Legislature was restrained in the temporary appointment to " *officers*" of the *United States.* They wished it to be at liberty to appoint others than such.

On the motion of Mr. RANDOLPH, as amended, it passed in the affirmative,—

New Jersey, Pennsylvania, Maryland, Virginia, South Carolina, Georgia, aye — 6; Massachusetts, Connecticut, Delaware, North Carolina, no — 4 ; New Hampshire, divided.

Mr. GERRY moved, " that in the election of President by the House of Representatives, no State shall vote by less than three members; and where that number may not be allowed to the State, it shall be made up by its Senators; and a concurrence of a majority of all the States shall be necessary to make such choice." Without some such provision, five individuals might possibly be competent to an election, these being a majority of two-thirds of the existing number of States; and two-thirds being a quorum for this business.

Mr. MADISON seconded the motion.

Mr. READ observed, that the States having but one member only in the House of Representatives would be in danger of having no vote at all in the election: the sickness or absence either of the Representatives, or one of the Senators, would have that effect.

---

* In the printed Journal this amendment is put into the original motion.

Mr. MADISON replied, that if one member of the House of Representatives should be left capable of voting for the State, the States having one Representative only would still be subject to that danger. He thought it an evil, that so small a number, at any rate, should be authorized to elect. Corruption would be greatly facilitated by it. The mode itself was liable to this further weighty objection, that the representatives of a *minority* of the people might reverse the choice of a *majority* of the *States* and of the *people.* He wished some cure for this inconvenience might yet be provided.

Mr. GERRY withdrew the first part of his motion; and on the question on the second part, viz: "and a concurrence of a majority of all the States shall be necessary to make such choice," to follow the words, "a member or members from two-thirds of the States," it was agreed to, *nem. con.*

The second Section (see the 4th of Sept., page 655,) requiring that the President should be a natural born citizen, &c., and have been a resident for fourteen years, and be thirty-five years of age, was agreed to, *nem. con.*

The third Section, "The Vice President shall be *ex-officio* President of the Senate," being then considered.

Mr. GERRY opposed this regulation. We might as well put the President himself at the head of the Legislature. The close intimacy that must subsist between the President and Vice President makes it absolutely improper. He was against having any Vice President.

Mr. GOUVERNEUR MORRIS. The Vice President then will be the first heir apparent that ever loved his father. If there should be no Vice President, the President of the Senate would be temporary successor, which would amount to the same thing.

Mr. SHERMAN saw no danger in the case. If the Vice President were not to be President of the Senate, he would be without employment; and some member, by being made President, must be deprived of his vote, unless when an equal division of votes might happen in the Senate, which would be but seldom.

Mr. RANDOLPH concurred in the opposition to the clause.

Mr. WILLIAMSON observed, that such an officer as Vice President was not wanted. He was introduced merely for the sake of a valuable mode of election, which required two to be chosen at the same time.

Colonel MASON thought the office of Vice President an encroachment on the rights of the Senate ; and that it mixed too much the Legislative and the Executive, which, as well as the Judiciary department, ought to be kept as separate as possible. He took occasion to express his dislike of any reference whatever, of the power to make appointments, to either branch of the Legislature. On the other hand, he was averse to vest so dangerous a power in the President alone. As a method of avoiding both, he suggested that a Privy Council, of six members, to the President, should be established; to be chosen for six years by the Senate, two out of the Eastern, two out of the Middle, and two out of the Southern quarters of the Union; and to go out in rotation, two every second year; the concurrence of the Senate to be required only in the appointment of ambassadors, and in making treaties, which are more of a legislative nature. This would prevent the constant sitting of the Senate, which he thought dangerous; as well as keep the departments separate and distinct. It would also save the expense of constant sessions of the Senate. He had, he said, always considered the Senate as too unwieldy and expensive for appointing officers, especially the smallest, such as tide-waiters, &c. He had not reduced his idea to writing, but it could be easily done, if it should be found acceptable.

On the question, shall the Vice President be *ex officio* President of the Senate ? —

New Hampshire, Massachusetts, Connecticut, Pennsylvania, Delaware, Virginia, South Carolina, Georgia, aye — 8; New Jersey, Maryland, no — 2; North Carolina, absent.

The other parts of the same Section were then agreed to.

The fourth section, to wit: "The President, by and with the advice and consent of the Senate, shall have power to make treaties," &c., was then taken up.

Mr. WILSON moved to add, after the word "Senate," the words, "and House of Representatives." As treaties, he said, are to have the operation of laws, they ought to have the sanction of laws also. The circumstance of secrecy in the business of treaties formed the only objection; but this, he thought, so far as it was inconsistent with obtaining the legislative sanction, was outweighed by the necessity of the latter.

Mr. SHERMAN thought the only question that could be made was, whether the power could be safely trusted to the Senate. He thought it could; and that the necessity of secrecy in the case of treaties forbade a reference of them to the whole Legislature.

Mr. FITZSIMONS seconded the motion of Mr. WILSON; and on the question,—

Pennsylvania, aye — 1; New Hampshire, Massachusetts, Connecticut, New Jersey, Delaware, Maryland, Virginia, North Carolina, South Carolina, Georgia, no — 10.

The first sentence, as to making treaties, was then agreed to, *nem. con.*

On the clause, "He shall nominate, &c. — appoint ambassadors," &c., —

Mr. WILSON objected to the mode of appointing, as blending a branch of the Legislature with the Executive. Good laws are of no effect, without a good Executive, and there can be no good Executive, without a responsible appointment of officers to execute. Responsibility is in a manner destroyed by such an agency of the Senate. He would prefer the Council proposed by Colonel MASON; provided its advice should not be made obligatory on the President.

Mr. PINCKNEY was against joining the Senate in these appointments, except in the instances of ambassadors, who he thought ought not to be appointed by the President.

Mr. GOUVERNEUR MORRIS said, that as the President was to nominate, there would be responsibility; and as the Senate was to concur, there would be security. As Congress now make appointments, there is no responsibility.

Mr. GERRY. The idea of responsibility in the nomination to offices is chimerical. The President cannot know all characters, and can therefore always plead ignorance.

Mr. KING. As the idea of a Council, proposed by Col. MASON, has been supported by Mr. WILSON, he would remark, that most of the inconveniences charged on the Senate are incident to a Council of advice. He differed from those who thought the Senate would sit constantly. He did not suppose it was meant that all the minute officers were to be appointed by the Senate, or any other original source, but by the higher officers of the departments to which they belong. He was of opinion, also, that the people would be alarmed at an unnecessary creation of new corps, which must increase the expense as well as influence of the Government.

On the question on these words in the clause, viz.: "He shall nominate, and, by and with the advice and consent of the Senate, shall appoint, ambassadors, and other public ministers and consuls, and Judges of the Supreme Court," it was agreed to, *nem. con.*, the insertion of "and consuls" having first taken place.

On the question on the following words: "and all other officers of the United States," —

New Hampshire, Massachusetts, Connecticut, New Jersey, Delaware, Maryland, Virginia, North Carolina, Georgia, aye — 9; Pennsylvania, South Carolina, no — 2.

On motion of Mr. SPAIGHT, that "the President shall have power to fill up all vacancies that may happen during the recess of the Senate, by granting commissions which shall expire at the end of the next session of the Senate," it was agreed to, *nem. con.*

The fourth section. " The President by and with the advice and consent of the Senate shall have power to make treaties. *But no treaty shall be made without the consent of two-thirds of the members present*," being considered and the last clause being before the House, —

Mr. WILSON thought it objectionable to require the concurrence of two-thirds, which puts it into the power of a minority to control the will of a majority.

Mr. KING concurred in the objection; remarking that as the Executive was here joined in the business, there was a check which did not exist in Congress, where the concurrence of two-thirds was required.

Mr. MADISON moved to insert, after the word "treaty," the words " except treaties of peace; " allowing these to be made with less difficulty than other treaties. It was agreed to, *nem. con.*

Mr. MADISON then moved to authorize a concurrence of two-thirds of the Senate to make treaties of peace, without the concurrence of the President. The President, he said, would necessarily derive so much power and importance from a state of war, that he might be tempted, if authorized, to impede a treaty of peace.

Mr. BUTLER seconded the motion.

Mr. GORHAM thought the security unnecessary, as the means of carrying on the war would not be in the hands of the President, but of the Legislature.

Mr. GOUVERNEUR MORRIS thought the power of the President in this case harmless; and that no peace ought to be made without the concurrence of the President, who was the general guardian of the national interests.

Mr. BUTLER was strenuous for the motion, as a necessary security against ambitious and corrupt Presidents. He mentioned the late perfidious policy of the Stadtholder in

Holland; and the artifices of the Duke of Marlborough to prolong the war of which he had the management.

Mr. GERRY was of opinion that in treaties of peace a greater rather than a less proportion of votes was necessary, than in other treaties. In treaties of peace the dearest interests will be at stake, as the fisheries, territories, &c. In treaties of peace also, there is more danger to the extremities of the continent, of being sacrificed, than on any other occasion.

Mr. WILLIAMSON thought that treaties of peace should be guarded at least by requiring the same concurrence as in other treaties.

On the motion of Mr. MADISON and Mr. BUTLER,— Maryland, South Carolina, Georgia, aye—3; New Hampshire, Massachusetts, Connecticut, New Jersey, Pennsylvania, Delaware, Virginia, North Carolina, no — 8.

On the part of the clause concerning treaties, amended by the exception as to treaties of peace,—New Hampshire, Massachusetts, Connecticut, Delaware, Maryland, Virginia, North Carolina, South Carolina, aye — 8; New Jersey, Pennsylvania, Georgia, no — 3.

The clause, " and may require the opinion in writing of the principal officer in each of the Executive Departments, upon any subject relating to the duties of their respective offices," being before the House,—

Col. MASON * said, that in rejecting a Council to the President, we were about to try an experiment on which the most despotic government had never ventured. The Grand Seignor himself had his Divan. He moved to postpone the consideration of the clause in order to take up the following:

" That it be an instruction to the Committee of the States to prepare a clause or clauses for establishing an Executive Council as a Council of State for the President of the United States ; to consist of six members, two of which

---

* In the printed Journal, Mr. Madison is erroneously substituted for Colonel Mason.

from the Eastern, two from the Middle, and two from the Southern States ; with a rotation and duration of office similar to those of the Senate ; such Council to be appointed by the Legislature or by the Senate."

Doctor FRANKLIN seconded the motion. We seemed, he said, too much to fear cabals in appointments by a number, and to have too much confidence in those of single persons. Experience shewed that caprice, the intrigues of favorites and mistresses, were nevertheless the means most prevalent in monarchies. Among instances of abuse in such modes of appointment, he mentioned the many bad Governors appointed in Great Britain for the Colonies. He thought a Council would not only be a check on a bad President, but be a relief to a good one.

Mr. GOUVERNEUR MORRIS. The question of a Council was considered in the Committee, where it was judged that the President, by persuading his Council to concur in his wrong measures, would acquire their protection for them.

Mr. WILSON approved of a Council, in preference to making the Senate a party to appointments.

Mr. DICKINSON was for a Council. It would be a singular thing, if the measures of the Executive were not to undergo some previous discussion before the President.

Mr. MADISON was in favor of the instruction to the Committee proposed by Col. MASON.

The motion of Col. MASON was negatived, —

Maryland, South Carolina, ·Georgia, aye — 3 ; New Hampshire, Massachusetts, Connecticut, New Jersey, Pennsylvania, Delaware, Virginia, North Carolina, no — 8.

On the question of authorizing the President to call for the opinions of the Heads of Departments, in writing, it passed in the affirmative, New Hampshire only being, no.*

The clause was then unanimously agreed to.

Mr. WILLIAMSON and Mr. SPAIGHT moved, " that no treaty of peace affecting territorial rights should be made

* Not so stated in the printed Journal ; but conformable to the result afterwards appearing.

vithout the concurrence of two-thirds of the members of the Senate present."

Mr. KING. It will be necessary to look out for securities 'or some other rights, if this principle be established ; he moved to extend the motion to " all present rights of the United States."

Adjourned.

SATURDAY, SEPTEMBER 8TH.

In Convention,— The last Report of the Committee of Eleven (see the fourth of September) was resumed.

Mr. KING moved to strike out the exception of treaties of peace, from the general clause requiring two-thirds of the Senate for making treaties.

Mr. WILSON wished the requisition of two-thirds to be struck out altogether. If the majority cannot be trusted, it was a proof, as observed by Mr. GORHAM, that we were not fit for one society.

A reconsideration of the whole clause was agreed to.

Mr. GOUVERNEUR MORRIS was against striking out the exception of treaties of peace. If two-thirds of the Senate should be required for peace, the Legislature will be unwilling to make war for that reason, on account of the fisheries, or the Mississippi, the two great objects of the Union. Besides, if a majority of the Senate be for peace, and are not allowed to make it, they will be apt to effect their purpose in the more disagreeable mode of negativing the supplies for the war.

Mr. WILLIAMSON remarked, that treaties are to be made in the branch of the Government where there may be a majority of the States, without a majority of the people. Eight men may be a majority of a quorum, and should not have the power to decide the conditions of peace. There would be no danger, that the exposed States, as South Carolina or Georgia, would urge an improper war for the Western territory.

Mr. WILSON.   If two-thirds are necessary to make peace, the minority may perpetuate war, against the sense of the majority.

Mr. GERRY enlarged on the danger of putting the essential rights of the Union in the hands of so small a number as a majority of the Senate, representing perhaps, not one-fifth of the people.   The Senate will be corrupted by foreign influence.

Mr. SHERMAN was against leaving the rights established by the treaty of peace, to the Senate; and moved to annex a proviso, that no such rights should be ceded without the sanction of the Legislature.

Mr. GOUVERNEUR MORRIS seconded the ideas of Mr. SHERMAN.

Mr. MADISON observed that it had been too easy, in the present Congress, to make treaties, although nine States were required for the purpose.

On the question for striking out, "except treaties of peace,"—

New Hampshire, Massachusetts, Connecticut, Pennsylvania, Virginia, North Carolina, South Carolina, Georgia, aye — 8; New Jersey, Delaware, Maryland, no — 3.

Mr. WILSON and Mr. DAYTON moved to strike out the clause, requiring two-thirds of the Senate, for making treaties; on which, Delaware, aye — 1; New Hampshire, Massachusetts, New Jersey, Pennsylvania, Maryland, Virginia, North Carolina, South Carolina, Georgia, no — 9; Connecticut, divided.

Mr. RUTLEDGE and Mr. GERRY moved that "no treaty shall be made without the consent of two-thirds of all the members of the Senate "— according to the example in the present Congress.

Mr. GORHAM.   There is a difference in the case, as the President's consent will also be necessary in the new Government.

On the question,—

North Carolina, South Carolina, Georgia, aye — 3;

New Hampshire, Massachusetts, (Mr. GERRY, aye,) Connecticut, New Jersey, Pennsylvania, Delaware, Maryland, Virginia, no — 8.

Mr. SHERMAN moved that "no treaty shall be made without a majority of the whole number of the Senate"

Mr. GERRY seconded him.

Mr. WILLIAMSON. This will be less security than two-thirds, as now required.

Mr. SHERMAN. It will be less embarrassing.

On the question, it passed in the negative,—

Massachusetts, Connecticut, Delaware, South Carolina, Georgia, aye — 5; New Hampshire, New Jersey, Pennsylvania, Maryland, Virginia, North Carolina, no — 6.

Mr. MADISON moved that a quorum of the Senate consist of two-thirds of all the members.

Mr. GOUVERNEUR MORRIS. This will put it in the power of one man to break up a quorum.

Mr. MADISON This may happen to any quorum.

On the question, it passed in the negative,—

Maryland, Virginia, North Carolina, South Carolina, Georgia, aye — 5; New Hampshire, Massachusetts, Connecticut, New Jersey, Pennsylvania, Delaware, no — 6.

Mr. WILLIAMSON and Mr. GERRY moved " that no treaty should be made without previous notice to the members, and a reasonable time for their attending."

On the question,— all the States, no; except North Carolina, South Carolina, and Georgia, aye.

On a question on the clause of the Report of the Committee of Eleven, relating to treaties by two-thirds of the Senate — all the States were, aye; except Pennsylvania, New Jersey, and Georgia, no.

Mr. GERRY moved, that "no officer shall be appointed but to offices created by the Constitution or by law." This was rejected as unnecessary,—

Massachusetts, Connecticut New Jersey, North Carolina, Georgia, aye — 5; New Hampshire, Pennsylvania, Delaware, Maryland, Virginia, South Carolina, no — 6.

The clause referring to the Senate the trial of impeachment against the President, for treason and bribery, was taken up.

Colonel MASON. Why is the provision restrained to, treason and bribery only? Treason, as defined in the Constitution, will not reach many great and dangerous offences. Hastings is not guilty of treason. Attempts to subvert the Constitution may not be treason, as above defined. As bills of attainder, which have saved the British constitution, are forbidden, it is the more necessary to extend the power of impeachments. He moved to add, after "bribery," "or maladministration." Mr. GERRY seconded him.

Mr. MADISON. So vague a term will be equivalent to a tenure during pleasure of the Senate.

Mr. GOUVERNEUR MORRIS. It will not be put in force and can do no harm. An election of every four years, will prevent maladministration.

Col. MASON withdrew "maladministration;" and substituted, "other high crimes and misdemeanours against the State."

On the question, thus altered,—

New Hampshire, Massachusetts, Connecticut, Maryland, Virginia, North Carolina, South Carolina,* Georgia, aye — 8; New Jersey, Pennsylvania, Delaware, no — 3.

Mr. MADISON objected to a trial of the President by the Senate, especially as he was to be impeached by the other branch of the Legislature; and for any act which might be called a misdemeanour. The President under these circumstances was made improperly dependent. He would prefer the Supreme Court for the trial of impeachments; or rather, a tribunal of which that should form a part.

Mr. GOUVERNEUR MORRIS thought no other tribunal than the Senate could be trusted. The Supreme Court were too few in number, and might be warped or corrupted. He was against a dependence of the Executive on the Leg-

---

* In the printed Journal, South Carolina, no.

islature, considering the Legislative tyranny the great danger to be apprehended; but there could be no danger that the Senate would say untruly, on their oaths, that the President was guilty of crimes or facts, especially as in four years he can be turned out.

Mr. PINCKNEY disapproved of making the Senate the court of impeachments, as rendering the President too dependent on the Legislature. If he opposes a favorite law, the two Houses will combine against him, and under the influence of heat and faction throw him out of office.

Mr. WILLIAMSON thought there was more danger of too much lenity, than of too much rigor, towards the President, considering the number of cases in which the Senate was associated with the President.

Mr. SHERMAN regarded the Supreme Court as improper to try the President, because the Judges would be appointed by him.

On motion by Mr. MADISON, to strike out the words, "by the Senate," after the word "conviction,"—

Pennsylvania, Virginia, aye — 2; New Hampshire, Massachusetts, Connecticut, New Jersey, Delaware, Maryland, North Carolina, South Carolina, Georgia, no — 9.

In the amendment of Col. MASON just agreed to, the word "State," after the words, "misdemeanours against," was struck out; and the words, "United States," unanimously inserted, in order to remove ambiguity.

On the question to agree to the clause, as amended, — New Hampshire, Massachusetts, Connecticut, New Jersey, Delaware, Maryland, Virginia, North Carolina, South Carolina, Georgia, aye — 10; Pennsylvania, no — 1.

On motion, the following: "The Vice President and other civil officers of the United States, shall be removed from office on impeachment and conviction, as aforesaid," was added to the clause on the subject of impeachments.

The clause of the Report made on the fifth of September, and postponed, was taken up, to wit: "All bills for raising revenue shall originate in the House of Representa-

44

tives; and shall be subject to alterations and amendments by the Senate. No money shall be drawn from the Treas ury but in consequence of appropriations made by law."

It was moved to strike out the words, "and shall be subject to alterations and amendments by the Senate;" and insert the words used in the Constitution of Massachusetts on the same subject, viz: "but the Senate may propose or concur with amendments, as in other bills;" which was agreed to, *nem. con.*

On the question on the first part of the clause, "all bills for raising revenue shall originate in the House of Representatives," * —

New Hampshire, Massachusetts, Connecticut, New Jersey, Pennsylvania, Virginia, North Carolina, South Carolina, Georgia, aye — 9; Delaware, Maryland, no — 2.

Mr. GOUVERNEUR MORRIS moved to add to the third clause of the Report made on the fourth of September, the words, "and every member shall be on oath;" which being agreed to, and a question taken on the clause, so amended, viz: "The Senate of the United States shall have power to try all impeachments; but no person shall be convicted without the concurrence of two-thirds of the members present; and every member shall be on oath,"—

New Hampshire, Massachusetts, Connecticut, New Jersey, Delaware, Maryland, North Carolina, South Carolina, Georgia, aye — 9; Pennsylvania, Virginia, no — 2.

Mr. GERRY repeated his motion above made, on this day, in the form following: "The Legislature shall have the sole right of establishing offices not heretofore provided for;" which was again negatived,— Massachusetts, Connecticut and Georgia, only, being aye.

Mr. McHENRY observed, that the President had not yet been any where authorized to convene the Senate, and moved to amend Article 10, Section 2, by striking out the words, "He may convene them [the Legislature] on extraor-

---

* This was a conciliatory vote, the effect of the compromise formerly alluded to. See note, page 666.

dinary occasions;" and inserting, "He may convene both, or either of the Houses, on extraordinary occasions." This, he added, would also provide for the case of the Senate being in session, at the time of convening the Legislature.

Mr. WILSON said, he should vote against the motion, because it implied that the Senate might be in session when the Legislature was not, which he thought improper.

On the question,— New Hampshire, Connecticut, New Jersey, Delaware, Maryland, North Carolina, Georgia, aye —7; Massachusetts, Pennsylvania, Virginia, South Carolina, no — 4.

A committee was then appointed by ballot, to revise the style of, and arrange, the articles which have been agreed to by the House. The Committee consisted of Mr. JOHNSON, Mr. HAMILTON, Mr. GOUVERNEUR MORRIS, Mr. MADISON, and Mr. KING.

Mr. WILLIAMSON moved, that, previous to this work of the Committee, the clause relating to the number of the House of Representatives should be reconsidered, for the purpose of increasing the number.

Mr. MADISON seconded the motion.

Mr. SHERMAN opposed it. He thought the provision on that subject amply sufficient.

Col. HAMILTON expressed himself with great earnestness and anxiety in favor of the motion. He avowed himself a friend to a vigorous government, but would declare, at the same time, he held it essential that the popular branch of it should be on a broad foundation. He was seriously of opinion, that the House of Representatives was on so narrow a scale, as to be really dangerous, and to warrant a jealousy in the people, for their liberties. He remarked, that the connection between the President and Senate would tend to perpetuate him, by corrupt influence. It was the more necessary on this account that a numerous representation in the other branch of the Legislature should be established.

On the motion of Mr. WILLIAMSON to reconsider, it was negatived,*—

Pennsylvania, Delaware, Maryland, Virginia, North Carolina, aye — 5; New Hampshire, Massachusetts, Connecticut, New Jersey, South Carolina, Georgia, no — 6.

Adjourned.

_____

MONDAY, SEPTEMBER 10TH.

In Convention,— Mr. GERRY moved to reconsider Article 19, viz: " On the application of the Legislatures of two-thirds of the States in the Union, for an amendment of this Constitution, the Legislature of the United States shall call a Convention for that purpose," (see the sixth of August,— page 461.)

This Constitution, he said, is to be paramount to the State Constitutions. It follows, hence, from this article, that two-thirds of the States may obtain a Convention, a majority of which can bind the Union to innovations that may subvert the State Constitutions altogether. He asked whether this was a situation proper to be run into.

Mr. HAMILTON seconded the motion; but, he said, with a different view from Mr. GERRY. He did not object to the consequences stated by Mr. GERRY. There was no greater evil in subjecting the people of the United States to the major voice, than the people of a particular State. It had been wished by many, and was much to have been desired, that an easier mode of introducing amendments had been provided by the Articles of the Confederation. It was equally desirable now, that an easy mode should be established for supplying defects which will probably appear in the new system. The mode proposed was not adequate. The State Legislatures will not apply for alterations; but with a view to increase their own powers. The National Legislature will be the first to perceive, and will be most sensible to, the necessity of amendments; and ought also to be empow-

_____

* This motion and vote are entered on the printed Journal of the ensuing morning

ered, whenever two-thirds of each branch should concur, to call a Convention. There could be no danger in giving this power, as the people would finally decide in the case.

Mr. MADISON remarked on the vagueness of the terms, " call a Convention for the purpose," as sufficient reason for reconsidering the article. How was a Convention to be formed ? — by what rule decide ? — what the force of its acts ?

On the motion of Mr. GERRY to reconsider,—

Massachusetts, Connecticut, Pennsylvania, Delaware, Maryland, Virginia, North Carolina, South Carolina, Georgia, aye — 9 ; New Jersey, no — 1 ; New Hampshire, divided.

Mr. SHERMAN moved to add to the article : " or the Legislature may propose amendments to the several States for their approbation; but no amendments shall be binding until consented to by the several States."

Mr. GERRY seconded the motion.

Mr. WILSON moved to insert, " two-thirds of," before the words, " several States ;" on which amendment to the motion of Mr. SHERMAN,—

New Hampshire, Pennsylvania, Delaware, Maryland, Virginia, aye — 5 ; Massachusetts, Connecticut, New Jersey, North Carolina, South Carolina, Georgia, no — 6.

Mr. WILSON then moved to insert, " three-fourths of," before " the several States ;" which was agreed to, *nem. con.*

Mr. MADISON moved to postpone the consideration of the amended proposition, in order to take up the following

" The Legislature of the United States, whenever two-thirds of both houses shall deem necessary, or on the application of two-thirds of the Legislatures of the several States, shall propose amendments to this Constitution, which shall be valid to all intents and purposes as part thereof, when the same shall have been ratified by three-fourths, at least, of the Legislatures of the several States, or by conventions in three-fourths thereof, as one or the other mode of ratification may be proposed by the Legislature of the United States."

Mr. HAMILTON seconded the motion.

Mr. RUTLEDGE said he never could agree to give a power by which the articles relating to slaves might be altered by the States not interested in that property, and prejudiced against it. In order to obviate this objection, these words were added to the proposition: * "provided that no amendments, which may be made prior to the year 1808 shall in any manner affect the fourth and fifth sections of the seventh article." The postponement being agreed to,—

On the question on the proposition of Mr. MADISON and Mr. HAMILTON, as amended,—

Massachusetts, Connecticut, New Jersey, Pennsylvania, Maryland, Virginia, North Carolina, South Carolina, Georgia, aye — 9 ; Delaware, no -- 1 ; New Hampshire, divided.

Mr. GERRY moved to reconsider Articles 21 and 22 ; from the latter of which " for the approbation of Congress," had been struck out. He objected to proceeding to change the Government without the approbation of Congress, as being improper, and giving just umbrage to that body. He repeated his objections, also, to an annulment of the confederation with so little scruple or formality.

Mr. HAMILTON concurred with Mr. GERRY as to the indecorum of not requiring the approbation of Congress. He considered this as a necessary ingredient in the transaction. He thought it wrong, also, to allow nine States as provided by Article 21, to institute a new Government on the ruins of the existing one. He would propose, as a better modification of the two Articles (21 and 22) that the plan should be sent to Congress, in order that the same, if approved by them, may be communicated to the State

---

* The printed Journal, makes the succeeding proviso as to the fourth and fifth sections of the seventh article, moved by Mr. Rutledge, part of the proposition of Mr. Madison.

Legislatures, to the end that they may refer it to State Conventions ; each Legislature declaring, that, if the convention of the State should think the plan ought to take effect among nine ratifying States, the same should take effect accordingly.

Mr. GORHAM. Some States will say that nine States shall be sufficient to establish the plan; others will require unanimity for the purpose, and the different and conditional ratifications will defeat the plan altogether.

Mr. HAMILTON. No convention convinced of the necessity of the plan will refuse to give it effect, on the adoption by nine States. He thought this mode less exceptionable than the one proposed in the article: while it would attain the same end.

Mr. FITZSIMONS remarked, that the words, "for their approbation," had been struck out in order to save Congress from the necessity of an act inconsistent with the Articles of Confederation under which they held their authority.

Mr. RANDOLPH declared, if no change should be made in this part of the plan, he should be obliged to dissent from the whole of it. He had from the beginning, he said, been convinced that radical changes in the system of the Union were necessary. Under this conviction he had brought forward a set of republican propositions, as the basis and outline of a reform. These republican propositions had, however, much to his regret, been widely, and, in his opinion, irreconcileably, departed from. In this state of things, it was his idea, and he accordingly meant to propose, that the State conventions should be at liberty to offer amendments to the plan; and that these should be submitted to a second General Convention, with full power to settle the Constitution finally. He did not expect to succeed in this proposition, but the discharge of his duty in making the attempt would give quiet to his own mind.

Mr. WILSON was against a reconsideration for any of the purposes which had been mentioned.

Mr. KING thought it would be more respectful to Con-

gress, to submit the plan generally to them; than in such
a form as expressly and necessarily to require their approbation or disapprobation.   The assent of nine States he
considered as sufficient; and that it was more proper to
make this a part of the Constitution itself, than to provide
for it by a supplemental or distinct recommendation.

Mr. GERRY urged the indecency and pernicious tendency
of dissolving in so slight a manner, the solemn obligations
of the Articles of Confederation.   If nine out of thirteen
can dissolve the compact, six out of nine will be just as able
to dissolve the new one hereafter.

Mr. SHERMAN was in favor of Mr. KING's idea of submitting the plan generally to Congress.   He thought nine
States ought to be made sufficient; but that it would be
better to make it a separate act, and in some such form as
that intimated by Col. HAMILTON, than to make it a particular article of the Constitution.

On the question for reconsidering the two articles, 21
and 22,—

Connecticut, New Jersey, Delaware, Maryland, Virginia,
North Carolina, Georgia, aye — 7; Massachusetts, Pennsylvania, South Carolina, no — 3; New Hampshire, divided.

Mr. HAMILTON then moved to postpone Article 21, in
order to take up the following, containing the ideas he had
above expressed, viz:

" Resolved, that the foregoing plan of a Constitution
be transmitted to the United States in Congress assembled,
in order that if the same shall be agreed to by them, it may
be communicated to the Legislature of the several States, to
the end that they may provide for its final ratification, by
referring the same to the consideration of a Convention of
Deputies in each State, to be chosen by the people thereof;
and that it be recommended to the said Legislatures, in their
respective acts for organizing such Convention, to declare,
that if the said Convention shall approve of the said Constitution, such approbation shall be binding and conclusive
upon the State; and further, that if the said Convention

shall be of opinion that the same, upon the assent of any nine States thereto, ought to take effect between the States so assenting, such opinion shall thereupon be also binding upon such a State, and the said Constitution shall take effect between the States assenting thereto."

Mr. GERRY seconded the motion.

Mr. WILSON. This motion being seconded, it is necessary now to speak freely. He expressed in strong terms his disapprobation of the expedient proposed, particularly the suspending the plan of the Convention, on the approbation of Congress. He declared it to be worse than folly, to rely on the concurrence of the Rhode Island members of Congress in the plan. Maryland had voted, on this floor, for requiring the unanimous assent of the thirteen States to the proposed change in the Federal system. New York has not been represented for a long time past in the Convention. Many individual deputies from other States, have spoken much against the plan. Under these circumstances can it be safe to make the assent of Congress necessary? After spending four or five months in the laborious and arduous task of forming a Government for our country, we are ourselves, at the close, throwing insuperable obstacles in the way of its success.

Mr. CLYMER thought that the mode proposed by Mr. HAMILTON would fetter and embarrass Congress as much as the original one, since it equally involved a breach of the Articles of Confederation.

Mr. KING concurred with Mr. CLYMER. If Congress can accede to one mode they can to the other. If the approbation of Congress be made necessary, and they should not approve, the State Legislatures will not propose the plan to Conventions; or if the States themselves are to provide that nine States shall suffice to establish the system, that provision will be omitted, every thing will go into confusion, and all our labor be lost.

Mr. RUTLEDGE viewed the matter in the same light with Mr. KING.

On the question to postpone, in order to take up Colonel HAMILTON's motion,—

Connecticut, aye — 1; New Hampshire, Massachusetts, New Jersey, Pennsylvania, Delaware, Maryland, Virginia, North Carolina, South Carolina, Georgia, no —10.

A question being then taken on the Article 21, it was agreed to unanimously.

Colonel HAMILTON withdrew the remainder of the motion to postpone Article 22; observing that his purpose was defeated by the vote just given.

Mr. WILLIAMSON and Mr. GERRY moved to reinstate the words, "for the approbation of Congress," in Article 22; which was disagreed to, *nem. con.*

Mr. RANDOLPH took this opportunity to state his objections to the system. They turned on the Senate's being made the court of impeachment for trying the Executive — on the necessity of three-fourths instead of two-thirds of each House to overrule the negative of the President — on the smallness of the number of the Representative branch — on the want of limitation to a standing army — on the general clause concerning necessary and proper laws — on the want of some particular restraint on navigation acts — on the power to lay duties on exports — on the authority of the General Legislature to interpose on the application of the *Executives* of the States — on the want of a more definite boundary between the General and State Legislatures — and between the General and State Judiciaries — on the unqualified power of the President to pardon treasons — on the want of some limit to the power of the Legislature in regulating their own compensations. With these difficulties in his mind, what course, he asked, was he to pursue? Was he to promote the establishment of a plan, which he verily believed would end in tyranny? He was unwilling, he said, to impede the wishes and judgment of the Convention, but he must keep himself free, in case he should be honored with a seat in the Convention of his State, to act according to the dictates of his judgment.

The only mode in which his embarrassment could be removed was that of submitting the plan to Congress, to go from them to the State Legislatures, and from these to State Conventions, having power to adopt, reject, or amend; the process to close with another General Convention, with full power to adopt or reject the alterations proposed by the State Conventions, and to establish finally the Government. He accordingly proposed a resolution to this effect.

Doctor FRANKLIN seconded the motion.

Colonel MASON urged, and obtained that the motion should lie on the table for a day or two, to see what steps might be taken with regard to the parts of the system objected to by Mr. RANDOLPH.

Mr. PINCKNEY moved, "that it be an instruction to the Committee for revising the style and arrangement of the articles agreed on, to prepare an address to the people, to accompany the present Constitution, and to be laid, with the same, before the United States in Congress."

* The motion itself was referred to the Committee, *nem. con.*

* Mr. RANDOLPH moved to refer to the Committee, also, a motion relating to pardons in cases of treason; which was agreed to, *nem. con.*

Adjourned.

TUESDAY, SEPTEMBER 11TH.

In Convention,— The Report of the Committee of style and arrangement not being made, and being waited for, The House adjourned.

WEDNESDAY, SEPTEMBER 12TH.

In Convention,— Doct. JOHNSON, from the Committee of style, &c., reported a digest of the plan, of which printed

---

*These motions are not entered in the printed Journal.

copies were ordered to be furnished to the members. He also reported a letter to accompany the plan to Congress.

REPORT.*

We the people of the United States, in order to form a more perfect union, to establish justice, insure domestic tranquillity, provide for the common defence, promote the general welfare, and secure the blessings of liberty to ourselves and our posterity, do ordain and establish this Constitution for the United States of America:

ARTICLE I.

Sect. 1. All Legislative powers herein granted shall be vested in a Congress of the United States, which shall consist of a Senate and House of Representatives.

Sect. 2. The House of Representatives shall be composed of members chosen every second year, by the people of the several States, and the electors in each State shall have the qualifications requisite for electors of the most numerous branch of the State Legislature.

No person shall be a Representative who shall not have attained to the age of twenty-five years, and been seven years a citizen of the United States, and who shall not, when elected, be an inhabitant of that State in which he shall be chosen.

Representatives and direct taxes shall be apportioned among the several States which may be included within this Union, according to their respective numbers, which shall be determined by adding to the whole number of free persons, including those bound to servitude for a term of years, and excluding Indians not taxed, three-fifths of all other persons. The actual enumeration shall be made within three years after the first meeting of the Congress of the United States, and within every subsequent term of ten

---

* This is a literal copy of the printed Report. The copy in the printed Journals contains some of the alterations subsequently made in the House.

years, in such manner as they shall by law direct. The number of Representatives shall not exceed one for every forty thousand, but each state shall have at least one Representative; and until such enumeration shall be made, the State of New Hampshire shall be entitled to choose three; Massachusetts, eight; Rhode Island and Providence Plantations, one; Connecticut, five; New York, six; New Jersey, four; Pennsylvania, eight; Delaware, one; Maryland, six; Virginia, ten; North Carolina, five; South Carolina, five; and Georgia, three.

When the vacancies happen in the representation from any State, the Executive authority thereof shall issue writs of election to fill such vacancies.

The House of Representatives shall choose their Speaker and other officers; and they shall have the sole power of impeachment.

Sect. 3.   The Senate of the United States shall be composed of two Senators from each State, chosen by the Legislature thereof, for six years; and each Senator shall have one vote.

Immediately after they shall be assembled in consequence of the first election, they shall be divided [by lot*], as equally as may be, into three classes.   The seats of the Senators of the first class shall be vacated at the expiration of the second year, of the second class at the expiration of the fourth year, and of the third class at the expiration of the sixth year; so that one-third may be chosen every second year; and if vacancies happen by resignation, or otherwise, during the recess of the Legislature of any State, the Executive thereof may make temporary appointments, until the next meeting of the Legislature.

No person shall be a Senator who shall not have attained to the age of thirty years, and been nine years a citizen of the United States, and who shall not, when elected, be an inhabitant of that State for which he shall be chosen.

---

* The words, "by lot," were not in the Report as printed; but were inserted in manuscript as a typographical error, departing from the text of Report referred to the Committee of style and arangement.

The Vice President of the United States shall be President of the Senate, but shall have no vote, unless they be equally divided.

The Senate shall choose their other officers, and also a President *pro tempore*, in the absence of the Vice President, or when he shall exercise the office of President of the United States.

The Senate shall have the sole power to try all impeachments. When sitting for that purpose, they shall be on oath. When the President of the United States is tried, the Chief Justice shall preside; and no person shall be convicted without the concurrence of two-thirds of the members present.

Judgment in cases of impeachment shall not extend further than to removal from office, and disqualification to hold and enjoy any office of honour, trust or profit under the United States; but the party convicted shall nevertheless be liable and subject to indictment, trial, judgment and punishment, according to the law.

Sect. 4. The times, places and manner of holding elections for Senators and Representatives, shall be prescribed in each State by the Legislature thereof; but the Congress may at any time by law make or alter such regulations.

The Congress shall assemble at least once in every year; and such meeting shall be on the first Monday in December, unless they shall by law appoint a different day.

Sect. 5. Each House shall be the judge of the elections, returns and qualifications of its own members; and a majority of each shall constitute a quorum to do business; but a smaller number may adjourn from day to day, and may be authorized to compel the attendance of absent members, in such manner, and under such penalties, as each House may provide.

Each House may determine the rules of its proceedings, punish its members for disorderly behaviour, and, with the concurrence of two-thirds, expel a member.

Each House shall keep a journal of its proceedings, and

from time to time publish the same, excepting such parts as may in their judgment require secrecy; and the Yeas and Nays of the members of either House on any question shall, at the desire of one-fifth of those present, be entered on the Journal.

Neither House, during the session of Congress, shall, without the consent of the other, adjourn for more than three days, nor to any other place than that in which the two Houses shall be sitting.

Sect. 6. The Senators and Representatives shall receive a compensation for their services, to be ascertained by law, and paid out of the Treasury of the United States. They shall in all cases, except treason, felony and breach of the peace, be privileged from arrest during their attendance at the session of their respective Houses, and in going to and returning from the same; and for any speech or debate in either House they shall not be questioned in any other place.

No Senator or Representative shall, during the time for which he was elected, be appointed to any civil office under the authority of the United States, which shall have been created, or the emoluments whereof shall have been increased during such time; and no person holding any office under the United States shall be a member of either House during his continuance in office.

Sect. 7. The enacting style of the laws shall be, "Be it enacted by the Senators and Representatives in Congress assembled."

All bills for raising revenue shall originate in the House of Representatives; but the Senate may propose or concur with amendments, as on other bills.

Every bill which shall have passed the House of Representatives and the Senate, shall, before it become a law, be presented to the President of the United States. If he approve, he shall sign it; but if not, he shall return it, with his objections, to that House in which it shall have originated, who shall enter the objections at large on their

Journal, and proceed to reconsider it. If after such reconsideration two-thirds of that House shall agree to pass
the bill, it shall be sent, together with the objections, to the
other House; by which it shall likewise be reconsidered;
and if approved by two-thirds of that House, it shall become law.   But in all such cases the votes of both Houses
shall be determined by Yeas and Nays, and the name of the
persons voting for and against the bill, shall be entered on
the Journal of each House, respectively.   If any bill shall
not be returned by the President within ten days (Sundays
excepted) after it shall have been presented to him, the
same shall be a law, in like manner as if he had signed it,
unless the Congress by their adjournment prevent its return, in which case it shall not be a law.

Every order, resolution, or vote, to which the concurrence of the Senate and House of Representatives may be
necessary (except on a question of adjournment), shall be
presented to the President of the United States; and before
the same shall take effect shall be approved by him, or, being disapproved by him, shall be repassed by three-fourths*
of the Senate and House of Representatives, according to
the rules and limitations prescribed in the case of a bill.

Sect. 8. The Congress may by joint ballot appoint a
Treasurer.   They shall have power —

To lay and collect taxes, duties, imposts and excises, to
pay the debts and provide for the common defence and
general welfare of the United States.

To borrow money on the credit of the United States.

To regulate commerce with foreign nations, among the
several States, and with the Indian tribes.

To establish an uniform rule of naturalization and uniform laws on the subject of bankruptcies throughout the
United States.

To coin money, regulate the value thereof, and of foreign coin, and fix the standard of weights and measures.

---

* In the entry of this Report in the printed Journal " two thirds " are substituted
for " three-fourths."   This change was made after the Report was received.

To provide for the punishment of counterfeiting the securities and current coin of the United States.

To establish post offices and post roads.

To promote the progress of science and useful arts, by securing for limited times to authors and inventors the exclusive right to their respective writings and discoveries.

To constitute tribunals inferior to the Supreme Court.

To define and punish piracies and felonies committed on the high seas, and [punish]* offences against the law of nations.

To declare war, grant letters of marque and reprisal, and make rules concerning captures on land and water.

To raise and support armies; but no appropriations of money to that use shall be for a longer term than two years.

To provide and maintain a navy.

To make rules for the government and regulation of the land and naval forces.

To provide for calling forth the militia, to execute the laws of the Union, suppress insurrections, and repel invasions.

To provide for organizing, arming and disciplining the militia, and for governing such part of them as may be employed in the service of the United States; reserving to the States, respectively, the appointment of the officers, and the authority of training the militia according to the discipline prescribed by Congress.

To exercise exclusive legislation, in all cases whatsoever, over such district (not exceeding ten miles square) as may, by cession of particular States, and the acceptance of Congress, become the seat of government of the United States; and to exercise like authority over all places purchased by the consent of the Legislature of the State in which the same shall be, for the erection of forts, magazines, arsenals, dock-yards, and other needful buildings. And—

To make all laws which shall be necessary and proper for carrying into execution the foregoing powers, and all

---

*Punish, a typographical omission in the printed Report.

other powers vested by this Constitution in the Government of the United States, or in any department or officer thereof.

Sect. 9. The migration or importation of such persons as the several States now existing shall think proper to admit, shall not be prohibited by the Congress prior to the year one thousand eight hundred and eight; but a tax or duty may be imposed on such importation, not exceeding ten dollars for each person.

The privilege of the writ of Habeas Corpus shall not be suspended, unless when, in cases of rebellion or invasion, the public safety may require it.

No bill of attainder shall be passed, nor any *ex post facto* law.

No capitation tax shall be laid, unless in proportion to the census hereinbefore directed to be taken.

No tax or duty shall be laid on articles exported from any State.

No money shall be drawn from the Treasury, but in consequence of appropriations made by law.

No title of nobility shall be granted by the United States. And no person holding any office of profit or trust under them shall, without the consent of the Congress, accept of any present, emolument, office or title, of any kind whatever from any king, prince, or foreign State.

Sect. 10. No State shall coin money, or emit bills of credit, or make any thing but gold or silver coin a tender in payment of debts, or pass any bills of attainder, or *ex post facto* laws, or laws altering or impairing the obligation of contracts; or grant letters of marque and reprisal, or enter into any treaty, alliance or confederation, or grant any title of nobility.

No State shall, without the consent of Congress, lay imposts or duties on imports or exports; or with such consent, but to the use of the Treasury of the United States; or keep troops or ships of war in time of peace; or enter into any agreement or compact with another State, or with any foreign power; or engage in any war, unless it shall be actually invaded by enemies, or the danger of invasion be so imminent as not to admit of delay until the Congress can be consulted.

ARTICLE II.

Sect. 1. The Executive power shall be vested in a President of the United States of America. He shall hold his office during the term of four years, and, together with the Vice President, chosen for the same term, be elected in the following manner:

Each State shall appoint, in such manner as the Legislature thereof may direct, a number of Electors, equal to the whole number of Senators and Representatives to which the State may be entitled in Congress; but no Senator or Representative shall be appointed an Elector, nor any person holding an office of trust or profit under the United States.

The Electors shall meet in their respective States, and vote by ballot for two persons, of whom one at least shall not be an inhabitant of the same State with themselves. And they shall make a list of all the persons voted for, and of the number of votes for each; which list they shall sign and certify, and transmit, sealed, to the seat of the General Government, directed to the President of the Senate. The President of the Senate shall, in the presence of the Senate and House of Representatives, open all the certificates, and the votes shall then be counted. The person having the greatest number of votes shall be the President, if such number be a majority of the whole number of Electors appointed; and if there be more than one who have such majority, and have an equal number of votes, then the House of Representatives shall immediately choose by ballot one of them for President; and if no person have a majority, then from the five highest on the list the said House shall in like manner choose the President. But in choosing the President, the votes shall be taken by States, and not *per capita*, the representation from each State having one vote.

A quorum for this purpose shall consist of a member or members from two-thirds of the States, and a majority of all the States shall be necessary to a choice. In every case, after the choice of the President by the Representatives, the person having the greatest number of votes of the Electors shall be the Vice President. But if there should remain two or more who have equal votes, the Senate shall choose from them, by ballot, the Vice President.

The Congress may determine the time of choosing the Electors, and the time in which they shall give their votes; but the election shall be on the same day throughout the United States.

No person except a natural born citizen, or a citizen of the United States at the time of the adoption of this Constitution, shall be eligible to the office of President; neither shall any person be eligible to that office who shall not have attained to the age of thirty-five years, and been fourteen years a resident within the United States.

In case of the removal of the President from office, or of his death, resignation, or inability to discharge the powers and duties of the said office, the same shall devolve on the Vice President, and the Congress may by law provide for the case of removal, death, resignation or inability, both of the President and Vice President; declaring what officer shall then act as President; and such officer shall act accordingly, until the disability be removed, or the period for choosing another President arrive.

The President shall, at stated times, receive a fixed compensation for his services, which shall neither be increased nor diminished during the period for which he shall have been elected.

Before he enter on the execution of his office, he shall take the following oath or affirmation: "I, ———, do solemnly swear (or affirm) that I will faithfully execute the office of President of the United States, and will, to the best of my judgment and power, preserve, protect and defend the Constitution of the United States."

Sect. 2. The President shall be commander in-chief of the army and navy of the United States, and of the militia of the several States, when called into the actual service of the United States. He may require the opinion, in writing, of the principal officer in each of the Executive departments, upon any subject relating to the duties of their respective offices. And he shall have power to grant reprieves and pardons for offences against the United States, except in cases of impeachment.

He shall have power by and with the advice and consent of the Senate, to make treaties, provided two-thirds of the Senators present concur ; and he shall nominate, and, by and with the advice and consent of the Senate, shall appoint, ambassadors, other public ministers and consuls, judges of the supreme court, and all other officers of the United States whose appointments are not herein otherwise provided for.

The President shall have power to fill up all vacancies that may happen during the recess of the Senate, by granting commissions which shall expire at the end of their next session.

Sect. 3. He shall from time to time give to the Congress information of the state of the Union, and recommend to their consideration such measures as he shall judge necessary and expedient. He may, on extraordinary occasions, convene both Houses, or either of them, and in case of disagreement between them, with respect to the time of adjournment, he may adjourn them to such time as he shall think proper ; he shall receive ambassadors and other public ministers ; he shall take care that the laws be faithfully executed, and shall commission all the officers of the United States.

Sect. 4. The President, Vice President, and all civil officers of the United States, shall be removed from office on impeachment for, and conviction of, treason, bribery, or other high crimes and misdemeanours.

Article III.

  Sect. 1. The Judicial power of the United States, both in law and equity, shall be vested in one Supreme Court, and in such inferior courts as the Congress may from time to time ordain and establish. The judges both of the supreme and inferior courts, shall hold their offices during good behaviour ; and shall at stated times, receive for their services a compensation, which shall not be diminished during their continuance in office.

  Sect. 2. The Judicial power shall extend to all cases, both in law and equity, arising under this Constitution, the laws of the United States, and treaties made, or which shall be made, under their authority. To all cases affecting ambassadors, other public ministers and consuls. To all cases of admiralty and maritime jurisdiction. To controversies to which the United States shall be a party. To controversies between two or more States ; between a State, and citizens of another State ; between citizens of different States ; between citizens of the same State claiming lands under grants of different States ; and between a State, or the citizens thereof, and foreign States, citizens or subjects.

  In cases affecting ambassadors, other public ministers and consuls, and those in which a State shall be a party, the Supreme Court shall have original jurisdiction. In all the other cases before mentioned, the Supreme Court shall have appellate jurisdiction, both as to law and fact, with such exceptions, and under such regulations, as the Congress shall make.

  The trial of all crimes, except in cases of impeachment, shall be by jury; and such trial shall be held in the State where the said crimes shall have been committed ; but when not committed within any State, the trial shall be at such place or places as the Congress may by law have directed.

  Sect. 3. Treason against the United States shall consist only in levying war against them, or in adhering to their enemies, giving them aid and comfort. No person shall be convicted of treason unless on the testimony of two witnesses to the same overt act, or on confession in open court.

The Congress shall have power to declare the punishment of treason, but no attainder of treason shall work corruption of blood, nor forfeiture, except during the life of the person attainted.

Article IV.

Sect. 1. Full faith and credit shall be given, in each State, to the public acts, records, and judicial proceedings of every other State. And the Congress may, by general laws, prescribe the manner in which such acts, records and proceedings shall be proved, and the effect thereof.

Sect. 2. The citizens of each State shall be entitled to all privileges and immunities of citizens in the several States.

A person charged in any State with treason, felony, or other crime, who shall flee from justice, and be found in another State, shall, on demand of the executive authority of the State from which he fled, be delivered up, and removed to the State having jurisdiction of the crime.

No person legally held to service or labor in one State, escaping to another, shall, in consequence of regulations subsisting therein, be discharged from such service or labor; but shall be delivered up, on claim of the party to whom such service or labor may be due.

Sect. 3. New States may be admitted by the Congress into this Union; but no new States shall be formed or erected within the jurisdiction of any other State; nor any State be formed by the junction of two or more States, or parts of States; without the consent of the legislatures of the States concerned, as well as of the Congress.

The Congress shall have power to dispose of and make all needful rules and regulations respecting the territory or other property belonging to the United States: and nothing in this Constitution shall be so construed as to prejudice any claims of the United States, or of any particular State.

Sect. 4. The United States shall guarantee to every State in this Union a republican form of government; and shall protect each of them against invasion; and, on application of the Legislature or Executive, against domestic violence.

ARTICLE V.

The Congress, whenever two-thirds of both Houses shall deem necessary, or on the application of two-thirds of the Legislatures of the several States, shall propose amendments to this Constitution ; which shall be valid to all intents and purposes, as part thereof, when the same shall have been ratified by three-fourths at least of the Legislatures of the several States, or by conventions in three-fourths thereof, as the one or the other mode of ratification may be proposed by the Congress: Provided, that no amendment which may be made prior to the year 1808 shall in any manner affect the ——— and ——— sections of the ——— article.

ARTICLE VI.

All debts contracted, and engagements entered into, before the adoption of this Constitution, shall be as valid against the United States under this Constitution as under the Confederation.

This Constitution, and the laws of the United States which shall be made in pursuance thereof ; and all treaties made, or which shall be made under the authority of the United States, shall be the supreme law of the land; and the judges in every State shall be bound thereby, anything in the Constitution or laws of any State to the contrary notwithstanding.

The Senators and Representatives beforementioned, and the members of the several State Legislatures, and all executive and judicial officers, both of the United States and ɔf the several States, shall be bound by oath, or affirmation, to support this Constitution; but no religious test shall ever be required as a qualification to any office or public trust under the United States.

ARTICLE VII.

The ratification of the Conventions of nine States shall be sufficient for the establishment of this Constitution between the States so ratifying the same.

LETTER.

" We have now the honor to submit to the consideration of the United States, in Congress assembled, that Constitution which has appeared to us the most advisable.

" The friends of our country have long seen and desired, that the power of making war, peace, and treaties; that of levying money, and regulating commerce, and the correspondent executive and judicial authorities, should be fully and effectually vested in the general government of the Union. But the impropriety of delegating such extensive trust to one body of men is evident. Thence results the necessity of a different organization. It is obviously impracticable, in the federal government of these States, to secure all rights of independent sovereignty to each, and yet provide for the interest and safety of all. Individuals entering into society must give up a share of liberty, to preserve the rest. The magnitude of the sacrifice must depend as well on situation and circumstances, as on the object to be obtained. It is at all times difficult to draw with precision the line between those rights which must be surrendered, and those which may be reserved. And on the present occasion this difficulty was increased by a difference among the several States, as to their situation, extent, habits, and particular interests.

" In all our deliberations on this subject, we kept steadily in our view that which appeared to us the greatest interest of every true American, the consolidation of our union, in which is involved our prosperity, felicity, safety, perhaps our national existence. This important consideration, seriously and deeply impressed on our minds, led each State in the Convention to be less rigid in points of inferior magnitude, than might have been otherwise expected. And thus the Constitution which we now present is the result of a spirit of amity, and of that mutual deference and concession, which the peculiarity of our political situation rendered indispensable.

"That it will meet the full and entire approbation of every State is not, perhaps, to be expected. But each will doubtless consider, that had her interest alone been consulted, the consequences might have been particularly disagreeable and injurious to others. That it is liable to as few exceptions as could reasonably have been expected, we hope and believe; that it may promote the lasting welfare of that country so dear to us all; and secure her freedom and happiness, is our most ardent wish."

Mr. WILLIAMSON moved to reconsider the clause requiring three-fourths of each house to overrule the negative of the President, in order to strike out three-fourths and insert two-thirds. He had, he remarked, himself proposed three-fourths instead of two-thirds; but he had since been convinced that the latter proportion was the best. The former puts too much in the power of the President.

Mr. SHERMAN was of the same opinion; adding that the States would not like to see so small a minority, and the President, prevailing over the general voice. In making laws, regard should be had to the sense of the people, who are to be bound by them; and it was more probable that a single man should mistake or betray this sense, than the Legislature.

Mr. GOUVERNEUR MORRIS. Considering the difference between the two proportions numerically, it amounts, in one House, to two members only; and in the other, to not more than five; according to the numbers of which the Legislature is at first to be composed. It is the interest, moreover, of the distant States, to prefer three-fourths, as they will be oftenest absent, and need the interposing check of the President. The excess, rather than the deficiency, of laws was to be dreaded. The example of New York shows that two-thirds is not sufficient to answer the purpose.

Mr. HAMILTON added his testimony to the fact, that two-thirds in New York had been ineffectual, either where a popular object, or a legislative faction, operated; of which he mentioned some instances.

Mr. GERRY. It is necessary to consider the danger on the other side also. Two-thirds will be a considerable, perhaps, a proper, security. Three-fourths puts too much in the power of a few men. The primary object of the revisionary check of the President is, not to protect the general interest, but to defend his own department. If three-fourths be required a few Senators, having hopes from the nomination of the President to offices, will combine with him and impede proper laws. Making the Vice President Speaker increases the danger.

Mr. WILLIAMSON was less afraid of too few than of too many laws. He was, most of all, afraid that the repeal of bad laws might be rendered too difficult by requiring three-fourths to overcome the dissent of the President.

Colonel MASON had always considered this as one of the most exceptionable parts of the system. As to the numerical argument of Mr. GOUVERNEUR MORRIS, little arithmetic was necessary to understand that three-fourths was more than two-thirds, whatever the numbers of the Legislature might be. The example of New York depended on the real merits of the laws. The gentlemen citing it had no doubt given their own opinions. But perhaps there were others of opposite opinions, who could equally paint the abuses on the other side. His leading view was, to guard against too great an impediment to the repeal of laws.

Mr. GOUVERNEUR MORRIS dwelt on the danger to the public interest from the instability of laws, as the most to be guarded against. On the other side, there could be little danger. If one man in office will not consent where he ought, every fourth year another can be substituted. This term was not too long for fair experiments. Many good laws are not tried long enough to prove their merit. This is often the case with new laws opposed to old habits. The inspection laws of Virginia and Maryland, to which all are now so much attached, were unpopular at first.

Mr. PINCKNEY was warmly in opposition to three-fourths, as putting a dangerous power in the hands of a few Senators headed by the President.

Mr. MADISON. When three-fourths was agreed to, the President was to be elected by the Legislature, and for seven years. He is now to be elected by the people, and for four years. The object of the revisionary power is two-fold, — first, to defend the Executive rights; secondly, to prevent popular or factious injustice. It was an important principle in this and in the State Constitutions, to check legislative injustice and encroachments. The experience of the States had demonstrated that their checks are insufficient. We must compare the danger from the weakness of two-thirds, with the danger from the strength of three-fourths. He thought on the whole, the former was the greater. As to the difficulty of repeals, it was probable that in doubtful cases, the policy would soon take place, of limiting the duration of laws, so as to require renewal instead of repeal.

The reconsideration being agreed to,—

On the question to insert two-thirds in place of three-fourths,—

Connecticut, New Jersey, Maryland, (Mr. McHENRY, no,) North Carolina, South Carolina, Georgia, aye — 6; Massachusetts, Pennsylvania, Delaware, Virginia, (General WASHINGTON, Mr. BLAIR, Mr. MADISON, no; Colonel MASON, Mr. RANDOLPH, aye,) no — 4; New Hampshire, divided.

Mr. WILLIAMSON observed to the House, that no provision was yet made for juries in civil cases, and suggested the necessity of it.

Mr. GORHAM. It is not possible to discriminate equity cases from those in which juries are proper. The Representatives of the people may be safely trusted in this matter.

Mr. GERRY urged the necessity of juries to guard against corrupt judges. He proposed that the Committee last appointed should be directed to provide a clause for securing the trial by juries.

Colonel MASON perceived the difficulty mentioned by Mr. GORHAM. The jury cases cannot be specified. A general principle laid down, on this and some other points, would be sufficient. He wished the plan had been prefaced with a Bill of Rights, and would second a motion if made for the purpose. It would give great quiet to the people; and with the aid of the State Declarations, a bill might be prepared in a few hours.

Mr. GERRY concurred in the idea, and moved for a Committee to prepare a Bill of Rights.

Colonel MASON seconded the motion.

Mr. SHERMAN was for securing the rights of the people where requisite. The State Declarations of Rights are not repealed by this Constitution; and being in force are sufficient. There are many cases where juries are proper, which cannot be discriminated. The Legislature may be safely trusted.

Colonel MASON. The laws of the United States are to be paramount to State Bills of Rights.

On the question for a Committee to prepare a Bill of Rights,—

New Hampshire, Connecticut, New Jersey, Pennsylvania, Delaware, aye — 5; Maryland, Virginia, North Carolina, South Carolina, Georgia, no — 5; Massachusetts, absent.

The clause relating to exports being reconsidered, at the instance of Colonel MASON,— who urged that the re-

strictions on the States would prevent the incidental duties
necessary for the inspection and safe keeping of their produce, and be ruinous to the staple States, as he called the
five Southern States,— he moved as follows: "provided,
nothing herein contained shall be construed to restrain any
State from laying duties upon exports for the sole purpose
of defraying the charges of inspecting, packing, storing
and indemnifying the losses in keeping the commodities in
the care of public officers, before exportation." In answer
to a remark which he anticipated, to wit, that the States
could provide for these expenses, by a tax in some other
way, he stated the inconvenience of requiring the planters
to pay a tax before the actual delivery for exportation.

Mr. MADISON seconded the motion. It would at least be
harmless; and might have the good effect of restraining the
States to *bona fide* duties for the purpose, as well as of
authorizing explicitly such duties; though perhaps the best
guard against an abuse of the power of the States on this
subject was the right in the General Government to regulate trade between State and State.

Mr. GOUVERNEUR MORRIS saw no objection to the motion. He did not consider the dollar per hogshead laid on
tobacco in Virginia, as a duty on exportation, as no draw-
back would be allowed on tobacco taken out of the ware-
house for internal consumption.

Mr. DAYTON was afraid the proviso would enable Pennsylvania to tax New Jersey under the idea of inspection
duties of which Pennsylvania would judge.

Mr. GORHAM and Mr. LANGDON thought there would be
no security, if the proviso should be agreed to, for the
States exporting through other States, against these
oppressions of the latter. How was redress to be obtained,
in case duties should be laid beyond the purpose expressed?

Mr. MADISON. There will be the same security as in
other cases. The jurisdiction of the Supreme Court must
be the source of redress. So far only had provision been
made by the plan against injurious acts of the States. His

own opinion was, that this was insufficient. A negative on the State laws alone could meet all the shapes which these could assume. But this had been overruled.

Mr. FITZSIMONS. Incidental duties on tobacco and flour never have been, and never can be, considered as duties on exports.

Mr. DICKINSON. Nothing will save the States in the situation of New Hampshire, New Jersey, Delaware, &c., from being oppressed by their neighbours, but requiring the assent of Congress to inspection duties. He moved that this assent should accordingly be required.

Mr. BUTLER seconded the motion.

Adjourned.

<hr>

THURSDAY, SEPTEMBER 13TH.

In Convention,—Col. MASON. He had moved without success for a power to make sumptuary regulations. He had not yet lost sight of his object. After descanting on the extravagance of our manners, the excessive consumption of foreign superfluities, and the necessity of restricting it, as well with economical as republican views, he moved that a committee be appointed to report articles of association for encouraging, by the advice, the influence, and the example, of the members of the Convention, economy, frugality, and American manufactures.

Doctor JOHNSON seconded the motion; which was, without debate, agreed to, *nem. con.;* and a committee appointed, consisting of Colonel MASON, Doctor FRANKLIN, Mr. DICKINSON, Doctor JOHNSON and Mr. LIVINGSTON.*

Col. MASON renewed his proposition of yesterday on the subject of inspection laws, with an additional clause giving to Congress a control over them in case of abuse, — as follows:

"Provided, that no State shall be restrained from im-

<hr>

* This motion, and appointment of the committee, do not appear in the printed Journal. No report was made by the Committee.

posing the usual duties on produce exported from such State, for the sole purpose of defraying the charges of inspecting, packing, storing, and indemnifying the losses on such produce, while in the custody of public officers; but all such regulations shall, in case of abuse, be subject to the revision and control of Congress."

There was no debate, and on the question,—

New Hampshire, Massachusetts, Connecticut, Maryland, Virginia, North Carolina, Georgia, aye — 7 ; Pennsylvania, Delaware, South Carolina, no — 3.

The report from the Committee of style and arrangement was taken up, in order to be compared with the articles of the plan, as agreed to by the House, and referred to the committee, and to receive the final corrections and sanction of the Convention.

Article 1, Section 2. On motion of Mr. RANDOLPH, the word "servitude" was struck out, and "service" unanimously * inserted, the former being thought to express the condition of slaves, and the latter the obligations of free persons.

Mr. DICKINSON and Mr. WILSON moved to strike out, "and direct taxes," from Article 1, Section 2, as improperly placed in a clause relating merely to the constitution of the House of Representatives.

Mr. GOUVERNEUR MORRIS. The insertion here was in consequence of what had passed on this point ; in order to exclude the appearance of counting the negroes in the *representation*. The including of them may now be referred to the object of direct taxes, and incidentally only to that of representation.

On the motion to strike out, "and direct taxes," from this place,—

New Jersey, Delaware, Maryland, aye — 3 ; New Hampshire, Massachusetts, Connecticut, Pennsylvania, Virginia, North Carolina, South Carolina, Georgia, no — 8.

---

* See page 372 of the printed Journal.

Article 1, Section 7 — " if any bill shall not be returned by the President within ten days (Sundays excepted) after it shall have been presented to him," &c.

Mr. MADISON moved to insert, between " after," and " it," in Article 1, Section 7, the words, " the day on which," in order to prevent a question whether the day on which the bill be presented ought to be counted, or not, as one of the ten days.

Mr. RANDOLPH seconded the motion.

Mr. GOUVERNEUR MORRIS. The amendment is unnecessary. The law knows no fractions of days.

A number of members being very impatient, and calling for the question,—

Pennsylvania, Maryland, Virginia, aye — 3 ; New Hampshire, Massachusetts, Connecticut, New Jersey, Delaware, North Carolina, South Carolina, Georgia, no — 8.

Doctor JOHNSON made a further report from the Committee of Style, &c., of the following resolutions to be substituted for Articles 22 and 23.

" Resolved, that the preceding Constitution be laid before the United States in Congress assembled ; and that it is the opinion of this Convention, that it should afterwards be submitted to a Convention of Delegates chosen in each State by the people thereof, under the recommendation of its Legislature, for their assent and ratification ; and that each convention assenting to and ratifying the same, should give notice thereof to the United States in Congress assembled."

" Resolved, that it is the opinion of this Convention, that as soon as the Conventions of nine States shall have ratified this Constitution, the United States in Congress assembled should fix a day on which Electors should be appointed by the States which shall have ratified the same; and a day on which the Electors should assemble to vote for the President; and the time and place for commencing proceedings under this Constitution: That after such publication the Electors should be appointed, and the Senators

46

and Representatives elected: That the Electors should meet on the day fixed for the election of the President, and should transmit their votes, certified, signed, sealed and directed, as the Constitution requires, to the Secretary of the United States in Congress assembled: That the Senators and Representatives should convene at the time and place assigned: that the Senators should appoint a President for the sole purpose of receiving, opening and counting the votes for President, and that after he shall be chosen, the Congress, together with the President, should, without delay, proceed to execute this Constitution.

Adjourned.

FRIDAY, SEPTEMBER 14TH.

In Convention, — The Report of the Committee of style and arrangement being resumed, —

Mr. WILLIAMSON moved to reconsider, in order to increase the number of Representatives fixed for the first Legislature.   His purpose was to make an addition of one-half generally to the number allotted to the respective States; and to allow two to the smallest States.

On this motion, — Pennsylvania, Delaware, Maryland, Virginia, North Carolina, aye — 5; New Hampshire, Massachusetts, Connecticut, New Jersey, South Carolina, Georgia, no — 6.

Article 1, Section 3, the words "by lot," * were struck out, *nem. con.*, on motion of Mr. MADISON, that some rule might prevail in the rotation that would prevent both the members from the same State, from going out at the same time.

"*Ex officio,*" struck out of the same section as superfluous, *nem. con.;* and, "or affirmation," after "oath," inserted, — also unanimously.

Mr. RUTLEDGE and Mr. GOUVERNEUR MORRIS moved,

---

* "By lot," had been reinstated from the Report of the Committee of five made on the sixth of August, as a correction of the printed Report by the Committee of style, &c. See pages 451, and 701.

"that persons impeached be suspended from their offices, until they be tried and acquitted."

Mr. MADISON. The President is made too dependent already on the Legislature by the power of one branch to try him in consequence of an impeachment by the other. This intermediate suspension will put him in the power of one branch only. They can at any moment, in order to make way for the functions of another who will be more favorable to their views, vote a temporary removal of the existing magistrate.

Mr. KING concurred in the opposition to the amendment.

On the question to agree to it, —

Connecticut, South Carolina, Georgia, aye — 3; New Hampshire, Massachusetts, New Jersey, Pennsylvania, Delaware, Maryland, Virginia, North Carolina, no — 8.

Article 1, Section 4, "except as to the places of choosing Senators," was added, *nem. con.* to the end of the first clause, in order to exempt the seats of government in the States from the power of Congress.

Article 1, Section 5. "Each House shall keep a journal of its proceedings, and from time to time, publish the same, excepting such parts as may in their judgment require secrecy."

Col. MASON and Mr. GERRY moved to insert, after the word "parts," the words, "of the proceedings of the Senate," so as to require publication of all the proceedings of the House of Representatives.

It was intimated, on the other side, that cases might arise where secrecy might be necessary in both Houses. Measures preparatory to a declaration of war, in which the House of Representatives was to concur, were instanced.

On the question, it passed in the negative, —

Pennsylvania, Maryland, North Carolina, aye — 3; New Hampshire, Massachusetts, Connecticut, New Jersey, Delaware, Virginia, Georgia, no — 7; South Carolina, divided.

Mr. BALDWIN observed, that the clause, Article 1, Section 6, declaring that no member of Congress, "during the time for which he was elected, shall be appointed to any civil office under the authority of the United States which shall have been created, or the emoluments whereof shall have been increased, during such time," would not extend to offices *created by the Constitution;* and the salaries of which would be created, *not increased,* by Congress at their first session. The members of the first Congress consequently might evade the disqualification in this instance. He was neither seconded nor opposed, nor did any thing further pass on the subject.

Article 1, Sect. 8. The Congress "may by joint ballot appoint a Treasurer,"—

Mr. RUTLEDGE moved to strike out this power, and let the Treasurer be appointed in the same manner with other officers.

Mr. GORHAM and Mr. KING said that the motion, if agreed to, would have a mischievous tendency. The people are accustomed and attached to that mode of appointing Treasurers, and the innovation will multiply objections to the system.

MR. GOUVERNEUR MORRIS remarked that if the Treasurer be not appointed by the Legislature, he will be more narrowly watched, and more readily impeached.

Mr. SHERMAN. As the two Houses appropriate money, it is best for them to appoint the officer who is to keep it; and to appoint him as they make the appropriation, not by joint, but several votes.

General PINCKNEY. The Treasurer is appointed by joint ballot in South Carolina. The consequence is, that bad appointments are made, and the Legislature will not listen to the faults of their own officer.

On the motion to strike out, —

New Hampshire, Connecticut, New Jersey, Delaware, Maryland, North Carolina, South Carolina, Georgia, aye -- 8; Massachusetts, Pennsylvania, Virginia, no — 3.

Article 1, Sect. 8, — the words "but all such duties,

imposts and excises, shall be uniform throughout the United States," were unanimously annexed to the power of taxation.

On the clause, " to define and punish piracies and felonies on the high seas, and punish offences against the law of nations,"—

Mr. GOUVERNEUR MORRIS moved to strike out "punish," before the words, "offences against the law of nations," so as to let these be *definable*, as well as punishable, by virtue of the preceding member of the sentence.

Mr. WILSON hoped the alteration would by no means be made. To pretend to *define* the law of nations, which depended on the authority of all the civilized nations of the world, would have a look of arrogance, that would make us ridiculous.

Mr. GOUVERNEUR MORRIS. The word *define* is proper when applied to *offences* in this case; the law of nations being often too vague and deficient to be a rule.

On the question to strike out the word "punish," it passed in the affirmative, —

New Hampshire, Connecticut, New Jersey, Delaware, North Carolina, South Carolina, aye — 6; Massachusetts, Pennsylvania, Maryland, Virginia, Georgia, no — 5.

Doctor FRANKLIN * moved to add, after the words, " post roads," Article 1, Sect. 8, a power " to provide for cutting canals where deemed necessary."

Mr. WILSON seconded the motion.

Mr. SHERMAN objected. The expense in such cases will fall on the United States, and the benefit accrue to the places where the canals may be cut.

Mr. WILSON. Instead of being an expense to the United States, they may be made a source of revenue.

Mr. MADISON suggested an enlargement of the motion, into a power " to grant charters of incorporation where the interest of the United States might require, and the legis-

---

* This motion by Doctor FRANKLIN not stated in the printed Journal, as are some other motions.

lative provisions of individual States may be incompetent."
His primary object was, however, to secure an easy communication between the States, which the free intercourse now
to be opened seemed to call for. The political obstacles
being removed, a removal of the natural ones as far as possible ought to follow.

Mr. RANDOLPH seconded the proposition.

Mr. KING thought the power unnecessary.

Mr. WILSON. It is necessary to prevent *a State* from
obstructing the *general* welfare.

Mr. KING. The States will be prejudiced and divided
into parties by it. In Philadelphia and New York, it will
be referred to the establishment of a bank, which has been
a subject of contention in those cities. In other places it
will be referred to mercantile monopolies.

Mr. WILSON mentioned the importance of facilitating
by canals the communication with the Western settlements.
As to banks, he did not think with Mr. KING, that the
power in that point of view would excite the prejudices and
parties apprehended. As to mercantile monopolies, they
are already included in the power to regulate trade.

Col. MASON was for limiting the power to the single
case of canals. He was afraid of monopolies of every
sort, which he did not think were by any means already
implied by the Constitution, as supposed by Mr. WILSON

The motion being so modified as to admit a distinct
question specifying and limited to the case of canals,—

Pennsylvania, Virginia, Georgia, aye — 3; New Hampshire, Massachusetts, Connecticut, New Jersey, Delaware,
Maryland, North Carolina, South Carolina, no — 8.

The other part fell of course, as including the power
rejected.

Mr. MADISON and Mr. PINCKNEY then moved to insert,
in the list of powers vested in Congress, a power "to
establish an University, in which no preferences or distinctions should be allowed on account of religion."

Mr. WILSON supported the motion.

Mr. Gouverneur Morris. It is not necessary. The exclusive power at the seat of government, will reach the object.

On the question,—

Pennsylvania, Virginia, North Carolina, South Carolina, aye — 4 ; New Hampshire, Massachusetts, New Jersey, Delaware, Maryland, Georgia, no — 6 ; Connecticut, divided, (Doctor Johnson, aye; Mr. Sherman, no.)

Colonel Mason, being sensible that an absolute prohibition of standing armies in time of peace might be unsafe, and wishing at the same time to insert something pointing out and guarding against the danger of them, moved to preface the clause (Article 1, Sect. 8), "to provide for organizing, arming and disciplining the militia," &c., with the words, "and that the liberties of the people may be better secured against the danger of standing armies in time of peace."

Mr. Randolph seconded the motion.

Mr. Madison was in favor of it. It did not restrain Congress from establishing a military force in time of peace, if found necessary; and as armies in time of peace are allowed on all hands to be an evil, it is well to discountenance them by the Constitution, as far as will consist with the essential power of the Government on that head.

Mr. Gouverneur Morris opposed the motion, as setting a dishonorable mark of distinction on the military class of citizens.

Mr. Pinckney and Mr. Bedford concurred in the opposition.

On the question,—

Virginia, Georgia, aye — 2; New Hampshire, Massachusetts, Connecticut, New Jersey, Pennsylvania, Delaware, Maryland, North Carolina, South Carolina, no — 9.

Colonel Mason moved to strike out from the clause (Article 1, Sect. 9,) "no bill of attainder, nor any *ex post facto* law, shall be passed," the words, "nor any *ex post facto* law." He thought it not sufficiently clear that the prohibition meant by this phrase was limited to cases of a criminal nature; and no Legislature ever did or can altogether avoid them in civil cases.

Mr. GERRY seconded the motion; but with a view to extend the prohibition to "civil cases," which he thought ought to be done.

On the question, all the States were no.

Mr. PINCKNEY and Mr. GERRY moved to insert a declaration, "that the liberty of the press should be inviolably observed."

Mr. SHERMAN. It is unnecessary. The power of Congress does not extend to the press.

On the question, it passed in the negative,—

Massachusetts, Maryland, Virginia, South Carolina, aye — 4; New Hampshire,* Connecticut, New Jersey, Pennsylvania, Delaware, North Carolina, Georgia, no — 7.

Article 1, Section 9. "No capitation tax shall be laid, unless," &c.

Mr. READ moved to insert after "capitation," the words, "or other direct tax." He was afraid that some liberty might otherwise be taken to saddle the States with a readjustment, by this rule, of past requisitions of Congress; and that his amendment, by giving another cast to the meaning, would take away the pretext.

Mr. WILLIAMSON seconded the motion, which was agreed to.

On motion of Col. MASON, the words "or enumeration," were inserted after, as explanatory of "census,"— Connecticut and South Carolina, only, no.

At the end of the clause, "no tax or duty shall be laid on articles exported from any State," was added the following amendment, conformably to a vote on the 31st of August, (p. 647,) viz: "no preference shall be given, by any regulation of commerce or revenue, to the ports of one State over those of another: nor shall vessels bound to or from one State, be obliged to enter, clear, or pay duties, in another."

* In the printed Journal, New Hampshire, aye.

Col. MASON moved a clause requiring, "that an account of the public expenditures should be annually published."

Mr. GERRY seconded the motion.

Mr. GOUVERNEUR MORRIS urged that this would be impossible, in many cases.

Mr. KING remarked, that the term expenditures went to every minute shilling. This would be impracticable. Congress might indeed make a monthly publication, but it would be in such general statements as would afford no satisfactory information.

Mr. MADISON proposed to strike out "annually" from the motion, and insert "from time to time," which would enjoin the duty of frequent publications, and leave enough to the discretion of the Legislature. Require too much and the difficulty will beget a habit of doing nothing. The articles of Confederation require half yearly publications on this subject. A punctual compliance being often impossible, the practice has ceased altogether.

Mr. WILSON seconded and supported the motion. Many operations of finance cannot be properly published at certain times.

Mr. PINCKNEY was in favor of the motion.

Mr. FITZSIMONS. It is absolutely impossible to publish expenditures in the full extent of the term.

Mr. SHERMAN thought "from time to time," the best rule to be given. "Annually" was struck out, and those words inserted, nem. con.

The motion of Col. MASON, so amended, was then agreed to, nem. con., and added after "appropriations by law," as follows: "and a regular statement and account of the receipts and expenditures of all public money shall be published from time to time."

The first clause of Article 1, Sect. 10, was altered so as to read, "no State shall enter into any treaty, alliance or confederation; grant letters of marque and reprisal; coin money; emit bills of credit; make anything but gold and silver coin a tender in payment of debts; pass any bill of attainder, *ex post facto* law, or law impairing the obligation of contracts, or grant any title of nobility."

Mr. GERRY entered into observations inculcating the importance of public faith, and the propriety of the restraint put on the States from impairing the obligation of contracts; alleging that Congress ought to be laid under the like prohibitions. He made a motion to that effect. He was not seconded.

Adjourned.

SATURDAY, SEPTEMBER 15TH.

In Convention,—Mr. CARROLL reminded the House that no address to the people had yet been prepared. He considered it of great importance that such an one should accompany the Constitution. The people had been accustomed to such, on great occasions, and would expect it on this. He moved that a committee be appointed for the special purpose of preparing an address.

Mr. RUTLEDGE objected, on account of the delay it would produce, and the impropriety of addressing the people before it was known whether Congress would approve and support the plan. Congress, if an address be thought proper, can prepare as good a one. The members of the Convention can, also, explain the reasons of what has been done to their respective constituents.

Mr. SHERMAN concurred in the opinion that an address was both unnecessary and improper.

On the motion of Mr. CARROLL,—

Pennsylvania, Delaware, Maryland, Virginia, aye — 4; New Hampshire, Massachusetts, Connecticut, New Jersey, South Carolina,* Georgia, no — 6; North Carolina,* absent.

Mr. LANGDON. Some gentlemen have been very uneasy that no increase of the number of Representatives has been admitted. It has in particular been thought, that one more ought to be allowed to North Carolina. He was

----

* In the printed Journal, North Carolina, no; South Carolina, omitted.

of opinion that an additional one was due both to that State, and to Rhode Island; and moved to reconsider for that purpose.

Mr. SHERMAN. When the Committee of eleven reported the appointments, five Representatives were thought the proper share of North Carolina. Subsequent information, however, seemed to entitle that State to another.

On the motion to reconsider,—

New Hampshire, Connecticut, Delaware, Maryland, Virginia, North Carolina, South Carolina, Georgia, aye — 8 ; Massachusetts, New Jersey, no — 2 ; Pennsylvania, divided.

Mr. LANGDON moved to add one member to each of the representations of North Carolina and Rhode Island.

Mr. KING was against any change whatever, as opening the door for delays. There had been no official proof that the numbers of North Carolina are greater than before estimated, and he never could sign the Constitution, if Rhode Island is to be allowed two members, that is, one-fourth of the number allowed to Massachusetts, which will be known to be unjust.

Mr. PINCKNEY urged the propriety of increasing the number of Representatives allowed to North Carolina.

Mr. BEDFORD contended for an increase in favor of Rhode Island, and of Delaware also.

On the question for allowing two Representatives to Rhode Island, it passed in the negative,—

New Hampshire, Delaware, Maryland, North Carolina, Georgia, aye — 5 ; Massachusetts, Connecticut, New Jersey, Pennsylvania, Virginia, South Carolina, no — 6.

On the question for allowing six to North Carolina, it passed in the negative,—

Maryland, Virginia, North Carolina, South Carolina, Georgia, aye — 5 ; New Hampshire, Massachusetts, Connecticut, New Jersey, Pennsylvania, Delaware, no — 6.

Article 1, Sect. 10, (the second paragraph) " No State shall, without the consent of Congress, lay imposts or duties on imports or exports ; nor with such consent, but to the use of the Treasury of the United States."

In consequence of the proviso moved by Colonel MASON, and agreed to on the 13th of Sept., (Page 719,) this part of the Section was laid aside in favour of the following substitute, viz : "No State shall, without the consent of Congress, lay any imposts or duties on imports or exports, except what may be absolutely necessary for executing its inspection laws ; and the nett produce of all duties and imposts, laid by any State on imports or exports shall be for the use of the Treasury of the United States ; and all such laws shall be subject to the revision and control of the Congress."

On the motion to strike out the last part, "and all such laws shall be subject to the revision and control of the Congress," it passed in the negative, —

Virginia, North Carolina, Georgia, aye — 3 ; New Hampshire, Massachusetts, Connecticut, New Jersey, Delaware, Maryland, South Carolina, no — 7 ; Pennsylvania, divided.

The substitute was then agreed to, — Virginia alone being in the negative.

The remainder of the paragraph being under consideration, viz : " nor keep troops nor ships of war in time of peace, nor enter into any agreement or compact with another State nor with any foreign power, nor engage in any war, unless it shall be actually invaded by enemies, or the danger of invasion be so imminent as not to admit of delay until Congress can be consulted," —

Mr. McHENRY and Mr. CARROLL moved, that " no State shall be restrained from laying duties of tonnage for the purpose of clearing harbours and erecting light-houses."

Col. MASON, in support of this, explained and urged the situation of the Chesapeake, which peculiarly required expenses of this sort.

Mr. GOUVERNEUR MORRIS. The States are not restrained from laying tonnage, as the Constitution now stands. The exception proposed will imply the contrary, and will put the States in a worse condition than the gentleman (Col. MASON) wishes.

Mr. MADISON.   Whether the States are now restrained from laying tonnage duties, depends on the extent of the power "to regulate commerce."   These terms are vague, but seem to exclude this power of the States.   They may certainly be restrained by treaty.   He observed that there were other objects for tonnage duties, as the support of seamen, &c.   He was more and more convinced that the regulation of commerce was in its nature indivisible, and ought to be wholly under one authority.

Mr. SHERMAN.   The power of the United States to regulate trade being supreme, can control interferences of the State regulations, when such interferences happen; so that there is no danger to be apprehended from a concurrent jurisdiction.

Mr. LANGDON insisted that the regulation of tonnage was an essential part of the regulation of trade, and that the States ought to have nothing to do with it.

On motion, "that no State shall lay any duty on tonnage without the consent of Congress,"—

New Hampshire, Massachusetts, New Jersey, Delaware, Maryland, South Carolina, aye — 6; Pennsylvania, Virginia, North Carolina, Georgia, no — 4; Connecticut, divided.

The remainder of the paragraph was then remoulded and passed, as follows, viz.:   "No State shall, without the consent of Congress, lay any duty of tonnage, keep troops or ships of war in time of peace, enter into any agreement or compact with another State, or with a foreign power, or engage in war, unless actually invaded, or in such imminent danger as will not admit of delay."

Article 2, Sect. 1, (the sixth paragraph) the words, "or the period for choosing another President arrive," were changed into, "or a President shall be elected," conformably to a vote of the seventh of September.

Mr. RUTLEDGE and Doctor FRANKLIN moved to annex

to the end of the seventh paragraph of Article 2, Sect. 1,
" and he (the President) shall not receive, within that
period, any other emolument from the United States or any
of them."

On which question,—

New Hampshire, Massachusetts, Pennsylvania, Maryland, Virginia, South Carolina, Georgia, aye — 7; Connecticut, New Jersey, Delaware, North Carolina, no — 4.

Article 2, Sect. 2.   " He shall have power to grant
reprieves and pardons for offences against the United
States," &c.

Mr. RANDOLPH moved to except " cases of treason.   The
prerogative of pardon in these cases was too great a trust.
The President may himself be guilty.   The traitors may be
his own instruments.

Col. MASON supported the motion.

Mr. GOUVERNEUR MORRIS had rather there should be no
pardon for treason, than let the power devolve on the Legislature.

Mr. WILSON.   Pardon is necessary for cases of treason,
and is best placed in the hands of the Executive.   If he be
himself a party to the guilt, he can be impeached and
prosecuted.

Mr. KING thought it would be inconsistent with the constitutional separation of the Executive and Legislative
powers, to let the prerogative be exercised by the latter.   A
legislative body is utterly unfit for the purpose.   They are
governed too much by the passions of the moment.   In
Massachusetts, one assembly would have hung all the insurgents in that State; the next was equally disposed to
pardon them all.   He suggested the expedient of requiring
the concurrence of the Senate in acts of pardon.

Mr. MADISON admitted the force of objections to the
Legislature, but the pardon of treasons was so peculiarly
improper for the President, that he should acquiesce in the
transfer of it to the former, rather than leave it altogether
in the hands of the latter.   He would prefer to either, an

association of the Senate, as a council of advice, with the President.

Mr. RANDOLPH could not admit the Senate into a share of the power. . The great danger to liberty lay in a combination between the President and that body.

Col. MASON. The Senate has already too much power. There can be no danger of too much lenity in legislative pardons, as the Senate must concur; and the President moreover can require two-thirds of both Houses.

On the. motion of Mr. RANDOLPH,—

Virginia, Georgia, aye — 2; New Hampshire, Massachusetts, New Jersey, Pennsylvania, Delaware, Maryland, North Carolina, South Carolina, no — 8; Connecticut, divided.

Article 2, Section 2, (the second paragraph). To the end of this Mr. GOUVERNEUR MORRIS moved to annex, "but the Congress may by law vest the appointment of such inferior officers as they think proper in the President alone, in the courts of law, or in the heads of departments."

Mr. SHERMAN seconded the motion.

Mr. MADISON. It does not go far enough, if it be necessary at all. Superior officers below heads of departments ought in some cases to have the appointment of the lesser offices.

Mr. GOUVERNEUR MORRIS. There is no necessity. Blank commissions can be sent.

On the motion, — New Hampshire, Connecticut, New Jersey, Pennsylvania, North Carolina, aye — 5; Massachusetts, Delaware, Virginia, South Carolina, Georgia, no — 5; Maryland, divided.

The motion being lost, by an equal division of votes, it was urged that it be put a second time, some such provision being too necessary to be omitted ; and on a second question, it was agreed to, *nem. con.*

Article 2, Sect. 1. The words, "and not *per capita*," were struck out, as superfluous ; and the words, "by the Representatives," also, as improper, the choice of President being in another mode, as well as eventually by the House of Representatives.

Article 2, Sect. 2. After the words, "officers of the United States whose appointments are not otherwise provided for," were added the words, "and which shall be established by law."

Article 3, Sect. 2, (the third paragraph.) Mr. PINCKNEY and Mr. GERRY moved to annex to the end, "and a trial by jury shall be preserved as usual in civil cases."

Mr. GORHAM. The constitution of juries is different in different States, and the trial itself is *usual* in different cases in different States.

Mr. KING urged the same objections.

General PINCKNEY also. He thought such a clause in the Constitution would be pregnant with embarrassments.

The motion was disagreed to, *nem. con.*

Article 4, Sect. 2, (the third paragraph,) the term "legally" was struck out; and the words, "under the laws thereof," inserted after the word "State," in compliance with the wish of some who thought the term *legal* equivocal, and favoring the idea that slavery was legal in a moral view.

Article 4, Sect. 3. "New States may be admitted by the Congress into this Union : but no new State shall be formed or erected within the jurisdiction of any other State ; nor any State be formed by the junction of two or more States, or parts of States, without the consent of the Legislatures of the States concerned, as well as of the Congress."

Mr. GERRY moved to insert, after, "or parts of States," the words, "or a State and part of a State ;" which was disagreed to by a large majority ; it appearing to be supposed that the case was comprehended in the words of the clause as reported by the Committee.

Article 4, Sect. 4. After the word "Executive," were inserted the words, "when the Legislature cannot be convened."

Article 5. "The Congress, whenever two-thirds of both

Houses shall deem necessary, or on the application of two-thirds of the Legislatures of the several States, shall propose amendments to this Constitution, which shall be valid to all intents and purposes as part thereof, when the same shall have been ratified by three-fourths at least of the Legislatures of the several States, or by Conventions in three-fourths thereof, as the one or the other mode of ratification may be proposed by the Congress : provided, that no amendment which may be made prior to the year 1808 shall in any manner affect the first and fourth clauses in the ninth Section of Article 1."

Mr. SHERMAN expressed his fears that three-fourths of the States might be brought to do things fatal to particular States ; as abolishing them altogether, or depriving them of their equality in the Senate. He thought it reasonable that the proviso in favor of the States importing slaves should be extended, so as to provide that no State should be affected in its internal police, or deprived of its equality in the Senate.

Colonel MASON thought the plan of amending the Constitution exceptionable and dangerous. As the proposing of amendments is in both the modes to depend, in the first immediately, and in the second ultimately, on Congress, no amendments of the proper kind, would ever be obtained by the people, if the Government should become oppressive, as he verily believed would be the case.

Mr. GOUVERNEUR MORRIS and Mr. GERRY moved to amend the Article, so as to require a Convention on application of two-thirds of the States.

Mr. MADISON did not see why Congress would not be as much bound to propose amendments applied for by two-thirds of the States, as to call a Convention on the like application. He saw no objection, however, against providing for a Convention for the purpose of amendments, except only that difficulties might arise as to the form, the quorum, &c., which in constitutional regulations ought to be as much as possible avoided.

47

The motion of GOUVERNEUR MORRIS and Mr. GERRY was agreed to, *nem. con.*

Mr. SHERMAN moved to strike out of Article 5, after "legislatures," the words, "of three-fourths," and so after the word "Conventions," leaving future Conventions to act in this matter like the present Convention, according to circumstances.

On this motion,—

Massachusetts, Connecticut, New Jersey, aye — 3; Pennsylvania, Delaware, Maryland, Virginia, North Carolina, South Carolina, Georgia, no — 7; New Hampshire, divided.

Mr. GERRY moved to strike out the words, "or by Conventions in three-fourths thereof." On which motion,—

Connecticut, aye — 1; New Hampshire, Massachusetts, New Jersey, Pennsylvania, Delaware, Maryland, Virginia, North Carolina, South Carolina, Georgia, no — 10.

Mr. SHERMAN moved, according to his idea above expressed, to annex to the end of the Article a further proviso "that no State shall, without its consent, be affected in its internal police, or deprived of its equal suffrage in the Senate."

Mr. MADISON. Begin with these special provisos, and every State will insist on them, for their boundaries, exports, &c.

On the motion of Mr. SHERMAN,—

Connecticut, New Jersey, Delaware, aye — 3; New Hampshire, Massachusetts, Pennsylvania, Maryland, Virginia, North Carolina, South Carolina, Georgia, no — 8.

Mr. SHERMAN then moved to strike out Article 5 altogether.

Mr. BREARLY seconded the motion; on which,—

Connecticut, New Jersey, aye — 2; New Hampshire, Massachusetts, Pennsylvania, Maryland, Virginia, North Carolina, South Carolina, Georgia, no — 8; Delaware, divided.

Mr. GOUVERNEUR MORRIS moved to annex a further

proviso, " that no State, without its consent, shall be deprived of its equal suffrage in the Senate."

This motion, being dictated by the circulating murmurs of the small States, was agreed to without debate, no one opposing it, or, on the question, saying, no.

Colonel MASON, expressing his discontent at the power given to Congress, by a bare majority to pass navigation acts, which he said would not only enhance the freight, a consequence he did not so much regard, but would enable a few rich merchants in Philadelphia, New York and Boston, to monopolize the staples of the Southern States, and reduce their value perhaps fifty per cent., moved a further proviso, " that no law in the nature of a navigation act be passed before the year 1808, without the consent of two-thirds of each branch of the Legislature. On which motion,—

Maryland, Virginia, Georgia aye — 3; New Hampshire, Massachusetts, Connecticut, New Jersey, Pennsylvania, Delaware, South Carolina, no — 7; North Carolina, absent.

Mr. RANDOLPH, animadverting on the indefinite and dangerous power given by the Constitution to Congress, expressing the pain he felt at differing from the body of the Convention on the close of the great and awful subject of their labours, and anxiously wishing for some accommodating expedient which would relieve him from his embarrassments, made a motion importing, " that amendments to the plan might be offered by the State conventions, which should be submitted to, and finally decided on by, another general convention." Should this proposition be disregarded, it would, he said, be impossible for him to put his name to the instrument. . Whether he should oppose it afterwards, he would not then decide; but he would not deprive himself of the freedom to do so in his own State, if that course should be prescribed by his final judgment.

Col. MASON seconded and followed Mr. RANDOLPH in animadversions on the dangerous power and structure of the Government, concluding that it would end either in monarchy, or a tyrannical aristocracy; which, he was in doubt, but one or other, he was sure. This Constitution had been formed without the knowledge or idea of the people. A second convention will know more of the sense of the people, and be able to provide a system more consonant to it. It was improper to say to the people, take this or nothing. As the Constitution now stands, he could neither give it his support or vote in Virginia; and he could not sign here what he could not support there. With the expedient of another Convention, as proposed, he could sign.

Mr. PINCKNEY. These declarations from members so respectable, at the close of this important scene, give a peculiar solemnity to the present moment. He descanted on the consequences of calling forth the deliberations and amendments of the different States, on the subject of government at large. Nothing but confusion and contrariety will spring from the experiment. The States will never agree in their plans, and the deputies to a second convention, coming together under the discordant impressions of their constituents, will never agree. Conventions are serious things, and ought not to be repeated. He was not without objections as well as others, to the plan. He objected to the contemptible weakness and dependence of the Executive. He objected to the power of a majority, only, of Congress, over commerce. But apprehending the danger of a general confusion, and an ultimate decision by the sword, he should give the plan his support.

Mr. GERRY stated the objections which determined him to withhold his name from the Constitution: 1, the duration and re-eligibility of the Senate; 2, the power of the House of Representatives to conceal their Journals; 3, the power of Congress over the places of election; 4, the unlimited power of Congress over their own compensation; 5, that Massachusetts has not a due share of representatives allotted to her; 6, that three-fifths of the blacks are to be represented, as if they were freemen; 7, that under the power over commerce, monopolies may be established; 8, the Vice

President being made head of the Senate. He could, however, he said, get over all these, if the rights of the citizens
were not rendered insecure — first, by the general power
of the Legislature to make what laws they may please to
call " necessary and proper;" secondly, to raise armies and
money without limit; thirdly, to establish a tribunal without juries, which will be a Star Chamber as to civil cases.
Under such a view of the Constitution the best that could
be done, he conceived, was to provide for a second general
Convention.

On the question, on the proposition of Mr. RANDOLPH,
all the States answered, no.

On the question to agree to the Constitution, as
amended, all the States, aye.

The Constitution was then ordered to be engrossed,
and the House

Adjourned.

MONDAY, SEPTEMBER 17TH.

In Convention.— The engrossed Constitution being
read,—

Doctor FRANKLIN rose with a speech in his hand, which
he had reduced to writing for his own convenience, and
which Mr. WILSON read in the words following.

" Mr. PRESIDENT:

" I confess that there are several parts of this Constitution which I do not at present approve, but I am not sure I
shall never approve them. For having lived long, I have
experienced many instances of being obliged by better information, or fuller consideration, to change opinions even
on important subjects, which I once thought right, but
found to be otherwise. It is therefore that, the older I
grow, the more apt I am to doubt my own judgment, and
to pay more respect to the judgment, of others. Most men,
indeed, as well as most sects in religion, think themselves
in possession of all truth, and that wherever others differ

from them, it is so far error. Steele, a Protestant, in a
dedication, tells the Pope, that the only difference between
our churches, in their opinions of the certainty of their
doctrines, is, 'the Church of Rome is infallible, and the
Church of England is never in the wrong.' But though
many private persons think almost as highly of their own
infallibility as of that of their sect, few express it so naturally as a certain French lady, who, in a dispute with her
sister, said, 'I don't know how it happens, sister, but I
meet with nobody but myself, that is always in the right
—*il n'y a que moi qui a toujours raison.*'

"In these sentiments, sir, I agree to this Constitution,
with all its faults, if they are such; because I think a General Government necessary for us, and there is no form of
government, but what may be a blessing to the people if
well administered; and believe further, that this is likely
to be well administered for a course of years, and can only
end in despotism, as other forms have done before it, when
the people shall become so corrupted as to need despotic
government, being incapable of any other. I doubt, too,
whether any other Convention we can obtain may be able
to make a better Constitution. For when you assemble a
number of men to have the advantage of their joint wisdom, you inevitably assemble with those men all their
prejudices, their passions, their errors of opinion, their
local interests and their selfish views. From such an assembly can a perfect production be expected? It therefore
astonishes me, sir, to find this system approaching so near
to perfection as it does; and I think it will astonish our
enemies, who are waiting with confidence to hear that our
councils are confounded, like those of the builders of Babel;
and that our States are on the point of separation, only to
meet hereafter for the purpose of cutting one another's
throats. Thus I consent, sir, to this Constitution, because
I expect no better, and because I am not sure, that it is not
the best. The opinions I have had of its errors I sacrifice
to the public good. I have never whispered a syllable of

them abroad. Within these walls they were born, and here they shall die. If every one of us, in returning to our constituents, were to report the objections he has had to it, and endeavour to gain partizans in support of them, we might prevent its being generally received, and thereby lose all the salutary effects and great advantages resulting naturally in our favor among foreign nations as well as among ourselves, from our real or apparent unanimity. Much of the strength and efficiency of any government, in procuring and securing happiness to the people, depends on opinion — on the general opinion of the goodness of the government as well as of the wisdom and integrity of its governors. I hope, therefore, that for our own sakes, as a part of the people, and for the sake of posterity, we shall act heartily and unanimously in recommending this Constitution (if approved by Congress and confirmed by the Conventions) wherever our influence may extend, and turn our future thoughts and endeavours to the means of having it well administered.

"On the whole, sir, I cannot help expressing a wish that every member of the Convention who may still have objections to it, would with me, on this occasion, doubt a little of his own infallibility, and to make manifest our unanimity, put his name to this instrument." He then moved that the Constitution be signed by the members, and offered the following as a convenient form, viz: "Done in Convention by the unanimous consent of *the States* present, the seventeenth of September, &c. In witness whereof we have hereunto subscribed our names."

This ambiguous form had been drawn up by Mr. Gouverneur Morris, in order to gain the dissenting members, and put into the hands of Doctor Franklin, that it might have the better chance of success.

Mr. Gorham said, if it was not too late, he could wish, for the purpose of lessening objections to the Constitution, that the clause, declaring that "the number of Representatives shall not exceed one for every forty thousand," which had produced so much discussion, might be yet reconsidered, in order to strike out "forty thousand," and insert "thirty thousand." This would not, he remarked, establish that as an absolute rule, but only give Congress a greater latitude, which could not be thought unreasonable.

Mr. KING and Mr. CARROLL seconded and supported the ideas of Mr. GORHAM.

When the President rose, for the purpose of putting the question, he said, that although his situation had hitherto restrained him from offering his sentiments on questions depending in the House, and, it might be thought, ought now to impose silence on him, yet he could not forbear expressing his wish that the alteration proposed might take place. It was much to be desired that the objections to the plan recommended might be made as few as possible. The smallness of the proportion of Representatives had been considered, by many members of the Convention an insufficient security for the rights and interests of the people. He acknowledged that it had always appeared to himself among the exceptionable parts of the plan ; and late as the present moment was for admitting amendments, he thought this of so much consequence, that it would give him much satisfaction to see it adopted.*

No opposition was made to the proposition of Mr. GORHAM, and it was agreed to unanimously.

On the question to agree to the Constitution, enrolled, in order to be signed, it was agreed to, all the *States* answering, aye.

Mr. RANDOLPH then rose, and with an allusion to the observations of Dr. FRANKLIN, apologized for his refusing to sign the Constitution, notwithstanding the vast majority and venerable names that would give sanction to its wisdom and its worth. He said, however, that he did not mean by this refusal to decide that he should oppose the Constitution without doors. He meant only to keep himself free to be

---

* This was the only occasion on which the President entered at all into the discussions of the Convention.

governed by his duty, as it should be prescribed by his future judgment. He refused to sign, because he thought the object of the Convention would be frustrated by the alternative which it presented to the people. Nine States will fail to ratify the plan, and confusion must ensue. With such a view of the subject he ought not, he could not, by pledging himself to support the plan, restrain himself from taking such steps as might appear to him most consistent with the public good.

Mr. GOUVERNEUR MORRIS said, that he too had objections, but considering the present plan as the best that was to be attained, he should take it with all its faults. The majority had determined in its favor, and by that determination he should abide. The moment this plan goes forth, all other considerations will be laid aside, and the great question will be, shall there be a National Government, or not? and this must take place, or a general anarchy will be the alternative. He remarked that the signing, in the form proposed, related only to the fact that *the States* present were unanimous.

Mr. WILLIAMSON suggested that the signing should be confined to the letter accompanying the Constitution to Congress, which might perhaps do nearly as well, and would be found satisfactory to some members* who disliked the Constitution. For himself he did not think a better plan was to be expected, and had no scruples against putting his name to it.

Mr. HAMILTON expressed his anxiety that every member should sign, A few characters of consequence, by opposing, or even refusing to sign the Constitution, might do infinite mischief, by kindling the latent sparks that lurk under an enthusiasm in favor of the Convention which may soon subside. No man's ideas were more remote from the plan than his own were known to be; but is it possible to deliberate between anarchy and convulsion on one side, and

---

* He alluded to Mr. Blount for one.

the chance of good to be expected from the plan on the other?

Mr BLOUNT said, he had declared that he would not sign so as to pledge himself in support of the plan, but he was relieved by the form proposed, and would, without committing himself, attest the fact that the plan was the unanimous act of the States in Convention.

Doctor FRANKLIN expressed his fears, from what Mr. RANDOLPH had said, that he thought himself alluded to in the remarks offered this morning to the House. He declared, that, when drawing up that paper, he did not know that any particular member would refuse to sign his name to the instrument, and hoped to be so understood. He possessed a high sense of obligation to Mr. RANDOLPH for having brought forward the plan in the first instance and for the assistance he had given in its progress; and hoped that he would yet lay aside his objections, and, by concurring with his brethren, prevent the great mischief which the refusal of his name might produce.

Mr. RANDOLPH could not but regard the signing in the proposed form, as the same with signing the Constitution. The change of form, therefore, could make no difference with him. He repeated, that, in refusing to sign the Constitution, he took a step which might be the most awful of his life; but it was dictated by his conscience, and it was not possible for him to hesitate,— much less, to change. He repeated, also, his persuasion, that the holding out this plan, with a final alternative to the people of accepting or rejecting it *in toto*, would really produce the anarchy and civil convulsions which were apprehended from the refusal of individuals to sign it.

Mr. GERRY described the painful feelings of his situation, and the embarrassments under which he rose to offer any further observations on the subject which had been finally decided. Whilst the plan was depending, he had treated it with all the freedom he thought it deserved. He now felt himself bound, as he was disposed, to treat it with the respect due to the act of the Convention. He hoped he should not violate that respect in declaring, on this occasion, his fears that a civil war may result from the present crisis of the United States. In Massachusetts, particularly, he saw the danger of this calamitous event. In that State there are two parties, one devoted to De- mocracy, the worst, he thought, of all political evils; the other as violent in the opposite extreme. From the collision of these in opposing and resisting the Constitution, con- fusion was greatly to be feared. He had thought it neces- sary, for this and other reasons, that the plan should have been proposed in a more mediating shape, in order to abate the heat and opposition of parties. As it had been passed by the Convention, he was persuaded it would have a contrary effect. He could not, therefore, by signing the Constitution, pledge himself to abide by it at all events. The proposed form made no difference with him. But if it were not otherwise apparent, the refusals to sign should never be known from him. Alluding to the remarks of Doctor FRANKLIN, he could not, he said, but view them as levelled at himself and the other gentlemen who meant not to sign.

General PINCKNEY. We are not likely to gain many converts by the ambiguity of the proposed form of signing. He thought it best to be candid, and let the form speak the substance. If the meaning of the signers be left in doubt, his purpose would not be answered. He should sign the constitution with a view to support it with all his influence, and wished to pledge himself accordingly.

Doctor FRANKLIN. It is too soon to pledge ourselves, before Congress and our constituents shall have approved the plan.

Mr. INGERSOLL did not consider the signing either as a mere attestation of the fact, or as pledging the signers to support the Constitution at all events; but as a recommenda- tion of what, all things considered, was the most eligible.

On the motion of Doctor FRANKLIN, —

New Hampshire, Massachusetts, Connecticut, New Jersey, Pennsylvania, Delaware, Maryland, Virginia, North Carolina, Georgia, aye — 10; South Carolina, divided.*

Mr. KING suggested that the Journals of the Convention should either be destroyed, or deposited in the custody of the President. He thought, if suffered to be made public, a bad use would be made of them by those who would wish to prevent the adoption of the Constitution.

Mr. WILSON preferred the second expedient. He had at one time liked the first best; but as false suggestions may be propagated, it should not be made impossible to contradict them.

A question was then put on depositing the Journals and other papers of the Convention, in the hands of the President; on which, —

New Hampshire, Massachusetts, Connecticut, New Jersey, Pennsylvania, Delaware, Virginia, North Carolina, South Carolina, Georgia, aye — 10; Maryland,† no — 1.

The President having asked, what the convention meant should be done with the Journals, &c. whether copies were to be allowed to the members, if applied for, it was resolved, *nem. con.* "that he retain the Journal and other papers, subject to the order of Congress, if ever formed under the Constitution."

The members then proceeded to sign the Constitution, as finally amended, as follows:

We the people of the United States, in order to form a more perfect union, establish justice, insure domestic tranquillity, provide for the common defence, promote the general welfare, and secure the blessings of liberty to ourselves and our posterity, do ordain and establish this Constitution for the United States of America.

---

*General PINCKNEY and Mr. BUTLER disliked the equivocal form of signing, and on that account voted in the negative.

† This negative of Maryland was occasioned by the language of the instructions to the Deputies of that State, which required them to report to the State the *proceedings* of the Convention.

ARTICLE I.

Sect. 1. All legislative powers herein granted; shall be vested in a Congress of the United States, which shall consist of a Senate and House of Representatives.

Sect. 2. The House of Representatives shall be composed of Members chosen every second year, by the people of the several states; and the electors in each State shall have the qualifications requisite for electors of the most numerous branch of the State Legislature.

No person shall be a representative who shall not have attained to the age of twenty-five years, and been seven years a citizen of the United States, and who shall not, when elected, be an inhabitant of that State in which he shall be chosen.

Representatives and direct taxes shall be apportioned among the several States which may be included within this Union, according to their respective numbers, which shall be determined by adding to the whole number of free persons, including those bound to service for a term of years and excluding Indians not taxed, three-fifths of all other persons. The actual enumeration shall be made within three years after the first meeting of the Congress of the United States, and within every subsequent term of ten years, in such manner as they shall by law direct. The number of representatives shall not exceed one for every thirty thousand, but each State shall have at least one representative; and until such emuneration shall be made, the State of New Hampshire shall be entitled to choose three, Massachusetts eight, Rhode Island and Providence Plantations one, Connecticut five, New York six, New Jersey four, Pennsylvania eight, Delaware one, Maryland six, Virginia ten, North Carolina five, South Carolina five, and Georgia three.

When vacancies happen in the representation from any State, the Executive authority thereof shall issue writs of election to fill such vacancies.

The House of Representatives shall choose their Speaker and other officers; and shall have the sole power of impeachment.

Sect. 3. The Senate of the United States shall be composed of two Senators from each State, chosen by the Legislature thereof, for six years; and each Senator shall have one vote.

Immediately after they shall be assembled in consequence of the first election, they shall be divided, as equally as may be, into three classes. The seats of the Senators of the first class shall be vacated at the expiration of the second year, of the second class at the expiration of the fourth year, and of the third class at the expiration of the sixth year, so that one-third may be chosen every second year; and if vacancies happen, by resignation, or otherwise, during the recess of the Legislature of any State, the Executive thereof may make temporary appointments until the next meeting of the Legislature, which shall then fill such vacancies.

No person shall be a Senator who shall not have attained to the age of thirty years, and been nine years a citizen of the United States, and who shall not, when elected, be an inhabitant of that State for which he shall be chosen.

The Vice President of the United States shall be President of the Senate, but shall have no vote, unless they be equally divided.

The Senate shall choose their other officers, and also a president pro tempore, in the absence of the Vice President, or when he shall exercise the office of President of the United States.

The Senate shall have the sole power to try all impeachments. When sitting for that purpose, they shall be on oath or affirmation. When the President of the United States is tried, the Chief Justice shall preside; and no person shall be convicted without the concurrence of two-thirds of the members present.

Judgment, in cases of impeachment, shall not extend

further than to removal from office, and disqualification to hold and enjoy any office of honor, trust, or profit, under the United States; but the party convicted shall nevertheless be liable and subject to indictment, trial, judgment, and punishment, according to law.

Sect. 4. The times, places, and manner of holding elections for Senators and Representatives, shall be prescribed in each State by the Legislature thereof; but the Congress may, at any time, by law, make or alter such regulations, except as to the places of choosing Senators.

The Congress shall assemble at least once in every year, and such meeting shall be on the first Monday in December, unless they shall by law appoint a different day.

Sect. 5. Each House shall be the judge of the elections, returns, and qualifications of its own members, and a majority of each shall constitute a quorum to do business; but a smaller number may adjourn from day to day, and may be authorized to compel the attendance of absent members, in such manner, and under such penalties as each House may provide.

Each House may determine the rules of its proceedings, punish its members for disorderly behaviour, and with the concurrence of two-thirds, expel a member.

Each House shall keep a Journal of its proceedings, and from time to time publish the same, excepting such parts as may in their judgment, require secresy, and the yeas and nays of the members of either House, on any question, shall, at the desire of one-fifth of those present, be entered on the Journal.

Neither House, during the session of Congress, shall, without the consent of the other, adjourn for more than three days, nor to any other place than that in which the two Houses shall be sitting.

Sect. 6. The Senators and Representatives shall receive a compensation for their services, to be ascertained by law, and paid out of the Treasury of the United States. They shall, in all cases, except treason, felony, and breach of the

peace, be privileged from arrest during their attendance at
the session of their respective Houses, and in going to or
returning from the same, and for any speech or debate in
either House, they shall not be questioned in any other
place.

No Senator or Representative shall, during the time for
which he was elected, be appointed to any civil office under
the authority of the United States, which shall have been
created, or the emoluments whereof shall have been increased, during such time ; and no person holding any
office under the United States, shall be a member of either
House during his continuance in office.

Sect. 7. All bills for raising revenue shall originate in
the House of Representatives ; but the Senate may propose
or concur with amendments, as on other bills.

Every bill which shall have passed the House of Representatives and the Senate, shall, before it become a law, be
presented to the President of the United States. If he
approve, he shall sign it ; but if not, he shall return it,
with his objections, to that House in which it shall have
originated, who shall enter the objections at large on their
Journal, and proceed to reconsider it. If, after such reconsideration, two-thirds of that House shall agree to pass the
bill, it shall be sent, together with the objections, to the
other House, by which it shall likewise be reconsidered,
and if approved by two-thirds of that House, it shall
become a law. But in all such cases, the votes of both
Houses shall be determined by yeas and nays, and the
names of the persons voting for and against the bill, shall
be entered on the Journal of each House respectively. If
any bill shall not be returned by the President within ten
days (Sundays excepted) after it shall have been presented
to him, the same shall be a law, in like manner as if he had
signed it, unless the Congress by their adjournment prevent
its return ; in which case it shall not be a law.

Every order, resolution, or vote, to which the concurrence of the Senate and House of Representatives may be

necessary, (except on a question of adjournment,) shall be presented to the President of the United States ; and before the same shall take effect, shall be approved by him, or being disapproved by him, shall be repassed by two-thirds of the Senate and House of Representatives, according to the rules and limitations prescribed in the case of a bill.

Sect. 8. The Congress shall have power —

* To lay and collect taxes, duties, imposts, and excises; to pay the debts and provide for the common defence and general welfare of the United States; but all duties, imposts, and excises, shall be uniform throughout the United States.

To borrow money on the credit of the United States:

To regulate commerce with foreign nations, and among the several States, and with the Indian tribes:

To establish a uniform rule of naturalization, and uniform laws on the subject of bankruptcies throughout the United States:

To coin money, regulate the value thereof, and of foreign coin, and fix the standard of weights and measures:

To provide for the punishment of counterfeiting the securities and current coin of the United States:

To establish post offices and post roads:

To promote the progress of science and useful arts, by securing, for limited times, to authors and inventors, the exclusive right to their respective writings and discoveries:

To constitute tribunals inferior to the Supreme Court:

To define and punish piracies and felonies committed on the high seas, and offences against the law of nations:

To declare war, grant letters of marque and reprisal, and make rules concerning captures on land and water:

---

* That " To lay and collect taxes, duties, imposts, and excises," ought not to be a separate clause from " to pay the debts," &c. ; see in the printed Journal of the Convention, the report of the Committee of Eleven, September 4th — also copy of the draft of the Constitution as it stood Sept. 12th, printed by the Convention for the use of the members, now in the Department of State — also copy of the Constitution, as agreed to and signed, printed in sheets at the close of the Convention. The proviso " but all duties, imposts, and excises, shall be uniform,"&c., by its immediate reference, suggests the same view of the text.

To raise and support armies; but no appropriation of money to that use shall be for a longer term than two years:

To provide and maintain a navy·

To make rules for the government and regulation of the land and naval forces:

To provide for calling forth the militia to execute the laws of the Union, suppress insurrections, and repel invasions:

To provide for organizing, arming, and disciplining the militia, and for governing such part of them as may be employed in the service of the United States — reserving to the States respectively, the appointment of the officers, and the authority of training the militia according to the discipline prescribed by Congress:

To exercise exclusive legislation in all cases whatsoever, over such district, (not exceeding ten miles square,) as may, by cession of particular States, and the acceptance of Congress, become the seat of government of the United States, and to exercise like authority over all places purchased, by the consent of the Legislature of the State in which the same shall be, for the erection of forts, magazines, arsenals, dock-yards, and other needful buildings: and,

To make all laws which shall be necessary and proper for carrying into execution the foregoing powers, and all other powers vested by this Constitution in the government of the United States, or in any department or officer thereof.

Sect. 9. The migration or importation of such persons as any of the States, now existing, shall think proper to admit, shall not be prohibited by the Congress prior to the year 1808, but a tax or duty may be imposed on such importation, not exceeding ten dollars for each person.

The privilege of the writ of habeas corpus shall not be suspended, unless when, in cases of rebellion or invasion, the public safety may require it.

No bill of attainder, or ex post facto law, shall be passed.

No capitation or other direct tax shall be laid, unless in proportion to the census or enumeration herein before directed to be taken.

No tax or duty shall be laid on articles exported from any State. No preference shall be given by any regulation of commerce or revenue to the ports of one State over those of another: nor shall vessels bound to or from one State, be obliged to enter, clear, or pay duties in another.

No money shall be drawn from the Treasury, but in consequence of appropriations made by law: and a regular statement and account of the receipts and expenditures of all public money shall be published from time to time.

No title of nobility shall be granted by the United States: and no person holding any office of profit or trust under them, shall, without the consent of the Congress, accept of any present, emolument, office, or title of any kind whatever, from any king, prince, or foreign State.

Sect. 10. No State shall enter into any treaty, alliance, or confederation; grant letters of marque and reprisal; coin money; emit bills of credit; make any thing but gold and silver coin a tender in payment of debts; pass any bill of attainder, ex post facto law, or law impairing the obligation of contracts, or grant any title of nobility

No State shall, without the consent of the Congress, lay any imposts or duties on imports or exports, except what may be absolutely necessary for executing its inspection laws; and the net produce of all duties and imposts, laid by any State on imports or exports, shall be for the use of the Treasury of the United States, and all such laws shall be subject to the revision and control of the Congress. No State shall, without the consent of Congress, lay any duty of tonnage, keep troops or ships of war in time of peace, enter into any agreement or compact with another State, or with a foreign power; or engage in war, unless actually invaded, or in such imminent danger as will not admit of delay.

ARTICLE II.

Sect. 1. The Executive power shall be vested in a President of the United States of America. He shall hold his office during the term of four years, and, together with the Vice President, chosen for the same term be elected as follows:

Each State shall appoint, in such manner as the Legislature thereof may direct, a number of Electors, equal to the whole number of Senators and Representatives to which the State may be entitled in the Congress; but no Senator or Representative, or person holding any office of trust or profit under the United States, shall be appointed an Elector.

The Electors shall meet in their respective States, and vote by ballot for two persons, of whom one at least shall not be an inhabitant of the same State with themselves. And they shall make a list of all the persons voted for, and of the number of votes for each; which list they shall sign and certify, and transmit sealed to the seat of the Government of the United States, directed to the President of the Senate. The President of the Senate shall, in the presence of the Senate and House of Representatives, open all the certificates, and the votes shall then be counted. The person having the greatest number of votes shall be the President, if such number be a majority of the whole number of Electors appointed; and if there be more than one who have such majority, and have an equal number of votes, then the House of Representatives shall immediately choose, by ballot, one of them for President; and if no person have a majority, then, from the five highest on the list, the said House shall, in like manner, choose the President. But, in choosing the President, the votes shall be taken by States, the representation from each State having one vote; a quorum for this purpose shall consist of a member or members from two-thirds of the States, and a majority of all the States shall be necessary to a choice. In every case, after the choice of the President, the person having the greatest number of votes of the Electors, shall be the Vice President. But if there should remain two or more who have equal votes, the Senate shall choose from them, by ballot, the Vice President.

The Congress may determine the time of choosing the Electors, and the day on which they shall give their votes; which day shall be the same throughout the United States.

No person, except a natural born citizen, or a citizen of the United States at the time of the adoption of this Constitution, shall be eligible to the office of President, neither shall any person be eligible to that office, who shall not have attained to the age of thirty-five years, and been fourteen years a resident within the United States.

In case of the removal of the President from office, or of his death, resignation, or inability to discharge the powers and duties of the said office, the same shall devolve on the Vice President, and the Congress may, by law, provide for the case of removal, death, resignation, or inability, both of the President and Vice President, declaring what officer shall then act as President, and such officer shall act accordingly, until the disability be removed, or a President shall be elected.

The President shall, at stated times, receive for his services a compensation, which shall neither be increased nor diminished during the period for which he shall have been elected, and he shall not receive within that period any other emolument from the United States, or any of them.

Before he enters on the execution of his office, he shall take the following oath or affirmation:

" I do solemnly swear (or affirm) that I will faithfully execute the office of President of the United States, and will to the best of my ability, preserve, protect, and defend, the Constitution of the United States."

Sect. 2. The President shall be commander-in-chief of the army and navy of the United States, and of the militia of the several States, when called into the actual service of the United States; he may require the opinion, in writing, of the principal officer in each of the Executive Departments, upon any subject relating to the duties of their respective offices; and he shall have power to grant reprieves and pardons for offences against the United States except in cases of impeachment.

He shall have power, by and with the advice and consent of the Senate, to make treaties, provided two-thirds of the senators present concur; and he shall nominate, and, by and with the advice and consent of the Senate, shall appoint ambassadors, other public ministers and consuls, Judges of the Supreme Court, and all other officers of the United States, whose appointments are not herein otherwise provided for, and which shall be established by law. But the Congress may, by law, vest the appointment of such inferior officers as they think proper in the President alone, in the courts of law, or in the heads of departments.

The President shall have power to fill up all vacancies that may happen during the recess of the Senate, by granting commissions which shall expire at the end of their next session.

Sect. 3. He shall, from time to time, give to the Congress information of the state of the union, and recommend to their consideration such measures as he shall judge necessary and expedient; he may, on extraordinary occasions, convene both Houses, or either of them, and in case of disagreement between them, with respect to the time of adjournment, he may adjourn them to such time as he shall think proper; he shall receive ambassadors and other public ministers; he shall take care that the laws be faithfully executed; and shall commission all the officers of the United States.

Sect. 4. The President, Vice President, and all civil officers of the United States, shall be removed from office on impeachment for, and conviction of, treason, bribery, or other high crimes and misdemeanors.

Article III.

Sect. 1. The Judicial power of the United States shall be vested in one Supreme Court, and in such inferior courts as the Congress may, from time to time, ordain and establish. The Judges, both of the supreme and inferior courts, shall hold their offices during good behaviour; and shall, at stated times, receive for their services a compensation which shall not be diminished during their continuance in office.

Sect. 2. The judicial power shall extend to all cases in law and equity, arising under this Constitution, the laws of the United States, and treaties made, or which shall be made, under their authority; to all cases affecting ambassadors, other public ministers and consuls; to all cases of admiralty and maritime jurisdiction; to controversies to which the United States shall be a party; to controversies between two or more States; between a State and citizens of another State; between citizens of different States; between citizens of the same State, claiming lands under grants of different States; and between a State, or the citizens thereof, and foreign States, citizens, or subjects.

In all cases affecting ambassadors, other public ministers and consuls, and those in which a State shall be a party, the Supreme Court shall have original jurisdiction. In all the other cases before mentioned, the Supreme Court shall have appellate jurisdiction, both as to law and fact, with such exceptions, and under such regulations, as the Congress shall make.

The trial of all crimes, except in cases of impeachment, shall be by jury; and such trial shall be held in the State where the said crimes shall have been committed; but when not committed within any State, the trial shall be at such place or places as the Congress may by law have directed.

Sect. 3. Treason against the United States shall consist only in levying war against them, or in adhering to their enemies, giving them aid and comfort. No person shall be convicted of treason unless on the testimony of two witnesses to the same overt act, or on confession in open court.

The Congress shall have power to declare the punishment of treason; but no attainder of treason shall work corruption of blood, or forfeiture, except during the life of the person attainted.

ARTICLE IV.

Sect. 1. Full faith and credit shall be given in each State to the public acts, records, and judicial proceedings of every other State. And the Congress may, by general laws, prescribe the manner in which such acts, records, and proceedings, shall be proved, and the effect thereof.

Sect. 2. The citizens of each State shall be entitled to all privileges and immunities of citizens in the several States.

A person charged in any State with treason, felony, or other crime, who shall flee from justice, and be found in another State, shall, on demand of the executive authority of the State from which he fled, be delivered up, to be removed to the State having jurisdiction of the crime.

No person held to service or labor in one State, under the laws thereof, escaping into another, shall, in consequence of any law or regulation therein, be discharged from such service or labor; but shall be delivered up, on claim of the party to whom such service or labor may be due.

Sect. 3. New States may be admitted by the Congress into this Union; but no new State shall be formed or erected within the jurisdiction of any other State; nor any State be formed by the junction of two or more States, or parts of States; without the consent of the legislatures of the States concerned, as well as of the Congress.

The Congress shall have power to dispose of and make all needful rules and regulations respecting the territory or other property belonging to the United States: and nothing in this Constitution shall be so construed as to prejudice any claims of the United States, or of any particular State.

Sect. 4. The United States, shall guarantee to every State in this Union, a republican form of government, and shall protect each of them against invasion ; and, on application of the Legislature or the Executive, (when the Legislature cannot be convened,) against domestic violence.

Article V.

The Congress, whenever two-thirds of both Houses shall deem it necessary, shall propose amendments to this Constitution ; or, on the application of the Legislatures of two-thirds of the several States, shall call a Convention for proposing amendments, which, in either case, shall be valid to all intents and purposes, as part of this Constitution, when ratified by the Legislatures of three-fourths of the several States, or by conventions in three-fourths thereof, as the one or the other mode of ratification may be proposed by the Congress ; Provided, that no amendment which may be made prior to the year 1808, shall in any manner affect the first and fourth clauses in the ninth section of the first article ; and that no State, without its consent, shall be deprived of its equal suffrage in the Senate.

Article VI.

All debts contracted, and engagements entered into, before the adoption of this Constitution, shall be as valid against the United States under this Constitution, as under the Confederation.

This Constitution, and the laws of the United States which shall be made in pursuance thereof, and all treaties made, or which shall be made, under the authority of the United States, shall be the supreme law of the land ; and the judges in every State shall be bound thereby ; anything in the Constitution or laws of any State to the contrary notwithstanding.

The Senators and Representatives beforementioned, and the members of the several State Legislatures, and all executive and judicial officers, both of the United States, and of the several States, shall be bound by oath, or affirmation, to support this Constitution ; but no religious test shall ever be required as a qualification to any office or public trust under the United States.

ARTICLE VII.

The ratification of the conventions of nine States shall be sufficient for the establishment of this Constitution between the States so ratifying the same.

Done in Convention, by the unanimous consent of the States present, the 17th day of September, in the year of our Lord 1787, and of the independence of the United States of America, the twelfth. In witness whereof, we have hereunto subscribed our names.

GEORGE WASHINGTON, *President*,
and Deputy from Virginia.

New Hampshire.
JOHN LANGDON,
NICHOLAS GILMAN.

Massachusetts.
NATHANIEL GORHAM,
RUFUS KING.

Connecticut.
WILLIAM SAMUEL JOHNSON,
ROGER SHERMAN.

New York.
ALEXANDER HAMILTON.

New Jersey.
WILLIAM LIVINGSTON,
DAVID BREARLY,
WILLIAM PATTERSON,
JONATHAN DAYTON.

Delaware.
GEORGE READ,
GUNNING BEDFORD, Jr.,
JOHN DICKINSON,
RICHARD BASSETT,
JACOB BROOME.

Maryland.
JAMES McHENRY,
DANIEL of ST. THOMAS JENIFER,
DANIEL CARROLL.

Virginia.
JOHN BLAIR.
JAMES MADISON, Jr.

North Carolina.
WILLIAM BLOUNT,
RICHARD DOBBS SPAIGHT,
HUGH WILLIAMSON.

Pennsylvania.	*South Carolina.*
BENJAMIN FRANKLIN,	JOHN RUTLEDGE,
THOMAS MIFFLIN,	CHARLES COTESWORTH PINCKNEY,
ROBERT MORRIS,	CHARLES PINCKNEY,
GEORGE CLYMER,	PIERCE BUTLER.
THOMAS FITZSIMONS.	
JARED INGERSOLL,	*Georgia.*
JAMES WILSON,	WILLIAM FEW.
GOUVERNEUR MORRIS.	ABRAHAM BALDWIN.

Attest:

WILLIAM JACKSON, *Secretary.*

The Constitution being signed by all the members, except Mr. RANDOLPH, Mr. MASON and Mr. GERRY, who declined giving it the sanction of their names, the Convention dissolved itself by an adjournment sine die.

Whilst the last members were signing, Doctor FRANKLIN, looking towards the President's chair, at the back of which a rising sun happened to be painted, observed to a few members near him, that painters had found it difficult to distinguish in their art, a rising, from a setting, sun. I have, said he, often and often, in the course of the session, and the vicissitudes of my hopes and fears as to its issue, looked at that behind the President, without being able to tell whether it was rising or setting; but now at length, I have the happiness to know, that it is a rising, and not a setting sun.

INDEX,

GENERAL AND ANALYTICAL,

TO

MADISON'S JOURNAL OF THE CONSTITUTIONAL CONVENTION.

CONTRIBUTIONS—Continued.

of States, to be in proportion to freemen and three-fifths of slaves, 164.

CONTROVERSIES, decision of those between States, about territory or jurisdiction, 69, 455, 599.

CONVENTION of Eastern States and New York proposed, 43.

at Annapolis, 37, 45.

proposals for Federal, 37, 39, 43.

character of Federal, 51.

members who attend it, 53, 55, 58, 72, 78, 84, 89, 108, 136, 142, 199, 209, 311, 449.

assembles at Philadelphia, 53.

elects General Washington President, 54.

elects William Jackson Secretary, 55.

adopts rules, 56, 58.

commences main business, 59.

extent of powers, 74, 167, 171, 176, 187, 282.

importance of decision, 241, 244, 246.

determines to adopt national, in preference to federal system, 196.

goes into Committee of the Whole, 72.

Committee of the Whole reports series of propositions, 160.

determines not to go again into Committee of the Whole, 163, 462.

clashing opinions endanger dissolution, 259.

prayers in it proposed, 260.

appoints committee of one from each State, to suggest compromise between large and small States about representation, 285.

secession threatened by some members, 297, 357.

adjourns, for opportunity of making compromise between large and small States, 359.

informal meeting, relative to representation of large and small States, 359.

appoints Committee of Detail, to draught Constitution, 418.

its resolutions, as adopted after discussion, 444.

refers resolutions, as adopted, to Committee of Detail, 444.

refers plans of Mr. Pinckney and Mr. Randolph to Committee of Detail, 449.

refers amended draught of Constitution to Committee of Revision, 691.

second draught of Constitution reported to it, 699.

adopts final draught of Constitution, 748.

gives directions as regards journals, 748.

provision for expenses, 660, 663.

CONVENTIONS OF STATES, Constitution to be submitted to, 64, 111, 150, 162, 176, 199, 410, 448, 461, 640, 645, 713, 721, 739, 741, 762.

Congress to call one, to amend Constitution, 461, 640, 712, 737, 738, 739, 741, 761.

CONVICTION of treason, 68, 454, 567, 688, 710, 759.

of President of malpractice or neglect, 98, 161, 392, 447, 688.

of President of treason, bribery, or corruption, 458, 656, 688, 709, 758.

under impeachment, 459, 654, 688, 689, 690, 702, 750.

pardon before it, 613.

CONVICTS, introduction of those from abroad, 610.

COPPER, legal tender, 71.

COPYRIGHT, powers of Congress in regard to, 550, 661, 705, 753.

CORPORATIONS, power of Congress, under Constitution, in regard to, 549, 725.

United States to be one, 559.

CORRESPONDENCE between the President and State Executives, 90, 457, 612.

CORRUPTION, President to be removed for, 70, 393, 458, 613, 688, 709, 758.

Heads of Departments to be removed for, 561.

of State Legislatures, 521, 526.

of blood not to be worked by attainder, 454.

of British government, 103, 105, 222.

influence of, 178.

COUNCIL, EXECUTIVE, 86, 101, 123, 553, 560, 585, 613, 656, 679, 683.

COUNCIL OF REVISION to consist of Executive and convenient number of Judiciary, 62, 101, 104, 107, 121, 123, 398, 533.

COUNCIL OF STATE, 560.

COUNSELLORS in France receive no salary, 94.

COUNTERFEITING, Congress to legislate upon, 68, 454, 545, 705, 753.

pardon of, 613.

COURTS—See Judiciary, Supreme Court, Inferior Courts.

interfered with by State laws during Confederation, 47.

COURT MARTIAL, 589.

CREDENTIALS of members of Federal Convention, 55.

CREDIT, emission of bills of, by Congress, 67, 454, 541.

bills of, not to be emitted by States, 71, 459, 620, 706, 755.

to be given by States to records and judicial proceedings of each other, 72, 460, 625, 649, 711, 760.

that of Confederation to be secured by Constitution, 550, 569, 587, 596, 599, 605, 712, 761.

CREDITORS, public, unprovided for in 1787, 46.

injured by State laws during the Confederation, 47.

CRIME, and criminals, to be tried in State where committed, 70, 459, 619, 710, 759.

to be tried in State courts, 191.

to be defined by Congress, 545.

CRIMINALS, fugitive, to be delivered up to one another by States, 71, 460, 624, 711, 760.

CROMWELL, 104.

CURRENCY, pretext for one of paper cut off, 543.

DAMAGES, provision for those on bills of exchange, 624.

DAVIE, WILLIAM R., attends Federal Convention, 54.

proposes an impeachment of President for malpractice or neglect, 98.

considers impeachment of President an essential provision, 392.

his views relative to duration of Executive term, 422, 436.

his views on ratio of representation, 277, 302.

insists on slaves being included in ratio of representation, 335.

DAYTON, JONATHAN, attends Federal Convention, 209.

objects to joint ballot in Congress to elect President, 600.

desires an equal vote of States in Congress for President, 602.

LANSING, JOHN — Continued.

opposes going into Committee of the Whole, 163.

objects to propositions of Mr. Randolph as amended and adopted, 167.

thinks Convention limited to amendment of Confederation, 167, 200.

proposes that power of legislation be vested in Congress, 200.

opposes negative of Congress on State laws, 201.

proposes equal vote of States in House of Representatives, 253.

wishes some plan for compromise on question of representation, 289.

LAWS—See Acts.

LAW OF NATIONS not sufficiently protected under Confederation, 60.

Congress to legislate on offences against, 68, 454, 705, 753.

LEE, RICHARD H., views in regard to the Federal Constitution, 44.

LEGISLATURE—See Congress of the Constitution; States.

LEVYING WAR, evidence of, in cases of treason, 68, 454, 564, 711, 759.

LIGHTHOUSES, States to levy duties to erect them, 732.

LIMITATION relative to continuance of revenue laws, 585.

on suspension of writ of habeas corpus, 619, 706, 754.

LIVINGSTON, WILLIAM, attends Federal Convention, 108.

reports provisions relative to public debt and militia, 568.

reports provisions relative to slaves, navigation, and capitation taxes, 598.

LOANS to be made by Congress under the Constitution, 67.

LORDS, HOUSE OF, impossible in America, 97, 231, 234.

considered noble institution, 182.

Senate should be like it, 125.

not a model for Senate, 158, 231.

negative on the Commons, 274.

LYCIAN LEAGUE, 275.

M'CLURG, JAMES, attends Federal Convention, 54.

proposes Executive term to be during good behavior, 369.

desires some specific provision relative to exercise of Executive powers by President, 397.

M'HENRY, JAMES, attends Federal Convention, 55.

remarks on subterfuges adopted to avoid provision in regard to money-bills, 519.

proposes to raise taxes by requisitions, 572.

desires prohibition in regard to attainders and ex post facto laws, 586.

desires regulation in regard to trade between States, 611, 648.

views as to mode of ratifying Constitution, 643.

desires provision for President to convene Senate separately, 690.

signs Constitution, 762.

MADISON, JAMES, (1784) becomes member of House of Delegates of Virginia, 34.

(1786) appointed delegate to Convention at Annapolis, 35, 37,

draws act of Virginia appointing delegates to Federal Convention, 43.

remarks on ancient Confederacies, 29.

remarks on colonies before Revolution, 30.

MADISON, JAMES—Continued.

wish to remedy evils of Confederation, 34.

prepares to take reports of debates in Federal Convention, 49.

attends Federal Convention, 53.

thinks powers of National Government should not be too much limited, 117, 255.

wishes to protect minority from oppression by majority, 118.

his general views of National as compared with a Federal Government, 187, 263.

his objections to Mr. Patterson's plan, 187.

effect of breach of compact by member of Confederacy, 188, 416.

remarks on violations of articles of Confederation by States, 189.

views of defects of Confederation, 190.

remarks on effect of mere Confederacy on small States, 193.

remarks on scheme for equalizing States, 195.

remarks on danger of encroachments by States and National Government on each other, 211, 255, 264.

his general views as to ends to be sought in forming Constitution, 241, 254.

fears more from power of States than of General Government, 264.

opposes committee to prepare plan of compromise between large and small States, relative to representation, 289, 292.

his course towards small States complained of, 297.

objects to distinctions between new and old States, 329.

urges importance of preserving mutual independence of great departments of government, 399, 402.

thinks preponderance of Legislature is chiefly to be guarded against, 399, 402.

views on general power of President, 86, 121.

opposes removal of President by Congress, on application of States, 96.

opposes absolute negative in Executive, 103, 121.

wishes Judiciary united with Executive to revise laws, 122, 399, 402, 532, 536, 716.

urges necessity of making Executive and Legislature independent of each other, 370.

views on impeachment of President, 393, 688, 689, 723.

views on election of President, 387, 427, 428, 429, 657, 665, 666, 667, 674, 677.

thinks ballot in Congress for President should be joint, 601.

desires provision to prevent President from appointing to offices not previously created by law, 604.

suggests exercise by Council of Executive powers during vacancy, 613.

objects to equal suffrage being allowed to all States, 77, 254, 276.

thinks Senate and Judiciary should not be chosen immediately by people, 80.

opposes division of Union into Senatorial districts, 82.

thinks Judiciary should be appointed by Senate, 109, 157.

advocates small Senate, 125.

advocates proportional representation in Senate, 126, 276, 280, 291, 351.

objects to election of Senators by State Legislatures, 128.

suggests negative on State laws being given to Senate, 135.

792

INDEX.

OFFICERS — Continued.

not to accept presents or titles, 593, 706, 755.

none to be appointed to offices not previously created by law, 604.

not to be appointed electors of President, 397, 668, 675, 707, 756.

to be removed, on conviction, under impeachment, 689, 702, 750.

OPINIONS of Judges to be given to President and Congress, 558.

of members of Council to be given to President, 561.

of Heads of Departments to be given to President, 656, 683, 709, 758.

ORIGINATION of acts to belong to each branch of Legislature, 62, 83, 445, 453.

of money-bills must be in House of Representatives, 65, 158, 290, 291, 303, 356, 447, 450, 480, 484, 505, 512, 524, 531, 570, 661, 689, 703, 752.

PAPER MONEY, new emissions by States feared, 47.

difficulties under Confederation, 34, 47, 60.

emission of, by Congress, 67, 454, 541, 543.

prohibited to States, 71, 132, 191, 459, 619, 706, 755.

PARDON, granted by President, 70, 457, 613, 709, 734, 758.

not to extend to impeachments, 70, 457, 612, 709, 758.

in cases of treason, 698, 699.

PATENTS, power of Congress in regard to, 550, 661, 705, 753.

PATTERSON, WILLIAM, attends Federal Convention, 53.

urges settlement of proportion of representation, 110.

thinks proper object of Convention mere revision and extension of articles of Confederation, 139.

wishes to preserve efficiency of State Governments, 140.

offers plan in series of resolutions, 163.

his plan compared with that of Mr. Randolph, 167, 189.

thinks plan of Mr. Randolph beyond authority of Convention, 168.

contends for States having an equal vote, 169, 170.

wishes laws of Confederation to be acted upon through State Judiciaries, 170.

his plan rejected, 196.

wishes New Hampshire delegates sent for, 270.

complains of course pursued towards small States, 296, 358.

insists on equal vote of States in Senate, 309, 358.

objects to proportional representation in either House, 314.

proposes election of President by electors appointed by States, 387.

signs Constitution, 762.

PAY, of President, 62, 70, 93, 161, 397, 437, 447, 457, 708, 757.

that of President not to be increased or diminished during his term, 62, 70, 104, 437, 447, 458, 708, 757.

of President to be paid out of National Treasury, 397, 437.

of electors of President, 398.

of Senators, 61, 67, 156, 160, 247, 287, 445, 452, 494, 495, 527, 703, 751.

of Senators to be paid by States, 156, 248, 452, 530.

PAY — Continued.

of Representatives, 61, 67, 152, 160, 217, 223, 445, 452, 495, 528, 703, 751.

of members of Congress to be paid out of National Treasury, 153, 160, 217, 223, 528.

of members of Congress to be paid by States, 193, 218, 452.

how that of members of Congress should be fixed, 495, 529.

that of Judges, 62, 110, 162, 377, 447, 458, 614, 710, 759.

no increase or diminution of that of Judges during their term, 63, 110, 162, 377, 447, 458, 615, 710, 759.

it ought to be adequate, 78, 220, 616.

struggles to obtain it, 95.

it ought to be fixed, 153, 219, 528, 530.

PAYMENT, no tender to be authorized by States but gold or silver, 71, 459, 706, 755.

PEACE, members of Congress may be arrested for breach of, 66, 452, 703, 751.

when troops may be kept during, 71, 459, 559.

ought not to depend on Executive, 85.

cases affecting national, to be tried by National Judiciary, 157, 379, 448.

to be made by Congress, 549.

PENNSYLVANIA, arbitrary conduct of its Colonial Governors, 102, 104.

violates articles of Confederation, 190.

sends delegates to Federal Convention, 53, 55.

proposes General Washington as President of Convention, 54.

objects to equal vote of large and small States in Convention, 57.

desires proportional representation in both branches of Congress, 239.

proportion of electors of President, 389, 391.

proportion of representation in Senate before census, 66.

proportion of representation in House of Representatives before census, 65, 312, 316, 355, 446, 450, 701.

PENSIONERS, disqualification of, as members of Congress, 442.

PEOPLE to elect Representatives, 61, 78, 445, 450, 700, 749.

of several States to ratify Constitution, 64, 111, 410, 448, 713, 762.

ought to be represented in House of Representatives, 78.

to elect Senators, 82.

to elect Executive, 88, 89, 92, 365, 368.

of States establish Constitution, 449, 462, 700, 748.

their sentiments on new Constitution, 171.

PIERCE, WILLIAM, attends Federal Convention, 78.

in favor of representation of people in House of Representatives, 120.

in favor of States being represented in Senate, 120.

proposes three years as Senatorial term, 155.

PINCKNEY, CHARLES, attends Federal Convention, 54.

appointed on Committee to prepare rules for Convention, 55.

submits plan of Constitution, 64.

plan referred to Committee of Whole, 72.

general views on nature of Constitution, position of people of Union, and objects to be sought, 228.

SHERMAN, ROGER — Continued.

thinks that amendments of Constitution should be assented to by several States, 693.

prefers to submit Constitution to Congress of Confederation, but not to require their assent, 696.

views on mode of ratifying Constitution, 641, 642, 644.

signs Constitution, 762.

SHIPS of war, not to be kept by States during peace, 71, 459, 706, 755.

SLAVERY, 476, 478, 577, 608.

SLAVES, three-fifths of, included in ratio of representation, 147, 161, 165, 302, 312, 356, 446, 455, 700, 749.

to be included in apportionment of representation according to numbers, 324, 332, 356, 476.

three-fifths to be included in ratio of direct taxation, 336, 339, 356, 446, 455, 476, 700, 749.

provision in regard to emancipation, 418, 623.

power of Congress to tax or prohibit their migration or importation, 455, 577, 599, 608, 694, 706, 754.

compromise between Northern and Southern States relative to, 582, 599, 694.

fugitive to be delivered up, 624, 631, 711, 760.

SMALL STATES contend for equal vote in Congress, 32.

SMITH, MERIWETHER, appointed delegate to Convention at Annapolis, 35.

SOLDIERS—See Army, Military.

SOUTH CAROLINA adopts exclusive commercial regulations, 47.

sends delegates to Federal Convention, 54.

proportion of representation in House of Representatives before census, 65, 312, 316, 355, 700, 749.

proportion of representation in Senate before census, 66.

proposal to increase proportion of representation, 318.

proportion of electors of President, 389, 391, 707, 756.

SOVEREIGNTY, jealousies of States about, 60.

how far should be given up, 140, 141, 167, 169, 174, 180, 186, 196, 209, 238, 252.

people attached to that of States, 177.

how far retained and yielded by States, 198, 209, 214, 251, 267, 282, 285.

effect of separation from Great Britain upon it, 197, 204.

of States represented in Senate, 512.

of States in cases of treason, 564.

SPAIGHT, RICHARD D., attends Federal Convention, 54.

proposes rules to regulate discussions of Convention, 58.

urges election of Senate by State Legislatures, 81.

proposes seven years for Senatorial term, 154.

in favor of reconsidering decision, to choose President by electors appointed by State Legislatures, 418.

objects to requiring more than majority to pass navigation act, 628.

suggests seven years for Executive term, 671.

signs Constitution, 762.

SPARTA, 173, 233, 256, 534.

SPEAKER, to be member of Executive Council, 585.

to fill vacancy in Presidency, 70, 458.

SPEAKER — Continued.

to be elected by Representatives, 451, 701, 750.

SPEECH, freedom of, 66, 452, 703, 752.

STADTHOLDER, intrigues to increase his power, 106.

STAGES, regulation of, on post-roads, 551, 553.

STAMPS, duties to be laid by Congress, 164.

STANDARD of weights and measures may be fixed by Congress, 68, 454, 541, 704, 753.

STATE, Council of, 560.

Secretary of, 561.

STATES (under the Confederation), a revenue system can only be made by mutual accommodation, 32.

will not pay their quotas of taxes, 34.

infractions of British treaty, 47.

address of Congress on necessity of harmony and yielding local considerations, 32.

keep troops and make compacts without consent of Congress, 47.

violate contracts by internal administration, 47, 59.

jealousy between each other, 60, 208, 263.

encroach on Congress, 60, 133, 177, 190, 208, 251.

difficulties in adopting Confederation, 32.

differ as to suffrage in Confederation, 32.

differ in regard to public lands in Confederation, 33.

violate treaties of Confederation, 47, 60.

differ in regard to taxes on imports in Confederation, 33, 46.

conflicting commercial regulations during Confederation, 35, 47, 59.

five, send delegates to Convention at Annapolis, 37.

all except Rhode Island send delegates to Federal Convention, 45.

proceedings in regard to Federal Convention, 55, 57, 76, 163.

STATES (under the Constitution), proposal to do them away, 149, 263.

sovereignty, 139, 142, 167, 169, 197.

efforts to increase their own power, 177.

must be swallowed up by National Government, 180.

not necessary for any of main purposes of government, 181.

to be thrown into one mass and divided again, 169, 195.

ought not to be swallowed up by National Government, 196, 204, 205, 209, 214.

effect of separation from Great Britain upon sovereignty, 198.

effect of union on large and small, comparatively, 199, 244, 255, 262, 281.

situation will prevent combinations of large against small, 255.

to be preserved by Constitution but rendered subordinate, 282.

alliance of small ones with foreign powers threatened, 282, 283.

plan of compromise between large and small ones, on question of representation, 269, 278, 285, 289, 290, 355, 357.

people of, establish Constitution, 449, 462, 700, 749.

not to be unnecessarily encroached upon, 83, 130, 169, 362.

powers of Government ought to be left with them as much as possible, 116, 120, 127, 130, 139, 166, 169, 204, 235, 238, 251, 362, 585.

INDEX. 803

TRADE—Continued.

Convention at Annapolis to regulate it, 36.

between States, under Confederation, 39, 45, 46.

regulation of, by Congress, 69, 164, 453, 610, 704, 753.

between States, 610, 618, 626, 647, 718, 728, 732.

with Indians, 549, 585, 654, 704, 753.

TREASON, members of Congress may be arrested for, 66, 452, 703, 751.

definition and punishment of, 68, 454, 563, 710, 759.

President to be removed for, 70, 458, 613, 688, 709, 758.

pardon in cases of treason, 698, 699.

TREASURER may be appointed by Congress by ballot, 68, 454, 544, 704, 724.

TREATY, commercial one with Dutch, 47.

operation of, on the States under the Confederation, 46, 60.

infractions of British treaty, 47, 60,

violations of, by States during Confederation, 47, 60.

infractions of that with France, 47.

President to have an agency in them, 596.

to be made by Senate, 69, 186, 246, 455, 531, 596.

to be made by President, with advice of Senate, 185, 655, 680, 709, 758.

not to be made by States, 71.

to be Supreme law, 69, 166, 364, 445, 455, 593, 610, 617, 712, 761.

to be enforced by Congress, 68, 166, 454, 594.

ratification of them, 596, 656, 682.

power of Senate in regard to, 69, 185, 246, 455, 531, 596, 656, 682, 685, 709, 758.

laws of States contravening them to be negatived by Congress, 62, 161.

plans of, to be prepared by Secretary of Foreign Affairs, 560.

not to be published in journal of Senate, 502.

how far they are to be considered as laws, 463, 617.

between States, without consent of Congress, 190, 459.

between States and Indians, 190.

between States not sufficient for union, 73, 188.

effect of violation on rights of parties, 189.

TRIAL to be in State where crime is committed, 70, 459, 619, 719, 759.

of impeachments, 585, 619, 654, 688, 690, 698, 702, 750.

TROOPS, not to be kept by States during peace, 71, 459, 559, 706, 732, 733, 755.

TUCKER, ST. GEORGE, appointed to Convention at Annapolis, 35, 37.

TYLER, MR., proposes appointment of delegates to Convention at Annapolis, 36.

UNIFORMITY of commercial regulations, object of Convention at Annapolis, 36.

as to bankruptcy and naturalization needed during Confederation, 47.

of regulations relative to trade between States, 611, 618, 627, 647, 718, 728, 732, 739.

of regulations relative to bankruptcy, 624, 649, 650, 704, 753.

UNION, a more lasting one than that of Confederation desired, 31, 41, 43.

commercial regulations necessary to preserve it, 35.

UNION—Continued.

endangered by conflicting regulations of States, 35.

gloomy prospects of, in 1787, 46-48.

division of, desired by some, 48.

dangerous situation, in 1787, 60.

merely Federal not sufficient, 73.

to be divided into Senatorial districts, 82.

objects of it, 116.

how to be dissolved, 188.

nature of, 189.

necessity of, 194, 261, 262, 265, 266, 294.

proposed, by throwing States into one mass, and dividing them anew, 169, 181, 195.

UNITED STATES Government, to be so styled, 64, 449, 462, 700, 748.

to form corporation, 559.

treason against them, as distinguished from that against individual States, 564.

UNITY of Executive, 85, 98, 99, 123, 161, 165, 173, 365, 420, 447, 457, 600, 707, 756.

UNIVERSITY, establishment of, by Congress, 68, 550, 726.

VACANCY, in House of Representatives, 65, 451, 701, 749.

in Senate, 66, 451, 482, 701, 750.

in Executive, 70, 458, 613, 655, 656, 677, 708, 757.

VALUATION—See Land.

VETO—See Negative.

See Revision.

VICE PRESIDENT, election of, 654, 676, 707, 756.

powers and duties of, 655, 656, 676, 702, 750.

impeachment and removal of, 689.

VIRGINIA prohibits importation of various articles, 47.

averse to extending power of Congress of Confederation, 35.

appoints delegates to Convention at Annapolis, 35, 38.

passes law appointing delegates to Federal Convention, 42.

prefers revision of Confederation by Convention instead of Congress, 41.

proceedings relative to Federal Convention, 41.

sends delegates to Federal Convention, 53.

advocates equal vote of large and small States in Convention, 57.

looked to for plan for new government, 59.

proportion of representation in House of Representatives before census, 65, 312, 316, 355, 446, 450, 700, 749.

proportion of representation in Senate before census, 66.

desires proportional representation in both branches of Congress, 239.

proportion of electors of President, 389, 391, 707, 756.

VOTE, difficulties in regard to, in Confederation, 32.

equality of, insisted on by Delaware for each State, 55.

equality of, in Convention objected to, 57.

of two-thirds in Congress required in certain cases, 123, 455, 500, 656.

required to re-enact laws returned by President, 62, 67, 101, 107, 447, 453, 704, 752.

equality of, in Congress, 77, 134, 169, 251, 253, 356.

on money-bills to be in proportion to contribution, 279.

CPSIA information can be obtained
at www.ICGtesting.com
Printed in the USA
BVOW08*2350151216

470988BV00002B/3/P